41: *Afro-American Poets Since 1955*, edited by Trudier Harris and Thadious M. Davis (1985)

42: *American Writers for Children Before 1900*, edited by Glenn E. Estes (1985)

43: *American Newspaper Journalists, 1690-1872*, edited by Perry J. Ashley (1986)

44: *American Screenwriters*, Second Series, edited by Randall Clark, Robert E. Morsberger, and Stephen O. Lesser (1986)

45: *American Poets, 1880-1945*, First Series, edited by Peter Quartermain (1986)

46: *American Literary Publishing Houses, 1900-1980: Trade and Paperback*, edited by Peter Dzwonkoski (1986)

47: *American Historians, 1866-1912*, edited by Clyde N. Wilson (1986)

48: *American Poets, 1880-1945*, Second Series, edited by Peter Quartermain (1986)

49: *American Literary Publishing Houses, 1638-1899*, 2 parts, edited by Peter Dzwonkoski (1986)

50: *Afro-American Writers Before the Harlem Renaissance*, edited by Trudier Harris (1986)

51: *Afro-American Writers from the Harlem Renaissance to 1940*, edited by Trudier Harris (1987)

52: *American Writers for Children Since 1960: Fiction*, edited by Glenn E. Estes (1986)

53: *Canadian Writers Since 1960*, First Series, edited by W. H. New (1986)

54: *American Poets, 1880-1945*, Third Series, 2 parts, edited by Peter Quartermain (1987)

55: *Victorian Prose Writers Before 1867*, edited by William B. Thesing (1987)

56: *German Fiction Writers, 1914-1945*, edited by James Hardin (1987)

57: *Victorian Prose Writers After 1867*, edited by William B. Thesing (1987)

58: *Jacobean and Caroline Dramatists*, edited by Fredson Bowers (1987)

59: *American Literary Critics and Scholars, 1800-1850*, edited by John W. Rathbun and Monica M. Grecu (1987)

60: *Canadian Writers Since 1960*, Second Series, edited by W. H. New (1987)

61: *American Writers for Children Since 1960: Poets, Illustrators, and Nonfiction Authors*, edited by Glenn E. Estes (1987)

62: *Elizabethan Dramatists*, edited by Fredson Bowers (1987)

63: *Modern American Critics, 1920-1955*, edited by Gregory S. Jay (1988)

64: *American Literary Critics and Scholars, 1850-1880*, edited by John W. Rathbun and Monica M. Grecu (1988)

65: *French Novelists, 1900-1930*, edited by Catharine Savage Brosman (1988)

66: *German Fiction Writers, 1885-1913*, 2 parts, edited by James Hardin (1988)

67: *Modern American Critics Since 1955*, edited by Gregory S. Jay (1988)

68: *Canadian Writers, 1920-1959*, First Series, edited by W. H. New (1988)

69: *Contemporary German Fiction Writers*, First Series, edited by Wolfgang D. Elfe and James Hardin (1988)

70: *British Mystery Writers, 1860-1919*, edited by Bernard Benstock and Thomas F. Staley (1988)

71: *American Literary Critics and Scholars, 1880-1900*, edited by John W. Rathbun and Monica M. Grecu (1988)

72: *French Novelists, 1930-1960*, edited by Catharine Savage Brosman (1988)

73: *American Magazine Journalists, 1741-1850*, edited by Sam G. Riley (1988)

74: *American Short-Story Writers Before 1880*, edited by Bobby Ellen Kimbel, with the assistance of William E. Grant (1988)

75: *Contemporary German Fiction Writers*, Second Series, edited by Wolfgang D. Elfe and James Hardin (1988)

76: *Afro-American Writers, 1940-1955*, edited by Trudier Harris (1988)

77: *British Mystery Writers, 1920-1939*, edited by Bernard Benstock and Thomas F. Staley (1988)

78: *American Short-Story Writers, 1880-1910*, edited by Bobby Ellen Kimbel, with the assistance of William E. Grant (1988)

79: *American Magazine Journalists, 1850-1900*, edited by Sam G. Riley (1988)

(Continued on back endsheets)

Dictionary of Literary Biography • Volume One Hundred Four

British Prose Writers, 1660-1800
Second Series

Dictionary of Literary Biography • Volume One Hundred Four

British Prose Writers, 1660-1800
Second Series

8479

Edited by
Donald T. Siebert
University of South Carolina

A Bruccoli Clark Layman Book
Gale Research Inc.
Detroit, London

Printed in the United States of America

Published simultaneously in the United Kingdom
by Gale Research International Limited
(An affiliated company of Gale Research Inc.)

The paper used in this publication meets the minimum requirements
of American National Standard for Information Sciences—Permanence
Paper for Printed Library Materials, ANSI Z39.48-1984. ∞™

ISBN 0-8103-4584-6
91-6630 CIP

For my daughters,
Suzannah and Maggie

Contents

Plan of the Series

. . . Almost the most prodigious asset of a country, and perhaps its most precious possession, is its native literary product—when that product is fine and noble and enduring.

Mark Twain*

The advisory board, the editors, and the publisher of the *Dictionary of Literary Biography* are joined in endorsing Mark Twain's declaration. The literature of a nation provides an inexhaustible resource of permanent worth. We intend to make literature and its creators better understood and more accessible to students and the reading public, while satisfying the standards of teachers and scholars.

To meet these requirements, *literary biography* has been construed in terms of the author's achievement. The most important thing about a writer is his writing. Accordingly, the entries in *DLB* are career biographies, tracing the development of the author's canon and the evolution of his reputation.

The purpose of *DLB* is not only to provide reliable information in a convenient format but also to place the figures in the larger perspective of literary history and to offer appraisals of their accomplishments by qualified scholars.

The publication plan for *DLB* resulted from two years of preparation. The project was proposed to Bruccoli Clark by Frederick G. Ruffner, president of the Gale Research Company, in November 1975. After specimen entries were prepared and typeset, an advisory board was formed to refine the entry format and develop the series rationale. In meetings held during 1976, the publisher, series editors, and advisory board approved the scheme for a comprehensive biographical dictionary of persons who contributed to North American literature. Editorial work on the first volume began in January 1977, and it was published in 1978. In order to make *DLB* more than a reference tool and to compile volumes that individually have claim to status as lit-

erary history, it was decided to organize volumes by topic, period, or genre. Each of these freestanding volumes provides a biographical-bibliographical guide and overview for a particular area of literature. We are convinced that this organization—as opposed to a single alphabet method—constitutes a valuable innovation in the presentation of reference material. The volume plan necessarily requires many decisions for the placement and treatment of authors who might properly be included in two or three volumes. In some instances a major figure will be included in separate volumes, but with different entries emphasizing the aspect of his career appropriate to each volume. Ernest Hemingway, for example, is represented in *American Writers in Paris, 1920-1939* by an entry focusing on his expatriate apprenticeship; he is also in *American Novelists, 1910-1945* with an entry surveying his entire career. Each volume includes a cumulative index of subject authors and articles. Comprehensive indexes to the entire series are planned.

With volume ten in 1982 it was decided to enlarge the scope of *DLB*. By the end of 1986 twenty-one volumes treating British literature had been published, and volumes for Commonwealth and Modern European literature were in progress. The series has been further augmented by the *DLB Yearbooks* (since 1981) which update published entries and add new entries to keep the *DLB* current with contemporary activity. There have also been *DLB Documentary Series* volumes which provide biographical and critical source materials for figures whose work is judged to have particular interest for students. One of these companion volumes is entirely devoted to Tennessee Williams.

We define literature as the *intellectual commerce of a nation:* not merely as belles lettres but as that ample and complex process by which ideas are generated, shaped, and transmitted. *DLB* entries are not limited to "creative writers" but extend to other figures who in their time and in their way influenced the mind of a people. Thus the series encompasses historians, journalists, publishers, and screenwriters. By this means readers of *DLB* may be aided to perceive litera-

---

*From an unpublished section of Mark Twain's autobiography, copyright © by the Mark Twain Company.

ture not as cult scripture in the keeping of intellectual high priests but firmly positioned at the center of a nation's life.

DLB includes the major writers appropriate to each volume and those standing in the ranks immediately behind them. Scholarly and critical counsel has been sought in deciding which minor figures to include and how full their entries should be. Wherever possible, useful references are made to figures who do not warrant separate entries.

Each *DLB* volume has a volume editor responsible for planning the volume, selecting the figures for inclusion, and assigning the entries. Volume editors are also responsible for preparing, where appropriate, appendices surveying the major periodicals and literary and intellectual movements for their volumes, as well as lists of further readings. Work on the series as a whole is coordinated at the Bruccoli Clark Layman editorial center in Columbia, South Carolina, where the editorial staff is responsible for accuracy of the published volumes.

One feature that distinguishes *DLB* is the illustration policy—its concern with the iconography of literature. Just as an author is influenced by his surroundings, so is the reader's understanding of the author enhanced by a knowledge of his environment. Therefore *DLB* volumes include not only drawings, paintings, and photographs of authors, often depicting them at various stages in their careers, but also illustrations of their families and places where they lived. Title pages are regularly reproduced in facsimile along with dust jackets for modern authors. The dust jackets are a special feature of *DLB* because they often document better than anything else the way in which an author's work was perceived in its own time. Specimens of the writers' manuscripts are included when feasible.

Samuel Johnson rightly decreed that "The chief glory of every people arises from its authors." The purpose of the *Dictionary of Literary Biography* is to compile literary history in the surest way available to us—by accurate and comprehensive treatment of the lives and work of those who contributed to it.

The *DLB* Advisory Board

Foreword

In Great Britain the literary period from about 1740 to 1800 has often been called the Age of Johnson and, more recently, the Age of Hume and Johnson to acknowledge the dominating presence of that other great thinker and seminal figure, the English Johnson's Scottish counterpart. No such rubric, however, can do justice to an age so rich in literary and intellectual prose. Leo Damrosch notes that "the later eighteenth century produced some of the highest achievements in our language" and names David Hume, Edward Gibbon, Edmund Burke, Samuel Johnson, and James Boswell as respectively "the greatest British philosopher, historian, political philosopher, critic-moralist, and biographer." All these authors of the first rank appear in this volume of the *Dictionary of Literary Biography*, and they are joined by many other important writers, including Adam Smith, who might well be termed Britain's greatest economic theorist. Matthew Arnold may have slighted the eighteenth century by calling it an age of prose, an invidious and tenuous label to be sure, but even were it so, it was decidedly an age of prose giants. In that favorite paradigm of eighteenth-century theory, the notion of recurring cycles of great ages, this was surely one of those cultural apexes.

No generalization could possibly characterize the achievement of this group of "giants after the flood," as it were, and that of the many other important writers represented here. One might, however, view most of them as engaged in an effort to systematize human knowledge, to discover the basis of societies and civilizations and chart their development, and to understand human nature—all in the belief, or at least the hope, that human life is perfectible and that the idea of civilization is not merely an ideal. In any event, there are few authors featured in this volume who did not contribute to some such Enlightenment goal: besides the giants mentioned already, one would have to name Godwin, Goldsmith, Kames, Percy, Reynolds, Robertson, the Wartons, Warburton, and Wollstonecraft as salient examples, with others such as Chesterfield, Smollett, and Wesley sharing in that endeavor. And one

might single out one common thread in the systematizing of knowledge that is especially noteworthy of this period—the ordering of the arts of poetry, painting, and music. In this volume Johnson, Hawkins, Reynolds, Walpole, and Joseph and Thomas Warton were part of that effort.

Nevertheless, it is important to emphasize as well that diversity most characterizes the intellectual and artistic achievement of this whole period in the British Isles, an age traditionally spanning a century and a half, from the Restoration through the eighteenth century. It was an age of the multifaceted individual, an age when literary people were involved in affairs of state and extended their interests, and in many cases their expertise as well, into the other arts—painting, music, architecture, landscape gardening, for instance—and into fields such as science: it was a time when the notion of two cultures, one of science and the other of art, could not have been comprehended.

Nor did the typical writer specialize. Oliver Goldsmith, a major author in this book, also claims a place in the three other volumes of the *Dictionary of Literary Biography* devoted to this period—those dealing with drama, poetry, and the novel. As Samuel Johnson justly pronounced, Goldsmith touched nothing that he did not adorn. Yet Goldsmith's versatility—not to say what he adorned—is in many respects eclipsed by that of Johnson himself, whom Donald Greene identifies in this volume as "poet, dramatist, journalist, satirist, biographer, essayist, lexicographer, editor, translator, critic, parliamentary reporter, political writer, story writer, sermon writer, travel writer and social anthropologist, prose stylist, conversationalist, Christian." Johnson may have rather playfully referred to himself as a poet (at least in terms of linguistic idealism) "doomed at last to wake a lexicographer," but he did not, nor did his age, undervalue his *Dictionary of the English Language* (1755). And the versatility and range of many others represented here deserve honorable mention. No one in the eighteenth century would have thought it unusual that the great philosopher David Hume would also have published essays on everything from manners, fine taste, and tragedy to political science and economics, or that he would also have written a voluminous *History of England* (1754-1762) that would be the standard well into the next century.

Not only did many writers of this age work effectively in a variety of principal genres, but they did so in genres that in the twentieth century we may not normally think of as "literary" forms. The diary or journal, the memoir or autobiography, and the familiar letter are prominent examples. Indeed, the letter stands out in particular, for when Alexander Pope managed (with some trickery) to get his personal correspondence published, that literary event seems to have initiated a new form of belles lettres for eighteenth-century England, one that every writer would henceforth regard as a necessary accomplishment. After Pope it is rare to discover a distinguished writer in major genres who did not leave a body of correspondence well worth reading, both for what it reveals about the writer's life and times and for its high level of writing per se. Of authors represented here one thinks immediately of Horace Walpole, Lord Chesterfield, and William Cowper, as well as both Johnson and Hume. And in James Boswell one discovers not only a delightful correspondent but arguably the preeminent diarist of all time.

The familiar letter is related to an assumption about life itself that one could regard as fundamental to eighteenth-century culture. We think of this age as one in which polite and worldly values predominated—a stereotype in fact of elaborate costumes, powdered wigs, witty repartee, indeed an overall pattern of highly stylized behavior, whether in the elaboration of minuets, duels, levees, or even in the salutes and exchanges of the most ordinary personal relations: "I am, Sir, your most obedient and humble servant." There is some degree of truth in this popular image, but perhaps more of untruth. The vast majority of the population never had the chance to indulge themselves so, nor did they have any direct connection with letters and the arts, much less with high life. Moreover, could we revisit those times, we might be shocked at the repellent grossness and social ineptitude of many a lord or lady.

Still, the image does suggest something that rightly belongs to the literature of the age: namely, the assumption that life, at least ideally, should be cultivated as a fine art in itself. Thus a great deal of eighteenth-century writing is biographical in the broad sense of the term, as if it were an age of the "how-to" manual in the art of living. History in Lord Clarendon and Bishop Burnet begins as autobiography and remains almost fixated on the biographical. In Hume the "character" of any great historical figure serves to make sense of that figure's actions, to be sure, but such an analysis remains of great interest in and of itself: what lessons are there, Hume implies, about how best to live? Johnson freely admitted that the biographical part of literature was what he loved most. Moreover, he maintained that even the life of a relatively obscure man, if well told, would have immense value. In a letter to a friend he notes, "[Your uncle's] art of life certainly deserves to be known and studied. He lived in plenty and elegance upon an income which to many would appear indigent and to most, scanty. How he lived therefore every man has an interest in knowing." And in Johnson's *Lives of the Poets* (1779, 1781) the long critical biographies (say of Alexander Pope or Joseph Addison) have the "character" at their very center. The biographical first part leads into the "character," and the critical examination of the works follows it; the "character" becomes in a sense both the moral encapsulation of a life and the determinant of a writer's achievement. The same central concern about how best to live might be found throughout the nonfiction writing of this period, whether it be sermons, philosophical or political discourses, periodical essays, literary criticism, satire, or even hack journalism. The diary and the letter are but the most obvious manifestations.

As was observed in the foreword to *British Prose Writers, 1660-1800: First Series* (DLB 101), if the prose writers of the Restoration and eighteenth century are somewhat different from those of more modern times in their typical range and emphases, they are much more similar to modern writers than to their Renaissance predecessors in one important respect—prose style. That rather colloquial plain style, recommended in the later seventeenth century by the proponents of the New Philosophy (that is, what we call science), becomes almost the norm among eighteenth-century writers of prose. Jonathan Swift may have satirized its theoretical extremes, but he nonetheless wrote in a plainer style than did his mentor Sir William Temple, who, for all his allegiance to the ancients in preference to the moderns, wrote in a plainer, much more gentlemanly style than did his forebears in the Renaissance. It is true that Johnson's prose in *The Rambler* (1750-1752) might be characterized as almost baroque, although years later in his *Lives of the Poets* he wrote in much shorter, less formally structured sentences, and chose more ordinary words. In any case, if it is difficult to find many examples of plain style in the prose of the earlier seventeenth century, it is equally difficult to find a great deal of formally structured prose in the later seventeenth century and into the following one.

In many respects a down-to-earth style is the vehicle of down-to-earth ideas, and one might hazard without too much risk the argument that the prose of ideas in this period is a prose devoted in the main to the practical, the obviously useful, whether it be the examination of one's personal life and how it might best be understood and lived—the moral dimension, broadly conceived—or the pursuit of means by which it might be materially improved—the political on the one hand and the scientific and technological on the other. Once again the spirit of the empirical and the utilitarian is pervasive among the writers represented here. That great French encyclopedist Denis Diderot might be cited in this regard, because it is well to remember that the phenomenon being considered is not limited to Great Britain; it is one of the hallmarks of the Enlightenment:

> Place on one side of the scales the actual advantages of the most sublime sciences and the most honored arts, and on the other side the advantages of the mechanical arts, and you will find that esteem has not been accorded to the one and to the other in just proportion to the benefits they bring. . . . How strangely we judge! We expect everyone to pass his time in a useful manner, and we disdain useful men. . . . Let us finally render artists [that is, artisans] the justice that is their due. The liberal arts have sung their own praise long enough; they should now raise their voice in praise of the mechanical arts.

Perhaps in this statement, and indeed in many assumptions about the purpose and style of writing, we see the essential modernity of the intellectual prose of the Restoration and eighteenth century.

The reader of this volume might ask what dictated the inclusion of the writers treated here. In planning such a project, especially one limited by the constraints of volume size, an editor has to be selective. Clearly there is not room for a hundred authors, however interesting they might be in some special sense. In determining inclusion, I have asked myself the following questions as a rationale of selection: (1) has the writer produced a considerable body of significant or distinguished nonfiction prose—significant intellectually (that is, in being innovative or seminal), or otherwise distinguished by its enduring quality and effectiveness as literature (despite how meaningless a term such as "literature" might be regarded in so-called postmodern criticism); (2) has the writer been widely quoted or otherwise recognized by contemporaries or by later readers, critics, and scholars?

Another editor might well have fashioned a somewhat different table of contents from mine. In the final analysis the perception of significance is a function of those genetic and environmental determinants that make the perceiver unique, as one authority included in this volume noted long ago in very different language. Even after allowing for the variability and unreliability of our choices—in his otherwise incisive essay "Of the Standard of Taste" (1757)—David Hume poses the rhetorical question of who in his right mind could prefer John Bunyan to Joseph Addison. Among Hume's contemporaries anyone who might have preferred Bunyan would have deserved a place in the Hospital of St. Mary of Bethlehem—that is to say, Bedlam. Yet one notices in recent decades that at least as much appreciative criticism has been devoted to Bunyan as to Addison.

—Donald T. Siebert

Acknowledgments

This book was produced by Bruccoli Clark Layman, Inc. Karen L. Rood, senior editor for the *Dictionary of Literary Biography* series, was the in-house editor.

Production coordinator is James W. Hipp. Systems manager is Charles D. Brower. Photography editors are Edward Scott and Timothy Lundy. Permissions editor is Jean W. Ross. Layout and graphics supervisor is Penney L. Haughton. Copyediting supervisor is Bill Adams. Typesetting supervisor is Kathleen M. Flanagan. Information systems analyst is George F. Dodge. Charles Lee Egleston is editorial associate. The production staff includes Rowena Betts, Reginald A. Bullock, Teresa Chaney, Patricia Coate, Sarah A. Estes, Robert Fowler, Mary L. Goodwin, Ellen McCracken, Kathy Lawler Merlette, Laura Garren Moore, John Myrick, Pamela D. Norton, Cathy J. Reese, Laurrè Sinckler-Reeder, Maxine K. Smalls, and Betsy L. Weinberg.

Walter W. Ross and Timothy D. Tebalt did the library research at the Thomas Cooper Library of the University of South Carolina with the assistance of the following librarians: Gwen Baxter, Daniel Boice, Faye Chadwell, Jo Cottingham, Cathy Eckman, Rhonda Felder, Gary Geer, David L. Haggard, Jens Holley, Jackie Kinder, Thomas Marcil, Laurie Preston, Jean Rhyne, Carol Tobin, Virginia Weathers, and Connie Widney.

Dictionary of Literary Biography • Volume One Hundred Four

British Prose Writers, 1660-1800
Second Series

Dictionary of Literary Biography

James Boswell

(29 October 1740 - 19 May 1795)

John J. Burke, Jr.
University of Alabama

BOOKS: *Observations, Good or Bad, Stupid or Clever, Serious or Jocular, on Squire Foote's Dramatic Entertainment, Intituled, The Minor. By a Genius* (Edinburgh, 1760; London: Printed for J. Wilkie, 1761);

An Elegy on the Death of an Amiable Young Lady. With an Epistle from Menalcas to Lycidas [i.e., Lycidas to Menalcas] (Edinburgh: Printed by A. Donaldson & J. Reid for Alex Donaldson, 1761);

An Ode to Tragedy. By a Gentleman of Scotland (Edinburgh: Printed by A. Donaldson & J. Reid for Alex Donaldson, 1661 [i.e., 1761]);

The Cub, at Newmarket: A Tale (London: Printed for R. & J. Dodsley, 1762);

Critical Strictures on the New Tragedy of Elvira, Written by Mr. David Malloch, by Boswell, Andrew Erskine, and George Dempster (London: Printed for W. Flexney, 1763);

Letters between the Honourable Andrew Erskine, and James Boswell, Esq. (London: Printed by Samuel Chandler for W. Flexney, 1763);

Disputatio juridica, ad Tit. X. Lib. XXIII. Pand. de supellectile Jegata quam . . . publicae disquisitioni subjicit Jacobus Boswell (Edinburgh: Apud Alexandrum Kincaid, 1766);

Dorando, A Spanish Tale (London: Printed for J. Wilkie, sold also by J. Dodsley, T. Davies, and by the booksellers of Scotland, 1767);

The Essence of the Douglas Cause (London: Printed for J. Wilkie, 1767);

An Account of Corsica, the Journal of a Tour to that Island; and Memoirs of Pascal Paoli (Glasgow:

James Boswell (portrait by Sir Joshua Reynolds; National Portrait Gallery, London)

Printed by Robert & Andrew Foulis for Edward & Charles Dilly, London, 1768);

A Letter to Robert Macqueen, Lord Braxfield, on His Promotion to Be One of the Judges of the High Court of Justiciary (Edinburgh: Sold by all the booksellers, 1780);

A Letter to the People of Scotland, on the Present State of the Nation (Edinburgh: Printed & sold by all the booksellers, 1783; London: Printed for C. Dilly, 1784);

A Letter to the People of Scotland on the Alarming Attempt to Infringe the Articles of the Union, and Introduce a Most Pernicious Innovation, by Diminishing the Number of the Lords of Sessions (London: Printed for Charles Dilly, 1785);

The Journal of a Tour to the Hebrides with Samuel Johnson, LL.D. (London: Printed by Henry Baldwin for Charles Dilly, 1785);

Ode by Dr. Samuel Johnson to Mrs. Thrale, upon Their Supposed Approaching Nuptials (London: Printed for R. Faulder, 1784 [i.e., 1788]);

A Conversation between His Most Sacred Majesty George III. and Samuel Johnson, LL.D. Illustrated with observations by James Boswell, Esq. (London: Printed by Henry Baldwin for Charles Dilly, 1790);

No Abolition of Slavery; or, The Universal Empire of Love (London: Printed for R. Faulder, 1791);

The Life of Samuel Johnson, LL.D. (2 volumes, London: Printed by Henry Baldwin for Charles Dilly, 1791; revised and augmented, 3 volumes, 1793);

The Principal Corrections and Additions to the First Edition of Mr. Boswell's Life of Johnson (London: Printed for C. Dilly, 1793);

Boswelliana: The Commonplace Book of Boswell, edited by Charles Rogers (London: Grampian Club, 1874);

Private Papers of James Boswell from Malahide Castle; in the Collection of Lt.-Colonel Ralph Heyward Isham, 18 volumes: volumes 1-6 edited by Geoffrey Scott, volumes 7-18 edited by Scott and Frederick A. Pottle (Mount Vernon, N.Y.: Privately printed by W. E. Rudge, 1928-1934);

The Yale Edition of the Private Papers of James Boswell:

Boswell's London Journal, 1762-1763, edited by Pottle (New York: McGraw-Hill, 1950; London: Heinemann, 1950);

Boswell in Holland, 1763-1764, Including His Correspondence with Belle de Zuylen (Zélide), edited by Pottle (New York: McGraw-Hill, 1952; London: Heinemann, 1952);

Boswell on the Grand Tour: Germany and Switzerland, 1764, edited by Pottle (New York: McGraw-Hill, 1953; London: Heinemann, 1953);

Boswell on the Grand Tour: Italy, Corsica, and France, 1765-1766, edited by Frank Brady and Pottle (New York: McGraw-Hill, 1955; London: Heinemann, 1956);

Boswell in Search of a Wife, 1766-1769, edited by Brady and Pottle (New York: McGraw-Hill, 1956; London: Heinemann, 1957);

Boswell for the Defense, 1769-1774, edited by W. K. Wimsatt and Pottle (New York: McGraw-Hill, 1959; London: Heinemann, 1960);

Boswell's Journal of a Tour to the Hebrides with Samuel Johnson, LL.D., edited by Pottle and Charles H. Bennett (1936), revised by Pottle (New York: McGraw-Hill, 1961; London: Heinemann, 1963);

Boswell: The Ominous Years, 1774-1776, edited by Charles Ryskamp and Pottle (New York: McGraw-Hill, 1963; London: Heinemann, 1963);

Boswell in Extremes, 1776-1778, edited by Charles McC. Weis and Pottle (New York & London: McGraw-Hill, 1970; London: Heinemann, 1971);

Boswell: Laird of Auchinleck, 1778-1782, edited by Joseph W. Reed and Pottle (New York & London: McGraw-Hill, 1977);

Boswell: The Applause of the Jury, 1782-1785, edited by Irma S. Lustig and Pottle (New York & London: McGraw-Hill, 1981);

Boswell: The English Experiment, 1785-1789, edited by Lustig and Pottle (New York & London: McGraw-Hill, 1986);

Boswell: The Great Biographer, 1789-1795, edited by Marlies K. Danziger and Brady (New York & London: McGraw-Hill, 1989).

Editions: *Boswell's Life of Samuel Johnson, Together with Boswell's Journal of a Tour to the Hebrides and Johnson's Diary of a Journey into North Wales*, 6 volumes, edited by George Birkbeck Hill, revised by L. F. Powell (Oxford: Clarendon Press, 1934-1964);

The Journal of a Tour to Corsica; and Memoirs of Pascal Paoli, edited by Morchard Bishop (London: Williams & Norgate, 1951).

James Boswell is important for several reasons. His biography of Samuel Johnson is undoubtedly his most celebrated work, and for it he has traditionally been assigned pride of place among biographers. *The Life of Samuel Johnson, LL.D.* (1791) is often said to mark the boundary between old and new biography just as surely as the contemporary revolution in France marked the boundary between old and new political arrangements. But Boswell the writer did much more than just create the most significant biography in modern times. He electrified Great Britain in 1768 with an account of the revolutionary events then taking place on the Mediterranean island of Corsica and later played a significant role in helping Gen. Pasquale di Paoli set up a government in exile in London. In 1785 he enlarged the dimensions of travel literature significantly when he published his *Journal of a Tour to the Hebrides*, a work that recounts a trip he had taken with Johnson through Scotland and some of her western islands in 1773. But Boswell's most striking achievement may be the private journals that he kept during most of his adult life. They were discovered only in the twentieth century, and are only now fully published. Taken together they constitute the greatest diary ever written in English.

Apart from his stunning literary achievements, Boswell's life was often characterized by frustration and disappointment. He was born to Alexander and Euphemia Erskine Boswell in Edinburgh on 29 October 1740. He was raised in a Whiggish household that adhered to the strict Presbyterian tenets of the Church of Scotland. When he was eight the family moved to Auchinleck, the ancestral estate in the western part of the Scottish lowlands, not far from Glasgow and Ayr. When he was thirteen he entered the University of Edinburgh, where he studied for the next five years, before going on to the University of Glasgow (1759-1760). Apart from his early love of literature, there were no signs that he was an exceptional student. While at the University of Edinburgh, though, he was to meet other young men who would later play a significant part in his life, most notably William Johnston Temple and John Johnstone of Grange. The young Boswell, if anything, was far more interested in becoming a swashbuckling soldier, and his desire for a military career was only one of many youthful conflicts with his stern and proper father. Alexander Boswell, Lord Auchinleck, wanted his son to follow his own path, to become a lawyer and settle down on their ancestral estate in Ayrshire as the next laird of Auchinleck.

Young James Boswell's response to his father's demands was to flee to London, some four hundred miles to the south, first in 1762 and again in 1763. Boswell's early journals have an intoxicating sense of freedom about them. In London he became acquainted with the people who would make such a difference in his life, John Wilkes, David Garrick, Edmund Burke, Joshua Reynolds, Topham Beauclerk, Bennet Langton, and above all, Samuel Johnson. Late in the summer of 1763 Boswell moved to Holland ostensibly to study law at the University of Utrecht but

actually to be in an appropriate place for beginning a Grand Tour of the Continent that would bring him to Germany, Switzerland, Italy, Corsica, and France, and would include interviews with Jean-Jacques Rousseau, Voltaire, and Pasquale di Paoli.

Boswell returned home in 1766, shortly after his mother died, to the insistent demands from his father that he settle down. Before he could do that, though, he had to decide about a wife. He spent some time on this endeavor, finally settling his affections upon his first cousin Margaret Montgomerie. This decision may have been the best one he ever made, but from his father's point of view it was the worst. Margaret Montgomerie had barely a penny to her name. To underscore his paternal displeasure Alexander Boswell did not attend the ceremony and arranged to marry a second time, on 25 November 1769, the very day his son took Margaret for his bride. However, Margaret Boswell was to prove a loving and devoted wife, a true companion and friend to someone who would have exasperated even a saint. Together they had five children: Veronica (born in 1773), Euphemia (born in 1774), Alexander (born in 1775), James, Jr. (born in 1778), and Elizabeth (born in 1780).

Boswell's father died in 1781, and James succeeded him as laird of Auchinleck with an income that has been estimated as £1,600 a year, though most of that amount was tied up in paying for the expenses that came with the position he now had in society. The story of the rest of James Boswell's life is the story of ceaseless efforts to augment his income so that he could support his life-style and the ever-expanding needs of his five children. He enjoyed some success as a lawyer with the Scottish bar (to which he had been admitted in 1766), but the sums he earned were so modest that he determined to move himself and his family to London so that he could try his hand at the English bar (to which he was admitted in 1786). That proved to be a disastrous decision. Margaret died in 1789 from tuberculosis, and from that time on Boswell had to face life as a widower. He had enjoyed some success with the publication of his *Account of Corsica* in 1768 and *The Journal of a Tour to the Hebrides* in 1785, but neither publication brought in the kind of money that would leave him financially secure. To remedy this situation, he sought preferment. Yet, except for a brief stint as recorder for Carlisle, he failed to get a position that would bring in the additional income he so desperately

Boswell's parents: Alexander Boswell, Lord Auchinleck (painting by Allan Ramsay); and Euphemia Erskine Boswell, Lady Auchinleck (painting by an unknown artist). Both portraits are in the collection of Sir Arthur Eliott of Stobs, Bart.

needed. To be sure, there was a moment of glory in 1791 when he published his *Life of Samuel Johnson*, which had been seven years in the making. Nevertheless, Boswell's last years were by and large a gloomy affair, marked by various bouts of illness, constant financial difficulties, and psychological depression. He died in London on 19 May 1795. Three weeks later he was laid to rest in the family vault on his ancestral estate in Scotland.

Boswell did publish three major works during his lifetime, and they were sufficient to give him a measure of literary immortality. The publication of his *Account of Corsica* in 1768 first brought him to the attention of the public at large. The spirit of revolution that would become so palpable as the century came to a close was most apparent then in a backward island off the coasts of Italy and France. At that time Corsica was claimed by Genoa. However, a hardy group of native Corsicans, led by the virtuous and courageous Pasquale di Paoli, was struggling to throw off the Genoese yoke. Boswell, then only twenty-four years old, had visited with Jean-Jacques Rousseau. He was well acquainted with the conclusion to chapter 10 in part 2 of *The Social Contract*

(1762), which pointed to Corsica as a shining example of what other European countries could become if they threw off the chains of tyranny. Boswell, then on his Grand Tour, was scheduled to spend almost all of 1765 in Italy, but he could not resist the chance to go to Corsica. He wanted to see for himself what this movement of national liberation was all about. He got aboard a boat in Leghorn that brought him to the Corsican coast, then made the rugged journey into the interior. He eventually made his way to the small village of Sollacarò, where he was able to spend almost a week in Paoli's company. After returning to Britain in 1766 he began to write an account from the notes he had taken at the time; then he added some two hundred pages of Corsican history digested from the work of others; at the end he attached a sketch of his meetings and conversations with Paoli. The book was published on 18 February 1768.

Boswell's *Account of Corsica* forces us to revise some commonly mistaken notions. It is easy enough when reading or hearing about Boswell's journals to come away with the impression that he was a frivolous character who was always chasing women or getting drunk. But whatever Boswell's follies, there was clearly an underlying seriousness in his character that makes him stand out from his contemporaries in a completely admirable light. It was not unusual in the eighteenth century for a young man of Boswell's class to go on a Grand Tour of the Continent, but it certainly was unusual for a young man to take the time and trouble to visit a backwater place such as Corsica on the chance that he might find something interesting there. On such a journey Boswell had to endure primitive living conditions, extreme physical pain, and serious danger to his life. It would be hard to think of a Horace Walpole or a Thomas Gray making such a trip. However, the young James Boswell did, and the burning curiosity that drove him on remains one of his most attractive qualities.

It also becomes clear from studying this work that Boswell would have achieved some measure of renown if he had never met Samuel Johnson. We can recognize in his portrait of Paoli many of the features that were to be used to much better effect in the later *Life of Johnson*, but which still win our admiration in their early form. There are, for instance, the deft verbal portraits, with an emphasis on dramatizing his material, often with sly humor. He vividly conveys the first moments of his meeting with Paoli, which are at once naive and uneasy; only later does he reveal that Paoli at first thought the preposterous figure who had come among them was a Genoese spy. There is also his record of conversation. It is clear enough from this work that Boswell was already interested in learning how to record conversation and that he could do so creditably. There is also the matter of autobiography. In *An Account of Corsica* there is a Paoli's Boswell, just as there is a Johnson's Boswell in *The Journal of a Tour to the Hebrides* and in *The Life of Samuel Johnson*. The important thing to notice about Boswell's autobiographical portraits is that they are rhetorical. Boswell did not use his published works as a way of shamelessly flaunting himself before an uneager and uninterested world. The autobiography grounds the reality of the events in Boswell's personal experience, as is right and proper. Moreover, it provides the artistic contrast that allows us to get a better gauge of who Pasquale di Paoli is.

Boswell's *Account of Corsica* is a remarkable achievement by almost any count. It is certainly one of the few occasions when a literary figure actually shaped events in the world outside the world of letters. Boswell certainly was not able to

prevent the Genoese from crushing Paoli's rebellion. They achieved that by turning the island over to the French. Nevertheless, Boswell's book aroused considerable support for Paoli in England. He would later be given a pension of £1,200 a year by the government, and he would run a government in exile in London until his unfortunate decision to return to Corsica in 1790. If Paoli had been successful, if he had become the liberator of his people and the father of one of the first true republics in Europe, he would loom much larger today on the historical scene, and what Boswell had written about him would necessarily be of more interest. However, posterity is rarely interested in those on the losing sides of conflicts in the distant past. To a very real extent the fortunes of Boswell's first major work were tied to the declining fortunes of the man he wrote about. As Paoli has continued to shrink in significance, so too has Boswell's *Account of Corsica*.

That was not, however, to be the fate of the subject of Boswell's next major book, *The Journal of a Tour to the Hebrides with Samuel Johnson, LL.D.*, first published near the end of September 1785, some ten months after Johnson's death on 13 December 1784. *The Journal of a Tour to the Hebrides* may well be the most important single work in Boswell's canon; yet it does not have a fixed identity. It is often printed separately as a piece of travel literature, which it is. But it is also a portion of the *Life* which would be published in 1791, more than six years later, and is in fact printed as a part of the *Life* (volume 5) in the Hill and Powell edition, the single most important edition of Boswell's works. As remarkable as *The Journal of a Tour to the Hebrides* might seem to be at first, it is actually a culmination of what Boswell had been doing for years. Thanks to the documents recovered from Malahide Castle, we now know that Boswell had been keeping a journal well before he met Samuel Johnson. If we did not have his private journals, we would still know from *An Account of Corsica* that he kept a journal at times, just as we would know that he was adept at recording conversation and that he had an eye for significant details and a gift for dramatizing his materials. What is new in *The Journal of a Tour to the Hebrides* is the figure of Samuel Johnson, and that seems to have been difference enough.

But why Johnson and not someone else? To understand Boswell's attraction to Johnson, we must attend to the serious side of his character.

James Boswell (engraving by E. Finden after a portrait by G. Langton)

he was sipping tea in the room behind Tom Davies's bookshop. Their first meeting was not auspicious. Boswell was a callow youth of twenty-two and much too bent on making a good impression, while Johnson at fifty-three was not the kind to be easily impressed under the best of circumstances. He certainly was not ready to be told by a youngster, and a Scots youngster at that, how he should handle his relations with David Garrick.

The real story of their relationship probably begins with the follow-up meeting at Johnson's quarters in the Inner Temple. There the two discovered that they enjoyed one another's company, undoubtedly with Boswell seeing in Johnson the kind of father figure he had always wanted, while Johnson saw in Boswell the son he had never had. Those, of course, are overtones in their relationship, but they were never prisoners of narrow psychological roles. First and foremost, they became friends, in the deepest and truest sense of that word. For a while that friendship could only be continued by letter, because Boswell was to set off on a Grand Tour that would take him through Germany, Italy, France, and, of course, to Corsica, and therefore away from Great Britain for more than two years. When Boswell returned there was a noticeable improvement in his ability to record Johnson's conversations, something he could not do so easily at first. Recording conversation is no easy matter. It is an art that has to be learned, and one that can be improved through practice. Boswell practiced his art in his journals, and gradually got better.

His growing skill at recording conversation made the idea of a trip to Scotland by Johnson all the more pivotal. The eighteenth century, as is so often noted, was an age of travel; travel was a tool for exploration and investigation and thus an important part of the intellectual debates of the time. The thirst for knowledge could well be Johnson's most conspicuous trait, but limited by circumstances and also by poverty, he had not been able to travel to any significant extent. A trip to Scotland, and particularly to the Hebrides, offered him the opportunity to do something he had always wanted to do, to travel about and test for himself the current social theories, particularly those that argued for the superiority of primitive societies. With Boswell for a traveling companion he knew he would have somebody with him who would make the journey as enjoyable as possible. For Boswell it was an opportunity to be in Johnson's company on an uninterrupted basis. It

Boswell's initial acquaintance with Johnson was apparently through Johnson's *Rambler* papers (1750-1752), and they are not usually thought of as fare for the light-headed or light-hearted. From the beginning Johnson represented to Boswell something that he wanted and needed in his own life, a firm sense of direction, a rational control over the riotous urges of fancy and emotion. Of course, Johnson was also famous, and Boswell was always curious about the people he read and heard about. Following the publication of Johnson's *Dictionary* in 1755 Boswell heard more and more of Johnson. That is undoubtedly why he wanted to meet him as early as his first jaunt to London in 1762, and why he had asked first Thomas Sheridan and then Andrew Erskine to arrange a meeting for him. Boswell was not, of course, to meet Johnson by those means, but instead almost incidentally on 16 May 1763, while was also to be a kind of experiment. He would get to see what this literary lion would be like away from the familiar circumstances of London.

We do not know exactly when Boswell decided that his way to literary fame would be as Johnson's biographer. According to Marshall Waingrow, the first written evidence occurs in 1769 when Boswell asked Johnson if it would be all right to publish his letters after his death. Boswell first indicated that he had something far grander in mind on 31 March 1772, when he wrote in his journal: "I have decided to write Johnson's biography, but I have not told him yet." By 31 March 1772 Boswell had also obtained Johnson's agreement to come to Scotland. The journey was to be delayed, but Johnson came on 19 August 1773, after first accompanying his friend Robert Chambers to Newcastle.

Johnson's visit to Scotland was successful beyond Boswell's wildest dreams. It gave him time to know Johnson better than ever because he had 101 days in his company without any significant interruptions. It allowed him to see Johnson in a variety of circumstances: from poking about inside a smoky hut on the edge of Loch Ness to elegant dining with the duke and duchess of Argyle; from the salty company of illiterate boatmen as they sailed from isle to isle to that of cerebral university dons in Glasgow; from spirited conversations with such intellectually sophisticated figures as William Robertson and James Burnett, Lord Monboddo, to heated political arguments with Lord Auchinleck, Boswell's stubbornly Whiggish father. On land and on sea, through valleys and over mountains they traveled, but above all they talked: talked about trees, talked about turnips, talked about Ossian, talked about social theories, talked about government. It was out of the record of these days that Boswell, with help from Edmond Malone, would carve out *The Journal of a Tour to the Hebrides* that he published in 1785. More important, it was at this moment that he decided he had whatever it would take to write the "life" of Samuel Johnson. Nevertheless, writing a "life" necessarily involved a much larger scale than the limited dimensions of a "tour" or "journey," so Boswell faced an immensely more difficult and daunting task.

Boswell worked on shaping and refining his *Life of Johnson* for the better part of the six and a half years that passed between the death of Johnson on 13 December 1784 and its publication on 16 May 1791. By almost all measures it is an admirable achievement, one of the greatest books to be published in eighteenth-century England, and undoubtedly the most famous biography in the English-speaking world. It is a remarkable achievement even by what could be described as the scientific standards of biography. The basic arrangement of the *Life* is chronological, and that is because Boswell more than any other single person established the chronology of the events in Johnson's life. There have been some notable modern successes at filling in the gaps in that chronology—for example, Johnson's secret collaboration with Robert Chambers on the Vinerian Law Lectures in the late 1760s—but the basic chronology that Boswell established has not been seriously challenged. Boswell also added to the dimensions of the Johnson canon, giving emphasis to the many unsigned pieces Johnson published during his first years in London. There have been other additions to the canon. We have learned, for instance, that Johnson was responsible for the sections on foreign books and foreign history in the *Gentleman's Magazine*, that he wrote electoral addresses for Henry Thrale, and that he helped Bishop Thomas Percy with the *Reliques of Ancient English Poetry* (1765). None of these, however, have substantially altered our picture of his interests and achievements, though they have enlarged it.

Boswell's *Life* also contains a substantial collection of Johnson's letters, 344 in all. This is particularly important to Boswell's method because he had claimed that he adopted the example of William Mason in his *Memoirs of the Life and Writings of Thomas Gray* (1775)—that is, he intended to let Johnson speak in his own voice so that where and when possible he would be telling his own story. This is a clear advantage, for instance, over Sir John Hawkins, who, though he quoted generously from Johnson's writings in his biography, quoted only sparingly from letters because he had so few to quote from. In 1788, the year after Hawkins's biography appeared, Hester Thrale Piozzi published an edition of Johnson's letters, mostly to herself. Boswell's contribution would of course include a generous number of letters to and from himself, but it also includes many letters to and from other correspondents, including the well-known letter to Philip Dormer Stanhope, Lord Chesterfield, as well as letters to and from Bennet Langton, Charles Burney, Sir Joshua Reynolds, and Thomas Warton, among others. The fact that he could publish these letters is powerful testimony about his industry and his diligence.

(568.)

this morning with the illustrious
Donaldson. In the evening I went
to Temple's; he brought me ac:
quainted with a Mr Claxton a
very good sort of a young man tho
reserved at first. Mr Nicholos was
there too. Our conversation was
sensible & lively. I wish I could
spend my time allways in such company.

Monday 16 May.
Temple & his Brother breakfas:
ted with me. I went to Love's
to try to recover some of the mo:
ney which he owes me. But alas
a single guinea was all I could
get. He was just going to dinner,
so I stayed & eat a bit; tho' I was
angry at myself afterwards.
I drank tea at Davies's in Russ:
el Street and about seven came
in the great Mr Samuel John:
son, whom I have so long wished
to see. Mr Davies introduced
me to him. As I knew his mortal
antipathy at the Scotch, I said
to

Description of Boswell's first meeting with Samuel Johnson, from Boswell's journal entry for 16 May 1763 (Yale University Library)

(569)

to Davies; don't tell where I come
from. However he said From Scotland.
Mr Johnson said I indeed I come
from Scotland, but I cannot help
it. Sir replied he. That I find
is what a very great many of
your countrymen cannot help.
Mr Johnson is a man of a most
dreadfull appearance. He is a
very big man is troubled with sore
eyes, the Palsy & the King's
evil. He is very slovenly in
his dress & speaks with a
most uncouth voice. yet his
great knowledge, and strength
of expression command vast
respect and render him very
excellent company. He has
great humour and is a worthy
man. But his dogmatical rough:
:ness of manners is disagreable.

Boswell's *Life of Johnson*, like any biography, is basically a record of facts. The excellence of a biography is measured first by the accuracy with which it records the facts of its subject's life. It must, however, be more than accurate; it must also be full; that is, it must record all the facts that we would want to know. To assess Boswell's *Life of Johnson* as a record of facts properly requires an understanding of the nature of the task Boswell faced as he set out to account for the whole of Johnson's life. Boswell was certainly acquainted with him during the later part of his life, but he had no personal knowledge of Johnson during his early years or even when he first became a celebrated public figure.

The first problem then was lack of information on the period of Johnson's life before Boswell met him in 1763. Johnson's early years were particularly obscure. Since only about one-fifth of the *Life* is devoted to the first fifty-three years of Johnson's life, which included his schooling up through his thirteen months at Pembroke College, Oxford, his several failed attempts at finding a way to earn a living, his marriage to the widowed Elizabeth Porter, his early literary successes, his triumph as a public figure with the *Dictionary*, and the granting of his pension, it is clear enough that Boswell did not fully succeed with the task he had set for himself. Modern scholars have understandably focused on the early and middle years as the areas where the Boswellian record might be improved, and they have drawn attention to some obvious gaps and occasional mistakes.

It has been argued, and argued rightly, that we do not learn all we might need to know or all we would like to know about Johnson from the pages of Boswell's biography. Certainly we have only an imperfect notion of how Johnson was formed by family life, what his relationships must or could have been with his father, Michael; his mother, Sarah; and his brother, Nathaniel. It is also true that we have little sense of Johnson as a married man, though he was married for more than seventeen years. We can develop a somewhat better sense of his intellectual development, but even here there is much more that we would like to know. Boswell reported correctly that Johnson had left Oxford before taking a degree, but he did make a mistake in relying on information he had received from the Reverend William Adams, who was the master of Pembroke College when Boswell knew him. As a result Boswell left the young Samuel Johnson at Pembroke for "lit-

tle more than three years," when, according to the information supplied by Pembroke's buttery books, Johnson actually resided at Oxford for only thirteen months before returning to Lichfield. There are mistakes in Boswell's *Life*, but they are not numerous. More important, what mistakes there are not of the kind that would dramatically alter our understanding of Johnson.

What is all too easily forgotten when enumerating Boswell's relatively few lapses is how much he got right. Just how much he did get right becomes readily apparent when Boswell's work is compared with that of other of his contemporaries. Between Johnson's death on 13 December 1784 and the publication of Boswell's *Life* on 16 May 1791, roughly sixteen biographical accounts of Johnson were published. At least two of them—Hester Thrale Piozzi's *Anecdotes of the Late Samuel Johnson*, published in 1786, and Sir John Hawkins's *Life of Samuel Johnson*, published in 1787—can be considered major works. If we compare what we learn from them about Johnson's early years, including how long he attended Pembroke College, we quickly see that Boswell stands out as the most reliable of the early biographers. We learn about his family—father, mother, and brother—from all the major biographers. We learn from each of them, for instance, that young Samuel contracted scrofula from his wet nurse and that his mother brought him to London so that he could be touched by the queen. But both Hawkins and Piozzi repeat the story of a three-year-old child prodigy composing verses on a duck, while we learn from Boswell that the verses were really composed by Johnson's father. Hester Thrale Piozzi retells some anecdotes about Johnson's days at Oxford but is vague about the details of his residence there, while Sir John Hawkins leaves Johnson at Oxford just as long as Boswell did. Hawkins noted that Johnson had left Oxford for Lichfield in December of 1729, but he was sure that he had returned to Oxford and "made up the whole of his residence in the university, about three years." If Boswell is occasionally unreliable, so are his chief rivals. It is in the early years that modern scholars have been most successful in adding to and completing the Boswellian record, but that is largely because the Boswellian record has always been so reliable to begin with.

Johnson's middle years represent a different problem. The middle years refer to the time when Johnson became a public figure and acquired the reputation of being the greatest liter-

Boswell in Rome, 1765 (painting by George Willison; Scottish National Portrait Gallery)

ary figure in England, in other words, the time of *The Rambler* (1750-1752) and the *Dictionary* (1755), of *Rasselas* (1759) and *The Idler* (1758-1760). The middle years are usually dated from 1749, the year when Johnson published *The Vanity of Human Wishes*, the first publication to have his name on the title page, to the year 1763, when he first met Boswell. Boswell was not, of course, personally acquainted with Johnson during those years either, but many of the people he knew best were, and he relied upon them for accurate information. This is part of the importance, for instance, of Sir Joshua Reynolds, Frank Barber, Oliver Goldsmith, David Garrick, Dr. Charles Burney, Arthur Murphy, William Maxwell, Topham Beauclerk, and Bennet Langton. Boswell collected information from each of these, and fleshed out his record with their testimony.

Boswell's method can be illustrated in his reconstruction of the events that led up to Johnson's quarrel with Lord Chesterfield just be-

fore the publication of his *Dictionary* on 15 April 1755. The origins of that quarrel were in Johnson's dedication of his original *Plan of a Dictionary* to Lord Chesterfield in August 1747. Johnson, young and still relatively unknown, hungry and poor, undoubtedly expected further interest and favors for his work from the earl. Chesterfield meanwhile believed that he had shown all the interest and encouragement that was appropriate with a gift of ten pounds to the starving author. Somehow, contrary to expectations, Johnson pushed on and eventually completed his work on the *Dictionary*, and according to all the reports had completed it brilliantly. The earl of Chesterfield, hearing those reports, and with a clear and distinct memory of the dedication of the *Plan* still in his head, near the end of 1754 composed two highly flattering essays on the approaching publication of Johnson's *Dictionary* for a periodical called the *World*. Johnson responded to the essays in the *World* with his now-famous letter rejecting Lord Chesterfield's flatteries as belated attempts to have the *Dictionary* dedicated to him: "Is not a Patron, my Lord, one who looks with unconcern on a man struggling for life in the water, and, when he has reached ground, encumbers him with help?"

To appreciate Boswell's achievement in this account we need only compare his version with the mangled versions we find in all other contemporary biographies. All of Johnson's first biographers were aware that there had been a serious quarrel between Johnson and Lord Chesterfield, and most of them knew that there had been some kind of letter, though they were not sure when the letter was sent, nor what it said. Almost everybody believed that the quarrel had been started when Lord Chesterfield had snubbed Johnson for Colley Cibber, a man with a reputation as the prince of dunces. Some of the early biographers, though not all, mention the publication of the two essays in the *World*, but for the most part they thought the essays were published after the quarrel rather than before it. This led them to see the essays in the *World* as Lord Chesterfield's failed attempt to patch up the quarrel, whereas actually they were what triggered it. The principal source for Boswell's account in the *Life* is unimpeachable because it was Johnson himself. He denied that Lord Chesterfield had ever preferred Colley Cibber before him, and in fact denied that there had ever been a single incident that had brought about the rupture between them. It was Boswell who persuaded Johnson to dictate from memory a copy of the letter he had written to Lord Chesterfield in the first week of February 1755 repudiating his patronage. It was Boswell who first published that letter along with suitable excerpts from Lord Chesterfield's essays in the *World*. Boswell fleshed out some of the details from Johnson's friend the Reverend William Adams, who was residing in London at the time. He may also have relied on, directly or indirectly, Robert Dodsley, who played a part, too, in these events. It is much in the same vein that he reconstructed other key events during Johnson's middle years, such as the death of his wife and the awarding of his pension.

If Boswell as Johnson's biographer had done no more than what he did for Johnson's early and middle years, he would undoubtedly have won some form of immortality. But it is his account of the later years, the last twenty-one years of Johnson's life, that earned him literary greatness and forever changed the meaning of

Pasquale di Paoli, leader of the Corsican independence movement (engraving by John Raphael Smith, from a painting commissioned by Boswell from Henry Benbridge). Paoli's conversations with Boswell during his visit to Corsica in October and November 1765 inspired Boswell to write An Account of Corsica.

what constitutes a biography. He did this because of his record of conversations, the most celebrated part of his *Life of Johnson* and Boswell's most distinctive contribution to the art of biography. Any just estimate of his artistic stature must make this a center of concern because here Boswell was doing what nobody else had ever done. It is not even an exaggeration to add that this part of his achievement has never yet been matched, and that it may not ever be done so well again.

The key to Boswell's ability to record conversation was his habit of keeping a journal. Often but not always he would write up daily accounts of what had happened to him. He had begun recording conversation before he ever met Johnson. One of the most memorable moments in the *London Journal* occurs in January of 1763. Boswell, after gaining all that he had wished from an actress he calls "Louisa," discovers that he has a bad case of gonorrhea. He is at once angry, frustrated, and deflated by the realization that he had been deceived. He decides that he must confront Louisa and make her face her guilt. He records the moment of that confrontation in his journal as a dialogue or conversation between the two of them.

Of course, he also recorded his first meeting with Johnson on 16 May 1763 in his journal. What we see in the journal are the elements of what will later appear in the *Life* in more polished form. According to the *London Journal*:

> I drank tea at Davies's in Russell Street, and about seven came in the great Mr. Samuel Johnson, whom I have so long wished to see. Mr. Davies introduced me to him. As I knew his mortal antipathy at the Scotch, I cried to Davies, "Don't tell where I come from." However, he said, "From Scotland." "Mr. Johnson," said I, "indeed I come from Scotland, but I cannot help it." "Sir," replied he, "that, I find, is what a very great many of your countrymen cannot help."

Boswell goes on to describe Johnson's "dreadful appearance" and to register his distaste for his "dogmatical roughness of manners," but then goes on to record what he remembers of Johnson's conversation on that day. What he has recorded consists of Johnson talking about how much authors are like other men and how little real distinction they enjoy in modern times; a favorable but qualified comment on *The Elements of Criticism* (1762) by Henry Home, Lord Kames; his dislike of some of the recent behavior of John Wilkes; his distaste for the cant of liberty; and brief critical comments on both Thomas Sheridan and Samuel Derrick.

Changes were made when this entry was transferred into the *Life of Johnson*. Most noticeably, the remarks about Johnson's unpleasant, even frightening, appearance have been eliminated and replaced by a statement about how much Sir Joshua Reynolds's portrait of Johnson had prepared him for his first glimpse of the living man. What may be more significant is that there is no explicit statement expressing Boswell's resentment against his dogmatic roughness. The preparation for their first exchange is more elaborate, with a greater effort at painting the scene, establishing, for instance, a dramatic parallel with *Hamlet* to fix such nonverbal elements as tone, gesture, and expression.

> At last, on Monday the 16th of May, when I was sitting in Mr. Davies's back-parlour, after having drunk tea with him and Mrs. Davies, Johnson unexpectedly came into the shop; and Mr. Davies having perceived him through the glass-door in the room in which we were sitting, advancing towards us,—he announced his aweful approach to me, somewhat in the manner of an actor in the part of Horatio, when he addresses Hamlet on the appearance of his father's ghost, "Look, my Lord, it comes."
>
> . . . .
>
> Mr. Davies mentioned my name, and respectfully introduced me to him. I was much agitated; and recollecting his prejudice against the Scotch, of which I had heard much, I said to Davies, "Don't tell where I come from."—"From Scotland," cried Davies, roguishly. "Mr. Johnson, (said I) I do indeed come from Scotland, but I cannot help it." I am willing to flatter myself that I meant this as a light pleasantry to sooth and conciliate him, and not as a humiliating abasement at the expence of my country. But however that might be, this speech was somewhat unlucky; for with that quickness of wit for which he was so remarkable he seized the expression "come from Scotland," which I used in the sense of being of that country; and, as if I had said that I had come away from it, or left it, retorted, "That, Sir, I find, is what a very great many of your countrymen cannot help."

This more polished version illustrates something important about Boswell's record of conversation. It can be naively thought that for the Boswellian record to pass muster, Boswell had to have functioned as a kind of eighteenth-century tape recorder, and that only the words, the very words that Johnson and his interlocutors spoke can be accepted as an accurate and authentic account of what actually happened. But that would be a naive view of conversation in general and of Boswell's record of Johnson's conversation in particular. A transcript of any ordinary, everyday conversation in the eighteenth century would not look like the polished dialogue in an eighteenth-century play. Sentences in conversation are not always perfectly formed, and diction is often far from exact. There are pauses, stumblings, coughs, throat clearings, smiles. Much of the meaning in most spoken exchanges is in fact conveyed by nonverbal means, through the eyes, movements of the head, and gestures with the hands. None of these can appear as such on the printed page.

Moreover, even if it were possible to have a completely faithful transcript of a conversation, the bare printed words could easily be subject to misinterpretation. Part of what we notice when we compare the version in the *Journal* with the version in the *Life* are the efforts Boswell makes to see that neither he nor Johnson is misinterpreted. He wants to assure his fellow Scots that he was not slighting his native land when he begged Tom Davies not to tell Johnson that he was from Scotland. He also provides commentary on Johnson's reply to show it as an example of wit rather than of dogmatic roughness. The adverb "roguishly" is added to Davies's reply, and helps us better catch the tone of teasing that evidently was part of the interaction between Boswell and Tom Davies.

The rest of the entry is more interesting. It reveals that from the very start, even one as inauspicious as this, Boswell is captivated by Johnson's talk and feels compelled to record what he said, but not all of what he said. Johnson walked in at seven, and Boswell was forced to leave at ten because of a prior appointment. What appears in Boswell's journal clearly does not represent three hours of conversation. The art of recording conversation necessarily begins with selection and requires judgment from the recorder. The six topics Boswell recorded at their first meeting reflect what he found most interesting in those three hours of talk. Lord Kames, a Scotsman who sat with Boswell's father on the Court of Sessions, was clearly one of them. It is worth noting the slight modifications in this entry as it passed from his journal into the text of the *Life*. In the journal what reads as "Lord Kames's *Elements* is a pretty essay and deserves to be held in some estimation, though it is chimerical" becomes " 'Sir, this book ("The Elements of Criticism," which he had taken up,) is a pretty essay, and deserves to be held in some estimation, though much of it is chimerical.' " In the later version Boswell tells us that Johnson "had taken up" a copy of Lord Kames's *Elements of Criticism* before making his remark. This added touch provides us with a context that tells us how Kames's book became a topic of conversation. He also has the words "much of " before "it is chimerical," undoubtedly having noticed that there would be no good reason to hold it "in some estimation" if the book were totally chimerical. There might be some who would argue that such changes are distortions of the original record, but it seems more reasonable to see them as part of an honest effort to provide a faithful record of what was actually said.

It is also worth noting that John Wilkes was one of the topics of conversation at this first meeting between Johnson and Boswell. Earlier in his journal, Boswell had mentioned having seen Wilkes, but he had not yet actually met and talked with him. He would do that for the first time eight days later, on 24 May 1763, and he would find himself completely charmed by Wilkes. On 16 May 1763, however, Wilkes was a topic of conversation because of the attacks he had been making upon the royal family in the *North Briton*. Boswell had been following these events and had even gone out on one occasion to observe the commotion Wilkes was causing, so he was bound to be interested in what Johnson had to say on these matters. It seems prescient that Wilkes should figure so immediately in the relationship between the two men, given the fairly large part he would later play in both their lives and given the very large one he would play in the greatest single scene in the *Life of Johnson*.

What the record in the *London Journal* indicates is that Boswell had already acquired considerable skill in recording conversation but that he was not yet at the peak of his ability in this difficult art. After presenting us with his record of Johnson's conversation during June and early July of 1763, he says: "Let me here apologize for the imperfect manner in which I am obliged to exhibit Johnson's conversation. In the early part of my acquaintance with him, I was so wrapt in admiration of his extraordinary colloquial talents, and so little accustomed to his peculiar mode of expression, that I found it extremely difficult to recollect and record his conversation with its genuine vigour and vivacity. In progress of time, when my mind was, as it were, *strongly impregnated with the Johnsonian aether*, I could with much more facility and exactness carry in my memory and commit to paper the exuberant variety of his wisdom and wit."

Boswell did gain more facility and exactness as time went on, in part because of his habit of writing down the important events of each day in his journal and in part because he grew accustomed to Johnson's characteristic manner of speaking. The transition from journeyman to master would occur during the 101 days they spent together when touring Scotland and her western islands in 1773. During that time Boswell let Johnson read what he was writing in his journal. He tells us that Johnson made a few small corrections but for the most part seemed genuinely impressed with Boswell's record of his talk and satisfied with its accuracy. Boswell's full mastery of the art of recording conversation is probably seen most

James and Margaret Boswell with their three eldest children, Alexander, Veronica, and Euphemia (painting by Henry Singleton; Scottish National Portrait Gallery)

easily in the unusually full record he kept during 1778. Here he is not just recording Johnson talking, or even two speakers talking with one another, but actually recording the conversation of several speakers. On 9 April 1778, for instance, he and Johnson dined at Sir Joshua Reynolds's, where the guests included Dr. Shipley, the Bishop of St. Asaph, and Allan Ramsay, who had just returned from a trip to Italy where he had visited Horace's villa. Here is Boswell's rendition of how the conversation evolved:

The Bishop said, it appeared from Horace's writings that he was a cheerful contented man. JOHNSON. "We have no reason to believe that, my Lord. Are we to think Pope was happy, because he says so in his writings? We see in his writings what he wishes the state of his mind to appear. Dr. Young, who pined for preferment, talks with contempt of it in his writings, and affects to despise every thing that he did not despise." BISHOP OF ST. ASAPH. "He was like other chaplains, looking for vacancies: but that is not peculiar to the clergy. I remember when I was with the army, after the battle of Lafeldt, the

officers seriously grumbled that no general was killed." BOSWELL. "How hard is it that man can never be at rest." RAMSAY. "It is not in his nature to be at rest. When he is at rest, he is in the worst state that he can be in; for he has nothing to agitate him."

This picture of civilized talk is a large part of the reason Boswell's *Life of Johnson* has entranced generation after generation of readers. It is in fact so graceful and so entrancing that it is easy to forget just how much skill was necessary to record it and then render it in a way that would be comprehensible to people who were not there.

There are other features which set Boswell's *Life of Johnson* apart and which belong more to its art than to its science. One of these is Boswell's Boswell. This refers to the Boswell who appears as a character in the *Life*, a Boswell that is quite different from Boswell the narrator or Boswell the author of the *Life*. To those who feel that it is the biographer's duty to efface him- or herself from the biography in the interests of objectivity, Boswell's method of including himself in the story will seem to be little more than an exercise in vanity, the biographer using the biography as a means for drawing attention to himself. But a careful look at when and how Boswell appears in the *Life* reveals that Boswell's Boswell is intended to serve the interests of objectivity. Boswell, after all, was part of Johnson's *Life*, and his presence is a reminder of his credentials for writing this biography, for he is someone who, in Johnson's words, "had eaten," "drunk," and "lived in social intercourse" with the subject about whom he was writing, as Johnson had required he should. If conversations were to be presented as taking place between people, the interlocutors were often enough Johnson and Boswell. The conversations are more meaningful because we hear them as exchanges between two very different men whom we have come to know in the process of reading the book. Boswell often disagrees with Johnson, in his opinion on Henry Fielding, or on slavery, or on the justice of the American cause, but those disagreements are important too. They help us to mark the boundary between Boswell and Johnson, and reassure us that Boswell has made an effort to be objective, that the Johnson he presents to us is not a Johnson who simply thinks and acts like himself.

Another creative aspect of Boswell's *Life* is revealed in those moments when Boswell's very presence produces something that might not otherwise have taken place. This can be as small and as trivial as Boswell asking Johnson why a fox's tail is bushy, or as large and revealing as coaxing Johnson into stating his serious thoughts on marriage or government. For lack of a better word, these could be called Boswell's "experiments" referring to events arranged by Boswell, events that would not have occurred if he had not been there, but because he was there and did arrange them they became part of Johnson's biography. Boswell's tactics were not without their risk, but when they do work they represent the grandest moments of the *Life*. The tour of Scotland and the Hebrides could, in fact, be described as one grand experiment. Johnson would never have made that trip if Boswell had not made the arrangements and graciously served as his host and traveling companion. And who would want to argue that the life and the *Life* of Johnson are not the richer for the 101 days he spent in Scotland?

All of these features, those that belong to the art of the *Life*, are clearly evident in one of the supreme moments in Boswell's biography, the meeting between Johnson and Wilkes at Dilly's on 15 May 1776. This moment in the *Life* proceeded from a kind of scientific curiosity on Boswell's part, a desire to see what would happen if he put one element of a possibly explosive compound into contact with another. It was necessarily a high-risk strategy. It was always possible that an experiment might blow up in his face. He experienced a taste of what might happen when on 22 September 1777 he had unwisely expressed a desire to see Johnson and the Whiggish Catharine Macaulay together. Johnson had turned on him with a stinging rebuke, "No, Sir, you would not see us quarrel, to make you sport. Don't you know that it is very uncivil to *pit* two people against one another?"

The possibility of an explosive quarrel in a meeting between Johnson and Wilkes was even more palpable. As Boswell himself says of them without much exaggeration, "two men more different could perhaps not be selected out of all mankind": Johnson the sturdy Tory, Wilkes the arch-Whig; Johnson the stoic, Wilkes the epicurean; Johnson the moralist and devout believer, Wilkes the rake, thoroughly secular and almost certainly an agnostic. Moreover, the differences between the two had taken a sharply personal turn in the past. Wilkes had had little difficulty turning Johnson's eccentricities into ridicule, while Johnson had leveled an attack of breathtaking ferocity on Wilkes and his supporters in *The False Alarm*, a political pamphlet he had published in 1770. Incredible as it may seem, Boswell had been on very friendly terms with both men for more than a decade, and somehow had managed to keep these two different parts of his life totally separate. Now, however, he conceived, as he says, "an irresistible wish" to bring the two of them together.

Boswell set about his task as though he were writing a script, though it was a script where the denouement could not be foreseen. A chance had come his way when he learned that his friend Edward Dilly would be hosting a dinner to which Wilkes had been invited. Boswell then persuaded Dilly to invite Johnson to the dinner too. Once he had the invitation in hand, he then had to persuade Johnson to attend, and that was no easy task. His strategy was to play upon the pride Johnson took in his good manners, slyly suggesting that Johnson might not want to attend a dinner where there might be people in attendance he did not like. Johnson caught the innuendo exactly as Boswell had hoped he would,

Engravings from Thomas Rowlandson's Picturesque Beauties of Boswell *(1786), caricatures illustrating passages from Boswell's* Journal of a Tour to the Hebrides*: Boswell at Auchinleck; Samuel Johnson and Boswell beginning their tour, accompanied by Boswell's manservant, Joseph Ritter; Boswell doing a Highland dance; Johnson discovering Boswell with a headache after a night of drinking, and commenting, "What, drunk yet?"; Boswell holding a rope to keep him out of the sailors' way during a storm; Boswell's father and Johnson exchanging Whig and Tory views on Oliver Cromwell and Charles I (Boswell reports the argument as heated but nonviolent)*

and quickly responded that he would never be so ill-mannered as to dictate who the other guests might be.

At this point all was going according to script. But when Boswell appeared at Johnson's door on the evening of the dinner party he found that Johnson had forgotten about the invitation from Dilly and had agreed instead to have dinner with his housemate, the blind Anna Williams. All seemed lost. Boswell, though, ever resourceful, begged permission from the peevish Mrs. Williams for Johnson to attend the dinner at Dilly's. When she gave it, Johnson called out for a clean shirt, and Boswell had regained the victory he had just been about to lose.

Total triumph, however, was not yet in hand. The most dangerous moment lay ahead at Dilly's. When Johnson entered the room he realized immediately he did not fit in with the company. As soon as he caught sight of Wilkes, he picked up a book and withdrew. A breakthrough only became possible when dinner was announced. At this point Boswell lets himself disappear from the picture and keeps our eyes on the two major actors. Wilkes sat down next to Johnson and started to win him over by helping him to some fine veal, a process Boswell dramatizes vividly in the following conversation: " 'Pray give me leave, Sir:—It is better here—A little of the brown—Some fat, Sir—A little of the stuffing—Some gravy—Let me have the pleasure of giving you some butter—Allow me to recommend a squeeze of this orange;—or the lemon, perhaps, may have more zest'—'Sir, Sir, I am obliged to you, Sir,' cried Johnson, bowing, and turning his head to him with a look for some time of 'surly virtue,' but, in a short while, of complacency."

Boswell has just brought off the most brilliant truce, as Edmund Burke would say, in the history of world diplomacy. The scene continues for several more pages, and Boswell records the various topics of their conversation, the buffoonery of Foote, Garrick's reputation for avarice, the interpretation of a difficult line in Horace, jokes about Scotland, and a considerable amount of kidding at Boswell's expense. Finally, the tables are completely turned when Johnson gets in some sly pokes at the libertine life-styles of both Boswell and Wilkes: " 'You must know, Sir, I lately took my friend Boswell and shewed him genuine civilised life in an English provincial town. I turned him loose at Lichfield, my native city, that he might see for once real civility: for you know he lives among savages in Scotland, and among

rakes in London.' WILKES. 'Except when he is with grave, sober, decent people like you and me.' JOHNSON (smiling). 'And we ashamed of him.' "

Not only is this arguably Boswell at his best, it is also an instance of when the phrase "Boswell's Johnson" has its most accurate meaning. The meeting between Johnson and Wilkes would never have taken place if Boswell had not been there to arrange it. Thus in a very real sense he was not only recording Johnson's life: he was actually creating it. It seems fair enough to say that Johnson surprises us with his good-natured response and by the resourcefulness with which he turns the tables on his creator. It is clear enough that Boswell's purpose in this scene is not to draw attention to himself, but to help us see something that is very much to Johnson's credit.

The achievement of the *Life* is realized in moments such as the dinner with Wilkes, but it can also be experienced in its cumulative effect. The chief virtue of the *Life* is its variety, a sense of roundedness, a sense that if we can ever come to know a fellow human being through a book, we have come to know Samuel Johnson through Boswell's great biography. It has been said that Boswell's *Life* leads us to hero worship, but that of course is nonsense. There are too many moments—Johnson quarreling, Johnson whining, Johnson being grumpy, Johnson acting strangely—when Boswell's Johnson is in short merely acting like the rest of us. The obverse argument is that Boswell's *Life* subtly debunks Johnson, making him look narrow-minded and foolish when he was no such thing. These critics lay particular stress on the seeming emphasis in the *Life* on Johnson's explosive High Church zeal or his hot-headed Toryism.

But it ought to be crystal clear that Boswell's purpose was no more to discredit Johnson than it was to exalt him beyond the dimensions of the human. Being human can mean being thoughtful, kind, warm, and generous, but it can also mean being testy, grouchy, inconsiderate, lazy, and selfish. Boswell's Johnson is by turn all of these because Boswell wanted to present him to us as fully human. The nature of Boswell's intentions in the *Life* can perhaps be clarified by the testimony of Fanny Burney, someone who is not likely to be numbered among his admirers. She recorded in her diaries a moment when, much to her embarrassment, Boswell approached her, hoping to secure her help for the biography

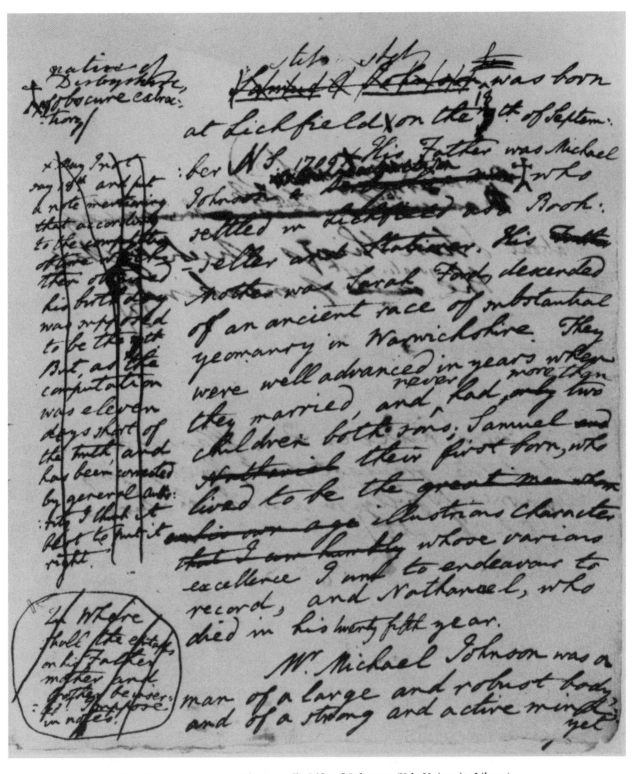

Page from the manuscript for Boswell's Life of Johnson *(Yale University Library)*

he was then writing: "Yes, madam; you must give me some of your choice little notes of the Doctor's; we have seen him long enough upon stilts; I want to show him a new light. Grave Sam, and great Sam, and solemn Sam, and learned Sam,— all these he has appeared over and over. Now I want to entwine a wreath of the graces across his brow; I want to show him as gay Sam, agreeable Sam, pleasant Sam; so you must help me with some of his beautiful billets to yourself." These are not the words of a debunking biographer nor are they the words of a hero worshiper. They serve rather as unambiguous evidence about Boswell's intentions in the *Life*. Fanny Burney's testimony on this matter is all the more persuasive both because she is recording an exchange that had taken place spontaneously and because it was recorded by someone who was not at all friendly to Boswell's interests.

The Life of Johnson was the last work to be published by Boswell during his lifetime, and the one most responsible for his enduring literary reputation. Yet Boswell's reputation in the twentieth century is no longer tied to a single work, and that is the result of one of the most astounding stories in the annals of literary scholarship. As Richard Altick retells the story in *The Scholar Adventurers* (1950), one day in 1850 in the French town of Boulogne-sur-mer an English gentleman otherwise unknown to history came away from a small shop with some purchases wrapped in old paper. When unwrapping one of the parcels he happened to notice the name of James Boswell was signed to the end of a letter. This chance occurrence was to lead to the publication in 1856 of Boswell's letters to the Reverend William Temple, and the revelation of a James Boswell who existed quite apart from his role as the biographer of Samuel Johnson.

Just how much of that James Boswell existed would become even more visible with further discoveries. When Boswell died in 1795 he had left behind an enormous store of papers. He had appointed the Reverend William Temple, Edmond Malone, and Sir William Forbes as his literary executors and had left them the charge of determining what if anything from this huge store of papers could be published for the benefit of his children. Some of those papers were stored at the Boswell home in Auchinleck, and a part of them in an ebony cabinet mentioned in Boswell's will. Others were stored at the home of Sir William Forbes, who after he had examined them under the terms of the will had kept them

by him, and never had an opportunity to return them to Auchinleck. Wherever the papers were, though, they were inaccessible to outsiders.

Eventually the papers stored at Auchinleck, including those in the ebony cabinet, were moved to Ireland, to Malahide Castle just outside of Dublin, where the last direct descendant of James Boswell had taken up residence. In 1927 James Boswell Talbot, sixth Lord Talbot de Malahide, agreed to sell the Boswell papers in his possession to Lt. Col. Ralph Heyward Isham, an American collector, with the understanding that the papers would be kept together and would be published in a dignified scholarly edition. This original purchase included some of Boswell's letters and a few leaves from the manuscript version of the *Life*, but most important were the journals that Boswell had kept for almost thirty-three years. These would form the basis of the elegant eighteen-volume edition of *Private Papers of James Boswell* that was privately printed for Colonel Isham between 1928 and 1934.

But even as Isham's edition was going forward under the editorship first of Geoffrey Scott and then of Frederick Pottle, new discoveries were being made. In April 1930 the Talbot family discovered more papers in a croquet box, papers that included the manuscript version of Boswell's *Journal of a Tour to the Hebrides*. Later in the same year Claude Colleer Abbott, working independently of all the others, came across a new cache of Boswell papers at Fettercairn House in Kincardineshire, nowhere near the ancestral Boswell home at Auchinleck. A substantial portion of Boswell's papers had come to be stored at Fettercairn because this house had become the residence of the direct descendants of Sir William Forbes, one of the three men Boswell had named as his literary executors, and who had physical possession of some of the papers. Abbott came upon hundreds of letters, originals and copies, that testify to Boswell's vast correspondence. Among them were the letters of Temple to Boswell, the other side of the correspondence that had been found in Boulogne in 1850. There were also letters from Johnson to various correspondents. And, perhaps most important, the manuscript of what would become known as *Boswell's London Journal, 1762-1763*, thus bridging what had been an awkward gap in the documentary record.

There is a gap in the chronology here that had awkward implications for modern scholarship. Though Abbott made these discoveries in the late fall and early winter of 1930, he did not make them public until 1936. This delay was going to prove embarrassing to two monuments of modern scholarship, Colonel Isham's edition of the *Private Papers* and the Hill and Powell edition of Boswell's *Life*. Both had in good faith represented themselves as the latest in Boswell scholarship, but the latest in Boswell scholarship was without their knowledge already something different from what they were presenting to the public because of the new discoveries at Fettercairn.

Incredibly enough, the story of these discoveries does not even end here. In March 1937 Colonel Isham, with permission from the Talbots, made another search of the residence at Malahide and came upon more papers in a tin dispatch box. This find included Johnson's diary and the register of the letters Boswell had sent and received between 1782 and 1790. In the fall of 1940 the Talbots were to find yet more Boswell papers, this time stored in the hayloft of an old barn that had not been used for more than twenty years. This find recovered a large number of letters, including more letters from Temple to Boswell, and the sketch Boswell had written of his own life for Rousseau in Switzerland in 1764.

Colonel Isham somehow managed to keep the collection of the Boswell papers intact, in spite of the financial hardships brought on by the constant stream of new discoveries and the burden of the complex legal wranglings that were to follow. In 1949 Colonel Isham turned his collection over to his alma mater, Yale University. As a result, Yale now houses what is beyond doubt the world's finest single collection of Boswell's papers. Yale's collection has formed the basis of what is referred to as the trade edition of Boswell's journals, an edition that began with the publication of the *London Journal* in 1950 and is now complete with the publication in 1989 of the last volume of the journals, entitled *Boswell: The Great Biographer*.

The publication of the journals has affected Boswell's literary reputation in the twentieth century more than anything else. The journals are, of course, invaluable for source studies. We now have the means, for instance, to compare the public versions of events in *The Journal of a Tour to the Hebrides* and in the *Life* with what was originally entered into the journals. What we have found has for the most part increased our esteem for Boswell's intelligence and deepened our respect for his integrity. Some scholars are more in awe than ever of the industry he employed in writing, collecting, and preserving so much.

Above all, Boswell can no longer be seen as the author of one great book. He is now the author of absorbing and vivid journals, someone who set a new standard in the genre of autobiography, or, as some would have it, someone who is responsible for the greatest diary ever written. In other words, Boswell's Boswell is now as important as Boswell's Johnson, and with good reason. In the journals we see better than ever what battles must be fought in the effort to be human in the modern world. Moreover, Boswell is a ready-made example for postmodernism with its emphasis on the role of writing in our lives. He seems to embody as well as anyone our struggle to overcome emptiness and meaninglessness through a heroic will to write.

Curiously enough, we do not know where Boswell got his original notion to keep a journal, nor what precedent if any he had in mind. What we do know is that at first he kept some diaries, but to quote Frederick Pottle, whose familiarity with the Boswell papers was nonpareil, "to judge from the surviving specimens [from the diaries], they had all been concise and unambitious." However, not long before his twenty-second birthday, on 14 September 1762, more than two months before he would set out for London, Boswell began something which he titled "Journal of My Jaunt, Harvest 1762." It was, says Pottle, "consciously begun as prologue to and training for the swelling act which he planned to record in London. It was the inception of an elaborate literary journal which he was to keep without the gap of a single day at least to the end of January 1765—nearly two thousand quarto pages of careful manuscript. It is the first of his writings in which he demonstrates his power to write so that others must read what he has written."

Perhaps the first and most striking impression we have when we begin to read in the journals is how different this Boswell is from the Boswell we thought we knew from the *Life* or from the *Tour*. Those of us who have formed our picture of Boswell on those books cannot help but think of him as someone who followed a great man around, trying to record whatever wit or wisdom he was willing to utter. It comes as a surprise to learn that Boswell led a full existence quite apart from Samuel Johnson. Perhaps this comes through most forcefully in the *London Journal*, which records that time in his life—Boswell was only twenty-two—before he even met Samuel Johnson. His relish for London is obvious. His rebellion against his father is smoldering. More

Auchinleck House, the ancestral home Boswell inherited after his father's death in 1781

than anything he wants a career as a soldier in the guards, but he is never successful in winning the appointment that he seeks.

Most of all, though, Boswell is interested in women, or at least in recording his interest in women. Whether or not Boswell was more highly sexed than other men may be open for question. What is clear is that he found sanction, or thought he found sanction, from the company of men, for believing that a man was entitled to, or even required to, seek relief with a woman several times a week. What may be most significant is a note of boasting in his description of his sexual intrigues. That note makes it hard to escape the inference that he wrote these down fully believing that his record of his encounters with prostitutes would win the approval of his fellow males, and perhaps even their grudging admiration. This may tell us a good deal about how men talked to one another "off the record" in the eighteenth century, but it does not seem to be all that different from how they talk among themselves in the twentieth.

The most memorable moments in the *London Journal* come during Boswell's intrigue with an actress he calls "Louisa." It is formed like a min-

iature play. In the first two acts, we find Boswell scheming and plotting to win the lady's favor. After some complications he finally wins what he has been seeking. He performs in bed as a prodigy of nature, pleasing Louisa by coming to a climax five times in a single night. It would seem as though life could not be better. Then comes the downturn. Shortly after his night of lovemaking he begins to experience familiar symptoms. The realization slowly grows that, prodigy of nature though he may be, he has just contracted a very ordinary case of gonorrhea. Venereal disease means being bedridden for at least a month, and considerable expense for the attentions of a physician. In the final act he chooses to confront Louisa with the facts of her duplicity and corruption. She protests her innocence, but this time he does not fall for the bait. There is a somewhat unexpected twist at the end when the two guineas he had earlier "lent" Louisa are returned to him wrapped in plain paper, without a note of explanation or apology. It is vivid writing, and we might even note that the confrontation scene is rendered in dialogue. Yet despite its theatrical elements or perhaps because of them, it is hard to shake off the sense that we come extraordinarily

Boswell's ebony cabinet, in which some of his papers were stored at Auchinleck House. During the first decade of the twentieth century the papers and cabinet were taken to Malahide Castle, near Dublin, Ireland, where they remained inaccessible to scholars until Lt. Col. Ralph Heyward Isham bought them from Boswell's descendants in 1927 and published them as Private Papers of James Boswell *(1928-1934).*

close to the experience of day-to-day life in the eighteenth century in this journal, and the taste proves to be rather tart.

There are other moments in the journals that have become part of our legend and lore, but none perhaps more celebrated than Boswell's interviews with Rousseau and Voltaire. He reveals in these many of the same qualities that he would later employ in the *Life of Johnson,* and to much the same effect. The theatrical element is undoubtedly the most important. We know from Boswell's own testimony early in the journal that he had every intention of stopping to see both Rousseau and Voltaire, two of Europe's most famous men, when he began his Grand Tour. Both men lived near the border between France and Switzerland, and thus on his route south from Germany into Italy. He had even secured a letter of introduction to Rousseau from George Keith, Earl Marischal, but in December 1764, when Boswell got close to Rousseau's home near Neuchâtel, he learned that the great man was suffering badly from several physical ailments and that he was constantly plagued by visitors. This meant that he might not get to see Rousseau, letter or no letter.

Boswell decided that he had to do something that would win Rousseau's interest, so he sat down and composed a letter that contained a portrait of his life and explained why at twenty-four he needed the guidance of an older, wiser man. It turned out that Rousseau, then fifty-two, was captivated by such unusual tactics. Boswell won permission to visit, and ended up winning the affection of both his host and his host's mistress, Thérèse le Vasseur.

Boswell would follow a similar strategy to gain entrance to Voltaire's mansion at Ferney, just outside of Geneva. Boswell spent his first day at Voltaire's residence on 24 December 1764. He started up a conversation with the great man in the afternoon, talking with him about Johnson and Lord Kames, especially about Kames's *Elements of Criticism,* in part because Boswell suspected Voltaire did not like it. He had to break off his visit in order to get back to Geneva before five o'clock when the gates of the city were shut for the night. As a result he decided to write a letter to Voltaire's niece Madame Denis, asking for permission to stay overnight at Ferney. Permission was quickly granted because Boswell had made such a positive impression upon the seventy-two-year-old Voltaire.

The success of both interviews depends upon the sense of drama. That drama in turn depends upon Boswell himself. He becomes a kind of stand-in for all of us, slowly laying the groundwork for his meetings with both men. In both cases Boswell's youthful exuberance proves irresistible to the older men, and they find themselves charmed by an unlikely source. There are exchanges of views which are interesting in themselves, but the most interesting are those that come in the confrontations over religion. With Rousseau, the question is the character of his religious beliefs, when Boswell, looking steadily into his eye, asks him: "But tell me sincerely, are you a Christian?" With Voltaire, he approaches the same subject a bit more indirectly, but once the subject does come up he reports with some satisfaction how Voltaire did "rage," eventually falling back exhausted upon his chair and holding his head. Under further prodding from Boswell Voltaire finally acknowledges the deistic beliefs for which he was famous: the existence of a supreme being, but without any necessity for churches and a clergy, nor for any of the doctrines of supernatural revelation. Boswell is particularly horrified when Voltaire expresses his indifference to the notion of personal immortality. This was the religious doctrine that mattered most to Boswell. But his wavering confidence in the doctrine of immortality provides no more of an explanation for his bizarre religious behavior than any other.

Anyone who reads in Boswell's journals is bound to feel jolted by the experience of reading in one paragraph how nothing seems to matter more than the exalted devotion he feels at a liturgy or a sermon, only to find him roaring about in search of a whore in the next. Boswell's religious practices, like so much else in his life, were part of his rebellion against his father. He was of course raised according to the strict Presbyterian practices of his parents. Almost as soon as he was on his own, he converted to Roman Catholicism, only to recant shortly after, due to pressure from his family. Despite his recantation he retained an attraction to Catholicism, and perhaps even a sympathy with it. That would explain why he was so much at ease and so well accepted as a traveler in Italy, France, and Corsica. Ultimately, in line with his Anglophilia, Boswell found his richest satisfactions in the religious practices of High Church Anglicanism, and this was to provide yet another bond between him and Samuel Johnson.

There are other moments in the journals that have acquired a fame of their own. Many find themselves fascinated with Boswell's complex relationship with Belle de Zuylen, a captivating woman known as Zélide, whom he came to know while in Holland. His relationship with Margaret Montgomerie, the woman who would become his wife and mother of his five children, has its own attraction. His efforts in behalf of the sheep stealer John Reid are deeply moving and a convincing evidence that there was more to Boswell than a foolish pride in his aristocratic rank. His interview in 1778 with Margaret Caroline Rudd, the woman who charmed her way out of a capital conviction for forgery, is a revelation of yet another side of that nature.

The later journals, though always interesting, are less engaging and somewhat less full. By and large they recount Boswell's disastrous decision to pursue a career at the English bar and later to seek political advancement by means of favor from the powerful. Eventually they recount the painful story of the wasting away of his wife, Margaret, who had contracted tuberculosis. Her premature death adds another sorrowful burden to the growing gloom of his final years. Near the end we see Boswell shamed and humiliated when younger men steal his wig, forcing him to travel a dozen miles in order to appear properly attired before the imperious Sir James Lowther, Lord Londsdale. Later still we hear about a drunken Boswell being mugged and rolled while on his way home late at night. His last days are the story of the disintegration of what had once been a superbly healthy body, one that had withstood incredible amounts of abuse. Eventually, though, even Boswell's body proved to be mortal. He died on 19 May 1795, his death the result of a kidney infection that could be traced easily enough to multiple incidents of venereal disease.

A recounting of the sad events at the close of Boswell's life should serve as a reminder about the nature of Boswell's journals. Autobiography ought not to be confused with biography. While Boswell is recording instance after instance of his personal decline and degradation, he is at work producing one of the glories of English literature. The discrepancy between this idea of himself and the reality we know to be true, between his sense of himself as a failure and the success he was then creating in *The Life of Samuel Johnson* is something that surely ought to interest scholars and critics alike. We cannot and should not equate the flesh-and-blood Boswell with the Boswell of the journals. As much as Boswell recorded about himself, he clearly did not record all, nor even much, of what we might find most interesting about him. It will be the business of his future biographers to take more careful note of these discrepancies, to investigate them, and to debate how we might account for them. When we do, we may have a better understanding of the curious combinations of weakness and strength that can constitute genius.

Letters:

Letters of James Boswell, Addressed to the Rev. W. J. Temple, edited by Sir Philip Francis (London: Bentley, 1857 [i.e., 1856]);

The Letters of James Boswell, 2 volumes, edited by Chauncey Brewster Tinker (Oxford: Clarendon Press, 1924);

The Correspondence of James Boswell and John Johnston of Grange, edited by Ralph S. Walker (New York: McGraw-Hill, 1966; London: Heinemann, 1966);

The Correspondence and Other Papers of James Boswell Relating to the Making of the "Life of Johnson," edited by Marshall Waingrow (New York: McGraw-Hill, 1969; London: Heinemann, 1969);

Boswell's Correspondence with Certain Members of the Club, edited by Charles N. Fifer (New York: McGraw-Hill, 1976; London: Heinemann, 1976);

The Correspondence of James Boswell with David Garrick, Edmund Burke, and Edmond Malone, edited by George M. Kahrl, Rachel McClellan, Thomas W. Copeland, Peter S. Baker, and James M. Osborn (London: Heinemann, 1987; New York: McGraw-Hill, 1988).

Bibliographies:

Frederick A. Pottle, *The Literary Career of James Boswell, Esq., Being the Bibliographical Materials for a Life of Boswell* (Oxford: Clarendon Press, 1929);

Anthony E. Brown, *Boswellian Studies*, second edition, revised (Hamden, Conn.: Archon, 1972);

Marion S. Pottle, *Catalogue of the Papers of James Boswell at Yale University* (New York: McGraw-Hill, forthcoming).

Biographies:

Frederick A. Pottle, *James Boswell: The Earlier Years, 1740-1769* (New York: McGraw-Hill, 1966);

Frank Brady, *James Boswell: The Later Years, 1769-1795* (New York: McGraw-Hill, 1984);

Iain Finlayson, *The Moth and the Candle: A Life of James Boswell* (London: Constable, 1984).

References:

Harold Bloom, ed., *Dr. Samuel Johnson and James Boswell*, Modern Critical Views (New York: Chelsea House, 1986);

Bloom, ed., *James Boswell's "Life of Samuel Johnson,"* Modern Critical Interpretations (New York: Chelsea House, 1985);

Bertrand Bronson, "Boswell's Boswell," in his *Johnson and Boswell*, University of California Publications in English, volume 4, no. 9 (Berkeley: University of California Press, 1944); republished as *Johnson Agonistes & Other Essays* (Berkeley & Los Angeles: University of California Press, 1965), pp. 53-99;

David Buchanan, *The Treasure of Auchinleck: The Story of the Boswell Papers* (New York: McGraw-Hill, 1974);

John J. Burke, Jr., "The Documentary Value of Boswell's *Journal of a Tour to the Hebrides*," in *Fresh Reflections on Samuel Johnson*, edited by Prem Nath (New York: Whitston, 1987), pp. 349-372;

James L. Clifford, ed., *Twentieth Century Interpretations of Boswell's "Life of Johnson"* (Englewood Cliffs, N.J.: Prentice-Hall, 1970);

Greg Clingham, *Boswell: The Life of Johnson* (Cambridge: Cambridge University Press, 1991);

Clingham, ed., *New Light on Boswell: Critical and Historical Essays on the Occasion of the Bicentenary of the "Life of Johnson"* (Cambridge: Cambridge University Press, 1991);

William C. Dowling, *The Boswellian Hero* (Athens: University of Georgia, 1979);

Joseph Foladare, *Boswell's Paoli* (Hamden, Conn.: Archon, 1979);

Mary Hyde, *The Impossible Friendship: Boswell and Mrs. Thrale* (Cambridge, Mass.: Harvard University Press, 1972);

Allan Ingram, *Boswell's Creative Gloom: A Study of Imagery and Melancholy in the Writings of James Boswell* (New York: Barnes & Noble, 1982);

Donald Kay, "Boswell in the Green Room," *Philological Quarterly*, 57 (Spring 1978): 195-212;

Irma S. Lustig, "Fact into Art: James Boswell's Notes, Journals, and the *Life of Johnson*," in *Biography in the Eighteenth Century*, edited by John D. Browning (New York: Garland, 1980), pp. 128-146;

Maximillian Novak, "James Boswell's *Life of Johnson*," in *The Biographer's Art: New Essays*, edited by Jeffrey Meyers (London: Macmillan / New York: New Amsterdam, 1989), pp. 31-52;

Frederick A. Pottle, "James Boswell, Journalist," in *The Age of Johnson: Essays Presented to Chauncey Brewster Tinker* (New Haven: Yale University Press, 1949), pp. 15-25;

Pottle, "The Power of Memory in Boswell and Scott," in *Essays on the Eighteenth Century Presented to David Nichol Smith* (Oxford: Clarendon Press, 1945), pp. 168-189;

Pottle, *Pride and Negligence: The History of the Boswell Papers* (New York: McGraw-Hill, 1982);

William S. Siebenschuh, *Form and Purpose in Boswell's Biographical Works* (Berkeley & Los Angeles: University of California Press, 1972);

John A. Vance, ed., *Boswell's "Life of Johnson": New Questions, New Answers* (Athens: University of Georgia Press, 1985).

Papers:

Most of the Boswell papers are at Yale University. That they are for the most part in one place is due largely to the heroic efforts of Lt. Col. Ralph Isham to keep the collection together, and to the noble way Yale has continued to carry out its responsibilities as custodian. After Yale, to quote the words of David Buchanan in *The Treasure of Auchinleck*, "the largest and finest Boswellian collection in the world is to be found in the Hyde Library at Four Oaks Farm in New Jersey." There are also important Boswell papers at the National Library of Scotland.

Edmund Burke

(12 January 1729? - 9 July 1797)

Elizabeth R. Lambert
Gettysburg College

SELECTED BOOKS: *The Reformer*, 13 numbers (Dublin: Printed for & sold by J. Cotter, 28 January-21 April 1748);

A Vindication of Natural Society (London: Printed for M. Cooper, 1756);

A Philosophical Enquiry into the Origin of Our Ideas of the Sublime and Beautiful (London: Printed for R. & J. Dodsley, 1757; enlarged, 1759);

A Short Account of a Late Short Administration (London: Published for J. Wilkie, 1766);

Observations on a Late State of the Nation (London: Printed for J. Dodsley, 1769);

Thoughts on the Cause of the Present Discontents (London: Printed for J. Dodsley, 1770);

Mr. Edmund Burke's Speeches at His Arrival at Bristol, and at the Conclusion of the Poll (London: Printed for J. Wilkie, 1774);

Speech of Edmund Burke, Esq. on American Taxation (London: Printed for J. Dodsley, 1775; New York: Printed by J. Rivington, 1775; Philadelphia: Printed & sold by Benjamin Towne, 1775);

The Speech of Edmund Burke, Esq., on Moving his Resolutions for Conciliation With the Colonies (London: Printed for J. Dodsley, 1775; New York: Printed by J. Rivington, 1775);

A Letter from Edmund Burke, Esq.; One of the Representatives in Parliament for the City of Bristol, to John Farr, and John Harris, Esqrs., Sheriffs of that City, on the Affairs in America (Bristol: Printed by William Pine, 1777);

Speech of Edmund Burke, Esq. Member of Parliament for the City of Bristol, On Presenting to the House of Commons (on the 11th of February, 1780) a Plan for the Better Security of the Independence of Parliament, and the Oeconomical Reformation of the Civil and Other Establishments (London: Printed for John Hay, 1780);

Ninth Report from the Select Committee, Appointed to Take into Consideration the State of the Administration of Justice in the Provinces of Bengal, Bahar, and Orissa (London, 1783);

Eleventh Report from the Select Committee, Appointed to Take into Consideration the State of the Adminis-

Edmund Burke, 1776 (mezzotint by J. Jones, from the portrait by George Romney)

tration of Justice in the Provinces of Bengal, Bahar, and Orissa (London, 1783);

Mr. Burke's Speech, on the 1st December 1783, upon the Question for the Speaker's Leaving the Chair, in order for the House to Resolve itself into a Committee on Mr. Fox's East India Bill (London: Printed for J. Dodsley, 1784);

Mr. Burke's Speech on the Motion Made for Papers Relative to the Directions for Charging the Nawab of Arcot's Private Debts to Europeans, on the Revenues of the Carnatic (London: Printed for J. Dodsley, 1785);

Articles on Charges of High Crimes and Misdemeanours, Against Warren Hastings, 4 parts (London: Printed for John Stockdale, 1786);

Reflections on the Revolution in France and on the Proceedings in Certain Societies in London Relative to that Event (London: Printed for J.

Dodsley, 1790; New York: Printed by Hugh Gaine, 1791);

Lettre de M. Burke, à un membre de l'Assemblée nationale de France (Paris: L'Assemblée nationale, chez Artaud, 1791), republished as *Letter from Mr. Burke to a Member of the National Assembly in answer to some Objections to his book on French Affairs* (London: Printed for J. Dodsley, 1791; New York: Printed by Hugh Gaine, 1791);

Appeal from the New to the Old Whigs (London: Printed for J. Dodsley, 1791; New York: Printed by Childs & Swaine, 1791);

A Letter from the Right Hon. Edmund Burke, M.P. in the Kingdom of Great Britain to Sir Hercules Langrishe, Bart. M.P. on the Subject of Roman Catholics in Ireland (Dublin: Printed by P. Byrne, 1792; London: Printed for J. Debrett, 1792);

A Letter from the Right Honorable Edmund Burke to a Noble Lord, on the Attacks Made upon Him and His Pension (London: Printed for J. Owen and F. & C. Rivington, 1796; New York: Printed for T. Allen & A. Drummand, 1796; Philadelphia: Printed for B. Davies, H. & P. Rice, and J. Ormrod, 1796);

Thoughts on the Prospect of a Regicide Peace [unauthorized edition] (London: Printed for J. Owen, 1796); republished as *Two Letters Addressed to a Member of Parliament, on the Proposals for Peace with the Regicide Directory of France* [authorized edition] (London: Printed for F. & C. Rivington, 1796; Philadelphia: Printed for William Cobbett & J. Ormrod, by Bioren & Madan, 1797);

A Third Letter to a Member of the Present Parliament, on the Proposals for Peace with the Regicide Directory of France (London: Printed for F. & C. Rivington, sold also by J. Hatchard, 1797);

Three Memorials on French Affairs (London: Printed for F. & C. Rivington, sold also by J. Hatchard, 1797);

Thoughts and Details on Scarcity (London: Printed for F. & C. Rivington, and J. Hatchard, by T. Gillet, 1800);

The Works of the Right Honourable Edmund Burke, 16 volumes, edited by Walter King and French Laurence (London: F. & J. Rivington, 1803-1827)—includes "An Essay Towards an Abridgment of the English History," "Tracts on the Popery Laws," and "Letter on the Affairs of Ireland";

The Writings and Speeches of the Right Honorable Edmund Burke, 12 volumes (Boston: Little, Brown, 1901);

A Note-Book of Edmund Burke: Poems, Characters, Essays and other Sketches in the Hands of Edmund and William Burke, edited by Henry V. F. Somerset (Cambridge: Cambridge University Press, 1957);

The Writings and Speeches of Edmund Burke, 3 volumes to date, edited by Paul Langford and others (Oxford: Clarendon Press, 1981-   ).

Ordinarily one approaches the writings of practicing politicians without anticipating any benefit other than that of becoming informed—that is, unless they are the writings of Edmund Burke. Burke is so knowledgeable about political systems and ideas; so much a master of style, diction, and metaphor; and so much a student of human nature that his works merit the designation of literature. Moreover, as William Roscoe wrote to William Petty, Lord Shelburn, in a letter of 7 November 1796: "Mr. Burke is himself so conspicuous a part of his work that it is impossible to avoid him." Burke's persona, speaking across the centuries, still has the ability to engage the reader's mind and emotions. However, the complexity of Burke's thought defies neat categorization. He was a Rockingham Whig; yet some, like the nineteenth-century Thomas Carlyle, have labeled him a Tory; he has been designated "The Father of Conservatism"; yet many see him as a liberal.

While certain problems Burke responded to as an eighteenth-century practicing politician are past history—the American Revolution, British control of India, the French Revolution, the penal laws in Ireland—certain aspects of these issues are as vital today as they were during Burke's lifetime. And so it is that one rarely leaves off reading Burke with a feeling of indifference; a reader is more likely to quarrel with him, to heartily agree with him, or to be of both minds at once. That is the interesting thing about Burke: he is as controversial today as he was in the eighteenth century.

Born in Dublin on 12 January in 1729 or 1730, Edmund Burke was the second son of four surviving children of Richard Burke, attorney of His Majesty's Court of Exchequer, and Mary Nagle Burke. When the young Edmund showed signs of lung trouble, his parents sent him to live with his Catholic relatives, the Nagles, on their farm in the south of Ireland. Those years in County Cork and in a happy, religious family

*This painting of Burke may be the early portrait by Thomas Worlidge (1700-1766) that Burke mentioned
in a 13 July 1774 letter (Collection of Dr. Brendan O'Brien, Dublin).*

had a lifelong effect on Burke. There he acquired a love of the land and farming. He also studied Latin with a well-intentioned but slightly inept schoolmaster by the name of O'Halloran and Irish lore and legends with his Nagle cousins.

At the age of twelve Edmund was sent, with his elder brother, Garrett, and his younger brother Richard, to a school in Ballitore conducted by the Quaker Abraham Shackleton. At Ballitore Edmund formed a lifelong friendship with Richard Shackleton, the schoolmaster's son. After three years Burke left Ballitore to enter Trinity College in Dublin. Thus, by the time Edmund was sixteen he had been exposed to three different ways of life and three different ways of thinking, all of which left a deep and lasting impression on him.

Burke entered Trinity College on 14 April 1744; what we know of his college years comes from the letters he wrote to Richard Shackleton.

He speaks humorously of his consecutive forays into science, logic, history, and literature as his "furor Mathematicus," "furor logicus," "furor historicus," "furor poeticus"—each of which was abandoned as soon as another interest came along. In 1747 Burke began to put into writing his observations stemming from reading Longinus and others on the sublime. He told Richard Shackleton that he was drafting an "odd" piece on the subject. Burke also seems to have been a typical eighteenth-century Trinity student in his interest in the Dublin theater scene. In his case it took the form of an unfinished "Essay on the Drama"; in writing a play supposedly submitted to Thomas Sheridan (father of Richard Brinsley Sheridan) but which was never produced; and active participation in the Dublin theater riots of 1746-1747.

In a more productive way Burke formed the Student's Debating Society, a weekly club instituted "for the formation of our minds and manners for the functions of Civil Society," and to provide opportunities for "correcting our taste, regulating and enriching our judgment, brightening our wit, and enlarging our knowledge and of being serviceable to others in the same things." To achieve these ends, the members debated, declaimed, and read papers. Several of the topics Burke would meet again some thirty years later in the House of Commons. In the record of these debates we find Burke espousing ideas which are hallmarks of his philosophy. For example, in one meeting when he argued against the repeal of a law imposing the death penalty for stealing sheep, he demonstrated veneration for tradition and suspicion of sudden change that would deeply alter or eliminate long-standing traditions: "When we are to repeal a standing law we are not to do it lightly; our Ancestors saw the wisdom of this Law, or they would not enact it." One of the reasons he gave reflects his experiences on the Nagle farm and a basic concept of property: "a man's property's his life . . . he that seizes my property would seize my life." According to the records of the society, there were also indications of Burke's future behavior on the floor of Commons—some of the members charged him with being "damned absolute."

The debating club was undertaken in conjunction with others; an offshoot of the club was a weekly, *The Reformer*, titled and written by Burke himself. The thirteen issues he published dealt with such subjects as the theater, religion, the arts, and poverty in Ireland. As the title indicated, Burke had a didactic purpose in mind. The summer recess made further publication impracticable. Although Burke intended to resume publication the following winter, he never did.

While producing *The Reformer* Burke took his A.B. degree on 28 February 1748 but continued to occupy his rooms at Trinity as he was entitled to do. Before leaving Trinity for England and Middle Temple, where he had been enrolled since 1747, Burke seems to have become part of a local political fracas. Charles Lucas, a formidable critic of political corruption in Ireland, was running for the Irish Commons in a by-election. There is evidence that Burke wrote several pamphlets supporting Lucas, but the exact nature of Burke's participation in the tumult surrounding the election is not clear.

In accordance with his father's wishes, Burke went to London in the spring of 1750 to study law at Middle Temple. In leaving Ireland Burke left not only a homeland but also a sense of place. In Dublin he had been known as the talented son of a prominent attorney; he had achieved recognition as a student at Trinity, and he had made his presence felt in Dublin arts and politics through his writings. England was a different matter. The penal laws against Irish Catholics cast their shadows over every Irishman of whatever religious persuasion who traveled the waters between Ireland and England. From first to last Burke's brogue, which he never made any attempt to modify, betrayed his origins and put him on the fringes of English society. Adding to the young man's uneasiness was the discrepancy between Burke's literary ambitions and his father's plans that he study law. His arrival in England plunged him into obscurity in both the personal and historical sense.

What we know of his life from 1750 to 1756 comes from five letters to Richard Shackleton and a few anecdotes recounted years later by those who knew him at the time. These sources tell us that he attended classes at Middle Temple with ever-increasing distaste for a legal career, that he suffered from uncertain health, and that his friends were, for the most part, from the diverse Irish community in London. One of the sureties who signed Burke's bond at Middle Temple was a man named John Burke, whose son William became an intimate friend of Edmund's. They shared thoughts, ambitions, and eventually, it is rumored, love for the same woman, although William stepped aside when Jane Nugent's preference was clearly for Edmund.

As students, Edmund and William kept a notebook which is a compilation of character sketches, observations, essays, and poems. Some of the entries are clearly Edmund's and others are identified as William's. The attributions of others are doubtful. The first item, dated November 1750, was written by Edmund. "The Muse Divorced" describes "the fatal Itch" that makes "scribbling" more attractive than the study of law. Other items by Burke reflect on the nature of true genius, the relationship between morality and religion, and a collection from his papers labeled "Several Scattered Hints Concerning Philosophy and Learning." He also wrote "A Plan for Arguing" which reflects his later practice.

The *Note-Book* is significant for the insight it gives into Burke's characteristic habits of thought as a young man. The observations look both back to his speculations in *The Reformer* and forward to his work in the *Annual Register*. It is here that we find him trying out extended character sketches, which he later embedded into his writings on America, India, and France.

The *Note-Book* has biographical significance in that various pieces were written when Burke was a patient in the home of Doctor Christopher Nugent, a noted Irish physician practicing in Bath. In the course of Burke's stay in the Nugent household, the doctor's daughter, Jane, became the focus of his attention. They were married on 12 March 1757; Jane was an extremely competent, loving woman who became indispensable to both Burke's career and his personal life. Jane and Edmund had two sons: Richard (named after Burke's younger brother and commonly called Richard, Jr., to distinguish him from his uncle) and Christopher, who died in early childhood.

At some point in the mid 1750s, Burke's growing estrangement from the study of law became a total separation. His father did not take kindly to Edmund's change of plans and his infatuation with writing; in fact, it occasioned a breach between them which was healed only in 1760.

In 1756 Burke emerged from obscurity to publish *A Vindication of Natural Society*, followed the next year by *A Philosophical Enquiry into the Origin of Our Ideas of the Sublime and Beautiful*. He also intended to write a history of England but finished only a brief account, "An Essay Towards an Abridgement of the English History," published posthumously in 1812.

The essay is short, and its importance is controversial. Some think it has little value as an expression of Burke's political thought, but others contend that it is important for what it tells us about his early perceptions of the historical process, his tendency to link morality and politics, and his view of the prescriptive nature of the English Constitution. For example, he rejects the notion that "would settle the ancient Constitution in the most remote times exactly in the same form in which we enjoy it at this day" and notes that changes in manners and customs over the ages are considerable enough to produce changes in laws and in the forms governments take. It is believed that Burke discontinued the history when David Hume published his. Years later contemporaries urged Burke to write a history of his own times, but Burke protested that "he did not yet know enough of the springs of action in his own times to write the history."

A Vindication of Natural Society, Burke's first significant publication, was a philosophical satire on the ideas of the deist Henry St. John, Vis-

Jane Burke (portrait by Sir Joshua Reynolds; from Sir Philip Magnus, Edmund Burke: A Life, *1939)*

count Bolingbroke, whose works had been published posthumously two years earlier and caused consternation because of the irreligious tone. Burke made a mockery of Bolingbroke's argument against religion by using Bolingbroke's language and style to mount an argument against social institutions. Burke's argument runs thus: the history of mankind is found to be a history of its wars. Governments, law, religion, and organized society are corrupt and cause hatred and division among peoples. Therefore, Burke ironically concludes, one can find satisfaction only in a natural state—"Life is simple, and therefore it is happy."

The imitation was too perfect; Burke's impersonation of Bolingbroke's style was not recognized as such, and consequently, the irony was lost. Nevertheless, that he was able to pull off a perfect imitation is a tribute to the young man's talents. At the time *A Vindication of Natural Society* was published Burke did not enlighten his readers, but nine years later when he saw his chance to come into Parliament, he published a second edition with a preface assuring readers that his design was to "show that . . . the same engines which were employed for the destruction of religion, might be employed with equal success for the subversion of government; and that specious arguments might be used against those things which they, who doubt of everything else, will never permit to be questioned." In April 1757 Burke published a treatise on aesthetics which he had begun in his undergraduate days at Trinity: *A Philosophical Enquiry into the Origin of Our Ideas of the Sublime and Beautiful.*

A Philosophical Enquiry was an outcome of Burke's study of Longinus and other aestheticians as well as Burke's observations of the workings of human emotion. In the preface he notes that the terms "sublime" and "beautiful" as applied to aesthetic principles are frequently "inaccurate" and too inclusive. As a way of making clear the distinctions between the two terms, Burke proposes to examine their origins in the human psyche. His examination, Burke writes, will cover three areas: the passions of an individual; the qualities of things which incite these passions; and the laws of nature governing the first two. This done, Burke concludes, "the rules deductible from such an enquiry might be applied to the imitative arts, and to whatever else they concerned, without much difficulty." In effect, Burke follows other aestheticians by examining the qualities of the object which evokes the response but goes beyond them by examining the nature of the aesthetic experience as it affects the body and the emotions. Burke's approach allows psychological and even physiological explanations for the aesthetic experience.

Burke also stands out from other aestheticians in his linking the emotion of terror with the sublime: "terror is in all cases whatsoever, either more openly or latently the ruling principle of the sublime." Here Burke, no doubt, has in mind contemporary interest in poetry and fiction which played upon a fundamental fascination for haunted castles, graveyards at midnight, and bare ruined choirs in abbey churches. In addition, he postulates that nature is cause for the astonishment that is the effect of the sublime in its highest degree: "A level plain of a vast extent on land is certainly no mean idea . . . but can it ever fill the mind with any thing so great as the ocean itself ?" Thus Burke's sensationist line of thought traces human responses to the qualities of obscurity, power, vastness, and infinity to the imagination and not to the reasoning faculty.

In his discussion of the sublime, Burke also rejects Locke's "pleasure/pain theory," which asserts that there are only two states of being—pain and pleasure—and that the diminution of one causes the other. Burke argues that pain and pleasure are "each of a positive nature, and by no means necessarily dependent on each other for their existence. The human mind is often, and I think it is for the most part, in a state neither of pain nor pleasure, which I call a state of indifference."

The second part of *A Philosophical Enquiry* deals with the origins of the human response to beauty. Here, too, Burke takes on contemporary theory connecting beauty to proportion, utility, and goodness (or perfection). Specifically he objects to the classical theory that connects proportion in architecture to proportion in the human body and beauty with "the fitness of parts for their several purposes." For Burke, the response to beauty is centered in the emotions: "beauty demands no assistance from our reasoning; even the will is unconcerned; the appearance of beauty as effectually causes some degree of love in us, as the application of ice or fire produces the ideas of heat or cold."

In the second edition (1759) Burke found it necessary to respond to certain criticisms. In some places he had to "explain, illustrate and enforce" his theory. He also added an essay on taste as "it leads naturally enough to the principal enquiry." In defining taste, Burke was adhering to the tradition of Joseph Addison, David Hume, and others who conducted the same inquiry into the psychological responses to an aesthetic experience. Burke believed that taste operates by "fixed principles" which are the same for all individuals. Thus it was possible to set certain standards and for individuals to improve their taste by improving their judgment.

Contemporary criticism of *A Philosophical Enquiry* either condemned it vigorously or acknowledged it to be "an example of true criticism," as did Samuel Johnson. Those of Johnson's mind responded positively to Burke's empirical approach. However, some philosophical writers objected to his linking the sublime with terror and to his sensationism. Their objections, however, indicate that they took his ideas seriously. On a more pedestrian level, references to Burke's ideas concerning the sublime and the beautiful in contemporary diaries and letters indicate the extent to which they had filtered into conversation and contemporary thinking. Twentieth-century critics and theorists see in Burke's sensationist approach to aesthetics a revolt against neoclassic principles and hence a harbinger of the Romantic movement. Few would be so rash as to term Burke a "Romantic," for he is rooted firmly in his empirical age. Modern scholars also see interesting parallels between Burke's aesthetic theory and his political thought.

With the publication of *A Philosophical Enquiry into the Origin of Our Ideas of the Sublime and Beautiful*, Burke's reputation as an author was established. Nevertheless, the treatise, and especially Burke's linking the sublime with terror, gave a sense of respectability to the burgeoning Gothic literature. It may also have been the means of reconciling Burke with his father, who had never quite forgiven him for abandoning a law career. Tradition holds that Burke sent his father a copy of the treatise, and the father was so pleased that he sent a present of one hundred pounds.

Thus, in the closing years of the 1750s Burke had established a significant reputation as a writer. He was one of the founding members of Johnson's literary club and could count among his friends Samuel Johnson, Sir Joshua Reynolds, David Garrick, and Elizabeth Montagu and the Bluestocking circle. He obviously was proud of his reputation as a writer. Meeting him in 1761, Horace Walpole wrote to a friend about Burke: "He is a sensible man, but has not worn off his authorism yet—and thinks there is nothing so charming as writers and to be one—he will know better one of these days."

In 1758 Burke was contracted by the publishers Robert and James Dodsley to edit the new *Annual Register*—a yearly summary and analysis of politics, science, and the arts and a review of recent books. Although Burke was not aware of it at the time, his work as editor of the *Annual Register* was an excellent preparation for his political career.

The significant feature of the publication was the history section, which consisted of a historical essay concerning the ongoing Seven Years' War in Europe, a chronological diary of interesting and curious events in Britain during the year past, and a collection of state papers, which were official documents having to do with the policies of Britain. Culling information from state papers, correspondence, and individual accounts, Burke wrote the history section as one connected narrative. The events themselves were known to the public; Burke added a human-interest element by dramatizing the facts. As was his habit, he focused on personal accounts whenever possible and embellished them with his considerable narra-

tive skill. For example, in summarizing the military actions of 1757, Burke wrote: "perhaps in all the records of time, the compass of a single year, on the scene of a single country, never contained so many striking events, never displayed so many revolutions of fortune.... Six pitched battles fought. Three great armies annihilated. The French army reduced and vanquished without fighting. The Russians victorious and flying as if they had been vanquished."

As Burke became more politically involved, the history section of the *Annual Register* reflected his changing interests. In addition to the dramatic narration of events, Burke began to focus on the background to those events and to situations. When he became active in the affairs of America and interested in India, these situations merited in-depth treatment and reflected Burke's own study of the problems. Moreover, his political involvement is also reflected in the tone of the history section. In the beginning he had tried to maintain an impartial voice; by the mid 1760s Burke's tone had decidedly partisan implications.

Scholarly concern with Burke's association with the *Annual Register* centers on the length of time he was involved with it, and, by extension, how long the *Annual Register* continued to reflect Burke's thoughts and reactions to political events in Britain. Stylistic and thematic analysis of the history section indicates Burke's strong presence from 1758 until 1767. In 1765 there is evidence of another hand. Thereafter Burke's actual work on the *Annual Register* becomes problematic as does the extent of his influence upon opinions voiced in it.

Although Burke was writing, he had published only two significant pieces under his own name; the editor of the *Annual Register* was not publicized. Aside from undergraduate attempts to write poetry and probably drama, he seems to have had no inclination for creative forms of literature. Or perhaps he soon recognized that his particular talents were not in that direction. Many years later he characterized himself as a writer: "[I am] used only to have some substantial matter of Praise or blame, to express according to my powers, with force and clearness; but as to ... pretty turned Phrases, I never had any hand at them."

In 1761 Burke was head of a household and father of two children; he needed some employment that would give him a steady income and at the same time enable him to continue with the *Annual Register* and other writings. With some

An unfinished portrait of Charles Watson Wentworth, Marquis of Rockingham, and his secretary, Edmund Burke (Fitzwilliam Museum, Cambridge). Sir Joshua Reynolds began this painting in 1766 but discontinued work on it sometime during 1767.

reluctance Burke turned from full-time writing when he accepted a position as secretary to William Gerard Hamilton, chief secretary to George Montagu Dunk, Earl of Halifax, lord lieutenant of Ireland.

As secretary to Hamilton, Burke returned to Ireland. There he found widespread discontent because of the penal laws restricting the material wealth of Irish Catholics and their participation in the public life. Burke made his observations on the condition of Irish Catholics the essence of a piece which was not published until after his death. "Tracts on the Popery Laws" are fragments, but they are enough to illustrate the depth of Burke's feelings concerning the injustice of the penal laws.

In the few extant pieces of the first part of the tract, Burke proposes to show how the "Popery laws in general" were the "one leading cause of the imbecility of the country." In the second chapter, which is virtually complete, he examines each of the laws, among which were laws prohibiting the rights of inheritance, laws encouraging

children to conform to the established church and thereby be eligible to sue their Catholic parents for maintenance, laws forbidding Catholics the ownership of land, laws forbidding Catholics entrance to universities and to the professions, and laws against free exercise of religion. In the third chapter Burke deals with the effects of the penal laws and their "unhappy influence on the prosperity, the morals and the safety" of the Irish. Finally, he confronts and refutes specific arguments for supporting the penal laws. For example, many feared that if the Catholics had too much freedom, the pope would invade England; Burke describes this fear as "a wild chimera" and assures his readers that the papacy had long ago abandoned such a policy—"To encourage revolt in favor of foreign princes is an exploded idea in the politics of that [the papal] court."

The "Tracts on the Popery Laws" are significant, for it is here that Burke sets forth several of his basic principles concerning civil law. He states that the essence of law "requires that it be made as much as possible for the benefit of the whole."

Thus, given the fact that the Catholic population was two-thirds of the Irish people, Burke asserts: "The happiness or misery of multitudes can never be a thing indifferent. A law against the majority of the people is in substance a law against the people itself. . . ." Furthermore, such laws do not have authority because "the remote or the efficient cause of the law is the consent of the people, either actual or implied." When people consent to be governed they give up their judgment but not their rights. In effect, people "are presumed to consent to whatever the Legislature ordains for their benefit." However, all laws are subject to a higher law; if the people made a law prejudicial to the whole community, it would be invalid because it is made against the principle of superior law: "I mean the will of Him who gave us our nature, and in giving impressed an invariable law upon it." God's "invariable law" is the Natural Law. Belief in the Natural Law—the universal ethical norm which is accessible to reason and which binds all mankind—was part and parcel of Burke's early religious training and is implicit or explicit in all his writings.

Although not published during his lifetime and incomplete as we have them, "Tracts on the Popery Laws" demonstrate Burke's concern for his native country. His was a personal concern. While his father raised Edmund and his two brothers as Protestants, and his wife, Jane, was raised in the Presbyterian faith of her mother, Burke's mother, sister, and his father-in-law were Catholics, as were his favorite Nagle relations. In eighteenth-century Britain, his was guilt by association. From the time he entered public life there were always accusations that Burke was not only a Catholic but had been in a Jesuit seminary in France. Caricaturists more often than not picture him in priest's robes or at least wearing the Jesuit's baretta. Burke made it a practice never to answer these charges, but he knew that whatever he did for Ireland was going to be given a double meaning by his enemies.

In 1765 Burke became private secretary to Charles Watson Wentworth, Marquis of Rockingham, who had just become first lord of the treasury. Within a few months Ralph, Lord Verney, offered the vacancy for his borough, Wendover, to Burke. Although the results of the election were a foregone conclusion, Burke had to go through the motions. By the time he celebrated his thirty-sixth birthday in January, he was firmly entrenched in a political career. In throwing his lot in with the Rockingham Whigs, Burke was destined to be in the opposition for all but a short period in his political life. Burke's service to his party took several forms: party contact with special interest groups, minor negotiations with members of other groups, and literary services. His duties in the last category included drafting petitions and circulars, going over the drafts of pamphlets other members wrote, and framing letters. As a defender of the party, he proved himself invaluable; however, in 1769 Burke was not the dominant influence in the Rockingham party that he would become later. He had a great personal loyalty to Lord Rockingham, whom he loved and idealized. However, Burke's loyalty did not make him a hanger-on or one of those who attended Rockingham in his social life. Business done; Burke left. He recognized that his middle-class Irish origins would always give him a certain "pro forma" place outside aristocratic circles. He neither aspired to nor wanted more; his close and loyal circle of family and friends made his personal life full and rich. He truly was, as he described himself, "a plain man."

On 7 July 1766 the first Rockingham administration ended when the king dismissed the ministry. In a publication entitled *A Short Account of a Late Short Administration*, Burke defends the achievements of the Rockingham administration. Three years later, he was again at the bar to defend the Rockingham party against attacks in *The Present State of the Nation*, a pamphlet written by William Knox. Burke's *Observations on a Late State of the Nation* deals with Knox's charges point by point. However, Burke's most enduring contribution to political thought is in the more philosophical second part, where he sets forth several important themes: morality and politics are inseparable; party government is a natural consequence of a mixed constitution and a free state; and honor must be restored to politics through party. These general ideas were not unusual in eighteenth-century political thought; what was unusual was the identification of these themes with any specific political party, and this Burke did in associating "a large body of men, steadily sacrificing ambition to principle" with the Rockingham Whigs.

Later in 1769, when the Rockingham Whigs were engaged in a power struggle with William Pitt, Lord Chatham's party for leadership in the opposition, Burke enlarged upon the themes set forth in his *Observations*. The publication, *Thoughts on the Cause of the Present Discontents* (1770), became an official manifesto for the

The Seat of the Rt. Honble Edmund Burke at Beconsfield Bucks.
Pub. by J. Sewell, Cornhill.

Gregories, the estate Burke bought in 1768

Rockingham Whigs and a document of primary importance in the history of political parties.

In the years he had been a member of the Rockingham Whigs, Burke had learned much about the importance of political parties and the useful function opposition might perform. Burke first set down his thoughts on the subject in July 1769. He circulated a draft among party members and asked Rockingham to comment on it. In November he told Rockingham that he was "very far from confident, that the doctrines avowed in this piece . . . will be considered as well founded; or that they will be at all popular"; therefore he wanted to make sure that "it should be truly the Common Cause." One of his concerns was that other opposition groups would think that he had undermined their cause. He was also worried that the press would increase their attacks on him; at the time he was accused of being Junius, a vitriolic anonymous political writer.

The first and most controversial part of the *Thoughts on the Cause of the Present Discontents* discusses a "double cabinet" or an unofficial body of advisers to the king who were the real power behind the throne. Burke details the effects of this "shadow cabinet" on the king, the court system,

Parliament, and the nation. He speaks of "a faction ruling by the private inclinations of a court, against the general sense of the people."

Burke and, by extension, the Rockingham Whigs have been severely criticized for their double-cabinet theory. Sir Louis Namier and others have charged that the theory of a bogus court faction was set up to explain certain unexpected administrative changes. More recent scholarship, using original documents, discounts "evil intent" on the part of Burke and the Rockingham Whigs and affirms that the "myth" of the double cabinet was a sincerely held belief of the Rockingham Whigs several years before Burke came on the scene and that he "inherited" the idea.

The second part of the *Thoughts on the Cause of the Present Discontents* is Burke's unique contribution to theories concerning the necessity, the nature, and the use of political parties. For Burke, individuals achieve their highest potential as members of a group; therefore, membership in a political party is consistent with the nature of an individual as a social being. He defines party as "a body of men united for promoting by their joint endeavors the national interest upon some particular principle in which they are all agreed." Burke certainly does not have in mind the modern two-party democratic system; Burke's party is a parliamentary group whose leadership is assumed by a member of the aristocracy. He sees the party out of office—the opposition—as occupying a useful place as equalizers. Parties in opposition are necessary for balanced legislation and as instruments of representative government. In effect Burke perceives party as fundamental to good constitutional government. Burke's immediate object in writing the *Thoughts on the Cause of the Present Discontents* was to demonstrate the difference between the Rockingham Whigs and other factions such as the Bedfords and the Grenvilles. The Rockingham Whigs, Burke argues, adhered to the traditional principles of the Whigs. The pamphlet goes beyond Burke's original partisan intention in that it became the official statement of his party. Although, as noted above, critics argue about the validity of some of Burke's statements, in its analysis of the contemporary political situation and in its assumptions concerning the social nature of individuals, his pamphlet is a primary document in the history of political parties.

Feeling that he had attained professional security as a Rockingham Whig, Burke decided that the time had come, as he told an Irish friend, Richard Shackleton, "to cast a little root in this Country" (1 May 1768), and in 1768, with financial aid from his brother Richard and from William Burke, he purchased, for twenty thousand pounds, an estate near the town of Beaconsfield in Buckinghamshire—the midpoint in the journey between London and Oxford. The estate, called Gregories, had been in the family of the poet Edmund Waller since 1558; with the house Burke also acquired about six hundred acres of land and a significant collection of pictures, marble busts, and statues. In years to come, the estate provided Burke with an outlet for his love of farming and a release from the pressures of political life. The country estate also became the gathering place for friends, political allies, and Irish relations. Life at Beaconsfield was never dull; even in financially lean times it had a certain gusto; the same horses that were used to pull Burke's coach in London were put to the plow at the estate, and when the house was robbed of all the silver and plate, Jane Burke told a correspondent, "all our friends, must bring their Knives and forks in their pockets, as the French do. Well, if we are poor, we are honest" (3 November 1784).

Burke's maiden speech in the House of Commons, made on 19 April 1774, just three days after his entry, made him a figure to be reckoned with. William Pitt commended him as "a very able advocate," and noted that Rockingham was fortunate to have such a man in his party. The subject of Burke's speech, which so impressed his listeners, was the American colonies.

As editor of the *Annual Register* Burke had made himself knowledgeable about American affairs. In 1771 he became even more familiar with the problems of the colonies when he was made agent for the colony of New York. The compilations of his ideas are found in two publications: the *Speech on American Taxation* and the more familiar *Speech on Conciliation With the Colonies*, both published in 1775.

Even a cursory reading of these works will disprove the easy generalization that "Burke supported the American Revolution." From first to last Burke's quarrel with the measures taken by the British government in the management of the North American colonies was not that the strictures were inherently repressive and unjust but that they were unjust measures because they were used against British subjects who happened to live across the Atlantic.

The first of his lengthy speeches on the American question was made a few months after the Boston Tea Party (16 December 1773). Burke spoke for two hours against proposed retaliatory legislation. One of the measures, among those named the "Intolerable Acts," was the Boston Port Bill, which closed Boston Harbor until the owners of the destroyed tea had been compensated. In response to numerous requests, the speech was published on 10 January 1775.

The *Speech on American Taxation* is not a defense of the colonial spirit manifested in throwing some three hundred casks of tea into Boston Harbor but is rather an attack on colonial policy and on the Boston Port Bill as meanspirited. In the course of discussion Burke, well aware of the House's impatience with any more capitulation to the colonies, mounts a defense of the Rockingham party's repeal of the Stamp Tax in 1766 when, Burke argues, the colonists were content with concessions made. He argues that this new scheme of taxation has revived colonial dissatisfaction.

Although Burke was well aware that Parliament was not going to concede its right to tax, he did not deal with the essential question: how long do you continue to repeal measures which are

The portrait of Burke that Sir Joshua Reynolds painted for Henry and Hester Thrale in 1774
(National Gallery of Ireland)

not to the liking of the colonists? Burke's refusal to handle that question indicates that he underestimated the feelings of the colonists with respect to taxation—no amount of capitulation to separate incidents would satisfy them.

The *Speech on American Taxation* was admired at the time, and still is, for the scope of Burke's analysis and for the character portrayals of George, Viscount of Townshend, George Grenville, and William Pitt, Earl of Chatham, that it contains. For example, his description of Chatham's surrounding himself with "yes-men" is a masterpiece of metaphor: "he put together a piece of joinery, so cross indented and whimsically dove-tailed; a cabinet so variously inlaid; such a piece of diversified Mosaic; such a tesselated pavement without cement; here a bit of black stone, and there a bit of white; patriots and courtiers, king's friends and republicans; whigs and tories; treacherous friends and open ene-

mies; that it was indeed a very curious show, but utterly unsafe to touch, and unsure to stand on."

Burke's rhetoric evoked admiration but no action. He was fighting a losing battle to convince the administration that their American policy was, as he later wrote his friend Richard Campion, bringing England "with hasty strides to its utter ruin" (1 December 1777).

However, Burke was not one to give up easily. A year after his *Speech on American Taxation* he came back to the subject; this time he had a proposal for conciliation. In the opening statements of *Speech on Conciliation With the Colonies*, delivered on 22 March 1775, Burke puts two questions before the House: "First, whether you ought to concede; and secondly, what your concession ought to be." By way of demonstrating the need for concession, Burke argues from the particular circumstances and from the nature "of the object we have before us." The first circumstance takes in the commerce, geography, and agricultural way of life in the colonies. He enforces his argument with specific figures: in sixty-eight years England's trade with America has increased twelvefold; as a matter of fact, "the commerce of your colonies is out of all proportion beyond the numbers of the people." In describing the expanding agriculture and industry of the country, he notes that it is the same spirit of enterprise that makes "a love of freedom the predominating feature which marks and distinguishes the whole."

Interwoven throughout Burke's argument are repeated reminders that the people of the colonies are descendants of Englishmen; as such their ideas of freedom and liberty bear the stamp of their English heritage: "They are therefore not only devoted to liberty, but to liberty according to English ideas and on English principles." "Principles" and "ideas" are abstractions easily dismissed, Burke warns his audience: "Abstract liberty, like other mere abstractions, is not to be found." If so, the moot point becomes not "whether their spirit deserves praise or blame" but "what, in the name of God, shall we do with it?" Moving forward with his argument, Burke cites another reality: "Three thousand miles of ocean lie between you and them. No contrivance can prevent the effect of this distance in weakening government. Seas roll, and months pass, between the order and the execution; and the want of a speedy explanation of a single point is enough to defeat an whole system."

Concluding his argument on the futility of dealing with the colonies by changing them, Burke offers another equally futile alternative— "prosecute that spirit in its overt acts as criminal." That too is impossible: "I do not know the method of drawing up an indictment against an whole people." According to his argument, the only viable alternative is conciliation.

Burke disposes of the taxation question by affirming that Parliament has the *right* to tax, but then he takes the issue to higher ground: "My idea, therefore, without considering whether we yield as matter of right or grant as matter of favor, is, *to admit the people of our colonies into an interest in the Constitution,* and, by recording that admission in the journals of Parliament, to give them as strong an assurance as the nature of the thing will admit that we mean forever to adhere to that solemn declaration of systematic indulgence." Burke then discusses similar cases where conciliation was effective: Ireland, Wales, Chester, and Durham. Finally Burke offers thirteen

specific resolutions, among them repeal of the Tea Act and the Intolerable Acts, which included the Boston Port Bill.

There were a great many people who took exception to Burke's portrayal of the American colonists as well-intentioned lovers of liberty. His friend Samuel Johnson argued that in choosing to leave the mother country, an individual also chooses to relinquish certain privileges—such as representation—that come with residence in that country. Another critic, Josia Tucker, wrote an answer in the form of a letter to Burke. Tucker objected to each of Burke's six factors contributing to "spirit of liberty" in the colonies. Among other points of disagreement was Tucker's statement that the early Americans were religious "enthusiasts" who were bigoted and who had no compunction about taxing "the Ungodly." He concluded that Britain would be better off without the burden of the American colonies because the Americans would then pay their debts to Great Britain as they did to other countries.

In the fall of 1774 Burke lost his seat for Wendover and was tempted to resign from Parliament in favor of William Burke. While Rockingham voiced admiration for Edmund's "principles," he admonished, "I am sure both for M Wm Burke and all your family concerns, yourself being in parliament, is the principal thing necessary." Burke took Rockingham's advice and spent the next months in a grueling campaign; in the middle of October he went six hundred miles in eight days by coach and on horseback to secure a place for himself in the Bristol poll. Safely elected by 8 November 1774, he wrote a candidate's perennial complaint to his wife, Jane: "I begin to breathe, though my Visits are not half over. However I dispatch them at a great Rate. . . . Now my dearest Jane I entertain some glimpse of hope that I shall see you shortly."

In 1777 Burke wrote a public letter to the sheriffs of Bristol attacking Lord North's bill partially suspending the Habeas Corpus Act in Britain. He attacks the bill on the ground that, for the first time, distinctions are made among the people of the realm—"the bare suspicion of the crown" can put an individual outside the law. Burke sees North's action as evidence of the way that American troubles are "productive of many mischiefs. . . . Not only our policy is deranged, and our empire distracted, but our laws and our legislative spirit appear to have been totally perverted by it." He imputes the troubles in America to government mismanagement: "*General* rebel-

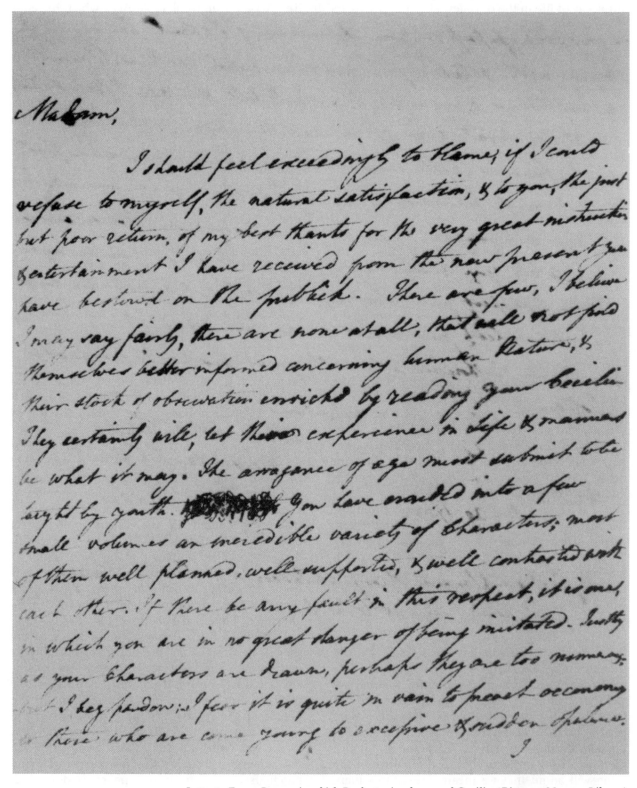

Letter to Fanny Burney in which Burke praises her novel Cecilia *(Pierpont Morgan Library)*

I might [illegible] or your delicacy if I should fill my letter to you with what I fill my conversation to others. I should be troublesome to you alone, if I should tell you all I feel & think, on the natural vein of humour, the tender pathetic, the comprehensive & noble moral; & the sagacious observation, that appear quite throughout that extraordinary performance. In an age distinguished by producing extraordinary Women, I should love to tell you where my opinion would place you amongst them— I respect your modesty, that will not endure the commendations which your merit forces from every body.

I have the honour to be with great gratitude, respect, & Esteem,

*Madam
Your most obedient
& most humble Servt.
Edm Burke*

*Whitehall
July 29. 1782.*

My best compliments & congratulations to Doctor Burney on the great honour acquired to his family.

lions and revolts of an whole people never were *encouraged*, now or at any time. They are always *provoked*. . . ." He points to his plan of conciliation as still viable and defines a free government as "for any practical purpose, . . . what the people think so—and that they, and not I, are the natural, lawful, and competent judges of this matter." *A Letter to the Sheriffs of Bristol* provoked a mixed reaction. Burke's definition of a free government was a point for ridicule; others resented his attack on speculative thinkers.

In 1774, when Burke was elected to represent Bristol, the influential merchants there agreed with his American policy. At the time they had no quarrel with his perception of his duty as their representative as described in his acceptance speech: "It is [the duty of your representative] to sacrifice his repose, his pleasure, his satisfactions to theirs—and above all, ever and in all cases, to prefer their interest to his own. But his unbiased opinion, his mature judgement, his enlightened conscience, he ought not to sacrifice to you, to any man, or to any set of men living. These he does not derive from your pleasure,—no, nor from the law and the Constitution. They are a trust from Providence, for the abuse of which he is deeply answerable." The Bristol merchants did not understand the full implications of his statements until their local interests collided with the Irish trade interests that affected the empire. Thus, in 1780 when Burke went to Bristol to campaign for reelection, he was aware of dissatisfaction with his stands as their representative, and on 9 September he declined the poll. Rockingham, aware of Burke's discouragement with public life, wrote to William Henry Cavendish Bentinck, Duke of Portland, that they had to contrive something for him as "I think in every view, it is right and necessary that he should be in Parliament, both in respect to the publick and to himself." In November Burke was elected to Malton, a rotten borough in Rockingham's control; he was to represent Malton until he retired from Parliament in 1794.

When war between the American colonies and England broke out, Burke focused his attention on the political disturbances in Ireland with the view of being effective there. Working quietly and sometimes indirectly, he urged acceptance of a Catholic Relief Bill which relaxed the Penal Laws respecting the ownership and inheritance of property. The bill first passed in England and Scotland; by 1780 Catholics in Ireland were voted the same privileges. According to the bill, Catholics were able to lease land for a period of 999 years and were able to sell and inherit lands under the same conditions as Protestants.

The passage of the bill was not accepted by certain Protestant associations, and on 2 June 1780 Lord George Gordon led an angry crowd to the House of Commons, where they were refused a hearing. On the evening of 5 June they attacked the home of Sir George Savile, who sponsored the bill, and it was rumored that the mob intended to burn Burke's house. In a 13 June letter to Richard Shackleton, Burke described the riots: "For four Nights, I kept watch at Lord Rockinghams, or Sir George Savilles, whose houses were Garrisond by a strong body of Soldiers, together with Numbers of [true] friends of the first rank, who were willing to share their danger. . . ." On the fifth day of the riots he took to the streets—"I thought, that if my Liberty was once gone, and that I could not walk the Streets of this Town with tranquility, I was in no condition to perform the duties for which I ought alone to wish for Life. I therefore resolved, they should see, that, for one, I was neither to be forced nor intimidated from the straight line of what was right. . . ." Burke did confront the mob, but fortunately they decided that he was "a gentleman" and made way for him. These incidents, no doubt, came to his mind ten years later when he described in vivid detail the early days of the French Revolution.

At the same time Burke expended significant efforts to change certain financial practices in government. These efforts are detailed in his *Speech on Economical Reform*, delivered on 11 February 1780. In his reform plan Burke advocates specific changes in civil and domestic expenditures of the crown which would reduce the influence of the crown and strengthen the role of Parliament in the constitution. However, Burke characteristically cautions, such changes are not to be made quickly. To be viable, reforms needed to be made prudently and with a temperate approach which, for him, always had the principle of growth. The primary focus of his plan was the reduction and reorganization of the civil list. Other measures include giving Treasury the responsibility for all civil list expenditures. In addition to these core proposals, Burke set out others which were given due attention in the following years.

Two years later Burke had the opportunity to put his suggested reforms into practice when he was made paymaster general of the forces in the second Rockingham administration of 1782.

In that capacity, Burke was able to get a civil-list act through Parliament that reformed the pay office by consigning the balances to the Bank of England rather than keeping them in the personal possession of the paymaster. In this area he had accomplished what he set out to do, and he turned his attention to another part of the British empire: India.

The problem of British rule in India is such a complex tapestry of economics, politics, native customs, and individual responsibilities that to take one part in isolation is to risk missing the complexity of the whole. That Burke was able to penetrate this morass, discern the various entities, and see each in its relation to the total picture attests to the power of his intellect.

While Burke had written on India when he was editor of the *Annual Register*, his official Indian writings begin a few years after the American Revolution and continue into the French—a period of some fourteen years. During those years he "looked at everything that could throw light on the subject," talked to people who had been to India, and corresponded with those who were still there. At first his view of India was objective and distant; as its affairs became daily intellectual fare, he told a friend, "they engross my whole heart, and in truth cost me some sleepless nights."

The general cause of Burke's sleepless nights—and the source of trouble in British India—was the East India Company, a trading company incorporated by royal charter in 1600. Through territorial wars, the company had established itself as the ruling body in British India, placed its own nominee on the throne, and ruled through a governor. In 1771 the governor of Bengal was Warren Hastings, who became the first governor general in 1774.

Criticism of the company's administration led to a call for a select committee to look into Indian affairs. In 1771 Burke and the Rockingham Whigs objected to such an investigation because they feared that the outcome would put more power and influence into the hands of the king and his ministers. However, by 1781 Burke's sympathies were with the natives. He had been elected to a select committee constituted in response to a petition by certain members of the East India Company and a committee of British subjects living in Bengal for an investigation into abuses.

Contemporaries and historians have faulted Burke for his about-face with respect to the East India Company. They accuse him of self-interest because he owned stock in it and of being misled by William Burke, his kinsman, and Philip Francis, member of the Council of Bengal and enemy of Hastings. That Burke was manipulated by William or by Philip Francis is highly improbable; he came to his conclusions after years of detailed investigation and knew more about it than the other two men together.

The select committee issued eleven reports unfavorable to the directors of the East India Company and to Governor-General Warren Hastings. (Burke wrote the ninth and the eleventh and assisted in preparing others.) There was increasing speculation as to whether legislation was enough or whether criminal prosecution was called for. Parliament had ordered the recall of Hastings when Lord Rockingham died on 1 July 1782. The king appointed a Hastings supporter, William Petty, Lord Shelburn, prime minister, but the Rockingham Whigs refused to serve under him. Under this arrangement, Burke was again in the opposition, and Hastings was temporarily saved from recall. In February Charles Fox and Frederick, Lord North, set aside personal animosities to form a coalition ministry, and Shelburn resigned. In the coalition ministry Burke took up his former position as paymaster general of the forces.

The chief product of the coalition government—and the cause of its downfall—was Fox's East India Bill. Although it had Fox's name attached to it, most of the bill was written by Burke. The most striking feature was the proposal to replace the East India Company directors with a commission, nominated by Fox, of seven members from the House of Commons. This commission would rule India for four years and be responsible to (but not removable by) the House of Commons. A storm erupted over any interference in the affairs of the East India Company. Because the interests and fortunes of people both in England and in India were involved, organized protests were formed to influence votes against Fox's bill. On 1 December 1783 Burke defended the bill in a three-hour speech.

In his opening remarks Burke establishes his persona as one who "has thought himself obliged by the research of years" to defend the proposed measures. Burke reminds his listeners that "this business cannot be indifferent to our fame. It will turn out a matter of great disgrace or great glory to the whole British nation." He notes that objections to the bill did not stem

Charles James Fox and Edmund Burke (portrait by Angelica Kauffmann; National Gallery of Ireland)

from the "efficiency, the vigor, or the completeness of the scheme" but from the effects "which this plan of reform for Indian administration may have on the privileges of great public bodies in England."

Throughout the carefully reasoned speech Burke reminds his listeners that political power and commercial privilege are trusts for which one is held accountable. Commercial companies and governments have a responsibility to those under their control. He speaks to the objection that "the bill is an attack on the chartered rights of men" by distinguishing between chartered rights and natural rights. While not directly mentioning natural law in conjunction with natural rights, he implies that they are linked. Legal rights, which include charters, are "artificial" in that they must conform to the primary natural rights of man. Citing the East India charter as one which establishes monopoly and creates power, Burke concludes that "political power and commercial monopoly are *not* the rights of men;

and the rights to them derived from charters it is fallacious and sophistical to call 'the chartered rights of men.' "

Because the East India Company abused its power, it was the duty of Parliament, as the agency which gives the company its charter, to redress these abuses. Reverting again to the responsibilities of those in power, Burke admits that differences of language and custom make governing India difficult. Nevertheless, Providence has placed Britain in the situation, "and we must do the best we can. . . . The situation of man is the preceptor of his duty."

Burke's speech had the desired effect in Commons, and that body passed Fox's East India Bill, but when it came before the House of Lords, the king circulated a letter saying that he would regard as an enemy anyone who voted for it. On 17 December 1783 the bill was defeated in the House of Lords; the following day the king dismissed the coalition ministry. On 19 December Burke received notice that his majesty had no further need for his services as paymaster general of the forces. Although Burke went back into opposition, his work on the select committee was not affected by the change in ministry.

In the 1784 election which followed, Burke easily won reelection to Parliament as representative of Malton, but others who supported the coalition government were not as fortunate. Roughly one hundred coalition supporters lost their seats and, in popular parlance, became "Fox's martyrs."

In April Burke went to Glasgow, where he had been elected lord rector of the university, a politically significant as well as honorary post. When the new Parliament went into session, he discovered that his position had changed significantly. The membership was younger; two hundred fifty were under forty years of age. Burke felt himself to be playing "a captive part in a triumphal procession" as these new and old enemies staged coughing fits and tried to shout him down when he spoke. The end of the year brought additional sorrow when he was first pallbearer at the funeral of his old friend Samuel Johnson.

Fox's India bill had called for an investigation into the nawab of Arcot's debts, which were the result of corrupt practices of the East India Company. Pitt had included the same issue in the bill he submitted after becoming minister. There was a cursory examination, and then a payment plan was set up whereby the nawab's creditors would be paid what they claimed with no questions asked. Seeing intimations of the corruption he had always feared would come to Britain through the unscrupulous dealings of the East India Company, Burke delivered and published a speech on the nawab of Arcot's debts.

Delivered on 28 February 1785, the speech is primarily an accusation against specific people who had a role in the settling of the nawab's debts: Henry Dundas, chairman of the Secret Committee on India Affairs and author of the settlement; William Pitt and other ministers; Paul Benfield, member of the East India Company who profited handsomely from his position there and who bribed his way into the House of Commons; and Richard Atkinson, Benfield's agent. Its topicality makes the speech difficult going for one not versed in eighteenth-century Indian affairs. With typical thoroughness Burke details the misuse of monies and follows each of the principals "over that field of deception, clearing what he has purposely obscured, and fairly stating what it was necessary for him to misrepresent."

While the details may elude the modern reader, Burke's imagery and his characterization of central participants make it one of his greatest speeches. Burke's Swiftean imagery, here and in other speeches dealing with India, was calculated to make real the corruptions that he saw. Henry Dundas is "exposed like the sow of imperial augury, lying in the mud with all the prodigies of her fertility about her, as evidence of her delicate amours." Paul Benfield, "that minion of the human race," is labeled as "a criminal, who long since ought to have fattened the region kites with his offal." Benfield's playing fast and loose with positions in the House of Commons is "the golden cup of abominations—the chalice of the fornications of rapine, usury, and oppression" held out by the "gorgeous Eastern harlot." Nor does Burke spare his auditors the horrors of war precipitated by greed: "The miserable inhabitants, flying from their flaming villages, in part were slaughtered; others, without regard to sex, to age, to the respect of rank or sacredness of function . . . were swept into captivity in an unknown and hostile land."

Paul Benfield's letters, with their repeated references to Burke as "the damn'd Paddy" and "the Malevolent Paddy," reflect the hatred felt for Burke by those who were the objects of his investigation. In spite of Burke's rough treatment of Dundas, the two were able to work together later in the prosecution of the governor general of India, Warren Hastings. That unfortunate gentleman finally arrived in England in June; two months later Burke's *Speech on the Nawab of Arcot's Debts* was published and set the stage for one of the greatest spectacles of the latter half of the eighteenth century—the impeachment trial of Warren Hastings.

That Burke was able to convince Pitt and the House of Commons to impeach Hastings was a feat of no little significance. It is even more significant that Burke never thought Hastings would actually be declared guilty. He wished to prove "*a general evil intention*, manifested through a long series and a great variety of acts." In essence, the issue was not legal but moral and concerned the use of power. In Warren Hastings Burke saw the personification of rapacious power.

In the plethora of paper that was generated from start to finish of the India/Hastings business, Burke sounds the issues of empire that he confronted in the American crises ten years earlier. Once again Burke is dealing with arbitrary rule of a colony, and once again he comes down on the side of humanitarian government which bases its strictures on the particular nature and circumstances of the colony in question. When Hastings argued that "actions do not bear the same moral qualities which the same actions would bear in Europe," Burke counters with an appeal to Natural Law: "the laws of morality are the same everywhere . . . there is no action which would pass for an act of extortion, of peculation, of bribery, and of oppression in England, that is not an act of extortion, of peculation, of bribery, and oppression in Europe, Asia, Africa, and all the world over."

The theme running through all of his speeches and writings on India is that conquest carries with it moral duties: "this nation never did give a power without annexing to it proportionable degree of responsibility . . . to observe the laws, rights, usages, and customs of the natives and to pursue their benefit in all things: for this duty was inherent in the nature, institution, and purpose of the office which they received." He laments the fact that England, as represented by the East India Company, had done nothing for the natives—"has erected no churches, no hospitals, no palaces, no schools; England has built no bridges, made no highroads, cut no navigations, dug out no reservoirs. . . ."

Seeing in the East India Company's arbitrary rule of India a foreshadowing of the same results as Britain's dictatorial rule of America, Burke fears for the empire. He argues that the political and economic systems of a colony must be allowed to function naturally; that is, according to the customs of the country. Let alone, the result would be harmony between the mother country and her colony; in this case, India— "if we are not able to contrive some method of governing India *well*, which will not of necessity become the means of governing Great Britain *ill*, a ground is laid for their eternal separation."

Critics have faulted Burke's approach to the India problem on several counts. They say that he viewed the Indians no more realistically than he did the Americans in 1775—he idealized their society and their government, and he misjudged their desire to remain a British colony. They see him as a utilitarian, not a humanist, and charge him with obscuring pragmatic, partisan concerns behind the smoke screen of morality. Perhaps more than any of these, Burke is criticized for his single-minded prosecution of Warren Hastings, an affable man who seemed unaware that he had

committed crimes for which he should be impeached. The viability and seriousness of these charges continue to be debated; meanwhile we have Burke's own perceptions of his case—"If I am wrong, it is not for want of pains to know what is right." His perceptions of the situation also include his estimation of the place "the India business" occupies in his life's work. A year before his death, he wrote to his executor: "Let my endeavours to save the Nation from that Shame and guilt, be my monument; The only one I ever will have. Let every thing I have done, said, or written be forgotten but this."

The impeachment trial of Warren Hastings ran an extraordinary length of time—seven years; 148 sittings. The press, never gentle where Burke was concerned, harshly condemned him in prose and in caricature for the intensity with which he ran the prosecution and blamed him for the length of the trial. The journals of the trial exonerate Burke and the managers. Moreover, it certainly was not Burke's wish that it continue. He had to postpone his retirement from the House of Commons, and he was worn out in body and mind. The fatigue of "reading, comparing, and extracting Mountains of Papers" over a long period of time affected his health—"I am not well," he told a friend; "I eat too much; I drink too much; I sleep very little." To Gen. John Burgoyne, a fellow committee member, he enumerated the stumbling blocks to a timely end to the impeachment: "we have to deal with partial judges, unwilling and prevaricating witnesses, mangled records, a reluctant House of Commons, and an indifferent publick" (4 May 1788). Moreover, even among Burke's friends Hastings had his sympathizers, who thought him an "injured and innocent man." In the beginning, the trial was a spectacle in the mode of a coronation—the galleries of Westminster Hall were filled with the notable, the interested, and the curious. As the trial dragged on, Burke found himself on center stage in a one-man show. His party had become sick of the whole business, and by 1792 even the attendance of the managers was sparse, and on 6 June 1792 only Burke was present at the appointed time. At last, on 20 June 1794 the impeachment trial of Warren Hastings came to an end when the case was sent to the House of Lords for judgment. The following day Burke tendered his resignation from the House of Commons to William, Earl Fitzwilliam.

During the seven years that he was preoccupied with the Hastings business, Burke's life continued in other directions. For one thing, the situation in the neighboring country across the channel nudged itself into his consciousness. In August 1789 he wrote to Lord Charlemont: "As to us here our thoughts of everything at home are suspended, by our astonishment at the wonderful Spectacle which is exhibited in a Neighboring and rival Country—England gazing with astonishment at a French struggle for Liberty and not knowing whether to blame or to applaud!"

On 4 November 1789 Burke received a letter from a young Frenchman, Charles Jean-François Depont, who had visited the Burkes in London and in Beaconsfield. Depont asked Burke for his opinion of recent developments in France. Burke jotted a brief reply and then seems to have laid it aside. Coincidentally, on that same day Richard Price, a Dissenting preacher and member of a radical group called The Revolution Society, gave a sermon commemorating the Glorious Revolution of 1688. Price rejoiced in the fall of the Bastille the preceding July and declared that "Civil governors are properly the servants of the public; and a King is no more than the first servant of the public, created by it, maintained by it, and responsible to it. . . ." Among the three principles of the revolution which his society upheld was that of the "right to chuse our own governors; to cashier them for misconduct; and to frame a government for ourselves." Burke did not read Price's sermon until a few days before Parliament resumed in January. He was alarmed enough to "throw down a few notes." His uneasiness was increased when, in February, Charles James Fox, leader of the Whigs, political ally, and friend, praised the French Revolution. A week later Burke wrote to a correspondent that he felt "obliged to *act*. . . . As far as my share of a public trust goes, I am in *trust* religiously to maintain the rights and properties of all descriptions of people. . . ." By this time Burke had framed several replies to Depont; the third letter became the *Reflections on the Revolution in France*. The full title—*Reflections on the Revolution in France and on the Proceedings in Certain Societies in London Relative to that Event*—indicates Burke's center of concern. The book was not written with the intention of influencing events in France; Burke's aim was to halt any incursion of French ideas or actions into England.

The intellectual climate of France had disturbed Burke when he visited there in 1773; earlier, in 1769, he had predicted disaster from its economic situation. Then he had a visit from

Thomas Paine, who told him, with great enthusiasm, about the revolutionary stirrings which he had seen in France. Price's sermon, and a publication arguing for complete separation of church and state written by Presbyterian minister Joseph Priestly, made Burke aware of a significant feeling in England in favor of the French Revolution. From the start he realized that the direction of this revolution was toward political and social turmoil and not toward reform.

Using the letter form, which allowed for a personal tone and more open structure, Burke begins by disassociating himself from the Revolution Society and the other pro-French group, the Constitutional Society. He then quickly moves to an attack on those in the radical movement in England and a refutation of their claims to be heirs of the 1688 revolution. Price comes in for a whipping as "a man much connected with literary caballers and intriguing philosophers; with political theologians and theological politicians both at home and abroad." In castigating Price's "Bill of Rights"—to choose "our own governors, cashier them for misconduct and frame a government for ourselves"—Burke explains the significance of the English revolution of 1688, which, he says, was a constitutional method of making important changes in civil society.

In the second and longest part of the *Reflections on the Revolution in France* Burke uses the English constitution as a model for the way the French could have needed reforms and still keep the ancien regime intact. "You might, if you pleased, have profited of our example. . . . Your privileges, though discontinued, were not lost to memory. . . . you might have repaired those walls; you might have built on those old foundations." Burke assures his reader that he respects France's particular national character; he does not expect France to be a constitutional replica of England. He defends the ancien regime but does not do so uncritically: "there was no question but that abuses existed, and that they demanded a reform . . . the true question at present is, Whether those who would have reformed, or those who have destroyed, are in the right?" Change is necessary for continued existence, but precipitous change is dangerous; change that does not look back to history is ephemeral; and change that aims for perfection is doomed to failure in a finite world.

Burke then gives a detailed critique of the composition of the National Assembly and its reforms of the clergy, the military, and public fi-

The POLITICAL-BANDITTI assailing the SAVIOUR of INDIA.

James Gillray's Tory view of the impeachment proceedings against Warren Hastings, governor general of India: Burke fires a blunderbuss at Hastings while Fox attacks him with a knife and Frederick, Lord North, steals a moneybag.

nances. He wonders aloud how "an handful of country clowns who have seats in that Assembly, some of whom are said not to be able to read and write," have the experience to govern a nation. Forging his counterrevolution, Burke deals with each French reform by comparing it with a like situation in England. He concludes: "The improvements of the national assembly are superficial, their errors fundamental." In conclusion Burke warns his young correspondent that, before a final settlement is reached, France "may be obliged to pass, as one of our poets says, 'through great varieties of untried being,' and in all its transmigrations to be purified by fire and blood."

While echoing concepts Burke expresses elsewhere, the *Reflections on the Revolution in France* has a brilliance all its own. Familiar themes appear and reappear in multiple contexts; flashes of irony intersperse reasoned discussions, and sub-

lime heights are scaled as Burke soars to the reaches of the Gothic and the pathetic.

One recognizes a familiar theme in his treatment of speculators and metaphysicians who "are so taken up with their theories about the rights of man, that they have totally forgot his nature." He has always held that human nature is complex; therefore he cannot praise anything which relates to human concerns "on a simple view of the object . . . in all the nakedness and solitude of metaphysical abstraction." For Burke terms such as *liberty*, *equality*, and *fraternity* in the abstract are meaningless. "Circumstances . . . give in reality to every political principle its distinguishing colour, and discriminating effect." But Burke is not antirationalist. In fact, a deeply reflective, "sagacious, powerful and combining mind" is necessary in one who is to govern. Such an individual tests a theory by the way it works in practical circumstances. Even then, a powerful mind is not enough—once again Burke links politics and morality: "All persons possessing any portion of power ought to be strongly and awfully impressed with an idea that they act in trust; and that they are to account for their conduct in that trust to the one great master, author and founder of society."

Burke believes that a hierarchical class structure is natural to society and that European civilization has depended "for ages" upon "the spirit of a gentleman." That spirit resides in the landed gentry who have a sense of responsibility for civil society. In the hierarchical class structure that Burke speaks of, property plays a significant role. Ownership and protection of property are natural instincts; the "professors of the rights of men" had not learned that "the first and original faith of civil society" is pledged "to the property of the citizen." Society is continued by "the power of perpetuating our property in our families." It follows that loyalty to the state comes from loyalty to small groups—"To be attached to the subdivision, to love the little platoon we belong to in society, is the first principle . . . of public affections." Finally, the hereditary principle also applies to governments.

Burke had long held that prescription—authority sanctioned by long-standing usage—gave title to political authority. Thus the form a government took was not something to be decided anew by each generation. However, government did not gain authority simply by lasting a long time but by how well it had worked over a long period. Yes, Burke agrees, "society is indeed a contract." However, he attacks revolutionaries who would dissolve this most serious of contracts "as nothing better than a partnership agreement in a trade of pepper and coffee. . . . it is a partnership in all science . . . art . . . every virtue . . . all perfection." In essence Burke comes round again to the moral basis of political authority—society is to provide for the intellectual and moral life of its members. Moreover this partnership does not function only for the present generation: "but between those who are living, those who are dead, and those who are to be born." Present government depends upon wisdom accreted over the centuries. The British constitution, Burke informs his French reader and reminds his British audience, is a prescriptive one that has a moral basis. "We have an inheritable crown; an inheritable peerage; and an house of commons and a people inheriting privileges, franchises, and liberties, from a long line of ancestors. This policy appears to me to be the . . . happy effect of following nature. . . ."

Where do individual rights fit into prescriptive government? "The *real* rights of men," Burke contends, are the right to justice, to labor and to the fruits of labor, to inheritance, to feed and to educate one's children and "to instruction in life, and to consolation in death." Thus, while "all men have equal rights" it is "not to equal things." To presume that all men are fit to govern is to toy with the nature of things.

With the publication of the *Reflections on the Revolution in France* in November 1790, Burke found that his friends and enemies did an about-face. Those who recently had been against him in the Hastings business found themselves aligned with his view of the French Revolution. Fanny Burney, a Hastings supporter, wrote to a friend that the *Reflections on the Revolution in France* was the "noblest, deepest, most animated and exalted work that I think I have ever read." The king, who had often been the object of Burke's satire, said that every gentleman should read it, and even the independent press gave it favorable treatment. Letters and diaries give evidence of the overwhelming support Burke received for his views of the situation in France.

However, the opposition was formidable. Satirists and caricaturists found the *Reflections on the Revolution in France* good game. A typical example is a print depicting Burke as Don Quixote wearing a Jesuit's baretta and paying court to Marie Antoinette. Slightly behind him, a weeping Jane Burke is pictured. Burke is saying, "Jesus Christ what an ass I have been a number of Years, to have doted on an old woman—Heavens! what's her bacon and eggs to the delicious Dairy of this celestial Vision." In a sense, the print is a backhanded compliment to Burke's devotion to his wife.

Most of the pamphlet attacks on the *Reflections on the Revolution in France* contend that the will of the people is supreme. Others attack Burke for his lack of judgment, for being reactionary, for misrepresenting the Glorious Revolution of 1688, for an imperfect understanding of French affairs, and for being intolerant of religious dissent. There were many who saw Burke's view of the French Revolution as inconsistent with his "approval" of the American Revolution. In fact, Burke never "approved of the American Revolution"; he approved of the colonists' struggle to be given the privileges of British subjects. Others gave wholesale condemnation to the "hys-

DON DISMALLO, AFTER AN ABSENCE OF SIXTEEN YEARS, EMBRACING HIS BEAUTIFUL VISION!

Burke embracing Marie Antoinette as his wife weeps, a political cartoon reflecting the widely held opinion that Burke had abandoned political allies when he supported the French monarchy in his Reflections on the Revolution in France

terical" tone of the *Reflections on the Revolution in France*. These inevitably refer to the passage where Burke describes the mob invading Marie Antoinette's bedchamber as evidence that "the age of chivalry is gone. That of sophisters, economists and calculators has succeeded."

In terms of intellectual and analytical acumen, James Mackintosh's *Vindiciae Gallicae* (1791) ranks above other pamphlet replies. However, the most familiar reply to Burke is Thomas Paine's *Rights of Man* (1791). Paine's view of the French Revolution differs completely from Burke's. Paine believed that the situation in France would resolve itself as did the American Revolution—in an orderly system of representative government. As noted, Burke saw that the character of the French Revolution was more in-

clined to destroy than to build and would result in bloodshed and anarchy. Paine's book is a personal attack on Burke and a condemnation of the institutions that Burke held sacred: the monarchy, the state, the church, and the constitution. Paine's judgment of Burke's passage on Marie Antoinette's sufferings is well known: "He pities the plumage but forgets the dying bird." Paine did not recognize rhetorical exaggeration. This is not to say that Burke was posturing his sorrow for the French queen's plight, but in the context of the passage she is a symbol for a world that seems doomed. Moreover, the passage is atypical of Burke's style throughout his book. The ideological dispute between Paine and Burke went on for several years. As a matter of fact, writing to a friend in 1795, Burke complains that the Paine/

Priestly sympathizers "will have it . . . [that] Citizen Paine only moves as I drag him along."

Modern critics of the *Reflections on the Revolution in France* discuss Burke's ideas on many levels—historical, economical, political, and philosophical. One basis of contention centers on Burke's meaning of "prescriptive government"; others juxtapose the arguments of Burke and Karl Marx as a way of understanding contemporary politics. One sees the *Reflections on the Revolution in France* as Burke indirectly upholding his Irish countrymen; another sees Burke's ideas as reflective of the Scottish school of political economy. Some assert that the book is yet another proof that Burke does not have a political philosophy. Others maintain that Burke's ideas in the *Reflections on the Revolution in France* are thoroughly rooted in the Natural Law tradition. One thing is certain: the *Reflections on the Revolution in France* continues to challenge readers of every generation, who somehow discover that Burke is saying something to them.

Responses to the *Reflections on the Revolution in France* also came from France itself. A member of the National Assembly, François Louis-Thibault de Menonville, wrote to Burke protesting his judgments against members of the National Assembly. De Menonville, a moderate, was afraid Burke's vehemence would agitate extremists. Burke sent a reply to de Menonville. He also alerted the French to the possibility of war by suggesting that the "act of power" to restore control in France would have to "come from abroad." When Burke heard that de Menonville had published his letter, he prepared it for publication in England under the title *Letter to a Member of the National Assembly in answer to some Objections to his book on French Affairs.*

Many still felt that Burke was an alarmist. He found himself on the margins of political life and, most acutely, an outsider in his own party. The final break did not come until May, and, when it did, it occurred in the House of Commons. On 15 April Charles Fox ended a debate on Russia with a panegyric on the French Revolution. Burke was not able to reply until three weeks later when Fox publicly repeated his support for the "rights of man." Burke exploded, and in the presence of the assembled House told Fox, "I have done my duty at the price of my friend: our friendship is at an end." The emotional scene ended with Fox in tears and Burke still enraged.

Acted out in the public forum, the quarrel was fair game for the press, who announced the following day that "Mr Burke retires from Parliament." Burke, who had no such intentions until Hastings's trial was ended, was bitter and felt that he had been publicly condemned.

The argument between Burke and his party leaders concerning the legitimacy of the French Revolution centered on their interpretations of the revolution of 1688. The Foxite Whigs believed that the 1688 revolution was simply a triumph of the people's will; that sovereignty constantly and unalienably resides in the people. Burke held that the 1688 revolution prevented any change and thus more firmly established an inherited monarchy limited by the balance of Lords and Commons.

During the summer of 1791 he set down his position in a work which he titled *Appeal from the New to the Old Whigs*. Although the pamphlet was published anonymously and supposedly was written by a person who believed in Burke's principles, it was clear that Burke wrote it. The "Old Whigs" of the title refer to those, like Burke, who felt themselves to be in the tradition of the Whigs of 1688; the "New Whigs" were those who had aligned themselves with Thomas Paine and Richard Price. In addition to being a defense of Burke's position, *Appeal from the New to the Old Whigs* is also an answer to Paine's *Rights of Man*, for the culpable "they" in the pamphlet refers specifically to those who have adopted Paine's views. Without ever mentioning Paine's name ("this great teacher of the rights of man") or quoting directly from *Rights of Man*, Burke castigates Paine and his book.

Appeal from the New to the Old Whigs is important as a clarification of Burke's basic ideas concerning the English constitution and revolution as expressed in the *Reflections on the Revolution in France*. The form is more structured and the rhetoric more subdued, but the familiar flashes of irony are there. Burke's argument is based upon his metaphysics as well as his politics. In essence he argues that obedience to the constitution is part of the duties a social being incurs by virtue of living in a civil society. Moreover, civil obligations are linked to other moral obligations: "We have obligations to mankind at large, which are not in consequence of any special voluntary pact. They arise from the relation of man to man, and the relation of man to God, which relations are not matters of choice." According to Burke, these obligations do not require our consent; he uses

Edmund Burke (portrait by James Barry; National Gallery of Ireland)

the analogy of the parent-child relationship. "Parents may not be consenting to their moral relation; but, consenting or not, they are bound to a long train of burdensome duties towards those with whom they have never made a convention of any sort. Children are not consenting to their relation; but their relation . . . implies their consent, because the presumed consent of every rational creature is in unison with the predisposed order of things."

Two problems stem from this line of reasoning. First, how does one equate the universal moral order with the constitution of a particular country—a fallible thing? Burke's answer rests on the moral outcome of political actions as they affect concrete circumstances: "The practical consequences of any political tenet go a great way in deciding upon its value. Political problems do not primarily concern truth or falsehood. They relate to good or evil. What in the result is likely to produce evil is politically false; that which is productive of good, politically true." The second problem with Burke's argument concerns needed change: does prescriptive government allow for viable change? Burke answers that change is justified "*only* upon the *necessity* of the case" and that

change must follow the direction set by "our ancestors [who] . . . went on insensibly drawing this Constitution nearer and nearer to its perfection, by never departing from its fundamental principles, nor introducing any amendment which had not a subsisting root in the laws, Constitution, and usages of the kingdom."

In *Appeal from the New to the Old Whigs* Burke takes time to refute charges that he is inconsistent and defies his critics to find evidence of his "inconsistency" anywhere in his writings. Once again refuting the charge that he defended the American colonists, he asserts that he "would have thought very differently of the American cause" if he believed that they rebelled "because they thought they had not enjoyed liberty enough." Burke quotes Benjamin Franklin's opinion, given in a long conversation with him, during which Franklin "lamented, and with apparent sincerity," the separation which he feared was inevitable between Great Britain and her colonies. Franklin had said that "America . . . would never again see such happy days as she had passed under the protection of England."

Appeal from the New to the Old Whigs was published in August 1791, and within two weeks a third edition was in preparation. Many felt that it was superior to the *Reflections on the Revolution in France* in its more closely reasoned argument. However, Burke still had not won over those within the party who thought he had misrepresented their case and who still disagreed with his interpretation of the 1688 revolution. That interpretation is a point of contention among historians even today, and Burke's description of "natural aristocracy," which he identifies with intelligent and moral men of rank, sits uneasily with members of modern democratic societies. In spite of these theoretical and elitist problems, Burke's *Appeal from the New to the Old Whigs* continues to be relevant to discussions concerning the source and the nature of an individual's political obligations.

Within two months Burke had begun another essay on the French Revolution. The occasion was Louis XVI's acceptance of the new constitution. Burke drew up a lengthy argument for the ministry stating that the new French government was illegal. In "Thoughts on French Affairs," first published in *Three Memorials on French Affairs* (1797), Burke attributes a "large share" of the blame for French affairs to Louis XVI, who "with his own hand . . . pulled down the pillars which upheld his throne; and this he did, because he could not bear the inconveniences which are attached to everything human. . . ." Burke concludes his argument by stating that he has done "with this subject, I believe, forever" and expresses the fear that in God's providence the French Revolution was to succeed.

After completing "Thoughts on French Affairs" in December 1791, Burke certainly was not "done with the subject forever." The French Revolution was to haunt his thoughts and dog his footsteps until the day he died. Its effects, literally, lived in his home, for as French emigres sought shelter in England, they came to the doorstep of the man who so forcefully defended their cause. At one point, Jane Burke, who did not speak French, was spending "whole days with those who could not speak a word of English." It is to Burke's credit that he recognized how exceptional his wife was in this respect. On 5 September 1794 he wrote to Abbé François-Marie de la Bintinaye, "This, I will venture to say, was what would not have been endured by any other woman in the world; and it required great force of Mind. . . ."

Burke also founded a school for the children of French emigrants at Penn, three miles from his Beaconsfield estate. The school caused Burke more than one headache as he suddenly found himself trying to control admissions, tuition payments, curricular matters, hiring, and teacher relations, as those who meant well either tried to take over the school or just left everything up to him. He arranged for the school to be supported out of the British treasury until the restoration of the monarchy in France; Penn School functioned until 1820. He took an active interest in the school and personally supervised it until his health failed.

While his duties with Hastings's trial and other Parliamentary matters took up Burke's time during the stressful years of the early 1790s, he found time out to relax with friends and to discuss such subjects as Milton's poetry. At Margate, where he wrote *Appeal from the New to the Old Whigs*, he answered his friend James Boswell's request for his opinion of *The Life of Samuel Johnson* (1791). The Burke-Boswell relationship was a strange mixture; Burke's lifelong obsession with keeping the details of his personal life private collided with Boswell's lifelong obsession with making his public. It was a tribute to their friendship, then, when Burke wrote to Boswell that, conversing with the king about the *Life of Johnson*, "I said, what I thought, that I had not read any

thing more entertaining; though I did not say to his Majesty, what nothing but the freedom of friendship could justify my saying to yourself, that many particulars [concerning Johnson's private life] there related might as well have been omitted; However in the multitude of readers perhaps some would have found a loss in their omission" (20 July 1791).

Many years before, Burke had written, concerning the Penal Laws in Ireland, that rebellions are produced by persecution. With the French Revolution Burke's concern about the political stability of Ireland became acute; he could foresee the consequences for Britain and Ireland if French revolutionary theory caught on in Ireland. His interest was made personal when his son Richard, in his professional capacity as a lawyer, was appointed agent of the Catholic Committee.

The Catholic Committee was seeking four revisions to the Penal Laws concerning Catholic membership in the civil professions and Catholic ownership of property as entitlement to the franchise. When Richard went to Ireland, Edmund supported his efforts by a letter to Sir Hercules Langrishe, a longtime friend and member of the Irish House of Commons. Burke intended his letter to Langrishe to be made public.

Burke's main point in *A Letter to Sir Hercules Langrishe* is that religion should be kept out of the question at hand. He argues that admitting Catholics to the franchise is not the same thing as admitting them to membership in the government. "In our Constitution there has always been a difference between *a franchise* and *an office*, and between the capacity for the one and for the other. Franchises were supposed to belong to the *subject*, as *a subject*, and not *as a member of the governing part of the state*." He further points out that excluding Catholics from the vote excludes them from the British constitution: they cannot "think themselves in an *happy* state, to be utterly excluded from all its direct and all its consequential advantages."

In 1761 Burke had argued against the Penal Laws on the basis of natural rights. Since an appeal to the rights of man had become tainted by association with the French Revolution, Burke, in 1792, now argues against the Penal Laws by invoking prudence: "Are we to be astonished, when, by the efforts of so much violence in conquest . . . that, whenever they came to act at all, many of them would act exactly like a mob, without temper, measure, or foresight?" With great de-

"Pity the Sorrows of a Poor old Man."

James Gillray's caricature of Burke begging at the door of Bedford House reflects the Tory view that Burke's pension was excessive.

tail he demonstrates that there is nothing in the British constitution or the coronation oath that forbids giving these concessions to the Catholics. As he did in 1761, Burke deals with the fears of those who would refuse the franchise to Irish Catholics because of a "papal invasion." "I do not believe that discourses of this kind are held, or that anything like them will be held, by any who walk about without a keeper."

One who is familiar with Burke's argument against oppression of Catholics and his impatience with those who oppress Irish Catholics will recognize the similarity between the "Tracts on the Popery Laws" and his *Letter to Sir Hercules Langrishe*. He states as much in the closing of his letter to Langrishe: "Since I could think at all, those have been my thoughts. You know that thirty-two years ago they were as fully matured in my mind as they are now."

The year 1793 had hardly begun when events in France vindicated Burke's perception of the path the revolution would take. On 21 January Louis XVI was executed; in February France declared war on Britain; in September occurred the unspeakable horrors that accompanied the murder of some twelve hundred people in what came to be known as the "September Massacres"; and on 16 October Marie Antoinette was guillotined.

In England the ministry began to listen more closely to Burke's advice on French affairs. To him, it was a war against an ideology, not against France; he felt that European civilization was at risk. He sent a memorial to the ministry in October—titled "Remarks on the Policy of the Allies" when it was published in *Three Memorials on French Affairs*—stating in detail the implications of his policy. "In an address to France, in an attempt to treat with it, or in considering any scheme at all relative to it, it is impossible we should mean the geographical, we must always mean the moral and political country." Throughout the piece Burke stresses European commonality built upon the pillars of religion and property. In this emergency Burke urged that denominational differences be overlooked. In an attached appendix there are excerpts from Emmerich von Vattel's *Law of Nations* which complement Burke's views of international law.

After seven years, the impeachment trial of Warren Hastings at last drew to a close in June 1794. Having spoken on the opening days of the trial, Burke gave the speeches closing it. He spoke to each of the charges, reiterating the themes that had been invoked throughout the many sessions, and at the end reminded his listeners that no man was above the law. "No doubt princes have violated the law of this country: they have suffered for it. Nobles have violated the law: their privileges have not protected them from punishment. Common people have violated the law: they have been hanged for it. . . . There is but one law for all, namely, the law of humanity, justice, equity—the Law of Nature and of Nations." After the managers of the trial finished their case against Hastings on 16 June 1794 and received the thanks of the House of Commons on the twentieth, Burke saw his way to retirement was clear. The following day he wrote to Earl Fitzwilliam that his "engagement with the publick is fulfilled." In his reply Fitzwilliam acknowledges that Burke's letter came as no surprise and expresses his gratitude "for the credit and reputation you have confer'd upon me by receiving that seat at my hands—the House of Commons has now lost not only its brightest ornament, but what is more essential, the source of its greatest wisdom . . . " (26 June 1794).

Burke was not in Westminster Hall a year later when Hastings was acquitted of the articles of impeachment. On the surface it certainly appeared that he had spent seven years in a wasted cause. In a larger sense, though, he had not. Posterity recognizes and appreciates his efforts in behalf of an oppressed people and his demand that those who govern must realize theirs is a sacred trust. At the time there was a feeling that Hastings's acquittal ended disputes on the subject. However, the contrary has happened, for debate still goes on as to the validity of Burke's charges, his motives, and the long-term effects of his counsels concerning imperial administration.

Burke's enjoyment of the retired life at Beaconsfield was to be short-lived, for, within a few months of each other, his beloved brother and his son died of consumption. The last two volumes of his correspondence and various publications attest to the power of his mind, his concern with the affairs of state, and his continual sense of responsibility for them. These things also are a testament to a spirit that was not defeated by the intense sorrow of personal loss. That his letters were answered, his advice was requested, and his young followers were in attendance is evidence of his continuing influence in the politics of Britain.

There was reason for his ongoing involvement. Irish politics continued to be troublesome, and the war against French aggression appeared doomed to end without the monarchy being restored. Nor did Burke's personal enemies allow him a quiet retirement. Francis Russell, Duke of Bedford, and James Maitland, Earl of Lauderdale, publicly attacked his pension on the grounds that it was excessive and that it conflicted with the principles of economy espoused by Burke himself. Many rose in Burke's defense, but the most eloquent response to Bedford's attack was Burke's own, written in the form of a public letter to Earl Fitzwilliam. Burke's *Letter to a Noble Lord* (1796) is an eloquent defense of his political life. It is an apologia for the life of a self-made man and ranks as one of the most moving autobiographical statements in our literature.

Burke defends his pension on the grounds that it is just and is "a demonstration of gratitude." He has not asked for it, he assures Bedford; the pension had been granted in view of his immeasurable service to the public. One of these services, he reminds the duke, was to support "with great zeal . . . those old prejudices which buoy up the ponderous mass of his nobility, wealth, and titles" which the French would reduce without hesitation. Then Burke sums up the work of his public career: "to obtain liberty for the municipal country in which I was born . . . ; to support with unrelaxing vigilance every right, every privilege, every franchise in this my adopted . . . country; and to preserve those rights . . . in every land, in every climate . . . under the protection of the British Crown."

Burke's concern that the bloodshed of the French Revolution would become England's fate was not an idle one. Bad harvests, wartime cutbacks, and rising prices made for political as well as economic unrest. In October 1795 the king's

This portrait of Burke was commissioned from John Hoppner by Trinity College, Dublin, in 1795
(Trinity College, Dublin).

carriage was stoned by people crying "Bread" and "No War." The government fixed its attention on economic problems, and Burke sent a paper to William Pitt in which he linked economic and political theory to the principle that government should not interfere with the economy. The paper was intended only for Pitt, but others heard of it and urged Burke to publish it. He would not, but it was published by his executors under the title *Thoughts and Details on Scarcity* (1800). To those who are accustomed to the humanist Burke, his statements on a free market, private property, and employer-employee relationships seem harsh and out of place in our time: "The great use of government is as a restraint ... to provide for us in our necessities is not in the power of government. ... Labor is a commodity like every other, and rises or falls according to the demand. This is in the nature of things."

Again Burke speaks in terms of prescriptive government, which originally was a term concerning landed property. Thus his references to the employer-employee relationship are in terms of the farmer and his hired man who have identity of interests: "Their interests are always the same, and it is absolutely impossible that their free contacts can be onerous to either party." He addresses the problem of justice—what does one do in case of calamity? "Whenever it happens that a man can claim nothing according to the rules of commerce and the principles of justice, he passes out of that department and comes within the jurisdiction of mercy."

In *Thoughts and Details on Scarcity* Burke comes across as unfeeling: "The laboring people are only poor because they are numerous. Numbers in their nature imply poverty." Moreover, to state that "it is absolutely impossible" that the farmer and his hired hand should have different interests sounds absurdly idealistic for a man of Burke's experience. In his defense, Burke's supporters point to the fact that in actual practice no one was more ready to relieve the distresses of the poor and to put himself out in their cause. The poor of Beaconsfield were the immediate recipients of his charity. During the last two years of his life, when the price of corn was high, Burke had a windmill on his property grind corn for the poor. He established several benefit societies for the aged and infirm and visited the poor of the parish.

In the summer of 1795 the king announced that England wished to begin peace negotiations with France. Burke was now a private citizen, but "a sense of duty" that he could not resist made him pick up his pen—"the only weapon I have left"—to write what amounted to four public letters; the so-called "Fourth Letter" was written first but not published until after his death, in volume 5 (1812) of the quarto edition of Walter King and French Laurence's edition of Burke's works.

The *Letters on a Regicide Peace* play upon all the themes of the *Reflections on the Revolution in France* and other antirevolutionary writings. Burke asserts that the regicide directory is not the legitimate French government; there remains an unbridgeable gap between the manners, morals, and religion of England and that of atheistic France. He states that the security of England requires the total destruction of the regicide government. The themes expressed in these letters are not new, but the stridency of Burke's tone in them has been a cause of criticism. His cries are harsh, but they are the cries of a dying prophet-figure. One of his last writings was a "Letter on the Affairs of Ireland," in which he repeated his long-held beliefs concerning peace in Ireland.

The last months of Burke's life were spent in the pain of stomach cancer, but his energy in behalf of the empire never flagged. He dictated letters from his couch and discussed further publications. Surrounded by those he loved, Burke died on 9 July 1797 at his Beaconsfield estate. He chose as his final resting place not the splendor of Westminster Abbey, to which he was entitled, but the small parish church of St. Mary's All Saints, Beaconsfield.

There is a certain paradox to Edmund Burke's life and work. The leaders of his party relied on him to put their policies and their positions into language that would command atten-

tion and win support; yet he never had a cabinet post when his party was in power. Members of the House of Commons listened to him with undisguised interest, applauded his oratory, and then voted against the measures he was advocating. An older generation in the House sat spellbound as he pulled metaphor after metaphor out of the air, and they laughed with him even when the irony was at their expense. A younger generation shouted him down and derided him as "the dinner bell" of Commons as they walked out on his speeches. Yet today it is Burke who has stood the test of time while his detractors, with a few exceptions, have become footnotes in the pages of history.

Many quarrel with the contention that Burke is a political philosopher. Certainly he is not in the sense that John Locke and David Hume are; yet, in another sense, Burke's ideals—principles—have the timeless aura of philosophical tenets. He believed that politics and morality are of a piece; that one generation cannot afford to ignore the advances and errors of preceding ones; that humanity is linked by an unwritten moral code governing social and political conduct; that practical politicians need to refer to concrete circumstances and not to abstractions which ignore the realities of human behavior. These principles are viable not just in the eighteenth century; they resurface whenever the political process is examined.

Thus posterity recognizes the vitality of Burke's ideas; it also responds to the man himself, for there is a perennial appeal about a self-made man who never shirked his duty; about a man alone in the face of what he perceived to be cosmic forces that would rend his world. On the opposite side of that coin, Burke also generates a sympathetic response when he speaks of his love of family and of the land, and when his sympathies for the poor and unfortunate make him respond emotionally as well as intellectually. Burke cannot be said to have changed his world, but he never claimed to do so. In the end, he acknowledged credit "not for what I did as for what I prevented from being done."

Letters:

The Correspondence of the Right Honourable Edmund Burke; Between the year 1744 and the period of his decease, in 1797, 4 volumes, edited by Charles William, Earl Fitzwilliam, and Sir Richard Bourke (London: F. & J. Rivington, 1844);

The Correspondence of Edmund Burke, 10 volumes, edited by Thomas W. Copeland and others (Chicago: University of Chicago Press / Cambridge: Cambridge University Press, 1958-1978).

Bibliographies:

William B. Todd, *A Bibliography of Edmund Burke* (London: Rupert Hart-Davis, 1964);

Clara I. Gandy and Peter J. Stanlis, *Edmund Burke: A Bibliography of Secondary Studies to 1982* (New York: Garland, 1983).

Biographies:

Sir James Prior, *Memoir of the Life and Character of the Right Hon. Edmund Burke*, fifth edition, revised (London: H. G. Bohn, 1854);

Peter Burke, *The Public and Domestic Life of the Right Hon. Edmund Burke* (London: Nathaniel Cooke, 1854);

Thomas MacKnight, *History of the Life and Times of Edmund Burke*, 3 volumes (London: Chapman & Hall, 1858-1860);

Arthur P. I. Samuels and Arthur Warren Samuels, *The Early Life, Correspondence and Writings of the Rt. Hon. Edmund Burke* (Cambridge: Cambridge University Press, 1923);

Robert H. Murray, *Edmund Burke: A Biography* (Oxford: Oxford University Press, 1931);

John Morley, *Burke* (London: Macmillan, 1936);

Donald C. Bryant, *Edmund Burke and His Literary Friends* (St. Louis: Washington University Press, 1939);

Dixon Wecter, *Edmund Burke and His Kinsmen: A Study of the Statesman's Financial Integrity and Private Relationships* (Boulder: University of Colorado Press, 1939);

Sir Philip Magnus, *Edmund Burke: A Life* (London: Murray, 1939);

Thomas W. Copeland, *Our Eminent Friend Edmund Burke* (New Haven: Yale University Press, 1949);

Russell Kirk, *Edmund Burke: A Genius Reconsidered* (New Rochelle: Arlington House, 1967).

References:

Ruth Anita Bevan, *Marx and Burke: A Revisionist View* (La Salle, Ill.: Open Court, 1973);

Francis P. Canavan, *Edmund Burke: Prescription and Providence* (Durham: Duke University Press, 1987);

Gerald W. Chapman, *Edmund Burke: The Practical Imagination* (Cambridge, Mass.: Harvard University Press, 1967);

Ian R. Christie, "Myth and Reality in Late Eighteenth Century British Politics," in his *Myth and Reality in Late Eighteenth Century British Politics and Other Papers* (Berkeley: University of California Press, 1970), pp. 27-54;

Alfred Cobban, *Edmund Burke and the Revolt Against the Eighteenth Century* (London: Allen & Unwin, 1960);

Carl B. Cone, *Burke and the Nature of Politics: The Age of the American Revolution* (Lexington: University of Kentucky Press, 1957);

Cone, *Burke and the Nature of Politics: The Age of the French Revolution* (Lexington: University of Kentucky Press, 1964);

John R. Dinwiddy, "Utility and Natural Law in Burke's Thought: A Reconsideration," *Studies in Burke and His Time*, 16 (Winter 1974-1975): 105-128;

Michael Freeman, *Edmund Burke and the Critique of Political Radicalism* (Oxford: Blackwell, 1980);

Ross J. S. Hoffman, *Edmund Burke, New York Agent* (Philadelphia: American Philosophical Society, 1956);

Thomas H. D. Mahoney, *Edmund Burke and Ireland* (Cambridge, Mass.: Harvard University Press / London: Oxford University Press, 1960);

Harvey C. Mansfield, Jr., *Statesmanship and Party Government: A Study of Burke and Bolingbroke* (Chicago: University of Chicago Press, 1965);

Timothy O. McLoughlin, *Edmund Burke and the First Ten Years of the 'Annual Register' 1758-1767*, Rhodesia Series in Humanities, Occasional Paper no. 1. (Salisbury: University of Rhodesia Press, 1975);

Frank O'Gorman, *Edmund Burke: His Political Philosophy* (Bloomington: Indiana University Press, 1973);

J. G. A. Pocock, "Burke and the Ancient Constitution—A Problem in the History of Ideas," *Historical Journal*, 3, no. 2 (1960): 125-143;

Earl A. Reitan, "Burke, Trevelyan, and Ashley: The Meaning of the Glorious Revolution of 1688-89," *Studies in Burke and His Time*, 11 (Winter 1969-1970): 1463-1470;

Robert A. Smith, "Burke's Crusade against the French Revolution: Principles and Prejudices," in *Edmund Burke: the Enlightenment and the Modern World*, edited by Peter J. Stanlis (Detroit: University of Detroit Press, 1967), pp. 27-44;

Leo Strauss, *Natural Right and History* (Chicago: University of Chicago Press, 1953);

Richard M. Weaver, "Edmund Burke and the Argument from Circumstance," in his *The Ethics of Rhetoric* (Chicago: Regnery, 1953), pp. 55-84;

John C. Weston, "Edmund Burke's Wit," *Review of English Literature*, 4 (July 1963): 95-107.

Papers:

The largest collection of Burke manuscripts is in the Sheffield Central Library, Sheffield, England; the second largest is in the Northamptonshire Record Office, Delapre Abbey, Northampton, England. The most extensive Burke collection in the United States is in the Osborn Collection at the Beinecke Library of Yale University. The rest are widely dispersed.

Philip Dormer Stanhope, Fourth Earl of Chesterfield

(22 September 1694 - 24 March 1773)

Alan T. McKenzie
Purdue University

BOOKS: *Letters Written by the Late Right Honourable Philip Dormer Stanhope, Earl of Chesterfield, to his Son, Philip Stanhope, Esq; Late Envoy Extraordinary at the Court of Dresden: Together with Several Other Pieces on Various Subjects. Published by Mrs. Eugenia Stanhope, From the Originals Now in Her Possession* (2 volumes, London: Printed for J. Dodsley, 1774; 4 volumes, New York: Printed by J. Rivington & H. Gaine, 1775);

Miscellaneous Works of the Late Philip Dormer Stanhope, Earl of Chesterfield: Consisting of Letters to his Friends, Never Before Printed, and Various Other Articles. To Which are Prefixed, Memoirs of his Life Tending to Illustrate the Civil, Literary, and Political, History of His Time. By M. Maty, M.D., 2 volumes, edited by J. O. Justamond (London: Printed for Edward & Charles Dilly, 1777, 1778);

Letters from Lord Chesterfield, to Alderman George Faulkner, Dr. Madden, Mr. Sexton, Mr. Derrick, and the Earl of Arran. Being a supplement to His Lordship's Letters (London: Printed for John Wallis, 1777);

Characters of Eminent Personages of His Own Time (Holburn: Printed for William Flexney, 1777); enlarged as *Characters by Lord Chesterfield Contrasted with Characters of the Same Great Personages by Other Respected Writers. Also letters to Alderman George Faulkner, Dr. Madden, Mr. Sexton, Mr. Derrick, and the Earl of Arran. Intended as an Appendix to His Lordship's Miscellaneous Works* (London: Printed for Edward & Charles Dilly, 1778);

Miscellaneous Works of the Late Philip Dormer Stanhope, Earl of Chesterfield; Consisting of Letters, Political Tracts, and Poems. Volume the Third; Completing the Edition of His Lordship's Works, Began by Dr. Maty, edited by Benjamin Way (London: Printed by & for T. Sherlock, and for J. Williams, T. Evans, and J. Ridley, 1778);

Letters from a Celebrated Nobleman to His Heir. Never Before Published (London: Printed by J. Nichols, for J. Bowen, 1783);

Supplement to the Letters Written by the Late Right Honourable Philip Dormer Stanhope, Earl of Chesterfield, to his Son, Philip Stanhope, Esq. (London: Printed for J. Dodsley, 1787);

The Letters [and Works] of Philip Dormer Stanhope, Earl of Chesterfield, 5 volumes, edited by

Philip Dormer Stanhope, fourth Earl of Chesterfield, circa 1742 (portrait after William Hoare; National Portrait Gallery, London)

Lord Mahon (London: Richard Bentley, 1845, 1853; Philadelphia: Lippincott, 1892);

Letters of Philip Dormer, Fourth Earl of Chesterfield, to his Godson and Successor, edited by the Earl of Carnarvon (Oxford: Clarendon Press, 1890);

The Letters of Philip Dormer Stanhope, Earl of Chesterfield, with the Characters, 3 volumes, edited by John Bradshaw (London: Swan Sonnenschein, 1892; New York: Scribners, 1892);

The Letters of Philip Dormer Stanhope, 4th Earl of Chesterfield, 6 volumes, edited by Bonamy Dobrée (London: Eyre & Spottiswoode / New York: Viking, 1932);

Some Unpublished Letters of Lord Chesterfield, edited by S. L. Gulick, Jr. (Berkeley: University of California Press, 1937);

Characters (1778, 1845), introduction by Alan T. McKenzie, Augustan Reprint Society Publication, no. 259-260 (Los Angeles: William Andrews Clark Memorial Library, 1990).

OTHER: "Five Unpublished Letters by Lord Chesterfield," edited by Cecil Price, *Life and Letters*, 59 (October 1948): 3-10.

Philip Dormer Stanhope, fourth Earl of Chesterfield, was perhaps the politest man in an age that took its manners seriously and one of the wittiest in an age that specialized in that rare, volatile, and exasperating commodity. When an old friend, Solomon Dayrolles, came to pay his last respects to Chesterfield on his deathbed, the earl asked his servant, in a final, polite gesture, to "Give Dayrolles a chair." These last words confirmed a lifetime devoted to the cultivation of ease, the expression of attention, the imparting of instruction, and the solicitation of goodwill. In the pursuit of these ends Chesterfield delivered speeches, composed essays, and conducted an extensive correspondence, most notably a long series of letters on polite behavior addressed to his illegitimate son—the work for which he is still best known.

While Chesterfield's wit and integrity still shine through the polish he put on everything he said and wrote, his importance to subsequent ages rests on the exemplary and active life that he lived, on the high political positions he held (higher than any other writer in his, or most other, ages), and, especially, on his comments on the politics and manners of his times. These comments, always graceful, instructive, and authoritative, reflect Chesterfield's considerable powers of observation, discernment, and judgment, as well as his unillusioned insight into human nature and behavior.

If his writings are not the creation of his imagination, they serve as a useful reminder that literature has other, insufficiently regarded sources. His prose combines the skills of the conversationalist and the essayist rather than those of the novelist and the poet. His talents and background enabled him to enter, indeed to preside over, the drawing rooms, committee rooms, and political offices that most of his contemporaries could only imagine, often with the peculiar inaccuracy of envy. Inasmuch as these were the places in which much of the public life of the eighteenth century was lived, Chesterfield remains an important source for those who want to look into that age. He enables us to see it from a lofty and unusually well-informed point of view, and, given the clarity of his mind and the elegance of his prose, to understand it as well as to enjoy it.

The family into which Philip Dormer Stanhope was born had been powerful and well connected for centuries: his grandfather's grandfather was created an earl in 1628; his mother, Lady Elizabeth Savile Stanhope, was the daughter of George Savile, Marquis of Halifax; and numerous other titles adorned his family tree. By the time his mother died in 1708, his father, Lord Philip Stanhope (later the third Earl of Chesterfield), who was morose, stingy, and partial to his second son, had consigned his eldest son, Philip, to his maternal grandmother. The sophisticated and gracious Gertrude, Lady Halifax, shaped him into a polite, confident, and richly articulate (in both French and English) young man. Good as this lineage was, Chesterfield never allowed himself or any of his family to be overly impressed by the "merely fortuitous advantages" of blood or titles—their own or anyone else's. Under a painting of a man and woman and two boys with the Stanhope arms in the corner he wrote, with characteristic wit and self-deprecation: "Adam Stanhope of Eden Garden and Eve Stanhope his wife, with their two sons Cain Stanhope and Abel Stanhope."

Educated at first by private tutors, Philip then spent two years (1712-1714) at Trinity Hall, Cambridge, where he took up smoking and drinking to be genteel, and anatomy, classics, and rhetoric to be successful. As he later wrote to his son:

> I remember, so long ago as when I was at Cambridge, whenever I read pieces of eloquence (and indeed they were my chief study) whether ancient or modern, I used to write down the shining passages, and then translate them, as well and as elegantly as ever I could; if Latin or French, into English; if English, into French. This, which I practised for some years, not only improved and formed my style, but imprinted in my mind and memory the best thoughts of the best authors. The trouble was little, but the advantage I have experienced was great.

This was once the usual procedure for developing style: emulating excellent models, practicing translation, stocking the memory, and schooling the judgment. This method seems to have worked for Chesterfield, whose writings exhibit more of the uniform polish and clarity evident in that extract than the "shining passages" it mentions.

Having acquired a considerable stock of Cicero, Horace, Martial, and Ovid, together with a touch of pedantry and a taste for argumentation,

Philip left Cambridge to polish his manners in Antwerp, The Hague, and Paris, where he perfected the arts of speaking and behaving so as to please the polite. He also developed an aptitude and a fondness for the manners and language, but not the chauvinism or the absolutism, of the French, and learned, to his eternal regret, the expensive pleasures of the gambling table.

In 1715 he returned to England where, thanks to his family connections, he became a Member of Parliament—a Whig who voted his conscience—and gentleman of the bedchamber to George, Prince of Wales. This was the beginning of a long career at court, a career somewhat hampered by his independence and integrity of mind, hatred of bribes and other forms of dishonesty, and perhaps most by his gift for ridicule. He displayed contempt for Robert Walpole, a man neither honest nor polite, and he expressed it for Caroline, Princess of Wales, who thereafter hated him bitterly.

Upon his father's unlamented death in 1726, he became fourth earl of Chesterfield and a member of the House of Lords, where his talents could truly shine. The next year the Prince of Wales became George II, and Chesterfield was eventually appointed ambassador to The Hague, over the objections and delays of his enemies, Queen Caroline and Walpole, prime minister in everything but name.

At The Hague Lord Chesterfield, as he now was, exercised his talents for pleasing and sharpened his eye for the foibles of human nature. His official letters to the secretary of state, Charles, Lord Townshend, from this period are full of edged deference to the king, accounts of the lavish hospitality he provided his colleagues and friends, and elaborate details of diplomatic maneuvering. As one would expect, Chesterfield was effective as an ambassador, well able to sort out the personal and political complexities of the several contending empires that decided the fate of Europe in this era. Lord Townshend described him as "dextrous, vigilant, and zealous." He negotiated Britain's way into the Treaty of Vienna, and he arranged the marriage between Anne, the Princess Royal, and William, the Prince of Orange. For these services he was, again over the objections of his enemies, appointed lord steward of the king's household and made a knight of the garter (18 June 1730).

Among the diversions from state business at The Hague was Mademoiselle Elizabeth du Bouchet, a reasonably well-born French Hugue-

Dear Boy   Bath. Nov: 9 c e th 1739

I am glad to hear that you went to see the Lord Mayor's shoni, for I suppose it amus'd you, and besides, I would have you see every thing. It is a good way of getting knowledge, especially if you enquire carefully (as I hope you always do) after the meaning, and the particulars of every thing you see. You know then, to be sure, that the Lord Mayor is the Head of the city of London, and that there is a new Lord Mayor chosen every year. That the city is govern'd by the Lord Mayor, the Court of Aldermen, and the common councill. There are six and twenty Aldermen, who are the most considerable tradesmen of the city; the Common councill is very numerous, and consists likewise of Tradesmen, who all belong to the several companys, that you saw march in the procession, with their colours and Streamers. The Lord Mayor is chosen every year out of the Court of Aldermen. There are but two Lord Mayors in England; one for the city of London, and the other for the city of York. The Mayors of other Towns, are only call'd Mayors, not Lord Mayors. People, who have seen little, are apt to stare sillily, and wonder at every new thing they see; but a Man, who ████ has been bred in the world, looks at every thing with coollness and sedateness, and makes proper observations, upon what he sees.

Page from one of Chesterfield's more than four hundred letters to his son Philip Stanhope, who was seven when this letter was written (Pierpont Morgan Library) not, who became the mother of the son to whom Chesterfield wrote the letters for which he is still best known. Philip Stanhope, as he was called, was born in 1732, after his father returned to England. The next year Lord Chesterfield married Melusina de Schulemberg, Countess of Walsingham and Baroness of Aldborough, the daughter of George I and the duchess of Kendal, one of his mistresses. Chesterfield's wife brought him mature elegance, financial security, and domestic comforts. As he wrote to a friend, Frederik Willem, Baron Torck, on 2 January 1733: "il m'en faudrait une qui à tous égards se contentât de donner beaucoup, et de recevoir peu; et qui dans un mot s'accommoderait d'un corps délabré, et raccommoderait des affaires délabrées...." (I had to have [a woman] who in all respects would be content to give much, and to receive little; and who in a word, would put up with a dilapidated body and repair a dilapidated financial condition....)

During this period Chesterfield became so entangled in the Opposition to Walpole and the king that he was obliged to give up his post as lord steward. In one of the clever social and political essays he wrote for Opposition periodicals (*Fog's Journal*, 17 January 1736), he urged the king to create an army of wax figures set in motion by clockwork, as a replacement for the actual army, which was expensive, incompetent, and a threat to liberty. In the seventeen numbers of *Common Sense* usually attributed to him (5 February 1737 - 27 January 1739) Chesterfield brought his grace and gentility to bear on the usual periodical topics of the period: the follies of his contemporaries, especially their rage for foreign fashion, affectations, taste, feeble conversation, trivial social ceremonies, and operas; and such political vices as factionalism, bribery, and fiscal extravagance. His recurrent themes are liberty, wit, and the obligation of the upper class to set a good example. His devices consist of indicting native customs by analogous exotic ones, citations from Horace and Cicero, and occasional sexual innuendo. The freshest and wittiest of these essays is number 36 (8 October 1737—misnumbered 37 in Maty's and Mahon's editions), which disposes of the periodicals of the rival party by asserting the evident superiority of the wit and eloquence in *Common Sense*.

Chesterfield took for granted the intricate and hereditary social structure of his age and shared that age's assumption about the social place of women. In *Common Sense* number 31 (10 September 1737—misnumbered 33 in Maty's edition) he wrote: "Women are not formed for great cares themselves, but to soothe and soften ours: their tenderness is the proper reward for the toils we undergo for their preservation; and the ease and chearfulness of their conversation, our desirable retreat from the labors of study and business. They are confined within the narrow limits of domestic offices; and, when they stray beyond them, they move excentrically, and consequently without grace." This attitude also informs, or infects, his correspondence, which includes this notorious passage in his 5 September 1748 letter to his son: "Women, then, are only children of a larger growth; they have an entertaining tattle and sometimes wit; but for solid, reasoning good-sense, I never in my life knew one that had it, or who reasoned or acted consequentially for four-and-twenty hours together."

He writes on general follies and types with the detachment that his age required—a detachment that precluded the manifestations of sincerity and individuality that have since come to be expected of authors. When Chesterfield picked up his pen it was to divert and instruct others rather than to express his own emotions, ideals, or uncertainties. In most of his periodical essays he operates at a level of manners deepened by reading and experience and elevated by thought and style.

The best of these essays are informed by keen observation of manners and behavior—observations rooted in Chesterfield's age, but still resonant: "But if, when he approaches them, they pull up their gloves, adjust their tucker, and count the sticks of their fan, let them despair, for they are further gone [in love] than they imagine" (*Common Sense*, no. 51, 15 January 1758). The political principles put forth here are equally well conceived—they too were, after all, based on extensive and significant experience. They are also well expressed and, some of them, still relevant: "nothing is so much to be dreaded in a government, as a minister without virtue or merit, who gains the favour of his prince ..." (*Common Sense*, no. 15, 14 May 1737—misnumbered 16 in Maty's edition).

Chesterfield returned to the same topics in twenty-three numbers of *The World* (3 May 1753 - 7 October 1756). The two best-known of these essays, numbers 100 (28 November 1754) and 101 (5 December 1754), drew a fierce and indignant rebuttal from Samuel Johnson, who felt condescended to and taken advantage of by Chester-

Engraving of Chesterfield House, in the Mayfair section of London. Chesterfield had begun construction of this mansion by 1747 and was able to move in, with some work still unfinished, in 1749. The house was demolished in 1934.

field's belated support of his *Dictionary* (1755). Nevertheless, these two essays express very well the nature and uses of a dictionary, the rich dependence of English on borrowed words, the glory of English authors, and Johnson's own talent for lexicography. Number 101 does indicate a preference for polished English that must have added to Johnson's annoyance, even though the distinction between polished and fashionable language ought to have appealed to the lexicographer.

Chesterfield says what is usually said on these topics, but he does so with elegance, wit, and ease and an unusually good eye for social codes and behavior. He was determined to write for a wide audience without condescending, and he succeeded. Thus his essay on the folly of dueling (number 113, 27 February 1755) adds to the usual arguments an account of a duel between a man and an Irish greyhound (the greyhound won) and the suggestion that the protocol of duels be revised so that only adversaries of equal weight meet, even if they have to wait until one adversary has lost weight and the other gained it. The best of these essays for *The World* is number 148 (30 October 1755), where Chesterfield is in his element, distinguishing, both linguistically and socially, between civility and good breeding: "To sacrifice one's own self-love to other people's is a short, but, I believe, a true definition of CIVILITY: to do it with ease, propriety, and grace, is

GOOD-BREEDING. The one is the result of good-nature; the other of good-sense, joined to experience, observation, and attention."

The shrewd eloquence in his speeches and essays, rather than his genealogy and his manners, underlay Chesterfield's emergence as a leader of the Opposition. His speeches to the House of Lords are well informed and well expressed, if not sufficiently removed from the occasions that provoked them to be of lasting interest. Some of their eloquence, clarity, and wit survives in their printed versions. His speech on the Licensing Bill (1737) opposed the restraint on the liberty of the stage with an informed survey of stage and political history, the threat that wit was about to become subject to an excise tax, and an intriguing and enlightened analogy: "Wit, my lords, is a sort of property: it is the property of those who have it, and too often the only property they have to depend on." John, Lord Hervey, no admirer of Chesterfield, said that this speech was "one of the most lively and ingenious speeches against [that bill] I ever heard in Parliament, full of wit, of the genteelest satire, and in the most polished, classical style that the Petronius of any time ever wrote. It was extremely studied, seemingly easy, well delivered, and universally admired. On such occasions nobody spoke better than Lord Chesterfield. . . ."

Chesterfield's 1743 speeches opposing the financing of the war by collecting more taxes on gin were public-spirited, unusually scathing even for Chesterfield, and ineffectual. (Some of the wit for which Chesterfield has been credited was actually the creation, in one of the most delicious of all literary ironies, of Samuel Johnson, who reconstructed the Parliamentary debates for the *Gentleman's Magazine*.) The one speech that accomplished all that Chesterfield could have wished brought the replacement of the Julian calendar, then used in England, with the more accurate Gregorian calendar employed on the Continent. To accomplish this feat Chesterfield sharpened his talents with his contempt. As he wrote his son on 18 March 1751, he had to persuade his audience that he

> knew something of the matter, and also to make them believe that they knew something of it themselves, which they do not. . . . I gave them, therefore, only an historical account of calendars, from the Egyptian down to the Gregorian, amusing them now and then with little episodes; but I was particularly attentive to the choice of my words, to the harmony and roundness of my periods, to my elocution, to my action. This succeeded, and ever will succeed; they thought I informed, because I pleased them; and many of them said, that I had made the whole very clear to them, when, God knows, I had not even attempted it.

In 1744 Chesterfield returned briefly to The Hague to induce the Dutch to prosecute the war of the Austrian Succession more vigorously. Then he went to Ireland to take up the important and difficult post of lord lieutenant. When the king tried to withhold several of the privileges associated with these appointments, Chesterfield insisted, with characteristic independence, forcefulness, and imprudence, on his privileges. He expressed his indignation and determination so forcibly in a letter to Thomas Pelham Holles, Duke of Newcastle (13 April 1745) that the king was obliged to relent. The mind that drove Chesterfield's pen was uncompromising.

In late August 1745 Chesterfield took up residence in Dublin, whence he administered Ireland with toleration, elegance, and efficiency, in the face of truculence, resentment, and the Jacobite (and Catholic) rebellion under way just across the Channel. By both precept and example he encouraged Irish manufacture and discouraged gambling and drunkenness. The Irish were

especially susceptible to his candor, his elegance, and his banter, and when he left Ireland on 24 April 1746, he was escorted by the people of Dublin and cheered by the poor. It was his last truly successful government post.

Soon after his return to London Chesterfield was persuaded, against his better judgment, to accept the position of secretary of state, a post he was supposed to divide with the duke of Newcastle, but the duke would not share power, and Chesterfield could not subordinate himself. His principled opposition to continuing the war combined with the quality of his information from and understanding of the political circumstances in the Low Countries to render him unable to agree with Newcastle's policies. As he wrote to his old friend Solomon Dayrolles on 25 August 1747, "I let them go on quietly, being convinced that events will soon show who is in the right and who in the wrong." Events proved Chesterfield right, and even the king was forced to admit that he had been so. But Chesterfield was tired, unwell, and preoccupied with his son. He had never had a gift for compromise, the patience to deal with less able or less eloquent men, or the ambition necessary for political success in any age, so he removed himself from the lofty stage on which he had played so many important roles. On 23 February 1748 he wrote to Dayrolles, "I have been behind the scenes, both of pleasure and business. I have seen all the coarse pulleys and dirty ropes, which exhibit and move all the gaudy machines; and I have seen and smelt the tallow-candles which illuminate the whole decoration, to the astonishment and admiration of the ignorant audience." The images here are both striking and effective; the passage conveys the eighteenth century's fascination with the theater and mechanical devices as well as Chesterfield's lordly contempt for the gaping multitude.

Now that he was retired, Chesterfield turned in earnest to a project he had begun in 1736, the education and exhortation of his young son by correspondence. His early letters, though largely playful, were still full of information and commands. He had advised his son, only five at the time, to learn ancient history and mythology so that he could understand poetry. These early letters, usually in French, sought to school the boy in early and recent history and to animate him in Roman virtue by heroic examples.

In letter after letter (more than four hundred survive, and as many more seem to have disappeared) he sought to shape his son's intellec-

A 1922 photograph of the library at Chesterfield House, with Chesterfield's collection of paintings of authors hanging as he placed them circa 1749

tual and social character, to instill in him attention, industry, and the desire to please, and, always, to polish his manners. The letters bristle with instructions, explanations, exhortations, and maxims: "The characteristic of a well-bred man is, to converse with his inferiors without insolence, and with his superiors with respect and ease" (17 May 1748); "Whoever is in a hurry, shows that the thing he is about is too big for him" (10 August 1749). The exhortations are often repeated and sometimes accompanied by a still-unsettling combination of threats and promises, disappointment and encouragement: "I expect you to make prodigious improvements in your learning, by the time I see you again; for now that you are past nine years old, you have no time to lose; and I wait with impatience for a good account of you from Mr. Maittaire [Philip's tutor]: I dare not buy anything for you till then, for fear I should be obliged to keep it myself. But if I should have a very good account, there shall be very good rewards brought over" (30 May 1741). These letters constitute an essential

and eloquent compendium of what one active, intelligent, and powerful man thought his son needed to know in order to make his way in the courts by which Europe was governed in the eighteenth century. They abound with observations, distinctions, and instructions such as the following, written from Paris on 4 November 1741:

> This place is, without dispute, the seat of true good breeding; the people here are civil without ceremony, and familiar without rudeness. They are neither disagreeably forward, nor awkwardly bashful and shame-faced; they speak to their superiors with as little concern, and as much ease, though with more respect, as to their inferiors; and they speak to their inferiors with as much civility, though less respect, as to their superiors.

While clearly composed with an eye to the present and expected behavior of the recipient, that passage reflects the observed, indeed scrutinized, behavior of the French court, as well as the social values, abstract vocabulary, and periodic syntax of the eighteenth century.

Chesterfield's well-balanced pen was always at the service of his judicious assessments of the manners he observed:

> Dancing is in itself a very trifling, silly thing; but it is one of those established follies to which people of sense are sometimes obliged to conform; and then they should be able to do it well. . . . dress is a very foolish thing; and yet it is a very foolish thing for a man not to be well dressed, according to his rank and way of life; and it is so far from being a disparagement to any man's understanding, that it is rather a proof of it, to be as well dressed as those whom he lives with . . . (19 November 1745).

Lord Chesterfield did not make the social rules by which he had lived and his son would be judged, nor did he set out to reform or ridicule those rules. But he did understand and express them, clearly and intelligently. And he expected his (utterly dependent) son, in learning to obey these rules, to exceed them and conform to a higher ideal: "I tell you very seriously, that I both expect and require a great deal from you, and if you should disappoint me, I would not advise you to expect much from me. I ask nothing of you but what is entirely in your own power; to be an honest, a learned, and a well-bred man" (23 March 1746). Notice, in addition to the severity of that remark, its clarity and its sequence, which move it well beyond manners into the realm of character and intelligence.

From retirement, then, Lord Chesterfield continued to supervise his son's itinerary, enunciation, epistolary style, diplomatic career, and dental hygiene, and to give sensible directions as to what to read and see while in Germany and Italy. Thus a letter of 20 September 1748 instructs Philip to inquire into the Crusades and the ancient religious and military orders, of which Chesterfield took a quite cynical view, and one of 19 April 1749 to "extract the spirit of every place you go to. In those places, which are only distinguished by classical fame, and valuable remains of antiquity, have your Classics in your hand and in your head; compare the ancient geography, and descriptions, with the modern; and never fail to take notes." He expected his son to become fluent, even elegant, in French, German, and Italian, without losing the Latin and Greek he had learned from his tutors. It was not an easy, nor merely social, curriculum that Chesterfield had in mind, nor was it simply an academic one: "I do by no means advise you to throw away your time in ransacking, like a dull antiquarian, the minute and unimportant parts of remote and fabulous times. Let blockheads read what blockheads wrote" (1 November 1750).

Many of these late letters include what amount to small essays: on the frivolity and ill manners of the English abroad; the necessity of dissimulation and concomitant viciousness of simulation; Italian literature; how to treat "the old Pretender" with prudent civility (one of the most intriguing letters, 5 September 1749); French fashions and manners; handwriting; and epics. Some of them are more generally reflective—that of 22 February 1748, for example, on proud and injudicious pedantry and that of 10 May 1748, on the duplicity, flattery, and uses of the court: "In Courts, a versatility of genius, and a softness of manners, are absolutely necessary, which some people mistake for abject flattery, and having no opinion of one's own: whereas it is only the decent and genteel manner of maintaining your own opinion, and possibly of bringing other people to it." Others direct his son to study treaties, perfect his grammar, and seek a mistress. Chesterfield's critics have made too much of the advice that his son should seek a sexual liaison with a woman of quality as part of his civilizing process (the advice is repeated or alluded to only eight times in 430 letters, according to Dobrée's count) and too little of such insights as his essential distinction between dissimulation (without which, Chesterfield insists, and most readers will be obliged to acknowledge, no business can be done) and simulation (which, he equally insists, is mean and criminal).

From the beginning to the end of this correspondence, no theme is more often or more urgently insisted on than that of "attention," in both its intellectual and social senses: "For my own part, I would rather be in company with a dead man than with an absent [inattentive] one; for if the dead man gives me no pleasure, at least he shows me no contempt; whereas the absent man, silently indeed, but very plainly, tells me that he does not think me worth his attention" (22 September 1749).

As Philip grew older his father's letters turned increasingly from manners to history and philosophy, displaying a heartening willingness to discuss military strategy, domestic politics, and European affairs. Some of them even praise Philip's increasing knowledge of history. Thus a letter of 30 August 1748 supplies a long, well-informed political dissertation on the failure of the European powers to support one another in Flanders.

Chesterfield's gift for constructing maxims out of his own experience never deserted him: "A little prince in the neighbourhood of great ones, must be alert, and look out sharp, if he would secure his own dominions; much more still if he would enlarge them. He must watch for conjunctures, or endeavor to make them. No princes have ever possessed this art better than those of the House of Savoy . . ." (27 April 1749). He shrewdly read the signs of revolution in France as early as 25 December 1753: "in short, all the symptoms which I have ever met with in history, previous to great changes and revolutions in Government, now exist, and daily increase in France," and to deplore his country's treatment of the American colonies: "For my part, I never saw a froward child mended by whipping; and I would not have the mother country become a step-mother. Our trade to America brings in, *communibus annis*, two millions a-year . . ." (27 December 1765).

The retired statesman did what he could to further his son's career. While he was unable to get him appointed resident at Venice because the king objected to his illegitimacy, he managed in 1756 to secure his appointment as resident at Hamburg. But his son's failing health, more, perhaps, than his failings in polish and attention, hampered his career. After 1765 the letters show a sad and genuine concern with his son's health, rather than his own. This concern, as always, took the form of advice.

In all of his letters Chesterfield tries, without evident success, to inculcate in his son that penetrating observation and knowledge of the world that his own correspondence exhibits:

> Search, therefore, with the greatest care, into the characters of all those whom you converse with; endeavour to discover their predominant passions, their prevailing weaknesses, their vanities, their follies, and their humours; with all the right and wrong, wise and silly springs of human actions, which make such inconsistent and whimsical beings of us rational creatures. A moderate share of penetration, with great attention, will infallibly make these necessary discoveries. This is the true knowledge of the world . . . (2 October 1747).

This is the sort of knowledge that made some of Chesterfield's contemporaries (especially Henry Fielding) great novelists, dramatists, and essayists.

It made him an excellent statesman and correspondent; whether it also made him a good father is by no means clear. Chesterfield managed his role of father quite deliberately and quite candidly: "Nineteen fathers in twenty, and every mother who had loved you half as well as I do, would have ruined you; whereas I always made you feel the weight of my authority, that you might one day know the force of my love. Now, I both hope and believe, my advice will have the same weight with you from choice, that my authority had from necessity" (29 September 1752).

All his life Chesterfield had worked hard, sometimes as long as fourteen hours a day, at this and his other correspondence, all of which exhibits ease and grace, rather than the labor that must have gone into it. He wrote weekly or more frequently to friends, colleagues, relatives, and various dukes and lords—Dobrée's edition of his surviving correspondence fills six large volumes and includes more than 2,600 letters. In them Chesterfield sorted out and conveyed, from successive vantage points in The Hague, Dublin, the House of Lords, and Chesterfield House, the complex mercantile, marital, and military maneuvers of the Dutch, the Spanish, the Austrians, the Prussians, the French, and the Jacobites. His sources (both official and unofficial), his social access, and his connections were so good and his prose is so clear that the intricacies of his numerous negotiations remain intelligible, instructive, and diverting. His grasp of Dutch politics was especially fine—better, perhaps, than that of the court in his own country, where he continued to be held suspect. While he was always alert to and fluent in the language of diplomatic nicety, his impatience with ceremony and delay occasionally ruffled the smooth surface of his reports and requests.

Letters to other members of the Opposition convey opinions and news, offer advice and strategy, and look behind the events of the period. For example, the letter of 27 August 1734 to Alexander Hume Campbell, Earl of Marchmont, discusses Opposition strategy in the House of Lords, and that of 12 November 1737 to George Lyttelton gives instructions on how to manage the Prince of Wales. Numerous letters to Baron Torck on national and European politics prove that he retained his insights into current events, prominent personalities, and the French language all his life. His letters from Ireland, mainly to Newcastle, reflect Chesterfield's continued interest in affairs on the Continent, his firm

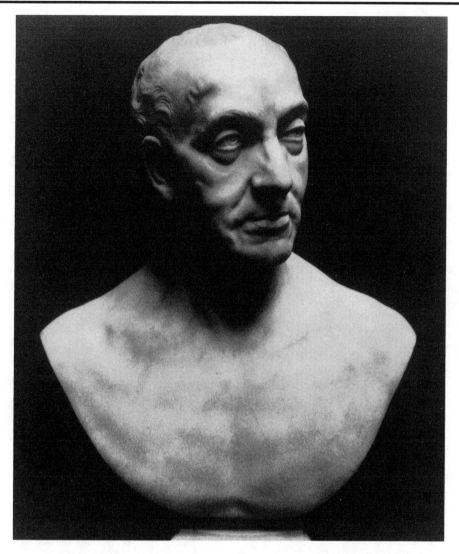

Chesterfield in 1757 (marble bust by Joseph Wilton; British Museum)

control of Ireland in the face of the rebellion in Scotland, and his fair disbursing of posts in the Church of Ireland. His letters as secretary of state include details of statecraft, finance, military matters, and diplomatic finagling that attest to his patience as well as his skill. He is, for example, well able to instruct John Montagu, Earl of Sandwich, on how to placate the Hapsburgs and bemuse the Dutch.

Many readers find his letters to his friend and dependent Dayrolles (the man to whom he paid his last civility) among Chesterfield's best, combining, as they do, warmth, information, reciprocal favors, business, and civility with instructions for raising Dayrolles's son and reports on Chesterfield's own health. Even on this last subject Chesterfield's civility and wit enabled him to write well, that is, with candor, grace, and good

sense: "Deaf men and dead men differ very little except in one point, which is, that letters from the dead would be very curious, and probably very instructive; whereas those from the deaf must necessarily be very dull" (4 February 1755). The letter of 10 June 1763, on Dayrolles's gout, is a small masterpiece, as are several to Richard Chenevix, Bishop of Waterford, on how patiently Chesterfield copes with his own failing health: "My state of health, which you are always kindly inquisitive about, is just as you left it. I am too old to expect it to mend, and thank God it declines but gently, and I rather glide than tumble down hill" (17 May 1766).

Some of his mildly flirtatious French correspondence with Mme. Cécile-Thérèse de Monconseil, especially his letter of 8 September 1747, could be cited to prove that he took

Dear Phil.   Aug. ?. [1762]

Though I generally write to you upon
those subjects which you are now chiefly employed
in, such as History, Geography and French, yet I must
from time to time remind you of two much more important dutys which I hope you will never forget, nor
neglect. I mean your duty to God, and your duty to Man.
God has been so good as to write in all our hearts, the
duty that he expects from us; which is adoration.
and thanksgiving, and doing all the good we can to
our fellow creatures. Our conscience, if we will but
consult and attend to it, never fails to remind us of
those dutys. I dare say that you feel an inward
pleasure when you have learned your book well,
and have been a good boy, as on the other hand I am
sure you feel an inward uneasyness when you
have not done so. This is called conscience, which
I hope you will always consult and follow. You
owe all the advantages you enjoy to God, who can
and who probably will, take them away, whenever
you are ungratefull to him, for he has justice as

Chesterfield's 2 August 1762 letter to his godson Philip Stanhope, later the fifth Earl of Chesterfield (by permission of the Lilly Library, Indiana University)

well as mercy. Get by heart the four following and
excellent lines of Voltaire, and retain them in your
mind as long as you live.

> Dieu nous donna les biens, il veut qu'on en jouïsse,
> Mais n'oubliés jamais leur cause et leur Auteur;
> Et quand vous goutez sa Divine faveur,
> O mortels, gardez vous d'oublier sa Justice.

Your duty to Man is very short and clear, it is only to do to him
whatever you would be willing that he should do to you. And
remember in all the business of your life, to ask your conscience
this question; Should I be willing that this should be done
to me? If your conscience, which will always tell you truth,
answers, NO, do not do that thing. Observe these rules, and
you will be happy in this world, and still happier in the next.
Bon soir mon petit bout d'homme.

Chesterfield

women seriously as a source of ideas as well as manners. His correspondence with Henrietta Howard, Countess of Suffolk, maintained a high level of wit and thoughtfulness for over fifty years, beginning with playful letters to her lapdog in 1716 and continuing through two very clever, very polite, letters purporting to be from his footman in 1766.

Chesterfield devoted that portion of his retirement not occupied by his voluminous correspondence to building one lavish house and rebuilding another. He gave special care to his library, his art collection, and his garden, where he cultivated exotic melons and dignified ease, disturbed only by his increasing deafness. That affliction and the death of his son on 16 November 1768 put an end to his plans and his lessons. This must have been both a disappointment and a relief, as his son would not take the only kind of polish that Chesterfield knew how to apply. Soon after word of his son's death reached him, he learned that Philip had married a woman by no means in keeping with his plans for him. The news must have been something of a shock. Nevertheless, Chesterfield treated his unlooked-for daughter-in-law and his two grandsons warmly, generously, and without complaint.

Even before his son's death, Chesterfield had turned his attentions to another Philip Stanhope, his godson, distant relation, and heir. To this Philip he addressed another series of letters, nearly three hundred, every bit as polished and pedagogical as those to his son, but noticeably more indulgent. Again offering lessons in geography, French, history, and manners, they inculcate the necessity of attention and the duty of pleasing. Fourteen of them were published in the February-June 1744 issues of the *Edinburgh Magazine* as "The Art of Pleasing." In fact, these letters are often more pleasing than those to his own son, precisely because Chesterfield found so much more to commend in his godson, whose letters, compositions, deportment, manners, and character pleased the aging earl. Perhaps his best letter is the one to his godson that Chesterfield wrote for delivery after his death. It is tender, candid, and full of good sense, dignity, and, of course, advice.

One advisory maxim he offered to his godson was "Do you be sure never to speak of yourself, for yourself, nor against yourself; but let your character speak for you. Whatever that says, will be believed, but whatever you say of it, will not, and only make you odious or ridiculous" (14

January 1766). It seems fair to suggest that "character" was of as much significance and concern to the eighteenth century as "identity" is to the twentieth and that Chesterfield devoted his life to constructing his own, his son's, and his godson's, and to assessing the characters of others. He saw his letters as an extension of his own character across the sea or the city, but not through the ages; Chesterfield certainly never wrote with publication in mind. While he took considerable care in composing that character, he let it speak for itself, as it still does, to those who will read his correspondence attentively.

This lifelong attention to character expressed itself in twenty "Characters" that Chesterfield left in manuscript when he died. His grandfather Halifax had contributed to this once enormously popular genre. Chesterfield's characters are well observed, severely but impartially judged, and succinctly expressed. Densely antithetic, they add and subtract attributes and bristle with assessment and indictment. Here he is, with wit, malice, and accuracy, on Queen Caroline:

> She loved money, but could occasionally part with it, especially to men of learning, whose patronage she affected. She often conversed with them, and bewildered herself in their metaphysical disputes, which neither she nor they themselves understood. Cunning and perfidy were the means she made use of in business. . . .

On 24 March 1773 Philip Dormer Stanhope, fourth Earl of Chesterfield, died at the age of seventy-eight, extending his last courtesy and kindness to his friend Dayrolles. In his will, printed in part in the *Gentleman's Magazine* (1773), he expressed, one last time, his contempt for the worldly pomp he had mastered: "Satiated with the pompous follies of this life, of which I have had an uncommon share, I would have no posthumous ones displayed at my funeral, and therefore desire to be buried in the next burying place to the place where I shall die, and limit the whole expence of my funeral to £100." He left the mother of his son £500, which some have pronounced inadequate, and she declined to accept.

Chesterfield's gentility was exemplary in his own age, though it may well seem excessive in this one. His wit incorporated all the civility and attention he urged on his son, and displayed that awareness of audience, tone, language, and surprise that he advised his son to employ. In his *Apology for the Life of Mr. Colley Cibber* (1740) Colley Cib-

Chesterfield in 1769 (portrait by Thomas Gainsborough)

ber, the aging poet laureate, left an observant and appreciative account that invites contrast with several of Chesterfield's contemporaries, none more so than Samuel Johnson:

> In Conversation, he is seldom silent but when he is attentive, nor ever speaks without exciting the Attention of others; and tho' no Man might with less Displeasure to his Hearers engross the Talk of the Company, he has a Patience in his Vivacity that chuses to divide it, and rather gives more Freedom than he takes; his sharpest Replies having a mixture of Politeness that few have the command of; his Expression is easy, short, and clear; a stiff or studied Word never comes from him; it is in a simplicity of Style that he gives the highest Surprize, and his Ideas are always adapted to the Capacity and Taste of the Person he speaks to. . . . In a word, this Gentleman gives Spirit to Society the Moment he comes into it, and whenever he

leaves it they who have Business have then leisure to go about it.

Of the many bons mots that have been attributed to Chesterfield, perhaps the quickest, the best, and the most effective is his reply to George II when he refused to sign a commission that had already been written up: "the monarch angrily refused, and said, *I would rather have the devil.* With all my heart, replied the earl, I only beg leave to put your majesty in mind, that the commission is indited *to our right-trusty and well-beloved cousin.* This sally had its effect; the king laughed, and said, *My lord, do as you please.*"

His own character, as he himself told Lord Marchmont, lacked avarice and ambition, a refreshing and unusual absence in any courtier, and one that gave him a useful attitude toward the court, especially Walpole's court. Useful, that is, for someone content to comment on, rather than to thrive within, that court. And it is his comments that entitle his prose to more attention than it has received. His abilities enabled him to rise high and remain long, while his genius enabled him to express what he saw with clarity and vigor, in prose that is detached, elegant, unfussy, and solid—prose, in other words, of great civility.

It might also be kept in mind that in the course of his long, busy life, Chesterfield had known, visited, conversed with, written to, aided, and been admired by a remarkable list of important writers: Joseph Addison; Dr. John Arbuthnot; George Berkeley; Henry Fielding; John Gay; Alexander Pope; Jonathan Swift; Henry St. John, Viscount Bolingbroke; James Thomson; Soame Jenyns; James Hammond; David Hume; William Warburton; Tobias Smollett; David Garrick; even, late in life, Horace Walpole; and on the other side of the Channel, Bernard le Bouyer de Fontenelle, Charles de Secondat Montesquieu, Voltaire, and Francesco Algarotti, among others. These were not slight acquaintances. He had been Pope's guest at Twickenham, Gay's pall bearer, and Bolingbroke's intimate. He bestowed lavish hospitality on Montesquieu and Voltaire and maintained a long correspondence with them both.

Soon after he died, Chesterfield's letters to his son were published by his son's wife, much to the dismay of his family. They were enormously popular, going through more than twenty editions by the end of the century, and numerous extracts, abridgements, translations, and parodies were also published. Yet subsequent ages have failed to appreciate the prose and the man for various reasons. Some readers cannot abide so unillusioned an account of human nature, others deplore so calculating an appraisal of the ways of succeeding at court, and many are simply unnerved by so much gentility. It became fashionable for those who had not known him and would not read him attentively to deplore the immorality and the polish that Chesterfield inculcated and the good breeding he manifested and believed in.

Various clergymen and sentimentalists wrote rejoinders; William Cowper apostrophized him in "The Progress of Error" (1782) as a "Greybeard corrupter of our list'ning youth"; and Boswell's account of Chesterfield's supposed mistreatment of Johnson was most damaging. His Victorian "disciple," Chester in Charles Dickens's *Barnaby Rudge*, so far misjudged him as to find

him a source of hypocrisy, selfishness, and condescension, qualities not at all evident in his letters or his life.

That rehabilitation which ought to have been rendered unnecessary by Matthew Maty's memoir in volume 1 of *Miscellaneous Works* (1777) should have been inaugurated by C. A. Sainte-Beuve's *Causeries du Lundi* (1850; the French have always had an affinity for him), continued by the studies of Roger Coxon (1925) and Willard Connely (1939), and confirmed by Bonamy Dobrée's splendid biography and scholarly edition of the correspondence (1932). But it will probably have to wait until academic criticism has developed a tolerance for elegance and procedures for assessing expository prose, especially the subtle complexities of actual correspondence.

Bibliography:

Sidney L. Gulick, *A Chesterfield Bibliography to 1800*, second edition, revised (Charlottesville: Published for the Bibliographical Society of America by the University Press of Virginia, 1979).

Biographies:

Matthew Maty, "Memoirs of Lord Chesterfield," in volume 1 of *Miscellaneous Works of the Late Philip Dormer Stanhope, Earl of Chesterfield* (London: Printed for Edward & Charles Dilly, 1777);

Bonamy Dobrée, "The Life of Philip Dormer Stanhope, Fourth Earl of Chesterfield," in volume 1 of *The Letters of Philip Dormer Stanhope, 4th Earl of Chesterfield* (London: Eyre & Spottiswoode / New York: Viking, 1932);

Samuel Shellabarger, *Lord Chesterfield* (New York: Macmillan, 1935); slightly revised as *Lord Chesterfield and His World* (Boston: Little, Brown, 1951);

Willard Connely, *The True Chesterfield: Manners—Women—Education* (London: Cassell, 1939).

References:

Rex A. Barrell, *Chesterfield et la France* (Paris: Nouvelles Editions Latines, 1968);

S. M. Brewer, *Design for a Gentleman: The Education of Philip Stanhope* (London: Chapman & Hall, 1963);

John Churton Collins, "Lord Chesterfield's Letters," in his *Essays and Studies* (London: Macmillan, 1895), pp. 193-262;

Roger Coxon, *Chesterfield and his Critics* (London: Routledge, 1925);

Sidney L. Gulick, Jr., "Johnson, Chesterfield, and Boswell," in *The Age of Johnson: Essays Presented to Chauncey Brewster Tinker* (New Haven: Yale University Press, 1949), pp. 329-340;

Gulick, "The Publication of Chesterfield's *Letters to His Son*," *PMLA*, 51 (March 1936): 165-177;

Elizabeth Hedrick, "Fixing the Language: Johnson, Chesterfield, and *The Plan of a Dictionary*," *ELH*, 55 (Summer 1988): 421-442;

Paul J. Korshin, "The Johnson-Chesterfield Relationship: A New Hypothesis," *PMLA*, 85 (March 1970): 247-259;

Jacob Leed, "Johnson and Chesterfield: 1746-47," *Studies in Burke and His Time*, 12 (Fall 1970): 1677-1690; see also Paul J. Korshin, "Johnson and Literary Patronage: A Comment on Jacob Leed's Article, *Studies in Burke and His Time*, 12 (Winter 1970-1971): 1804-1811; and Leed, "Johnson, Chesterfield, and Patronage: A Response to Paul Korshin," *Studies in Burke and His Time*, 13 (Fall 1971): 2011-2015;

F. L. Lucas, "Lord Chesterfield," in his *The Search for Good Sense: Four Eighteenth-Century Characters* (London: Cassell, 1958), pp. 129-176;

J. H. Neumann, "Chesterfield and the Standard of Usage in English," *Modern Language Quarterly*, 7 (1946): 463-475;

David Piper, "The Chesterfield House Library Portraits," in *Evidence in Literary Scholarship: Essays in Memory of James Marshall Osborn*, edited by René Wellek and Alvaro Ribeiro (Oxford: Clarendon Press, 1979), pp. 179-195;

Cecil Price, " 'The Art of Pleasing': The Letters of Chesterfield," in *The Familiar Letter in the Eighteenth Century*, edited by Howard Anderson and others (Lawrence: University Press of Kansas, 1966), pp. 92-107;

C. A. Sainte-Beuve, "Lettres de Lord Chesterfield a son fils," in *Causeries du Lundi*, volume 2 (Paris: Garnier Frères, 1850), pp. 226-246; translated by Katharine P. Wormeley, in *Portraits of the Eighteenth Century: Historic and Literary* (New York: Putnam's, 1905), pp. 285-308;

James H. Sledd and Gwin J. Kolb, "Lord Chesterfield and Dr. Johnson," in their *Dr. Johnson's Dictionary: Essays in the Biography of a Book* (Chicago: University of Chicago Press, 1955), pp. 85-104;

Basil Willey, "Lord Chesterfield (1694-1773)," in his *The English Moralists* (London: Chatto & Windus, 1965), pp. 269-282;

Virginia Woolf, "Lord Chesterfield's Letters to His Son," in her *The Common Reader: Second Series* (London: Hogarth Press, 1932), pp. 86-92.

Papers:

Chesterfield's official papers and letters from the Netherlands are in the Ryks Archief, the Royal Library, and the Queen's Library at The Hague. Many of his other letters are in the Public Record Office or the manuscript room at the British Library in London. Others are in private collections, especially that of the earl of Sandwich. Those to the duchess of Marlborough are at Blenheim Palace, where they are inaccessible. The letters to his godson are at the Lilly Library, Indiana University; those to Lord Huntingdon are at the Henry E. Huntington Library (which has also acquired Gulick's extensive collection of Chesterfield's published works).

William Cowper

(15 November 1731 - 25 April 1800)

James King
McMaster University

BOOKS: *Olney Hymns, In Three Books,* by Cowper and John Newton (London: Printed & sold by W. Oliver, sold also by J. Buckland and J. Johnson, 1779);

Anti-Thelyphthora. A Tale, in Verse (London: Printed for J. Johnson, 1781);

Poems by William Cowper, Of the Inner Temple, Esq. (London: Printed for J. Johnson, 1782);

The History of John Gilpin (London: Printed for J. Fielding, 1785);

The Task, A Poem, in Six Books (London: Printed for J. Johnson, 1785);

Proposals for Printing by Subscription, A New Translation of the Iliad and Odyssey of Homer into Blank Verse (London: Printed for J. Johnson, J. Walter & J. Debrett, 1791);

The Iliad and Odyssey of Homer, Translated into English Blank Verse, 2 volumes (London: Printed for J. Johnson, 1791);

Poems Translated from the French of Madam de la Mothe Guion (Newport-Pagnel: Printed & sold by J. Wakefield, sold also by T. Williams, London, 1801);

Adelphi. A Sketch of the Character, and An Account of the Last Illness, of the Late Rev. John Cowper (London: Printed by C. Whittingham & sold by T. Williams, 1802);

Latin and Italian Poems of Milton Translated into English Verse, and a Fragment of a Commentary on Paradise Lost, By the Late William Cowper, Esqr. (Chichester: Printed by J. Seagrave for J. Johnson and R. H. Evans, London, 1808);

Memoir of the Early Life of William Cowper, Esq. Written by Himself (London: Printed for R. Edwards, 1816);

Memoirs of the Most Remarkable and Interesting Parts of the Life of William Cowper, Esq. of the Inner Temple (London: Printed for the editor and sold by E. Cox & Son, 1816).

Editions: *Poetical Works,* edited by H. S. Milford, fourth edition, with corrections and additions by Norma Russell (London: Oxford University Press, 1967);

The Letters and Prose Writings of William Cowper, 5 volumes, edited by James King and Charles Ryskamp (Oxford: Clarendon Press, 1979-1986);

The Poems of William Cowper, volume 1 (1748-1782), edited by John D. Baird and Ryskamp (Oxford: Clarendon Press, 1980).

William Cowper's letters are renowned for their seemingly effortless spontaneity. He once asked his young friend William Unwin: "If a Man may Talk without thinking, why may he not Write upon the same Terms?" (6 August 1780). Certainly, Cowper wrote letters quickly and decisively, his manuscripts showing little or no sign of hesitation or revision. Although the letters appear artless, Cowper claimed that the "familiar stile" was the most difficult in which to succeed. Yet, his fluent turns of phrase were obviously released at the moment pen was put to paper. Cowper facetiously commented on the virtues of haphazardness when he wryly asserted in a 5 April 1783 letter to John Newton: "When one has a Letter to write there is nothing more usefull than to make a Beginning. In the first place, because unless it be begun, there is no good reason to hope that it will ever be ended." In a more serious vein Cowper felt it essential that one not write without thinking "but always without premeditation." As a result, Cowper "speaks" to us in his letters, and his conversation is, by turns, filled with gossip, village news, advice, humorous anecdotes, and self-reflection. Above all, they display a lively mind monitoring itself and reporting its discoveries in a corresponding manner. Nevertheless, candor sometimes gives way to artfulness. There certainly are different selves in the letters. Young, self-confident Billy Cowper is a man of the world devoted to fashion in clothing, literature, and a mode of life. Later, during the short-lived heights of his Evangelical fervor, he writes with conviction of the power of God to transform his wicked self. In his best letters—those written from 1779 to 1786—Cowper distills a measure of

William Cowper, 1792 (portrait by L. F. Abbott; National Portrait Gallery, London)

intense joy from the constant sense of impending gloom which threatened to swallow him. And there are the final letters when, exhausted by his eternal battle against a hostile God and a consuming sense of worthlessness, he tells, sometimes too repetitiously and self-absorbedly, of the stark pathos which invades his every waking moment. In the end overpowering inner darkness prevails. Words, once the source of pleasure for himself and others, no longer have any power.

Cowper was born on 15 November 1731 at Berkhamsted, where his father, John, was the rector of St Peter's Church. From one of the first families of Hertfordshire, John Cowper was the son of Spencer Cowper, a judge who at the end of his career was puisne justice of the common pleas, and John's granduncle was William, first Earl Cowper, twice lord chancellor. Cowper's mother, Ann Donne, of Bedham Grange in Norfolk, was supposed to have been related to John Donne, the poet, though such descent was proba-

bly collateral. John and Ann were married in 1728, and their first child, Spencer, who died at five weeks, was born the following year. In his portrait of Ann Cowper, D. Heins depicts her as delicate and frail; during the nine years that she was married, only two children survived. Spencer was followed by twins, who died two days after birth. William was the fourth, but first surviving, child of the couple, and the young boy idolized his mother, whom he remembered as angelic. He was shattered when she died on 3 November 1737 of complications following the birth of John, her seventh, but second surviving, child. William never completely recovered from his mother's death, and melancholia invaded his being. As he said, her death was "ne'er forgot"; from that time, he claimed, his life "pass'd . . . but roughly."

Before the death of his mother, Cowper went to a dame school at Berkhamsted; in 1737 he went briefly to study with the rector at

Ann Cowper, the poet's mother (engraving by William Blake, from a miniature by D. Heins; courtesy of Special Collections, Thomas Cooper Library, University of South Carolina)

Aldbury and then to school at Markyate Street in Bedfordshire, where he was the victim of bullying. At the age of eight, when he was discovered to have weak eyes and to be in danger of losing one of them, he was sent to the home of Mrs. Disney, an oculist with whom he remained for about two years. He disliked Mrs. Disney, but her regimen may have done his eyes some good. Westminster had long been the Cowper family school when William matriculated there in April 1742. Part of John Cowper's ambition in sending his eldest son to his own school was, as William facetiously put it, to assist his intention "to beget a Chancellor." John also desired the strong Whig principles of Westminster (as opposed to those of its great Tory rival, Eton) to be instilled in his son from an early age. That ambition was realized, and Cowper also became an excellent student, a good athlete, and a desirable companion. He was eventually head of his house and third in the sixth form.

After Westminster Cowper spent nine months at home and then was sent, in 1750, to acquire the practice of law with an attorney, Mr. Chapman of Greville Street, in the heart of the London legal district. There he became a close friend of Edward Thurlow, a future lord chancellor. During his time at Chapman's, Cowper began to frequent his uncle Ashley Cowper's home in Southampton Row, where there were three attractive cousins: Harriot (later Lady Hesketh), Elizabeth (later Lady Croft), and Theadora. By the summer of 1752, he was infatuated with Thea, and during 1752 and 1753 they saw each other daily. After two years of seemingly idyllic courtship, the love affair began to go wrong. In about 1756 Ashley intervened and forbade marriage. Cowper's lack of a fixed income was the stated reason, but Ashley Cowper may have divined William Cowper's lack of wholehearted devotion to Thea. Earlier, in 1753, Cowper's first major depression had likely occurred as a result of a quarrel with Thea.

Cowper left Mr. Chapman's sometime in 1753 and was living at the Middle Temple by November of that year. As he had been admitted there in 1748, he soon fulfilled, in June 1754, the six years of membership required for a call to the degree of the Utter Bar. He had additional obligations for three more years, and on the day those requirements were met he resigned from the Middle Temple and transferred his membership to the more prestigious Inner Temple, where on 17 June 1757 he purchased a set of chambers. Cowper had little interest in the law, which had been his father's choice of profession. Instead Cowper wanted to be one of the literati. He was a member of the Nonsense Club, seven old Westminsters who dined together every Thursday, and it was in this assemblage that he began his apprenticeship in the arduous task of learning to write in an offhand, casual manner.

In Cowper's early as well as mature prose there is conviviality and ease. Simple elegance is the hallmark of all his writing, and it was during these London years that he learned the graceful use—and manipulation—of language, as in his "Dissertation on the Modern Ode" (*St. James's Magazine*, April 1763), when he lampoons the ode-making excesses of his time: such poems can come forth "with equal propriety on the death of a king or a tom-tit, on a great minister, or a common whore, on the ruin of a nation, or the fall of a tobacco-box." In his early prose writings, Cowper displayed an obvious affinity with Joseph Addison and Sir Richard Steele. In poetry, he looked upon Thomas Gray and William Mason with mild contempt for their attempts at a Miltonic manner. He admired Abraham Cowley, Samuel Butler, Matthew Prior, Charles Churchill, George Colman the Elder, and Robert Lloyd; in those days, he was not antagonistic to Alexander Pope.

In 1763 a severe psychic crisis overwhelmed Cowper. The only work which he had undertaken in a consistent fashion in the 1750s and 1760s was as a commissioner of bankrupts, a position which brought him sixty pounds a year. When his uncle Ashley forced him to become involved in the preparations to qualify as clerk of the journals in the House of Lords, Cowper, despite his legal training, felt unable to defend his claim to this sinecure before the bar of the House. The prospect of a public appearance terrified him, becoming the focus of incredible anxiety. He was plunged into a nightmarish world:

"The feelings of a man when he arrives at the place of execution are probably much like what I experienced every time I set my foot in the office." Cowper escaped in August 1763 to Margate, where he encountered Ashley and Theadora. Ashley told Cowper that he could marry Thea if he obtained the post at the House of Lords. Cowper "recovered" his spirits during the next two months, but upon his return to London in late October he still had to face an audience at the House of Lords. He hoped madness would overtake him, and he thought constantly of suicide, at which he made several attempts. When he tried to hang himself, he fell to the floor and was discovered by a servant. Eventually, Cowper's brother, John, a fellow of Corpus Christi College, Cambridge, was summoned, and he determined that his brother be hospitalized at the Collegium Insanorum of the kindly Nathaniel Cotton at St Albans, where he remained until 1765.

As the intensity of his depression waned, Cowper became more and more aware in 1764 of a God who cherished him and desired his redemption. He became convinced of the truths of Evangelicalism. Cowper's conversion reached a heightened pitch and then subsided. He was Evangelical in his espousal of the truths of the inner heart and in his insistence on experiencing and describing the emotional effects of God's goodness. For a decade, his devotion became a bulwark against the depressions he had experienced in London. Cotton, who was not Evangelical, was concerned "lest the sudden transition from despair to joy should terminate in a fatal frenzy." Cowper remained with him until June 1765, when John obtained rooms for his brother at Huntingdon, sixteen miles from Cambridge.

At Huntingdon, Cowper, who always lived as a gentleman and expected others to assist him in maintaining the style to which he had become accustomed, imprudently spent in three months what should have lasted a year. As a partial solution to this difficulty, he became a boarder on 11 November 1765 at the home of the Reverend Morley Unwin, his wife, Mary, and their children, Susanna and William. At once, Cowper was drawn to Mary Unwin, being overcome with "anxious thoughts." The friendship flowered quickly, and Morley Unwin was jealous of Cowper's hold on his wife. For Cowper, Mary Unwin was a maternal figure who, he told a friend, Margaret King, on 12 March 1790, "supplied to me the place of my own mother, my own invaluable mother,

Gent.Mag. June 1804. Pl.II.p.505.

A LANDSCAPE from a DRAWING by M^r. COWPER the POET.

Engraving of a landscape drawn by Cowper (from the Gentleman's Magazine, *June 1804; courtesy of Mills Memorial Library, McMaster University)*

these six and twenty years. Some sons may be said to have had many fathers, but a plurality of mothers is not common." Mrs. Unwin, however, may have been sexually attracted to Cowper; there was unfounded talk at Huntingdon of improprieties. After Morley Unwin died suddenly in June 1767, Cowper and Mrs. Unwin decided to leave Huntingdon for Olney.

The move was made at the instigation of the Evangelical curate John Newton, who had introduced himself to Cowper and Mrs. Unwin on 6 July 1767. Newton, an aggressive, boisterous man, urged Cowper to become involved in his ministry, and later the two men collaborated on *The Olney Hymns* (1779). Cowper, known in the town as "Sir Cowper" or the "Esquire," was an outsider to rural Buckinghamshire, and to a large extent his power to evoke this pastoral landscape in his letters and poems was derived from his "foreign" sensibility. Keenly aware of idiosyncrasy in behavior and speech, Cowper wrote letters that are repositories of amusing, colorful anecdotes about the town and its inhabitants. His quiet life at Olney was disrupted when his brother became ill in 1769 and died the following year. He nursed John and assisted his conversion to Evangelicalism.

In 1767 Cowper had written a spiritual autobiography; three years later, he wrote an account of John's final days, which he then joined to the earlier segment. The timid William Cowper of the earlier narrative is remarkably different from the confident William Cowper in the second. Throughout *Adelphi* (The Brothers, 1802), Cowper demonstrates a remarkable power to appropriate symbolical meaning to events which might seem merely coincidental, improbable, or fantastic. In contrast Cowper's letters from 1764 to 1778 lack subtlety; they are replete with biblical quotation and paraphrase. There is a great deal of religious fervor in these missives, but very little of Cowper's personality.

Cowper's "delicacy of sentiment" in religion began to decline after three or four years at Olney. Cowper's intense Evangelicalism had largely arisen as a defense against the feelings of self-loathing which had invaded him at the Temple. He could not sustain this commitment. In 1773, partially in response to Olney gossip about two unmarried people living together, Cowper and Mrs. Unwin became engaged. The possibility that through marriage he would lose his new mother was simply too much for him, and a depression, similar to the one of 1763, overtook him in January 1773. During that winter, he experienced a nightmare, "before the recollection of which, all consolation vanishes." In this dream, he heard the dreadful words: "Actum est de te, periisti" ("It is all over with thee, thou hast perished"). The engagement was broken, and Cowper became convinced he was the outcast of God. He never again attended public worship.

From 1774 to 1778 Cowper's animals and garden were his mainstays against depression. Late in the 1770s, he began including short poems, which he called "productions of the Lyric kind," in letters to William Unwin, then rector of Stock in Essex. Although an Evangelical, the Cambridge-educated Unwin was a considerably more worldly person than his mother or John Newton, and Cowper was at ease with his young friend. From 1778 to 1780 Cowper perfected in his correspondence with Unwin the artful candor and spontaneity which are characteristic of his finest letters. To Unwin, Cowper could playfully condemn the art of letter writing: "I wrote my last Letter to inform you that I had nothing to say, in Answer to which you have said Nothing" (31 October 1779). He could also be tartly frank with him about the vocation of poet: "I have no more Right to the Name of Poet, than a Maker of Mousetraps has to That of an Engineer. . . . Such a Talent in Verse as mine, is like a Child's Rattle, very entertaining to the Trifler that uses it, and very disagreeable to all beside" (circa 7 February 1779).

Although Newton left Olney in 1780 to become rector of St. Mary Woolnoth in London, he retained a strong hold over Cowper's emerging poetical talent. *Anti-Thelyphthora* (1781), Cowper's satirical attack on his cousin Martin Madan's advocacy of polygamy as a method of curbing prostitution, was written at Newton's instigation. The eight moral satires, which compose most of *Poems by William Cowper, Of the Inner Temple, Esq.* (1782), were also influenced by Newton. The reviewers of that book of verse reserved their praise for the short poems at the end of the volume, and Cowper, who paid close attention to such comments, realized that he should move away from the couplet to blank verse, from satire to autobiography, from imitation of Pope to a revitalization of Milton. Glimpses of this direction can be clearly seen in "Retirement," the last of the long poems in the 1782 collection.

A change in direction meant a new confidant, a role eagerly assumed by Unwin. Three

Harriot Cowper (later Lady Hesketh), the cousin to whom Cowper addressed some of his liveliest letters (portrait by Francis Cotes; from James King and Charles Ryskamp, eds., The Letters and Prose Writings of William Cowper, *volume 2, 1981)*

years later followed *The Task* (1785), the semi-autobiographical poem which made Cowper's name a household word for the next few decades. Here, Cowper merged Miltonic syntax and diction with spiritual autobiography to create a late-eighteenth-century *Paradise Lost*. *The Task* is a poem of enormous vigor in which Cowper wrote of what he knew best: his own contrary heart. Having confessed the secrets of that heart, he largely vanquished the need to write poetry.

At this time, Cowper's talent as a letter writer came to fruition. In October 1785 Cowper's cousin Harriot Hesketh wrote him, reviving a correspondence which had lapsed for almost twenty years. A cultivated person interested in literature, she congratulated her cousin on his success as a poet. Cowper received Lady Hesketh's letter with unmitigated joy. He had long been cut off from the society into which he had been born and in which he had lived for the first thirty-one years of his life. He had thrust his hand out to that world in his two volumes of verse, but Lady Hesketh's missive inaugurated a more direct involvement with the past. Her rich and varied gossip provided him with a view of a world he regarded with hostile eyes but whose enticements nevertheless attracted him. Cowper's "unspeakable pleasure in being still beloved" by Lady Hesketh is especially reflected in the letters he sent to her from October 1785 until her arrival at Olney on 21 June 1786, seven months after the renewal of their friendship. Bemusedly, he told her on 10 January 1786: "I am become the wonder of the Post Office in this town. They never sent so many letters to London in their lives." So steeped was Cowper with his affection for his Harriot that he could both truly and artfully say to her: "I love you my cousin . . . my very roses smell of thee" (1 February 1788). Earlier, Cowper's neighbor at Olney, Lady Austen, had been the muse of *The Task*; Lady Hesketh inspired his finest letters.

Cowper told Lady Hesketh on 12 October 1785 that when he found her letter at his breakfast table, "I said within myself, this is just as it should be; We are all grown young again, and the days that I thought I should see no more, are actually return'd." Cowper's power as a letter writer is derived to a considerable extent from the sense of rejuvenation he experienced in his friendships with William Unwin and Harriot Hesketh. In writing to them he reached back to his London days and composed letters about "the meagre produce of the land" in which he released his sparkling wit: these two persons were the audience which rekindled the finest moments in his life as a London sophisticate. Their worldly, inscribed presences elicited his finest prose. For Cowper style is not the man—style is vested in the response of a reader who calls up the remembrance of things past.

Cowper also said, in his 20 March 1786 letter to Lady Hesketh, that "method . . . is never more out of its place than in a letter." Nevertheless, there is more "method" in Cowper's letters than he admits. He habitually begins a letter with a humorous or incidental observation, moves to his proper subject in a second paragraph, and then returns to the ephemeral in a subsequent paragraph. The etiquette of letters is that of polite conversation. Another device—one Cowper was largely unaware of—is his tailoring of his letters to his recipient's personality. There are duty letters to his lawyer friend, Joseph Hill, pious missives to John Newton, and the vibrant, lively ones to William Unwin and Harriot Hesketh.

The success of *The Task* unleashed Cowper's ambition, and from 1785 to 1790 he was preoccupied with an attempt to gain literary immortality by surpassing Pope as a translator of Homer. In the late 1770s, from the stance of outsider, he had commented in his letters on the literary world; in the 1780s, he wanted to be an active participant in that world. Up to the publication of *The Task*, Cowper had been a gentleman who wrote verses, but with the translation of Homer he saw himself as a man of letters dedicated to reputation and royalties. The letters from late 1785 to 1791 are concerned with little more than the translation of Homer, and in those letters a very determined and sometimes acerbic William Cowper can be discerned. In employing blank verse Cowper was trying to forge a literary identity as if Pope had not existed. Such a stance made him anxious and ultimately deeply antagonistic to Pope. In a letter to the *Gentleman's Magazine* (August 1785) Cowper wrote: "The Iliad and Odyssey, in his hands, have no more of the air of antiquity than if he himself invented them. . . . Pope resembles Homer just as Homer resembled himself when he was dead. His figure and his features might be found, but their animation was all departed."

In November 1786 Cowper moved to the Lodge at Weston Underwood. At Olney he had lived in a house which fronted and was part of the market square; in the countrified atmosphere of Weston, his house was clearly demarcated from the road. Such a setting obviously befitted his new view of himself as a man of letters, but he experienced a severe depression from January to June 1787. After his recovery he soldiered on with the translation.

Cowper agreed in 1789 to write book reviews for his publisher Joseph Johnson's journal, the *Analytical Review*: ten were published in 1789-1790, one in 1793. In these reviews, Cowper aptly mixes praise and blame; he can be sarcastic, and he even jokes about suicide when he remonstrates against the phrase "*To finish life before that life expires*" from *Poetical Essays* by a "young Gentleman of Hertford College, Oxford": "The line distinguished by italics is a very alarming one, especially considering that it is written by a

Dereham —
Apr: 11 · 1799 ·

Dear Sir —

Your last letter so long unanswer'd may, and indeed
must, have proved sufficiently, that my state of mind is
not now more favourable to the purpose of writing than it
was when I received it; for had any alteration in that
respect taken place, I should certainly have acknowledged
it long since, or at whatsoever time the change had ~~taken~~ happen'd,
~~place~~, and should not have waited for the present call to
upon me to return you my thanks at the same time for the
letter and for the book which you have been so kind as to send
me. Mr Johnson has read it to me. If it afforded me any
amusement, or suggested to me any reflections, they were
only such as served to imbitter, if possible, still more the
present moment, by a sad retrospect to those days when
I thought myself secure of an eternity to be spent with the
spirits of such men as He whose life afforded the subject of it
But I was little aware of what I had to expect, and that a
storm was at hand which in one terrible moment would
darken, and in another still more terrible, blot out that
prospect for ever. —— Adieu Dear Sir, whom in those days
I call'd Dear friend, with feelings that justified the appellation —
I remain yours
Wm Cowper.

The last extant letter by Cowper, written to Reverend John Newton, the Evangelical curate at Olney, who had sent Cowper a book, per-
haps Newton's recently published Memoirs of the Late Rev. William Grimshaw *(Princeton University Library)*

lover mourning the death of his mistress. His tutor should watch him narrowly, and his bedmaker should every night take care to secure his garters" (*Analytical Review*, February 1790). The mixed success of the translation of Homer, when it was published in 1791, dismayed Cowper, but he nevertheless pressed on with an edition of and commentary on Milton.

Joseph Johnson had decided in August 1790 to publish a *Milton Gallery* which would rival John Boydell's *Shakespeare Gallery* (1789). Johnson asked Cowper in August 1791 to edit this book, and Cowper was excited at the prospect of passing through the "three gradations of authorship, Poet, Translator, and Critic" (letter to Walter Bagot, 6 September 1791). Cowper was certainly well qualified as poet and translator to render Milton's Latin and Italian poems into English, but he did not have the books at hand to consult notes by other scholars and to prepare extensive annotation. Also, the energy and devotion which he had been able to give to Homer were lacking, and domestic problems impinged mercilessly on his work. Despite his deep-seated admiration for Milton, whom he saw as a spiritual father, and the ensuing friendship with William Hayley brought about by this venture, Cowper eventually abandoned the project and was delighted to hear from Joseph Johnson at the end of 1793 that the project had been shelved.

In his unfinished commentary on *Paradise Lost*, Cowper paid close attention to Milton's technical adroitness in blank verse. He heartily disliked Samuel Johnson's *Life of Milton*, and he was therefore eager to present his favorable opinion on the virtuosity of Milton's metrical accomplishment. Cowper did not mention Samuel Johnson, but Johnson was his target in this series of notes, just as Cowper had continually kept Pope before him as the opponent he would have to surpass in rendering Homer into English. Although Cowper does not reveal any new directions for Milton criticism, he does provide a succinct testimonial to the English poet he most admired.

Cowper's mental condition worsened considerably after 1793, and in 1795 he and Mrs. Unwin were taken to Norfolk by his cousin John Johnson. Cowper's last five years were particularly sad. He heard voices and was unable, even momentarily, to subdue what he believed to be the wrath of an angry God. He died on 25 April 1800. During the long years of illness which consumed his life, he made many valiant efforts to quell his inner demons.

Cowper lamented in his 27 February 1780 letter to William Unwin: "Alas! what can I do with my Wit? I have not enough to do great things with.... I must do with it as I do with my Linnet, I keep him for the most part in a Cage, but now & then set open the Door that he may whisk about the Room a little, & then shut him up again." Despite the interior darkness which constantly invaded every aspect of his being, Cowper was sometimes able to escape excessive concern for self. At such moments his letters glisten with an immediacy and delicacy that place them among the finest in the English language.

Letters:

William Hayley, *The Life, and Posthumous Writings, of William Cowper, Esqr.*, 3 volumes (Chichester: Printed by J. Seagrave for J. Johnson, London, 1803-1804);

The Letters of the Late William Cowper, Esq. To His Friends, A New Edition. Revised by His Kinsman, J. Johnson, 3 volumes (London: Printed for Baldwin, Cradock & Joy, 1817);

Private Correspondence of William Cowper, Esq, with Several of His Most Intimate Friends, 2 volumes, edited by John Johnson (London: Printed for Henry Colburn and Simpkin & Marshall, 1824);

Volumes 3-7 of *The Works of William Cowper, Esq. Comprising His Poems, Correspondence, and Translations, With a Life of the Author, by the Editor*, 15 volumes, edited by Robert Southey (London: Baldwin & Cradock, 1835-1837);

The Correspondence of William Cowper, 4 volumes, edited by Thomas Wright (London: Hodder & Stoughton, 1904);

The Letters and Prose Writings of William Cowper, 5 volumes, edited by James King and Charles Ryskamp (Oxford: Clarendon Press, 1979-1986);

Selected Letters of William Cowper, edited by King and Ryskamp (Oxford: Clarendon Press, 1989).

Bibliography:

Norma Russell, *A Bibliography of William Cowper to 1837* (Oxford: Clarendon Press, 1963).

Biographies:

William Hayley, *The Life, and Posthumous Writings, of William Cowper, Esqr.*, 3 volumes (Chichester: Printed by J. Seagrave for J. Johnson, London, 1803-1804);

Robert Southey, volumes 1-3 of *The Works of William Cowper, Esq. Comprising His Poems, Correspondence, and Translations, With a Life of the Author, by the Editor*, 15 volumes (London: Baldwin & Cradock, 1835-1837);

Thomas Wright, *The Life of William Cowper* (London: T. F. Unwin, 1892; second edition, London: Farnscombe & Sons, 1921);

David Cecil, *The Stricken Deer* (London: Constable, 1929);

Maurice Quinlan, *William Cowper: A Critical Life* (Minneapolis: University of Minnesota Press, 1953);

Charles Ryskamp, *William Cowper of the Inner Temple, Esq.: A Study of His Life and Works to the Year 1768* (Cambridge: Cambridge University Press, 1959);

James King, *William Cowper: A Biography* (Durham: Duke University Press, 1986).

References:

William R. Cagle, "Cowper's Letters: Mirror to the Man," in *The Familiar Letter in the Eighteenth Century*, edited by Howard Anderson, Philip B. Daghlian, and Irvin Ehrenpreis (Lawrence: University of Kansas Press, 1966), pp. 210-223;

J. Copley, "Cowper on Johnson's *Life of Milton*," *Notes and Queries*, new series 24 (July-August 1977): 311-317;

Pierre Danchin, "Cowper's Poetic Purpose As Seen in his Letters," *English Studies*, 46 (June 1965): 235-244;

William Henry Irving, *The Providence of Wit in the English Letter Writers* (Durham: Duke University Press, 1955), pp. 328-359;

James King, "Cowper's *Adelphi* Restored: The Excisions to Cowper's Narrative," *Review of English Studies*, 30 (August 1979): 291-305;

John N. Morris, "The Uses of Madness: Cowper's *Memoir*," *American Scholar*, 34 (Winter 1964-1965): 112-126;

Bruce Redford, *The Converse of the Pen* (Chicago: University of Chicago Press, 1986), pp. 49-92;

Arthur Sherbo, "Cowper's *Connoisseur* Essays," *Modern Language Notes*, 70 (May 1955): 340-342.

Papers:

The late Professor Neilson C. Hannay of Boston University was an indefatigable collector of Cowper manuscripts (404 holograph letters), and his collection is the basis of the Princeton University Library collection, the largest holding of Cowper manuscripts and related documents. Other substantial holdings are in the possession of the Misses C. and A. Cowper Johnson, the British Library, the Hertford County Record Office (the Panshanger Collection), the Cowper and Newton Museum at Olney, and the Pierpont Morgan Library. Manuscript sources are listed in each volume of *The Letters and Prose Writings of William Cowper*, edited by James King and Charles Ryskamp.

Edward Gibbon
(8 May 1737 - 16 January 1794)

Patricia B. Craddock
University of Florida

BOOKS: *Essai sur l'Étude de la Littérature* (London: Chez T. Becket & P. A. De Hondt, 1761); translated as *An Essay on the Study of Literature* (London: Printed for T. Becket & P. A. De Hondt, 1764);

Mémoires Littéraires de la Grande Bretagne, Pour l'An 1767, by Gibbon and Georges Deyverdun (London: Chez T. Becket & P. A. De Hondt, 1768);

Mémoires Littéraires de la Grande Bretagne, Pour l'An 1768, by Gibbon and Deyverdun (London: Chez C. Heydinger et se vend chez P. Elmsley, 1769);

Critical Observations on the Sixth Book of the Aeneid (London: Printed for P. Elmsley, 1770);

The History of the Decline and Fall of the Roman Empire (6 volumes, London: W. Strahan & T. Cadell, volume 1, 1776; revised, 1777; volumes 2 and 3, 1781; volumes 4-6, 1788; 8 volumes, Philadelphia: Published by William Y. Birch & Abraham Small, Printed by Robert Carr, 1804-1805);

A Vindication of Some Passages in the Fifteenth and Sixteenth Chapters of the History of the Decline and Fall of the Roman Empire (London: Printed for W. Strahan & T. Cadell, 1779);

Mémoire Justicatif pour servir de Réponse à l'Exposé de la Cour de France (London, 1779);

Miscellaneous Works of Edward Gibbon, Esquire, with Memoirs of his Life and Writings, Composed by Himself, edited by John, Lord Sheffield (2 volumes, London: A. Strahan & T. Cadell, jun., and W. Davies, 1796; 5 volumes, augmented and revised, London: John Murray, 1814);

The Autobiographies of Edward Gibbon, edited by John Murray (London: John Murray, 1896);

Gibbon's Journal to January 28, 1763, edited by D. M. Low (London: Chatto & Windus, 1929);

Le Journal de Gibbon à Lausanne, edited by Georges A. Bonnard (Lausanne: F. Rouge, 1945);

Edward Gibbon, 1781 (engraving from a portrait by George Romney)

Miscellanea Gibboniana, edited by G. R. de Beer, Bonnard, and L. Junod (Lausanne: F. Rouge, 1952);

Gibbon's Journey from Geneva to Rome, edited by Bonnard (London & New York: Thomas Nelson, 1961);

The English Essays of Edward Gibbon, edited by Patricia B. Craddock (Oxford: Clarendon Press, 1972).

Editions: *The History of the Decline and Fall of the Roman Empire*, 7 volumes, edited by J. B. Bury (London: Methuen / New York: Macmillan, 1896-1900);

Memoirs of My Life, edited by Georges A. Bonnard (London: Nelson, 1966).

Edward Gibbon's *History of the Decline and Fall of the Roman Empire* (1776-1788) is generally acknowledged to be the best narrative history ever written in English, and it is arguably among the two or three greatest historical works in any language. A major contribution to eighteenth-century British literature both as a narrative and as a model of one kind of prose style, it is also an important document of the European Enlightenment, for two reasons: it permanently transferred the history of religious institutions to the context of social and civil history, and it provided proof that the recurrent polarities of historical writing, called in Gibbon's day "erudition" and "philosophy," could be reconciled, not only without prejudice to either but also with profit to both. Gibbon is in a sense a "one-book" author, though the six massive volumes of the *Decline and Fall* were published at three different times during a period of thirteen years and though his posthumously compiled memoirs have become a minor classic of that genre. Yet when an author's one book is immediately recognized as a classic, survives for more than a century as the major authority in its field, and is thereafter edited and annotated so that—even after it has been superseded in details or supplemented in approach—it can serve new generations as a classical document, one book suffices, as the author hoped and expected, to ensure the "immortality of [his] name and writings."

Gibbon was the eldest son of star-crossed lovers. Their marriage had received the reluctant consent of Gibbon's formidable paternal grandfather, who died a few months before Gibbon's birth, at some financial cost: not only was the estate entirely entailed, but descendants of a more profitable marriage, if such were ever to occur, would take precedence over those of the marriage that produced Gibbon himself. Edward and Judith Porten Gibbon, parents of the historian, were, moreover, so entirely devoted to each other that they left their sickly infant to the care of his mother's sister, Catherine Porten, "the true mother of [his] mind as well as of [his] health." He learned to read so early that he could not remember not knowing how, but he knew that it was his Aunt Kitty's "kind lessons" that gave him the "early and invincible love of reading, which [he] would not exchange for the treasures of India."

In an interval of health at the age of seven he enjoyed the tutelage of one John Kirkby, author of a grammar and of a philosophic romance, for some months; and in 1746 he suffered the advantages of the grammar school at Kingston-upon-Thames, where he was buffeted by his classmates for the "sins of his Tory ancestors" (the children's reaction to the Jacobite uprising of 1745) and "at the expence of many tears and some blood, . . . purchased the knowledge of the Latin syntax."

That year, 1746, was the last of his mother's life. After bearing and losing six more children, she died. The inconsolable father resigned his son to his sister-in-law's care, and the boy experienced a year of unfettered growth in the free range of his maternal grandfather's library. Throughout his youth, he was essentially an autodidact, learning most when he was least controlled by others, except by the interest and praise of an affectionate adult. Though he persuaded himself that he had no need to study languages, he gave some direction to his reading by an "early and rational application to the order of time and place." Two other attempts at formal education produced limited results; when Aunt Kitty began to support herself and her mother by becoming a "dame" (housemother and landlady) for the boys at Westminster School, her first resident pupil was her nephew, whose frequent illnesses permitted him few of the advantages, social or intellectual, of a public school, though he was at Westminster intermittently from January 1748, when he was almost eleven, to August 1750, with perhaps a brief further trial in January 1751. He was later temporarily the resident pupil of Philip Francis, a scholar and wit who lived in a healthy spot, Esher in Surrey, but who unfortunately left his students to the care of "a Dutch Usher, of low manners and contemptible learning."

With adolescence Gibbon's health problems disappeared, but thanks to his prodigious reading and interrupted studies he already possessed "a stock of erudition that might have puzzled a Doctor, and a degree of ignorance of which a school boy would have been ashamed." His father therefore sent him to Oxford, where, three and a half weeks before his fifteenth birthday, he thought himself a man. His disappointment with the "monks" of Magdalen and Oxford, "steeped in port and prejudice," did not entirely dampen his scholarly ardor; during the first long vacation, he wrote a "book," an attempt to solve a chro-

Silhouettes by Mrs. Brown (Add. MS. 34874, f. 140; British Library)

nological crux called, in imitation of Voltaire's very different work, "The Age of Sesostris." (This manuscript does not survive.) When he returned, he "bewildered himself into the errors of the Church of Rome" and declared himself a Catholic. Horrified by his son's adoption of the proscribed religion, Edward Gibbon the elder sent him, in July 1753, to Protestant Switzerland to be reconverted. It was the most fortunate disaster of Gibbon's life.

In Switzerland he was placed in the house and under the authority of a kind and educated man, Daniel Pavillard, who had the wit and generosity to recognize his pupil's extraordinary capabilities and to nurture them. In time, his gentle methods bore fruit. After renouncing Catholicism, acquiring French, and mastering Latin, Gibbon spent the next five years thoroughly educating himself (with Pavillard's help) in Latin classical literature and modern discussions, in both French and Latin, of both literary and philosophical issues. He also acquired some social graces and confidence and made two lifelong friends, one of whom, the beautiful Suzanne Curchod, might

have been much more. The classically educated only child of an erudite minister, she was the belle of Lausanne, but she apparently recognized the great mind in Gibbon's small body and the two became engaged. Not yet twenty-one, Gibbon again began to write a book, this one eventually to be completed and published under the title *Essai sur l'Étude de la Littérature* (1761). Both book and romance were interrupted by an unexpected summons to return to England.

He arrived in England in May 1758, three days before his coming-of-age. This was no coincidence; his father, who, during his long absence, had remarried, desired to break the entail on the family estates in order to deal with some of his creditors; and to do so, he needed the consent of the next heir, Gibbon. In return he offered his son an independent income of three hundred pounds, an income sufficient for life as a bachelor scholar in London and the country, or perhaps as a frugal married man, but certainly not as a married scholar. This distinction immediately became important, for as soon as he dared, Gibbon told his father about Suzanne.

Forgetful of his own romance, the father replied, "You are independent; marry your foreigner if you wish, but before you do so, remember that you are a son and a citizen." Then he expatiated on the cruelty of Gibbon's abandoning him and sending him early to his grave (he was not yet fifty-one), as well as the "baseness" of deserting his country. Confronted with this attack, in Gibbon's own phrase, he "sighed as a lover; but obeyed as a son." His resignation was perhaps assisted by the new charms of Suzanne's only but powerful rival in his affections, scholarship; when he wrote to tell Suzanne of his father's ultimatum, he had just sent his first real book to be copied (24 August 1758).

Written in French partly because that was the language in which Gibbon then felt most comfortable, partly because he wished to address the philosophes of Europe, and partly because of vanity, the *Essai sur l'Étude de la Littérature* was motivated originally by Gibbon's "desire of justifying and praising the object of a favourite pursuit . . . of proving by my own example as well as by my precepts that all the faculties of the mind may be exercised and displayed by study of ancient litterature." Fashionable scholarship unjustly sneered at erudition, Gibbon argued; it was simply a fashion, ignoring the importance of classical studies to cultural history and their practice not merely by dull compilers, but by great men. And, he continued, we all concede that classical literature remains beautiful, but we fail to notice that our taste for and appreciation of that beauty is dependent on our knowledge of the past, which is what the commentators offer us. It is true that some images, drawn from nature, need no elucidation, and that such images predominate in a few genres. But most images are drawn from human activities, and these, being specific to a particular age or nation, require knowledge external to the text.

Gibbon had finished the first part of the *Essai*, carrying his reader to this point in his text, before he left for England. He had just begun what might have been a final section dealing with "criticism," by which he meant "the art of judging writings and writers—what they have said, whether they have said it well, whether they have spoken truth," and by truth, he explains in a note, he means "Historic Truth"—the honesty and sincerity of the witnesses' testimony, not the reliability of their opinions. The *Essai* thus conceived would have been a clear if belated contribution to the famous "Querelle" between the an-

cients and the moderns; either in Lausanne or in England, he added further support for the ancients by arguing that progress in matters such as religion, politics, and warfare gave the modern a less poetic world to write about than the ancient had enjoyed and by illustrating at length the usefulness of antiquarian knowledge in the appreciation of even so "natural" a work as Virgil's *Georgics*.

When he returned to his concluding section, it was improved and clarified by revision, as he created a transition between the section on kinds of images and that on the nature of criticism. The new material describes the scope of criticism: "everything that man has been, everything that genius has created, everything that reason has pondered, all that labor has collected—that is the department of criticism." But by this point the *Essai* had really turned to the subject that naturally lay closest to Gibbon's heart, the nature of historical inquiry, and the subsequent developments and illustrations of this originally subordinate point give the little book an appearance of disorder and occasional obscurity, which was severely criticized by Gibbon himself and by some of his early critics. To modern readers, however, these are fortunate faults, for they permit Gibbon to make his earliest statements about historical research and writing; in particular, he outlines here, in the character of the "true critic," the special synthesis of antiquarian precision, thoroughness, and reliability with philosophic imagination and perspective that would later constitute a major contribution of the *Decline and Fall* to the history of historical writing. Another important contribution, the focus on cultural history even in the context of an apparently traditional political narrative, is also foreshadowed, for Gibbon not only attempts to point out the relevance of classical studies to all other bodies of knowledge, including natural science, but also he singles out religion as a sociological phenomenon. In the first draft (unpublished), it is even the transition from paganism to Christianity that he singles out; this section, however, was replaced in the final draft by the section that later pleased him most, a speculation on the origins of pagan religion. But this final draft was not written immediately; instead, after a somewhat frustrating encounter with the scholar from whom he sought advice about his book, Matthew Maty, Gibbon undertook other projects, including the reading of the histories of David Hume and William Robertson, his predecessors in the "triumvirate of British historians." He also attempted but did not complete a purely antiquarian treatise.

These projects in turn were interrupted by modern events. Gibbon and his father became active in local politics, and then, much to their surprise, found that the local militia, in which they had casually enrolled, had been called to active duty. From May 1760 to January 1763, Capt. Edward Gibbon, Jr., was third in command of the South Battalion of the Hampshire Militia. As neither the colonel nor the major (Edward Gibbon, Sr.) was active or efficient in military affairs, most of the day-to-day business fell to the young captain; "every memorial and letter relative to our disputes was the work of my pen; the detachments or courtmartials of any delicacy or importance were my extraordinary duties; and . . . I always exercised the Battalion in the field." It was during this period (in August 1761) that he began to keep a journal (published in 1929), prefacing it with a memorial account of the earlier years of his life that was much fuller than he had thought possible.

Gibbon enjoyed life in the militia sufficiently to consider becoming a career officer, but his feelings were always at best ambivalent. Though he entered fully into the duties and social life of the militia, he found it intellectually stifling and sought stimulation in his own reading and writing. At his father's insistence he briefly attempted to run for Parliament, but his most significant decision was to return to his *Essai* and, after extensive revisions, to publish it. The once-contemplated dedication to Suzanne was replaced by a dedication to his father, who had urged the young author to publish the book as a possible step toward a diplomatic appointment. The parliamentary attempt was abandoned on 1 April 1761; the book was sent to the press on 30 April. Gibbon received the first copy on 23 June. There were gratifying letters from the recipients of presentation copies, and some of the Continental journals, in particular, recognized the genius of the young author, but it was received with only mild approbation at home and did not provide the impetus to preferment for which Mr. Gibbon, at least, had hoped.

Undaunted, Gibbon began to look for another subject and to teach himself Greek. A letter from Lausanne described his former love, Suzanne Curchod, as the reigning belle, enjoying the attentions of many admirers. Gibbon, perhaps relieved, though he is boyishly cynical about fickle women in his journal, records several meetings with an interesting Miss Chetwynd, but nothing came of this or any other flirtation in Gibbon's life. He would meet Suzanne again, however, when, in 1763, he was allowed by his father to make the Grand Tour.

The first ten weeks were spent in Paris, where Gibbon was gratified to discover that his little book had gained him status as an author and where he enjoyed, about equally, fashion, cuisine, and "agreable and rational conversation" (his brief journal of his stay in Paris was published in *Miscellanea Gibboniana*, 1952), though he was shocked by the "intolerant zeal" of the philosophers there. He then returned to Lausanne, where he once more met Suzanne Curchod, who, now orphaned, wished to reinstate their romance. Gibbon's unwillingness to do so caused a temporary rift in their long friendship, but the long stay at Lausanne had a more favorable effect on his scholarly development. In preparing himself for his forthcoming tour of Italy, he reviewed the various epochs of Roman history, thus unconsciously preparing himself for his great work as well.

He kept a journal of his tour of Italy, but regrettably it ends shortly after he arrived in Rome, "in a dream of antiquity"—before what he represents in his memoirs as the most important single moment of his life: "It was at Rome on the fifteenth of October 1764, as I sat musing amidst the ruins of the Capitol while the barefooted fryars were singing Vespers in the temple of Jupiter, that the idea of writing the decline and fall of the City first started to my mind." The Capitol was not in ruins, the antiquarian Gibbon had consulted had mistakenly identified the temple of Juno as that of Jupiter, and it had rained on the morning of 15 October, so Gibbon may have the date wrong. But whatever the figurative or rhetorical content of this account, it is clear that the juxtaposition of pagan and Christian Rome had a powerful effect on Gibbon's imagination and was a necessary preliminary to the writing of the history.

After four months in Rome (broken by a visit to Naples) and a brief stay at Venice, Gibbon returned to England via Paris, reaching his father's house on 25 June 1765, four and a half years after his departure. Gibbon was now twenty-eight years old. For the next five and half years, however, he had to continue to play the role of son of the house, not an ungrateful role, since he was very fond of his stepmother and since he was allowed to welcome to his house his old friend

Gibbon's record of the inspiration for his History of the Decline and Fall of the Roman Empire *(Add. MS. 34874, f. 88; British Library)*

from Lausanne, Georges Deyverdun, and to pursue new friendships, notably that with one John Holroyd, later Lord Sheffield and Gibbon's literary executor. But his father's pressing debts, deteriorating health, and fretful temper made it both urgent and difficult for his friends and especially his son to stabilize his affairs. Gibbon would later regard this period as the most unprofitable of his life, for he was forced to set aside his inspiration and to labor at less rewarding tasks, both literary and economic.

The financial problems were not sufficiently settled to permit Gibbon to begin intensive work on his history until 1772, but beginning in the summer of 1765, Georges Deyverdun visited whenever Gibbon himself was in residence at the family home in Surrey, that is, during most of the summers. Gibbon turned to two literary projects in which he and his friend collaborated. One, an annual review volume comprising reviews in French of important English-language publications, was at first an equal collaboration and later principally the work of Deyverdun; the other was "a history of Swiss liberty," written entirely by Gibbon but heavily dependent upon the German translations of source works provided by Deyverdun.

Two volumes of the *Mémoires Littéraires de la Grande Bretagne*, for 1767 and 1768, were published in 1768 and 1769. In his memoirs Gibbon claimed that, for the most part, the collaboration was so close and cooperative that he did not remember what he had written and what was written by Deyverdun: "in our social labours we composed and corrected by turns." Gibbon acknowledged authorship of reviews of George, Lord Lyttelton's history of Henry II and of Horace Walpole's *Historic Doubts on the Life and Reign of King Richard the Third*; the two friends were fortunately able to procure also some comments on Walpole's book from the famous David Hume. In his memoirs Gibbon praises Deyverdun's remarkable feat of translating the comic poem *A New Bath Guide* into French prose. Other essays on historic topics in the volume are probably Gibbon's or partly Gibbon's; they provided him with an opportunity to think about the perils and principles of his chosen craft.

The first volume of the *Mémoires Littéraires* appeared in April 1768, stillborn. "I will presume to say that their merit was superior to their reputation," says Gibbon drily, "but it is not less true that they were productive of more reputation than emolument." Small though their fame, the profit was still less—in fact, the publisher refused to continue, and after the second volume also failed to find a public the two friends might have abandoned the project. In fact, however, they, or rather Deyverdun, continued to work on a third volume, until Deyverdun found a post as traveling tutor and left England.

Meanwhile, Deyverdun had finished the translations of Swiss sources that Gibbon needed to begin work on the Swiss history. It was not his first attempt at historical analysis, but it was his first attempt at historical narrative. The only modern scholar to evaluate it as history (H. S. Offler, in 1948) is kinder to it than Gibbon himself was to be. Later in life Gibbon condemned it as "superficial": "an abridgement rather than a history, a declamation rather than an abridgement." At the time, however, the finished section received the praise of David Hume, whose only major criticism was that the author should write in English. But the next critics to whom he submitted the manuscript, a "litterary society of foreigners," condemned it outright. Gibbon decided that their judgment was correct and abandoned the project.

His time for scholarly pursuits, though neither reading nor writing was entirely abandoned, was seriously limited in the late 1760s by the desperate state of his father's financial affairs, and the failing health of mind and body that made Mr. Gibbon both incapable of dealing with his own problems and difficult for others to assist. Gibbon's patient labors on these uncongenial tasks, and particularly the kindness with which he contrived to respect his father's dignity in these distresses, show him at his best. He was greatly assisted, practically speaking, by the acumen of a family connection, James Scott, and by his own friend John Holroyd. A compensation for Gibbon was the growing affection between him and his stepmother, who, like his beloved Aunt Kitty, gave him the kind of adoptive and therefore unthreatening family ties which he sought throughout his life. Surprisingly, in the midst of all this distress, Gibbon completed and published his first book in English.

The project was a reply to William Warburton's *Divine Legation of Moses Demonstrated* (1738-1765), which attempted to prove (among many other things) that Virgil effectively revealed the secret initiation ceremonies of the Eleusinian mysteries in the sixth book of the *Aeneid*. Gibbon's "accidental sally of love and resentment" refuted Warburton point by point, sometimes in a pert or sarcastic manner very unlike the dignified irony or playful wit that characterize Gibbon's later public and private writing. Fortunately, *Critical Observations on the Sixth Book of the Aeneid* (1770) is not all negative: it also involves positive appreciation of Virgil's achievement, and relevant interpretative distinctions. Of special interest to Gibbon's later work, however, is a key objection to Warburton's broader hypothesis (that enlightened pagans were informed, in the mysteries, of the fundamental truth that there was but one first cause). Gibbon found Virgil's theology, because of its materialism, both incompatible with Warburton's hypothesis and objectionable as a foundation for poetry. Despite the "sublime Poetry" of Virgil's description of the "mind of the universe," he is a materialist: "THE MIND of the UNIVERSE is rather a Metaphysical than a Theological Being. His intellectual qualities are faintly distinguished from the Powers of Matter, and his moral Attributes, the source of

Gibbon in 1774 (portrait by Walton; private collection)

all religious worship, form no part of Virgil's creed."

Gibbon's small (fifty-six-page) book received a brief but favorable notice in the *Monthly Review*, and the *Critical Review* honored it with eight pages of extracts, but it did not attract many readers or a second edition. Most gratifying to the author was the praise of the great German editor of Virgil, C. G. Heyne, whose comment Gibbon quotes in his memoirs. Classical scholars still occasionally take seriously Warburton's theory about the Eleusinian mysteries in Virgil, but it is hard to deny Gibbon's view that if Warburton is correct, Virgil has dishonorably betrayed what he had sworn to keep secret. Gibbon had little time to savor the reception of his critique; his father's illness became so acute in February 1770 (the month in which the *Critical Observations on the Sixth Book of the Aeneid* appeared) that he was no longer consulted in any business matters. On 12 November 1770 he died. Two further years largely devoted to "business" were required before Gibbon could settle down in his own house

and library in London to begin the actual writing of the *Decline and Fall of the Roman Empire*.

During this period, however, he was able to begin or continue the preliminary reading for the project. He tells us in a note to a chapter in the third volume of his history, a portion dealing with the late fourth and early fifth centuries, that "as early as 1771" he had expressed one of the points just made in "a rough draught of the present History." That draft probably took the form of an annotated chronological outline; one portion of such an outline, dealing with the years 800-1500, survives in manuscript. Before May 1774, probably in July or August 1773, he took another significant step toward the history: he wrote a considered thematic overview of his subject, or at least of the portion of it to which he at first committed himself. This essay, in revised form, he eventually published as the conclusion of his first three volumes, under the title, "General Observations on the Fall of the Empire in the West."

The essay indicates similarities and differences between Gibbon's perspective and those of his principal modern predecessors, Montesquieu and Voltaire. They also show his concern with internal and external causes of decline (Christianity and barbarism) and his dissent from simplistic accounts of causation. More subtly, they suggest his recognition that political history is interdependent with social and cultural history, his dissatisfaction with purely moral historical explanations, whether concerned with individuals or with a whole society, and, together with an assumption that history always adopts a double temporal perspective, his highly qualified assent to the idea of progress. Most of the positions taken in this early essay are relatively crude, compared to those of the history itself, and though it is often quoted, it is also often criticized, especially by readers unaware of its early date.

At least in its first version, moreover, this essay left unsolved for Gibbon the problem of what he calls "style," a very inclusive term that relates not only to word choice and rhetorical devices, but to tone, to attitude toward narrator, subject, and readers, and to large and small units of organization. He also had trouble deciding where to begin his account of the decline of the empire. He accepted the paradoxical position that the "decline" in a sense began with its establishment by Augustus, as Gibbon makes clear in his discussion of Augustus's effect on the Roman constitution in chapter 3. But the empire certainly had significant periods of power and apparent health, of maturity, that contrast with eras of more obvious decadence.

Gibbon wished to choose one era as a background for his portrayal of the decline, replacement, and relics of Roman civilization. He settled on a period identified by Voltaire as one of the four great ages in the history of humankind, the period in the second century A.D. when five good emperors ruled successively, especially the last forty-two years of the period, the age of the two Antonines, "possibly the only period of history in which the happiness of a great people was the sole object of government." The first three chapters of the *Decline and Fall*, then, portray at this peak of prosperity the geographical range and military establishment of the empire; its civil, religious, cultural, and economic state; and its constitution, which retained the image of a republic but was in reality a dictatorship. The composition of these three chapters cost Gibbon much labor: "Many experiments were made before I could hit the middle tone between a dull Chronicle and a Rhetorical declamation; three times did I compose the first chapter, and twice the second and third, before I was tolerably satisfied with their effect." Later chapters, for the most part, were composed more fluently—so much so, in fact, that he could send the original manuscript, without an intervening copy, to the press.

Most readers have regarded these first three chapters as among the most brilliant in the history, not only because of their style and their demonstration of an unprecedented range and depth of information, but because they establish the unique tone and theme of the history: the empire, replacing the republic, was itself both an improvement over and a decline from its predecessor; similarly, modern Europe, heir to the empire, both fails to live up to its predecessor and surpasses it. The *Decline and Fall* examines the process by which one civilization gives way to another and ponders the wasteful way in which some of the virtues of the older society are lost without compensating gains; and yet in many of the transitions some faults are cured; some new virtues are added; some old ones are preserved. Noting that some civilizations pass without a trace, Gibbon devotes his history not to them or to a glib theory of progress, but to the subject inspired by the ruins of the city of Rome, the human tendency to create by partially destroying what we have received from the past. Gibbon's reader must recognize both irony and elegy—must appreciate the magnificence of human achievements and abilities and respect and regret their loss, and at the same time recognize their limitations, their costs, and the benefits of what was made possible by their destruction.

After these first three chapters had been written and rewritten, Gibbon found that he "advanced with a more equal and easy pace" in the remainder of volume 1. Its composition was, however, interrupted by two momentous events: the distinguished publishing firm of Strahan and Cadell, who published Hume and were soon to publish Adam Smith, accepted the unfinished book of the virtually unknown historian, at their own risk; and Gibbon's cousin Edward Eliot offered him a seat in Parliament, which he was to hold without political obligation and on the easy financial terms of a later payment or legacy to Eliot's younger son. Gibbon took his new parliamentary responsibilities seriously, seeking out both books and experts on the most significant issues, listening to the leading men of both parties, and carefully planning his maiden speech, especially after he heard various other new members make fools of themselves with their efforts. He was never able to bring himself to deliver that or any other speech in Parliament, but he gained a reputation, in private conversation, for well-informed and independent thought, though he usually voted with the government of Frederick, Lord North. Still, it came as a distinct shock to Horace Walpole, among others, when the modest Mr. Gibbon published the *Decline and Fall*.

Much of the rest of the first volume varies between two kinds of content: absorbing and horrifying narratives of the changes of power in the Roman Empire, with occasional feeble and unavailing efforts by the senate to restore the republic; and synchronic accounts of other kinds of state and states of society in portrayals of Rome's enemies and rivals, the Germans and the Persians. Implicitly, then, four major perspectives are contrasted in the first fourteen chapters of the history: those of republican Rome, nomadic hunters such as the Germans, the eastern monarchies (and Gibbon represents Persia as a theocracy as well), and Rome in the age of the Antonines. The first volume, which might have been the only volume, climaxes with a portrayal of a fifth world order, the Christian—first the early Christian "republic," with its antisocial relationship to Roman society, and then, in the examination of the truth of the pagan persecution of the Christians, medieval and modern Christendom, particularly the religious wars in which Christians had slaughtered each other. These last two chapters, 15 and 16, were at once the most celebrated and the most notorious portions of the history.

The history was published 17 February 1776. It was not only hailed as an immediate classic but quickly became a best-seller. Gibbon wrote in his memoirs: "The first impression [1,000 copies] was exhausted in few days: a second and third Edition were scarcely adequate to the demand; and the bookseller's property was twice invaded by the pyrates of Dublin. My book was on every table, and almost on every toilette."

Although criticism from self-appointed defenders of Christianity began as soon as they had read the last two chapters (the first attack was published in October 1776), Gibbon was content to ignore them, or in one case, politely to agree to disagree. Instead, after a brief holiday from his task, in June of 1776 he began work on volume 2. Before the end of the year he had completed an account of a reign clearly critical to the history of the transfer of cultural and political power from pagan to Christian Rome, Constantine's. The chapter he had written was immensely long—fifty sheets (by way of comparison, chapters 15 and 16, without their notes, required only fourteen sheets). Dissatisfied, he set it aside and turned to Parliament and society, as well as to financial negotiations to sell off enough of his property to settle his father's debts and increase his own income to an amount comfortable for the life he wanted in London. In these negotiations throughout the rest of his life, his practical friend John Holroyd, later Lord Sheffield, was of enormous value to him, advising and overseeing all such transactions. But times were bad, especially for the sale of land, and it was only after the history was completed and Gibbon had retired to Switzerland that he finally achieved freedom from financial worry, albeit, of course, it was the worry of a bourgeois, not the desperate need of a poor man.

During the new session of Parliament, Gibbon came as close as he was ever to do to joining the ranks of the Opposition Whigs, those who took the American cause in the current conflict. But as Gibbon later made clear, he never thought their cause preferable in principle, though he agreed with them about some of the errors of Lord North's government in negotiating with the colonists and then in conducting the war. An effect of this rapprochement was that

Gibbon enjoyed friendly engagements with great men of all parties. Some of these men, such as Charles Fox, remained his friends for life, despite political differences.

In December 1776 Gibbon learned that a translation of his history, by a young man who had been Louis XVI's English tutor and was now one of his secretaries, was being published, and in 1777 he went to Paris, where he enjoyed the salons of Suzanne Curchod Necker and Walpole's friend Mme. du Deffand, opportunities to use the "public" libraries of the king and of the Abbey de St. Germain, and consultations with men of affairs who gave him information about revenue, population, and so on that he later incorporated in his history. This sojourn in Paris long represented for Gibbon the epitome of civilized living; he went far out of his way to praise it in his next volume: "If Julian could now revisit the capital of France, he might converse with men of science and genius, capable of understanding and of instructing a disciple of the Greeks: . . . and he must applaud the perfection of that inestimable art which softens and refines and embellishes the intercourse of social life."

Back in England, Gibbon returned to his history with renewed vigor. He rejected the long chapter on the reign of Constantine, producing instead a series of three chapters that provide structural ties backward and forward to the age of the Antonines and to other new establishments, such as Justinian's, in the long history of the empire. For this account Gibbon clearly and explicitly rejects chronological organization and begins to discuss with his reader the complex interplay between temporal perspectives and the historian's creative role that he had already recognized in practice in the first volume. "The age of the great Constantine and his sons is filled with important events," he tells us, "but the historian must be oppressed by their number and variety, unless he diligently separates from each other the scenes which are connected only by the order of time. He will describe the political institutions that gave strength and stability to the [Christianized] empire, before he proceeds to relate the wars and revolutions that hastened its decline." After the problem of beginning was solved, composition went smoothly and swiftly; in the next few months Gibbon wrote not only of Constantine and his sons but also of the apostate emperor Julian and the brave and powerful bishop Athanasius, with a balance and verve that im-

The pleasing and even Philosophical fiction
of the seven sleepers who in the year 250 retired
into a cave near Ephesus to escape the persecution
of Decius, and who awoke one hundred and eighty
seven years afterwards (see Assemann. Bib. Orient. Tom i
p.338) has been received with universal applause
It is remarkable enough that this prodigy
should be related by James Saruge who was
born only fifteen years after it is supposed to
have happened; and who died Bishop of Batne
in the year 521. (Assemann. Tom i p 289). From
the legends and offices of the Church of Syria
it was soon adopted by the Christian World: by
the Latins (Gregor Turon. de glor. Martyr. Li. C93
passio eorum quam Syro quodam interpretante
in Latinum transtulimus) by the Greeks (Phot.
Cod. 253) by the Russians (Menologium Slavo-
Russicum) and by the Abyssinians (Ludolf p 436)
Mahomet had probably heard it with plea:
sure when he conducted the camels of his mis
tress Cadigiah to the fairs of Syria. He inser:
ted it in the Koran and the story of the seven
sleepers is related and embellished by the Arabs
the Persians and all the nations who pro
fess the Mahometan Religion. (Renaudot Hist.
Patriarch Alexandrin. p 38-39) The seven sleepers
were discovered in a cave in Norway ——— (Paul.

Page from a notebook of supplemental notes, written before 28 April 1783, for already-published volumes of Gibbon's History of
the Decline and Fall of the Roman Empire *(MA 267, Pierpont Morgan Library). This page relates to a passage
in volume 3, chapter 33.*

pressed most readers as both stimulating and just.

But the composition of the *Decline and Fall* was far from being his only work in this fertile period. The "swarms of ecclesiastical critics" had continued to bite without stinging the historian, but in the spring of 1788 one Henry E. Davis, aged twenty-one and a recent graduate of Balliol, wrote a 284-page attack designed to prove that Gibbon was guilty of plagiarism and misrepresentation. This misguided and uninformed attack had the great value of provoking Gibbon into a response, *A Vindication of Some Passages in the Fifteenth and Sixteenth Chapters of the History of the Decline and Fall of the Roman Empire* (1779), his only sustained commentary on his practice as a historian. Gibbon begged his readers, once convinced of his innocence, to "forget [his] vindication." They have been unwilling to do so. "If he seriously hoped for [its] oblivion, he should have written different: with less irony, less appearance of relish, fewer of those majestic, devastating phrases," said Hugh R. Trevor-Roper in the introduction to a modern edition.

Gibbon's economic problems achieved a highly satisfactory resolution also: he was awarded a seat on the Board of Trade and Plantations, a body charged with overseeing foreign and colonial economic affairs, but with no real power or responsibilities. Though the board met frequently, the post was nearly a sinecure and it carried a salary of £750. It required that Gibbon not vote against the government that had appointed him, but since he had rarely done so anyway and regarded it as right in principle if sometimes unwise in practice, he was happy to agree. His cousin and patron, who was in the Opposition, consented to Gibbon's accepting this post while holding the seat of which he was the patron. All appeared to be smoothly and comfortably arranged.

The government, however, was engaged in debate with European powers about its struggle with its (former) colonies. Gibbon, distinguished author of a book in French as well as a great history in English, was asked first to correct and then to compose French statements on behalf of the government. The *Mémoire Justicatif* Gibbon composed in the summer of 1779 came well after his appointment to the Board of Trade, and, far from requiring it of him as a public servant, the government approached him very delicately, through his friend Lord Sheffield. Gibbon did not vouch for the content of this essay—"I spoke

as a lawyer from my brief "—but he thought it was received as effective by the "free and respectable tribunal" of European public opinion. And "the style and manner are praised by Beaumarchais himself." Public opinion in England, at least in Opposition circles, was much less favorable to both style and substance. "Cannot a single substantive escape without being compelled to marry an adjective?" moaned John Wilkes.

Despite these distractions, Gibbon's work on the new part of the *Decline and Fall* advanced swiftly in 1779. In fact, by September he realized that his new volume would be "twins"—two quartos, not one. The middle chapters of this pair of volumes deal with material that was entirely new to Gibbon's readers; the chapters contribute significantly to the contemporary and indeed long-lasting sense that his history was "indispensable" because it bridged the gap between the ancient and modern worlds in what seemed an extraordinarily novel and yet convincing way. This exotic material included unexpected heroes—women, barbarians, and popes, for example; and the non-narrative portions, such as the section on the "Manners of the Pastoral Nations," brought in both by association or analogy and by causal connection peoples far outside the Roman domain—the Huns, the Chinese, the people of Siberia. But what is perhaps most striking about the new volumes is the sense of the historian's mastery and conscious power over his materials. As he completed volume 3 in 1780, he was capable of truly audacious gestures, such as dismissing the last Western emperor in a parenthesis, lest he otherwise forget to mention his insignificant death.

But all was not going smoothly for Gibbon. Edmund Burke, in his celebrated bill for budgetary reform, proposed the elimination of the Board of Trade, despite its use as a nurse for the muses. Aware that the House of Lords was not enthusiastic about the bill, Gibbon remained calm in the face of this threat to his financial position. A more particular and personal threat was Edward Eliot's decision to offer the parliamentary seat Gibbon held to someone whose politics were more congenial. Like many others, Gibbon had to seek a new seat from those at the disposal of Lord North; unlike many, he could not afford to pay a large sum for it (or at any rate, not a *very* large sum), and he could not hold his place on the Board of Trade unless he was a Member of Parliament. In this crisis, he thought again of a favorite scheme of his youth: returning to Lausanne to live, near or with his old friend Dey-

Gibbon in 1785 (sketches by Lavinia, Countess Spencer; British Museum)

verdun. But that decision was not yet forced upon him: Lord North found another seat for Gibbon, and when the second and third volumes of the history appeared, their author was still Edward Gibbon, M.P.

While volumes 2 and 3, published on 4 April 1781, did not cause the storm of controversy of the first volume, the critics were even more certain of the classic status of the history when they appeared. The author believed that they had met the usual fate of sequels, and it took much longer to sell the edition of four thousand copies than it had the same number of copies in several editions of volume 1. Readers took longer not only to complete but even to begin their new "entertainment." Nevertheless, Gibbon had no difficulty in deciding to add to the history an account of the "decline"—that is, the one-thousand-year history—of the Eastern empire and its final fall to the Turks. After a year's sabbati-

cal, he set to work on volume 4.

The final chapter of volume 3, with the exception of the "General Observations," clearly looks forward to a further portion of the history. Indeed, it anticipates specifically the rise of Gothic kingdoms in the West that both preserved and rivaled fragments of the Roman civilization. At the beginning of volume 4, Gibbon might have been expected to portray the reign and establishment of Justinian, as a parallel to the accounts of the "Age of the Antonines" and the "Age of Constantine" with which the previous portions of his history had begun. But he refuses to grant that importance to Justinian. The first chapter of volume 4 is indeed a parallel to those earlier sections, but it is an ironic miniature, an account of the reign of the great Ostrogothic king of Italy, Theodoric, whose sole fault as king was that the bigotry of his subjects led him to a counterbigotry: "the life of Theodoric was too long, since he lived to condemn the virtue of Boethius and Symmachus." This chapter prepares us to see through the claims of Justinian to parity with the great emperors of the past; it leads to the other major subject of the second half of the history, the "republic of Europe," and it announces a not always realizable desire to privilege cultural and social history over political and especially over military history. Gibbon's view in volume 4 is that Justinian himself has only negative importance in "his" era and empire; he thwarts the efforts of his great general Belisarius and even limits the value of the most important monument of his age, the Justinian code of law. In this volume, a centerpiece is chapter 44, the famous account of the history of Roman law, and in all three of the new volumes, comparative law joins comparative religion as a recurrent topic in the history: legal history, Gibbon believes, is far from linear; progress and regress clearly accompany each other, in the present as in the past.

The same could be said of Gibbon's own life. Not only did the long-postponed reform bill eliminate his post at the Board of Trade, whose income made possible his life in London, but the fall of North's government eliminated Gibbon's hope of an alternative appointment. Though at his friends' urging he applied for a few governmental or diplomatic posts, he was well aware that the time required for these appointments would greatly hinder his progress on the *Decline and Fall*, and he pursued also an alternative: retirement to Lausanne, where his income, inadequate in England, would be comfortable; and where he could enjoy the companionship of his old friend Deyverdun and the style of society he had always preferred. As luck would have it, Deyverdun had recently inherited a house, La Grotte. As soon as the tenants could be removed, the two bachelors could settle down, each with his own suite of rooms, but with a common dining room and staff. Deyverdun could provide the house, Gibbon the housekeeping expenses. Gibbon moved permanently to Lausanne in September 1783.

There was a long delay before he could continue the composition of volume 4 (complete except for the final chapter) and turn to volumes 5 and 6. But when his books arrived and he could divide his days between study and society, in a comfortable house in a beautiful setting, with welcome appreciation from his neighbors and the pleasure of Deyverdun's conversation at every meal, he spent what he regarded as the happiest

four years of his life. Though this halcyon period was darkened by news of the death of his beloved Aunt Kitty and though he at first found great difficulty in dealing with the disparate materials of his final volumes, he completed the history triumphantly: "It was on the day or rather the night of the 27th of June 1787, between the hours of eleven and twelve that I wrote the last lines of the last page in a summerhouse in my garden." He describes almost lyrically the beautiful but silent scene. He was happy indeed to have completed his task and to anticipate the fame it might bring him. "But my pride was soon humbled, and sober melancholy was spread over my mind by the idea that I had taken my everlasting leave of an old and agreable companion, and that, whatsoever might be the future date of my history, the life of the historian must be short and precarious."

Volumes 5 and 6 are grouped topically, not chronologically, though within the topical arrangement there are long narrative sequences—the history of the Crusades, the biography of Muhammad, an account of the Mogul empire, Genghis Khan and Tamerlane, for example. Although, despite Gibbon's statement in the preface, it is far from true that Constantinople provides the point from which the action is viewed (as Rome had done for the earlier volumes), the stagnant or contracting domain of the Byzantine emperors is revisited concurrently, and the last of them is allowed truly heroic stature in the account of the fall of the last bastion of that empire, the city of Constantinople, the climax but not the conclusion of the history.

To conclude, Gibbon returns to the beginning, first to medieval Italy, which had a few brief resurgences of republican spirit, and finally to the fate of the city of Rome, his original subject. Its physical ruins are not to be blamed on climate, on barbarians, or even on religion; these agents have caused some damage, but the principal authors of destruction have been the citizens themselves, either fighting each other or raiding the ancient buildings for material for their own constructions. Not all that is new is bad, and not all that is old has been lost, but the change of civilization has clearly been accomplished at the cost of deplorable waste of human achievements and opportunities. The parable for Rome as a whole is clear enough.

In 1787, then, Gibbon returned to England for a long visit, to see his book—three volumes of it—through the press and to renew ties with

Gibbon's record of the completion of his History of the Decline and Fall of the Roman Empire *(Add. MS. 34874, f. 93; British Library)*

his English friends. He took with him the son of a Lausanne family who had joined Deyverdun and Lord Sheffield's family at the center of Gibbon's affections. This young man, Wilhelm de Sévery, was treated by Gibbon as his own son or nephew, and this adopted family relationship was a source of much happiness for the rest of his life.

The new volumes were published on Gibbon's fifty-first birthday, 8 May 1788. Again, critics recognized their classic standing, and buyers quickly completed their collections. Some carped

at the "indecency" of his account of Greek scandals (even in Greek); others found the style, or the nonchronological arrangement, unsatisfactory. "Yet upon the whole," said the author, "the history of the decline and fall seems to have struck a root both at home and abroad, and may, perhaps, an hundred years hence, still continue to be abused."

In July the contented author returned "home"—his appellation—to Lausanne. His enjoyment of his library was undercut by the serious and eventually fatal illness of his friend Deyverdun. Gibbon had thought of writing his memoirs and actually began the project before Deyverdun's death. But that melancholy event, his own illness, and ideas for other projects interrupted it. It was not until March of 1791 that he finally completed a draft of the memoirs, and this draft was in a very brief format, later called by his literary executor "annals," rather than memoirs, perhaps on Gibbon's own example. It was that executor, Lord Sheffield, to whom Gibbon eventually confided that he was attempting to narrate his own life; to him, early in 1793, Gibbon wrote that he had done little on the memoirs and was dissatisfied with that little. At that point he must have written all or nearly all that survives of his autobiographical sketches.

The winter of 1792-1793 was a hard one. Gibbon himself was ill, and his friend Salamon de Sévery was dying. Though the fear of an invasion from revolutionary France had subsided, Lausanne was full of refugees and conscious that its own tranquil, not to say smug, way of life was vulnerable. Gibbon decided to defer a planned visit to England. But his decision was reversed by the news that Lord Sheffield's wife, loved as a sister by Gibbon himself, had suddenly died. Gibbon immediately resolved to go to his friend. He stayed one extra day in Lausanne for the companionship of his friends the Séverys and then left his home, never to return.

In England Gibbon was somewhat disconcerted to discover that his friend was already planning to remarry. Nevertheless, their delight in each other's company was unabated, and Gibbon also enjoyed renewing other old friendships. He seized the opportunity to seek new information for his memoirs, the manuscript of which he had with him, but his only significant writing was the prospectus for a project he had long considered desirable, an edition of the ancient historians of England, to which Gibbon would have contributed prefaces but for which the major work would have been done by a young man named John Pinkerton. Gibbon's "Address" recommending Pinkerton and the project shows that his mental powers were undiminished; but his body was another matter. A long-neglected swelling in his groin had increased to enormous proportions. Gibbon could neither sit nor lie down in comfort. It had to be tapped and then, a few weeks later, tapped again. Most probably the tapping, in septic conditions, was the immediate cause of his death. After one painful night, he died at midday on 16 January 1794. Lord Sheffield arrived

too late to say farewell; as Gibbon's executor, he cared not only for his friend's body and estate but also for his memory, for it was he (with the help of his daughter and some friends) who patched together from the various drafts, some of Gibbon's letters, and his own words an account of the historian's life that long remained the standard version and a small classic in its own right. With these memoirs he also published selections from his friend's unfinished and unpublished works, selections that he later amplified in a new edition. Though his will forbade further publication of the Gibbon materials, his descendant decided in 1896 that the remainder should be released, beginning with the texts of the six separate drafts of Gibbon's memoirs.

In our own century, all of his journals, his extant letters, and his miscellaneous English works have been made available in modern editions. But the most remarkable circumstance has been the fate of the *Decline and Fall* itself. Like the work of Tacitus or Herodotus, Gibbon's has not been forgotten or superseded by subsequent historians; instead, it has been annotated and interpreted. In its first century, it continued to enjoy even factual authority; today, specialized studies provide far more information than the *Decline and Fall* even at its best, and some sections have been shown to be essentially incorrect. Gibbon's judgments and approaches could also be challenged by successors as wrong or incomplete or ill-chosen. Yet Gibbon's understanding of the past has continued at least to set the terms of many discussions, to challenge the temporary supremacy of one historical style or another. And no one—no group, even—has equaled his combination of range and precision. In the nineteenth century, in the midst of a golden age of German historiography, the German classicist Jacob Bernays wished for a nineteenth-century Gibbon, someone who could use modern methods and materials for a more complete history of the same range and depth. But in an age of essays and monographs, Bernays complained, no Gibbon was likely to be found. Therefore, in practice, "the eighteenth-century Gibbon remain[ed] indispensable," not only for amateurs but for professional historians. The twentieth century can say the same.

Letters:

Volume 1 of *Miscellaneous Works of Edward Gibbon, Esquire*, 2 volumes, edited by John, Lord

Sheffield (London: A. Strahan & T. Cadell Jun. and W. Davies, 1796);

Volumes 1 and 2 of *Miscellaneous Works of Edward Gibbon, Esq.*, 5 volumes, edited by Sheffield (London: John Murray, 1814);

The Private Letters of Edward Gibbon, 2 volumes, edited by R. E. Prothero (London: John Murray, 1896);

The Letters of Edward Gibbon, 3 volumes, edited by J. E. Norton (New York: Macmillan, 1956; London: Cassell, 1956).

Bibliographies:

H. M. Beatty, "Bibliography of Gibbon's History, Minor and Miscellaneous Works, and Letters; and of the Controversial Replies to the History," in *The History of the Decline and Fall of the Roman Empire*, volume 7, edited by J. B. Bury, second edition (London: Methuen, 1914);

J. E. Norton, *A Bibliography of the Works of Edward Gibbon* (New York & London: Oxford University Press, 1940);

Charles A. Watson, *The Writing of History in Britain: A Bibliography of Post-1945 Writings about British Historians and Biographers* (New York & London: Garland, 1982), pp. 233-262;

Patricia B. Craddock, *Edward Gibbon: A Reference Guide* (Boston: G. K. Hall, 1987).

Biographies:

J. Cotter Morison, *Gibbon*, English Men of Letters series (London: Macmillan, 1878);

John W. Robertson, *Gibbon* (London: Watts, 1925);

G. M. Young, *Gibbon* (London: Davies, 1932; New York: Appleton, 1933);

R. B. Mowat, *Gibbon* (London: Barker, 1936);

D. M. Low, *Edward Gibbon, 1737-1794* (London: Chatto & Windus, 1937);

Michael Joyce, *Edward Gibbon* (London & New York: Longmans, Green, 1953);

Gavin R. de Beer, *Gibbon and His World* (New York: Viking, 1968);

Patricia B. Craddock, *Young Edward Gibbon, Gentleman of Letters* (Baltimore: Johns Hopkins University Press, 1982); *Edward Gibbon, Luminous Historian* (Baltimore: Johns Hopkins University Press, 1989).

References:

Sheridan Baker, "Evil, Primitivism, and Progress in Gibbon's *Decline and Fall*," *Modern Language Studies*, 10 (Winter 1979-1980): 32-42;

Michel Baridon, *Edward Gibbon et le mythe de Rome* (Paris: Honoré Champion, 1977);

J. A. W. Bennett, *Essays on Gibbon* (Cambridge: Privately printed, 1980);

Jacob Bernays, "Edward Gibbon's Geschichtswerk: Ein Versuch zu einer Wurdigung," in *Gesammelte Abhandlungen*, edited by H. Usener (Berlin: Wilhelm Herz, 1885), II: 206-254;

Harold L. Bond, *The Literary Art of Edward Gibbon* (Oxford: Clarendon Press, 1960);

G. W. Bowersock, John Clive, and S. R. Graubard, eds., *Edward Gibbon and the Decline and Fall of the Roman Empire*, special issue of *Daedalus*, 105 (Summer 1976); republished (Cambridge, Mass.: Harvard University Press, 1977);

Leo B. Braudy, *Narrative Form in History and Literature* (Princeton: Princeton University Press, 1970);

Martine W. Brownley, "Gibbon's *Memoirs*: The Legacy of the Historian," *Studies on Voltaire and the Eighteenth Century*, 201 (1982): 209-220;

J. W. Burrow, *Gibbon*, Past Masters Series (Oxford: Oxford University Press, 1985);

W. B. Carnochan, *Gibbon's Solitude: The Inward World of the Historian* (Stanford: Stanford University Press, 1987);

M. et Mme. William de Charrière de Sévery, *La Vie de société dans le Pays de Vaud à la fin du dix-huitième siècle*, 2 volumes (Lausanne: Georges Bridel / Paris: Fischbacher, 1911-1912);

Patricia B. Craddock, "An Approach to the Distinction of Similar Styles: Two English Historians," *Style*, 2 (Spring 1968): 105-127;

L. P. Curtis, "Gibbon's 'Paradise Lost,'" in *The Age of Johnson: Essays Presented to Chauncey B. Tinker*, edited by F. W. Hilles (New Haven: Yale University Press, 1949), pp. 73-90;

Pierre Ducrey, ed., *Gibbon et Rome à la lumière de l'historiographie moderne* (Geneva: Droz, 1977);

Giorgio Falco, *La polemica sul medio evo* (Turin: Biblioteca della Societa storica subalpina, 1933);

James D. Garrison, "Lively and Laborious: Characterization in Gibbon's Metahistory," *Modern Philology*, 76 (November 1978): 163-178;

P. R. Ghosh, "Gibbon's Dark Ages: Some Remarks on the Genesis of the *Decline and Fall*," *Journal of Roman Studies*, 73 (1983): 1-23;

Giuseppe Giarrizzo, *Edward Gibbon e la cultura europea* (Naples: Istituto italiano per gli studi storici, 1954);

Lionel Gossman, *The Empire Unpossess'd* (Cambridge: Cambridge University Press, 1981);

Curt Hartog, "Gibbon and Locke," *Philological Quarterly*, 61 (Fall 1982): 415-429;

G. B. Hill, ed., *The Life of Edward Gibbon . . . by Himself* (London: Methuen, 1900);

J. W. Johnson, *The Formation of Neo-Classical Thought* (Princeton: Princeton University Press, 1967), pp. 193-251;

David P. Jordan, *Gibbon and His Roman Empire* (Urbana & London: University of Illinois Press, 1971);

Geoffrey Keynes, *The Library of Edward Gibbon* (London: Cape, 1940);

Arnaldo Momigliano, "Gibbon's Contribution to Historical Method," *Historia*, 2 (1954): 450-463; republished in his *Studies in Historiography* (London: Weidenfeld & Nicolson, 1966);

E. J. Oliver, *Gibbon and Rome* (New York & London: Sheed & Ward, 1958);

Richard N. Parkinson, *Edward Gibbon* (New York: Twayne, 1973);

J. G. A. Pocock, "Gibbon and the Shepherds: The Stages of Society in the *Decline and Fall*," *History of European Ideas*, 2 (1981): 193-202;

J. Meredith Read, *Historic Studies in Vaud, Berne, and Savoy*, 2 volumes (London: Chatto & Windus, 1897);

Patricia M. Spacks, *Imagining a Self: Autobiography and Novel in Eighteenth-Century England* (Cambridge, Mass.: Harvard University Press, 1976);

Joseph W. Swain, *Edward Gibbon the Historian* (New York: St. Martin's / London: Macmillan, 1966);

Arnold Toynbee, "A Critique of Gibbon's General Observations on the Fall of the Empire in the West," in volume 9 of his *A Study of History* (London: Oxford University Press, 1954), pp. 741-757;

Hugh R. Trevor-Roper, "History and Imagination," in *History and Imagination, Essays in Honor of H. R. Trevor-Roper*, edited by Hugh Lloyd-Jones and others (London: Duckworth, 1981; New York: Holmes & Meier, 1982);

C. V. Wedgwood, *Edward Gibbon*, Writers and Their Work (London & New York: Longmans, Green, 1955);

Lynn White, Jr., ed., *The Transformation of the Roman World: Gibbon's Problem after Two Centuries* (Berkeley & Los Angeles: University of California Press, 1966);

David Womersley, *The Transformation of The Decline and Fall of the Roman Empire* (Cambridge: Cambridge University Press, 1988);

Virginia Woolf, "The Historian and 'the Gibbon,'" in her *The Death of the Moth and Other Essays* (London: Hogarth Press, 1942).

Papers:

The most important collection of Gibbon papers is that in the British Library, formerly the property of Lord Sheffield. Another extensive collection, formerly the property of the Sévery family, is in the Archives Cantonales Vaudoises in Lausanne. Smaller but important are holdings in the Pierpont Morgan Library, New York City, and the Magdalen College Library, Oxford. An important collection of Lord Sheffield's papers, including the correspondence concerned with the publication of the *Miscellaneous Works* and an interleaved copy of the first edition, used in preparing the second, is at the Beinecke Library of Yale University. Other papers of Lord Sheffield are in the East Sussex Record Office. Many books once in Gibbon's library, a few with marginal annotations by the historian, are in the King's College Library, Cambridge University.

William Godwin

(3 March 1756 - 7 April 1836)

Elise F. Knapp
Western Connecticut State University

See also the Godwin entry in *DLB 39: British Novelists, 1600-1800.*

BOOKS: *The History of the Life of William Pitt, Earl of Chatham* (London: Printed for the author & sold by G. Kearsley, 1783);

A Defence of the Rockingham Party, in their Late Coalition with the Right Honorable Frederic Lord North (London: Printed for J. Stockdale, 1783); facsimile in *Four Early Pamphlets, 1783-1784,* introduction by Burton R. Pollin (Gainesville, Fla.: Scholars' Facsimiles and Reprints, 1966);

An Account of the Seminary that will be opened on Monday the Fourth Day of August, at Epsom in Surrey, for the Instruction of Twelve Pupils in the Greek, Latin, French, and English Languages (London: Printed for T. Cadell, 1783); facsimile in *Four Early Pamphlets, 1783-1784;*

The Herald of Literature; or, A Review of the Most Considerable Productions that will be made in the Course of the Ensuing Winter: With Extracts (London: Printed for J. Murray, 1784); facsimile in *Four Early Pamphlets, 1783-1784;*

Sketches of History, in Six Sermons (London: Printed for T. Cadell, 1784);

Instructions to a Statesman. Humbly inscribed to the Right Honorable George Earl Temple (London: Printed for J. Murray, J. Debrett & J. Sewell, 1784); facsimile in *Four Early Pamphlets, 1783-1784;*

Damon and Delia: A Tale (London: Printed for T. Hookham, 1784);

Italian Letters; or, The History of the Count de St. Julian, 2 volumes (London: Printed for G. Robinson, 1784);

Imogen: A Pastoral Romance. In Two Volumes. From the Ancient British (London: W. Lane, 1784);

History of the Internal Affairs of the United Provinces from the Year 1780, to the Commencement of Hostilities in June 1787 (London: Printed for G. G. & J. Robinson, 1787);

An Enquiry concerning Political Justice, and its influence on General Virtue and Happiness, 2 volumes (London: Printed for G. G. & J. Robinson, 1793); revised as *Enquiry concerning Political Justice, and its Influence on Morals and Happiness,* second edition, 2 volumes (London: Printed for G. G. & J. Robinson, 1796; Philadelphia: Printed for Bioren & Madan, 1796; revised again, third edition, 1798); facsimile of third edition, 3 volumes, with introduction and notes by F. E. L. Priestley (Toronto: University of Toronto Press, 1946);

Things as They Are; or, The Adventures of Caleb Williams (3 volumes, London: Printed for B. Crosby, 1794; 2 volumes, Philadelphia: Printed for H. & P. Rice and sold by J. Rice, Baltimore, 1795);

Cursory Strictures on the Charge delivered by Lord Chief Justice Eyre to the Grand Jury, October 2, 1794 (London: Printed for & sold by D. I. Eaton, 1794);

A Reply to an Answer to Cursory Strictures, supposed to be wrote by Judge Buller. By the Author of Cursory Strictures (London: Printed for & sold by D. I. Eaton, 1794);

Considerations on Lord Grenville's and Mr. Pitt's Bills, concerning Treasonable and Seditious Practices, and Unlawful Assemblies. By a Lover of Order (London: Printed for J. Johnson, 1795);

The Enquirer. Reflections on Education, Manners, and Literature. In a Series of Essays (London: Printed for G. G. & J. Robinson, 1797; Philadelphia: Printed for Robert Campbell by John Bioren, 1797);

Memoirs of the Author of a Vindication of the Rights of Woman (London: Printed for J. Johnson and G. G. & J. Robinson, 1798); republished as *Memoirs of Mary Wollstonecraft Godwin, Author of A Vindication of the Rights of Woman* (Philadelphia: Printed by James Carey, 1799);

St. Leon: A Tale of the Sixteenth Century, 4 volumes (London: Printed for G. G. & J. Robinson, R. Noble, printer, 1799; Alexandria, Va.:

William Godwin, 1801 (portrait by James Northcote; National Portrait Gallery, London)

Printed by J. & J. D. Westcott for J. V. Thomas, 1801);

Antonio: A Tragedy in Five Acts (London: Printed by Wilks & Taylor for G. G. & J. Robinson, 1800; New York: D. Longworth, 1806);

Thoughts. Occasioned by the Perusal of Dr. Parr's Spital Sermon, preached at Christ Church, April 15, 1800: being a Reply to the Attacks of Dr. Parr, Mr. MacKintosh, the Author of an Essay on Population, and Others (London: Printed by Taylor & Wilks and sold by G. G. & J. Robinson, 1801);

Life of Geoffrey Chaucer, the Early English Poet, including the Memoirs of his Near Friend and Kinsman, John of Gaunt, Duke of Lancaster: With Sketches of the Manners, Opinions, Arts and Literature of England in the Fourteenth Century, 2 volumes (London: Printed by T. Davison for R. Phillips, 1803);

Fleetwood: or, The New Man of Feeling (3 volumes,

London: Printed for R. Phillips, 1805; 2 volumes, Alexandria, Va.: Published by Cotton & Stewart, printed by Duane & Son, 1805; New York: I. Riley, printed by S. Gould, 1805);

Fables, Ancient and Modern. Adapted for the Use of Children, as Edward Baldwin (2 volumes, London: Printed for T. Hodgkins, at the Juvenile Library, 1805; 1 volume, Philadelphia: Johnson & Warner, 1811);

The Looking-Glass. A True History of the Early Years of an Artist; Calculated to awaken the Emulation of Young Persons of Both Sexes, in the Pursuit of Every laudable Attainment: particularly in the Cultivation of the Fine Arts, as Theophilus Marcliffe (London: Printed for T. Hodgkins at the Juvenile Library, 1805);

The Life of Lady Jane Grey, and of Lord Guildford Dudley, her Husband, as Theophilus Marcliffe (London: Printed for T. Hodgkins, 1806);

The History of England, For the Use of Schools and Young Persons, as Edward Baldwin (London: T. Hodgkins, 1806);

The Pantheon: or Ancient History of the Gods of Greece and Rome. Intended to facilitate the Understanding of the Classical Authors, and of the Poets in General, as Edward Baldwin (London: Printed for T. Hodgkins, 1806);

Faulkener: A Tragedy (London: Printed for R. Phillips by R. Taylor, 1807);

Essay on Sepulchres; or, A Proposal for erecting some Memorial of the Illustrious Dead in All Ages on the Spot where their Remains have been interred (London: Printed for W. Miller, 1809);

The History of Rome: From the Building of the City to the Ruin of the Republic, as Edward Baldwin (London: M. J. Godwin & Co., 1809);

Outlines of English Grammar, partly abridged from Hazlitt's New and Improved Grammar of the English Tongue, as Edward Baldwin (London: Printed for M. J. Godwin & Co., 1810);

Lives of Edward and John Philips. Nephews and Pupils of Milton. Including Various Particulars of the Literary and Political History of their Times (London: Longman, Hurst, Rees, Orme & Brown, 1815);

Letters of Verax, to the Editor of the Morning Chronicle, on the Question of a War to be commenced for the Purpose of putting an End to the Possession of Supreme Power in France by Napoleon Bonaparte (London: Printed by Richard & Arthur Taylor, 1815);

Mandeville. A Tale of the Seventeenth Century in England (3 volumes, Edinburgh: Printed for A Constable and Longman, Hurst, Rees, Orme & Brown, London, 1817; New York: Published by W. B. Gilley and C. Wiley & Co., printed by Clayton & Kingsland, 1818; Philadelphia: Published by M. Thomas, printed by J. Maxwell, 1818);

Letter of Advice to a Young American (London: Printed for M. J. Godwin by Richard & Arthur Taylor, 1818);

Of Population. An Enquiry concerning the Power of Increase in the Numbers of Mankind, being an Answer to Mr. Malthus's Essay on that Subject (London: Printed for Longman, Hurst, Rees, Orme & Brown, 1820);

History of Greece: From the Earliest Records of that Country to the Time in which it was reduced into a Roman Province, as Edward Baldwin (London: M. J. Godwin & Co., 1821);

History of the Commonwealth of England. From its Commencement, to the Restoration of Charles the Second, 4 volumes (London: Printed for H. Colburn, 1824-1828);

Cloudsley. A Tale (3 volumes, London: H. Colburn & R. Bentley, 1830; 2 volumes, New York: Printed by J. & J. Harper and sold by Collins & Hannay, Collins & Co., C. & C. & H. Carwill / Albany: O. Steele and Little & Cummings, 1830);

Thoughts on Man, his Nature, Productions and Discoveries. Interspersed with Some Particulars respecting the Author (London: Effinham Wilson, 1831);

Deloraine (3 volumes, London: R. Bentley, 1833; 2 volumes, Philadelphia: Carey, Lea & Blanchard, 1833);

Lives of the Necromancers: or, An Account of the Most Eminent Persons in Successive Ages, who have claimed for themselves, or to whom has been imputed by Others, the Exercise of Magical Power (London: F. J. Mason, 1834; New York: Harper, 1835);

An Essay on Trades & Professions by William Godwin, containing a Forcible Exposure of the Demoralizing Tendencies of Competition (Manchester: Heywood / London: Hetherington, 1842);

Essays Never Before Published, edited by C. Kegan Paul (London: H. S. King, 1873);

Uncollected Writings (1785-1822), edited by J. W. Marken and B. R. Pollin (Gainesville, Fla.: Scholars' Facsimiles & Reprints, 1968).

Editions: *The Adventures of Caleb Williams; or, Things as They Are,* edited by George Sherburn (New York: Rinehart, 1960);

Imogen: A Pastoral Romance from the Ancient British, edited by J. W. Marken (New York: New York Public Library, 1963);

Italian Letters; or, The History of the Count de St. Julian, edited by Burton R. Pollin (Lincoln: University of Nebraska Press, 1965);

Enquiry concerning Political Justice, edited by Isaac Kramnick (Harmondsworth & Baltimore: Penguin, 1976).

OTHER: Mary Wollstonecraft, *Posthumous Works of the Author of a Vindication of the Rights of Woman,* 4 volumes, edited by Godwin (London: Printed for J. Johnson and G. G. & J. Robinson, 1798);

Mary Shelley, *Valperga; or, The Life and Adventures of Castruccio, Prince of Lucca,* 3 volumes, extensively revised by Godwin (London: G. & B. W. Whittaker, 1823).

It was William Godwin's fate to rise suddenly to fame as a radical philosopher at the end of the eighteenth century and then to plunge almost as rapidly into opprobrium and neglect. Brought to public attention and approval by his daring concepts of individual freedom and the power of reason at the time of the French Revolution, he was vilified for his radical ideas after 1800, when Englishmen had become disillusioned by events in France beginning with the Terror of 1793-1794. Godwin was a writer of tremendous scope; in addition to his monumental treatise on political justice, he wrote letters, novels, plays, essays, children's books, textbooks, and legal arguments. He worked successfully with other writers in a variety of ways, editing the works of his wife, Mary Wollstonecraft, and revising books for his daughter, Mary Shelley. He made radical revisions in later editions of his own works as his theories evolved. While the range of his achievement—literary, personal, and political—was exceptional, in the twentieth century his influence is generally recognized in three limited areas: on younger poets of his own time, especially Percy Bysshe Shelley; on novelists, especially on Mary Shelley's *Frankenstein* (1818); and on later socialists, especially Robert Owen and his followers. He remains the acknowledged spokesman for radical philosophical anarchism.

William Godwin was born on 3 March 1756 in Wisbech, a prosperous market town and port in East Anglia. In politics the district had shown a staunch independence, providing supporters for Cromwell and eager listeners for the Levellers. Both Godwin's father and his grandfather were Dissenting ministers. Godwin's grandfather, Edward Godwin, distinguished himself as a scholar and writer, publishing sermons and hymns. A friend of other intellectuals, he offered Robert Blair criticism on his poem *The Grave* (1743) at the poet's request. Edward Godwin's achievement made a strong impression on his grandson.

William's father, John Godwin, was also a minister, although not an intellectual or ambitious man. He was strict, conscientious, and critical of his brilliant son, who recalled in an autobiographical piece that "one Sunday as I walked in the garden, I happened to take the cat in my arms. My father saw me, and seriously reproved my levity, remarking that on the Lord's-day he was ashamed to observe me demeaning myself with such profaneness." William's mother, the former Ann Hull, was a gentler, more affectionate

person, though no more a reader than her husband. Of their thirteen children, William was the only one with brilliant intellectual gifts; possibly the disparity between father and son in intellectual capacity explains William's later remark that though his father was "extremely affectionate toward the other children," he treated him with "ill humor and asperity."

The precocious boy's education began when his father's cousin Hannah taught him to read; by the time he was five he had read Bunyan's *Pilgrim's Progress* (1678), followed by the Old and New Testaments. He became intensely religious and resolved by the time he was eight to become a minister. Climbing into a child's high chair in the family kitchen, he would preach sermons to any listener he could attract. A weak and small child, he avoided sport and outdoor play, preferring to remain indoors reading. When he was eleven, he was sent on to Norwich to study under the Reverend Samuel Newton. There the cold criticism of his home was replaced by overt cruelty and sadism, which permanently marked the frail student. At the height of a bitter argument one day, Newton suddenly beat his pupil savagely. This episode and others suffered at the hands of this "most wretched of pedants" and his wife, "an animated statue of ice," set Godwin permanently against violence of any sort.

Newton's teaching left a strong impression, however. He was a Sandemanian, a member of a severe sect of Calvinism which stressed the depravity of man, rejected feeling and emotion, and emphasized reason as the only basis for action and belief. Godwin, too, became a Sandemanian, though he sought solace through reading—the novels of Henry Fielding, Samuel Richardson, Daniel Defoe, and Laurence Sterne, as well as the poetry of Edmund Spenser, Alexander Pope, and William Shakespeare.

In 1791 Newton sent his pupil off, claiming he had no more to teach him. Godwin was never to be free of Newton, however; he provided the model for tyrants and oppressors in many of Godwin's novels. From Norwich, Godwin went to Hoxton Academy near London, one of the best of the Dissenting academies. His tutor there was Alexander Kippis, a renowned scholar who inspired his student with a love of the classics, history, aesthetics, grammar, and oratory. He became familiar with Lockean psychology and Newtonian science. Godwin's belief in human perfectibility had its origin in this period.

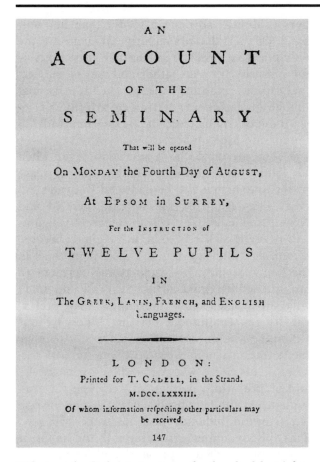

AN

ACCOUNT

OF THE

SEMINARY

That will be opened

On MONDAY the Fourth Day of AUGUST,

At EPSOM in SURREY,

For the INSTRUCTION of

TWELVE PUPILS

IN

The GREEK, LATIN, FRENCH, and ENGLISH
Languages.

LONDON:
Printed for T. CADELL, in the Strand.
M.DCC.LXXXIII.
Of whom information respecting other particulars may
be received.

147

*Title page for Godwin's prospectus for the school he tried to
start after he left the ministry and settled in London. Because
of low enrollment, the school never opened.*

During his five years at Hoxton, Godwin
felt lonely and persecuted by other students. The
themes of alienation and isolation which came to
dominate his novels reflect his own painful experience at this time. After leaving Hoxton in spring
1778, Godwin served as candidate minister in
small rural churches at Christchurch, Ware, and
Stowmarket. His ministry was a failure because
his sermons were too learned and philosophical
for the congregations, his manners too stiff and
unbending. He made a close friend of Joseph
Fawcett, later a noted poet and preacher. The
two young men would spend hours in theoretical
debate, arguing for as much as a day on topics
such as whether a motive is necessary for virtue.

At Stowmarket Godwin discovered the political writings of Jonathan Swift and was profoundly affected by both their style and philosophy. Swift had supported Irish independence
and had criticized the institution of monarchy.
The fourth book of *Gulliver's Travels* (1726), with
its model of ultimate rational behavior exhibited
in its portrayal of the Houyhnhms, especially influ-

enced Godwin. Swift "appears to have had a
more profound insight into the true principles of
political justice, than any preceding or contemporary author," he observed in his *Political Justice*.
The influence of Swift on Godwin's later writing
was pervasive; not only did Swift's ideas continue
to command his respect and support, but Swift's
use of many literary forms—letters, novels, essays, and political tracts—showed Godwin that political ideas could be expressed by many speakers
in a variety of modes. Godwin was to adopt both
Swift's values and his literary techniques.

A second literary acquaintance made at
Stowmarket was responsible for introducing Godwin to the French philosophes who were to alter
his views as significantly as Swift had done. Frederick Norman recommended that Godwin read
Claude-Arien Helvétius's *De L'ésprit* (1758), Paul
Thiry, Baron d'Holbach's *Système de la Nature*
(1770), and Jean-Jacques Rousseau's *Émile* (1762).
The impact of their works on the restless young
minister left him with diminished faith and new
questions about the nature of man and society.
He concluded that "human depravity originates
in the vices of the political constitution." In theoretical works and in fiction, Godwin always
traced crime to its source in social institutions
and conditions.

In 1782 Fawcett encouraged Godwin to give
up his work in the church and to take up a new career as a writer in London. Though he made one
last unsuccessful attempt as a minister, this time
in Beaconsfield, Godwin followed Fawcett's advice. He remained a preacher at heart for the
rest of his life, however. Most of his works had
strong didactic and moral tendencies. Godwin
began his writing career with *The History of the
Life of William Pitt, Earl of Chatham*, a biography
portraying the elder Pitt as an independent morally responsible leader. He published the work at
his own expense in 1783; although it produced
no financial return for its author, it was generally well received. Godwin boldly sent a copy to
Edmund Burke. There was no reply.

In the same year Godwin wrote his first
novel, *Damon and Delia* (1784). As he was to do
throughout his career, he wrote an intensely emotional, psychologically probing work at nearly the
same time that he was completing a rational, theoretical, or biographical study. The theme of
Damon and Delia is tragic love. The characters
and dialogue drew approval from the *English Review*, echoed by most critics. An autobiographical
thread in the novel appears in the character of a

virtuous and dedicated young minister whose best efforts are not appreciated by his insensitive congregation.

Busy at work in his new profession as writer, Godwin produced another political essay in 1783, *A Defence of the Rockingham Party, in their Late Coalition with the Right Honorable Frederic Lord North*. This work reveals two major aspects of Godwin's mature political philosophy: his belief that man is capable of immeasurable improvement through gradual degrees of change, and his conviction that practical considerations should dictate the direction of that change. Thus, taking a Whiggish position, Godwin argued that only the Rockingham party, with its conciliatory attitude toward the American colonies, could meet the needs of the nation. The pamphlet received praise for its polished style but drew mixed reviews for its political assertions.

Godwin now turned his efforts to supporting himself more adequately and arranged to set up an academy. In June 1783 he published the prospectus: *An Account of the Seminary that will be opened on Monday the Fourth Day of August, at Epsom in Surrey, for the Instruction of Twelve Pupils in the Greek, Latin, French and English Languages*. The prospectus was ignored by all except two journals, and low enrollment prevented the school from opening; yet the prospectus is of interest because it reveals basic concepts of Godwin's mature thinking: that social institutions are inevitably corrupt, that people can become free through education, and that man is naturally good and benevolent. History, language, and human nature are the proper subjects for a young person's education. Godwin rules out competition and force to maintain discipline. Above all, the imagination and intuition must be encouraged and developed by a sympathetic teacher, he asserts.

The years 1783 and 1784 were busy for Godwin, who wrote feverishly. He needed to test himself as a writer. He needed money. He published some of his sermons as *Sketches of History, in Six Sermons* (1784), where his characteristic condemnation of tyranny appears in a statement which drew critical disapproval as blasphemous: "God himself has not a right to be a tyrant." Aside from this objection, critical response was favorable.

Godwin was never far from Swift, both in his opposition to tyranny and in his adroitness in assuming masks and voices. Godwin's Swiftian genius appears clearly in *The Herald of Literature; or,*

A Review of the Most Considerable Productions that will be made in the Course of the Ensuing Winter: With Extracts (1784). This remarkable pamphlet is comprised entirely of passages from fictitious works, all written by Godwin but attributed to well-known writers such as Fanny Burney, William Hayley, and James Beattie. The entire work is a hoax. Godwin brings together "excerpts" from history, the novel, poetry, and drama, in an exhibition of pure virtuosity. The selections range from serious, sensuous, witty, and humorous, to poetic. Godwin's abiding concern for freedom and equality appears in praise for Thomas Paine. This pamphlet, amusing and impressive in its literary ingenuity, also points to the importance of considering all of Godwin's work—novels and plays as well as essays and treatises—in assessing his achievement.

Godwin published two more novels in 1784. In three weeks he completed *Italian Letters; or, The History of the Count de St. Julian*, an epistolary novel dealing with social issues. It explores the artificial values maintained by social class. Godwin received twenty guineas for the work, twice his usual payment. The novel was well received, in spite of its melodramatic plot and improbable characters.

Shortly after *Italian Letters* went to press, Godwin set to work on *Imogen: A Pastoral Romance. From the Ancient British*. Picking up on the current interest in ancient British folklore, Godwin set his novel in medieval Wales and made a shepherdess his heroine. For the modern reader, the novel's interest lies in the appealing interpretation of simple country life contrasted to the corruption of the court, vividly revealed in the character of Roderic, a magician bent on seducing Imogen. Godwin received ten pounds for *Imogen*, which contributed to his growing reputation as a writer.

Godwin became a regular contributor to the *English Review;* he also made translations and wrote contributions for the "British and Foreign History" section of the *New Annual Register* for 1783. In addition he wrote for a new Whig publication, the *Political Herald and Review*, where he expressed his distress at political repression in Ireland and India.

Lonely and restless during these early years in London, Godwin wrote to his sister Hannah asking her to recommend a wife for him. Hannah obliged, but her choice of a Miss Gay did not meet Godwin's expectations. He was drawn to strong and independent women. Gradually he found a social life in literary and publishing cir-

Thomas Holcroft and William Godwin attending the 1794 treason trial of John Thelwall, a leader of the London Corresponding Society (drawing by Sir Thomas Lawrence; collection of Dr. Kenneth J. Garlick)

cles, where he met Thomas Warton, the poet, Richard Brinsley Sheridan, the playwright, and William Wilberforce, the reformer, among many others. His most important and enduring friendship was with Thomas Holcroft, playwright, novelist, and correspondent for the *Morning Herald*. Holcroft was a resolute atheist; gradually his view eroded what remained of Godwin's religious belief.

In 1788 the anniversary of the Glorious Revolution sparked debate on the present state of the freedoms which had been sought a century earlier. Radical dissenting societies took shape to discuss issues of national and international concern—American independence, the Irish question, and unrest in France. After the fall of the Bastille in 1789, English interest rose to a high pitch. "My heart beat high with great swelling sentiments of Liberty," Godwin wrote. Reluctant at first to join the radical dissenting societies, he nevertheless attended a dinner at the Society for Commemorating the Glorious Revolution in November 1789 and listened with intense approval as Dr. Richard Price delivered *A Discourse on the*

Love of our Country. The lecture summarized views of dissenters and radical reformers: vice was seen as error brought on by social injustice; ignorance was a dangerous condition which universal education would correct; and liberty would spread to England from France. Godwin was impressed by Price's lecture; his ties to radical thinkers were made closer by Burke's *Reflections on the Revolution in France* (1790). Attacking the French Revolution, this eloquent book united radical English supporters of that struggle, Godwin among them. Burke drew spirited responses from the radicals. Mary Wollstonecraft wrote her *Vindication of the Rights of Men* (1790) and Thomas Paine his *Rights of Man* (1791). Godwin, with his friends Thomas Holcroft and the wealthy reformer Thomas Brand Hollis, helped Paine to arrange for publication of his pamphlet.

Godwin found himself caught up in a feverish spirit of political argument. In 1791 he proposed an ambitious treatise on political theory to the publisher George Robinson, who agreed to pay him expenses plus one thousand guineas. To prepare himself for the task, Godwin studied ancient historians, Thucydides, Plato, Livy, Sallust, and Plutarch; the French philosophes; and the English philosophers John Locke and Joseph Priestley. He selected Swift as an influential thinker and moralist. Among his friends, Holcroft and John Horne Tooke impressed Godwin deeply through their philosophical positions. Holcroft's condemnation of the institutions of marriage and of private property became Godwin's own.

The result of this study and consultation was the work on which Godwin's reputation today primarily rests, *An Enquiry concerning Political Justice, and its influence on General Virtue and Happiness,* published in 1793. In the first two books, man's social nature and origins are explored. Book 3 lays out the origins of government in history. Book 4 deals with individual rights, including the rights of individuals to reject government policies and positions. Man's natural benevolence will lead to virtuous actions. Book 5 weighs the merits of the executive and legislative branches of government and concludes that government is evil because it deprives individuals of their rights. Book 6 considers areas that government should stay clear of: identifying a national church or religion, supporting education, and providing employment. Godwin foresaw those areas as ones through which government could establish control or influence over its citizens. Book 7 considers crime and punishment, arguing that crime is the consequence of social conditions and concluding that persuasion rather than punishment is the proper treatment of criminals. Book 8 proposes sharp limits on the right to own private property. It discusses marriage and argues that marriage should not limit an individual's freedom. Throughout, Godwin asserts the perfectibility of man, or his capacity for virtually unlimited improvement. Government is shown to be a hindrance to human happiness. Vice is error, not inherent evil. Violence is condemned. Reform will result as reason prevails in the affairs of man. These bold concepts are presented in simple, aphoristic style.

Reception of *Political Justice* was strong and very favorable. Hazlitt wrote in his *Spirit of the Age* (1825): "No work of our time gave such a blow to the country as the celebrated *Enquiry*. . . . Tom Paine was considered for a time as Tom Fool to him; . . . Edmund Burke a flashy sophist. Truth, moral truth, it was supposed, had here taken its abode; and these were the oracles of thought." The work went through three editions in England in ten years and one each in Ireland and America. With its anarchistic precepts, it would almost certainly have been repressed by Pitt's government except for its high cost, three guineas, which presumably would restrict its exposure to the affluent. As it happened, the price did not limit sales; in hundreds of meeting places in England and Scotland subscribers bought copies and read them aloud. Godwin became the man of the hour.

Popular political agitation for reform grew after England declared war on France in 1793, but it met active resistance from the government. With increasing concern Godwin observed significant government repression of radicals. Habeas corpus was suspended. Twelve reformers, members of the radical London Corresponding Society, including Godwin's friend Holcroft, were charged with high treason and imprisoned in the Tower. In a closely reasoned effort to gain their release, Godwin, signing himself "A Lover of Order," wrote a pamphlet, *Cursory Strictures on the Charge delivered by Lord Chief Justice Eyre to the Grand Jury, October 2, 1794*. He argued that the judge, Sir James Eyre, Lord Chief Justice, had overstated the case for treason in charging the prisoners with conspiracy to overthrow the monarchy. Taking on the Swiftian persona of an objective barrister, Godwin methodically and logically showed the weakness in the prosecution's case in

an argument of acknowledged brilliance. The prisoners were released.

Immediately following the completion of *Political Justice,* Godwin threw himself into the composition of a novel, *Things as They Are; or, The Adventures of Caleb Williams* (1794), explaining that "It was the offspring of that temper of mind in which the composition of my *Political Justice* left me." Prosecution of his friends had shown Godwin that the times were dangerous ones for writers. In the preface to the 1795 edition, the author noted that "Terror was the order of the day; and it was feared that even the humble novelist might be shown to be a traitor."

The terror Godwin refers to appears in his novel in its theme of flight and obsessive pursuit. A gifted nobleman, Ferdinando Falkland, driven by his distorted notions of honor and reputation, pursues his young employee, Caleb Williams, after he learns that the young man knows of his secret murder of a vicious and contemptible man. Falkland's real crime, for the reader and for Caleb, is that he lets innocent men be tried and executed for the murder. In trying to escape from Falkland, Caleb is imprisoned and finds the law a travesty. Social institutions are entirely governed by the powerful ruling class, represented by Falkland. He and Caleb are both corrupted by their unequal relationship, an inevitable product of the authority of the privileged class. In the end Falkland dies, a victim of his own abuse of power.

Caleb Williams was extraordinarily successful. All classes of society found their causes sympathetically presented. The Prince of Wales, later King George IV, was reported to have read it more than once. Three editions came out by 1797; it appeared in America and Ireland and was translated into French and German. George Colman the Younger dramatized it in 1796 as *The Iron Chest*. Edmund Kean played Falkland, distinguishing himself and the play.

Godwin's reputation was at a peak. Recognized as a successful philosopher and novelist, he entered the happiest period of his life. He relished the company of his literary friends but found special enjoyment in the conversation of talented women. Favorites over many years were Amelia Alderson (later Opie), and Elizabeth Inchbald, a successful novelist, playwright, and actress. In 1796 he met Mary Wollstonecraft for the second time. In 1791, at a dinner in honor of Thomas Paine, he had found her tiresomely assertive. He had not been able to speak to Paine at all. His impressions were very different at the sec-

Diary pages on which Godwin recorded the birth of Mary Godwin on 30 August 1797 and the deteriorating health of his wife, Mary Wollstonecraft, who died of septicemia on 10 September (on deposit at the Bodleian Library, Oxford; collection of Lord Abinger)

ond meeting. A forceful and effective feminist, Wollstonecraft had written *A Vindication of the Rights of Men* (1790) and *A Vindication of the Rights of Woman* (1792). She was strikingly attractive and had a beautiful, expressive voice. Godwin's sympathy was aroused by the callous treatment she had suffered from Gilbert Imlay, an American radical who had deserted her and their daughter, Fanny. An exchange of notes followed the meeting, and before long the friends became lovers. They were close neighbors who continued to live separate lives twenty doors apart. They did not consider marriage, for that was condemned in Godwin's philosophy, but they saw each other often and exchanged notes to arrange their visits and to confide their discoveries of pas-

sionate love. The order of their lives was shaken when Mary found herself pregnant in 1796. Dreading the thought of another illegitimate child, she urged Godwin to marry her. He agreed, in spite of his theoretical opposition and his earlier statement that marriage was "the most odious of all monopolies." For Godwin, his general principle was much less important than the happiness of the woman he adored.

Their daughter Mary was born on 30 August 1797. At first both mother and daughter seemed to be well. Soon, however, the mother developed septicemia. She died on 10 September. Her shattered husband determined to bring his grief under control for the sake of the infant Mary and her half sister, Fanny Imlay. He set

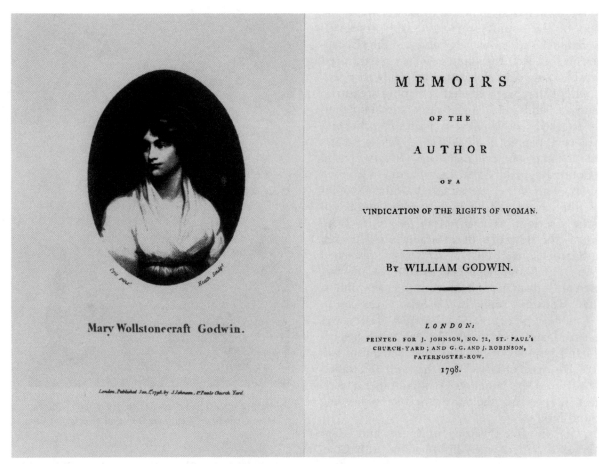

Frontispiece and title page for Godwin's biography of his first wife, whom he praised for her "exquisite sensibility, soundness of understanding, and decision of character"

about editing his wife's works and correspondence; his *Memoirs of the Author of a Vindication of the Rights of Woman* was published in 1798 and is a landmark in the art of biography, because it sensitively interprets her independent life, including her affairs with Gilbert Imlay and the painter Henry Fuseli. Like the portrait their friend John Opie painted of Mary, which for the forty remaining years of Godwin's life hung over his desk, the *Memoirs* show her sympathetically and fully. Many readers were offended by Godwin's frankness, judging the revelation of her affairs and her suicidal tendencies indecorous. Twentieth-century readers, however, find the book an invaluable source of information and interpretation.

Less controversial than his biographical writing at this time was Godwin's venture into the discursive mode. *The Enquirer. Reflections on Education, Manners, and Literature. In a Series of Essays* (1797) is a collection resembling *The Tatler* (1709-1711) and *The Spectator* (1711-1712, 1714) as well as Swift's *Polite Conversation* (1738) and *Di-*

rections to Servants (1745) in tone and choice of topic. Subjects range from "The Age of Queen Anne" and "Age of George II" to "Servants" and "Utility of Talents." One essay, "Of Avarice and Profusion," prompted the Reverend Thomas Malthus to write his highly influential reply, *Essay on the Principle of Population* (1798).

Characteristically, Godwin turned once again to the novel in 1798. *St. Leon: A Tale of the Sixteenth Century (1799)*, a Gothic novel, asserts familiar moral values but emphasizes the importance of the emotions and domestic affections. The preface clearly states that the "culture of the heart" is entirely compatible with commitment to justice. St. Leon is an aristocrat whose wealth and position, like Falkland's, isolates him. Marguerite, his wife, is based on Mary Wollstonecraft. The emphasis is on family ties and the value of love, a new element in Godwin's fiction. The novel was well received and earned its author four hundred guineas, though it was generally judged weaker than *Caleb Williams*.

Godwin's star fell after 1797, when the mood of the country turned sharply conservative. Samuel Taylor Coleridge attacked the philosopher in his lectures. James Gillray caricatured Godwin, Paine, and Holcroft in an elaborate drawing where they were labeled "creeping creatures, venomous and low." A chorus of amateur satirists attacked Godwin's rationalism. The sharpest mockery appeared in *St. Godwin: A Tale of the Sixteenth, Seventeenth, and Eighteenth Century* (1800), by Count Reginald de St. Leon, actually Edward Dubois. This burlesque attacked Godwin's opinions, the excesses of his plot, and the moral values he asserts in *St. Leon*. More painful to Godwin was the defection of an admired old friend, Dr. Samuel Parr, whose *Spital Sermon,* preached in April 1800 and published in 1801, clearly was aimed at Godwin when it attacked the "new philosophy." Godwin's reply, in *Thoughts. Occasioned by the Perusal of Dr. Parr's Spital Sermon* (1801), was measured and restrained. He defended his beliefs and pointed to the fact that Jacobinism was dead. He drily observed that his own reputation had suffered the same fate. His pamphlet had no effect in reversing the wave of criticism swelling around him.

Godwin found solace in Fanny and Mary and was gratified when his relations with Coleridge improved. Coleridge influenced him to modify his atheism, a shift that Mary Wollstonecraft had set in motion. Coleridge also introduced him to Charles Lamb. Godwin was writing a melodrama, *Antonio: A Tragedy in Five Acts* (1800), and Lamb helped to arrange its production. All critics united in condemning the play, which was a stark failure. Godwin was devastated. Though a later tragedy, *Faulkener* (1807), ran for six nights and drew some favorable reviews, drama was never Godwin's forte.

Increasingly reflective after critical battles and defeats, Godwin spent more and more time at home. One day in early May 1801 an attractive neighbor in her thirties called out to him, "Is it possible that I behold the immortal Godwin?" The neighbor, Mary Jane Clairmont, soon became the second Mrs. Godwin. She had a son, Charles, and a daughter, Jane "Claire" Clairmont. Godwin's loneliness and his need for a partner in caring for his girls explains his second marriage, which was devoid of affection if not of respect. Unpopular with Godwin's friends—Charles Lamb called her "that disgusting woman who wears green spectacles"—Mary Jane Clairmont was nevertheless a skilled linguist and author of

Portrait of a woman believed to be Mary Jane Clairmont, who became Godwin's second wife (location of original unknown)

a play Godwin admired. She was a good manager and housekeeper, but Mary Godwin and Fanny Imlay Godwin found in her the proverbial cruel stepmother. The only child of his second marriage was William, born 28 March 1803, whose death by cholera in 1832 contributed to his father's misery in his old age.

With Coleridge's encouragement, Godwin began to write a life of Chaucer. The project was originally conceived as a money-maker, but Godwin soon became immersed in fourteenth-century scholarship and did prodigious research before the two-volume *Life of Geoffrey Chaucer* appeared in 1803. Godwin treated both the fourteenth century and the poet's writing with care, stressing the importance of imagination and feeling in religion and social customs in Chaucer's day. *Chaucer* was well received by most critics; more than a thousand copies of the first edition sold out quickly. Although he was paid six hundred pounds by his publisher, Godwin considered the payment niggardly. He had five children to support and was constantly worried about finances.

His family's financial needs and the increasing unpopularity of radicalism led Godwin and his wife to launch a new publishing and writing venture in children's literature, the Juvenile Library. He dared not use his own name, as he bitterly observed: "Reviewers & old women of both sexes, have raised so furious a cry against me as a seditious man & an atheist that the tabbies who superintended schools either for boys or girls would have been terrified to receive a book under the name of Godwin." All his work on the Juvenile Library was therefore written under the pseudonyms of Edward Baldwin and Theophilus Marcliffe. Titles in the Juvenile Library included *Fables, Ancient and Modern* (1805), *The History of England* (1806), and *The Life of Lady Jane Grey* (1806); Godwin also wrote works on Greek mythology, English grammar, and histories of Greece and Rome. Most of the books were well received; ironically, the best notices often appeared in publications most hostile to William Godwin. The most popular and financially successful publication of the Juvenile Library was *Tales from Shakespeare* (1807), which Godwin commissioned from Charles and Mary Lamb. It became an instant classic.

In spite of its literary success, the Juvenile Library operated at a financial loss. Godwin was tormented by worries about money; in 1808 he narrowly escaped debtors' prison. While friends rallied and raised money to ease the crisis, Godwin lived in constant fear of creditors. That fear was to affect the important new relationship in his life, which began in 1812 when Godwin received a letter from Percy Shelley, a fervent admirer who at twenty shared Godwin's radical beliefs, unpopular as they had become. The two met and began to engage regularly in philosophical discussion. Shelley met Mary Godwin but took little notice of her until 1814, when the two fell in love; she was not yet seventeen. Shelley's wife, the former Harriet Westbrook, had two children and was pregnant with a third. When he learned of Shelley's plan to elope with Mary, Godwin tried vainly to bring about a reconciliation between the poet and Harriet. His efforts were in vain. On 28 July, Shelley, Mary, and Jane "Claire" Clairmont eloped to France. The resulting series of scandals was lurid and tragic: Harriet Shelley drowned herself in 1816; Claire Clairmont ran off with George Gordon, Lord Byron; and Fanny Imlay, depressed because these events made her unemployable at her aunt's school in Ireland, died after taking an overdose of laudanum.

Godwin at sixty (drawing by G. Harlow; location of original unknown)

His anguish drove Godwin to refuse to see Mary and Shelley when they returned from France; yet his financial straits moved him to borrow money from the wealthy young poet at the same time. Godwin's critics have been quick to point to the absurd inconsistency of his position; they overlook the circumstances. When Mary and Shelley were married, only a month after Harriet's suicide in 1816, Godwin became reconciled. Shelley's wealth increased after his grandfather's death, and Godwin's appeals for money from his son-in-law continued till the poet's death by drowning in 1822. Especially in the nineteenth century, these appeals tended to dominate critical discussion of Godwin and Shelley's relationship.

During these years of incredible emotional and financial strain, Godwin continued to write. Novels, especially, allowed him to vent emotion while earning some money. *Fleetwood: or, The New Man of Feeling* (1805) is a tragic tale of a Romantic misanthrope whose only solace is in family life. It was greeted favorably. *Mandeville. A Tale of the Seventeenth Century in England* (1817) gives a vivid account of political and religious developments during the Civil War in England. It also includes a study of mental disintegration and madness that Shelley admired but that the public rejected. *Cloudesley. A Tale* (1830) centers on a Romantic hero preoccupied by concerns over false notions of honor. The first edition sold out quickly and was followed by another. Godwin's friend Washington Irving saw to its publication in New York. Godwin's final novel, *Deloraine* (1833), returns to the theme of violent crime and revenge. Critics admired its exploration of human passion and its serious moral concerns. All of Godwin's novels after *Caleb Williams*, however, are less successful than that remarkable study of human passion. Godwin's increasing financial need, his anxiety about his extended family, and his failing health combine to explain the comparative weakness of his later efforts.

Among the last books Godwin wrote, his *History of the Commonwealth of England* (1824-1828), is most successful. First conceived as a hackwork, it became a thorough and definitive scholarly history in four volumes. Godwin consulted primary sources in the British Museum, looked at original documents in Parliament, and read contemporary tracts in preparation for writing the history. The work was the first scholarly account written from the republican point of view. A critical biography of Oliver Cromwell in the last volume is powerful and sympathetic. The history sold well, with reviewers predictably lined up on party lines.

Weakened by colds and fever during the winter of 1836, Godwin died quietly on 7 April, with his wife and beloved daughter Mary at his side. His wish to be buried next to Mary Wollstonecraft was honored by his daughter. Remains of her parents and of Mary Shelley were later placed with Shelley's heart in a vault in St. Peter's Church, Bournemouth, Hampshire.

Godwin was a man of his time. His life is a record of its energy, its idealism, and its faith in progress. His writing shows a deeply divided spirit; the extreme rationalism of his treatises and essays is in sharp contrast with the psychological studies of neurosis, obsession, and madness which appear in his novels and plays. His personal life reveals a revolution in emotional growth from his beginnings as a lonely child in a cold Calvinist household to his passionate and loving relationship with Mary Wollstonecraft; he was

willing to sacrifice his theoretical principles and endure ridicule for her sake. His position in twentieth-century literary history is fragmented. He is known variously as a radical anarchist, the husband of Mary Wollstonecraft, or the father of Mary Shelley. Only when the fragments are brought together can his achievement be fully realized. He then appears as an enabler whose influence can be noted in three areas. His radical philosophy and emphasis on progress and education influenced Robert Owen, later socialists, and the labor movement. His efforts as a novelist affected Mary Shelley's work, especially *Frankenstein*, which grew from her admiration of *Caleb Williams*. His ideas shaped much of Shelley's poetry and affected Coleridge, William Wordsworth, and Robert Southey in lesser degrees. These younger poets read both Godwin's theory and his fiction. The theory alone has been judged too rational, too deductive by twentieth-century critics; yet when Godwin's fiction is also taken into account, that imbalance is corrected. All Godwin's works form an ongoing dialogue between his intellect and his emotions, a dialogue which dramatizes the paradoxical and revolutionary period he epitomizes.

Letters:

Shelley and His Circle, 1773-1822, The Carl H. Pforzheimer Library, 8 volumes, volumes 1-4 edited by Kenneth Neill Cameron, volumes 5-8 edited by Donald H. Reiman (Cambridge, Mass.: Harvard University Press, 1961-1986);

Godwin & Mary: Letters of William Godwin and Mary Wollstonecraft, edited by Ralph M. Wardle (Lawrence: University of Kansas Press, 1966).

Biographies:

Charles Kegan Paul, *William Godwin: His Friends and Contemporaries,* 2 volumes (London: Henry S. King, 1876);

Ford K. Brown, *The Life of William Godwin* (London: Dent, 1926);

George Woodcock, *William Godwin: A Biographical Study with a Foreword by Herbert Read* (London: Porcupine Press, 1946);

Peter H. Marshall, *William Godwin* (New Haven & London: Yale University Press, 1984).

References:

H. N. Brailsford, *Shelley, Godwin, and Their Circle* (London: Williams & Norgate, 1913);

Marilyn Butler, "Godwin, Burke, and Caleb Williams," *Essays in Criticism,* 32 (July 1982): 237-257;

John P. Clark, *The Philosophical Anarchism of William Godwin* (Princeton: Princeton University Press, 1977);

David Fleisher, *William Godwin, a Study in Liberalism* (London: Allen & Unwin, 1951);

Rosalie Glynn Grylls, *William Godwin and His World* (London: Odhams Press, 1953);

Albert Goodwin, *The Friends of Liberty: The English Democratic Movement in the Age of the French Revolution* (Cambridge, Mass.: Harvard University Press, 1979);

William Hazlitt, *The Spirit of the Age: or Contemporary Portraits* (1825), in volume 11 of *The Complete Works of William Hazlitt,* 21 volumes, edited by P. P. Howe (London: Dent, 1932);

Chris Jones, "Godwin to Mary," *Keats-Shelley Review,* 1 (Autumn 1986): 61-74;

Don Locke, *A Fantasy of Reason: The Life and Thought of William Godwin* (London: Routledge & Kegan Paul, 1980);

D. H. Munro, *Godwin's Moral Philosophy, an Interpretation of William Godwin* (London: Oxford University Press, 1953);

John Middleton Murry, *Heaven——and Earth* (London: J. Cape, 1938);

Mitzi Myers, "Godwin's Memoirs of Wollstonecraft: The Shaping of Self and Subject," *Studies in Romanticism,* 20 (Fall 1981): 299-316;

Mark Philp, *Godwin's Political Justice* (Ithaca: Cornell University Press, 1986);

James Arthur Preu, *The Dean and the Anarchist,* Florida State University Studies, no. 33 (Tallahassee: Florida State University Press, 1959);

Henry Crabb Robinson, *Diary, Reminiscences, and Correspondence,* edited by Thomas Sadler, second edition (3 volumes, London: Macmillan, 1869; 2 volumes, Boston: Fields, Osgood, 1870);

Andrew J. Scheiber, "Falkland's Story: Caleb Williams' Other Voice," *Studies in the Novel,* 17 (Fall 1985): 255-266;

Elton Edward Smith and Esther Greenwell Smith, *William Godwin* (New York: Twayne, 1965);

George Watson, "The Reckless Disciple: Godwin's Shelley," *Hudson Review,* 39 (Summer 1986): 212-230;

Donald R. Wehrs, "Rhetoric, History, Rebellion: *Caleb Williams* and the Subversion of Eighteenth-Century Fiction," *Studies in English Literature, 1500-1900,* 28 (Summer 1988): 497-511.

Papers:

The Abinger Collection, on loan to the Bodleian Library, Oxford, includes Godwin's diaries and memoirs as well as manuscripts, notes, and correspondence. The Forster Collection in the Victoria and Albert Museum Library includes manuscripts for *Political Justice, Caleb Williams, Life of Geoffrey Chaucer,* and *History of the Commonwealth of England* as well as miscellaneous correspondence. The Carl H. Pforzheimer collection, now at the New York Public Library, includes the manuscript for *Fleetwood,* revisions for *St. Leon,* drafts, notes, and miscellaneous correspondence.

Oliver Goldsmith

(10 November 1730 or 1731 - 4 April 1774)

Samuel H. Woods, Jr.
Oklahoma State University

See also the Goldsmith entries in *DLB 39: British Novelists, 1660-1800* and *DLB 89: Restoration and Eighteenth-Century Dramatists*, Third Series.

BOOKS: *The Memoirs of a Protestant, Condemned to the Galleys of France for His Religion*, by Jean Marteilhe, translated by Goldsmith as James Willington, 2 volumes (London: Printed for R. Griffiths & E. Dilly, 1758);

An Enquiry into the Present State of Polite Learning in Europe (London: Printed for R. & J. Dodsley, 1759);

The Bee, nos. 1-8 (London, 6 October - 24 November 1759); republished as *The Bee. Being Essays on the most Interesting Subjects* (London: Printed for J. Wilkie, 1759);

The Mystery Revealed: Containing a Series of Transactions and Authentic Testimonials Respecting the Supposed Cock-Lane Ghost (London: Printed for W. Bristow, 1762);

The Citizen of the World; or, Letters from a Chinese Philosopher, Residing in London, to His Friends in the East, 2 volumes (London: Printed for the author & sold by J. Newbery & W. Bristow, J. Leake & W. Frederick, Bath; B. Collins, Salisbury; and A. M. Smart & Co., Reading, 1762; Albany, N.Y.: Printed by Barber & Southwick for Thomas Spencer, 1794);

Plutarch's Lives, Abridged from the Original Greek, Illustrated with Notes and Reflections, 7 volumes (London: Printed for J. Newbery, 1762);

The Life of Richard Nash, of Bath, Esq., Extracted Principally from His Original Papers (London: Printed for J. Newbery and W. Frederick, Bath, 1762);

An History of England in a Series of Letters from a Nobleman to His Son, 2 volumes (London: Printed for J. Newbery, 1764);

The Traveller; or, a Prospect of Society (London: Printed for J. Newbery, 1764; enlarged, 1765; Philadelphia: Printed by Robert Bell, 1768);

Essays. By Mr. Goldsmith (London: Printed for W. Griffin, 1765; enlarged, 1766);

Oliver Goldsmith (National Portrait Gallery, London). This painting is a copy, probably by Sir Joshua Reynolds or one of his students, of the portrait Reynolds painted for Henry and Hester Thrale.

Edwin and Angelina: A Ballad by Mr. Goldsmith, Printed for the Amusement of the Countess of Northumberland (London: Privately printed, 1765);

The Vicar of Wakefield: A Tale, 2 volumes (Salisbury: Printed by B. Collins for F. Newbery, London, 1766; second edition, revised, London: Printed for F. Newbery, 1766; Philadelphia: Printed for William Mentz, 1772);

A Concise History of Philosophy and Philosophers, by M. Formey, translated by Goldsmith (London: Printed for F. Newbery, 1766);

The Good Natur'd Man: A Comedy (London: Printed for W. Griffin, 1768);

The Roman History, from the Foundation of the City of Rome, to the Destruction of the Western Empire, 2 volumes (London: Printed for S. Baker & G. Leigh, T. Davies & L. Davis, 1769);

The Deserted Village: A Poem (London: Printed for W. Griffin, 1770; Philadelphia: Printed by William & Thomas Bradford, 1771);

The Life of Thomas Parnell, D.D. (London: Printed for T. Davies, 1770);

The Life of Henry St. John, Lord Viscount Bolingbroke (London: Printed for T. Davies, 1770);

The History of England, from the Earliest Times to the Death of George II, 4 volumes (London: Printed for T. Davies, Becket & De Hondt & T. Cadell, 1771);

Threnodia Augustalis: Sacred to the Memory of the Princess Dowager of Wales (London: Printed for W. Woodfall, 1772);

Dr. Goldsmith's Roman History, Abridged by Himself for the Use of Schools (London: Printed for S. Baker & G. Leitch, T. Davies & L. Davis, 1772; Philadelphia: Printed for Robert Campbell, 1795);

She Stoops to Conquer; or, The Mistakes of a Night: A Comedy (London: Printed for F. Newbery, 1773; Philadelphia: Printed & sold by John Dunlap, 1773);

Retaliation: A Poem (London: Printed for G. Kearsly, 1774);

The Grecian History, from the Earliest State to the Death of Alexander the Great (2 volumes, London: Printed for J. & F. Rivington, T. Longman, G. Kearsly, W. Griffin, G. Robinson, R. Baldwin, W. Goldsmith, T. Cadell & T. Evans, 1774; 1 volume, Philadelphia: Printed for Mathew Carey, 1800);

An History of the Earth, and Animated Nature (8 volumes, London: Printed for J. Nourse, 1774; 4 volumes, Philadelphia: Printed for Mathew Carey, 1795);

An Abridgement of the History of England from the Invasion of Julius Caesar to the Death of George II (London: Printed for B. Law, G. Robinson, G. Kearsly, T. Davies, T. Becket, T. Cadell & T. Evans, 1774; Philadelphia: Printed for R. Campbell, 1795);

The Comic Romance of Monsieur Scarron, translated by Goldsmith, 2 volumes (London: Printed for W. Griffin, 1775);

The Haunch of Venison: A Poetical Epistle to Lord Clare (London: Printed for J. Ridley & G. Kearsly, 1776);

A Survey of Experimental Philosophy, Considered in Its Present State of Improvement, 2 volumes (Lon-

don: Printed for T. Carnan & F. Newbery jun., 1776);

The Grumbler: A Farce, adapted by Goldsmith from Sir Charles Sedley's translation of David Austin de Brueys' *Le Grondeur,* edited by Alice I. Perry Wood (Cambridge: Harvard University Press, 1931).

Editions: *The Miscellaneous Works of Oliver Goldsmith, M.B.,* 4 volumes, edited by Thomas Percy (London: Printed for J. Johnson and others, 1801);

Collected Works of Oliver Goldsmith, 5 volumes, edited by Arthur Friedman (Oxford: Clarendon Press, 1966).

OTHER: Richard Brookes, *A New and Accurate System of Natural History,* preface and introductions to volumes 1-4 by Goldsmith, 6 volumes (London: Printed for J. Newbery, 1763-1764);

William Guthrie, John Gray, and others, *A General History of the World from the Creation to the Present Time,* preface to volume 1 by Goldsmith, 13 volumes (London: Printed for J. Newbery, R. Baldwin, S. Crowder, J. Coote, R. Withy, J. Wilkie, J. Wilson & J. Fell, W. Nicoll, B. Collins & R. Raikes, 1764);

C. Wiseman, *A Complete English Grammar on a New Plan,* preface by Goldsmith (London: Printed for W. Nicoll, 1764);

Poems for Young Ladies. In Three Parts. Devotional, Moral and Entertaining, edited by Goldsmith (London: Printed for J. Payne, 1767);

The Beauties of English Poesy, edited by Goldsmith, 2 volumes (London: Printed for William Griffin, 1767);

Charlotte Lennox, *The Sister: A Comedy,* epilogue by Goldsmith (London: Printed for J. Dodsley & T. Davis, 1769);

Thomas Parnell, *Poems on Several Occasions,* includes Goldsmith's biography of Parnell (London: Printed for T. Davies, 1770);

Henry St. John, Lord Viscount Bolingbroke, *A Dissertation upon Parties,* includes Goldsmith's biography of Bolingbroke (London: Printed for T. Davies, 1770);

Joseph Cradock, *Zobeide: A Tragedy,* prologue by Goldsmith (London: Printed for T. Davies, 1770).

During his short but remarkable literary career of only fifteen years, Oliver Goldsmith wrote individual essays, a pseudoletter essay series, biographies, poems, a novel, and plays—

every literary genre practiced in mid-eighteenth-century England. In all, his style showed such grace and charm that, when his friend Samuel Johnson wrote the epitaph for Joseph Nollekens's monument to Goldsmith in Westminster Abbey, he made special note of Goldsmith's versatility, adding that he had touched virtually every literary form, and he had touched none that he did not adorn. In one way or another Goldsmith commented on almost every social change that he and his contemporaries were living through: greater social mobility, the beginnings of the Agricultural and Industrial Revolutions, increasing urban growth and economic development, changing sexual customs, and even the early effects of British imperialism at home and abroad. Through the years since, his literary reputation has rested chiefly on *The Vicar of Wakefield* (1766), a novel both comic and romantic; *The Deserted Village* (1770), a pastoral poem nostalgic for a simpler, more innocent time; and *She Stoops to Conquer* (1773), now a classic comedy in the English dramatic repertory.

Goldsmith was born, probably in 1730, on 10 November at Pallas, County Longford, Ireland. His life falls into two almost equal periods, from his birth until his arrival in London in 1756 and then from 1756 until his premature death in 1774, the second covering his whole career as a professional writer. Considerable knowledge about the second half of his life survives and, of course, it demands our primary interest; reliable information about his early life is sketchy, although extremely important, because during his early years in Ireland, his personality and character received their definitive shape. He was the fourth child and second son of Charles Goldsmith, himself a younger son and a none too energetic Church of Ireland clergyman, and of Ann Jones, who also had several relatives that were clergymen. Her uncle was curate-in-charge of the parish of Kilkenny West in eastern County Longford and took Charles on as his assistant. The uncle died a short time after Oliver's birth, and Charles Goldsmith succeeded as curate-in-charge, moving to Lissoy, a few miles from the church. His income of about two hundred pounds a year meant relative prosperity for the family, and he lived the life of both priest and gentleman farmer.

Goldsmith's childhood in Lissoy was a happy one. Memories of it almost certainly helped him create the strong nostalgia that permeates *The Deserted Village* and appears in his other works as well. Though the family was financially secure after Charles was installed in Kilkenny West and could count themselves as members of the Anglo-Irish Establishment, or at least of its fringes, they lived with a family skeleton; a Goldsmith ancestor had been a Franciscan friar in the seventeenth century; he was converted to the established Church of Ireland and married, apparently in all sincerity. The family lived with this unpleasant secret at the same time that they followed the free and easy ways of the Protestant Ascendancy, and, if anything, the secret strengthened their identification with the Anglo-Irish, although unlike many of his contemporaries, Goldsmith never attacked the Roman Catholic church or its members in his writings. He could remember with pleasure and homesickness the family dairymaid singing "Johnny Armstrong's Last Good Night" at the family hearth, as he wrote his brother-in-law Daniel Hodson from London in 1757. His descriptions of the warm, cozy life that the Primroses lead in *The Vicar of Wakefield* almost certainly come more from memories of the simple pleasures of hospitality, country walks, tea parties, and picnics and from his knowledge of English country life rather than from the grim poverty of Ireland, but the Primroses' sense of family closeness surely recalls Goldsmith's own memories of his happy childhood. The relaxed easiness of the Anglo-Irish Ascendancy that permeated Goldsmith's childhood had a lasting effect on his own personality, and many of the traits his English friends later in life found bizarre and peculiar had their origin in the easygoing informality that dominated Ascendancy manners, all the more relaxed by the family's remoteness in the country, away from Dublin's more polished life. Both conversation and behavior continued to reflect the less constrained standards of the late seventeenth century rather than the creeping gentility that *The Spectator* (1711-1712, 1714) and books such as Daniel Defoe's *Family Instructor* (1715) were beginning to impose on middle-class English society.

Goldsmith's first teacher, his relative Mrs. Elizabeth Delap, found little promise of future talent in her three-year-old charge. When he was six, his father sent him to the village school, where Thomas Byrne was master. A retired soldier from the Marlborough wars, Byrne was easily diverted by his pupils into tales of his soldiering days, but Byrne could also extemporaneously translate Virgil's *Eclogues* into Irish verse. Goldsmith had almost certainly learned some Irish from playing with the children of his father's Celtic Irish tenants and may well have improved his knowledge of the language while Byrne was his teacher. Certainly, in some of his early newspaper essays, he discussed the native Celtic Irish culture and could well have heard some of the performances of Carolan, the last of the Irish bards, during his boyhood or adolescence. His maternal uncle and later patron, the Reverend Thomas Contarine, showed considerable interest in the old native culture and may well have taken his nephew along on some of his investigations.

Perhaps because of Byrne's interest in poetry, Goldsmith increased his own interest in Latin verse and built up his own confidence in himself enough so that he became a leader in schoolboy sports. He also had a severe case of smallpox that left his face severely scarred for life. After his early years with Byrne, his father sent him to three successive schools in the area— the diocesan school in Elphin, where he could live with relatives, then briefly to a school in Athlone, and finally to one in Edgeworthstown directed by a friend of his father's, who treated him with great kindness and stimulated his interest in Latin poetry even further. As his school days were ending, his future career worried the family. His father had originally intended him for a career in business since the family was already paying the expenses of his older brother, Henry, then studying at Trinity College, Dublin, intending him for a career in the established church. A college education for Oliver would strain their finances severely, but his mother believed his talents justified university study. His Uncle Contarine agreed and offered to pay some of his expenses, though Oliver would still have to go as a sizar, serving as a waiter at the Fellows' table, not as a gentleman commoner like Henry. He strongly resisted what he considered an indignity, but finally agreed, and entered Trinity on 11 June 1745.

Both Oxford and Cambridge had fallen into intellectual doldrums during the eighteenth century, but Trinity had somehow escaped. Goldsmith was not a distinguished student. He thought the emphasis on logic dull, as Jonathan Swift had, and he was never fully reconciled to being a sizar and having to wear the red cap that marked his inferior rank. In his academic work he found his tutor, Dr. Theaker Wilder, difficult to get along with. Unfortunately his father had arranged for him to have Wilder, a violent-tempered, sarcastic man, because his family lived

Statue of Goldsmith, by Foley, at the gate of Trinity College, Dublin

near the Goldsmiths. Goldsmith seems to have spent more time playing his flute than studying, and he reportedly increased his slender pocket money by selling ballads about events of the day, which he composed instead of preparing his lessons. Like most of his fellow students, he sampled much of the entertainment available in Dublin, then the second largest city in the British Isles, especially the theater and concerts. He probably began to gamble during his years at Trinity, an activity at which he never developed any real skill (throughout his life he was more often loser than winner). Accordingly, even in his later years when he earned very considerable sums of money, he was almost always short of ready cash and usually heavily in debt. During his second year at Trinity his father died, making his money troubles even more difficult. In May 1747 Goldsmith became involved in a serious riot, though he was not a ringleader, and was lucky to escape with a public reprimand rather than expulsion. A month later he won a small prize and celebrated his good fortune with a party in his college rooms that became noisy and disorderly enough to disturb his tutor, Wilder, who stopped the party abruptly, berating Goldsmith thoroughly and boxing his ears soundly. Goldsmith was so upset by the incident that he ran away from college, and only his brother Henry's persuasion convinced him to return. Finally, nearly five years after he entered Trinity, he met his degree requirements and received his B.A. in February 1750.

When Goldsmith returned to his family after his graduation, they had no doubts about his future career. On both sides of the family, tradition and influence virtually demanded that he find his future in the established church. He appears to have done some reading in theology as halfhearted preparation for holy orders, but very wisely Bishop Edward Synge of Elphin rejected his candidacy on the ground that he had not yet reached the canonical age. The legend that he presented himself for the interview in scarlet breeches seems apocryphal, but there is no evidence that the bishop urged him to return once he had reached the proper age, and he may well have believed that Oliver was not temperamentally suited to the clerical life, a belief that seems well founded. After his rejection he seemed to have no real plans and surely tried his mother's patience greatly with his idleness. Finally, his Uncle Contarine helped him find a job as tutor with a family in nearby County Roscommon, though a disagreement over cheating at cards soon ended that. He had saved some money and set out for Cork with America as his ultimate goal. Five weeks later he was back home with a sorry horse named Fiddleback and an elaborate but fanciful explanation. His mother's patience was now exhausted, and he moved in with the Daniel Hodsons, his brother-in-law and sister. Another family council convened to discuss his future, and Uncle Contarine put up fifty pounds for his passage money to London and first expenses in studying the law at the Temple. He gambled away the money in Dublin, completely destroying his mother's faith in his talent.

Of the learned professions only medicine remained for him to try, and the family gathered again to start him in this last remaining possibility. Once again, the family, mainly Uncle Contarine, provided his support. In September 1752 he sailed for Edinburgh and enrolled in several courses of lectures, including those of Alexander

Munro, the well-known professor of anatomy. On 8 May 1753 he wrote his uncle about his progress in his studies, praising Munro as the best of his teachers, and his name appears as a member of the Medical Society, then chiefly a student group, in January 1753. On 26 September 1753 he wrote his cousin Robert Bryanton to describe the dances he attended. Because Elizabeth, Duchess of Hamilton, was a famous Irish beauty, he enjoyed frequent dinners at the ducal table, although once he realized he was welcomed mainly as a kind of court jester, a role he found unworthy of his calling as a physician, he stopped going. In December 1753 he wrote his uncle, proposing to move on to Leyden the following year, and in May 1754 he wrote him again, proposing to finish his medical training and then return home. His letters to his uncle all seem calculated to present himself as a hardworking student, though their complete accuracy seems rather doubtful. Even so, when he did move on to Leyden in early 1754, he at least went through the motions of continuing his medical studies and praised the lectures of Gaubius, though he complained that except for those lectures, the quality of the teaching was vastly inferior to that in Edinburgh. His May 1754 letter to his uncle contains a long description of the Dutch and their country. The people he found stolid, dull, and fat, whether male or female, though he did admire the beauty of the country's towns: "Whenever I turn my Eye fine houses elegant gardens statues grottoes vistas present themselves but enter their towns and you are charmed beyond description. Nothing can be more clean or beautiful." He limited himself to these lovely features, even though, when he came to write *The Traveller* ten years later, he presented the country as one in which the love of riches has almost destroyed liberty:

> At gold's superior charms all freedom lies,
> The needy sell it, and the rich man buys
> A Land of tyrants, and a den of slaves
> Here wretches seek dishonourable graves,
> And calmly bent, to servitude conform
> Dull as their lakes that slumber in the storm.

Though in the first stages of decline as an imperial power and destined to yield its primacy to Britain, Holland very likely impressed Goldsmith as a society out of balance, in which the huge riches amassed by those engaged in commerce and trading upset the social equilibrium with the landed interest, with which Goldsmith's traditionalist sympathies naturally lay because of his own Irish rural experience. He repeatedly warned his English readers of the destruction of liberty that luxury had brought to those who had succumbed to its "silken sloth," contrasted with the moral magnificience of the uncorrupted English farmers:

> Pride in their port, defiance in their eye,
> I see the lords of human kind pass by.
>
> . . . .
>
> Fierce in their native hardiness of soul,
> True to imagin'd right, above control [.]

The probability that these ideas formed themselves fully in his mind while he was dividing his time between medical lectures and compulsive gambling is slight, but if we think of these as germs of future ideas incubating in the seedbed of his mind, blooming in their definitive form during his all-too-brief creative life of fourteen years, we shall not be far wrong.

A year after he had mentioned (to his uncle) leaving Edinburgh, he left Leyden, writing his uncle that he would finish up his study of medicine soon. (In May 1754, as he had begun his studies in Leyden, he had written his uncle that he was not sure how long he would stay there, but he hoped to be back in Ireland by the following March.) Goldsmith's travels through Europe may have covered much the same route as lordlings followed on their Grand Tours, but he performed them on foot, often depending on his flute to get him bed and board, in somewhat the same way that George Primrose describes his travels in *The Vicar of Wakefield*. His tour took him through Antwerp, Brussels, and Maestrecht, then on to Paris, Strasbourg, and Switzerland, where he saw a good bit of the Alps that summer. He then walked south through the Piedmont as far as Padua, where he spent six months, much of it in nearly total poverty. He wrote Daniel Hodson, begging for money to see him back to Ireland, money that Hodson collected as he could, though it never reached Goldsmith. Nearly destitute as he was, he made his way back through the principal north Italian cities and then turned northwest into France. How many of George Primrose's experiences we can accept as fact or near fact must remain uncertain, and especially doubtful is George's account of disputing theses at universities along the way in return for bed and board. By February 1756 Goldsmith had reached Calais and took the packetboat to Dover, landing there virtually penniless, still unprepared for any vocation at age twenty-five. Goldsmith's travels had shown him much of the practical side of life, even if at the lower end of the social scale rather than at the higher. His pride kept him from going back to Ireland and admitting his failure. Like Samuel Johnson and many others, he tried teaching school, and then he worked for an apothecary. One of his friends from Edinburgh days found him in the apothecary's shop and did what he could to help financially. Goldsmith briefly tried to establish a medical practice on London's Bankside in Southwark, but gave it up because his patients were, if anything, poorer than he was. After he had established himself as a writer, he was generally known as "Dr. Goldsmith," and the title pages of most of his signed work describe him as a bachelor of medicine. When or if he may have been granted any such degree remains an unsolved problem, and some have argued that he may have been granted an M.B. from Trinity College, Dublin, about 1756, but Bishop Thomas Percy, his friend from 1759 until his death and his first reliable biographer, expressed doubts that Goldsmith had ever received any medical degree.

Like Tobias Smollett and Johnson, Goldsmith had written a tragedy, now lost even in name, and he sought the help and influence of Samuel Richardson, but with no success. Richardson did, however, offer him work correcting proofs in his printing shop. In late 1756 one of Goldsmith's Edinburgh friends, named Milner, whose Presbyterian father, Dr. John Milner, kept a school in Peckham, was looking for a deputy to look after the school while his father was too sick to do so, and he invited Goldsmith to take charge of the school during his father's sickness. Goldsmith's management was haphazard at best since his pupils easily diverted him into singing songs and telling stories. He indulged in such practical jokes as tricking a servant boy into eating a candle by convincing him it was cheese. Except for his inability to manage his money, a lifelong problem, his time at Dr. Milner's school seems to have been reasonably happy, unlike his first experience as school usher immediately after his return from Europe, unhappiness almost certainly reflected by George Primrose's cousin in *The Vicar of Wakefield*, who described the tyranny of the headmaster, his wife's dislike of his ugly face, the schoolboys' obstreperousness, and his own lack of freedom for any social life of his own.

Dr. Milner, his ailing headmaster, did have a wide acquaintance, including influential friends who promised to help Goldsmith secure a physician's post with the East India Company at one of their stations near Coromandel in South India. Much more important, though, Milner introduced Goldsmith to Ralph Griffiths, the owner and publisher of the *Monthly Review*, founded in 1749, and then the only periodical in London exclusively devoted to reviewing books. Shortly afterward, Griffiths offered Goldsmith board and lodging at his house in Paternoster Row and one hundred pounds a year, which Goldsmith gladly accepted, though he lived with the Griffithses only about seven or eight months. Although he still clung to his scheme of going to India to make his fortune, Goldsmith had, without fully realizing it, found his niche. He gave Griffiths good value for his money: his long and largely favorable review (May 1757) of Edmund Burke's *Enquiry into the Origin of Our ideas of the Sublime and Beautiful* remains perhaps the best contemporary comment on that book. More important for his own future career, in his review (August 1757) of *Letters from an Armenian, to his Friends at Trebisonde*, he showed a clear understanding of this particular literary form, the pseudo-letter series:

> The Writer who would inform, or improve, his countrymen, under the assumed character of an Eastern Traveller, should be careful to let nothing escape him which might betray the imposture. If his aim be satirical, his remarks should be collected from the more striking follies abounding in the country he describes, and from those prevailing absurdities which commonly usurp the softer name of fashions. His accounts should be of such a nature, as we may fancy his Asiatic friend would wish to know,—such as we ourselves would expect from a Correspondent in Asia.

He faulted the supposed Armenian for his failure to maintain his pretended identity (though Goldsmith would change his mind about this point when he came to write his own *Citizen of the World* [1762]) and for devoting entirely too much space to trivial matters such as the doings of the wife of the Lord Mayor of Dublin. In September 1757 he confidently attacked Thomas Gray's *Odes* as directed to a coterie rather than the larger, general public he believed Gray had the ability to reach. He further attacked Gray's choice of unfamiliar Celtic subjects and unclear im-

agery, implicitly preferring the heroic couplet tradition and expository manner he would choose for his own *Traveller* in 1764.

Griffiths and Goldsmith quarreled in late 1758, and in January 1759 Goldsmith started contributing to Smollett's *Critical Review*, founded in 1756. He also translated Jean Marteilhe's *Mémoires d'un Protestant* (1758), signing it "James Willington," the name of one of his Trinity contemporaries. To finance his outfit for his Indian scheme, he contracted with Robert and James Dodsley to write a survey of belles lettres in Europe and England. In 1758 the East India Company confirmed his appointment, though he still had not found the money for his outfit and passage. Since the profit from his book for the Dodsleys remained uncertain, in December he underwent, but failed, an examination by the College of Surgeons that would have qualified him as a surgeon's mate, a post that would have paid his passage. With no more resources than his pen he found his financial affairs with Griffiths tangled. He avoided arrest for debt only by making over to Griffiths the copyright to a short life of Voltaire. His reviews had attracted the attention of the Reverend Thomas Percy, then chaplain to Hugh Smithson Percy, Earl (later Duke) of Northumberland, and Percy hunted him down in the slum of Green Arbour Court, where his room had only one broken chair and his bed. During their conversation, a neighbor's daughter interrupted them to ask for a chamberpot of coals. But the friendship thus begun with Percy lasted until Goldsmith's death in 1774. When the Dodsleys published his *Enquiry into the Present State of Polite Learning in Europe* in April 1759, he described from firsthand experience the difficult life of professional writers and their troubles with hard-hearted, greedy publishers, unsympathetic critics, and an uninterested public.

Goldsmith still held to his dream of making his fortune in India, but his writing skill and something like fate seemed to be pushing him toward a writing career. In March 1759 long-delayed news from India destroyed his dream of making his fortune there: the French had captured Coromandel a year before. Even though the British had recaptured it, fighting in the area continued and no assurances came of when normal life in the region could resume. Goldsmith saw that any future for him in India was far too uncertain to rely on and that he had best channel his energies into his developing career as a writer. Most of his reviews for Smollett's *Critical Review* show the same confident self-assurance of the reviews he wrote for Griffiths and concentrate on the merit or, more usually, the demerit of the books he was considering, now largely forgotten with the possible exception of his fellow Irishman Arthur Murphy's adaptation of Voltaire's play *The Orphan of China*. In his May 1759 review Goldsmith found far more faults than virtues, though he praised and republished one scene he did admire, concluding with praise of Voltaire as the first European who had praised English poetry, a point he had stressed in his "Memoirs of M. de Voltaire," written about this time but not published until two years later when it appeared in the February-November 1761 issues of the *Lady's Magazine*.

Even though Goldsmith's reviews for both Griffiths's *Monthly Review* and Smollett's *Critical Review* show little if any political bias, these two proprietors certainly did, with Griffiths showing strong Whig leanings and Smollett a strong Tory bias. In addition Griffiths had no reason to love Goldsmith since they had quarrelled over money matters, and he almost certainly looked on Goldsmith as a turncoat for writing for Smollett's rival magazine. Thus, when the Dodsleys published Goldsmith's *Enquiry into the Present State of Polite Learning in Europe* on 2 April 1779, even though the book appeared anonymously, Griffiths, like most insiders in the book trade, almost certainly knew Goldsmith was the author. He assigned the review to William Kenrick, who was fast gaining a reputation as a shrewd and partisan hack, able and willing to savage any book Griffiths wanted attacked. Kenrick went after Goldsmith with vigor, shrewdly snapping at one of Goldsmith's important strategies in the book: adopting the persona of a well-educated gentleman of leisure who was giving the reader his personal reflections. *An Enquiry into the Present State of Polite Learning in Europe* does not always reflect the self-confident air that Goldsmith had adopted in his reviews; at times it seems somewhat strained and inflated, lacking the easily informal, relaxed style he was to make his own. Though in no sense profound or original, the book does show many of Goldsmith's preoccupations that crop up again and again in his discursive writing: the sad plight of the author when the patronage system was dying and the modern system of royalty payments had not yet emerged, the importance of literature as an index to a society's cultural health, and the dangers of novelty for the sake of novelty at the expense of traditional literary forms.

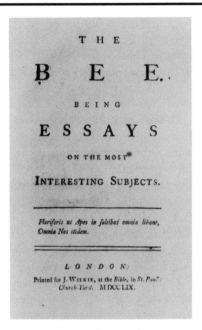

Title page for the collected edition of the weekly periodical Goldsmith wrote in 1759

With the publication of *An Enquiry into the Present State of Polite Learning in Europe* Goldsmith's reputation as a more than usually promising writer was growing, as was his circle of friendships. Because of his continuing reviews for the *Critical Review*, his friendship with his editor Smollett deepened; Percy had sought him out, and their friendship ripened; and probably about this time he met Johnson, very much a major figure in literary circles because of his monumental *Dictionary* (1755) and also his *Rambler* (1750-1752). In addition, as throughout his life, Goldsmith made close friends among his poor neighbors, especially with their children, and among the many Irishmen who, like him, had come to England dreaming of finding fame and fortune.

He slacked off work for the *Critical Review* because he had a new, promising project. He hoped to capitalize on the current popularity of the relatively new magazine format. Edward Cave's *Gentleman's Magazine* dated from 1731, but in the late 1750s a spate of magazines flowed from the publishers, most of them destined to die after only a few issues. The publisher John Wilkie hired Goldsmith to edit and provide almost all the copy for a new weekly, to be called *The Bee*. For Goldsmith the move from reviewer to editor-contributor was a step up the literary ladder. In the first number, Goldsmith presents a variation of the persona he had already used in his reviews and in *An Enquiry into the Present State of*

Polite Learning in Europe. No longer purporting to be the cultivated gentleman of leisure, he describes his shyness and social awkwardness but announces his intention, like the bee, to flit from subject to subject as his pleasure leads him; yet he promises also pleasant instruction, recalling for his contemporaries Swift's bee that provides sweetness and light. The first issue provides a reliable example of his typical subjects: the introduction establishing his persona; an essay on the theater praising French actors over their English contemporaries; a fable titled "Septimus and Alcander, taken from a Byzantine Historian," complete with a moral illustrating poetic justice; a translation from Voltaire; a pseudoletter from a traveler in Poland praising English freedom over the wretched life of the Poles; an essay on the French philosophe Pierre-Louis Moreau de Maupertius, who had died the preceding July; and two verse epigrams, one imitated from the Spanish and another Latin one in the same manner. By the fourth number, he wrote in his introductory essay that he had almost certainly aimed at too limited and cultivated an audience and should have sought the larger, less discriminating reading public. In all, he wrote eight numbers; all contain a great deal of material either adapted or translated from sources in French, especially the *Encyclopédie*; however, the seventh and eighth numbers include more material drawing on English sources. Even though *The Bee* failed, not surprisingly since Goldsmith wrote virtually everything printed in each thirty-two-page issue, he thought well enough of his effort to republish in his collected *Essays. By Mr. Goldsmith* (1765), with considerable revisions, eight of the forty-one pieces, and one reappeared with minor changes in *The Citizen of the World* (1762), even though Goldsmith did not use it as one of the Citizen of the World letters printed in the *Public Ledger*. Wilkie collected the unsold copies of *The Bee* and bound them up for sale in volume form (1759), but with no marked success. Enough copies remained unsold that after Goldsmith's death these were republished with a new, undated title page by the publisher W. Lane.

If Goldsmith was disappointed by the failure of *The Bee*, he hardly had time to mourn, since as he wound up *The Bee*, he was also writing for the *Busy Body*, the *Weekly Magazine*, the *Royal Magazine*, and Smollett's *British Magazine*, as well as the *Lady's Magazine*, published by Wilkie and edited for a time by Goldsmith. As he established a reputation for versatility and hard work,

his standing among the booksellers rose vastly, though to the public he remained just one more anonymous Grub Street writer, unknown and hence unrecognized.

The bulk of the pieces Goldsmith contributed to these newspapers and magazines are straightforward expository essays setting forth his opinions on various subjects, some of general and topical interest, such as "On the Present State of Our Theaters," published in the *Weekly Magazine* for 12 January 1760, attacking the theater managers for presenting more pantomimes than plays, especially plays by new authors; and "Some Remarks on the Modern Manner of Preaching," written for the *Lady's Magazine* for December 1760, urging preachers to show more liveliness and emotion in their sermons.

However, in Goldsmith's collection of his anonymously published pieces, *Essays. By Mr. Goldsmith* (1765), discursive essays predominate, but nearly one-third, eight of the twenty-seven pieces, use some kind of fictional device to make their discursive points. None of them is a short story in the modern sense of the term, but they are short fictions just as much as *Gulliver's Travels* is a fiction, even if it is not usually considered a novel in today's very elastic generic vocabulary. Goldsmith was, as usual, breaking no new literary ground here, since Addison had often resorted to allegories such as *Spectator* no. 159, "The Vision of Mirza," and Johnson frequently used fictional correspondents in *The Rambler*. Some of Goldsmith's fictive essays are little more than anecdotes, such as no. 15 in *Essays* (1765)—none of the pieces in the volume have titles—revised from the second number of *The Bee*, where it had the title "On Dress," in which an old bachelor pursues a fashionably dressed woman in St. James's Park, hoping for a romantic conquest. The lady, unfortunately, turns out to be his slightly older Cousin Hannah, and they spend the remainder of their time together criticizing the fashions of the day, as well as illustrating Goldsmith's main point that people often dress to conceal their faults and flaws, that clothing reveals appearances only, not reality, a point both Swift and Thomas Carlyle make at much greater length and far more elaborately.

Two of the best-known pieces Goldsmith chose to revise and reprint in *Essays* (1765) are no. 16, called "The Proceedings of Providence Vindicated. An Eastern Tale" when originally published in the *Royal Magazine* for December 1759, but also often called "Asem the Man-hater"; and no. 19, entitled "A Reverie at the Boar's-Head-Tavern in Eastcheap" when it appeared in the *British Magazine* for February, March, and April 1760. In the first Goldsmith burlesques the Oriental sublime allegory that had become a literary cliché by 1759, using the comic techniques of an overly inflated style, reductive and absurd illustrations, and a hurried, mechanical ending to attack the complacent optimism of contemporaries, such as Soame Jenyns, who argued that most human misery was divinely ordained. Using mock-sublime diction, Goldsmith relates how Asem, a wealthy young man from Segestan, has withdrawn into a life of solitary misanthropy near Mount Tauris. On the point of suicide he is stopped by a spirit later identified as the Genius of Conviction. Conviction tells him that Mohammed had once experienced a similar depression and that Allah had formed a world without vice or cruelty to show him that the ordinary world of men is really preferable. Conviction conducts him to a nearby lake and takes him below the surface to show him this alternate world, leading him through various stages of life in the Great Chain of Being: predatory animals are still predatory so that the land will not be overrun with noncarnivores. When Asem and Conviction encounter human beings, they find men fleeing from an army of squirrels, and dogs chasing another man. To answer Asem's objections Conviction replies that the men have no rational justification for attacking the animals, who have lately grown very powerful and troublesome. When they find a sick, starving man by the roadside, Conviction explains to Asem that in a perfectly rational world no one has more than just enough, so that no one practices charity without harming himself or his family. Asem then admits he showed only his own ignorance, praying that in the future he can avoid vice and pity in others, and he finds himself back on the lake shore. He quickly abandons his retreat, returns to his native Segestan, where his frugality brings wealth, and he ends his days surrounded by friends in affluence and ease. Thus, Goldsmith shows the sensitive reader his sturdy distrust of abstract philosophical systems that provide overly easy answers to the problem of evil. He uses the fiction of the Oriental allegory to set forth one of his chief themes, warning of the folly and danger in allowing generous impulses to outweigh prudence.

In the second, "A Reverie," Goldsmith's persona falls into a daydream induced by the Gothic architecture of the room, memories of Falstaff and Prince Hal, and a good bit of the landlord's wine. These influences all transform the landlord into Dame Quickly, who then tells him of the various purposes the tavern has served—a brothel, then a monastery in which the friars seduced maidens come for confession; then during the Reformation the monks were burned as schismatics, after which the building became a tavern once again, run by one of the king's cast-off mistresses, and in her hands the tavern once again became a lively, if none too decorous, place. Unfortunately she was ruined by courtiers who failed to pay their bills, and adventurers, pimps, and gamesters took over the place. The last landlady was burned for a witch, and since then the tavern has served by turns as a brothel, a meetinghouse for Dissenters, now a meeting place for Whigs, then a center for Tories. The persona interrupts her to complain: "you have really deceived me; I expected a romance and here you have been this half hour giving me only a description of the spirit of the times: if you have nothing more to communicate, seek some other hearer: I am determined to hearken only to stories." He awakens only to hear the landlord telling him about repairs he has made to the old inn. Though "A Reverie" is cast as a narrative, Goldsmith's point here, that human nature has changed very little over the centuries, is one commonly found among the conservative humanists of the time and is probably set forth most eloquently by Samuel Johnson in his *Preface to Shakespeare* (1765).

John Newbery, one of the most enterprising and innovative publishers of the time, had moved to London from publishing a successful newspaper in Reading and almost overnight established himself as a major force in the book trade. Along with Benjamin Collins of Salisbury, Newbery planned a new daily newspaper, the *Public Ledger*, a prototype of the London *Financial Times* and the *New York Wall Street Journal*, aimed primarily at the City merchants and traders. He signed Goldsmith on as a regular contributor at one hundred pounds a year, and Goldsmith's first trial effort consisted of two letters, the first to a London merchant from a Dutch trader introducing a Chinese traveling to observe Western manners and the second a letter from the Chinese himself, Lien Chi Altangi, to the Dutch merchant after his arrival in London. When these letters appeared together in the issue of 24 January 1760, they almost immediately found admiring readers. Very quickly, the letters took over the leading position on the first page and continued to hold it

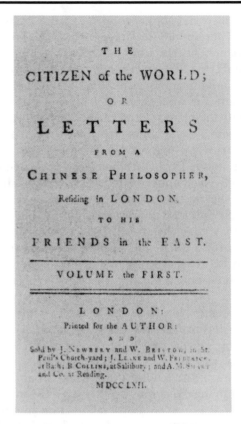

Title page for the collected edition of the essay series Goldsmith wrote for the Public Ledger *in 1760-1761*

until the series of 119 ended on 14 August 1761. Goldsmith collected the series, adding four to the original number, and Newbery with five other publishers, among them Benjamin Collins of Salisbury, published them in two volumes on 1 May 1762 with the title *The Citizen of the World*.

The Citizen of the World has always found admirers among Goldsmith's readers, some singling out individual letters as among the examples of Goldsmith's best writing. Wayne Booth considers the collection the best of all Goldsmith's achievements, surpassing *The Vicar of Wakefield*, *The Deserted Village*, and *She Stoops to Conquer*. Beyond any doubt *The Citizen of the World* is Goldsmith's first important literary work, but its popularity with twentieth-century readers—because its particular literary form, the pseudoletter series, no longer exists—has never been great. Only excerpted letters appear in anthologies, and the complete series exists only in older editions and in Arthur Friedman's magnificent *Collected Works* (1966), generally available only in research libraries. To appreciate Goldsmith's achievement fully, a reader must read the entire series.

As in all the literary forms that Goldsmith used, he adapted an already existing form, one quite popular among the readers of his time. The use of an oriental observing and commenting on Western customs had existed at least since Giovanni Paolo Marana's *L'Espion turc* (1684-1686) and was most widely known in Montesquieu's *Lettres persanes* (1721), which Goldsmith drew upon occasionally. He was much more heavily indebted to the 1755 English translation of Jean-Baptiste, Marquis d'Argens's *Lettres chinoises*, from which he took long passages, although none of his borrowings from d'Argens show that minor philosophe's almost obsessive attacks on the absolute monarchy of the Bourbons or on the corruptions of the monastic system for the very obvious reason that the English monarchy has always been a limited monarchy, at least in theory and certainly in practice since the Revolution of 1688. Henry VIII abolished the monastic foundations, and few of Goldsmith's readers had ever seen a monk or a nun unless they had traveled to France or Italy. As a result, Goldsmith used d'Argens's work chiefly for local color and avoided the Frenchman's militant atheism. His principal sources for Chinese matters were the two volumes of J. B. Du Halde's *Description of the Empire of China* (English translation, 1738) and Louis Le Comte's *Nouveaux Mémories sur l'état présent de la Chine* (third edition, 1697); he frequently acknowledged his use of these two works by Jesuit missionaries in his footnotes to his collected edition. He took his main Chinese character's name from Horace Walpole's pamphlet *A Letter from Xo Ho, a Chinese Philosopher at London to his friend, Lien Chi at Pekin* (1757).

By the time Goldsmith began writing his Chinese letters, the tide of taste for chinoiserie had already reached its highwater mark in the 1750s in literature, and the taste for pagodas and such in gardens and in Thomas Chippendale's adaptations of Chinese motifs in furniture was already well established. Thus Goldsmith realized that his primary audience of City merchants and traders knew and understood a fair amount about matters Chinese and that his Chinese traveler could ridicule many of the grosser deviations from real Chinese art, customs, and manners. He was confident enough of his own powers to realize that he need not worry too much about "betraying the imposture," as he had earlier described the problem in his review of the *Letters from An Armenian in Ireland, to his Friends at Trebisonde* (1757). As it pleased him, Goldsmith did keep his Chinese mask in place for gently satirical accounts of English social behavior and for serious matters such as religion and politics, as well as in reports of such leisure activities as the theater, the races, and the pleasure places such as Vauxhall Gardens. In letter 8, a prostitute robs Lien Chi, who mistakes her for one of the "well disposed daughters of hospitality," an experience that leads him to comment on the de facto polygamy of many Englishmen, though English law permits each man only one wife. Likewise, when he finds that Englishwomen lack the black teeth and tiny feet he so admires in Chinese women, we recognize Goldsmith's mocking his protagonist and raising the general question of the relativity of some cultural standards. As satirist, Lien Chi ridicules the prevalence of English hypochondria—the spleen and vapors so commonly mentioned by his contemporaries, and likewise notices in letter 69 the absurd fear of mad dogs, a short-lived epidemic terror in the 1760s—and the English love of strange sights and sideshow monsters. He can also praise Englishwomen for showing more restraint in gambling than his own countrywomen. In some letters Lien Chi's Chinese traits hardly figure, as Goldsmith uses him to speak out on some of the subjects dear to his heart: the booksellers' exploitation of poor authors; the advantages and, more important, the disadvantages of luxury; the benefits of the English limited monarchy in contrast to the absolutism in the Chinese empire; and the dangers of acquiring a colonial empire. Several letters comment on quite topical events: letter 43 eulogizes Voltaire, always one of Goldsmith's intellectual heroes, after a false report of his death in May 1760, and letter 53 severely attacks the first two volumes of *Tristram Shandy* as a work in which "Bawdry is often helped on by another figure, called Pertness." Even though Lien Chi never mentions Laurence Sterne's novel by name, the letter heading supplied in *The Citizen of the World* makes the identification clear.

One of the principal differences between such essay serials as *The Spectator* and *The Rambler* and the pseudoletter series is that while *The Spectator* and *Rambler* have little or no unity except for that provided by the central persona who purports to conduct the series, pseudoletter series such as the *Letters Persanes* and *The Citizen of the World* have some narrative element. Montesquieu's Persians, for example, inquire about life in Isfahan and hear reports of troubles among the women of the harem. Some literary critics have devoted discussions to the narrative ele-

ments in Goldsmith's series, but such discussions are brief, even fragmentary.

The narrative elements in *The Citizen of the World* play such an important role in the series that they may almost be called a frame story. Lien Chi has departed from China without imperial permission, so that the emperor has proscribed his entire family, all of whom die, except for his son Hingpo, whom his old friend and principal correspondent in China, Fum Hoam, hides and smuggles out of the empire. Hingpo determines to join his father in the West, but as he makes his way, Tartars capture him and sell him as a slave to a wealthy Persian. In the Persian's household he falls head over heels in love with a fellow slave, the beautiful Zelis, a European who returns his love. They escape from the Persian, who had determined to make Zelis one of his wives, when Tartars sack the Persian's palace. Both of them intend to make their way west via Moscow, though in the manner of the best romances they must endure separation before they eventually meet once more. Again, in the best romantic manner, Zelis turns out to be the niece of the Man in Black, Lien Chi's closest English friend.

Almost immediately after receiving Hingpo's series of letters about his enslavement and love for Zelis, Lien Chi writes his son, first giving him some rather heavy-handed fatherly advice about the conduct proper for a youth entering the world and then sending another extremely fatherly letter about how Catherina Alexowna won the heart of the Tsar Peter the Great by her humility, beauty, and virtue—qualities he makes quite clear Hingpo should look for in Zelis. These exchanges show Lien Chi's all-too-human doubts and fears over what he believes may be his son's infatuation with a woman of whom he knows virtually nothing and his, to us, amusing efforts to counsel prudence and caution, to help Hingpo see the difference between love and gratitude and the need to learn wisdom from living with other people. Besides these moralizing letters written to his son, Lien Chi's concern as a parent appears in letters to Fum Hoam. These touch more than incidentally on the need for prudence in life and on various aspects of marriage, such as the attack in letter 72 on the Marriage Act of 1753, which rumor reported might be revised and which Goldsmith criticized as making marriages across class lines too difficult. Thus, several letters not overtly related to Lien Chi's relationship with Hingpo show Lien Chi's mind is very full of his concerns about his son.

Lien Chi met the Man in Black on his visit to Westminister Abbey in letter 13, in which he shows Lien Chi splendid monuments erected to insignificant, but wealthy people; the collection of monuments in Poet's Corner, which includes no tablet to Alexander Pope; and the battered Coronation Chair with the legendary Stone of Scone. All these comments by the Man in Black reflect Goldsmith's rather acid views on the lottery of fame. The Man in Black, Mr. Drybone, who reappears in letters 26 and 27, tells Lien Chi his story, some elements of which have often been accepted as barely disguised autobiography, chiefly on the authority of Goldsmith's sister, Mrs. Daniel Hodson, a not always reliable source, especially when she recalled events in Goldsmith's London life for Bishop Percy shortly after Goldsmith's death in 1774. In letter 26 Lien Chi describes his friend as "an humourist in a nation of humourists," generously giving money to a beggar whose story he only half believes, just after he has railed against the poor: "imposters, every one of them; and rather merit a prison than relief." The Man in Black undoubtedly shares some traits with his creator, especially his willingness to give money to individual beggars, a trait Goldsmith shared with Samuel Johnson, even though he half knew his compassion was exploited. As the Man in Black explains, his father "told [his children] that universal benevolence was what first cemented society." Throughout his life Goldsmith was exceedingly skeptical about "universal benevolence" because it could not distinguish between the genuinely needy and those too lazy to work, and he also believed it could reduce anyone who practiced it to poverty too, as Mr. Drybone tells Lien Chi in his story of his own life, an account remarkably similar to Mr. Wilson's in Henry Fielding's *Joseph Andrews* (1742). Though personal appeals often overcame his theoretical objections, Goldsmith repeatedly advocated worldly prudence, the need to recognize the deceitful and dishonest, an insight which the Man in Black possesses but almost never practices, as Lien Chi describes his helping an old beggar, then a one-legged former naval officer, and finally a poor ragged woman ballad singer with two children. The Chinese clearly notes the inconsistency between his friend's theory and practice. Only when he came to write of Sir William Thornhill in *The Vicar of Wakefield* did Goldsmith present a character who has learned from experience, like

Fielding's Mr. Wilson, to live prudently in a world filled with imposture—though Sir William's own behavior is eccentric by any standard as he wanders about his estates disguised as Mr. Burchell.

Through the Man in Black, Lien Chi acquires a circle of London friends, such as Beau Tibbs and his wife, who pathetically burlesque the manners and language of the nobility, and the letters about these characters form the second narrative element in the series. Tibbs pesters both Lien Chi and the Man in Black with his transparently invented accounts of dinners with the Duchess of Picadilly and Lady Grogram and coach rides with Lord Muddler, though the Man in Black acutely but gloomily foretells Tibbs's future: "Condemned in the decline of life to hang upon some rich family whom he once despised, there to undergo all the ingenuity of studied contempt, to be employed only as a spy upon the servants, or a bugbear to fright the children into duty." In letter 55 Tibbs blithely invites Lien Chi and Drybone to the squalor of his garret, where his coy but slatternly wife orders them a dinner of ox cheek and bottled beer to be served two hours hence. Lien Chi pleads a prior engagement and escapes to satisfy his hunger elsewhere. Somewhat later on, in letter 73, the Man in Black invites Lien Chi to a supper at Vauxhall Gardens, together with the Tibbses and a pawnbroker's widow, whom Mr. Drybone is courting and for whom he turns out in superlative finery. The party marks one of the comic high points of the series, since the widow pines to see the waterworks display and Mrs. Tibbs is determined they shall have a genteel box for their supper, away from the view of the waterworks. After much prevailing from the company, most of it patently insincere, Mrs. Tibbs favors them with an almost interminable song, singing until the waterworks display is over, and the poor widow fails in her dearest wish and leaves in great displeasure, though the Tibbses assure everyone else the most fashionable hours are just beginning.

When Goldsmith wrote the letters for the *Public Ledger*, in the letter collected as number 116 in *The Citizen of the World* Lien Chi joins the Man in Black to argue with his unnamed niece that love is a fictitious passion. She had first appeared in London in what is collected as letter 99 (letter 97 in the *Public Ledger*), in which Lien Chi praises her exquisite beauty, manners, and intelligence. In the *Public Ledger* only two letters intervened between the debate between Lien Chi and the Man in Black's niece over the nature of love, and the letter collected as number 123, in which Hingpo is reunited with his father and recognizes the Man in Black's niece as Zelis, his beloved, and the various loose ends are tied into a happy ending for the major characters. The two intervening letters discuss the willingness of the Dutch to undergo any indignity to secure trading rights with Japan (letter collected as number 118) and the absurdity of some English titles (letter collected as number 120).

Goldsmith appears to have thought, or perhaps heard criticism, that the conclusion he gave the series of letters in the *Public Ledger* was hurried. At any rate, when he collected the letters for publication as *The Citizen of the World*, he added four letters to stretch his material between the debate over love and Hingpo's presentation of his beloved to his father. None of these letters touches upon the approaching resolution, and his dealing with other matters may help make the conclusion somewhat more credible. Letter 117 in *The Citizen of the World*, "A City Night-Piece," was originally published in the fourth number of *The Bee* (27 October 1759); letter 119, on the distresses of the poor, as shown by the career of a sentinel, was originally published in the *British Magazine* for June 1760; letter 121, written especially for *The Citizen of the World* compares the political fluctuation in Britain favorably with the stable tyranny of China; and letter 122, also written especially for *The Citizen of the World*, satirizes the overly minute, dull detail of recent travel books. Only then did Goldsmith use the letter which concludes the series in the *Public Ledger*. The material that appears in these insertions is not nearly so important as the fact that Goldsmith apparently realized that he needed several more letters before springing the grossly coincidental reunion between Zelis and Hingpo on his readers. His conclusion in *The Citizen of the World* still violates the most elementary canons of probability, but not nearly so strongly as the arrangement in the *Public Ledger* does. The sensible reader knows Goldsmith is pulling his leg in resorting to the conventions of romance, but after all, just as Goldsmith does not expect the reader to take Lien Chi seriously as a Chinese philosopher, so he does not expect the reader to take seriously either, the frame story in which Lien Chi acts. Both are parts of Goldsmith's tongue-in-cheek Irish humor.

Most critics and literary historians have underrated or ignored the two fictional threads that run throughout *The Citizen of The World*, usually dismissing the Hingpo-Zelis thread as romantic claptrap, though such romantic improbability is surely one of Goldsmith's objects of attack. The letters about Lien Chi's family, by Hingpo or by Lien Chi addressed to Hingpo, total twenty-three, although some of Lien Chi's to his son may seem to be completely discursive. However, most of Lien Chi's letters of this sort are actually fatherly advice, such as letter 66, distinguishing love and gratitude, clearly an appropriate subject for a father writing to a son newly enamored of a young woman about whom the father knows nothing. This letter is not primarily a discursive essay, but one written by a particularly concerned parent to a faraway son lacking parental guidance. In addition, whenever Goldsmith has Lien Chi or Hingpo write, shortly following is a letter, or even letters, treating the themes of love, marriage, parents and children, or similar topics, showing Lien Chi's concern for his son and his affairs, even if he may be writing to Fum Hoam in Pekin, his most usual correspondent. At least seven such letters show Lien Chi with the Man in Black or the other members of his circle. Clearly, in some of these, such as letter 28—Lien Chi's observation of the great number of old bachelors and maiden ladies—the Man in Black serves chiefly as a foil, explaining that neither the bachelors nor the old maids will surrender their independence. However, we can also see that this letter, not unreasonably, to some degree points to the romantic affairs of Hingpo and Zelis.

Some critics have seen *The Citizen of the World* as a work showing some elements of the novel and even moving toward the novel form. While forty-six letters, more than a third of the total number, do involve either the Hingpo-Zelis romance or Lien Chi's London circle, this view of the work as novelistic but not a full-blown novel seems influenced by the fact that Goldsmith's next prose work of any length is his novel *The Vicar of Wakefield*. Such discussions concentrate on The Man in Black, and the Tibbses, and hardly discuss the Hingpo-Zelis love affair and its intimate connection with the London circle letters. The view that in *The Citizen of the World* Goldsmith was developing skills such as characterization necessary for a novelist is partly true at best, and at worst mistaken. In Goldsmith's day there were several well-accepted forms of fiction, works not necessarily novels in the modern sense of the word. *Gulliver's Travels* is, of course, the best-known example. But the pseudoletter genre was also a com-

The Preface

In whatever light we regard the present war which has disturbed all Europe, we shall find it the most important of any recorded in modern history; whether we consider the power of the nations at variance, the number of the forces employ'd, or the skill of the generals conducting, we shall equally find matter for improvement or admiration. We shall see small kingdoms forced by the prudence of one man into an astonishing degree of power, and extensive countries scarce able to support their own rights or repel the invader.

But whatever these contentions may be thought of by others, they will never be regarded by Britons but as instances of her power, her bravery, and her greatness. In this war England will appear in greater splendour than in any period of the most boasted antiquity, it will be seen to poize the fates of Europe and bring its most potent and most ambitious states into the lowest degree of humiliation. This is a glory which should excite every lover of his country to celebrate as well as to share in.

The desolation of war, the insolent severity of victors, and the servitude of those who happen to be overcome have been often the topics of Declamation and employ'd the reasoner as well as the Rhetorician; but still I would doubt whether even wars have not their benefits, whether they do not serve as motion to waters, separate states of all a great number of vices contracted by long habits of peace. If we attentively examine the records of history we shall ever find that long indolence in any country was only productive of mischief, and that those very arts which were brought to perfection in peace often proved to introduce new vices with new luxury. The Roman state stood firm untill Italy had no longer any enemies to fear, contented with enjoying the fruits of victory they no more desired to obtain it, their wars were carried on by mercenary soldiers, their armies were levied in distant provinces, and those very provinces at length became their masters.

But to what purpose to cite ancient History when we have so recent and so near an instance in the Dutch. That people once brave, enthusiast in the cause of freedom, and able to make their state formidable to their neighbours, is by a long continuance of peace, divided into faction, set upon private interest, and neither able, nor willing to usurp its rights or revenge oppression. This may serve as a memorable instance of what may be the result of a total inattention to war, and an utter extirpation of martial ardour. Insulted by the French, threatened by the English, and almost universally despised by the rest of Europe. How unlike the brave peasants their Ancestors, who spread terror into either India, and always declared themselves the allies

Pages from the preface to "The Political View of the Result of the Present War with America upon Great Britain, France, Prussia, Germany, and Holland," a history of the Seven Years' War that Goldsmith compiled in 1761 from articles that had appeared in the Lady's Magazine *during 1756-1758 (HM176; Henry E. Huntington Library and Art Gallery). The history was published for the first time in 1837, as* Preface and Introduction to the History of the Seven Years's War.

of those who drew the sword in defence of freedom!

The friendship between the English and the Dutch was at first conceived to be insperable, they were termed in the stile of Politicians faithful friends, natural allies Protestant confederates, and by many other names of national endearment. Both had the same interest as opposed to France, and some resemblance of religion or of hord to popery, yet these were but slight ties with a nation whose only views were comerce, a rivalry in that will serve to destroy with them every conviction. No merely mercantile man, or mercantile nation has any friendship but for money, and an alliance between them will last no longer than their common safety or common profit is endangered, no longer than they have an enemy ready to deprive them of more, than they can be able to steal from each other.

A long continuance of property in the same channel is also very prejudicial to a nation, in such a state emulation is in some measure destroyed fortune seems to stand still with those who are already in possession of it they who are rich have no need of an exertion of their abilities in order to preserve their wealth, and the poor must rest in hopeless indigence, but war gives a circulation to the wealth of a nation, the poor have many opportunities of bettering their fortune, and the rich must labour in order to support the necessary expences required in defraying it. Thus all are in action, and emulative industry is the parent of every national virtue.

A long continuance of peace in England was never productive of advantageous consequences, upon such occasions, we have ever seen her divided into factions, her senates becoming venal, and her ministers even avowing corruption. But when a foreign enemy appears, private animosities cease, factions are forgotten, and party rage is united against the common foe. I am not an advocate for war, but it were happy if mankind did not require such a scourge to keep them within those bounds which they ought to observe with respect to their country and themselves. It is not likely however that the English should relax into the abject state of debility of a neighbouring nation, they will have ever cause of distrust while France continues to cherish views of ambition. A Nation that seems the enemy of Britain by nature. Different in Religion, government and disposition it is almost impossible they can ever be thoroughly reconciled, and perhaps this rivalry will continue to preserve them both in circumstances of vigour and power longer than any other nations recorded in history, since from the situation of each country it does not seem easy to conceive how the one will ever be able entirely to oppress the other.

The System of Politics at present pursued by the English may properly be said to have taken rise in the reign of Queen Elizabeth, at this time the protestant religion was established, which then allied us to those countries who embraced the mon and lively form, and the fact that we have no exact modern equivalent is no reason we should try to fit this, one of Goldsmith's finest works, on the procrustean bed of the novel, which it clearly is not, or on the equally unsuitable bed of the miscellaneous essay series exemplified by *The Spectator* or *The Rambler*, where it clearly will not fit, either, without losing essential characteristics of its form. We must take it for what it is, a pseudoletter series, easily the best in English literature, with more than a third of the letters devoted to one narrative strand or another, though many of these make important discursive points as well, and slightly more than half the letters discursively treat English follies in comparison with Chinese virtues but also celebrate English virtues in comparison with Chinese failings. Unfortunately, many of the best things in the series disappear when anthologists excerpt what they consider representative letters. The very real merits of *The Citizen of the World* reveal themselves best to readers of all the letters.

For six months after he collected the letters and Newbery published them in two volumes, Goldsmith continued writing for the *British Magazine* and various other publications controlled by Newbery. That summer he spent some time in Bath, though not vacationing. He gained access to Beau Nash's papers from Nash's literary executor, absorbed the flavor of the society Nash had done so much to establish there, and collected anecdotes from those who had known him before his death in February 1761. His *Life of Richard Nash* (1762), published by Newbery and W. Frederick of Bath, follows the model of Johnson's *Life of Richard Savage* (1744) in presenting the life of a man of middle social rank, avoiding excessive praise but showing the relative insignificance of Nash's position as "King of Bath" through its ironic, mock-heroic tone.

Back in London, Goldsmith found himself in money troubles, and his landlady had him arrested for his unpaid rent. Goldsmith sent word to Johnson for help. Johnson sent him a guinea and came to Wine Office Court as soon as he could. There he found Goldsmith beginning to console himself with a bottle of Madeira bought with part of the guinea, but otherwise taking no steps to solve his problem. Johnson promptly corked the wine, calmed Goldsmith as best he could, and asked if he had any unpublished manuscripts. Goldsmith gave him the manuscript for a novel he had been working on, and, after scanning it, Johnson set off for a publisher, almost

certainly John Newbery, returning with sixty pounds cash, more than enough both to settle the demands of the landlady, whom Goldsmith berated for her incivility, and to give him some pocket money. On 28 October 1762, Newbery sold a one-third share of the copyright to Benjamin Collins of Salisbury, his partner in the *Public Ledger*. The novel, of course, was *The Vicar of Wakefield*, though it would not be published for four more years.

After this embarrassment, Goldsmith very willingly put Newbery, his principal employer over the past three years, in charge of his financial affairs. Newbery promptly moved him from Wine Office Court, with its easy access to tavern life and gambling tables, to Islington, where the bookseller used Canonbury House as his own weekend and summer retreat. In the Canonbury Tower, he also housed and managed the affairs of his talented but unstable son-in-law, Christopher Smart, as well as Goldsmith's. Goldsmith was to write what Newbery directed, and Newbery in turn would keep him in pocket money but hold back most of his earnings to pay Goldsmith's bills, including his bed and board. Here in Islington, Goldsmith renewed work on the poem that would become *The Traveller*. For almost a year he was removed from the temptations of London, yet close enough to town that he could enjoy Christmas dinner with Thomas Davies, the actor turned bookseller, and Davies's other guests, Robert Dodsley, the publisher of Goldsmith's *Enquiry into the Present State of Polite Learning in Europe*, and the flighty young Scot James Boswell, then on his first visit to London.

In the late fall of 1764, Sir Joshua Reynolds, finding Johnson's company and often melancholy conversation something of a burden, began sounding out their mutual friends with the idea of a dining club that would meet every Monday evening at the Turk's Head Tavern in Soho. Besides Johnson and Reynolds, there were Edmund Burke; Sir John Hawkins, a lawyer with a strong interest in music; two young aristocrats, Bennet Langton and Topham Beauclerk; and two others interested in literary and cultural matters. Goldsmith was also chosen as a charter member, probably at Johnson's suggestion, though Reynolds knew him well too. Hawkins thought him little better than another Grub Street hack, but *The Citizen of the World*, if not a runaway best-seller, had been well received in 1762, as had his *Life of Nash* in the fall of the same year. Another anonymous work had appeared in June, *An History of En-*

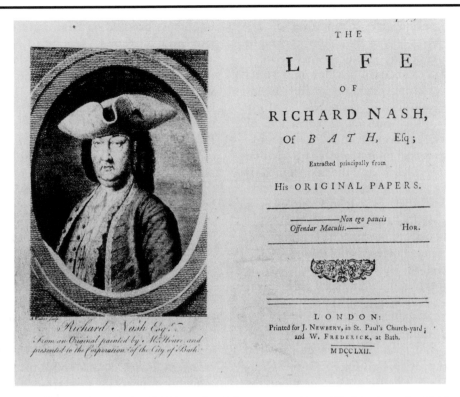

Frontispiece and title page for Goldsmith's biography of the supreme arbiter of Bath society, who, Goldsmith said, "had too much merit not to become remarkable, yet too much folly to arrive at greatness"

gland in a Series of Letters from a Nobleman to His Son, credited by some to Philip Dormer Stanhope, Lord Chesterfield, and by others to George, Lord Lyttelton, ascriptions that must have provided Goldsmith wry amusement. Indeed, he never acknowledged his authorship in any of the several editions published during his lifetime. Though all his work had so far been published anonymously and praised by literary insiders such as Johnson, Goldsmith was only then finishing up the first work that would bear his name on its title page, his discursive poem *The Traveller*, to be published in December 1764. Johnson not only read the poem in manuscript but helped Goldsmith by providing several couplets, including the final one. Thus, he was certainly convinced of Goldsmith's talent, and when the poem did appear Johnson described it in the *Critical Review* for December 1764 as "a production to which, since the death of Pope, it will not be easy to find anything equal." Though Goldsmith's fellow members might often treat him as a clown and make him the butt of their jokes, to those who knew, his literary talents amply justified him membership, and, during the ten years following, his literary works were ranked, by common consent, as the best for that decade.

In the tradition of the French philosophes, *The Traveller* surveys Italy, Switzerland, Holland, France, and England, relating the effects of climate to national traits but arguing that each country has lost its power and glory, usually through the baleful influence of luxury, which has overwhelmed national virtues. England appears as a country whose fate still remains undetermined and which may yet escape decline by maintaining the careful balance of a strong but limited monarchy, checking the influence of a power-hungry oligarchy, and balancing a healthy agriculture against the mercantile and trading interests that, like the magnates, endanger the social equilibrium by promoting luxury. Goldsmith's couplets show slightly more run-on lines than Pope's and avoid the Latinate diction of Johnson's couplet poems, but mainly they achieve their individuality through repeated words and phrases, a device he would exploit to achieve almost lyric effects in *The Deserted Village* six years later. He dedicated the poem to his brother Henry, a poor parish priest in Ireland, rather than seeking out some lord who would have gladly paid a good, round sum for the honor.

The Traveller confirmed Johnson's high opinion of Goldsmith's literary talent, and, as was customary in the period, the publication of his widely praised poem established him overnight as a major figure among contemporary writers, just as a strikingly successful novel would for a twentieth-century writer. Newbery and Goldsmith seized the opportunity to publish in June 1765, *Essays. By Mr. Goldsmith*, a collection of twenty-seven pieces previously published anonymously in newspapers, nine from *The Bee*, nine from *The Citizen of the World*, and the rest from various other places. This collection received wide praise for showing that his talent as an essayist was equal to his skill as a poet. He had emerged from general obscurity to become the leading literary lion of the time, flooded with dinner invitations from his fellow club members as well as from other major literary and social figures on the London scene, and he gloried in this new attention.

Despite his literary success, money troubles dogged him; he had received twenty guineas for *The Traveller* and a lesser sum for his *Essays*. Hoping to capitalize on his literary fame, he made his last, unsuccessful attempt to set up a medical practice. A second edition of *The Traveller*, with new lines (363-380) added, appeared in August 1765, with third and fourth editions of the enlarged poem also appearing in 1765. In 1766, a second edition of his *Essays* appeared, with two additional pieces. While Goldsmith received little money from these revised versions, they did keep his name before the public.

In the fall of 1764, Goldsmith had moved from Islington back to London, this time to 3 King's Bench Walk in the Temple. Apparently the revision Newbery wanted kept him busy and out of major difficulties. Newbery had plans for the manuscript of the novel he had bought in 1762, realizing no doubt that Goldsmith's name on it would guarantee a lively sale. The book appeared in two volumes in March 1766, printed by Benjamin Collins of Salisbury, who had bought one-third of the copyright back in 1762, for Francis Newbery, John Newbery's nephew. The original reviewers were mainly favorable but did not quite know what to make of it. Goldsmith's old enemies at the *Monthly Review* commented: "Through the whole course of our travels in the wild regions of romance, we never met with anything more difficult to characterize than the Vicar of Wakefield. . . ." But the *Critical Review* was more enthusiastic: "Genuine touches of nature, easy strokes of humor, pathetic pictures of domestic happiness and domestic distress (a

happiness proceeding from innocence and obscurity, and a distress supported with resignation and cheerfulness) are some of the methods here made use of to interest and move us." The reviewer deplored the piling up of Dr. Primrose's calamities in the second half and the hurried conclusion. Johnson disliked it, describing it to Fanny Burney as showing nothing of real life and little of nature. Excerpts appeared in several newspapers, and three London editions followed swiftly, the second of which contained extensive revisions by Goldsmith. A Dublin edition appeared in 1767 as well as French and German translations. The novel's great popularity really came only after Goldsmith's death in 1774, with more than twenty editions published in London before the end of the century. Throughout the nineteenth century at least two editions appeared almost every year, and additional translations into French, German, Italian, and Spanish continued. Johann Wolfgang von Goethe was heavily influenced by it during his youth and in his old age came to admire its wise irony. Both Sir Walter Scott and Washington Irving admired it, as did Leigh Hunt, Charles Dickens, William Makepeace Thackeray, George Eliot, and Henry James. Something of the novel's appeal to nineteenth-century audiences can almost certainly be attributed to Goldsmith's avoiding the racier and coarser pictures of eighteenth-century life in both Fielding and Smollett. More recently, as academic critics have freed themselves from the blinders of Romantic assumptions about literature, several critics have argued that the book, like much of Goldsmith's other writing, contains considerably more laughing irony and comic satire than most Romantic readers and critics— except Goethe—found, just as modern criticism of Swift and Pope differs radically from that of the nineteenth century. Modern critics have come to understand and stress the heavily rhetorical nature of virtually all writing before the Romantic period, and several have emphasized that Goldsmith's personas are not writing unalloyed autobiography. While Goldsmith the man becomes a less clearly defined figure, his literary creations become more sharply focused. As yet, critics have reached no consensus about many quite basic features of *The Vicar of Wakefield*, such as its prevailing tone—is it prevailingly comic, or comic and then sentimental?—or Goldsmith's attitude toward his narrator-protagonist—is he a wise and admirable religious man or an egotistical, imprudent erring human, perhaps still lovable or perhaps self-deceived and materialistic?

From the beginning, readers have noticed that the book falls into two almost equal parts, the first an almost unrelieved pastoral idyll and the second an almost equally unrelieved series of disasters that are finally reversed to present a happy ending. More-recent critics have argued that the novel's construction shows considerable care. The first three chapters serve as a prologue and are balanced by the final three chapters, in which the loose ends are tied up. The central part does fall into two roughly equal parts. In the first, we see the Primroses living an almost ideal life, their Eden threatened only by the villainous Squire Thornhill, though his evil nature is balanced by the virtue of Mr. Burchell, a wanderer with little or no fortune, whom Dr. Primrose charitably receives into the family circle. The second half plunges the Primroses into the sordid realities of the actual world, with George's tale of his misfortunes after leaving home, Olivia's apparent seduction, the burning of their house, the Vicar's dispossession and imprisonment, rumors of Olivia's death, Sophia's apparent abduction, and George's impending execution. Throughout, however, Goldsmith leaves clues for the observant reader: Mr. Burchell's slip of the tongue hints strongly that he may be someone other than the humble wanderer he seems; his ballad of Edwin and Angelina presents a happy ending and foreshadows the conclusion of the novel; and in the latter half a sharp reversal undoes the violence, cruelty, and wretchedness in the interpolated tale of Mathilda. Though the humor that dominates the first half dims during the second part, we recognize Goldsmith's reliance on the swift changes of fortune typical of romance conventions.

Goldsmith's most memorable character in the novel is certainly his narrator, the Vicar, Dr. Charles Primrose, who is sublimely convinced of his ability to govern his family according to traditional customs and received wisdom, though he patronizes his wife and daughters shamelessly for their social pretentions and homemade cosmetics. When faced with the very real evil of Squire Thornhill, the Vicar is easily duped, and Goldsmith shows his skill in handling his familiar theme of innocence undone by worldly wisdom, as Fielding often does too. Dr. Primrose, like Tom Jones, needs to temper his benevolence with worldly prudence, just as Sir William Thornhill has learned from his youthful experiences in a self-education strongly reminiscent of Mr. Wilson's in *Joseph Andrews*. Dr. Primrose's experiences in

Caricature of Goldsmith by Henry Bunbury (British Museum)

prison move him beyond Fielding' world, where Tom Jones could expect worldly happiness once he had learned to act prudently. The Vicar's almost unbelievable succession of disasters and his apparently hopeless position in prison lead him to abandon thoughts of relief in this world to prepare himself for eternity. His powerful sermon to the prisoners stresses faith over hope, that rewards and punishments belong to man's future state, not necessarily to this world. In the sermon, Dr. Primrose shows a radical change in his values, abjuring worldly prudence for Christian faith.

Just how lasting the Vicar's conversion is may well seem uncertain in the last three chapters, where a series of reversals occurs almost as incredible as the series of disasters that overtook him, and the family happiness and prosperity are restored. Olivia has not died a fallen woman after all. The squire's minion Jenkinson could not bring himself to ruin Olivia in a mock marriage and secured a genuine priest—though Olivia shows enough sense to live apart from the squire. Sir William Thornhill, abandoning his disguise as Mr. Burchell the lowly vagrant, reclaims the powers he had delegated to his rascally nephew. Sir William has also had ample opportunity to observe Sophia and to realize that she loves him for himself alone, not for his fortune. By happy chance, the embezzler who stole the Vicar's fortune is captured with the money largely intact.

Beginning with the reviewer for the *Critical Review*, critics have found these almost incredible disasters and reversals troublesome, but in more-recent years, some have seen them as Goldsmith's reliance on the conventions of romance as a way of giving his book a happy ending. Virtually all these critics see Sir William, finally revealed in his true identity after his long disguise as Mr. Burchell the penniless wanderer, as a character type also drawn from romance conventions.

Most recent critical disagreement lies in establishing Goldsmith's attitude toward Dr. Primrose: is he a self-deceived and often foolish man or is he Goldsmith's portrait of a clerical ideal, as the village preacher in *The Deserted Village* certainly is? These and other apparent problems in the novel depend on when Goldsmith finished work on it. Clearly the manuscript that Johnson sold was sufficiently finished that John Newbery, certainly no fool in money matters, was willing to purchase it, though that is not clear proof that the novel was ready for the press, however clearly Goldsmith had laid out the major framework. The advertisement to the novel, which argues that "the hero of this piece unites in himself the three greatest characters upon earth; he is a priest, a husbandman, and the father of a family," has usually been taken as a clear statement of Goldsmith's intention to portray his central character as an ideal type, but more than one episode in the book clearly shows him as a dupe, ill-equipped to cope with his adversary Squire Thornhill, and, without Sir William's intervention at the end, the Vicar's ability to cope with worldly problems seems improbable at best. The advertisement raises almost as many questions as it seems to answer. Primarily, we do not know when Goldsmith wrote it—in 1762 when fresh from writing *The Life of Richard Nash*, having just finished his mock-heroic celebration of the "King of Bath," or shortly before the novel's publication in 1766? The latter date, though by no means certain, seems more probable. Ever since *The Traveller* had appeared in 1764, Newbery had Goldsmith working almost incessantly revising the poem, then collecting the pieces that make up *Essays* (1764), and then enlarging that work by two

for *Essays* (1765). If, as seems likely, *The Vicar of Wakefield* was almost, but not quite finished in 1762, Goldsmith would have been pushed hard by Newbery to finish it up, see it through the press, and correct the proofs in time for its publication in March 1766. Presumably too, Newbery had physical possession of the manuscript from 1762 onward, so that even if Goldsmith had had time in his new fame after the publication of *The Traveller*, he could not have devoted considered thought and time to the kinds of problems that have bothered so many critics, such as the improbability that Sir William Thornhill and his nephew are approximately the same age. Thus, when finally published, the novel may very well represent two stages of composition, the first and most carefully constructed part written about 1761-1762, and a second, later part, how long we shall never know, but probably including the advertisement, written hastily to meet Newbery's 1766 deadline. How carefully Goldsmith reconsidered what he had composed around 1762, when most of the writing he had been doing was comic, remains a matter of speculation, but certainly the work he had done since 1764, especially *The Traveller* and his *History of England in a Series of Letters from a Nobleman to his Son* (June 1764), are both predominantly serious. Only his *Essays*, 1765 and 1766, contain more comic than serious writing, some of it the result of fairly careful revision.

Goldsmith was not entirely satisfied with the first edition of *The Vicar of Wakefield* and made extensive revisions for the second edition of May 1766, among them substituting the "Whistonean Controversy," a figment of Dr. Primrose's imagination, for the very real Bangorian Controversy of the first edition, although the latter had been largely a dead issue for nearly fifty years. If Goldsmith did intend to satirize Dr. Primrose, however gently, he did not apparently have time to insert additional signals, like the change to the "Whistonean Controversy," to suggest to the reader his own amiably ironic view of his protagonist. Undoubtedly Newbery pushed him hard for the revised copy, since the book sold only moderately well and both Newbery and Collins wanted to garner all possible profits from it. Whether or not Goldsmith would have corrected the improbabilities, objected to by critics who believe the novel is realistic, will remain forever moot, but, given the many conventions derived from romances of the time appearing in both halves of the book, such changes seem rather improbable. Though Johnson thought the book salable when he took it to Newbery, his later opinion that it contains little of real life and nothing of nature only shows his own misunderstanding of Goldsmith's probable intention, to burlesque romance so broadly that even lovers of that form could not fail to see that he was gently and amiably satirizing not only romantic type-characters but also implausible romantic plots. It would not be the first time an Englishman has failed to see the point of an Irishman's joke. That Johnson was not the only reader confused is amply shown by the way few nineteenth-century readers perceived this dimension of the book—Goethe almost alone seems to have grasped it—but also by the present disagreement among critics over interpreting the book. Whether or not a critical consensus will eventually emerge seems most uncertain at present, but even with some decline in its popularity, it remains, with *Gulliver's Travels* (1726) *Robinson Crusoe* (1719), and *Tristram Shandy* (1759-1767), one of the very few examples of eighteenth-century fiction to attract the attention of Johnson's common reader and enjoy some life outside the classroom.

Goldsmith was heartened by the success of the novel, even if the success were a modest one, but it brought him no money, and so he began to work on a play, since a successful play meant almost instant fortune. He offered Garrick *The Good Natur'd Man*, written during 1767, for Drury Lane, but Garrick put him off repeatedly, still remembering Goldsmith's sharp criticism of the theater managers in *An Enquiry into the Present State of Polite Learning in Europe* in 1759. He then turned to George Colman the Elder at Covent Garden, who accepted the play but delayed opening it until after Garrick presented Hugh Kelly's *False Delicacy*, a prime example of sentimental comedy. Goldsmith's play did open on 29 January 1768, bringing with it an author's share of four hundred pounds, and had a moderately successful run.

Goldsmith's success as a playwright reverses the pattern Henry Fielding had followed, since Fielding had learned from writing plays how to plot a story and to present believable characters who speak believable dialogue. For his plays Goldsmith drew on the character types he had used successfully in *The Citizen of the World* and *The Vicar of Wakefield*. In *The Good Natur'd Man*, Sir William Honeywood, the disguised manager of the other characters' lives, clearly derives from Sir William Thornhill; Lofty, the snobbish name dropper, comes from Beau Tibbs; and Miss Richland, the wise and patient heroine, develops from Sophia in *The Vicar of Wakefield*, though this character-type would not reach full flower until Kate Hardcastle in *She Stoops to Conquer*. Honeywood, the "Good Natur'd Man," is another of Goldsmith's universal benevolists like the Man in Black and Sir William Thornhill. Though Honeywood loses almost his entire fortune and also Miss Richland's through his rash imprudence, his worldly wise uncle saves him from utter destruction, though not from arrest for debt. He has to disguise, not very successfully, the bailiffs as his butler and footmen, but Miss Richland's loving compassion and wisdom bring about her happy marriage to the now responsible Honeywood. Many of the audience must have been confused by the play, since it burlesques sentimental comedy so subtly that at times it seems an example of that form, and almost certainly some of the audience failed to see the burlesque, while some understood Goldsmith's intent.

With the money from his play Goldsmith bought the lease on his last London home, rooms at no. 2 Brick Court, in the Temple. About this time, together with a Temple neighbor, he secured a country cottage out the Edgeward Road for a weekend and working retreat from the bustle of London. He also received word of his brother Henry's death in Lissoy, and perhaps out of his grief came the spark for *The Deserted Village* (1770). The last forty-six lines of *The Traveller* (1764) contain in embryo much of Goldsmith's best-known poem, and, as early as 1762, Goldsmith had written for *Lloyd's Evening Post* a scathing account of the disastrous effect the enclosure laws were having on English agricultural life, further upsetting the precarious traditional balance between agriculture and trade in English society. He put the blame on the increase in luxury, largely the result of enormous growth in the mercantile and trading interests. By the spring of 1769, he had finished the poem, and Griffin, who had also published *The Good Natur'd Man*, published the poem on 16 May 1770, with a dignified but somber dedication to Reynolds. The poem took the town by storm, with six editions printed by the end of the year and admiring reviews in both the *Monthly* and *Critical* reviews as well as praise in the *Gentleman's Magazine*. Then, as now, most readers have responded to the poem's nostalgia for a simpler time and place, an appeal made all the stronger by the social mobility the Industrial Revolution was bringing on. Its early readers sometimes saw Goldsmith's descrip-

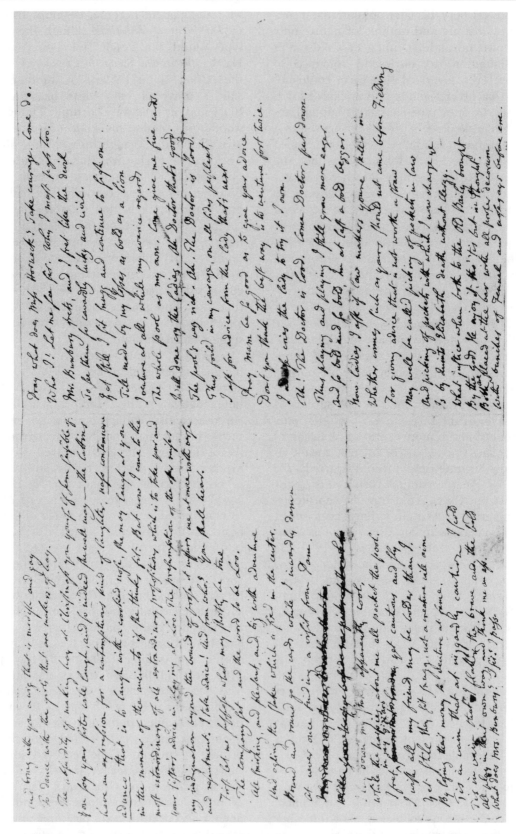

Pages from Goldsmith's circa 25 December 1773 response to Catherine Horneck Bunbury's verse epistle inviting him to Barton, Suffolk, her brother-in-law's home, for New Year's festivities (MA 1297; Pierpont Morgan Library)

tions of the now-vanished village life and the portraits of the preacher, the blacksmith, the schoolmaster, and the surviving widow as almost unchanged autobiographical memories of his father and brother and boyhood friends, a view strong in that part of County Longford, Ireland, even today. Blended with this strongly emotional nostalgia, Goldsmith preaches his favorite social doctrine, that the peasants were being driven from ancestral holdings by merchants who, enriched by their trade in luxuries, wanted to create imposing country seats with lavish gardens and noble landscape prospects, driving their former tenants to starve in the cities or to the wild and savage semitropical jungles of such colonies as Georgia. Several reviewers attacked Goldsmith's social protests as extreme and exaggerated, but certainly many old villages were being destroyed to make room for Georgian pleasure domes, though some were destroyed in the name of progress, as the English Agricultural Revolution moved relentlessly ahead. Goldsmith's criticism that the traditional combination of small farms and villages was being eliminated and that many of the country's best people were immigrating to the colonies is merely a highly memorable expression of social and political views he had long held and had shared with other conservatives, such as Samuel Johnson, another anti-imperialist. As far back as the 1730s, the decade of Goldsmith's birth, Jonathan Swift had bitterly criticized the Irish landlords who were replacing their farming tenants in the fertile central Irish plain with sheep and cattle herders. Today, the poem's continuing popularity owes less to its political and social ideas, though we may recall contemporary arguments over the American family farm, than to the strongly and skillfully evoked emotion of nostalgia and the belief that a largely rural past was better, especially among readers who find themselves living in a society in which traditional values, even those of the two-parent family, are badly shaken and seem to many to be at severe risk. *The Deserted Village* anglicizes the conventions of the classical pastoral and infuses them with new power, and Goldsmith convinces his readers of personal loss, as well as a whole community's irreparable loss. His repetition of words and phrases gives his heroic couplets a remarkable lyric strain. After more than two centuries the poem still marks its readers with its power and indelible effect.

From 1767, when *The Good Natur'd Man* brought him prosperity for the first time in his life, until a year or so before his death, Goldsmith's writing assured him a handsome income, usually around four hundred pounds a year, but his expensive habits—his generosity to the poor, especially poor Irishmen in London; his taste for expensive clothes; his hospitality in entertaining his friends; and especially his gambling losses—kept him always in debt to his publishers. His friendship with Reynolds had deepened profoundly, as his dedication of *The Deserted Village* shows, and through Reynolds he had met Mrs. Kane Horneck, a widow, and her two daughters, with whom he vacationed in Paris during the summer of 1770. He also met Robert Nugent, Viscount Clare, later Earl Nugent, an Irish peer who entertained him frequently in London, in Bath, and at his Essex country estate. Lord Clare once sent him a haunch of venison, and in return Goldsmith dashed off a thank-you poem, posthumously published in 1776, showing his talent for humorous anapestics that foreshadow his much finer and wiser, but unfinished *Retaliation*, published posthumously in 1774, a group of incisive character sketches of friends in the guise of imaginary epitaphs.

His life in the fashionable world was expensive, but he was working hard. During 1768 he compiled for 250 guineas his two-volume *Roman History, from the Foundation of the City of Rome, to the Destruction of the Western Empire*, published in May 1769 by Tom Davies. Davies had been much impressed by the sales of Goldsmith's epistolary *History of England* (1764) and believed correctly that there was a ready market among general readers for shorter, plainer histories than the far longer multivolume works of Smollett and David Hume. In June 1769 Goldsmith contracted with Davies to write a four-volume history of England for five hundred pounds, and the preceding February he had contracted with William Griffin to write an eight-volume natural history of animals at a hundred guineas a volume. As long as booksellers such as Griffin and Davies would offer him contracts, he apparently was willing to sign them and produce what they wanted. However, during the last two years before his death, the stress brought on by the need to fill these contracts undoubtedly affected his health. In April 1769 Reynolds had been knighted following his appointment as president of the Royal Academy, and in December he appointed Goldsmith Professor of Ancient History and Johnson Professor of Ancient Poetry in the Royal Academy, both unpaid, honorary positions, though for Goldsmith

Oliver Goldsmith (portrait by Benjamin West; from Temple Scott, Oliver Goldsmith Bibliographically and Biographically Considered, *1928)*

the appointment reflected his new importance in the contemporary cultural world. His lives of Thomas Parnell and of Henry St. John, Viscount Bolingbroke, both appeared in 1770, and the following year he did produce the four-volume history of England for which he had contracted with Davies in June 1769.

By 1773 Goldsmith had finished his second play, *She Stoops to Conquer*, and encountered the same problems with Colman and Garrick he had had with *The Good Natur'd Man*, but with the firm intervention of Johnson and other friends, Colman reluctantly presented the play on 15 March 1773, very late in the season for Goldsmith to expect a decent return. However, the play was an overwhelming success, and Goldsmith's share came to £502. As in his first play, he attacked the sentimental drama of the time although instead of burlesquing that fashionable form, he presented more directly laughing comedy. Before the play's production, Goldsmith had anonymously published "An Essay on the Theatre; or, a Comparison between Laughing and Sentimental Comedy" in the *Westminster Magazine* for January 1773. Arguing that the aim of comedy is to provoke laughter by showing the "Frailties of the Lower Part of Mankind" and invoking Aristotle by name, he clearly hoped to prepare

the ground for his soon-to-be produced play. Tony Lumpkin, a boorish, hard-drinking young country squire with an eye for the wenches, fulfills Goldsmith's and Aristotle's requirements, but the play belongs to Kate Hardcastle, Goldsmith's finest heroine, who exploits a misunderstanding created by Tony, and through her own skill and wit, ingeniously leads Marlow, her reluctant suitor—by her pretended roles as a barmaid and then as a poor relation—to what promises to be a triumphantly happy marriage. With a skill reminiscent of Viola in *Twelfth Night*, she conquers Marlow's shyness with fine ladies so skillfully he hardly knows what is happening to him. Probably Goldsmith's best single work, the play remains a solid and frequently revived part of the standard English dramatic repertory.

Following the custom that had worked so well for him in writing *She Stoops to Conquer*, Goldsmith spent his summers in the country, working on the two-volume *Grecian History, from the Earliest State to the Death of Alexander the Great*, and resumed work on his eight-volume natural history, both published posthumously by Griffin in 1774, the latter as *An History of the Earth and Animated Nature*. But his literary fame and livelier social life left him discontented, perhaps because of the pressure under which he was working. He physically attacked a newspaper editor who implied in print he was romantically involved with one of the Horneck sisters, but he was able to settle the matter out of court by contributing to the editor's favorite charity. His earlier friendship with Hugh Kelly had collapsed over the greater popularity of Kelly's *False Delicacy* and *School for Wives*, both of which Garrick had produced in competition with Goldsmith's two plays. He quarreled seriously with Reynolds over Reynolds's flattering portrait of James Beattie, a minor Scottish clergyman, who had been given a royal pension for his *Essay on Truth* (1770), which Goldsmith considered mere claptrap. Beattie's pension especially, and perhaps Johnson's earlier one, seemed to Goldsmith unfair, since he had certainly contributed to literature far more than Beattie had or was ever likely to.

Boswell's *Life of Johnson* for the years 1773 and 1774, the last year and a half of Goldsmith's life, shows Johnson often overpowering him, and most others, in conversation, never Goldsmith's strong suit. However, even when Boswell uses Goldsmith as a foil to Johnson in his generally unflattering presentation of Goldsmith, he does record Goldsmith's incisive comments on Johnson—

namely, that he had only the bear's rough skin and that in any fable Johnson might write, his fishes would all talk like whales. Johnson had proved a true and valuable friend to Goldsmith, at least from the time Johnson had sold the manuscript for *The Vicar of Wakefield* and extricated him from the clutches of his landlady. He had helped him by contributing key lines to both *The Traveller* and *The Deserted Village*; he browbeat Colman into producing *She Stoops to Conquer*; and, of course, he composed the inscription for the memorial table to Goldsmith in Poets' Corner, Westminister Abbey.

Goldsmith's hard work over the last several years had left him in precarious health, and after a relatively short illness he died in his Temple rooms on 4 April 1774, almost certainly of a kidney infection, complicated by his own stubborn insistence in taking large doses of Dr. James's Fever Powders, against the professional advice and strong objections of his doctors. Partly because of his relative youth—he was only forty-four—and his position as arguably the leading active writer of the time, his death produced almost universal shock and grief. In Reynolds' character sketch, discovered among Boswell's papers and published in 1952, Reynolds notes that "The literary world deplored his death more than could be expected, when it is considered how small a part of his works were wrote for fame, yet epigrams, epitaphs and monodies to his memory were without end." Johnson described him as "a very great man." But Goldsmith knew his own flaws, since with modest irony in *Retaliation* (1774) he describes himself as "Magnanimous Goldsmith, a goosbery fool," the pleasantly light dessert to the literary banquet in the poem. In this posthumously published, unfinished poem, he provides splendidly incisive but balanced character sketches in the form of imaginary epitaphs for such friends as Edmund Burke, Richard Cumberland, and David Garrick. Boswell's generally unflattering portrait in *The Life of Johnson* presents Goldsmith as a foolish man who wrote extremely well, ironically, a view very like Thomas Babington Macaulay's opinion of Boswell, and has, unfortunately, established what has remained the general opinion of Goldsmith's personality. However, Reynolds's prose character sketch presents Goldsmith in a far more sympathetic light, arguing that he often behaved like a fool on principle and more often than not may have mocked his sobersided English friends.

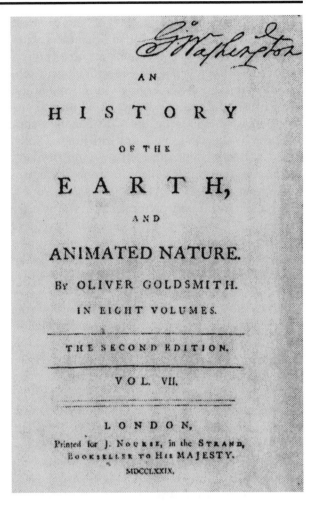

Title page for a volume of Goldsmith's natural history that once belonged to George Washington (auctioned by Sotheby's, 27 March 1985)

The most striking feature of Goldsmith's writing is his versatility: he produced memorable, even first-rate work in every literary form practiced in his lifetime—the individual essay, the pseudoletter series, the novel, poetry, history, and biography. Repeatedly, both in conversation and in his tributary Latin epitaph, Johnson showed that he believed Goldsmith was a first-rate writer who adorned all the forms in which he wrote. Running throughout all Goldsmith's writing is a strong moral strain, attacking cruelty and injustice, while allowing amply for flawed humanity's frailties and errors. Like Fielding, who heavily influenced his writing, Goldsmith strongly attacked perversions of the law that serve selfish, powerful interests. His conservative social and political ideas, formed as he grew up in Ireland, ally him with the Augustan humanists, such as Swift and Pope, as well as Johnson, with whom he also shared a largely rhetorical conception of literature, far more than with any of those whose ideas would coalesce into Romanticism. His sentiment remains sentiment, sometimes quite powerful, as in *The Deserted Village*. He strongly and consistently attacked the emerging sentimental ethos, just as his rural settings always show man as nature's steward, following the Christian humanist position. When Goldsmith satirizes human folly, he does so in a comic spirit; to use John Dryden's broad classifications, Goldsmith's approach is Horatian, not Juvenalian like Swift's or Pope's, though his social and political ideas are as close to theirs as they are to Johnson's. He may have learned something from the manner of Addison and Steele, but he despised and strongly condemned the Whiggery and sentimentality that figure so largely in their works.

His literary reputation was higher in the nineteenth century, among writers such as Dickens and Thackeray, than it probably is today, though *The Vicar of Wakefield* appears to have some life with the general reading public, and *She Stoops to Conquer* lives in the repertories of many community theaters as well as enjoying reasonably frequent professional revivals, most recently in London in 1984-1985. Most readers encounter *The Deserted Village* in classrooms, but many of them find that its nostalgia has a powerful appeal in an industrial society with few roots and virtually no traditional life. In a world where prose fiction is the overwhelmingly dominant form, Goldsmith's writings strongly attract students of literature. Students of narrative art find much to interest them in *The Citizen of the World* because of the way widely varied social comment relates to the narrative frame story. Because *The Vicar of Wakefield* consolidates many of the social, moral, religious positions common in the eighteenth century as well as most of the literary techniques used by Richardson, Fielding, Smollett, and even Sterne, the novel has aroused spirited debate in recent years. But, for those who would truly understand Goldsmith's beliefs in matters social, moral, and religious, his essays will always be the necessary beginning point.

Letters:

The Collected Letters of Oliver Goldsmith, edited by Katharine C. Balderston (Cambridge: Cambridge University Press, 1928).

Bibliography:

Temple Scott, *Oliver Goldsmith Bibliographically and Biographically Considered* (New York: Bowling Green Press, 1928).

Biographies:

Thomas Percy, Memoir of Goldsmith in volume 1 of *The Miscellaneous Works of Oliver Goldsmith, M.B.* (London: Printed for J. Johnson by H. Baldwin & Sons, 1801); modern edition of the memoir: *Thomas Percy's Life of Dr. Oliver Goldsmith*, edited by Richard L. Harp (Salzburg: Institut für Englische Sprache und Literatur, 1976);

Ralph M. Wardle, *Oliver Goldsmith* (Lawrence: University of Kansas Press, 1957).

References:

Sven Bäckman, *"This Singular Tale": A Study of "The Vicar of Wakefield" and Its Literary Background* (Lund, Sweden: Gleerup, 1971);

Martin C. Battestin, "Goldsmith: The Comedy of Job," in his *The Providence of Wit: Aspects of Form in Augustan Literature and the Arts* (Oxford: Clarendon Press, 1974), pp. 193-214;

Howard Bell, Jr., "*The Deserted Village* and Goldsmith's Social Doctrines," *PMLA*, 59 (September 1944): 747-772;

Wayne C. Booth, "Preconceptions about a Proper Structure: *The Citizen of the World*," in his *Critical Understanding: The Powers and Limits of Pluralism* (Chicago: University of Chicago Press, 1979), pp. 301-316;

Ronald S. Crane and Hamilton J. Smith, "A French Influence on Goldsmith's *Citizen of the World*," *Modern Philology*, 19 (August 1921): 83-92;

Curtis Dahl, "Patterns of Disguise in *The Vicar of Wakefield*," *English Literary History*, 25 (March 1958): 90-104;

Oliver W. Ferguson, "Oliver Goldsmith: The Personality of the Essayist," *Philological Quarterly*, 61 (Spring 1982): 179-191;

Morris Golden, "The Family-Wanderer Theme in Goldsmith," *English Literary History*, 25 (September 1958): 181-193;

Golden, "Goldsmith's Reputation in His Day," *Papers on Language and Literature*, 16 (Spring 1980): 213-238;

Robert H. Hopkins, *The True Genius of Oliver Goldsmith* (Baltimore: Johns Hopkins Press, 1969);

D. W. Jefferson, "Observations on *The Vicar of*

Wakefield," Cambridge Journal, 3 (1949-1950): 621-628;

Charles A. Knight, "Ironic Loneliness: The Case of Goldsmith's Chinaman," *Journal of English and Germanic Philology*, 82 (July 1983): 347-364;

Roger Lonsdale, " 'A Garden and a Grave': The Poetry of Oliver Goldsmith," in *The Author in His Work*, edited by Louis L. Martz and Aubrey Williams (New Haven & London: Yale University Press, 1978), pp. 3-30;

Patrick Murray, "The Riddle of Goldsmith's Ancestry," *Studies*, (Dublin), 63 (Summer 1974): 177-190;

Ricardo Quintana, *Oliver Goldsmith: A Georgian Study* (New York: Macmillan, 1967);

William Bowman Piper, "The Musical Quality of Goldsmith's *The Deserted Village*," *Studies in Eighteenth-Century Culture*, 14 (1984): 259-274;

Joshua Reynolds, *Portraits by Sir Joshua Reynolds. Character Sketches of Oliver Goldsmith, Samuel Johnson, and David Garrick, together with Other Manuscripts of Reynolds Discovered among the Boswell Papers and now First Published*, edited by Frederick W. Hilles (New York: McGraw-Hill, 1952), pp. 44-59;

G. S. Rousseau, ed., *Goldsmith; The Critical Heritage* (London & Boston: Routledge & Kegan Paul, 1974);

Samuel H. Woods, Jr., "Images of the Orient: Goldsmith and the *Philosophes*," *Studies in Eighteenth-Century Culture*, 16 (1985): 257-270;

Virginia Woolf, "Oliver Goldsmith," in her *The Captain's Death Bed and Other Essays* (New York: Harcourt, Brace, 1950), pp. 3-14.

Papers:

Literary manuscripts in Goldsmith's own hand are extremely rare, that of *The Haunch of Venison* in the New York Public Library being one of the few that survive. The largest concentration of Goldsmith manuscripts is in the British Library (Add. MSS 42515-42517). Margaret M. Smith has compiled a careful list of the surving autograph manuscripts, giving their present ownership and location, for the eighteenth-century volume of *The Index of English Literary Manuscripts*.

Sir John Hawkins

(9 April 1719 - 21 May 1789)

Bertram H. Davis
Florida State University

BOOKS: *The English Protestant's Answer to the Wicked Sophistry of Some Late Treasonable Papers* (London: Printed for J. Roberts, 1745);

Observations on the State of the Highways, and on the Laws for Amending and Keeping Them in Repair; with a Draught of a Bill for Comprehending and Reducing into One Act of Parliament the Most Essential Parts of All the Statutes in Force relating to the Highways, and for Making Provision for the More Easy and Effectual Repair of the Highways (London: Printed for J. Worrall, 1763);

A Charge to the Grand Jury of the County of Middlesex (London: Printed for J. Worrall & B. Tovey, 1770);

An Account of the Institution and Progress of the Academy of Ancient Music, with a Comparative View of the Music of the Past and Present Times. By a Member (London: Privately printed, 1770);

A General History of the Science and Practice of Music, 5 volumes (London: Printed for T. Payne & Son, 1776);

A Charge to the Grand Jury of the County of Middlesex (London: Printed for E. Brooke, 1780);

The Life of Samuel Johnson, LL.D. (London: Printed for J. Buckland and others, 1787).

Edition: *The Life of Samuel Johnson, LL.D.*, edited, abridged, with an introduction, by Bertram H. Davis (New York: Macmillan, 1961; London: Cape, 1961).

OTHER: John Stanley, *Six Cantatas, for a Voice and Instruments*, includes a preface and lyrics for five of the cantatas by Hawkins (London: Printed for J. Walsh, 1742);

Izaak Walton and Charles Cotton, *The Complete Angler, or, Contemplative Man's Recreation*, edited, with a life of Walton, by Hawkins and a life of Cotton, by William Oldys (London: Printed for T. Hope, 1760); revised and enlarged with Hawkins's life of Cotton replacing Oldys's (London: Printed for John, Francis & Charles Rivington, 1784);

The Works of Samuel Johnson, LL.D., Together with His Life, and Notes on His Lives of the Poets by Sir John Hawkins, Knt., 11 volumes (London: Printed for J. Buckland and others, 1787);

William Boyce, ed., *Cathedral Music*, second edition, includes a memoir of Boyce by Hawkins (London: Printed for J. Ashley, 1788).

SELECTED PERIODICAL PUBLICATIONS: "Essay on Honesty," *Gentleman's Magazine*, 9 (March 1739): 117-118;

"Remarks on the Tragedy of the Orphan," *Gentleman's Magazine*, 18 (November 1748): 502-506; (December 1748): 551-553;

Imitation of John Donne's "The Canonization," *Gentleman's Magazine*, 31 (October 1761): 472;

"Memoirs of the Life of Sig. Agostino Steffani," *Gentleman's Magazine*, 31 (November 1761): 489-492.

Sir John Hawkins has had the misfortune to be remembered for his unsociability, exemplified in the rudeness to Edmund Burke that led to his withdrawal from Samuel Johnson's best-known club. But Hawkins deserved better of posterity. As a magistrate he presided with integrity and devotion over the Middlesex part of London in the days when the justices of the peace in Quarter Sessions were its only unified local government. His history of music was the first to be completed in England, and his edition of Izaak Walton's *Compleat Angler*, for which he wrote a life of Walton and, later, a life of Charles Cotton, became the standard for the next century. His biography of Johnson, for whom he was one of the executors, was a full-length work that preceded Boswell's *Life of Johnson* (1791) by four years.

Born of a Welsh mother, Elizabeth Gwatkin Hawkins, and a City of London father, John Hawkins—a not very successful carpenter—the young John Hawkins seems to have been drawn early to the study of music, English, and Latin, the last of these probably at Samuel Watkins's acad-

Sir John Hawkins (portrait by James Roberts; Oxford Music Faculty)

emy in Spital Square, a nursery of writers for the *Gentleman's Magazine*. In 1737 he was articled to the attorney John Scott, and, during the five years prior to his admission to practice in the courts of common law, he rose regularly at four in the morning to read law and literature before being called to his daily chores. He also submitted essays and poems to the periodicals, his first identifiable effort being an "Essay on Honesty" published in the *Gentleman's Magazine* in March 1739. Thereafter literature, music, and the law were to shape much of the course of his life.

The "Essay on Honesty," which perhaps brought Hawkins into association with Johnson, was followed by others of a moral or social turn, along with a poem in imitation of John Donne's "The Canonization," remarkable only because Donne's poetry had few admirers in the eighteenth century. At the same time Hawkins was pursuing his musical interests by cultivating acquaintances with the composers William Boyce and John Stanley, both of whom set verses of his to music. For Stanley's *Six Cantatas, for a Voice and In-*

struments (1742), he wrote the lyrics for five of the cantatas and contributed a preface in which he deplored the popular taste that exalted foreign music to the neglect of the English. In the 1740s he joined the Madrigal Society and the Academy of Ancient Music, where George Frederick Handel was a frequent performer.

Of more substance than his earlier pieces were a thirty-page political pamphlet of 1745 and a two-part dramatic essay of 1748. Writing anonymously in *The English Protestant's Answer to the Wicked Sophistry of Some Late Treasonable Papers*, Hawkins lashed out at the Young Pretender's "manifesto" of 10 October 1745 and its alleged proofs of English grievances: "Is not every *Popish* Country under Heaven incomparably worse . . . than *England*?" he asked. But with dozens of pamphlets issuing from the press at this critical juncture in English history, Hawkins's effort probably attracted less notice than his "Remarks on the Tragedy of the Orphan," which was published in the November and December 1748 issues of the *Gentleman's Magazine*. Through a close examina-

Page from Hawkins's edition of Izaak Walton's Compleat Angler *(courtesy of the Strozier Library, Florida State University). Hawkins took this illustration from the* Book of Hawking, Hunting, and Fishing *published by Wynkyn de Worde at Westminster in 1496.*

tion of its plot, manners, and sentiments Hawkins found Thomas Otway's popular play wanting in moral purpose, its deficiencies a reflection of Otway himself: "to constitute a great Poet," he wrote, "the primary and essential qualification is TO BE A GOOD MAN." One of the more interesting pieces of dramatic criticism in that period, it may have been the deciding factor in Johnson's inviting Hawkins to join with him and seven others in a club which was to meet weekly at the King's Head in Ivy Lane.

Most of the Ivy Lane club members were young men with their fortunes still to make, including three doctors, a merchant, the bookseller John Payne, and Johnson's fellow writer for the *Gentleman's Magazine*, John Hawkesworth. After their first meeting, Johnson later recalled, Haw-

kins ate no supper and asked to be excused from paying his share. "We all scorned him, and admitted his plea," Johnson commented. ". . . Sir John was a most *unclubable* man!" But Hawkins stayed with this first Johnson club until it broke up about 1756, and in his biography of Johnson he left its only memorial.

On 24 March 1753 he married Sidney Storer of Highgate, who had inherited five thousand pounds from her father, a wealthy landowner whom Hawkins had assisted with his conveyancing. At their home in Austin Friars the Hawkinses held fortnightly musical assemblies, and with his newly acquired wealth Hawkins began to collect the early treatises on music that he was to present to the British Museum in 1778. A brief life of the composer Agostino Steffani that he printed for private distribution among his friends was submitted by one of them to the *Gentleman's Magazine* in November 1761. With his wife's inheritance increased by an estimated thirty thousand pounds after the death of her brother in 1759, Hawkins resolved to turn over his law practice to his young law clerk Richard Clark (later Lord Mayor of London) and devote his time wholly to literature and the arts.

But even before retirement became feasible he was at work on a time-consuming literary project. The year 1750 had seen a revival of Izaak Walton's *Compleat Angler* (1653) edited by Moses Browne, who had amended the text of Walton's fourth edition, including its verses, to suit his own taste; and Hawkins, unable to persuade Browne to change his practice in a projected new edition, moved ahead with one of his own based upon Walton's corrected fifth edition, with modifications only for spelling, capitalization, and punctuation. Browne's second edition was published in 1759 and Hawkins's first—advertised pointedly as a new and *correct* edition—in 1760. Infuriated, Browne vented his anger in two letters to the London newspapers in which he charged Hawkins with being too dull and lazy to file off the rust and refine the crudities of Walton's book. Hawkins responded only to the more hysterical second letter, but perhaps even that response was superfluous. For through his faithfully reproduced text and his introductory life of Walton, described by Johnson as "very diligently collected, and very elegantly composed," he had won the public by presenting the book as Walton might have wished. Himself an ardent angler, he supplemented Walton's comments on baits and the habits and haunts of fish and gave special attention to fly-fishing, in which Walton was not an expert. Learn to make your own flies, Hawkins advised his readers, for in imitating "these admirable creatures, there is little less pleasure than even in catching fish."

In 1760, after purchasing a house at Twickenham for summer occupancy, Hawkins moved from London with his wife and two infant children, shortly before the birth of a third child. At Twickenham he had good friends in Horace Walpole and sergeant-at-law Sir Samuel Prime, but in 1763 he alienated other neighbors when he sued Thomas Wallis and his gardeners for espaliering trees and vines to Hawkins's greenhouse wall—for making, according to the indictment, twenty thousand holes in the bricks and mortar with "certain Nails and Hammers." Hawkins won

the case, but in time he became uncomfortable because of the uneasiness this and other actions gave to his neighbors, and in 1771 he left Twickenham to reside the year round in London's Hatton Garden.

On 13 August 1761 he had been appointed to the Middlesex Commission of the Peace, and in 1763 he published *Observations on the State of the Highways*, an astute analysis of England's hodgepodge of antiquated highway laws, with a proposal for updating and consolidating them that Parliament acted upon in 1767. His leadership in that effort, and in turning back two attempts by the City of London to charge Middlesex with much of the cost of rebuilding and maintaining Newgate Prison, led to his unanimous election as chairman of the Middlesex Quarter Sessions in 1765. To this responsible position—Quarter Sessions was the local governing body for all of London except the City and Southwark and for the outlying districts along the west side of the Thames—he was reelected semiannually for the next fifteen years. During his chairmanship the justices were called into action frequently to suppress the riots that were common occurrences in that period, and his charges to the grand juries in the wake of the 1770 weavers' riots and the 1780 Gordon Riots were published at the request of the juries and his fellow justices. His major contribution as chairman was to establish and implement a procedure for investigating allegations of misconduct against the justices, with the result that several so-called trading justices were removed from the commission. In 1772 he was knighted in response to his request that he be accorded the same honor accorded to Sir John Fielding, chairman of the Westminster Quarter Sessions.

Hawkins's commitments to Quarter Sessions slowed up but did not halt his literary work. He contributed notes, most of them reflecting his musical and antiquarian interests, to Johnson's edition of Shakespeare (1765) and the Johnson-Steevens editions of 1773 and 1778. He wrote occasional short pieces that ended up in Francis Grose's *Antiquarian Repertory*. In 1764 he was invited to join with Johnson, Sir Joshua Reynolds, Edmund Burke, Oliver Goldsmith, and four others in a new club, later known as the Literary Club, and he remained a member until the coldness shown him by other members after his rudeness to Edmund Burke compelled him to withdraw. In 1770 he published an account of the Academy of Ancient Music in an effort to arrest the academy's declining fortunes following the deaths of Handel and the academy's founder, Johan Christopher Pepusch.

His most important work of the period was the five-volume *General History of the Science and Practice of Music*, published in 1776, eight months after the first volume of Charles Burney's *General History of Music*. Profusely illustrated with portraits, drawings, and musical scores, Hawkins's "magnificently conceived" history laid out the vast panorama of Western music, moving chronologically from ancient Greece and Rome through the various countries of Europe and stopping short only of any specific consideration of living contemporaries.

The history, to be sure, has some obvious shortcomings. Its intricate examination of the mathematical ratios of musical consonances and its lengthy extracts from early treatises have little interest for the general reader, although the extracts have proved an attraction for scholars, who have found the originals largely inaccessible. It slights contemporary music: the opera, which he considered "of all entertainments the most unnatural and absurd," and instrumental music, which he dismissed as "noise without harmony." Its style is at times pedestrian or legalistic, and Hawkins's fondness for anecdote and detail occasionally led him into absurdity himself, as in his extended note on the wonderful effect of music on mice and spiders.

Yet Hawkins's history has great strengths as well. Its style, on the whole lucid and readable, rises even to eloquence when Hawkins is inspired by a subject such as Handel's playing of the organ. In exalting the music of the sixteenth and seventeenth centuries—of Giovanni Pierluigi Palestrina, Claudio Monteverdi, the English madrigalists, and numerous others—Hawkins was well in advance of his age; and by and large his judgments have withstood the test of time. His final volume, with its intimate accounts not just of composers and compositions but of musical assemblies, societies, and rivalries, brings to life the vibrant activity of the England in which the young Hawkins acquired his knowledge and love of music. In their broad sweep his five volumes capture the richness and variety of Western music, setting with Burney's four volumes a standard for later historians to follow.

Although favorably reviewed in the *Gentleman's Magazine* and the *Critical* and *London* reviews, the history did not sell well, perhaps a consequence initially of its prohibitive six-guinea price.

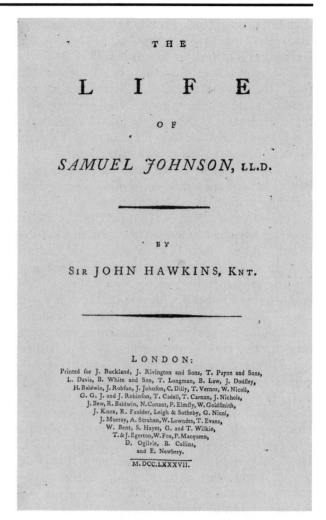

THE

L I F E

OF

SAMUEL JOHNSON, LL.D.

BY

Sir JOHN HAWKINS, Knt.

LONDON:

Printed for J. Buckland, J. Rivington and Sons, T. Payne and Sons, L. Davis, B. White and Son, T. Longman, B. Law, J. Dodsley, H. Baldwin, J. Robson, J. Johnson, C. Dilly, T. Vernor, W. Nicoll, G. G. J. and J. Robinson, T. Cadell, T. Carnan, J. Nichols, J. Bew, R. Baldwin, N. Conant, P. Elmsly, W. Goldsmith, J. Knox, R. Faulder, Leigh & Sotheby, G. Nicol, J. Murray, A. Strahan, W. Lowndes, T. Evans, W. Bent, S. Hayes, G. and T. Wilkie, T. & J. Egerton, W. Fox, P. Macqueen, D. Ogilvie, B. Collins, and E. Newbery.

M,DCC,LXXXVII.

Title page for Hawkins's biography of Samuel Johnson, with whom Hawkins was acquainted as early as 1739, twenty-four years before Johnson met his best-known biographer, James Boswell (courtesy of the Strozier Library, Florida State University)

But in a review that began after others were finished, it fell victim to the searing wit of William Bewley, a friend of Hawkins's rival Burney, who prodded Bewley to undertake a four-part article in the *Monthly Review* (February-August 1777) and supplied him with materials to sustain it. Whatever its effect on the sales of the book, Bewley's review, along with newspaper attacks by other Burney friends, set a pattern for the abuse of Hawkins that was to be followed by the wits of the next decade.

Hawkins's last major work was *The Life of Samuel Johnson, LL.D.*, which he undertook at the request of the booksellers almost immediately after Johnson's death on 13 December 1784. Based upon Johnson's works and surviving papers, published accounts of Johnson, information from friends, and Hawkins's own recollections of Johnson going back perhaps as far as 1739, the six-hundred-page book reflected a conscientious effort to present Johnson as Hawkins knew him and to place him in his milieu. Published in March 1787, both separately and as the first volume of the eleven-volume *Works of Samuel Johnson*, it was promptly pirated in Dublin, and it reached a second edition before the end of the year. This edition was to be its last publication for 174 years.

The long gap was a consequence partly of what one reviewer called "Sir John's way of writing" (*Country Magazine*, March 1787). His often legalistic style, his digressions beyond the need to portray Johnson's times, and his occasional harsh judgments of Johnson's contemporaries made the book a ready mark for wits such as George Steevens, Arthur Murphy, and Richard Porson. But the contemporary reaction would in time have been forgotten. The primary reason for the long neglect of Hawkins's biography was the publication of James Boswell's *Life of Johnson* in 1791. For Boswell—to whom Hawkins imprudently referred merely as "a native of Scotland"—not only eclipsed all previous efforts but pointedly attacked Hawkins for his digressions and what Boswell called his inaccuracy and the "dark uncharitable cast" of his treatment of Johnson.

Only in the last several decades, through the work of such scholars as James Clifford and Donald Greene, have the virtues of Hawkins's biography been adequately acknowledged. Inaccurate though it is at times, some of its information and analyses have proved more reliable than Boswell's. Hawkins was a more astute observer of Johnson's political development, for example, and he rejected the romantic interpretation of Johnson's marriage that Boswell embraced. Many of his characterizations and incidents are memorable: of Edward Cave, for example, who "had no great relish for mirth, but . . . could bear it," or of Johnson's all-night celebration for Charlotte Lennox and her novel. What seemed uncharitable in Hawkins was often only an effort, characteristic of the magistrate, to cast up the account of good and bad in order to reach the truth. But whatever his conclusions on individual matters, Hawkins never left any doubt about his admiration for Johnson's essential greatness.

Perhaps it was inevitable that a man like Sir John Hawkins—imprudent, moralistic, "unclubable," and too often unable to see himself as others saw him—would have no easy time of it in eighteenth-century literary London. But, though some may have risen higher, no scholar but Johnson in that age of extraordinary scholarship could match the variety of his achievements: a *Compleat Angler* that put an end to Moses Browne's "refining" process; a *History of Music* that survived the laughter of the wits to be twice reprinted in the nineteenth century; and a *Life of Johnson* that could emerge still vital after 174 years in the shadow of Boswell's towering *Life*. Although Hawkins did not merit a place with Johnson in Poets' Corner of Westminster Abbey, his burial in the North Cloister, not far from his friend, seems quite appropriate.

Biographies:
Percy A. Scholes, *The Life and Activities of Sir John Hawkins* (London: Oxford University Press, 1953);
Bertram H. Davis, *A Proof of Eminence: The Life of Sir John Hawkins* (Bloomington & London: Indiana University Press, 1973).

References:
Austin Dobson, "Sir John Hawkins, Knight," in his *Old Kensington Palace and Other Papers* (London: Chatto & Windus, 1910), pp. 112-139;
Laetitia-Matilda Hawkins, *Anecdotes, Biographical Sketches and Memoirs* (London: F. C. & J. Rivington, 1822);
Hawkins, *Memoirs, Anecdotes, Facts, and Opinions*, 2 volumes (London: Longman, Hurst, Rees, Orme, Brown & Green, 1824);
Lawrence Lipking, *The Ordering of the Arts in Eighteenth-Century England* (Princeton: Princeton University Press, 1970), pp. 229-268;
Roger Lonsdale, *Dr. Charles Burney: A Literary Biography* (Oxford: Clarendon Press, 1965);
Robert Stevenson, " 'The Rivals'—Hawkins, Burney, and Boswell," *Musical Quarterly*, 36 (January 1950): 67-82.

Papers:
Few Hawkins papers have survived, and most of those concern his work with the Middlesex Quarter Sessions. The largest group is housed in the Greater London Record Office. Most of the rest are in the Public Record Office. The locations of individual letters and other documents are recorded in Davis, *A Proof of Eminence*.

David Hume

(26 April 1711 - 25 August 1776)

Donald Livingston
Emory University

BOOKS: *A Treatise of Human Nature: Being an Attempt to Introduce the Experimental Method of Reasoning into Moral Subjects*, 3 volumes; volumes 1 and 2 (London: Printed for John Noon, 1739); volume 3 (London: Printed for Thomas Longman, 1740);

An Abstract of a Book Lately Published; Entitled, a Treatise of Human Nature, etc. Wherein the Chief Argument of That Book is Farther Illustrated and Explained (London: Printed for C. Borbet [i.e., Corbet], 1740);

Essays, Moral and Political, 2 volumes; volume 1 (Edinburgh: Printed for A. Kincaid, 1741; revised, 1742); volume 2 (Edinburgh: Printed for A. Kincaid, 1742); volumes 1 and 2 republished with *Three Essays, Moral and Political* (1748) as *Essays, Moral and Political*, third edition, corrected, with additions, 1 volume (London: Printed for A. Millar and for A. Kincaid, Edinburgh, 1748);

A Letter from a Gentleman to His Friend in Edinburgh: Containing Some Observations on a Specimen of the Principles Concerning Religion and Morality Said to be Maintain'd in a Book Lately Publish'd Intitled, A Treatise of Human Nature, etc. (Edinburgh, 1745);

A True Account of the Behaviour and Conduct of Archibald Stewart, Esq.; late Lord Provost of Edinburgh (London: Printed for M. Cooper, 1748);

Philosophical Essays Concerning Human Understanding (London: Printed for A. Millar, 1748; revised edition, London: Printed for M. Cooper, 1751); republished as *An Enquiry Concerning Human Understanding* in *Essays and Treatises on Several Subjects* (London: Printed for A. Millar and for A. Kincaid & A. Donaldson, Edinburgh, 1758);

Three Essays, Moral and Political (London: Printed for A. Millar and for A. Kincaid, Edinburgh, 1748);

An Enquiry Concerning the Principles of Morals (London: Printed for A. Millar, 1751);

Political Discourses (Edinburgh: Printed by R. Fleming for A. Kincaid & A. Donaldson, 1752);

Essays and Treatises on Several Subjects (4 volumes, London: Printed for A. Millar and for A. Kincaid & A. Donaldson, Edinburgh, 1753; revised, 1753-1756; revised again, 1 volume, 1758; revised again, 4 volumes, 1760; revised again, 2 volumes, 1764; revised again, London: Printed for A. Millar and for A. Kincaid, J. Bell & A. Donaldson, Edinburgh, and sold by T. Cadell, 1768; revised again, 4 volumes, London: Printed for T. Cadell and A. Kincaid & A. Donaldson, Edinburgh, 1770; revised posthumous edition, 2 volumes, with author's last corrections, London: Printed for T. Cadell and A. Donaldson & W. Creech, Edinburgh, 1777);

The History of Great Britain, Vol. I, Containing the Reigns of James I and Charles I (Edinburgh: Printed by Hamilton, Balfour & Neill, 1754; revised edition, London: Printed for A. Millar, 1759);

The History of Great Britain, Vol. II, Containing the Commonwealth, and the Reigns of Charles II and James II (London: Printed for A. Millar, 1757; revised, 1759);

Four Dissertations (London: Printed for A. Millar, 1757);

The History of England under the House of Tudor, 2 volumes (London: Printed for A. Millar, 1759);

The History of England, from the Invasion of Julius Caesar to the Accession of Henry VII, 2 volumes (London: Printed for A. Millar, 1762);

The History of England, from the Invasion of Julius Caesar to the Revolution in 1688 (6 volumes, London: Printed for A. Millar, 1762; revised, 8 volumes, 1763; posthumous edition with author's last revisions, London: Printed for T. Cadell, 1778);

Exposé succinct de la contestation qui s'est élévée entre M. Hume et M. Rousseau avec les pieces

David Hume, 1754 (portrait by Allan Ramsay; private collection; from David Daiches, Peter Jones, and Jean Jones, eds.,
A Hotbed of Genius: The Scottish Enlightenment, 1730-1790, *1986)*

justicatives (Paris, 1766); English edition: *A
Concise and Genuine Account of the Dispute between Mr. Hume and Mr. Rousseau* (London:
Printed for T. Becket & P. A. DeHondt,
1766);

The Life of David Hume, Esq. Written by Himself (London: Printed for W. Strahan & T. Caddell,
1777);

Two Essays (London, 1777);

Dialogues Concerning Natural Religion (London:
Printed for Robinson, 1779).

Editions: *The Natural History of Religion*, edited by
H. E. Root (Stanford: Stanford University
Press, 1957);

Dialogues Concerning Natural Religion, edited by
Norman Kemp Smith (Indianapolis: Bobbs-
Merrill, 1962);

*David Hume's Enquiries Concerning Human Under-
standing and Concerning the Principles of Morals*, edited by L. A. Selby-Bigge, third edi-

tion, revised by P. H. Nidditch (Oxford: Clarendon Press, 1975);

A Treatise of Human Nature, edited by Selby-Bigge,
second edition, with text revised and variant
readings by Nidditch (Oxford: Clarendon
Press, 1978);

*The History of England, From the Invasion of Julius
Caesar to the Abdication of James the Second,
1688* [1788 edition], 6 volumes (Indianapolis: Liberty Classics, 1983);

Essays, Moral, Political, and Literary, edited by
Eugene F. Miller (Indianapolis: Liberty Classics, 1985).

David Hume's literary work reveals an extraordinary range of interests and a mind of unusual scope and penetration. Recognized as one
of the greatest modern philosophers, he made
original contributions to the major areas of philo-

108

farther Preface, proceed to open up to you the present condition of my Health,
& to do that the more effectually shall give you a kind of History of my
Life, after which you will easily learn, why I keep my Name a Secret.

You must know then that from my earliest Infancy, I found alwise
a strong Inclination to Books & Letters. As our College Education in Scot:
land, extending little further than the Languages, ends commonly when we
are about 14 or 15 Years of Age, I was after that left to my own Choice
in my Reading, & found it encline me almost equally to Books of Reason:
ing & Philosophy, & to Poetry & the polite Authors. Every one, who is
acquainted either with the Philosophers or Critics, knows that there is nothing
yet establisht in either of these two Sciences, & that they contain little more
than endless Disputes even in the most fundamental Articles. Upon E:
:xamination of these I found a certain Boldness of Temper growing in me,
which was not enclin'd to submit to any Authority in these Subjects, but
led me to seek out some new Medium, by which Truth might be establisht.
After much Study & Reflection on this, at last, when I was about
18 Years of Age, there seem'd to be open'd up to me a new Scene of Thought,
which transported me beyond Measure, & made me with an Ardor natural
to young men, throw up every other Pleasure or Business to apply entire:
ly to it. The Law, which was the Business I design'd to follow appear'd
nauseous to me, & I cou'd think of no other way of pushing my Fortune
in the World, but that of a Scholar & Philosopher. I was infinitely
happy

Page from a 1734 letter to a physician, in which Hume provided "a kind of History of my Life" (RSE, I.30; Royal Society of Edinburgh)

sophical inquiry: epistemology, metaphysics, philosophy of mind, ethics, aesthetics, social and political philosophy, and philosophy of religion. Undergraduate textbooks in philosophy abound with examples of philosophical analyses derived from Hume: the riddle of induction, known as "Hume's problem of induction"; the "bundle" theory of the mind; the "is-ought" distinction between factual and moral judgments, known as "Hume's law"; the division of all judgments into those asserting matters of fact and those asserting relations of ideas, known as "Hume's fork." Several philosophical movements (often contrary to each other) have credited Hume with exerting a seminal influence. Immanuel Kant claimed that Hume awakened him from his "dogmatic slumbers," making possible his own highly influential philosophy of transcendental idealism; Edmund Husserl, the founder of phenomenology, confessed that Hume's philosophy of mind exercised a decisive influence on the formation of the phenomenological method; the logical positivists of the Vienna Circle claimed Hume and Ernst Mach as founders; and Jeremy Bentham credited Hume's moral and political philosophy with pointing the way to his own philosophy of utilitarianism. Hume's critical writings on religion give him claim to being the founder of the philosophy of religion. His essay "Of the Standard of Taste" is a classic in aesthetics. His writings on political economy form part of the foundation of modern economics and influenced his younger friend Adam Smith. Hume's political philosophy was used by French thinkers during and immediately after the French Revolution as a conceptual framework for criticizing revolution. Finally, Hume's political philosophy greatly influenced the Federalists James Madison and Alexander Hamilton and, through them, helped shape the U.S. Constitution.

In addition to these major philosophical achievements, Hume is one of the greatest historians of the modern period and one of the first to introduce scientific canons to the writing of history. During his lifetime he was known more as the author of *The History of England* (1754-1762) than as a philosopher, and he is still classed in the *British Library Catalogue* as "the historian." *The History of England* is about half of Hume's literary production. It was considered a classic during his lifetime and passed through seven editions. Hume's fellow historian Voltaire considered it "perhaps the best ever written in any language." Edward Gibbon greatly admired Hume's work and said

that Hume's 1776 letter praising the *Decline and Fall of the Roman Empire* "overpaid the labor of ten years." Hume made a small fortune from the *History*, as it was the best-selling history in English prior to Gibbon. It remained the standard history of England for nearly a century, until Thomas Babington Macaulay's began to replace it in 1849. Even so, it went through at least 175 posthumous editions and printings and was in print continuously down to the end of the nineteenth century. The young Winston Churchill learned English history from a student's edition of it, and one such edition was in print continuously from 1858 to 1910, with some printings of many more than 100,000 copies.

Hume was a writer's writer with a keen sense of how language both shapes and distorts thought. He experimented with many literary forms and was keen to correct and revise new editions of his works. He was a master of historical narrative, and he wrote philosophy in systematic form, as well as essays, narratives, dialogues, and eclectic combinations. His *Dialogues Concerning Natural Religion* (1779) are, next to Plato's dialogues, among the purest expressions of philosophical inquiry.

David Hume was born on 26 April 1711 in the eastern border country of Scotland, at the family estate of Ninewells. He was the youngest son of John Home and Katherine Falconer Home, both heirs to generations of strong-willed gentry-advocates. He had a brother, John, who was the eldest, and a sister, Katherine. The spelling of the family name was not fixed between the Anglicized "Hume" and the older "Home." David, who sought his fortune in the world of English letters, chose the former; John, who inherited the family estate and was a pioneer in introducing modern methods of agriculture in Scotland, chose the latter.

Hume was proud of his family, which, though never rich, had possessed the estate at Ninewells since the late fifteenth century. His father died when he was two, and he was raised by a strong, affectionate, and understanding mother, who, though attractive, never remarried. Hume was a person of strong affection and loyalty and was devoted to his family. Though absent from time to time in search of a career, Hume spent about half his years at Ninewells, and it was not until he was forty that he moved to Edinburgh to set up residence of his own. His sister, who, like Hume, never married, moved with him, and they remained together until his death.

Not much is known about Hume's early education. His family was devout, and Hume confessed that he was religious when young. As a boy he would have enjoyed the library one would expect to have been handed down from generations of advocates. He entered Edinburgh University 27 February 1723, shortly before he was twelve. He left in 1725 or 1726 without taking a degree and returned to Ninewells, where his family encouraged him to enter the law. He made an effort, but his own inclination was to literature and general learning. It was during this period before he was eighteen, when he was supposedly studying law, that Hume conceived the project of a philosophy of human nature.

By 1729 he had abandoned all pretense at legal studies and until 1734 did research for his projected *Treatise of Human Nature*. The work during this period was intense, and he was plagued, off and on, with depression. Medical regimens having failed, he finally sought relief by dropping his studies and taking a position with a wealthy merchant in Bristol. In a few months he was dismissed, having, among other things, quarreled with the merchant about the literary merits of his letters. But the brief experience of active life had its therapeutic effect. Hume immediately went to France in the summer of 1734 to compose what was to be his masterpiece, *A Treatise of Human Nature*.

Hume remained in France a little over three years. Most of *A Treatise of Human Nature* was composed near the Jesuit college of La Flèche, where René Descartes had been a student and which was a center of Cartesian studies. The *Treatise* bears a strong imprint of Cartesian influence. Hume's early retreat in France is a presage of the importance French culture was to have in his career. The Scots and French were connected by centuries of intermarriage and common policy against the English. The union of the Scottish and English parliaments occurred only four years before Hume's birth, but the union was not perceived as one of equals; and, although Scottish success in London was considerable, the union was often resented. Even educated Scots spoke and wrote English as virtually a foreign language. Hume eventually purged his writings of Scotticisms and even published a list for the benefit of his countrymen seeking to make it in an English world; but his speech, as he says, was "desperate and irreclaimable." He spoke broad Scots with a

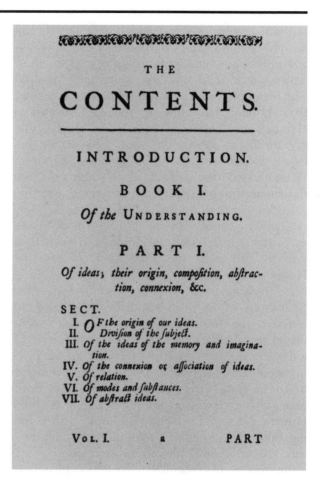

Page from Hume's first book, A Treatise of Human Nature, *written in France during 1734-1737*

rustic accent and could never feel at home in London. He stayed intermittently in London, for an amount of time that totalled only five years of his life. France was always his cultural home, and it was in France that his work was first appreciated. Hume's criticism of the chauvinism and backwardness that he perceived in the Whig literary and political establishment of England increased in violence as his career developed and was an important theme of the last decade of his life.

Hume returned to London in September 1737 to polish *A Treatise of Human Nature* and to look for a publisher. He cast the work in three books, one on the understanding, one on the passions, and one on morals. The first two were published early in 1739, the third late in 1740. The *Treatise*, as Hume said, "fell *dead-born from the press*." Although it was reviewed in scholarly journals in Britain, France, and Germany, the reviews showed no comprehension of the revolutionary philosophy Hume had worked out. The only favorable review was Hume's own, published anonymously in 1740 as *An Abstract of a Book Lately Published; Entitled, a Treatise of Human Nature, etc. Wherein the Chief Argument of That Book is Farther Illustrated and Explained.* Published in an edition of one thousand copies, the *Treatise* sold so poorly that the first edition was still being advertised in 1756, when Hume had achieved recognition as a writer.

Hume thought that the failure of the *Treatise* was due not to its content but to the manner in which it was written. But there was enough in the content itself to cause perplexity, for Hume sought to do two apparently inconsistent things in the *Treatise*: (1) he hoped to establish a universal science of human nature (the science of all sciences) on a secure foundation but (2) the foundation itself was supported only by a universal skepticism. This seemed to Hume's readers then and now as a case of building on quicksand. To this tension, if not contradiction, is added an ironic bantering tone characteristic of much of Hume's philosophical writing, which has led many to view Hume as a subversive thinker out to undermine commonsense beliefs in science, morals, and religion.

This was the interpretation of William Warburton, James Beattie, and John Stuart Mill. Many still read Hume this way. A heroic version of the negative, "subversive" reading is that, although Hume's thought ends in nihilism, it does so because Hume had the courage to carry the egocentric "way of ideas" of Descartes and John Locke to the bitter end. In doing so, he brilliantly exposes the limits of modern philosophy and opens the door to a deeper understanding. Hume is the Socratic gadfly of modern philosophy. This was the reading of Thomas Reid and Immanuel Kant.

The subversive reading, whether nihilistic or heroic, dominated until Norman Kemp Smith's *The Philosophy of David Hume* was published in 1941. Kemp Smith argued that the point of Hume's skepticism is to eliminate rationalism from critical thinking and to show that our deepest beliefs (in a world of causally connected objects independent of our perception, a self that remains the same over time, a moral order and the like) are determined by nonrational natural sources. The task of critical reflection is not to justify these beliefs; that is impossible since they are so fundamental that any purported justification would presuppose them. Kemp Smith concluded that Hume is not really a skeptic at all but a *naturalist*. Skepticism is merely a tool for showing us

what our inescapable natural beliefs are and these, not autonomous rational reflection, are the foundation of all critical thinking.

Kemp Smith's thesis that Hume is a naturalist was liberating. Its most important effect was that *A Treatise of Human Nature* could now be seen as a unity. Heretofore, philosophers had not gotten much beyond the skeptical arguments of book 1, which seemed to argue that objective thinking is impossible. If so, there seemed little point in trying to understand books 2 and 3, which abound in positive doctrines about the passions, morals, and government, many seeming to contradict fundamental doctrines of book 1 (for instance, in book 3 Hume insists that we have no idea of the self; in book 2 he says an idea of the self is ever present to us). In explaining the unity of *A Treatise of Human Nature* Kemp Smith enabled professional philosophers, for the first time, to read Hume as having positive doctrines of his own to teach.

Although the "subversive" reading of Hume lingers on, most commentary on Hume by philosophers is made through the broad interpretive framework provided by Kemp Smith. But that interpretation applied only to showing that the *Treatise* is a unity. The question remains of how to understand Hume's work as a whole: as epistemologist, philosopher of religion, and philosopher of the arts. In the last ten years an increasing number of books have been written exploring the full range of Hume's thought in all fields. And in the last twenty years more books have been written on Hume than in all years previously. Interest in Hume, as a philosopher, is now the greatest it has ever been.

Hume returned to Ninewells early in 1739 and remained there for the next six years. Though greatly disappointed at the failure of *A Treatise of Human Nature*, he immediately turned to recasting his thought in essay form. Within a year of publishing book 3 of the *Treatise*, he published the first volume of *Essays, Moral and Political*. A second volume appeared in 1742, and a revised edition of both volumes appeared in 1748. The *Essays* sold well. The first edition brought Hume one hundred and fifty to two hundred pounds, a welcome addition to his inheritance of around fifty pounds a year, on which he had been able to subsist, but nothing more. Bishop Joseph Butler, whose endorsement of the *Treatise* Hume had sought for in vain, warmly recommended the *Essays*. Henceforth Hume was to acknowledge himself as the author of his works.

A
LETTER
FROM A
GENTLEMAN
TO
His FRIEND in *Edinburgh*:

CONTAINING

Some OBSERVATIONS

ON

A Specimen of the Principles concerning
RELIGION and MORALITY,
said to be maintain'd in a Book lately publish'd, intituled, *A Treatise of Human
Nature*, &c.

EDINBURGH,
Pinted in the Year M. DCC. XLV.

*Title page for the pamphlet Hume wrote after he was refused
a position at the University of Edinburgh because* A Treatise
of Human Nature *was considered heterodox in matters
of religion*

He first did so in *Three Essays, Moral and Political* (1748), which was written to round off the second volume of *Essays, Moral and Political*. A third revised edition of both volumes as well as *Three Essays* was published in 1748 as *Essays, Moral and Political*. It was this edition that gained the unsolicited attention of the great Montesquieu, who wrote Hume a much welcomed letter of praise and encouragement. Hume entered the public world as an essayist.

In 1744 he sought and failed to secure the chair of moral philosophy at the University of Edinburgh. At a time when religious credentials were required for university posts, Hume's *Treatise of Human Nature* was considered religiously heterodox. This rejection called forth another anonymous pamphlet: *A Letter from a Gentleman to His Friend in Edinburgh* (1745), in which Hume tries to show that the principles of the *Treatise* logically pose no threat to religion and morality.

Though Hume's argument has seemed to many to be self-serving and disingenuous, there is no reason to doubt, as his later work shows, that he accepted the Pyrrhonian position that skepticism can accommodate itself with religious belief.

Having failed to secure the post at Edinburgh and being thirty-four, without a steady means of support other than his small annuity, Hume interrupted his studies at Ninewells early in 1745 to take a position as tutor to George, Marquess of Annandale, heir to one of the wealthiest families in Britain. The position paid three hundred pounds a year, and the duties were light, providing Hume with some leisure for writing and frequent visits to nearby London. It turned out, however, that the young marquess was mad, and Hume spent an unhappy year in the later stages of the marquess's breakdown. But the year was not without literary activity. Hume drafted a sixty-four-page sketch of the history of England from the Roman invasion to Henry II, a project he had entertained as early as the period of the *Treatise*. He also did work on the *Philosophical Essays Concerning Human Understanding*, which were published in 1748. These essays are a recasting of the epistemological issues dealt with in book 1 of the *Treatise*. The title was changed in 1758 to *An Enquiry Concerning Human Understanding*, a book which is today perhaps the most popular of Hume's philosophical writings. Hume also wrote three essays: "Of the Original Contract," "Of Passive Obedience," and "Of the Protestant Succession." These were written in response to the Jacobite rebellion which began July 1745, and ended with the massacre of the Highlanders at the Battle of Culloden 16 April 1746, the day Hume left the position at Annandale. The essays lay out the philosophical theories behind Jacobite claims for a restoration of the Stuarts as the legitimate regime and Whig claims about the legitimacy of the Glorious Revolution of 1688 and the present Hanoverian regime. Hume seeks to reconcile the issue by presenting the best case for each side, and also by showing that the practical behavior of both parties has more in common than their philosophical theories could allow. Hume had intended to publish all three of these essays in *Three Essays, Moral and Political*, but so violent was the Whig reaction to the Jacobite rebellion that he was persuaded to drop "Of the Protestant Succession" because of the strong case he had made there for the Jacobite cause. He substituted in its place "Of National Characters." This appears to be the first instance of what Hume felt as the oppressive hand of the Whig literary and political establishment. As a Scottish outsider (and a Whig of sorts himself), Hume sought the approval of the Whig establishment, but he became progressively alienated from it as his career developed.

Within a month after leaving Annandale, Hume accepted a position as secretary to his distant cousin Gen. James St. Clair, who was to command an expedition against the French in Canada. After months of ministerial indecision, St. Clair's troops were abruptly ordered to make an immediate diversionary raid on the coast of Brittany. They were forced to leave without adequate preparation, including maps (a tourist map was hastily purchased at a bookstore just as they left), and the invasion was an unrelieved disaster. The expedition to Canada was abandoned by the ministry in January of 1747. A year later Hume was again offered a position as secretary to St. Clair, this time on a secret military embassy to Vienna and Turin to persuade the queen of Austria and the king of Sardinia to keep their agreements to relieve British forces in Europe by invading southern France. Before leaving, he finished the *Philosophical Essays Concerning Human Understanding*. Although Hume enjoyed the mission, which lasted a little over a year, he had accepted it reluctantly and observed that it was the only extended period of his life in which his studies were disrupted. His two appointments with St. Clair, however, had increased his income to the point where he was now financially independent.

By the summer of 1749 Hume was back at Ninewells for two years of study and literary activity. A first draft of the *Dialogues Concerning Natural Religion* was completed, but the work did not see publication until 1779, three years after his death. He continued reading and note taking for his projected *History of England* and began recasting book 3 of *A Treatise of Human Nature* ("Of Morals") into what was to be published in 1751 as *An Enquiry Concerning the Principles of Morals*, a work which Hume judged by far his best. He also wrote another set of essays, *Political Discourses* (1752), which was his only book to be successful on first publication. It opened up his reputation at home and abroad.

Of the original twelve essays published in *Political Discourses*, eight have to do with issues in political economy: "Of Commerce," "Of Luxury," "Of Money," "Of Interest," "Of the Balance of Trade," "Of Taxes," "Of Public Credit," and "Of the Populousness of Ancient Nations." Hume argues for the public benefits of free trade and

Hume's brother, John Home of Ninewells (medallion by James Tassie, 1791; Scottish National Portrait Gallery)

against the mercantilists who urged state regulation of commerce and industry for the purpose of increasing the national supply of money. He argues that the wealth of a nation is not in the quantity of its money but in its people, their labor, ingenuity, and industry. In "Of Luxury" he challenges the popular view of those who thought that the emerging commercial society was decadent and longed for the rustic and virtuous simplicity of the ancient republics where people were governed by public spirit and not by the pursuit of private wealth. Hume observes that progress in knowledge, industry, and morals are internally connected and that modern commercial society is superior to ancient republics in political stability, humanity, and manners. In "Of the Populousness of Ancient Nations," he argues against the popular opinion that, because it was more virtuous, the ancient world was more populous. Hume contends that, under conditions of modern commercial society, the modern world is more populous and that if the mark of the virtue of a nation is a flourishing population, then modern commercial society is more virtuous than the societies of the ancient world. The debate about population and national virtue continued throughout the eighteenth century, culminating in Thomas Malthus's classical study *Essay on the Principles of Population* (1798). The basic principles of classical economics, which Hume's friend Adam Smith was to systematize in *The Wealth of Nations* (1776), are contained in Hume's *Political Discourses*.

The *Political Discourses* are also remarkable for the "Idea of a Perfect Commonwealth," in which Hume rejects the received opinion of ancient and modern political theory that republics are possible only in a small territory. Hume argues to the contrary that, although more difficult to establish, once a large commercial republic is established, it is not only possible but would be the best form of government. Hume then sketches out a federal hierarchy of republics within an extensive republic. It was this essay that encouraged Madison and Hamilton and helped to strengthen federalist arguments that a republic was possible in an extensive country such as America.

Due mainly to the increasing size of his brother's family, Hume left Ninewells for Edinburgh in the summer of 1751. Except for a year's stay in London (1758-1759) and a three-month jaunt to London in 1761, Hume remained in Edinburgh for the next twelve years. This was the most productive period of his career. When he left for London in 1763 to become secretary to the British embassy in Paris, his major literary work was complete.

In 1751 he again failed to secure a teaching post, this time the chair of logic at the University of Glasgow, recently vacated by Hume's friend Adam Smith, who had moved to the chair of moral philosophy. This position would have provided Hume with the library needed to begin writing his long-projected *History of England*, but this need was supplied the next year when Hume was elected by the Faculty of Advocates in Edinburgh as their librarian. He was now master of a library of thirty thousand volumes, but many were displeased with the appointment and trouble soon arose. Out of a list of seventy-four books Hume had purchased for the library, the curators ordered three to be removed from the shelves as too bawdy and frivolous for a learned library. Henceforth the responsibility of ordering books was taken out of Hume's hands and placed in the curators'. Though outraged and humiliated, Hume did not want to lose the use of the library. He saved face by retaining the office but giving

the blind poet Thomas Blacklock a bond of annuity for his salary of forty pounds a year.

Hume's reputation as a writer of European stature began in the early 1750s and grew with such rapidity that by 1757, after the death of Montesquieu in 1755, Hume's French translator, Abbé Jean-Bernard Le Blanc, could say that Hume was the only one in Europe who could replace Montesquieu. By 1764 Hume's London publisher, Andrew Millar, could take pride in telling a group of clergymen that he no longer numbered the editions of Hume's works because he considered them classics.

Although it was the *Political Discourses* that lifted Hume into the ranks of great European writers, his other philosophical writings had prepared the way. Within two years of publication, the *Political Discourses* had reached three editions, but *Philosophical Essays Concerning Human Understanding* was not far behind in reaching three editions within three years of its publication in 1748. Moreover, Hume began bringing out collected editions of his works in 1753 under the title *Essays and Treatises on Several Subjects*. The first edition was published in four volumes (1753), and the collection was in its fourth edition by 1764. It went through nine editions, including the posthumous edition of 1777, to which was prefixed an advertisement in which Hume repudiated *A Treatise of Human Nature* as a juvenile work and asked of the reader "that the following pieces may alone be regarded as containing his philosophical sentiments and principles." This repudiation was occasioned by James Beattie's *Essay on the Nature and Immutability of Truth*. Beattie, professor of moral philosophy and logic at Marischal College, Aberdeen, viewed Hume's philosophical writings as destructive of public morality and set out to refute those "unnatural productions, the vile effusion of a hard and stupid heart, that mistakes its own restlessness for the activity of genius, and its own captiousness for sagacity of understanding." Beattie was the first to launch the nihilistic, "subversive" reading of Hume. The work was enormously popular. Published in 1770, it went through five editions before Hume's death in 1776, earning the warm approval of Johnson, Burke, and George III, who awarded Beattie a pension of two hundred pounds a year.

Beattie's main object of abuse was *A Treatise of Human Nature*, as it was for others, such as Thomas Reid, who also believed Hume's philosophy to be subversive. Hume agreed that the style in which the *Treatise* was written made it vulnera-

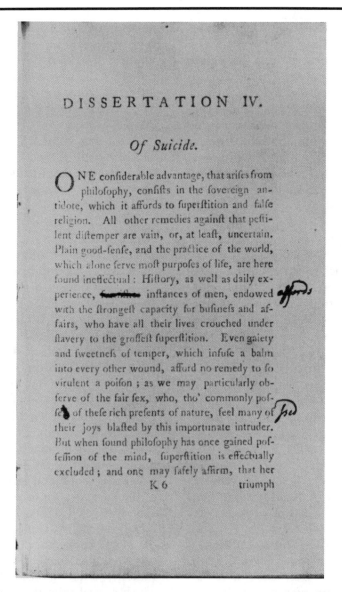

DISSERTATION IV.

Of Suicide.

ONE confiderable advantage, that arifes from philofophy, confifts in the fovereign antidote, which it affords to fuperftition and falfe religion. All other remedies againft that peftilent diftemper are vain, or, at leaft, uncertain. Plain good-fenfe, and the practice of the world, which alone ferve moft purpofes of life, are here found ineffectual: Hiftory, as well as daily experience, ~~furnifhes~~ inftances of men, endowed with the ftrongeft capacity for bufinefs and affairs, who have all their lives crouched under flavery to the groffeft fuperftition. Even gaiety and fweetnefs of temper, which infufe a balm into every other wound, afford no remedy to fo virulent a poifon; as we may particularly obferve of the fair fex, who, tho' commonly poffeff of thefe rich prefents of nature, feel many of their joys blafted by this importunate intruder. But when found philofophy has once gained poffeffion of the mind, fuperftition is effectually excluded; and one may fafely affirm, that her

K 6   triumph

Page from the printed sheets for the two dissertations that were suppressed from the book that was published in 1757 as Four Dissertations *(NLS, MS 509; National Library of Scotland). These sheets, with corrections in Hume's hand, are bound in Hume's copy of* Four Dissertations.

ble to such attack, and he described his public repudiation as "a compleat Answer to Dr. Reid and to that bigoted silly Fellow, Beattie." Although Hume never rejected the philosophical content of the *Treatise*, it is still true that he considered the *Essays and Treatises on Several Subjects* to be the more mature and better expression of his philosophical thinking. But most commentators have not followed him. One reason is that until fairly recently twentieth-century philosophers, especially in the English-speaking world, have worked within a fairly narrow conception of philosophy as a form of linguistic analysis. Being a systematic and fairly technical work, the *Treatise* has seemed a more congenial object to this way of thinking.

The result has been that some of the later philosophical works have not been perceived as *philosophical* works at all. Although this narrow conception of philosophy is not as popular as it once was, it will still be helpful in understanding Hume's philosophical achievement to make a brief comparison of the broad philosophical project of the *Treatise* with the later philosophical works.

This later philosophy was complete by 1757, with the publication of *Four Dissertations*, which were included in the 1758 edition and in all succeeding editions of *Essays and Treatises*. The four dissertations are "A Dissertation on the Passions," a vapid recasting of book 2 of *A Treatise of*

Human Nature ("Of the Passions"); "Of Tragedy" and "Of the Standard of Taste," two works which probably would have appeared in a projected, but unwritten, fourth book of the *Treatise* on criticism; and *The Natural History of Religion*, one of the early attempts in modern times to examine religion as a purely natural phenomenon. Hume had intended to title this volume "Five Dissertations" and to include "Of Suicide" and "Of Immortality." In "Of Suicide" he argues that natural reason does not prohibit suicide, nor do the scriptures. In "Of Immortality" he argues that natural reason provides no support for belief in immortality and that its sole support is in the revelation of the scriptures. "Five Dissertations" got to the stage of page proofs, which were read by Rev. William Warburton, who found parts of *The Natural History of Religion* and the two essays blasphemous and was able to prevail upon Hume, through his publisher, to suppress the two essays. They were replaced by "Of the Standard of Taste." Hume also made some slight changes in *The Natural History of Religion*, but not enough to satisfy Warburton, who published a blistering anonymous pamphlet: *Remarks on Mr. David Hume's Essay on the Natural History of Religion: Addressed to the Rev. Dr. Warburton* (1757).

Hume's later philosophy, published under the title *Essays and Treatises on Several Subjects*, was complete in one collection by 1758. It can be conveniently divided into three sets of works: (1) recasting of the three books of *A Treatise of Human Nature* as *An Enquiry Concerning Human Understanding* (the new title for *Philosophical Essays Concerning Human Understanding*), *A Dissertation on the Passions*, and *An Enquiry Concerning the Principles of Morals*; (2) *Essays Moral, Political, and Literary* (in which Hume combined the *Essays, Moral and Political* with the *Political Discourses* and "Of Tragedy" and "Of the Standard of Taste" taken from the *Four Dissertations*); and (3) *The Natural History of Religion*. The *Essays and Treatises* passed through nine editions, including a posthumous edition (1777) containing Hume's last revisions. Although Hume made frequent changes in these editions, most of the revisions are of a literary nature and none suggests a change in philosophical doctrine. To these works we may add the posthumously published *Dialogues Concerning Natural Religion*, "Of Suicide," and "Of Immortality," all of which Hume had intended to publish in the 1750s. In bulk the works of Hume's later philosophy are twice that of *A Treatise of Human Nature*, which runs some six hundred pages. Though the

philosophical principles of the *Treatise* and these later works are the same, there are important differences in style, rhetoric, and purpose. To appreciate how the later works are continuous with, yet different from, the *Treatise*, a brief statement of its central teaching concerning the nature of philosophy is required.

We may think of empiricism as philosophy which, having turned critical reflection on itself, discovers that knowledge is limited somehow to the sense or to introspection of consciousness. Locke, George Berkeley, and Hume are viewed as the triumvirate of modern empiricism, with Hume being the most radical of the three. But what is distinctive about Hume is not the radical character of his empiricism, but the radical character of his criticism of critical reflection itself. For Hume is the only one of the three to call himself a skeptic. Thus, it is questionable whether Hume should be considered an empiricist at all. But Hume is not a nihilistic skeptic; nor is he a methodological skeptic in the Cartesian sense of doubting all in order to discover what cannot be doubted. Hume's skepticism draws its inspiration from the ancient Greek skeptics, whose skepticism implies not doubt but *skeptikos*: unusually rigorous and determined inquiry about the good life. Though tailored to fit modern conditions of belief and sentiment, Hume's skepticism, like that of the ancients, is a form of wisdom.

In book 1 of the *Treatise* Hume used skeptical arguments to explode a fundamental principle of the entire ancient and modern philosophical tradition, namely that critical reflection is radically autonomous. The domain relative to which critical reflection is supposed to be autonomous is that unreflectively received order of opinion which Hume calls habit, custom, sentiment, prejudice, but most often common life. In this prereflective order (and Hume sought to show that we all inhabit this order), one follows a particular custom or tradition not because it is right but because it is the custom or tradition. If we say of a custom that it is followed because it is right, we are not acting out of custom as such but out of critical reflection. The only reason custom can give for following a custom is that it is the custom.

Now it is precisely this reflective order of existence from which the philosophical tradition has sought to emancipate itself and in opposition to which the autonomy of philosophical reason must be understood. Descartes is called the father of modern philosophy because he made especially clear what the autonomy of philosophical reflection means: methodologically, the entire unreflective order of custom is to be considered false until proven otherwise. This or that custom is to be considered false until proven otherwise. This or that custom may be rescued but only after certification by critical philosophical principles framed in a philosophical vacuum independent of all custom. This methodological principle of the autonomy of philosophical reflection has seemed overwhelmingly reasonable, not only to modern rationalists but to most of the Western philosophical tradition. For the alternative seems to be acceptance of some favorite prereflective custom at the beginning of inquiry, and that would turn philosophy into the handmaiden of theology, politics, or whatever the favored prejudice might be.

The skeptical arguments of book 1 of *A Treatise of Human Nature* assume the radical autonomy of philosophical reflection, but what Hume discovered is that if philosophical reflection is emancipated from the entire prereflective order, its critical principles will be vacuous. There would be no nonarbitrary way to apply them to the world. With a little logical ingenuity anything could be shown to confirm or disconfirm them. The result must be total skepticism. Philosophical autonomy, therefore, far from being self-certifying, subverts itself.

Philosophers, however, seldom end in skepticism because of a massive self-deception. They do not consistently follow the principle of radical autonomy but unknowingly smuggle in some favorite prejudice or custom which gives content to and hides what would otherwise be an entirely vacuous way of thinking. But this secret work of custom is never acknowledged; instead philosophers pompously display their custom-laden principles as the work of autonomous reason, unspotted by custom or what they are pleased to call prejudice. The point of Hume's skepticism is to expose this self-deception and to reform our conception of rational autonomy. Hume affirms what might be called the autonomy of custom: henceforth critical reflection must acknowledge the independent authority of prereflective custom. Any particular custom within the prereflective order can be criticized in the light of other customs and in the light of principles, models, and ideals abstracted from that order; but these principles must themselves bear the imprint of some particular order of custom. What must be ruled out, on pain of total skepticism or self-deception, is the attempt to frame critical principles independent of the prereflective domain of custom as a whole.

Hume did not see this as a form of philistinism or as a defense of irrationalism, though, of course, many have read him this way. On the contrary it was by assuming the strongest and most radical form of philosophical autonomy that Hume was able to win through to a criticism of it. The lesson is that there is no escaping the custom-laden character of human thought, even in philosophy, and that philosophers simply deceive themselves and others by not frankly acknowledging it. Critical reflection that recognizes this, Hume calls "true philosophy"; that which is still lost in the self-deception of a vain autonomy, he calls "false philosophy."

The philosophy framed in *A Treatise of Human Nature* has a positive, critical task and a negative, pathological task. The pathological task is to expose and to explain the illusions of a false philosophical reflection. The positive task is to bring to self-consciousness the prereflective customs of common life and to methodize and correct them. Hume understood common life to be an order of conventions. But he did not think of conventions as the result of conscious agreement. Humean conventions are prereflective and evolve spontaneously over time to satisfy human needs. The paradigm of a convention is language. The English language is not the result of conscious contrivance. No one planned or intended it; yet it is the work of men, and, through reflection, its rules, grammatical and aesthetic, can be brought to the level of critical awareness. The entire domain of human action can be viewed as a set of just such spontaneously evolving conventions: language, morals, government, art, science, religion. The task of true philosophy is to bring these to critical self-awareness and, since they are often in conflict, to render them mutually coherent.

There are several important differences between *A Treatise of Human Nature* and the later works. In the *Treatise* Hume had worked out a universal theory of the association of ideas to explain the origin and mechanism of human conventions of belief and sentiment. Although Hume never abandoned the possibility of such a theory, and, indeed, mentions it as a possibility in *An Enquiry Concerning Human Understanding* and in *Dissertation on the Passions*, he never again used it. Instead of adopting the stance of a theoretical *spectator* of human conventions, Hume adopts the position of a critical *participant* in the conventions themselves. Instead of trying to explain the deep

Engraving by S. C. Miger (1764), from a profile by Charles-Nicholas Cochin the Younger

causes underlying conventions, Hume sought to critically understand the rules, roles, and rationales of the conventions as understood by participants. He expressed this in *An Enquiry Concerning Human Understanding* as "mental geography"; that is, a study of the contours of the convention's surface rather than a study of a causal mechanism hidden from experience. This project of "unmasking" the surface of a convention by exposing its hidden causal structure occupied social and political theoreticians such as Antoine-Nicholas de Condorcet, Charles Fourier, Karl Marx, and Sigmund Freud. Hume was content to investigate the "surface" of the convention, that is, the rules and roles that participants spontaneously and unreflectively play out as participants, and he makes clearer in *An Enquiry Concerning Human Understanding* than he did in *A Treatise of Human Nature* that this is what he considers true philosophy to be: "philosophical decisions are nothing but the reflections of common life, methodized and corrected."

The move from theoretical spectator to critical participant is not merely a shift of emphasis but points the way to a change in methodology. Since the world of human conventions is made by men, men are capable of having a special understanding of this world which they cannot have

of the physical world. This is very like the doctrine of Giambattista Vico in the *New Science* (1725), that the true is the made: *verum et factum convertuntur*. To know something really as opposed to being merely a spectator of it is to have made it. Only God can know the world because he alone made it, but the historical world was made by man, so man can have genuine knowledge of it. On this view of knowledge the distinction between appearance and reality—so crucial to the theoretical spectator who is out to uncover the hidden structures of things—collapses. The Italian language, for example, really is whatever Italian speakers think it is. The special sort of knowledge that comes from participation in conventions (either directly or empathetically) rather than from speculation about them is affirmed by Hume in the *Essays Moral, Political, and Literary*: "though an appeal to general opinion may justly, in the speculative sciences of metaphysics, natural philosophy, or astronomy, be deemed unfair and inconclusive, yet in all questions with regard to morals, as well as criticism, there is really no other standard, by which any controversy can ever be decided." Like Vico, Hume held that the human sciences are more intelligible than the natural sciences. In *An Enquiry Concerning the Principles of Morals*, he contrasts natural science with "the practical and more intelligible sciences of politics and morals." The doctrine, first broached by Vico and Hume, that the human sciences frame a different sort of intelligibility than that of the natural sciences and so require a different sort of intelligibility than that of the natural sciences and so require a different methodology is an object of considerable debate today.

Another important difference between the later philosophical works and *A Treatise of Human Nature* is in rhetoric. The *Treatise* was cast in the form of a theoretical system, and is highly abstract and tightly reasoned. The author avoids the arts of persuasion and seeks to create a voice like that of a diffident Platonic spectator, willing to follow the argument wherever it leads. The systematic and abstract form drops out of the later works in favor of the essay, dialogue, and narrative. The later works are also more concrete. Philosophy proceeds more by description and examples, historical and fanciful, than by abstract reasoning. The rhetorical voice of the later works is that of a critical participant out to persuade other participants rather than the more detached tone of the treatise.

A moral and political mission informs much of the later writings. In the *Essays, Moral, Political and Literary*, political philosophy is not discussed merely in the abstract but in the context of British and European politics. In *An Enquiry Concerning the Principles of Morals* and in the *Essays*, ethics is not treated as an abstract science in search of a supreme moral principle, as modern moral philosophers tend to treat it, but as the question of what virtues one should develop. This was how the ancients thought of ethics, and in the essays "The Platonist," "The Stoic," and "The Sceptic," Hume explores the ancient question of what constitutes the good life. He defends an updated version of the wisdom of the ancient skeptics: a frank recognition of the limits of philosophical reflection, purged of custom, either to understand life or to guide it and, in light of this, reliance upon inclination, instinct, and that moderate critical reflection which works within custom and tradition and which Hume, in *A Treatise of Human Nature*, calls "true philosophy."

One task of true philosophy is to show how a false critical reflection can constrict and distort experience. This pathological task is a main source of the practical rhetoric of the later works. For example, *An Enquiry Concerning Human Understanding* is usually read as a recasting of the epistemological issues of book 1 of *A Treatise of Human Nature* ("Of the Understanding"), but it is much more than this. From beginning to end it is an attack on how religious philosophers undermine and distort common experience. In the first pages Hume isolates the object of the exercise: those religious philosophers who threaten to break in upon "every unguarded avenue of the mind, and overwhelm it with religious fears and prejudices." In the last, well-known paragraph of the book, he recommends, as the lesson of the whole, that we commit the books of these philosophers to the flames. A similar attack against religious philosophy runs throughout the *Essays, Moral, Political, and Literary*. Of special mention are "Of Superstition and Enthusiasm," which charts the baneful effects that traditionalistic Catholicism and Anglicanism (superstition) and puritanical Protestantism (enthusiasm) have on society and shows how, as natural phenomena, the civil magistrate may manipulate them to good use. In "Of National Characters," Hume analyzes the character of the clergy as a sociological type, arguing that hypocrisy is psychologically built into the very social role and character of the clergy and is one of its permanent liabilities. In

two chapters of *An Enquiry Concerning Human Understanding*, "Of a Particular Providence" (which contains the germ of the argument developed in the *Dialogues Concerning Natural Religion*) and "Of Miracles" (which was written during the period of *A Treatise of Human Nature* but not published in it) Hume undercut the possibility of any rational foundation for religious belief. "Of a Particular Providence" argues against the view of enlightened theists that inductive arguments from analogy can support belief in a providential deity. "Of Miracles" argues against proponents of revealed religion that the argument from human testimony is not by itself sufficient to establish the occurrence of a miracle (such as the Resurrection) which could be the foundation of a religious system.

The Natural History of Religion argues that the religious mind first arose out of fear and anxiety. Relief is sought by attempts to placate the intelligent invisible powers which are thought to be the cause of human misfortune. Humean psychology is such that the invisible powers must be thought of as having sensory properties, and so polytheism was the first religion. Theism evolves out of polytheism, not by rational reflection but by exalting one's particular deity over others to the point where it is thought of as being free of all sensory limits. But men cannot long contemplate a purely spiritual being, and so they create an order of sensory beings that mediate between man and the deity. These gradually usurp the devotion due to the theistic deity, and the swing begins back to polytheism only to be reversed at some point in the direction of theism. The lesson is that the religious mind is more concerned with the proper conceptualization of the deity and its own anxiety than it is with reason and morality.

The Natural History of Religion is a study of the psychology of popular religion. In Hume's picture of it, popular religion is the poison of society and resembles more the playsome whimsies of monkeys in human shape than serious endeavor. The case is otherwise with what Hume calls "pure theism," which arises not from fear but from an admiration of the order of the universe and which supports the sentiment of humanity and morals. Hume accepts a religion of this sort in *The Natural History of Religion* and in the *Dialogues Concerning Natural Religion*, though he does not think it could ever extend to more than an enlightened few and could never be institutionalized. Indeed, he observes in *The Natural History of Religion* that should such a secular moral religion ever become institutionalized, the interests of the institution itself and not reason and morality would be the chief concern of its adherents.

In the *Dialogues Concerning Natural Religion* Hume examines the belief, common to enlightened clergyman of his time, that at least a minimal form of theism admits of scientific proof. The question is explored by three characters: Demea, Cleanthes, and Philo. Hume allows the question to unfold dialectically, and he does so with such skill that it is difficult to say that any character represents entirely Hume's own view, though most have thought that the skeptic Philo comes closest. The *Dialogues Concerning Natural Religion* teach that there is no scientific support for even a minimal theism, but that such a belief naturally arises in men who have acquired the habit of viewing the universe in a scientific way. Philosophical theism, then, is no worse off than other fundamental beliefs, for, as Hume taught in *A Treatise of Human Nature* and in *An Enquiry Concerning Human Understanding*, our deepest beliefs, including those foundational to scientific thinking (that there are physical objects causally connected, and that there is a self identical over time) are incapable of rational support but arise spontaneously from nonrational sources.

Hume's attack on popular religion has a family resemblance to that of Enlightenment thinkers such as Voltaire and Hume's friends Paul Thiry, Baron d'Holbach; Denis Diderot; and Jean le Rond d'Alembert, but Hume differed from them in an important respect. The philosophes tended to view religion as the poison of society, the antidote of which is critical philosophical reflection. Religion, custom, and tradition are sources of darkness; philosophy is the source of light. Hume's distinction, within philosophy, between true and false forms of philosophical reflection never occurred to them. Yet as early as *A Treatise of Human Nature* Hume had argued that false philosophical reflection could alienate one from common life and pose as great a threat to society as religion. This thesis is expanded in the *Essays, Moral, Political, and Literary*, *An Enquiry Concerning Human Understanding*, and *An Enquiry Concerning the Principles of Morals*.

In the essay "Of Parties in General," Hume argues that the relation of religion and philosophy to society has not always been the same. In the ancient world, prior to the existence of philosophy, religion was polytheistic and consisted mainly of sacred stories that bound a community together; religions were different without being contrary; religious persecution was uncommon; and a spirit of religious pluralism prevailed. Fanaticism appeared when philosophy entered the scene. The reason is that philosophy is an inquiry that makes claims about what is thought to be ultimate reality. These claims are tested not by the social criterion of a tradition but by the autonomous reason of the individual thinker who must think of himself as deciding what is true not only for himself but for everyone else. As Plato taught, the very idea of philosophical inquiry entails that philosophers should be kings. And so Hume observes: "Sects of philosophy, in the ancient world, were more zealous than parties of religion." They caused less trouble to society because they were safely constrained to the private sector by the pagan civic religion, but, when Christianity appeared in the world, philosophy was well established, and the new religion was obliged to take on philosophic shape in order to defend itself among the learned. Christianity soon became the state religion, and the philosophical antagonism that had been confined to the private sphere by the civic pagan religion entered the public domain. In modern times the specifically philosophical element in Christianity has become more insistent and is in large part responsible for the "religious" wars that have racked Europe. When Hume attacks what he calls "modern religion," he always has in mind religion informed by a philosophical system.

The unholy union of Christianity and philosophy means that a rudimentary philosophical consciousness has existed throughout Christendom. In the Enlightenment the philosophical content of religion was coming more and more to the surface as religion demanded not only faith but philosophical respectability as well. Philosophical reflection, for good or ill, was becoming a mass phenomenon. One result was the emergence of a new kind of political party, one governed not by affection or interests but by metaphysical principle. Hume considered such parties unique to modern times, and he may lay claim to being one of the first critics of modern political ideologies: "Parties from *principle*, especially abstract speculative principle, are known only to modern times, and are, perhaps, the most extraordinary and unaccountable *phenomenon*, that has yet appeared in human affairs." In "Of the Original Contract" Hume laments the fact that "no party, in the present age, can well support itself, without a philosophical or speculative system of principles, annexed to its political or practical one." As his career developed, Hume began to see that critical philosophical reflection, crude though it may be, was entering public affairs. In *A Treatise of Human Nature* he had distinguished between true and false forms of critical philosophical reflection, showing how false philosophical reflection alienates from and distorts common experience. But in his later philosophical works this distinction takes on the shape of a moral and political mission: to purge public discourse of false philosophical consciousness in both its religious and secular forms. As a spokesman for the Enlightenment, Hume's criticism went deeper than that of the philosophes, for he saw clearly, as they did not, that the critical intellect itself could become a source of darkness as well as light.

The later works also manifest the positive task of true philosophy, namely the understanding of human conventions from the point of view of a critical participant. *An Enquiry Concerning Human Understanding* explores the convention of causal judgment, tracing it back to a nonrational psychological disposition, which men share with animals, to expect that constant conjunctions in experience will continue. Men, however, are reflective and, if purged of the illusion-making character of false philosophy, can, by trial and error, refine the judgments generated by this disposition into a science. *An Enquiry Concerning the Principles of Morals* explores the convention of morality, arguing that virtue reduces to qualities of character which are useful and agreeable to ourselves and others. In treating morality as a study of virtue, Hume was, and knew himself to be, running counter to the dominant method in moral philosophy. That method is to establish a supreme rule to guide conduct where the rule is established independent of the authority of established moral conventions. The paradigmatic modern examples here are Immanuel Kant, who sought an a priori ground for the moral rule, and John Stuart Mill, who sought an empirical ground. For both, virtue is peripheral to morals and is to be explained by the rule. But for Hume virtue is a set of dispositions rooted in established conventions and recognized by participants. On this view moral rules are derived from the virtues and not the other way. For Hume, moral thought, like all thought, is inescapably custom laden, though, as he takes great pains to show, this is compatible with objectivity. The modern liberal doctrine that there is a neutral point of view independent of custom from which to frame moral principles, though dominant, no longer has the grip it once had.

Since all standards are custom laden, Hume's conception of true philosophy requires a historical understanding of human conventions, and he was the first philosopher in modern times to give serious consideration to the historicity of human conventions. Hume's insights were first published in the *Essays, Moral, Political, and Literary* and are scattered throughout rather than systematically organized in particular essays. He makes the point that conventions evolve spontaneously, with little conscious reflection, and that much of the irony and tragedy of human existence is due to the fact that fundamental changes in conventions occur without participants being aware of what is happening. Although historians with hindsight can appreciate the ironies and tragedies of the past, no one can know what deep changes are or are not going on now. From this radical ignorance arise several historical illusions: that the present is a time of decline; that the present is merely the embryo of a new age that is dawning; and that attempts to preserve present forms are futile. Hume rejected the thesis defended by his friend Anne-Robert-Jacques Turgot (and by such later thinkers as Condorcet, Fourier, Auguste Comte, and Marx) that radical historical ignorance can be eliminated by discovering laws of history which would enable us to know in what direction the order of human conventions is evolving. In several of the *Essays, Moral, Political, and Literary* but especially in "Of Civil Liberty," "Whether the British Government Inclines More to Absolute Monarchy or to a Republic," and "Of Some Remarkable Customs," Hume warns against the attempt to discover the laws of history. The beginning of political wisdom is a frank recognition that radical historical ignorance cannot be overcome. The only remedy is moderation in politics and a deep historical understanding of the order of conventions in which one is a participant. This demand for historical self-knowledge, though implied in the philosophy of *A Treatise of Human Nature*, is one of the most important developments of Hume's later philosophical work.

Though laws of history are impossible, one can discover trends in the evolving conventions of which one is a part. In the *Essays, Moral, Political, and Literary* Hume seeks to make his readers aware of new conventions that have been emerging in the modern world over the last century or so: civil liberty and the rule of law, new economic relations which give promise of expanding wealth and prosperity to even poor countries, greater stability in government, a greater sense of humanity, and greater refinement in taste and the arts. Hume develops a rudimentary sociology of knowledge, arguing that improvements in commerce, manufacturing, science, morals, and the arts are internally connected: "We cannot reasonably expect, that a piece of woollen cloth will be wrought to perfection in a nation, which is ignorant of astronomy, or where ethics are neglected." Much of what Hume wrote in the *Essays* is a celebration of these emerging modern conventions which, he argues, are superior to those of the ancients in nearly every respect. In this he ran counter to a powerful current in his time, for many, including Jean-Jacques Rousseau, longed for the greater simplicity, integrity, and public spirit which they imagined to exist in the ancient republics. Hume, however, was no progressive in the nineteenth-century sense. In a frank exchange of correspondence with Turgot, Hume strongly criticized Turgot's belief in perpetual progress. His task was to bring these emerging modern conventions to self-awareness, explain their origins, how they work, what values they yield, and how they may be corrected. Throughout, Hume stresses the fragility of modern conventions, the fact that they are mostly the unintended consequences of acts, and how easily they may be lost by false historical and philosophical conceptions which distort and transform them into something they are not.

The Western philosophical tradition has had little place for history. Aristotle put it nicely when he said that poetry, being concerned with the universal, is more profound than history, which is concerned with the particular. Hume's *Treatise of Human Nature* has been typically viewed by philosophers as an ahistorical work, so it has seemed necessary to explain why Hume wrote *The History of England*. A popular explanation is that, having reached a skeptical impasse in the *Treatise* and having failed to gain public attention, Hume turned from philosophy to writing history for the purpose of achieving literary fame, which, Hume himself admitted, was his ruling passion. That this explanation will not do should now be obvious. Hume's distinction between true and false philosophy was aimed at the prevailing philosophical tradition, both ancient and modern. The reformation of philosophy proposed in the *Treatise* logically demands historical self-knowledge, but it is only in his later philosophical works that scattered attempts are made to provide such a reformation. Hume and Vico were

the first modern philosophers to conceive of philosophical understanding in such a way as to require historical knowledge. That Hume should write history should not appear surprising, and, as observed earlier, he had thought of writing a history of England as early as the period of the *Treatise* and actually wrote a sketch of English history in 1745.

After taking the position as keeper of the Advocates' Library in 1752, Hume immediately began his long *History of England*, the first volume of which was published in 1754. It covers the reigns of James I and Charles I. Reception was hostile, and it came from many quarters. In the first five weeks about 450 copies were sold in Edinburgh alone, but then sales dropped to 45 more for the entire year. It seemed to Hume that he had alienated almost everyone, and he was initially discouraged about continuing. But by 1757 he had published a second volume covering the Commonwealth, Cromwell's Protectorate, and the reigns of Charles II and James II. Hume then had to decide whether to bring the *History* up to the present or to write about pre-Stuart periods. He chose the latter, partly because he dreaded the political controversy that would be sure to arise if the *History* were brought closer to the present, but also because the materials necessary for a later history were centered in and around London, much of it in the family houses of the great Whig magnates, who would not be inclined to allow access to materials for the sort of history Hume might write. In 1759 Hume published two more volumes, carrying the *History* back through the house of Tudor. By 1762 the *History* was complete back to the invasion of Julius Caesar and was published in a complete edition in six volumes under the title *The History of England, from the Invasion of Julius Caesar to the Revolution of 1688*.

Despite the initial hostility to the first volume, the *History* sold well. By October of 1764, Hume's publisher Andrew Millar could report that about twenty-five hundred full sets of the quarto edition (1762), more than three thousand of the two Stuart volumes, and nearly two thousand of the octavo edition (1763) had been sold. The full set of *The History of England* went through 6 editions during Hume's lifetime, a posthumous one (1778) including his last corrections, and 175 later editions.

Two themes run throughout the *History*, both of which were first broached in the *Essays, Moral, Political, and Literary*. One is the story of

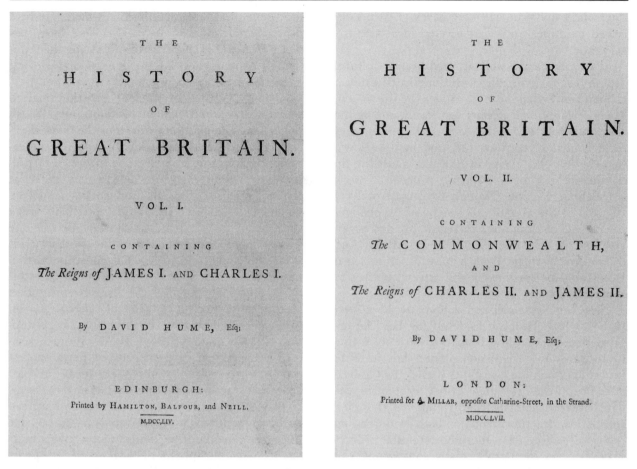

Title pages for the first two volumes of Hume's history, which presented a major challenge to the dominant Whig ideology in eighteenth-century Great Britain (courtesy of Special Collections, Thomas Cooper Library, University of South Carolina)

the rise of civilization in Britain—that is, the slow and painful evolution of those conventions and manners which make up the modern world, especially the convention of civil liberty. But the *History* is also a polemical work. In it Hume carries on a running battle with the Whig literary and political establishment, which had dominated British opinion since the late seventeenth century.

Hume thought that Whig ideology was moralistic, ahistorical, chauvinistic, and barbarous. It was a popular Whig view that the present constitution was simply a reenactment of an ancient constitution that stretched back to the Saxon forests. For them the story of English history was the story of attempts to overthrow the constitution by unpatriotic factions of all kinds, but especially in recent times by the Stuart kings. In the Glorious Revolution of 1688, the English again *restored* the ancient constitution as their ancestors before them had done. Along with this perception of an ancient liberty-loving English constitution went a

view of the Continent, and especially of France, as in a condition of slavery. Civil liberty, the Whigs believed, was a unique possession of the English and part of the national character. Some thought that the English had retained something like the manly virtue of the ancient republics. But that virtue was in danger of being lost because of the corrupting influences of the Continent. Thus the zealous Whig writer Catherine Macaulay, whose *History of England* (1763-1783) was written to counter Hume's, complained that British education does not train youth in the principles of free government. After they study a little Greek and Latin literature, she charged, their education is finished off with "what is called the tour of Europe, that is a residence for two or three years in the countries of France and Italy. This is the finishing stroke that renders them useless to all the good purposes of preserving the birthright of an Englishman." They soon become "caught with the gaudy tinsel of a superb court, the frolic levity of unreflecting slaves, and thus deceived by appearances, are riveted in a taste for servitude."

As a Scotsman who admired French culture, Hume had no sympathy with this sort of English chauvinism. What he had argued in the *Essays, Moral, Political, and Literary* (especially in "Of the Rise and Progress of the Arts and Sciences" and in "Of Civil Liberty") is reflected in his *History*, namely that civil liberty in England is just the tip of the iceberg of a civilizing process at work throughout Europe. Though the public political rhetoric of the absolute monarchy of France and the regime of Britain are different, life and property are as secure in France as in Britain. And the relatively rustic English have much to learn from the superior literary and artistic cultures of France and Italy.

In the first-published volume of the *History* (1754), which Hume considered the best, he argued that James I and Charles I were not trying to subvert an ancient constitution but were in fact defending the constitution they had inherited. Both were imprudent in not recognizing the gap between their inherited rights and changing conditions, but the actions of both in defending the constitution were morally defensible. Moreover, Charles even made many concessions, but the Puritans, though they talked of restoring their liberties, were not really interested in having grievances satisfied or reforms made in the constitution. The satisfaction of each demand produced a new one in a process governed by the inexorable logic of a theological ideal. For Hume the Puritans were not heroic patriots rescuing the constitution from the wicked designs of the Stuarts but revolutionaries out to establish a totally new order. They were motivated not by eighteenth-century concepts of civil liberty and the rule of law but by the most fanatical sort of bigotry, something that could not be placated by legal reforms. Ironically, the Puritans unintentionally jarred events into the shape of what was to be the eighteenth-century constitution of liberty—that envy of the world which Hume himself celebrated. So, ironically mimicking Whig panegyric, Hume could speak of the "wisdom of the English constitution, or rather the concurrence of accidents." Hume, therefore, grants to the Puritans a certain external narrative dignity because of the beneficent unintended consequences of their actions. But it was Charles, with all his faults, who possessed internal moral dignity and courage. In the Stuart volumes of the *History*, Hume exposed the general historical illusion which Herbert Butterfield made famous in *The Whig Interpretation of History* (1931): the error of reading the unintended consequences of the actions of historical agents back into their intentions.

The doctrine of ancient constitutionalism sets up a paranoid view of contemporary British politics, for the political world must be divided exclusively between those who threaten to undermine the constitution and those who seek to preserve it. All acts, events, and issues must be shaped by this scheme, including whatever evolving novelties may occur. Hume sought to break the grip of this doctrine by showing that, if one traces English history back to the Roman invasion, one finds not one ancient constitution that has evolved but at least four distinct constitutions. Hume agreed that the British constitution is the most perfect system of liberty known (though he doubted its stability). But his conception of it was quite different. He saw it not as a sacred reenactment of the deeds of heroic ancestors but the largely unintended result of past actions, a fragile instrument washed up by the interplay of contingent events and human nature—an instrument which, if cultivated, made possible unprecedented improvements in knowledge, morals, the arts, and prosperity. All could be lost by a failure in historical self-knowledge: by a paranoid reading of the past and present which, ironically, threatened to destroy the constitution of liberty in the name of liberty.

In 1763, a year after the completion of the *History*, Hume received an invitation from Francis Seymour Conway, Earl of Hertford, the new ambassador to France, to accompany him as his personal secretary. The religious animosity he experienced in Scotland, culminating in a move by the General Assembly of the Church of Scotland to excommunicate him, as well as the snobbery and growing anti-Scots sentiment in England following the Jacobite uprisings, inclined Hume to France, whose culture he had always admired and where he had written his first book.

Hume's works were well known in France, and upon arrival he was warmly greeted, became an idol in society, and a coveted member of the salons. Hume's appearance was not calculated to inspire such affection. He was tall and had become fat. In physical movements he was not graceful; he spoke with a rustic Scottish accent, and his spoken French was worse than his English. But he had a disarmingly naive, generous, and affectionate nature which women especially found charm-

Hume during his 1763-1766 stay in Paris (portrait by Carmontelle; Scottish National Portrait Gallery)

ing. He established many lasting friendships in France; among these were such well-known philosophes as Baron d'Holbach, d'Alembert, Diderot, and Turgot. Because of his good nature, he eventually became known among the French and throughout Europe as *le bon* David. While in France a love affair developed between Hume and Marie-Charlotte-Hippolyte de Campel de Saujéon, Comtesse de Boufflers-Rouverel, mistress of Louis-François de Bourbon, the Prince de Conti. But Hume was afraid to lose his independence, and Madame de Boufflers had ambitions to marry the prince; the relationship ripened into a lifelong friendship.

Hume was presented to the French court and met the young prince who was to become Louis XVI. He was only ten years old and amused Hume by shyly confessing himself to be an admirer of Hume's *History of England*. Throughout his life, Louis XVI was a close student of Hume and his *History*. As the Revolution gathered, he became obsessed with parallels between himself and Charles I. His secretary records that upon receiving the death sentence, he asked for Hume's volume on the death of Charles I. French conservatives, in the aftermath of the Revolution, used Hume's *History*, not Edmund Burke's *Reflections on the Revolution in France*, to understand what had happened. It was easy for them to see parallels between the destructive effects of Puritan revolutionary ideology and that of the Jacobins, between Charles I and Louis XVI, and between such revolutionary leaders as Cromwell and Robespierre. Hume's *History*

Hume and Jean-Jacques Rousseau, circa 1766, before Rousseau formed the paranoid delusion that Hume had brought him to England and secured him a royal pension only to discredit him

earned him the title of the "Scottish Bossuet" among the Catholic right in France.

Hume became embassy secretary in 1765 and on Lord Hertford's departure became chargé d'affaires in the few months that remained before a new ambassador arrived. Hume left for England in February 1766, taking with him Jean-Jacques Rousseau, whose writings had provoked increasing opposition by French and Genevan authorities. Hume found a country retreat in Derbyshire to satisfy Rousseau's desire for solitude and succeeded in securing, from the crown, a pension of a hundred pounds a year. From the first Rousseau had been loath to go to England.

He did not like the English, and he was suspicious of Hume, a man who actually liked the salons and the philosophes. Hume's naïveté, sociability, and vacant stare only aroused Rousseau's suspicion. The fear of persecution, which was to darken the remaining eight years of Rousseau's life, surfaced in the conviction that Hume's invitation was only a pretext for defaming him. Hume at first was shocked and angry. He asked for particular charges, and Rousseau eventually responded with a letter of eighteen folio pages written in a small neat hand, which made clear to Hume that Rousseau was not a villain but, rather, mad. Fearing that Rousseau was preparing to publish an account of the affair that would throw imputations on his morals and conduct, Hume broke a pledge he had made to himself never to reply to criticism in print. He assembled the relevant documents into a narrative which he distributed to the principal parties involved. D'Alembert, to whom Hume had given discretion to publish, produced a pamphlet containing Hume's narrative and a postscript of his own. The pamphlet appeared in Paris in 1766 under the title *Exposé succinct de la contestation qui s'est élévée entre M. Hume et M. Rousseau avec les pieces justicatives*. An English translation appeared in London the same year. In retrospect Hume regretted having allowed the account of the affair to be published.

Early in 1767, Hume became under secretary of state for the Northern Department, a post he held for eleven months. He lingered in London for another seven months, staying, as he usually did when in London, with Scottish friends. He received fellow Scots and, having good connections in government, assisted in securing patronage for them. The quandary he had been in since leaving France, of whether to take up residence in Paris or Edinburgh, was resolved. The call of his native country was too strong. Besides, Edinburgh, though remote from the centers of Europe, was not a backward place. It was the center of what has come to be known as the Scottish Enlightenment and contained a brilliant society of literary men, such as Adam Smith, Adam Ferguson (a founder of modern sociology), William Robertson (along with Hume, Gibbon, and Voltaire, one of the four great historians of the eighteenth century), Hugh Blair (holder of the newly created chair of rhetoric and belles lettres at the University of Edinburgh, which may be thought of as the first chair in English literature), Hume's cousin John Home the dramatist, Lord Kames, and many others. In such society Hume would have sufficient intellectual stimulation, as well as the intimacy which his nature demanded and which would be possible only in his native city.

In August of 1769 Hume was back in Edinburgh, where he spent the remaining seven years of his life. He built a house in the New Town (the most progressive urban plan in Europe), entertained his friends with dinners, revised and polished new editions of his works, and enjoyed what was always his central vanity and ambition, love of literary fame. Except for a late essay "Of the Origin of Government," written after 1774, Hume was done with all writing and ambition.

Hume's interest in political affairs, however, was as strong as ever. His political philosophy had grown out of British as well as European political experience and was intended to help shape that experience. His *History of England* was largely a political history designed to instruct his countrymen in the origins and inner workings of the constitution, but, surprisingly, his letters are relatively silent on political matters until around 1766, with the repeal of the Stamp Act. From then, until his death ten years later, there is a steady stream of political invective in the letters prompted by the Wilkes and Liberty riots and the American crisis. The views expressed in these letters constitute a comprehensive and prophetic criticism of British political order and, though complicated, are consistent with the central teachings in his philosophical and historical writings. Indeed, the despondent, urgent, and pessimistic tone of the letters is due to Hume's perception that what he had warned about earlier seemed to be coming to pass.

Hume resisted the Wilkes and Liberty movement and other attempts to extend republican and democratic institutions in Britain, and he firmly supported the government in attempts to suppress them. Yet, he supported the American colonies, arguing for complete independence as early as 1768. Few Americans thought of independence that early and even fewer in Britain. Even the "friends of America" in government, such as Burke, William Pitt, Earl of Chatham, and William Petty, Earl of Shelburne, did not seriously consider independence until after the battle of Saratoga in 1777, when they were forced to do so. Hume's position surprised his friends. In 1775 he disappointed his good friend William Mure of Caldwell who had asked him to draft a petition to the king on behalf of the freeholders of Renfrewshire asking for strong measures against

the Americans. Hume replied: "Besides, I am an American in my Principles, and wish we would let them alone to govern or misgovern themselves as they think proper."

Hume saw the Wilkes and Liberty riots as a case of how false philosophical and historical thinking of an entirely secular sort can yield a species of fanaticism and bigotry equal to anything religion had produced. John Wilkes had fled the country in 1763 on a charge of seditious libel and had the effrontery to return in 1768; as an outlaw he ran for Parliament and was elected by the county of Middlesex. He was rejected by Parliament. Three times he was reelected and three times rejected. "Wilkes and Liberty" became a rallying cry not only in London but throughout the far-flung dominions of the empire. Men in Jamaica, Carolina, London, and Yorkshire were ritualistically toasting Wilkes and Liberty with no clear or common grievance in mind which they wished to be corrected. The "Wilkes and Liberty" movement, if not the first, was one of the very early entirely secular mass-political "movements" in modern times. Hume thought it was unique and due entirely to those parties of "speculative" principle which he had examined in "Of Parties in General" and which he argued were peculiar to modern times.

In challenging the independence of Parliament, the Wilkes and Liberty movement (whatever merits it may have had) challenged the rule of law, and the government seemed powerless to suppress it. Hume taught that there is an internal struggle in every government between liberty and authority and that neither can absolutely prevail in the contest. He had always thought that the British constitution was too weak in authority. The main cause of this weakness was a disorder in opinion. The Whig literary and political establishment, which had ruled for nearly a century, had drummed into the national consciousness a false historical conception of the constitution (ancient constitutionalism) as well as a false philosophical theory of government (the contract theory of Locke, Algernon Sidney, and others). These historical and philosophical distortions of reality had produced a paranoid style in politics in which virtually anything could be see as a threat to liberty.

The fanaticism here was more absurd than that of the religious ideology which Hume thought was largely responsible for the English civil war. As he taught in *The Natural History of Religion*, one should expect absurdity in religion. But

A satiric engraving (August 1766) suggested by James Boswell, of the quarrel between Hume and Rousseau. Hume described this print in a 1767 letter to Madame de Boufflers: "M. Rousseau is represented as a Yahoo, newly caught in the woods; I am represented as a farmer, who caresses him and offers him some oats to eat, which he refuses in a rage; Voltaire and d'Alembert are whipping him up behind; and Horace Walpole making him horns of papier mâché. *The idea is not altogether absurd."*

absurdity in purely secular, and supposedly enlightened, historical and philosophical thought was something else. Part of the despondency manifest in the letters of the last decade of Hume's life is his awareness that the darkness in the religious intellect, ritualistically criticized by the Enlightenment, had suddenly appeared in the critical intellect itself.

In rejecting Wilkes and Liberty, Hume was not rejecting republican values. He always held to the republican ideal of government, though he did not make the mistake of Locke and other Whigs of confusing the ideal regime with the legitimate regime. Hume supported completely independent republican regimes in America, and he even wrote an essay explaining the possibility and desirability of a republican regime in a large territory. But Hume also held very early in his career that the peculiar historical circumstances of Britain were such that the only republic to be expected would be the oppressive sort experienced under Cromwell. Hume had argued as early as 1741, in "Whether the British Government Inclines More to Absolute Monarchy, or to a Republic," that Britain was poised to evolve into either

a republic or a civilized absolute monarchy. For the sake of liberty, he hoped it would become the latter.

Hume taught that republics, under conditions of modern commercial society, are more inclined to public debt than monarchies and are less able to extricate themselves by declaring bankruptcy than monarchies. In the *Essays, Moral Political, and Literary* Hume warned about the consequences of expanding public credit. In the letters of this period, he expressed the belief that public debt was reaching the critical point, brought on mainly by the bellicose mercantile policies of William Pitt. Using Whig ideology, Pitt had been able to present these policies under the noble aspect of national glory and liberty. Pitt's brilliant conduct of the Seven Years' War (1756-1763) had broken French sea power and left Britain with a vast empire to defend and a staggering public debt. It was for the purpose of paying for the empire that Britain sought to impose new forms of taxation on the American colonies.

Moreover, Hume had argued in "That Politics May be Reduced to a Science" (1741) that republican empires are more oppressive than mo-

Hume's 25 July 1766 letter to Madame La Presidente de Meinières, a Parisian friend, cataloguing his actions on Rousseau's behalf (MA 668; Pierpont Morgan Library) narchical ones. The monarch tends to view all his subjects as equal; whereas a republic will tend to see the colonies as serving the interests of the mother country and will contrive restrictions on trade and taxes to that end. Hume treated Britain as a virtual republic and, in the essay, contrasted the favorable treatment of Corsica by the absolute monarchy of France with the unfavorable treatment of Ireland by Britain. By 1765 it was clear to Hume that the British constitution was moving away from civilized absolute monarchy in the direction of a republic. The Stamp Act and other oppressive taxation schemes were simply concrete examples of Hume's maxim about oppressive republican regimes. It was in part for this reason that Hume urged independence for all British colonies.

After war between Britain and the colonies broke out in the spring of 1775, Hume argued that, no matter what resources Britain threw into it, the war simply could not be won and that little would be lost in trade if the colonies were given independence. Nowhere in the letters does Hume take a stand on the legal question of the *right* of the colonies to be taxed. Colonial leaders and Parliament (as well as George II) were all Whigs in this respect. Their political universe was an entirely constitutional and legalistic one. Hume, however, viewed norms, including legal ones, as expressions of established conventions. But legal conventions can change, and, when they do, adjustments in rights may be necessary. Hume viewed the conflict not legalistically but in causal terms: the colonies had been virtually self-governing from the beginning; after nearly a century they had come of age and were demanding that their own republican institutions be recognized. Independence had to be granted sooner or later, and it would be better to do it sooner.

In addition, Hume had an affection for the order of independence and liberty developing in America. He may even have written "Idea of a Perfect Commonwealth" (the theory that the most perfect form of government would be a federal republic in a large territory) with America in mind. He was a good friend of Benjamin Franklin, who stayed with Hume in his house in the New Town for nearly a month during the fall of 1771. He thought the colonies would one day be a flourishing empire which would eclipse Britain and possibly Europe. He urged the young Edward Gibbon, who had begun his career writing history in French (because it was the most polished and diffused language), to write in English. Assuming the continued expansion of the English-speaking colonies, English, not French, was likely to become the dominant language.

In 1772 Hume's health began to decline, apparently due to cancer of the bowels. By 1775 he had lost about seventy pounds and realized he was dying. The philosophical character he taught in all his writings (and with special eloquence in "The Skeptic"), that life is more a matter of carrying out the everyday routine than it is a serious endeavor, was played out in his dying. Four months before his death he penned a short autobiography, "My Own Life," which presents a picture of the philosopher dying with quiet dignity, calm, and cheerfulness. He even managed to respond with good humor to Boswell's morbid question of whether, as an unbeliever, he felt terror upon approaching death. Hume's good-natured negative response left Boswell disturbed. To the end he lived as he always had, concerned about public affairs in Edinburgh, eagerly reading the new books, and writing warm and witty letters to his friends. The last two weeks of his life were spent making final revisions for new editions of his works, preparing the *Dialogues* for posthumous publication, and writing brief letters of farewell to his friends. He died 25 August 1776, five days after the *Caledonian Mercury* of Edinburgh published the entire text of the American Declaration of Independence.

Letters:

Private Correspondence of David Hume with Several Distinguished Persons, between the Years 1761 and 1766 (London: Printed for Henry Colborn, 1820);

Letters of David Hume, and Extracts from Letters Referring to Him, edited by Thomas Murray (Edinburgh: Adam & Charles Black, 1841);

Life and Correspondence of David Hume. From Papers Bequeathed by His Nephew to the Royal Society of Edinburgh; and Other Original Sources by John Hill Burton, 2 volumes (Edinburgh: William Tate, 1846);

Letters of David Hume to William Strahan, edited by G. Birkbeck Hill (Oxford: Clarendon Press, 1888);

The Letters of David Hume, 2 volumes, edited by J. Y. T. Greig (Oxford: Clarendon Press, 1932);

New Letters of David Hume, edited by Raymond Klibansky and Ernest C. Mossner (Oxford: Clarendon Press, 1954).

Hume in 1766 (engraving by David Martin, after a portrait by David Ramsay)

Bibliographies:

T. E. Jessop, *A Bibliography of David Hume and of Scottish Philosophy, from Francis Hutcheson to Lord Balford* (London: Brown, 1938);

William B. Todd, "David Hume, A Preliminary Bibliography," in *Hume and the Enlightenment: Essays Presented to Ernest Campbell Mossner*, edited by Todd (Edinburgh: Edinburgh University Press, 1974), pp. 189-205;

Roland Hall, *Fifty Years of Hume Scholarship: A Bibliographical Guide* (Edinburgh: Edinburgh University Press, 1978);—updates by Hall, in November issues of *Hume Studies* (1977-   ).

Biographies:

T. E. Ritchie, *Account of the Life and Writings of David Hume* (London, 1807);

John Hill Burton, *Life and Correspondence of David Hume*, 2 volumes (Edinburgh: William Tate, 1846);

J. Y. T. Greig, *David Hume* (London: Cape, 1931);

Ernest Campbell Mossner, *The Life of David Hume*, second edition, revised (Oxford: Clarendon Press, 1980).

References:

Páll Ardal, *Passion and Value in Hume's Treatise* (Edinburgh: Edinburgh University Press, 1966);

Tom Beauchamp and Alexander Rosenberg, *Hume and the Problem of Causation* (Oxford: Oxford University Press, 1981);

Laurence Bongie, *David Hume, Prophet of the Counter-Revolution* (Oxford: Clarendon Press, 1965);

Nicholas Capaldi, *David Hume the Newtonian Philosopher* (Boston: Twayne, 1975);

Duncan Forbes, *Hume's Philosophical Politics* (Cambridge: Cambridge University Press, 1975);

J. C. A. Gaskin, *Hume's Philosophy of Religion* (London: Macmillan, 1978);

Peter Jones, *Hume's Sentiments, Their Ciceronian and French Context* (Edinburgh: Edinburgh University Press, 1982);

Donald W. Livingston, *Hume's Philosophy of Common Life* (Chicago: University of Chicago Press, 1984);

David Miller, *Philosophy and Ideology in Hume's Political Thought* (Oxford: Clarendon Press, 1981);

David F. Norton, *David Hume, Common-Sense Moralist, Sceptical Metaphysician* (Princeton: Princeton University Press, 1982);

Terence Penelhum, *Hume* (New York: St. Martin's Press, 1975);

Donald T. Siebert, *The Moral Animus of David Hume* (Newark: University of Delaware Press, 1990);

Norman Kemp Smith, *The Philosophy of David Hume: A Critical Study of its Origins and Central Doctrines* (London and New York: Macmillan, 1941);

John P. Wright, *The Sceptical Realism of David Hume* (Manchester: Manchester University Press, 1983).

Papers:

The largest and most important collection of Hume manuscripts and letters is the Hume Archives in the National Library of Scotland. This collection includes the massive amount of material bequeathed to the Royal Society of Edinburgh by Hume's nephew, Baron David Hume.

Samuel Johnson

(18 September 1709 - 13 December 1784)

Donald Greene
University of Southern California

See also the entries on Johnson in *DLB 39: British Novelists, 1660-1800* and *DLB 95: Eighteenth-Century British Poets*, First Series.

BOOKS: *A Voyage to Abyssinia by Father Jerome Lobo . . . and Fifteen Dissertations . . . by Mr. Le Grand. From the French* (London: Printed for A. Bettesworth & C. Hitch, 1735);

London: A Poem, in Imitation of the Third Satire of Juvenal (London: Printed for R. Doddesley, 1738);

Marmor Norfolciense: or an Essay on an Ancient Prophetical Inscription, In Monkish Rhyme, Lately Discover'd near Lynn in Norfolk. By Probus Britanicus (London: Printed for J. Brett, 1739);

A Compleat Vindication of the Licensers of the Stage, from the Malicious and Scandalous Aspersions of Mr. Brooke, Author of Gustavus Vasa . . . By an Impartial Hand (London: Printed for C. Corbett, 1739);

A Commentary on Mr. Pope's Principles of Morality, or Essay on Man. By Mons. Crousaz (London: Printed for A. Dodd, 1739);

An Account of the Life of Mr. Richard Savage, Son of the Earl Rivers (London: Printed for J. Roberts, 1744);

Miscellaneous Observations on the Tragedy of Macbeth: with Remarks on Sir T. H.'s Edition of Shakespear. To which is affix'd, Proposals for a New Edition of Shakeshear [sic] (London: Printed for E. Cave & sold by J. Roberts, 1745);

A Sermon Preached at the Cathedral Church of St. Paul, before the Sone of the Clergy, on Thursday the Second of May, 1745. by the Honourable and Reverend Henry Hervey Aston (London: Printed for J. Brindley & sold by M. Cooper, 1745);

Prologue and Epilogue, Spoken at the Opening of the Theatre in Drury-Lane 1747 (London: Printed by E. Cave, sold by M. Cooper & R. Dodsley, 1747);

The Plan of a Dictionary of the English Language; Addressed to the Right Honourable Philip Dormer, Earl of Chesterfield (London: Printed for J. & P. Knapton, T. Longman & T. Shewell, C. Hitch, A. Millar and R. Dodsley, 1747);

The Vanity of Human Wishes. The Tenth Satire of Juvenal, Imitated (London: Printed for R. Dodsley & sold by M. Cooper, 1749);

Irene: A Tragedy. As it is Acted at the Theatre Royal in Drury-Lane (London: Printed for R. Dodsley & sold by M. Cooper, 1749);

The Rambler, nos. 1-208 (London: Printed for J. Payne & L. Bouquet, (20 March 1750 - 14 March 1752); republished in 2 volumes (London: Printed for J. Payne, 1753);

A New Prologue Spoken by Mr. Garrick, Thursday, April 5, 1750. At the Representation of Comus, for the Benefit of Mrs Elizabeth Foster, Milton's Grand-Daughter, and only surviving Descendant (London: Printed for J. Payne & J. Bouquet, 1750);

A Dictionary of the English Language, 2 volumes (London: Printed by W. Strahan for J. & P. Knapton, T. & T. Longman, C. Hitch & L. Hawes, A. Millar, and R. & J. Dodsley, 1755);

An Account of an Attempt to Ascertain the Longitude at Sea. . . . By Zachariah Williams (London: Printed for R. Dodsley & J. Jeffries & sold by J. Bouquet, 1755);

Proposals for Printing, by Subscription, the Dramatick Works of William Shakespeare (London, 1756);

The Prince of Abissinia. A Tale, 2 volumes (London: Printed for R. & J. Dodsley and W. Johnston, 1759); American edition: *The History of Rasselas, Prince of Abissinia*, 1 volume (Philadelphia: Printed by Robert Bell, 1768);

The Idler, collected edition, 2 volumes (London: Printed for J. Newbery, 1761)—first published in the *Universal Chronicle, or Weekly Gazette* (15 April 1758 - 5 April 1760);

The Plays of William Shakespeare, in Eight Volumes, with the Corrections and Illustrations of Various

Samuel Johnson, 1756 (portrait by Sir Joshua Reynolds; National Portrait Gallery, London)

Commentators; to which are added Notes by Sam. Johnson (London: Printed for J. & R. Tonson and ten others, 1765); revised by Johnson and George Steevens (London, 1773);

The False Alarm (London: Printed for T. Cadell, 1770);

Thoughts on the Late Transactions Respecting Falkland's Islands (London: Printed for T. Cadell, 1771);

The Patriot. Addressed to the Electors of Great Britain (London: Printed for T. Cadell, 1774);

A Journey to the Western Islands of Scotland (London: Printed for W. Strahan & T. Cadell, 1775);

Taxation No Tyranny; an Answer to the Resolutions and Address of the American Congress (London: Printed for T. Cadell, 1775);

Prefaces, Biographical and Critical, to the Works of the English Poets, 10 volumes (London: Printed by J. Nichols for C. Bathurst and thirty-five others, 1779 [volumes 1-4]; 1781 [volumes 5-10]).

Editions: *Prayers and Meditations, composed by Samuel Johnson*, edited by George Strahan (London: Printed for T. Cadell, 1785);

The Works of Samuel Johnson, LL.D. volumes 1-11, edited by Sir John Hawkins (London: Printed for J. Buckland and forty others, 1787); volumes 12 and 13, *Debates in Parliament* (London: Printed for John Buckland, 1787); volume 14 (London: Printed for John Stockdale and G. G. J. & J. Robinson, 1788); "volume 15" (London: Printed for Elliot & Kay and C. Elliot, 1789);

The Lives of the English Poets [Prefaces, Biographical and Critical to the Works of the English Poets], 3 volumes, edited by G. B. Hill (Oxford: Clarendon Press, 1905);

The History of Rasselas, Prince of Abissinia, edited by R. W. Chapman (Oxford: Clarendon Press, 1927);

Samuel Johnson's Prefaces and Dedications, edited by Allen T. Hazen (New Haven: Yale University Press, 1937);

The Yale Edition of the Works of Samuel Johnson (12 volumes to date):

Volume 1: *Diaries, Prayers, and Annals*, edited by E. L. McAdam, Jr., with Donald and Mary Hyde (New Haven: Yale University Press / London: Oxford University Press, 1958);

Volume 2: *The Idler and The Adventurer*, edited by W. J. Bate, John M. Bullitt, L. F. Powell (New Haven & London: Yale University Press, 1963);

Volumes 3-5: *The Rambler*, edited by Bate and Albrecht B. Strauss (New Haven & London: Yale University Press, 1969);

Volume 6: *Poems*, edited by McAdam and George Milne (New Haven & London: Yale University Press, 1964);

Volumes 7 & 8: *Johnson on Shakespeare*, edited by Arthur Sherbo (New Haven & London: Yale University Press, 1968);

Volume 9: *A Journey to the Western Islands of Scotland*, edited by Mary Lascelles (New Haven & London: Yale University Press, 1971);

Volume 10: *Political Writings*, edited by Donald J. Greene (New Haven & London: Yale University Press, 1977);

Volume 14: *Sermons*, edited by Jean H. Hagstrum and James Gray (New Haven & London: Yale University Press, 1978);

Volume 15: *A Voyage to Abyssinia*, edited by Joel J. Gold (New Haven & London: Yale University Press, 1985);

The Life of Savage, edited by Clarence Tracy (Oxford: Clarendon Press, 1971);

Samuel Johnson, edited by Donald Greene, Oxford English Authors (Oxford & New York: Oxford University Press, 1984).

OTHER: *A Miscellany of Poems by Several Hands. Publish'd by J. Husbands*, includes Johnson's Latin verse translation of Alexander Pope's *Messiah* (Oxford: Printed by Leon. Lichfield, 1731);

Catalogus Bibliothecae Harleianae, 5 volumes, catalogue of the Harleian library, includes contributions by Johnson (London: Apud Thomas Osborne, 1743-1745);

Robert James, M.D., *A Medicinal Dictionary*, 3 volumes, written with the assistance of Johnson (London: Printed for T. Osborne & J. Roberts, 1743-1745);

The Harleian Miscellany, or a Collection of . . . Pamphlets and Tracts, 8 volumes, includes an introduction and annotations by Johnson (London: Printed for T. Osborne, 1744-1746);

Preface and "The Vision of Theodore, the Hermit of Teneriffe," in *The Preceptor: Containing a Course of General Education* (London: Printed for R. Dodsley, 1748);

William Lauder, *An Essay on Milton's Use and Imitation of the Moderns in His Paradise Lost*, includes a preface and a postscript by Johnson (London: Printed for J. Payne & J. Bouquet, 1750);

Charlotte Lennox, *The Female Quixote; or, the Adventures of Arabella*, includes a dedication by Johnson, who may also have written book 9, chapter 11 (London: Printed for A. Millar, 1752);

The Adventurer (London: Printed for J. Payne, nos. 1-140 (London, 7 November 1752 - 9 March 1754)—includes twenty-nine essays by Johnson;

Lennox, *Shakespear Illustrated: or the Novels and Histories on Which the Plays of Shakespear Are Founded*, includes a dedication by Johnson (London: Printed for A. Millar, 1753);

Sir Thomas Browne, *Christian Morals. . . . The Second Edition. With a Life of the Author by Samuel Johnson*, edited, with biography and annotations, by Johnson (London: Printed by Richard Hett for J. Payne, 1756);

Richard Rolt, *A New Dictionary of Trade and Commerce*, includes a preface by Johnson (London: Printed for T. Osborne & J. Shipton and four others, 1756);

The Greek Theatre of Father [Pierre] Brumoy. Translated by Mrs. Charlotte Lennox, includes a dedication and translations of two essays by Johnson (London: Printed for Mess. Millar, Vaillant, and six others, 1759);

Introduction on the history of early Portuguesse exploration, in *The World Displayed; or a Curious Collection of Voyages and Travels*, 20 volumes (London: Printed for J. Newbery, 1759-1761), I: iii-xxxii;

Proceedings of the Committee Appointed to Manage the Contributions begun at London Dec. xviii, MDCCLVIIII, for Cloathing French Prisoners of War, includes an introduction by Johnson (London: Printed by Order of the Committee, 1760);

John Gwynne, *Thoughts on the Coronation of His Present Majesty King George the Third, or, Reasons offered against confining the procession to the*

The market place at Lichfield in 1785 (engraving after a drawing by Stringer). Johnson was born in the building on the far right, which housed his father's bookshop on the ground floor.

usual track, and pointing out others more commodious and proper, much of the text written by Johnson (London: Printed for the Proprietor, and sold by F. Noble and three others, 1761);

"Author's Life" and dedication, in *The English Works of Roger Ascham . . . With Notes and Observations, and the Author's Life. By James Bennet*, edited in large part by Johnson (London: Printed for R. & J. Dodsley and J. Newbery, 1761);

Thomas Percy, ed., *Reliques of Ancient English Poetry*, includes a dedication by Johnson, who also provided general assistance (London: Printed for J. Dodsley, 1765);

Anna Williams, *Miscellanies in Prose and Verse* (London: Printed for T. Davies, 1766)—Johnson contributed the Advertisement, a short poem, "The Ant," possibly revisions to Miss Williams's poems, and *The Fountains: A Fairy Tale*;

The Convict's Address to His Unhappy Brethren. Delivered in the Chapel of Newgate, on Friday, June 6, 1777. By William Dodd, largely written by Johnson (London: Printed for G. Kearsley, 1777);

Poems and Miscellaneous Pieces, with a Free Translation of the Oedipus Tyrannus of Sophocles. By the Rev. Thomas Maurice includes a preface and possibly a dedication by Johnson (London: Printed for the Author and Sold by J. Dodsley and three others, 1779);

Dedication to the King, in *An Account of the Musical Performances in Westminster-Abbey and the Pantheon . . . in Commemoration of Handel. By Charles Burney* (London: Printed for the Benefit of the Musical Fund and sold by T. Payne and Son and G. Robinson, 1785);

Sir Robert Chambers, *A Course of Lectures on the English Law Delivered at the University of Oxford 1767-1773 by Sir Robert Chambers and Composed in Association with Samuel Johnson*, edited by Thomas M. Curley (Madison: University of Wisconsin Press, 1986; Oxford: Clarendon Press, 1986).

Samuel Johnson—poet, dramatist, journalist, satirist, biographer, essayist, lexicographer, editor, translator, critic, parliamentary reporter, political writer, story writer, sermon writer, travel writer and social anthropologist, prose stylist, conversationalist, Christian—dominates the eighteenth-century English literary scene as his contemporary, the equally versatile and prolific Voltaire, dominates that of France. Perhaps more: Voltaire had redoubtable rivals during his lifetime, Jean-Jacques Rousseau and Denis Diderot; Johnson had none. Alexander Pope, a greater poet (though Johnson was a fine one), and Jonathan Swift, a greater satirist (though Johnson's skill as a satirist has been underestimated), had died in the 1740s; Joseph Addison and Richard Steele, Johnson's precursors as popular essayists, still earlier. When Johnson's name began to be known, not long after the deaths of Swift and Pope, no challenger arose during the next forty years for the title of preeminent English man of letters.

That period has often been called the Age of Johnson. To be sure, he had notable contemporaries—Edmund Burke, David Hume, Edward Gibbon—but their literary abilities, formidable as they were, moved in a narrower circle of concerns. Henry Fielding, Samuel Richardson, and Laurence Sterne received and deserve great acclaim as the founding fathers of the English novel, but their contributions to other areas of writing are less noteworthy. Almost as prolific as Johnson and as varied in his interests was Horace Walpole, who sometimes expressed aristocratic disdain for the lowborn Johnson, though he never seems to have impinged greatly on Johnson's consciousness. Walpole might be argued to have made a greater impact than Johnson on the following century, in the form of those somewhat dubious legacies the "Gothic" romance and Victorian pseudo-Gothic architecture. But no one has ever suggested calling the later eighteenth century "the Age of Horace Walpole." It is not surprising that the standard bibliographies of studies in eighteenth-century English literature show Johnson to have been their most popular subject, followed at some distance by Swift and Pope, and at a longer one by Fielding, Daniel Defoe, John Dryden, and William Blake, with Walpole an also-ran.

Johnson's origins were humble, and much of his life was spent in not so genteel poverty. He once boasted, in reply to a complaint that he advocated preserving class distinctions, that he could hardly tell who his grandfather was. That grandfather seems to have been a small tenant farmer or day laborer, one William Johnson. William's son Michael, Samuel's father, was assisted by a charitable society to become apprenticed as a stationer. After serving his time he set up as a bookseller and, in a small way, publisher in the Midlands cathedral city of Lichfield. For a time he prospered, and attained minor civic office. In the poignant small fragment of an autobiography that has survived, Samuel recorded Michael's joy at his birth: "When he [the obstetrician] had me in his arms, he said, 'Here is a brave boy.' . . . My father being that year Sheriff of Lichfield, and to ride the circuit of the County the next day, he was asked by my mother, 'Whom he would invite to the Riding?' and answered 'All the town now.' "

Michael had married late. He was fifty-two and his wife forty when their first son was born on 18 September 1709 (N.S.). She was Sarah Ford, of a family of tradesmen and small landholders who thought themselves socially superior to the lowly Johnsons. "My father and mother had not much happiness from each other," Samuel recorded. "They seldom conversed, for my father could not bear to talk of his affairs, and my mother, being unacquainted with books, cared not to talk of any thing else." In spite of her no doubt strongly expressed advice, Michael's business deteriorated, and he died in the poverty from which he had briefly arisen. Sarah then took over the bookshop and ran it competently for the rest of her life. It was not a happy family. Sarah's bourgeois values were at odds with Michael's and Samuel's more intellectual interests, and recent scholars have attributed some of Samuel's later psychological problems to her lack of understanding or affection for the boy. A younger brother, Nathanael, seems to have suffered also; almost all that is known of him is a pathetic letter to Sarah written when he was twenty-four, accusing Samuel of turning his mother against him and giving a most gloomy picture of his own prospects. He died shortly afterward, and suicide has been suspected.

From childhood Samuel suffered from various physical ailments that plagued him throughout his life—near blindness in one eye, the tubercular infection scrofula (the "King's Evil," which even the royal touch of Queen Anne failed to cure), a persistent uncontrollable tic. But he grew up to be a strong, muscular man: his height of six feet was unusual in the eighteenth century, and, when he first sought employment in London as a writer, he was once advised rather to hire himself out as a public porter. He received

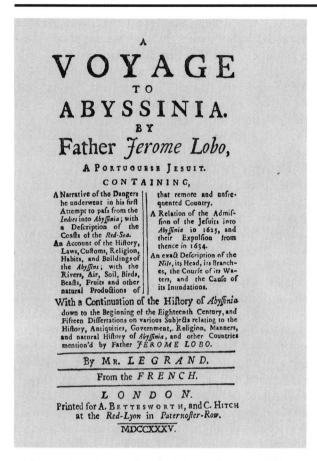

A
VOYAGE
TO
ABYSSINIA.
BY
Father *Jerome Lobo*,
A PORTUGUESE JESUIT.
CONTAINING,

A Narrative of the Dangers he underwent in his first Attempt to pass from the *Indies* into *Abyssinia*; with a Description of the Coasts of the *Red-Sea*.
An Account of the History, Laws, Customs, Religion, Habits, and Buildings of the *Abyssins*; with the Rivers, Air, Soil, Birds, Beasts, Fruits and other natural Productions of

that remote and unfrequented Country.
A Relation of the Admission of the Jesuits into *Abyssinia* in 1625, and their Expulsion from thence in 1634.
An exact Description of the *Nile*, its Head, its Branches, the Course of its Waters, and the Cause of its Inundations.

With a Continuation of the History of *Abyssinia* down to the Beginning of the Eighteenth Century, and Fifteen Dissertations on various Subjects relating to the History, Antiquities, Government, Religion, Manners, and natural History of *Abyssinia*, and other Countries mention'd by Father *JEROME LOBO*.

By MR. *LEGRAND*.

From the *FRENCH*.

LONDON.
Printed for A. BETTESWORTH, and C. HITCH at the *Red-Lyon* in *Paternoster-Row*.
MDCCXXXV.

Title page for Johnson's first book, a translation and adaptation of a book he had read at Oxford

the standard classical education in Latin and Greek at Lichfield grammar school, where he was regarded as something of a prodigy. He said that he caught his first enthusiasm for literature when, as a boy, searching for a cache of apples he thought Nathanael had hidden behind a shelf of books in their father's shop, he came across a volume of Petrarch (no doubt in Latin), and became so absorbed in it that he forgot about the apples. When he was sixteen, he transferred to the grammar school in nearby Stourbridge, where some of his Ford relations lived, and later paid tribute to the influence of his cousin Cornelius Ford, a polished intellectual, who encouraged the boy's love of books and ambition to write. While there, he began to compose boyish poetry—translations of Horace's odes, conventional love poems to young ladies, even one, the earliest that has survived, "On a Daffodil."

When he was seventeen, he returned to Lichfield and put in two no doubt reluctant years working in the bookshop, where, however, he had the opportunity to devour much of its contents; he

later said that he knew almost as much at eighteen as he did when he was in his fifties. The lad's learning and promise caused him to be taken up by the cultured Gilbert Walmesley, an official of the ecclesiastical court of the diocese, who used to invite Johnson and another younger Lichfield lad, the lively David Garrick, to dine with him and who encouraged Johnson's intellectual interests. Two years later a small legacy from a relation of Mrs. Johnson's enabled Samuel to enroll in Oxford University, where many of his less brilliant but more affluent schoolmates had already gone. When he entered Pembroke College, the breadth of the young man's reading is said to have made an impression on the dons. But the thirteen months he spent there before the money ran out were hardly successful ones. He found his tutors incompetent, and instead of attending lectures spent his time in such amusements as sliding on the ice and encouraging his fellow undergraduates in rebellious indiscipline. "I was rude and violent," he later said. "It was bitterness which they mistook for frolic. I was miserably poor, and I thought to fight my way by my literature and wit." Nevertheless it was at Oxford that he composed his first published work, a translation into Latin verse of Pope's long poem *Messiah* that appeared in a collection edited by an Oxford don (1731). Pope said it was so well done that it would be hard to tell whether his or the anonymous translator's was the original—a great compliment from the greatest poet of his time.

Leaving without a degree, Johnson returned to Lichfield for another two years, doing just what, no one knows—probably reading further in the bookshop and quarreling with the rest of his uncongenial family. Michael died in 1731, and presumably Samuel was told that he no longer need expect to be supported by the small income from the shop. He held one miserable teaching job for a few months and applied unsuccessfully for others where he was rejected because it was thought his strange appearance would cause him to be laughed at by the pupils. He went to live with a former schoolfellow in Birmingham, where he found occasional employment on the local newspaper, and published a set of proposals (1734, nonextant) for an edition of the poetry of the Italian Renaissance writer Politian, with a life of Politian, and a history of Renaissance Latin poetry from Petrarch to Politian. Nothing came of this, but a windfall of sorts was a commission to translate from the French *A Voyage to Abyssinia* by the Portuguese Jesuit Jerónimo

Lobo, with additional essays on the geography and customs of the country by Joachim Le Grand.

Published in 1735, this first book of Johnson's is of considerable interest. In the early seventeenth century, Portugal, in order to make its trade routes to India more secure, sponsored a Jesuit missionary expedition to Ethiopia, in the hope of converting its rulers from their ancient and, as the Jesuits thought, corrupt form of Christianity to Roman Catholicism and hence to bring the country more firmly under Portuguese influence. Lobo and Le Grand give a vivid account of this nearly unknown part of the world, supposedly the land of Prester John and the mysterious source of the Nile. Johnson's preface dwells on two themes that were to recur in his later work: he compliments Lobo on the honesty with which he, unlike other travel writers, has "described things as he saw them . . . copied nature from the life . . . consulted his senses, not his imagination," and he condemns the Portuguese and the Jesuits for trying to impose by force European domination on indigenous peoples, and justifying that force in the name of Christianity. The book had stirred up a heated controversy in Europe: Protestants maintained that the Ethiopian church was as legitimate a branch of Christianity as Roman Catholicism, perhaps even a purer one. Johnson makes it clear that he is on the Protestant side. His work is "by no means a translation, but an epitome": he does much skillful condensation and adaptation, often toning down the Catholic expressions in the text. His version runs to four hundred pages; for it young Johnson received five guineas (around two hundred dollars in present United States currency).

While living in Birmingham, Johnson met the merchant Henry Porter and his wife Elizabeth, née Jervis. Harry Porter died in September 1734, and on 9 July 1735 Johnson married his widow. Many eyebrows have been raised at this marriage between a penniless youth of twenty-five and a widow of forty-five with three fatherless children (after the wedding the children went to live with other relatives). But Johnson always praised her intellect and her beauty, and she was evidently intelligent enough to recognize the quality of Johnson's mind; at her death eighteen years later, he was devastated. She brought with her some six hundred pounds from her marriage settlement, and with it Johnson opened a boarding school at Edial, close to Lichfield. It attracted only a few pupils, one of them being

David Garrick. It soon closed, and Johnson, having tried in vain to earn a living in the Midlands by the use of his pen and his brains, decided to try his fate in the larger arena of London.

On 2 March 1737, Johnson, accompanied by young Garrick, set out to cover the hundred miles or so to London. They could afford only one horse and used the old method of "riding and tying." For the next twenty-five years Johnson was to earn a precarious living in London with his pen. Earlier he had written to Edward Cave, the enterprising publisher who had founded the first periodical to use the title "Magazine," the monthly *Gentleman's Magazine*. The word means simply a storehouse, and at first Cave's periodical consisted mostly of reprinted pieces from other London journals. It was to continue publication from 1731 to 1907, an astonishingly long life. Johnson suggested that there were numerous improvements that could be made to it if he were to contribute. Cave did not reply to this cheeky letter, but, after Johnson approached him in London, he began to use Johnson's services as a writer and used them more and more as time went on; there are times when Johnson seems to have been virtually in editorial control of the journal.

Johnson's long involvement with journalism is the most undeservedly neglected part of his career. He was one of its pioneers; after he joined Cave's staff, the *Gentleman's* was transformed into the prototype of the modern intellectual magazine, providing for the educated but not specialist reader a broad and thoughtful overview of events of current intellectual interest, reviewing important new books and printing original articles on the political scene, new literature, advances in science, religious controversy, and much else. Johnson contributed to its regular feature "Foreign History," reporting news from European capitals, battles in the War of the Austrian Succession, a massacre in Java, a coup d'état in Persia. He initiated a "Foreign Books" feature, reporting literary events in Europe. He did some "investigative reporting," uncovering the literary frauds of William Lauder, as he was later to do with "the Cock Lane ghost" affair and James Macpherson's "Ossian" imposture. In time he came to be regarded as the pundit of journalism, and was called on to write the opening manifestos for many new periodicals, in which he had wise things to say about the journalist's responsibility for the education of the thinking public, the need for truth in news reporting, the importance of timely correction or retraction of reports that have proved erroneous, and the dangers from fraudulent advertising.

The 1738 numbers of the *Gentleman's* carried, as well as some short pieces of verse by Johnson, his "Life of Sarpi." Paolo Sarpi's great *History of the Council of Trent* (1619), a classic of historiography, recounts, from an antipapal point of view, the events of this famous "ecumenical" council of the Roman Catholic church which, from 1545 to 1563, attempted to meet the growing challenge of Protestantism by tightening discipline and doctrine in the church. Sarpi was one of many Catholics who opposed the increase in centralized control. His much admired history had been translated into French, and Cave published a prospectus for a translation of this work into English by Johnson, who in fact completed a sizable portion of it. But a competing translation was announced, and Cave's project was abandoned. Johnson's succinct "Life" is presumably an attempt to salvage something from the project. Johnson's involvement with the *History of the Council of Trent* contradicts two legends about him, that he despised history and that his intellectual interests were the narrow ones of a "Little Englander," an archetypal John Bull. On the contrary, as his early dealings with Petrarch and Politian indicate, he was deeply interested in what happened in the rest of the world, and throughout his life was concerned to encourage his fellow countrymen to expand their intellectual horizons beyond the English Channel.

But the outstanding publishing event in the *Gentleman's Magazine* after Johnson arrived there in 1738 was the inauguration of a feature that was to continue for seven years and was greatly to increase its circulation and establish its lasting prosperity and authority. This was no less than the project of publishing reports of the debates in the British Parliament. Their publication had long been forbidden, politicians then as later being reluctant to have their doings scrutinized too closely, and in the spring of 1738 the House of Commons passed a resolution threatening offenders with "the utmost severity" if they attempted to do so. This was a blow to Cave. The prime minister, Sir Robert Walpole, had held office for sixteen years, and was now beleaguered by opponents intent on ousting him. For four more years the attacks on him in Parliament reached a pitch of violence seldom equaled in that always outspoken assembly, until Walpole was finally overthrown. The general public was keenly interested in the contest, and any periodical able to report the debates would see a great increase in its sales. Cave and his staff—some said primarily young Johnson—thought of a way around the ban. An article appeared in which the grandson of Lemuel Gulliver described a voyage he had recently made to the land of Lilliput, once visited by his famous grandfather. He discovered that the Lilliputian Parliament was debating issues very similar to those in London, and that opposition members such as the Urgol Ptit were hurling blistering attacks against Sir Retrob Walelop. He had brought back a shipload of reports of the debates of the Senate of Lilliput, which the *Gentleman's Magazine* thought might interest its readers during the unfortunate absence of reports of the debates in their own Parliament.

Throughout his life, Johnson was no friend to the preservation of official secrets. "The time is now come," he was later to write, "in which every Englishman expects to be informed of the national affairs, and in which he has a right to have that expectation gratified." For instance, one burning issue of the time was the charge that Walpole was weakly allowing Spain to maintain its embargo against English maritime trade with its South American possessions, a conflict which was presently to erupt in the so-called War of Jenkins's Ear. This gives the writer of the introduction to the Lilliputian debates the opportunity to reflect on the history of European exploitation of the New World: the Europeans "have made conquests and settled colonies in very distant regions, the inhabitants of which they look upon as barbarous, though in simplicity of manners, probity, and temperance superior to themselves; and seem to think they have a right to treat them as passion, interest, or caprice shall direct, without much regard to the rule of justice or humanity; they have carried this imaginary sovereignty so far that they have sometimes proceeded to rapine, bloodshed, and desolation."

The British record in North America is not spared: "When any of their people have forfeited the rights of society, by robberies, seditions, or other crimes," they are transported to America, "undoubtedly very much to the propagation of knowledge and virtue." These indictments Johnson was to repeat many times in his later writings. He concludes his account with a hair-raising description of how the Lilliputians, enraged by the corruptions of government in the time of Lemuel senior, "set fire to the palace" of the emperor, "and buried the whole royal family in its

St. John's Gate, London, where the office of the Gentleman's Magazine *was located*

ruins," together with the evil ministers who had fled there for protection. This was fifty years before the storming of the Bastille, and it is noteworthy that the implied threat is not only against Walpole and his associates but against the king he served, George II.

The Lilliputian debates occupied much of the *Gentleman's* space from 1738 to 1745 (Walpole was forced to resign in 1742, but an unsuccessful attempt to impeach him continued beyond that time). All the debates that appeared between July 1741 and March 1744, totaling around half a million words, are usually attributed to Johnson. Earlier and later debates are said to have been composed by others, perhaps with assistance or revision by Johnson, but there is no way of determining this. It used to be thought that they were entirely fictional compositions, but recent study shows, by comparing them with other extant reports, that their substance corresponds fairly well to what the speakers are supposed actually to have said, though the prose has undoubtedly been polished, as printed reports of parliamentary or congressional speeches still are. The quasi-official *Parliamentary History*, the predecessor of the official record, "Hansard," reprints them, and they are still sometimes quoted by historians unaware of Johnson's share in them as examples of the rhetorical ability of their supposed speakers. Johnson is once supposed to have said, "I took care not to let the Whig dogs have the best

of it," but most of those who ranted against Walpole were also Whigs. In fact, a careful reading of the debates will show that the honors for effectiveness are fairly equally divided between Walpole's supporters and his enemies, and on one occasion, the great debate in the House of Commons on 13 February 1741, on a motion calling for the removal of Walpole from office, Walpole is given a masterly final speech in reply. Other topics than the conduct of the Walpole administration are the subjects of extended debate: the state of the armed forces, foreign affairs, trade, the control of the sale of spirits, "urban renewal" (a bill for paving the streets of Westminster). Three or more years of reporting detailed discussion of such matters were a splendid apprenticeship for the general commentator on human affairs that Johnson was to become.

During these early years, Johnson published a good deal elsewhere than in the columns of the *Gentleman's*, publications with which Cave was also connected. In May 1738 a nineteen-page booklet appeared, containing a poem of 263 lines in heroic couplets (and one triplet) entitled *London*. It caused a mild stir and reached a second edition within a week. Pope, whose long poem *One Thousand Seven Hundred and Thirty Eight*, likewise a denunciation of life at that time and in that place, was published the same day, gave high praise to his unknown rival's work. *London* is subtitled *A Poem, in Imitation the Third Satire of Juvenal*, which was a diatribe against life in contemporary Rome. It is important to understand that an "imitation" is not a translation or even paraphrase of an original work, but rather what might be called a set of variations on a theme. Juvenal satirizes aspects of life in Rome which displease him, Johnson does the same with life in London; for instance, Juvenal condemns the baneful influence of Greek immigrants, Johnson of French. Both cities suffer from things that still plague metropolises—street hoodlums, jerry-built structures, corrupt politicians:

> Their ambush here relentless ruffians lay,
> And here the fell attorney prowls for prey;
> Here falling houses thunder on your head,
> And here a female atheist talks you dead.

There is enough humor in lines such as these to make one wonder just how serious much of the poem is in its denunciations. But the key line in the poem, which Johnson puts in capital letters, is serious enough: "SLOW RISES WORTH BY POVERTY DEPRESSED." The speaker in the poem is one Thales, whose talents and integrity the city has not recognized, and who is about to abandon it for the peaceful and virtuous life of the country. This has raised difficulties for those who recall Johnson's supposed saying that the man who is tired of London is tired of life. But that saying did not come until much later in Johnson's life—if he said it at all, and there is considerable doubt that he did—when he no longer suffered from poverty and obscurity. In 1738, like many another young man fresh from the provinces, he could well have been dismayed by the hectic confusion of the capital. Indeed, in the following year he returned to Lichfield for some months and once again tried to find a teaching position—and was once again turned down: worth rose no faster in the country than in the city. Then it was back to London's Grub Street once more, this time permanently.

London is heavily laced with the standard opposition propaganda of the time. The woes and the degeneracy of life in the capital are all due to the nefarious regime of Walpole and his minions; even his nominal master, King George, is lambasted for his frequent trips to visit his mistress in Hannover. The next year saw two long and violent prose pamphlets on the same theme—pseudonymously signed, of course, though even so, it was said that Johnson had to go into hiding for a time to avoid arrest. *Marmor Norfolciense*

(The Norfolk Stone) relates the discovery in Walpole's home county of an ancient boulder carved with a mysterious prophetic inscription, which a bumbling pedant, a Walpolian hanger-on, has great difficulty in explicating, though the reader has no trouble in seeing it as a rousing tirade against the many sins of the administration. Its satire is perhaps too heavily laid on for it to be very effective: Johnson seems to be trying to do what Swift had done in *The Windsor Prophecy* (1711), but he lacks Swift's control. In *A Complete Vindication of the Licensers of the Stage*, the satire is more skillfully handled. What is being "vindicated" is the action of the lord chamberlain's censors, appointed under the recently passed Stage Licensing Act, in refusing permission for a public performance of Henry Brooke's play *Gustavus Vasa*. It was a transparent piece of opposition propaganda, in which a noble "patriot" leads a revolt that liberates his country from the tyranny of a usurping king and his despicable prime minister. The act, the provisions of which remained in force until, incredibly, 1968, provided that no play could be publicly performed in London without the prior approval of the script by the lord chamberlain; it was of course designed to protect the administration from such criticism as Brooke's. Johnson's biting satire takes the form of a defense of the licensers by a stupid authoritarian government official, who goes on to propose that books too should be subjected to similar censorship, and, even better, that elementary schools should be abolished so that no one will be taught to read and so run the danger of being exposed to antigovernment views: "The nation will rest at length in ignorance and peace." It is as brilliant a piece of condemnation as has ever been written of the obscurantism fostered by dictatorial governments, a kind of prelude to *1984* (1949). Johnson's political thinking had, in fact, a good deal in common with George Orwell's.

Another publication of Johnson's in 1739, which until recently has been little studied, is his annotated translation, from the French, of Crousaz's *Commentary* on Pope's recently published *Essay on Man* (1733-1734). Jean-Pierre Crousaz, a Swiss clergyman and critic of some prominence, was much disturbed by Pope's poem, which seemed to him—as indeed it did to others—to deny Christian moral teaching and instead to advocate a form of deism. In the three-hundred-page work, Johnson stalwartly defends Pope's poem (with the exception of his theory of a "ruling passion"), and has no trouble showing that Crousaz, who, as he points out, knew no English, was misled by the many errors in the French translation that he used. Johnson makes his points by careful scrutiny of short passages of the poem and Crousaz's interpretation of them—the kind of "close reading" which was to be characteristic of Johnson's later literary criticism. As with Lobo and Sarpi, Johnson again demonstrates his concern with cultural events elsewhere than in Britain.

The *Gentleman's Magazine* between 1739 and 1744 contains much else by Johnson besides what has already been mentioned. Indeed there may be still more to be found; most journalism at that time was unsigned. Many of these pieces are short biographies, for the most part derived from earlier sources but enhanced by vivid and lucid prose and including frequent interpolations of pungent comment by Johnson. The lives of Sir Francis Drake, who in the reign of Elizabeth I circumnavigated the world and terrorized the Spanish fleet, and Robert Blake, Oliver Cromwell's admiral who defeated the Dutch, were no doubt inspired by the opposition line of castigating Walpole for Britain's failures in naval actions against the Spanish. The life of Herman Boerhaave praises the great Dutch medical scientist's championship of scientific empiricism against dogmatic theorizing, and his adherence to simple and pious Christianity. The sketches of the Dutch scholar Pieter Burman and the scholarly prodigy Jean-Philippe Barretier are, like the Boerhaave life, extended obituaries—all three had only recently died. The life of Thomas Sydenham, a famous medical innovator of the seventeenth century, and a translation of a eulogy of the French botanist Louis Morin by Fontenelle, secretary of the French Académie des Sciences, further demonstrate Johnson's interest in the sciences, as his translation of a long excerpt from the Frenchman J.-B. Du Halde's account of China indicates his interest in distant lands and cultures. A penetrating review of the memoirs of Sarah, Duchess of Marlborough, widow of the great duke and herself the close confidant and adviser—some said dominator—of Queen Anne, passes incisive judgments on the still controversial political events of the reigns of the last Stuarts and considers the problems of the historian: "Distrust is a necessary qualification of a student in history. Distrust quickens his discernment of different degrees of probability, animates his search after evidence, and perhaps heightens his pleasure at the discovery of

truth; for truth, though not always obvious, is generally discoverable."

In the later years of his connection with the *Gentleman's*, Johnson was also involved in the immense task of preparing a multivolumed catalogue of the great library of the Harleys, Earls of Oxford, an experience which gave him intimate familiarity with a huge number of pamphlets emanating from the political and religious controversies of sixteenth- and seventeenth-century England, some of which he annotated in the *Harleian Miscellany* (1744-1746), an eight-volume collection of reprints of some of them, and insight into the scholarly techniques needed to make proper use of them. His introduction to this miscellany is a splendid essay, "On the Origin and Importance of Small Tracts and Fugitive Pieces," which contains a rousing paragraph in praise of them as a manifestation of a free press in a free country:

> The form of our government, which gives every man that has leisure, or curiosity, or vanity the right of inquiring into the propriety of public measures, and, by consequence, obliges those who are entrusted with the administration of national affairs to give an account of their conduct to almost every man who demands it, may be reasonably supposed to have occasioned innumerable pamphlets which would never have appeared under arbitrary governments, where every man lulls himself in indolence under calamities of which he cannot promote the redress, or thinks it prudent to conceal the uneasiness of which he cannot complain without danger.

These early writings of Johnson have sometimes been disparaged as "hackwork." They were written to earn a living, to be sure, as a great deal of his later work was. But they are indispensable in showing us the foundations of the intellectual concerns and attitudes that persisted throughout his life, and the reader cannot neglect them without putting himself in danger of too shallow an understanding of Johnson's later writings.

Around 1744 Johnson's connection with the *Gentleman's Magazine* began to be more tenuous, but he and Cave collaborated on other projects. One of them was Johnson's most substantial piece of biography. In 1743 the writer who called himself Richard Savage died in a debtor's prison in Bristol. For many years he had made himself notorious in London by his ability to ingratiate himself with one patron after another, then to alienate him by extravagant antics, and to publish

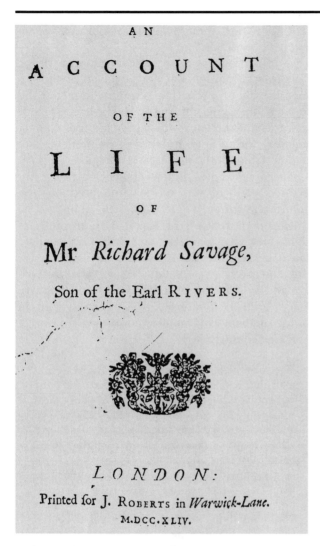

AN

ACCOUNT

OF THE

LIFE

OF

Mr *Richard Savage,*

Son of the Earl RIVERS.

LONDON:

Printed for J. ROBERTS in *Warwick-Lane.*

M.DCC.XLIV.

Title page for Johnson's biography of the poet who claimed to be the illegitimate son of Anne, Countess Macclesfield, and Richard Savage, Earl Rivers

satiric denunciations and complaints of the way so talented an individual as himself was ill-used by society—the paradigm of an "injustice collector" as one psychiatric critic calls him. At some time or other Johnson had known him and, like others, been attracted by his charismatic personality: Johnson related how, having not even the few pence needed for a bed in the meanest flophouse, they roamed the London streets together at night, inveighing against the crimes of the Walpole government, "reforming the world, dethroning princes, establishing new forms of government, and giving laws to the several states of Europe." Savage was thought to have provided the model for Thales in *London,* who, like Savage, went into exile in Wales.

On Savage's death Cave and Johnson saw that a biography of this well-known figure could be popular. Moreover, his strange career and personality offered Johnson a compelling challenge. Savage made much of the story he told very plausibly of his origin. According to him, he was the son of Anne, Countess of Macclesfield, by an adulterous affair with Richard Savage, Earl Rivers, and she freely proclaimed this to facilitate her divorce by her husband. After the divorce, Lady Macclesfield displayed the greatest hostility toward the child, would have nothing to do with him, and arranged to have him brought up in ignorance of his identity and in the humblest circumstances, even trying to have him shipped off to America. He went on to tell a pathetic story of how, after he learned his true identity, he used to haunt the street before her house hoping for a glimpse of her, and once, when the door was left open, ventured to enter and present himself to her, hoping for some token of affection. Instead, she screamed and ordered the servants to eject this intruder who had planned to murder her. Later, after Savage had been convicted of killing a man in a tavern brawl—he maintained that it was in self-defense—and sentenced to death, she intervened with the queen to try to prevent his being pardoned, though she was unsuccessful in doing so.

All this Lady Macclesfield denied, and indeed there is not a scrap of evidence of its truth other than Savage's assertions. History is full of impostors who have maintained that they were the long-lost and ill-used children of some celebrity. Johnson took this story from an earlier anonymous biography of Savage, the details of which were probably supplied by Savage himself, embellished them and obviously relished them: his dramatic prose makes his book a classic tearjerker. It has been suggested that his doing so throws some light on his suppressed feelings toward his own mother. Throughout the rest of the book, Johnson relates Savage's later ups and inevitable downs. He is fully aware of Savage's self-destructive and self-pitying nature. His account of Savage's furious indignation when some friends took up a collection to buy him a much needed suit of clothes and prudently gave the money to the tailor instead of to Savage himself, is reminiscent of an incident when Johnson was an undergraduate at Oxford, and his friends, noticing that his shoes were so dilapidated that he could not attend lectures, quietly placed a new pair before his door. As they stole away, the door opened and the shoes were hurled after them.

Gough Square, London, where Johnson lived during the years he worked on his Dictionary *(ceiling painting by Felix Kelly, in the Donald Hyde Rooms at the Houghton Library, Harvard University)*

The *Life of Mr. Richard Savage* (1744) is an astonishing work, perhaps the first "psychobiography" ever written. It alternates between passages of sympathetic description of Savage's woes, and analyses of the causes of them—Savage's irresponsibility and high opinion of his own importance, which Johnson clearly discerns and condemns. Yet it ends with this memorable apologia (though a paragraph was added, perhaps at Cave's insistence, emphasizing Savage's "want of prudence . . . negligence, and irregularity"): "Those are no proper judges of his conduct who have slumbered away their time on the down of plenty, nor will a wise man easily presume to say, 'Had I been in Savage's condition, I should have lived, or written, better than Savage.'" Perhaps this is also an apologia for the rebellious violence of some of young Johnson's early writings against "the establishment," and perhaps the writing of his friend's life had some kind of cathartic effect on his own bitterness about the world's neglect of his talents. At any rate he was later to retract his earlier denunciations of Walpole as the source of all the evil in his world: "He was a fine fellow. . . . He honoured his memory for having kept his country in peace many years, as also for his goodness and placability of his temper."

"Ambition is a noble passion," when properly directed, Johnson once declared, and wrote of Pope, "Self-confidence is the first requisite to great undertakings." Johnson was now in his mid thirties, and it became evident that he was intent on greater undertakings than those he had so far tried his hand on. The greatest challenge to an eighteenth-century man of letters was to edit Shakespeare, as Pope himself had done, with less than notable success. In 1745 Cave published a sheet of "Proposals for Printing"—by subscription—"a New Edition of the Plays of William Shakespeare," in ten volumes. The editor was to be "the Author of the Miscellaneous Observations on the Tragedy of Macbeth," a sixty-four-page pamphlet to which the proposals were appended. These "notes critical and explanatory" on *Macbeth* were intended as a sample of what might be expected in the edition, and were praised by William Warburton, who in his own edition of Shakespeare in 1747, said they were written by "a man of parts and genius"—a compliment for which the unknown Johnson was grateful, and which caused him to mitigate some of the very harsh criticism he bestowed on Warburton's edition when his own at last came out, twenty years later.

The 1745 proposals proved abortive; the rival bookseller Jacob Tonson declared that he was the sole proprietor of the copyright of Shakespeare's works, and threatened Cave with a lawsuit. The intervention turned out to be a blessing in disguise, for it deflected Johnson into another "great undertaking," which was to prove essential for the success of his own eventual edition. This was the first scholarly historical dictionary of the English language. The idea of preparing scholarly dictionaries of the new vernacular tongues that had replaced the Latin of the Roman Empire and the older Germanic tongues of its barbarian conquerors arose in the Renaissance. In Italy one of the recently founded scholarly academies, the Accademia della Crusca, had in 1612 published its *Vocabolario* of the new tongue of that country. In 1694 there appeared the *Dictionnaire* of the Académie Française, founded in emulation of the Italian academies.

These were not, like the ordinary "desk dictionary," intended merely for the casual user to check spelling and look up the meaning of "hard words," but were minutely detailed historical records of how the words in their language had hitherto been used, like the successor to Johnson's dictionary, the great *Oxford English Dictionary*. The function of his, Johnson wrote, was to facilitate "exactness of criticism and elegance of style." Johnson was also keenly aware that Britain in the eighteenth century was in the process of becoming a world power instead of the insignificant little island on the fringes of Europe that it had been, and that English would eventually become a world language. In his *Plan of a Dictionary* (1747) he expressed his hope that it would "fix" the language. But after he had completed his work on it, he confessed in its preface that this goal had been impossible—that language would inevitably suffer a process of change, and that his duty was not to "form, but register the language," not to "teach men how they should think, but relate how they have hitherto expressed their thoughts." At the same time the existence of such a record would inevitably result in a degree of stability, desirable in a language which was to be-

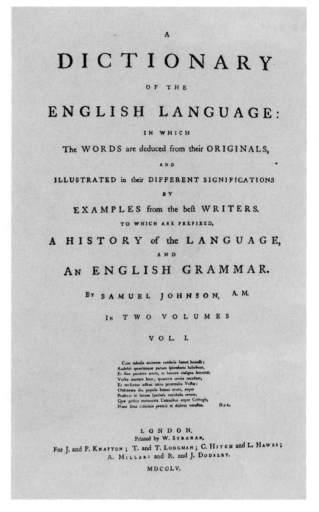

Title page for the first scholarly historical dictionary of the English language

come the means of communication among peoples in many parts of the world. The existence of Johnson's *Dictionary* and its successors did undoubtedly slow the rate of change of the language.

"Such as Chaucer is, shall Dryden be," Pope had lamented. Three hundred years after Chaucer wrote, his English was almost unintelligible except to the specially trained student; Dryden's, after the same period of three hundred years, remains perfectly lucid, virtually indistinguishable from that written in the twentieth century. It is presumably advantageous to be able to read Dryden as easily as a modern newspaper editorial, and for this we have Johnson and later lexicographers to thank.

Johnson acknowledged the great Italian and French dictionaries as his inspiration. They were produced over many years by teams of learned scholars, that of France being sponsored by the government itself. Johnson's was the result of private enterprise—that of a consortium of London publishers, with whom Johnson contracted in 1746 to produce it in three years, though in fact it took nine. The publishers agreed to pay him fifteen hundred guineas—modern equivalent around fifty thousand dollars. Out of this Johnson had to pay for the services of six assistants, who sat at tables in the attic of Johnson's rented house in Gough Square, London—still shown to visitors—taking dictation or assembling slips. The account given in James Boswell's *Life of Johnson* of how it was compiled is completely mistaken and was corrected not long afterward by Johnson's friend Thomas Percy. Johnson went about the task in a way not essentially different from the way modern dictionaries are constructed. He read through the books which he thought represented the best writing in standard modern English, marking words which seemed to exemplify various shades of meaning. The books so marked were given to the amanuenses, who noted the first letter of the marked word and copied on a slip of paper the sentence containing it. The slips were later assembled under the words so illustrated, and eventually arranged in alphabetical order (later lexicographers would use three-by-five-inch cards instead of slips, and still later, a computer program would do the recording and sorting). When this work had been done, Johnson would study the slips for a certain word, sort them out according to the different significations they seemed to convey in various contexts, formulate a definition to suit each of them, select quotations that supported that definition, arrange the definitions, along with the protocol quotations for each in an order that usually runs, roughly, from the more concrete to the more abstract or figurative, and send the result to the printer.

When the work was at last complete in 1755, it was at once recognized as England's greatest contribution to lexicography. Presentation copies were sent to the Italian and French academies and received with high compliment: "It was a very noble work, would be a perpetual monument of fame to the author, an honor to his own country in particular, and a general benefit to the republic of letters," said the president of the Accademia della Crusca. They sent presentation copies of their own dictionaries to Johnson in return. The two heavy folio volumes, priced at four pounds, ten shillings—around $150, about what a publication of that size would cost today—

contained some 40,000 word entries, with a total of around 115,000 supporting quotations; it was estimated that these were chosen from a total of twice that number collected for the purpose. The subtle discriminations between shades of meaning are impressive—the verb *to fall* is given 69 different significations, *to set* 88, *to take* 134; the *Oxford English Dictionary* has more, but it drew from a further century and a half of widespread use of English. Johnson, in his splendid preface, had named Francis Bacon, Richard Hooker, John Milton, and Robert Boyle, representing respectively philosophy, theology, poetry, and science, as models of the sources from which he had worked, but more mundane sources were also heavily drawn on, manuals of gardening, husbandry, military terminology, and other practical matters.

There was to be criticism of various definitions, some of it misplaced. The fact that *oats* were consumed by humans as well as by horses in Scotland had been noted by earlier commentators as an unusual phenomenon worth recording; the definition of *excise*—"a hateful tax levied upon commodities . . . "—a subject of much political controversy at the time, is no more hostile than the remarks on the subject in Sir William Blackstone's *Commentaries* (1765-1769), the great legal textbook of the century; the entry for *Whig*, which has been faulted for its tendentiously brief definition ("the name of a faction") contains a long and sympathetic description of Whig principles by Bishop Gilbert Burnet, a leading Whig. To be sure, Johnson very occasionally indulged his prejudices and his wit, as in the entry for *irony*, "A mode of speech in which the meaning is contrary to the words, as, *Bolingbroke* was a holy man"—the libertine Henry St. John, Viscount Bolingbroke, was one of Johnson's pet hates. The dictionary did not exclude down-to-earth words: *piss*, "To make water" not even stigmatized as "low" as Johnson did some less than elegant words—is wittily illustrated by a quotation from Sir Roger L'Estrange, "One ass pisses, the rest piss for company," an observation which Johnson as well as its author no doubt thought had some relevance to human as well as quadruped behavior. Four editions of the complete work were published in Johnson's lifetime, the last, in 1773, being extensively revised by Johnson himself. There were numerous later editions and abridgments; it was superseded as the standard authority on English vocabulary only by the *Oxford English Dictionary*, published between 1884 and 1928.

It might be thought that Johnson's work on this vast project, extending over nearly a decade, would have consumed all his available time and energy. But the fifteen hundred guineas advanced by his publishers by no means covered all his expenses, and had to be supplemented. Philip Dormer Stanhope, Earl of Chesterfield, the *grand seigneur* of the intellectual world at the time, had allowed Johnson to dedicate the *Plan of a Dictionary* to him in 1747; he gave Johnson ten pounds and then ignored him. When at last the work was ready for publication in 1755, Chesterfield hastened to get on the bandwagon by publishing two condescending essays praising it. He received a letter from Johnson that contained the most famous snub in the history of literature; Carlyle called it "the death-knell of patronage."

Meanwhile David Garrick, Johnson's pupil and companion on the road to London, had quickly made a name for himself in the theater, and was soon to become the most celebrated English actor of the century—perhaps of any century. In 1747, he was appointed manager of the Theatre Royal, Drury Lane, and called on his old teacher to write a prologue to be recited at its opening, one of Johnson's finest short poems, briefly surveying the history of English drama and calling on it to use its capacity for "useful mirth and salutary woe" in the service of truth and virtue. When Johnson and Garrick had traveled to London ten years before, Johnson brought with him a draft of a piece he had been working on in the Midlands, a tragedy in blank verse called *Irene* (three syllables—"I-rē-nē"). The then standard way for an ambitious young writer to make a name for himself was to have a successful play performed on the London stage. Johnson's tragedy at first received no encouragement from producers, but at last, in 1749, Garrick put it on at Drury Lane, doing all he could to make it succeed, with a galaxy of leading actors in the cast, and himself playing the principal male role. It ran for nine nights, a moderate success at the time, and brought Johnson three hundred pounds (around twelve thousand dollars).

The play was not, however, revived and has received some harsh criticism, not all of it deserved. The plot, which is based on a historical incident, deals with the classic conflict between duty and inclination; it more closely resembles works such as Pierre Corneille's *Cid* (1637) and Jean Racine's *Bérénice* (1670) than it does most English attempts at tragic drama. The story had been used by earlier dramatists. Irene, a beautiful young Greek, captured at the fall of Constantinople to the Turks in 1453, is passionately loved by the victorious Sultan Mohammed. He wishes to make her his sultana, but she must renounce her Christianity and become a convert to Islam. She is strongly tempted by the grandeur of the position and the power it will give her to do good to the vanquished Greeks. Her friend Aspasia, another Greek maiden, pleads with her not to abandon her religion. In the end, after much inward struggle, she succumbs and agrees to the marriage. But she is unwittingly caught up in an intrigue involving disaffected Turkish officers and Greek captives planning to overthrow Mohammed, and is accused of taking part in a plot to assassinate him. This is a lie, but Mohammed believes it and orders her to be put to death. Too late a messenger comes with proof that Irene has been loyal and indeed tried to prevent Mohammed's murder. It is conceivable that, with brilliant acting and direction, *Irene* might still succeed on the stage. It is handicapped, however, by the somewhat monotonous rhythm of the blank verse traditionally used for English verse tragedy; Johnson would have been more at home writing in heroic couplets, which he always preferred. The stories of Johnson's later mourning, "I thought it had been better" and saying, when a Mr. Pot was reported as having praised it highly, "If Pot says so, Pot lies" are of dubious authenticity.

A month before the first performance of *Irene*, Johnson published his greatest poem, *The Vanity of Human Wishes. The Tenth Satire of Juvenal, Imitated.* Of it and *London*, T. S. Eliot was to write, "Both of them seem to me to be among the greatest verse satires of the English or any other language," and "If lines 189-220 of *The Vanity of Human Wishes*"—the passage on Charles XII of Sweden—"are not poetry, I do not know what is." As used in connection with the Roman poets Juvenal, Persius, and Horace, who inaugurated the genre, "verse satire" was an informally organized address in verse, very often to an intimate friend. Horace's were labeled *sermones*, which means not "sermons" but something like a one-sided conversation, on some subject of contemporary interest, for instance, as in *London*, the current problems of life in that city. *Satura* or *satira* means a mixture, a hodgepodge—any things that strike the speaker's mind, in no particular order. It is almost identical with "dramatic monologue," popular with Robert Browning and T. S. Eliot ("Prufrock," "Gerontion," much of *The Waste*

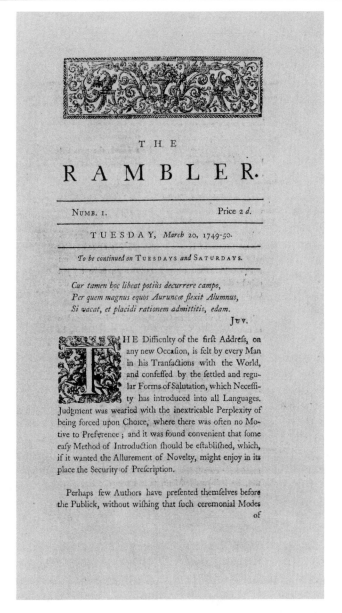

THE

RAMBLER.

NUMB. I.   Price 2 d.

TUESDAY, March 20, 1749-50.

To be continued on TUESDAYS and SATURDAYS.

Cur tamen hoc libeat potiùs decurrere campo,
Per quem magnus equos Auruncæ flexit Alumnus,
Si vacat, et placidi rationem admittitis, edam.
JUV.

THE Difficulty of the first Address, on any new Occasion, is felt by every Man in his Transactions with the World, and confessed by the settled and regular Forms of Salutation, which Necessity has introduced into all Languages. Judgment was wearied with the inextricable Perplexity of being forced upon Choice, where there was often no Motive to Preference; and it was found convenient that some easy Method of Introduction should be established, which, if it wanted the Allurement of Novelty, might enjoy in its place the Security of Prescription.

Perhaps few Authors have presented themselves before the Publick, without wishing that such ceremonial Modes of

The first number of Johnson's first series of periodical essays, through which he hoped to give "ardour to virtue and confidence to truth"

Land). It gives the impression of being casual and haphazard, but when successful, it will have a careful though inconspicuous dramatic organization.

The speaker in Johnson's poem begins with the exhortation to his listener to "Let Observation, with extensive view, / Survey mankind from China to Peru," and discover how much needless unhappiness is caused the human race by pursuing fallacious objects of desire that are thought to lead to happiness, but do not. The opening couplet does not, as has been asserted, say, "Let observation with extensive observation observe mankind extensively." As the critic George Saintsbury pointed out, observation (here personified) may be intensive or extensive; Johnson specifies the latter. It may observe various things, nature, governments, mankind; Johnson specifies the last. China, in the northeast corner of a map of the world with Britain at its center, was regarded in the eighteenth century as the home of a peaceful and enlightened civilization, superior to that of war-torn Europe. Peru, in the diagonally opposite corner, had been not long before the scene of the massacres and oppression inflicted on the native population by Francisco Pizarro and his Spanish invaders. The two places represent the two contrasting poles of potential human activity, from the best to the worst.

The poem continues with accounts of how the pursuit of merely human values leads in the end not to the expected happiness but to misery; how desire for political power destroyed Thomas Wolsey; George Villiers, first Duke of Buckingham; Thomas Wentworth, Earl of Strafford; and Edward Hyde, Earl of Clarendon; how the reward of ambition for scholarly fame may be "Toil, envy, want, the garret, and the jail"—after Johnson's encounter with Chesterfield, "garret" was changed to "patron"; for military glory, the inglorious end of the young King Charles XII of Sweden and the humiliations of Xerxes of Persia and Charles Albert of Bavaria; how he who yearns for a long life may end it in senile impotence; how the young woman who thinks physical beauty and desirability the be-all and end-all at last finds only contempt and infamy. Or, as it has been more succinctly put, "Be careful of what you wish for when you are young, for you may get it."

Does this gloomy recital mean, as some have thought, that human life is inevitably destined to be miserable? Not at all: the poem asserts not the vanity of human *life* but the vanity of merely human *wishes*; if one wants to avoid self-inflicted misery, adopt another set of values than those of wealth, power, glory, and the rest. Perhaps one should start reading the poem with its final twenty-five lines. If the pursuit of the objects described has resulted only in disillusion and grief, "Where then *shall* hope and fear their objects find?" Is the answer the Stoic and fatalist one, "Hope and fear nothing: refuse to get emotionally involved with anything"? "Must dull Suspense corrupt the stagnant mind? / Must helpless man, in ignorance sedate, / Roll darkling down the torrent of his fate?" "Enquirer, cease," the listener is abruptly told: there *are* things to be hoped and ceaselessly sought for which will not in the end produce such sterile and frustrated lives as those that have been described—not the "human" wishes for power, wealth, beauty, but those derived from a more than human source, the heavenly values of love, patience, faith ("faith, hope, charity"). "With these celestial Wisdom calms the mind," the poem ends, "And *makes* the happiness she does not *find*." This is an optimistic, not a pessimistic, view of life.

The plan of the poem is curiously close to that of *The Waste Land* ("waste" and "vanity" come from the same Latin root, *vanus*, empty). The first four sections of Eliot's poem (1922) give a most depressing picture of life in an emotionally sterile world; the last presents the remedy, "give, sympathize, control," and ends with an evocation of "the peace which passeth understanding." Like Eliot's, Johnson's poem is a difficult one. Garrick said rightly that when Johnson was younger, and "saw a good deal of what was passing in life, he wrote his *London*, which is lively and easy"—so much so that its exuberance gives the impression that, however many faults may be found with the London of the 1730s, life in it was at least exciting. "When he had become more retired"—as he must have done when beginning work on the *Dictionary*—"he gave us his *Vanity of Human Wishes*, which is as hard as Greek." Anyone who wishes to test this assertion might try a close reading of lines 135-156, sorting out the close-packed and bewilderingly varied imagery in the description of the young scholar's "quest."

After 1755 Johnson became widely known as "Dictionary Johnson." But before that time, and indeed after it, he was often referred to as "the Author of *The Rambler*," the great series of essays he published every Tuesday and Saturday from March 1750 to March 1752. The periodical essay is a form almost exclusively to be found in eighteenth-century Britain. It was made immensely popular by *The Tatler* and *The Spectator* of Steele and Addison from 1709 to 1714. It looked like something easy to write, and hundreds of imitations were begun by ambitious young authors during the following decades. But to turn out without interruption six carefully written essays a week, as with *The Spectator*, or twice a week, as with *The Rambler*, or even once a week, as with Johnson's *The Idler*, was a grueling task, and the great majority of them ceased after a few numbers. The genre demands different abilities from the "occasional essay," such as Montaigne, Francis Bacon, and Charles Lamb wrote when some subject took their fancy. Perhaps the closest modern analogy is with the work of the popular syndicated newspaper columnist, who also is required to produce his copy at stated times, and has certain topics and points of view his readers come to expect. The columnist signs his actual name, or sometimes an easily penetrated pseudonym. The author—or authors, for they were sometimes jointly written—of the periodical essay adopted the name of a persona, "Mr. Tatler," "Mr. Spectator," "Mr. Rambler," which he sometimes but by no means always paid lip service to in his writing; but, as with the columnist, the author of the periodical essay gave his reader some assurance of a certain amount of consistency in

The first number of Johnson's second essay series, which includes far more political commentary than The Rambler

the subjects he might expect to read about and the views about them he might expect to encounter.

Johnson closed his last *Rambler* with the assertion that his intention in the series had been to give "ardour to virtue and confidence to truth." The subjects of the essays, as in other such series, are highly diverse, and the same rich variety is to be found in his later essay series, *The Adventurer* (1752-1754), a collaboration of four authors, and *The Idler* (1758-1760). There is much on writing itself—journalism, biography, diction, versifica-

tion, translation. There are a large number about social evils: denunciation of imprisonment of debtors, the harshness of the criminal law (Johnson's plea that capital punishment be restricted to cases of murder is far ahead of his time), vivisection, the social conditions that give rise to prostitution, the tyranny of country squires—attitudes that nowadays would cause him to be considered a thoroughgoing "liberal." Many—a familiar device of the genre—consisted of letters supposedly written to Mr. Rambler or Mr. Idler asking for his advice about personal problems. There are memorable satires of would-be literary critics and fanatically partisan politicians.

Contemporary (and later) readers sometimes complained about the "heavy" prose style of *The Rambler*, and compared it unfavorably with the lighter touch of *The Spectator*. It is true that the papers—like *The Vanity of Human Wishes*—are closely written and require careful and sensitive reading in order to follow their sometimes intricate exposition of an abstract moral question. It was reported, although no concrete evidence was cited, that they had a circulation of only five hundred, compared with that of *The Spectator*, at its height, of ten thousand. But it has also been shown that of the current series of periodical essays *The Rambler* was the most frequently reprinted by the provincial press. *The Idler*, printed, unlike *The Rambler*, as a "column" in a weekly journal, the *Universal Chronicle*, generally has a lighter touch in its prose, but contains some of Johnson's most blistering comments on political matters—the tremendous denunciation in *Idler* 81 of the history of European oppression of the native population of the Americas, and *Idler* 22 (in the original numbering—it was omitted from the collected editions, perhaps because of its bitterness), in which a family of vultures observes the scene of gore left on a human battlefield and speculate what motives these strange creatures can have for slaughtering each other to provide a feast for vultures.

The presence of such political commentary in *The Idler* is accounted for by the fact that a great international war—a world war—had broken out in 1756, between Britain and Prussia on one side and France and Austria, later joined by Spain, on the other. This, the Seven Years' War, was to lead to the acquisition by Britain of Canada and India, and, indirectly, to the American Revolution. When the *Dictionary* was at last published in 1755, the fifteen hundred guineas from its publishers had long gone, and Johnson had at once to turn to other projects to earn a living. In the spring of 1756 he became editor of a new monthly, the *Literary Magazine*, which, in spite of its title, was largely devoted, under Johnson's editorship, to foreign affairs and, in particular, the course of the new war, the official declaration of which he printed in full in its first number. He was not inexperienced in such matters. His involvement in the "Foreign History" feature in the *Gentleman's* had familiarized him with the events of the War of the Austrian Succession and helped him with the background for a long biographical account in the *Literary Magazine* of Frederick "the Great" of Prussia, Britain's ally in the later war.

That war was very popular in Britain, especially when it became clear, after some early reverses, that the British were on the winning side, and that their success in it would lead to the establishment of a worldwide empire, with greatly increased opportunities for British trade. From the beginning Johnson expressed the strongest hostility to this enterprise, and published in his new journal what was planned to be a series of long articles giving a most uncomplimentary history of British involvement in colonization and consequent embroilment with foreign powers. Why shed blood for the possession of Canada, "a cold, uncomfortable, uninviting region, from which nothing but furs and fish were to be had"? In North America his sympathies are all with the natives, whom the European invaders have robbed of their lands: "The American dispute between the French and us is . . . only the quarrel of two robbers for the spoils of a passenger." When the French capture the island of Minorca, Johnson's attitude is "good riddance"; it would be well to get rid of Gibraltar as well. When Admiral John Byng was court-martialed and executed for the loss of Minorca, an action which Johnson maintained was only a cover-up for the administration's incompetence, he is as vociferous as his French counterpart Voltaire in its condemnation. That Johnson had been put in charge of the journal may have been due only to the fact that its proprietors were supporters of William Pitt, who at the time was in opposition to the administration. When, after five numbers of the journal had been published, Pitt was returned to power and took over the running of the war, Johnson's antiwar and antiadministration efforts were no longer in demand. The magazine adopted a stridently "patriotic" position, and, except for a few later articles, there is no further sign of Johnson's hand in it.

The *Literary Magazine*, however, contains some brilliant journalism by Johnson. There is close coverage of the war and foreign relations, including the printing in full of public documents concerned with them, and much incisive book reviewing. One long review is superb. A wealthy dilettantish dabbler in politics, literature, and theology, Soame Jenyns, had published *A Free Enquiry into the Nature and Origin of Evil*, purporting to answer the age-old question, how, given a God who is both omnipotent and benevolent, can we account for the presence of evil in the world which He has created? Jenyns explains this by use of the well-worn device of "the great chain of being": if one takes the long view, what appears to be evil to the individual who suffers pain or loss or poverty is really for the overall good of the whole of creation. In any case, God has mercifully provided alleviation for these evils by keeping the poor ignorant: there are some who would foolishly bestow education on the poor, but this would only increase their sensitivity to the ills they are exposed to. Ignorance is the opiate of the poor, Jenyns asserts. Johnson, who had had firsthand experience of poverty in a way Jenyns had not, has no difficulty demolishing such arguments.

Johnson's wife had died in 1752, and he poignantly records the loss and his loneliness at the end of his preface to the *Dictionary*. A year later he hoped to marry a second time; the lady who was apparently his choice, the learned and pious Hill Boothby, was already ill and died shortly afterward. Johnson's mother followed in 1759. For all that she had lived almost ninety years and that Johnson's relations with her may not always have been satisfactory—he did not see her during the last twenty years of her life—her death was another blow. To pay for the expenses of her last illness, he wrote, "in the evenings of a week," *The History of Rasselas, Prince of Abyssinia*, a *conte philosophique* like Voltaire's *Candide* (which appeared at almost the same time), rather than a romance or a novel. It opens in "The Happy Valley," surrounded by high mountains, where the younger relations of the Emperor of Abyssinia are immured for life so they can offer no danger to his rule. (This had been a historical custom in Ethiopia, except that the place of imprisonment was a mountain rather than a valley; Johnson had read many travelers' accounts of that distant land as well as that of Father Lobo.) Among its inmates is the fourth son of the emperor, Rasselas—"Ras" is an Ethiopian title meaning "prince" or "chief."

Although the Happy Valley is provided with everything to satisfy the physical wants of its inhabitants—the ultimate "welfare state"—the young prince is not happy (nor, it transpires, are its other dwellers, in spite of all the sensual gratification they receive). Why? Because he has nothing to hope and long for, nothing to feed "that hunger of imagination which preys incessantly upon life, and must be always appeased by some employment." Man's nature is such that he must al-

ways strive for something beyond his reach; to rest content with what he has is to deny that nature. The theme is remarkably close to that of Johann Wolfgang von Goethe's *Faust* (1808), where Faust agrees that his soul will be forfeit to Mephistopheles if, no matter how his human wishes are gratified—Johnson had written a poem about them—the day should come when he can say, "I am content." It never does. An old teacher of Rasselas reproaches him: if he knew the miseries of the outside world, he would appreciate life in the Happy Valley. Now at last Rasselas has something to desire—to see that outside world. He tunnels through the rocks, and is joined by an older man, the poet Imlac, who tells the story of his eventful life in the outside world, where, like Candide, he has constantly met with disillusion—and yet he is bored by the stultification of the Happy Valley. They are unexpectedly joined at the last moment by Rasselas's highly intelligent sister, the Princess Nekayah, and her lady companion Pekuah.

They emerge from the tunnel and set out on their search for a solution to the problem of "the choice of life," as Johnson originally entitled the tale. They sample the busy life of Cairo and the solitary life of a hermit, the pastoral life and the life of the rich and powerful, none of which leads to happiness. Nekayah makes a special study of married life, and comes to the conclusion "Marriage has many pains, but celibacy has no pleasures." Rasselas attends the lectures of learned philosophers, one of whom informs him that the answer lies in Stoic detachment—never allow yourself to be emotionally involved with anything outside yourself—and then breaks down at the news of his daughter's death. Another informs him that the secret is "to live according to Nature," but when Rasselas asks him, cannot explain how to go about this. While the others explore the Great Pyramid and wonder what can have possessed its builders to erect so enormous and useless a structure—it was the incessant human hunger of imagination, Imlac explains—Pekuah is carried off by a handsome Arab sheikh, who bears her away to his harem. This turns out to be another Happy Valley: the women have no outlets for *their* imagination and live frivolous and discontented lives; Pekuah wonders how the sheik can endure these bored and boring creatures. It is of course Pekuah's lively intelligence that attracts him; he too is an intelligent and honorable person and at length returns Pekuah to her companions. But intelligence in itself is not enough to ensure happiness. They visit a famous astronomer, who, after many years of studying the heavenly bodies in solitude, becomes paranoid and convinces himself that it is he who controls their movements. The astronomer is eventually cured of his "dangerous prevalence of imagination"—the dangerous condition when fantasy prevails over contact with reality—by being gradually weaned away from his solitary existence and brought into contact with his fellow human beings, especially—a nice touch—with the feminine charms of Nekayah and Pekuah.

They discuss death and the arguments for the immortality of the soul. At last they feel they have come to the end of their searches, and it is time to make their choices of life. They decide to return to their native Abyssinia—though not to the Happy Valley, where the one thing guaranteed is unhappiness—and to enter on the occupations which most attract their imaginations: for Rasselas, government; for Nekayah, education; for Pekuah, the administration of a convent of pious young women (perhaps a reaction to her observation of the life of the harem). They set high ideals for themselves in these, though knowing that those ideals will never be fully realized. As Johnson put it at the end of *Adventurer* 84, "Some deficiency must be forgiven all, for all are men. . . . It is, however, reasonable to have perfection in our eye, that we may always advance towards it, though we know it never can be reached." *Rasselas* has always been popular: hundreds of editions and dozens of translations have been and continue to be published.

The death in 1760 of George II, aged seventy-seven, whom Johnson had so often denounced along with the Whig ministries the king had supported, and the accession to the throne of his grandson George III, aged twenty-two, seemed to many, including Johnson, to give hope of a "new deal" in British politics. The new king was a conscientious and idealistic youth, as suspicious as Johnson of the old Whig oligarchy. George II and Walpole had been much condemned for failing to encourage literature and the arts; George III's first administration seemed to give notice of a change by awarding Johnson in 1762 an annual government pension of three hundred pounds. Such pensions to impecunious writers and scholars were not uncommon, but Johnson's came at an unfortunate time, when George was evidently intent on freeing himself from the old Whig ascendancy and bringing in

new ministers unconnected with it, such as the Scottish John Stuart, third Earl of Bute. Johnson's powerful blasts against the old political regime were well known; moreover, the practice of rewarding minor political hangers-on of the administration with pensions had impelled him to define *pension* in the *Dictionary* as "pay given to a state hireling for treason to his country." Hitherto most published comment on Johnson's work had been laudatory or at least respectful. Now he was subjected by those hostile to the political innovations of the new regime to a furious tirade of condemnation as a hireling lackey of the tyrannical administration of George III, and for the rest of his life abuse continued not only of his alleged political stance, but of his physical appearance, his personality, his prose style, his *Dictionary*, and almost everything else he wrote. Much of this abuse was repeated in the next century by that dedicated Whig propagandist Thomas Babington Macaulay, and traces of it still linger in modern comment on Johnson.

Johnson paid little heed; for the first time in his life he was free of pressing financial need. His way of life continued to be modest, but to assuage his loneliness he maintained a household of individuals whom his more fashionable friends tended to look down their noses at: the blind, but cultured, Anna Williams, a close friend of his dead wife; Elizabeth Desmoulins, daughter of his godfather Samuel Swynfen of Lichfield; an unqualified medical practitioner, Robert Levett, who worked with London slum dwellers too poor to pay the fee for regular medical attendance; his black servant, Frank Barber, born a slave in Jamaica, whom Johnson tried without great success to educate and was to make the residuary legatee of his estate. He could now become less "retired" than when he was slaving at journalism or lexicography. He paid his first visit in twenty years to his native Lichfield, finding "the streets much narrower and shorter than I had left them, inhabited by a new race of people to whom I was very little known." In the following years he made extended visits to Oxford and the Midlands to see old friends, his stepdaughter Lucy Porter and his old schoolfellow John Taylor, and others from time to time; to Cambridge, Devonshire, Lincolnshire, and Northamptonshire; and, in the 1770s, long trips to Scotland, Wales, and France.

In London he engaged in an active social life, dining out often with such friends as the artist Sir Joshua Reynolds, the musician Charles Burney, the scholar and future bishop Thomas

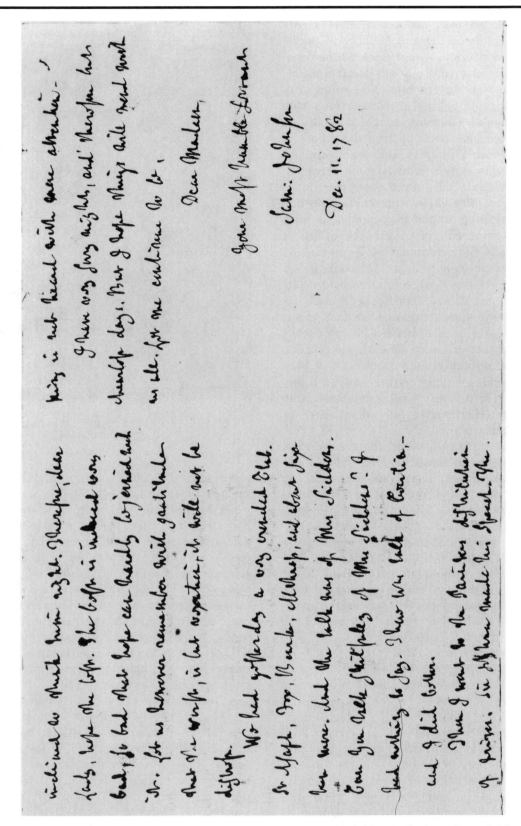

Pages from a letter to Hester Thrale, including a report on a Club meeting—attended by Charles James Fox and Edmund Burke, among others—where actress Sarah Siddons and Fanny Burney's novel Cecilia *were discussed (MA 204; Pierpont Morgan Library). The letter also mentions Sir Joshua Reynolds's most-recent prize-day discourse at the Royal Academy.*

Percy, above all with his new friends Henry Thrale, a wealthy brewer and Member of Parliament, and his vivacious wife, Hester, whose country home, Streatham Place, south of London, became a second home for him. The young Scot James Boswell, in search of famous men with whom to claim acquaintance, sought him out and from time to time, on trips from his home in Edinburgh, called on him and made copious notes of his conversation. Johnson gained a reputation for conversational wit and sometimes rather rough repartee, though, as with other celebrities, many jests floating around in the public domain were illicitly fathered on him. The role in his life of the famous Club, founded by Reynolds and Johnson, has perhaps been exaggerated. It was not, as some readers think, a modern men's club, with a clubhouse to which members regularly resort in the evenings for casual chat. It was a small group, only nine to begin with, which met for dinner at a tavern twice a month when Parliament was in session, around November to May, and, in the years for which records have been preserved, often had a very small attendance, with Johnson himself averaging only about three or four attendances a year.

Johnson's first obligation, after the award of the pension, was to finish his long delayed edition of Shakespeare. The 1745 proposals, we have seen, were withdrawn. But in 1756, after the *Dictionary* had been completed, new proposals were published. Tonson, who had blocked the earlier project, now agreed to print eight octavo volumes of the plays by subscription, with one guinea, half the subscription, to be paid in advance. Johnson dawdled and is even said to have lost the list of subscribers. He was twitted in satiric verse—"He for subscribers baits his hook, / And takes your cash; but where's the book?" The book finally appeared in 1765.

Like everything else of his after the pension, it received some violent attacks, but there is no question that it was by far the best edition of Shakespeare yet published. In the noble preface, as well as much memorable general literary criticism, Johnson states his principles of textual editing, so important in dealing with the difficult text of the early printings of the plays. Earlier editors, such as Pope and Warburton, when confronted by some word or expression unfamiliar to them, simply asserted that it must be a silly printer's mistake, and changed it to something closer to their own vocabulary. Not only was Johnson the first editor of Shakespeare to have access

Johnson in 1769 (mezzotint by James Watson, after a portrait by Sir Joshua Reynolds)

to a historical dictionary of the English of Shakespeare's time, he had compiled it himself. Thus when he sees that some word whose meaning had been forgotten in the eighteenth century makes sense in the signification it had in the sixteenth, he retains it, with an explanatory note. Johnson's is the first "variorum" edition of the plays—that is, it not only includes the present editor's comment on a passage, but republishes the notes of earlier editors which he finds helpful or which contain a misreading that he thinks should be corrected. It has been said that in modern variorum editions, when one wants the clearest and most convincing explanation of an obscure passage, one turns first to Johnson's note on it.

At the end of each play, Johnson makes a general observation on its effectiveness. As always, his criticism begins with his own personal reaction: those reactions are often strong and he has no false modesty about describing them: at the end of *King Lear*, "I was many years ago so shocked by Cordelia's death that I know not whether I ever endured to read again the last scenes of the play till I undertook to revise them as an editor," and of *Julius Caesar*, though many passages in it have been praised, "I have never been strongly agitated in perusing it and think it somewhat cold and unaffecting." Such frankness shocked the bardolaters of the nineteenth century, for whom Shakespeare could do nothing wrong. "Others abide our question; thou art free," wrote Matthew Arnold. To Johnson Shakespeare was a supremely great writer, nevertheless one not superhuman and immune to questioning. In 1773 Johnson published an extensively revised edition of his work in which he was assisted by George Steevens, who played a greater role in the edition of 1778. Nearly all later editions of Shakespeare owe something to these.

For three or four years from 1766 onward, Johnson was involved in another major work, the full details of which have only recently become known. This was his secret collaboration with Sir Robert Chambers, Vinerian Professor of English Law at Oxford University, on a series of lectures introducing undergraduates to the fundamentals of the common law—secret apparently to all Johnson's friends except Mrs. Thrale. Johnson had met Chambers in 1754 when Chambers was only seventeen and had just arrived from his native Newcastle to enroll as a law student at the Middle Temple in London, where Johnson was living at the time, and to matriculate at Lincoln College, Oxford. All who knew Chambers testified to his modesty and amiable disposition, and Johnson seems to have become a kind of surrogate father to him, advising him on his studies, getting him to write an article for his *Literary Magazine*, writing a recommendation when Chambers applied for one of the fellowships endowed by Charles Viner for the advancement of the study of English law, a new subject at Oxford. This fellowship brought Chambers into contact with the first Vinerian Professor, Sir William Blackstone, whose lectures were published as his famous *Commentaries on the Law of England*, throughout the eighteenth and nineteenth centuries the standard textbook for beginning law students in Britain and America.

When Blackstone resigned his chair in 1766, Chambers, only twenty-nine, was appointed to succeed him. He was understandably nervous about having to prepare a lecture series to compete with that of his eminent predecessor, so much so that he found it hard even to begin, and he forfeited a good deal of his stipend for failing to deliver the required number of lectures. He called on Johnson for assistance, and Johnson spent much time in Oxford and London working with him. Eventually a full series was completed,

running to some 450,000 words, which has only recently been published in its entirety. How much of this series comes from Johnson's own hand awaits further study. But certainly there are passages in it which sound very much like Johnson's prose and convey views on history, government, and political morality with which Johnson would certainly have agreed. It was another "great enterprise" almost in the class of the *Dictionary* and the edition of Shakespeare, and its potential for influencing British (and American) legal and political thinking was great.

The early 1770s found Johnson's style of political controversy as vigorous as it had been in the days of Walpole and his cohorts. John Wilkes, a witty and unscrupulous demagogue, after being elected Member of Parliament for the county of Middlesex, had been convicted on a charge of seditious libel and obscene publishing, and sentenced to a fine and imprisonment, whereupon the House of Commons expelled him from its membership. Wilkes was then twice reelected by the voters of Middlesex. The House then passed a resolution declaring him ineligible to sit, and instead seated his opponent, who had obtained only a minority of the votes, as the only qualified candidate in the election. Elected legislative bodies, including the American House of Representatives, still jealously guard their right to expel members whose conduct they disapprove, but the seating of Wilkes's opponent caused a nationwide hullabaloo by the opposition, who trumpeted that democracy was imperiled by this "alarming crisis," and raised the cry of "Wilkes and liberty." Early in 1770, Johnson, who, with his friend Henry Thrale M.P., was on the side of the administration in this, published *The False Alarm*, arguing the case for the House of Commons and sarcastically denouncing Wilkes's supporters as self-seeking rabble-rousers. It is worth noticing that, though Johnson has been denominated an undeviatingly partisan Tory, he denounces the "frigid neutrality" of "the Tories" in this affair.

The next year saw a preview of the struggle over the Falkland Islands that broke out again in 1982. Since the sixteenth century, Spain and Britain had squabbled about which, through early exploration and settlement, had the prior claim to sovereignty of this bleak archipelago in the south Atlantic. In 1770 the governor of Buenos Aires, then a Spanish colony, sent a naval expedition to the islands, which captured the small English settlement there. The British government protested to Madrid against this violation of its sovereignty,

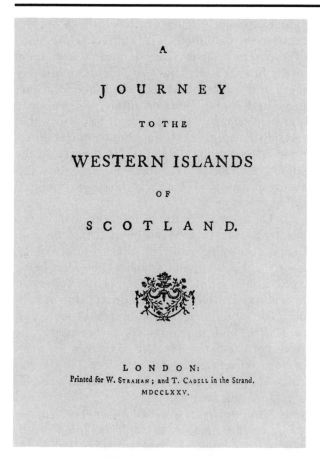

A

JOURNEY

TO THE

WESTERN ISLANDS

OF

SCOTLAND.

LONDON:
Printed for W. Strahan; and T. Cadell in the Strand.
MDCCLXXV.

Title page for Johnson's book about his 1773 visit to the Hebrides with James Boswell

and it seemed that a war might be imminent. The ministry, however, now headed by the young Frederick, Lord North, skillfully used diplomatic negotiations to avert a conflict, and the Spanish eventually agreed to withdraw their forces from the islands, though without prejudice to their claim of sovereignty over them. The opposition in Britain was furious: they had seen in the incident an opportunity to oust North and his ministry, and they accused it of cowardice and of sullying Britain's honor in not making war on Spain. Johnson's *Thoughts on the Late Transactions Respecting Falkland's Islands* (1771) gives a most lucid account of the early history of the islands and the sequence of events that led up to the incident—he had been given access by the government to the official documents concerning it—and has no difficulty in defending the ministry's actions, accusing the opposition of warmongering in order to fill the pockets of their supporters, the defense contractors.

The Patriot (1774) is a short but hard-hitting pamphlet designed to help reelect Thrale as M.P.

in the general election of 1774. It recapitulates the matters discussed in the two earlier pamphlets, and sharply distinguishes between true patriotism and that of the self-proclaimed "patriots" of the opposition: "Patriotism," Johnson was to say in a memorable remark, "is the last refuge of a scoundrel." It introduced a subject which Johnson enlarged on the next year in *Taxation No Tyranny*, a formal answer to the resolutions and address to the British people promulgated by the first Continental Congress, which had met in Philadelphia a few months earlier. Probably the movement for independence in the Thirteen Colonies had by this time gone too far for any attempt at appeasement to be successful. Johnson makes no such attempt. He controverts the American arguments so forcefully that the North ministry, which had more or less sponsored the pamphlet, toned it down considerably at the printer's, much to Johnson's disgust. The main thrust is stated in its title: for a government to collect taxes from a people in order to finance the benefits which that people are receiving from it is not tyranny—in the case of the Americans, the benefits especially of the defense afforded them by the British army and navy, which, at great expense to the British taxpayer, had freed them from the French threat to their north. Yet much of Johnson's lack of sympathy for the American settlers came from the fact that their land had been taken by force from its Indian possessors. As for the lack of American representation in the taxing body, the House of Commons, a large number of British taxpayers had no representation there either. The cry that the British government is planning further oppression by permitting the inhabitants of Quebec to practice their traditional Roman Catholicism, he says, comes oddly from those who are agitating for "freedom of conscience." He gets in another bitter jibe at southern American patriots in "How is it that we hear the loudest yelps for liberty from the drivers of Negroes?" On the right of secession of the Thirteen Colonies from the British empire, Johnson takes the position that Abraham Lincoln was to take eighty-six years later and was to result in a far bloodier war than that of 1775 to 1783: no such right exists. The pamphlet was highly controversial at the time, and still is. But it is vividly written and clearly argued, and cannot be casually dismissed without an attempt to counter those arguments.

An incidental result of Johnson's writing *Taxation No Tyranny* was the award to Johnson by Oxford University, of which Prime Minister Lord

North was the chancellor, of the honorary degree of Doctor of Civil Law (D.C.L.). Ten years earlier, the University of Dublin (Trinity College) had made him Doctor in Utroque Jure (J.U.D.: doctor of both canon and civil law). When the *Dictionary* was published in 1755, strings were pulled to have him awarded an honorary master of arts degree; it was thought that the appearance of "M.A." on the title page would enhance the work's respectability and sales. It is ironic that later writers, though not so many as there once were, have insisted on referring to him as "Doctor Johnson" or "the Doctor," for he thought very little of this title; like most sensible writers holding an honorary doctorate, he never used it, and scolded Boswell for arguing that it ought to be used. Hawkins reported that, after receiving the degree from Dublin, he resented being called "Doctor." Nor was there great distinction in having received the Oxford degree. Two years before, North had on a single occasion conferred sixty-eight honorary doctorates, many of them on minor political hangers-on of his, such as Henry Thrale, M.P., whom no one ever seems to have thought of calling "Doctor Thrale." In his *Journey to the Western Islands of Scotland*, after describing his visit to Aberdeen University, Johnson gives a scathing criticism of the proliferation of doctorates: Aberdeen had given one to William Kenrick, a scurrilous hack writer who had published a violent attack on Johnson's edition of Shakespeare. In the manuscript of his journal of the Scottish tour, which Johnson had read and praised, Boswell always refers to his companion as "Mr. Johnson," but when, after Johnson's death, he put it into print as *The Journal of a Tour to the Hebrides with Samuel Johnson, LL.D.* (1785), he changed all the "Mr.'s" to "Dr.'s" and, in the title of the work, added to Johnson's name the inaccurate "LL.D." One wonders why. At any rate, there seems no more point in a modern reader referring to "Doctor Johnson" than to "Doctor Wordsworth" or "Doctor Einstein," who also held honorary doctorates from Oxford. All three had earned enough distinction by their achievements not to need any more identification than their surnames.

It might seem that by his sixty-sixth year, Johnson had dealt with almost every possible genre of writing. His readers were to be surprised in 1775 to find him dealing successfully with a new one, that of the "travel book"—*A Journey to the Western Islands of Scotland*. "I had desired to visit the Hebrides, or Western Islands of Scot-

land, so long that I scarcely remember how the wish was originally excited," it begins. The notion of Johnson's being an insular and bigoted John Bull, uninterested in any place beyond his constricted London parish, is entirely mistaken. When he was only twenty, discontented with Oxford, he was overheard muttering to himself, "Well, I have a mind to see how they go on in other places of learning. I'll go see the universities abroad. I'll go to France and Italy. I'll go to Padua. . . . For an Athenian"—read "Oxonian"—"blockhead is the worst of all blockheads." He eventually got to France, with Mr. and Mrs. Thrale, in the same year his *Journey to the Western Islands of Scotland* was published. Most of this two-month tour was spent in or near Paris, where he saw all the most famous sights, including young King Louis XVI and Marie Antoinette at dinner. In 1774 he had made, with the Thrales, a three-month tour of the English Midlands and north Wales, in which they visited such great country houses as Chatsworth, Blenheim, and Kedleston, and Mrs. Thrale's native Welsh haunts. For the next year, 1775, an extended tour of Italy with the Thrales was planned, but at the last minute young Harry Thrale, their only son, died, and in their distress they did not feel like going. Johnson was deeply disappointed: more than any other place, he had longed to visit Italy, the cradle of the Renaissance, where his early heroes Petrarch and Politian had played their part in "the revival of learning." In the last year of his life, it was thought that the warmth of Italy might help him live through the winter, and plans were made for him to go there, but by that time he was too ill to travel.

Johnson's records of the trips to Wales and France remained in the form of brief diary notes. But those of the tour of Scotland provided the material for a substantial and readable book. From various places on the route he jotted down his observations in long letters to Mrs. Thrale, which he later used when putting the book together. His companion on the tour was James Boswell, who left his own record of it in *The Journal of a Tour to the Hebrides with Samuel Johnson, LL.D.* It has often been remarked that, whereas Johnson's book is about Scotland, Boswell's is about Johnson. Johnson's is much more than the bare record of an itinerary: it has been called a pioneering work of social anthropology. The rugged hills of the Highlands and the life lived there by the clansmen, not long removed from a feudal existence and speaking a tongue of their own, were

Page from the manuscript for Johnson's "Preface to Pope," written in 1780 and published the next year (MA 205; Pierpont Morgan Library) almost as much a mystery to the English and the Lowland Scots as those of Ethiopia, and Johnson wanted to explore that mystery.

The travelers set out from Edinburgh on 18 August 1773. For the first ten days their route lay along the North Sea coast, still part of the "civilized" Lowland culture, where Johnson was received and honored at the Universities of St. Andrews and Aberdeen and where they were welcomed at the homes of Scottish nobles and gentry. At Inverness they bade farewell to roads and wheeled vehicles and continued across the rugged terrain on horseback, accompanied by a sturdy servant and local guides. Johnson talked to the natives he met, questioning them closely about their way of life, and noting details of their occupations, their dwellings, their language, and their food. They crossed the water to Skye, the largest and most settled of the Hebrides, where they were entertained by various Macdonalds and Macleods, the two great clans of the island, with Highland dancing and song and bagpipe music. They clambered among the rocks in the rain, and Johnson had his first and probably only drink of Scotch whisky.

Three matters particularly concerned Johnson. One was the breakdown of the old clan system, and, connected with this, the widespread emigration from the Hebrides to America. He was ambivalent about this change: the orderliness of the clan organization, and the loyalty of the clansmen to their chiefs, appealed to him; yet at the same time he could understand why a Highlander should be willing to endure the hardships of starting a new life in a distant and largely unsettled land in order to have land of his own rather that to hold it at the pleasure of the chief. The other matter was the authenticity of the "Ossian" poems, a best-seller of the time, which James Macpherson proclaimed were translated from orally transmitted poems in Gaelic. After much inquiry, Johnson could find no evidence of the existence of such originals, and denounced them as a hoax, to Macpherson's anger. The travelers experienced some hair-raising journeys by boat to other islands during the stormy autumn season. They reverently visited Iona, where Christianity had first come to Great Britain after the barbarian invasions, and eventually made their way back to Edinburgh on 9 November. Forty years earlier Johnson had written in the dedication of his version of Lobo's *Voyage to Abyssinia*, "A generous and elevated mind is distinguished by nothing more certainly than an eminent degree of curiosity, nor is that curiosity more agreeably or usefully employed than in examining the laws and customs of foreign nations." *A Journey to the Western Islands* shows how agreeably and usefully such a mind can be employed.

Considering how frequently Johnson complained in his letters and diaries of ill health, one is surprised by all this activity in his mid sixties. He never seems to have suffered any incapacitating illness on his strenuous journeys, and one feels strongly tempted to conclude that, like his similarly energetic contemporary Voltaire, he was a considerable hypochondriac. Even more surprising is to find him, on his seventieth birthday in 1779, busily engaged in his last "great undertaking," begun two years before and to continue for another two years. This project was initiated by the London booksellers, a group for which Johnson, himself a bookseller's son, usually had high praise. Alarmed at the rumor that an Edinburgh publisher was bringing out a collection of works of English poets, and wishing to establish what they thought their copyright in these, they projected a multivolume anthology of the works of fifty-two English poets, most of them published between 1650 and 1750. They asked Johnson to write prefaces to the works of each poet. Johnson gladly agreed, asking only two hundred pounds; the delighted publishers at once raised this to three hundred, and later added another hundred.

Probably they expected no more than the perfunctory few pages a modern publisher envisions when he engages a celebrity to provide some desultory comments to be prefaced to a republication of a familiar work, to help publicity and sales; and indeed Johnson's prefaces to the poems of the many minor and forgettable versifiers included among the fifty-two *are* short and perfunctory. But when faced with such challenges as Milton, Dryden, and Pope, Johnson could not resist giving free rein to his pen, and the result was long, pamphlet-length essays. Possibly because of scheduling difficulties in printing so vast a work—it ran to sixty-eight volumes in all—Johnson's contributions did not at first precede the poetry they are supposed to introduce, but were printed separately, four volumes in 1779 and a further six volumes in 1781, although in later editions of the collection, edited by Alexander Chalmers and Robert Anderson, the works were so prefaced. It is important to remember that their original title, *Prefaces, Biographical and Critical, to the Works of the English Poets*, accurately describes their intended

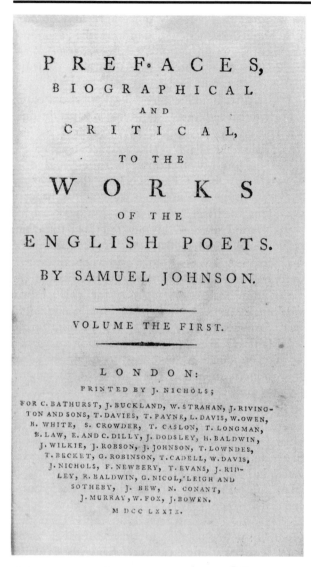

PREFACES,
BIOGRAPHICAL
AND
CRITICAL,
TO THE
WORKS
OF THE
ENGLISH POETS.
BY SAMUEL JOHNSON.

VOLUME THE FIRST.

LONDON:
PRINTED BY J. NICHOLS;
FOR C. BATHURST, J. BUCKLAND, W. STRAHAN, J. RIVING-
TON AND SONS, T. DAVIES, T. PAYNE, L. DAVIS, W. OWEN,
B. WHITE, S. CROWDER, T. CASLON, T. LONGMAN,
B. LAW, E. AND C. DILLY, J. DODSLEY, H. BALDWIN,
J. WILKIE, J. ROBSON, J. JOHNSON, T. LOWNDES,
T. BECKET, G. ROBINSON, T. CADELL, W. DAVIS,
J. NICHOLS, F. NEWBERY, T. EVANS, J. RID-
LEY, R. BALDWIN, G. NICOL, LEIGH AND
SOTHEBY, J. BEW, N. CONANT,
J. MURRAY, W. FOX, J. BOWEN.
M DCC LXXIX.

Title page for the first volume of essays that Johnson wrote as prefaces to a multivolume anthology of the works of fifty-two English poets. Because of delays in printing the anthology, Johnson's prefaces were first published separately.

function. The later popular title, *The Lives of the Poets*, which was not devised by Johnson, is misleading. They are not biographies, and their organization makes this clear: there is first a sketch of the life of the author, and then a critical essay on his writings. In the longer prefaces, there intervenes between these two sections what was called a "character" of the writer—an attempt to sum up and comment on what are perceived as the most important traits in his psychology and behavior.

The biographical parts of the *Prefaces* make delightful reading, at least for those who do not demand a hero-worshiping approach to famous writers, as some of their early readers did, expressing their outrage that Johnson should approach

such celebrities as fallible human beings. Johnson treats them much more in the vein of Lytton Strachey than of Thomas Carlyle. Johnson detests Milton's egocentricity and "left-wing" politics, remarking of his dictatorial treatment of his family, "It has been observed that they who most loudly clamour for liberty do not most liberally grant it" (the observer having been Samuel Johnson, who two years before had written, "How is it that we hear the loudest yelps for liberty from the drivers of Negroes?"). His distaste for Swift has puzzled many; after all, it is argued, they were both strong Tories. Perhaps; but there may be different kinds of Tories, and moreover, Swift called himself a Whig. Johnson's disrespect in referring to George, Lord Lyttelton, as "poor Lyttelton" nearly ruptured his friendship with the magnificent Mrs. Elizabeth Montagu, who admired Lyttelton. There is considerable dry irony at the expense of the somewhat ostentatiously pious Addison (Johnson's irony, for which he had a considerable talent, is often so subtle that casual readers tend not to notice it). Even Pope, to whom he devoted the longest of the biographical sketches and whose poetry he so greatly admired, is not spared, and his numerous human failings are not glossed over.

But in recording the foibles of his subjects, Johnson never becomes indignant. He fully appreciates, to quote the great modern biographer of James Joyce, that artistic grandeur can live with human weakness. In his *Rambler* 60, almost a manifesto of modern biographical theory, he firmly rejects the older view, that the function of biography is to teach morality by presenting either saintly and heroic figures to be imitated or deplorable ones whose vices are to be avoided. Like Strachey after him, he believed, "Human beings are too important to be treated as mere symptoms of the past. They have a value which . . . must be felt for its own sake." "I have often thought," he wrote, "that there has rarely passed a life of which a judicious and faithful narrative would not be useful." And the most telling parts of such a narrative are not of how the subject achieved worldly fame, "not how any man became great, but how he was made happy; not how he lost the favour of his prince, but how he became discontented with himself." Such a narrative will record the small, concrete details of how a life was lived: "Nothing is too little for so little a creature as man." And so we are given such details as the poignant account of Pope's having to be helped by a maid to dress because of his physical weakness, and that he wore three pairs of stockings to make his shrunken legs look more presentable; that Swift used to attend church daily, but as early as possible in the morning so that no one would see him and think him ostentatiously devout; that when Addison "suffered from vexation" by his wife, the haughty Charlotte, Countess of Warwick, he would escape to a tavern and console himself by drinking too much. Sometimes the *Prefaces* are enlivened by personal reminiscences by Johnson himself: how his father reported that Dryden's *Absalom and Achitophel* (1681) had been the second-best-selling item in the history of his bookshop; how the boys of Lichfield grammar school, which Addison had attended, used to engage in the practice of "barring out" the master from admission. The short life of the minor poet Edmund "Rag" Smith—so named from his shabby dress—gives Johnson an opportunity to express his grateful memory of Walmesley's courteously entertaining Lichfield boys such as himself and David Garrick, whose recent death, he laments, "has eclipsed the gaiety of nations, and impoverished the public stock of harmless pleasure."

Thoughtful and readable as the biographical sketches are, so much more scholarly investigation of the lives of figures such as Milton, Dryden, Swift, and Pope has taken place since Johnson's time that the serious student would be foolish to rely on them as definitive. Indeed, some of their most memorable stories have been discredited, such as the one that Swift's animosity toward Dryden can be accounted for by Dryden's having remarked, after reading Swift's early poems, "You will never be a poet, cousin Swift." But the massive body of literary criticism contained in the *Prefaces* remains as valid and thought provoking as ever. Like most other great critics—Dryden, Samuel Taylor Coleridge, Matthew Arnold, T. S. Eliot—Johnson never attempted to construct some all-embracing critical theory: he has little use for those who "judge by principles rather than perception." To try to confine his wide-ranging talent for critical perception in some pigeonhole labeled "neoclassicism" or the like is a waste of time. But certain generalizations about it can be made. Horace had said that poetry—that is, imaginative literature—should either please or instruct. Johnson corrects this prescription to "The end of poetry is to instruct *by* pleasing." "Works of imagination excel by their allurement and delight; by their power of attracting and detaining the attention. That book is

good in vain which the reader throws away." *Imagination* and *imagery* are among the terms Johnson most frequently uses in the *Prefaces*; he is always concerned to assess the skill of the poet in the use of effective images, which called up "pictures to the mind."

The starting point for Johnson's judgment of a work of literature is always the impression it makes on himself. We have seen that his never having been "strongly agitated" by *Julius Caesar* cancels out praise that others have given it. Similarly, *Lycidas* fails to please him: its use of the hackneyed pastoral genre, its blasphemous introduction of pagan mythology into a Christian setting, and, above all, what seems to him the callousness of using the death of a friend as a stage on which to exhibit technical virtuosity makes it impossible for him to respond to the work with anything but repulsion. The language of poetry, he believes (as William Wordsworth was to do), should be contemporary, "a selection of the language really spoken by men," if contemporary readers are to be able to respond to it emotionally. He despises the pedantic and affected use of archaic diction and convoluted sentence order in Thomas Gray and William Collins. The "generality" in literature that he praises, through the mouth of Imlac in chapter 10 of *Rasselas*, means the accessibility of its content to the experience of its readers; it does not mean "abstract," a word Johnson never uses as a critical term. Again, the "instruction" the reader receives through the pleasure a work gives him does not mean the inculcation of moral precepts. A modern interpretation of literature's "instructing by pleasing" might be "by involving the reader emotionally—by 'attracting and detaining his attention'—literature effects desirable changes in the patterns in his nervous system." It is a concept close to Aristotle's *katharsis*, or to Lionel Trilling's description of the function of the modern novel, "the most effective agent of the moral imagination in our time; its greatness and its practical usefulness [lie] in its unremitting work of involving the reader himself in the moral life, inviting him to put his own motives under examination, suggesting that reality is not as his conventional education has led him to see." And literature is and must be "practical" in that sense; it has to do with real human experience or it is nothing. "The only end of reading," Johnson tells Soame Jenyns, "is to enable the readers better to enjoy life, or better to endure it."

Johnson in 1783 (portrait by John Opie; National Galleries of Scotland)

The last few years of Johnson's life were marked by the death of old friends—Garrick, Anna Williams, his companion of so many years, and Robert Levett, whom, in 1783, he mourned in an exquisite elegiac poem. Most disturbing of all were the death of Henry Thrale and the decision of his widow, on whom he had so long depended for sympathy and care—he was surely more than a little in love with her—to marry again, this time the Italian musician Gabriel Piozzi, younger and more attractive than the stolid Henry, whose unfaithfulness to Hester was notorious. Johnson wrote her a letter of terrible denunciation; she replied with an equally spirited one, and communication between them ceased.

A few months before Johnson's death on 13 December 1784, of cardiovascular deterioration,

he had undergone what, in his last prayer, asking God to forgive its lateness, he called his "conversion." A full discussion of Johnson's religious life would be impossible in a short space, and what has been published on it by modern scholars has not been very helpful. But it may be affirmed that, theologically, he was a sincere and orthodox Anglican, displaying an ecumenical tolerance to the theology of other branches of Christianity; he gives, for example, the highest praise to the *Paradise Lost* of the arch-Puritan Milton, and asserts that he appears "to have been untainted by any heretical peculiarity of opinion." The episode of the conversion is related in detail by his old friend and biographer Sir John Hawkins. Hawkins called on Johnson one day, and found him in deep depression. He was suffering from severe edema (dropsy; accumulation of fluid in the tissues), which no medical attention seemed to be able to relieve, and knew that death was near. What concerned him was his spiritual state; he was in agony because he had no confidence of his salvation. Hawkins tried to reassure him by calling attention to the purity of his life and to all that his writings had done for the cause of human virtue. These were of no value, Johnson replied; all that counted was wholehearted faith in God, and this, he felt, he was without. He proposed to spend the next day in seclusion and in prayer and meditation.

On the following day Hawkins called again, and found Johnson now at peace with himself; he reported that after prolonged prayer and deep meditation, there had been a sudden copious evacuation of fluid, and he believed that this was a sign of his acceptability to God. From then until his death, his prayers reflect this new confidence. This incident has puzzled some scholars, but it is perfectly in accordance with the Anglican and general Protestant doctrine of justification by faith alone; mere "good works" in themselves can contribute nothing to an individual's salvation. The doctrine is clearly stated not only in the Anglican Book of Common Prayer, but in one of Johnson's sermons, in which he remarks that, although one may practice the outward forms and ceremonies of a religious life, "To give the heart to God, and to give the whole heart, is very difficult; the last, the great effort of long labour, fervent prayer, and diligent meditation." A recent medical study argues that the diuretic medication Johnson was taking for his dropsy, when accompanied by a state of intense emotion, may result in such a discharge as he experienced.

No doubt because of general concern with psychological matters in recent decades, a good deal has been written attempting to associate Johnson's religious beliefs with the periods of depression which he suffered throughout much of his adult life. The extent of these may have been exaggerated: most literary and other artists have so suffered, many of them to a worse degree than Johnson and with more serious consequences. It is well to keep in mind the opening sentence of one classic biography: "Samuel Johnson was a pessimist with an enormous zest for living," and that pessimism, as his greatest poem makes clear, was directed not toward life itself but toward false values in life. Taking the teachings of Christianity seriously may of course involve the Christian in psychological struggle, in "mental

fight," as very many "spiritual autobiographies," such as Bunyan's, demonstrate. Johnson followed the practice which for many centuries was recommended to Christians, of periodically making a close examination of his spiritual state. He did so each New Year's Day, during Easter week, and on his birthday, vehemently condemning himself for his sloth and other failures to live up to the Christian ideal, asking God's pardon for them, and praying for divine help in self-improvement. Sometimes he reproached himself for laxity in churchgoing, though he once excused himself on the grounds that his partial deafness made it difficult to hear the sermons, and, on one occasion, that when he could hear them, the mouthings of "ignorant and affected" preachers detracted from a religious frame of mind.

The mention of Johnson as a sermon writer is a reminder of what a great deal of his writing even so long an article as this lacks the space to deal with adequately. Sixteen of a reported forty sermons which he composed (for an honorarium of five pounds each) for clerical friends to deliver have survived. They deal lucidly and forcefully with familiar religious topics, and are in the straightforward and somewhat austere style of Anglican homiletics of the time. Johnson was also a skilled letter writer: more than fifteen hundred of his survive, in a great variety of tones, from the charming ones he wrote to Mrs. Thrale's little daughters, the intimate and humorous ones to Mrs. Thrale herself, formal ones to the somewhat intimidating Mrs. Montagu, informal and sometimes ironic ones to James Boswell, to masterpieces of denunciation such as those to Chesterfield and Macpherson and the unforgivable one to Mrs. Thrale on her marriage to Piozzi. There have been collected some fifty anonymous prefaces and dedications he wrote, often to help the sales of works by friends. He polished and added lines to poems by his friend Goldsmith, by George Crabbe, and by others. A good deal of his own best poetry is in Latin, at the time a more frequent medium for poetry of personal reflection and introspection than English. He wrote many more short biographies, reviews, essays, journalistic features and published more editorial work and translation than there has been room to describe here.

After his death, Johnson received many honors. He was buried in Westminster Abbey, near the memorial to Shakespeare, and a fine larger-than-life statue stands prominently in St. Paul's Cathedral, its Roman costume displaying his muscular frame; it gives a very different impression from the most often reproduced portrait of him by Reynolds, which gives him puffy cheeks and a decided pout. A general admiration of Johnson's achievement was the rule until the mid nineteenth century, when the historian Macaulay, in two widely circulated essays, picked up the themes of detraction of the partisans of Johnson's own time and improved on them. Many traits of this caricature were still current in the late twentieth century: Macaulay's account continued to be published in the *Encyclopaedia Britannica* until the 1960s.

Probably no major writer has ever been the subject of more misrepresentation than Johnson. It may be useful to list, in order that the student may avoid them, some of the most widespread errors about Johnson, errors that have long been exploded by serious scholars and careful readers of Johnson's writings. He was not a pigheaded adherent to "Toryism," whatever "Toryism" in the eighteenth century may have been. He was not an authoritarian or a blind devotee of monarchs and monarchism; few of his contemporaries were more devastating in their criticism of the monarchs under whom he lived and the ministries which they appointed. He was not an insular "John Bull"; he loved travel and was an enthusiastic student of foreign cultures. He did not despise history; he did not distrust modern science, but was a dedicated student of it. His *Dictionary* was a landmark in the study of the English language, as his *Shakespeare* was a landmark in the history of the editing of that writer. He was a fine poet, as T. S. Eliot has testified. He was a superb critic, as Edmund Wilson and other modern critics have insisted. He was a magnificent prose stylist: Macaulay's attack on what he called "Johnsonese" is based on an untrue story told by Boswell that once, after saying, "It has not wit enough to keep it sweet," Johnson immediately "translated" it into "It has not vitality enough to preserve it from putrefaction"; there is no record of his ever having done anything of the kind. He was in fact capable of an immense range of stylistic effects. He could use long and erudite Latinate words when it suited his artistic purpose; he could also effectively use short "Anglo-Saxon" ones. One scholar, praising a lovely sentence in *Rasselas*—"No man can taste the fruits of autumn while he is delighting his scent with the flowers of the spring: no man can, at the same time, fill his cup from the source and the mouth of the Nile"—pointed out that of its forty words, thirty-seven are monosyllables. The sentence also gives the lie to the myth that Johnson was addicted to generalities and abstractions in two beautiful images he has vividly concretized the abstract generalization "One must choose between two mutually exclusive sources of happiness." It is no doubt true, as Macaulay is fond of pointing out, that Johnson's physical appearance and such traits as his nervous tics were unattractive, that his clothing was shabby, and that his table manners and tastes in food were often bizarre—to which one can only reply, "So what?" His conversational wit could sometimes be acerbic; but many of the best-known insults and wisecracks attributed to him, by Boswell and others, are apocryphal, derived from popular joke books and in the public domain. He was not a literary dictator, a "Great Cham"; he affirmed his reluctance to pass judgment on contemporary literary productions, and the evidence supports him.

Despite the longevity of the mythical construct of Macaulay, the real Johnson continues to attract more students than any other English writer of his time. Why? Perhaps two Latin tags contain the answer, one applicable to the immense variety of Johnson's concerns, the other to his skill as a writer. One is Terence's "Homo sum; humani nil a me alienum est"—"I am a man; nothing human is irrelevant to me." The other is the splendid epitaph that Johnson composed for his friend Goldsmith and could justly serve as his own: "Nullum fere scribendi genus non tetigit, nullum quod tetigit non ornavit"—"Almost no form of writing was not touched by his pen, and he touched nothing that he did not adorn."

Letters:
The Letters of Samuel Johnson, with Mrs. Thrale's Genuine Letters to Him, 3 volumes, edited by R. W. Chapman (Oxford: Clarendon Press, 1952).

Bibliographies:
William P. Courtney and D. Nichol Smith, *A Bibliography of Samuel Johnson* (Oxford: Clarendon Press, 1915);

R. W. Chapman and Allen T. Hazen, "Johnsonian Bibliography: A Supplement to Courtney," *Proceedings of the Oxford Bibliographical Society*, 5 (1939), 119-166;

Donald Greene, "The Development of the Johnson Canon," in *Restoration and Eighteenth-Century Literature*, edited by Carroll Camden (Chicago: University of Chicago Press, 1963), pp. 407-427;

James L. Clifford and Donald J. Greene, *Samuel Johnson: A Survey and Bibliography of Critical Studies* (Minneapolis: University of Minnesota Press, 1970);

Donald Greene and John A. Vance, *A Bibliography of Johnsonian Studies, 1970-1985*, University of Victoria English Literary Studies, no. 39 (Victoria, B.C.: 1987).

Biographies:

Hester Lynch Piozzi (Mrs. Thrale), *Anecdotes of the Late Samuel Johnson, LL.D. During the Last Twenty Years of His Life* (London: Printed for T. Cadell, 1786); republished in *Memoirs of the Life and Writings of the Late Dr. Samuel Johnson* [by William Shaw]. *Anecdotes of the Late Samuel Johnson* [by Mrs. Piozzi], edited by Arthur Sherbo, Oxford English Memoirs and Travels (Oxford: Oxford University Press, 1974);

Sir John Hawkins, *The Life of Samuel Johnson, LL.D.*, volume 1, of *The Works of Samuel Johnson, LL.D.* (London: Printed for J. Buckland and forty others, 1787); republished (slightly abridged), edited by Bertram H. Davis (New York: Macmillan, 1961);

James Boswell, *The Life of Samuel Johnson, LL.D.*, 2 volumes, (London: Printed by Henry Baldwin for Charles Dilly, 1791); republished in *Boswell's Life of Johnson, Together with Boswell's Journal of a Tour to the Hebrides and Johnson's Diary of a Journey into North Wales*, 6 volumes, edited by G. B. Hill, revised and enlarged by L. F. Powell (Oxford: Clarendon Press, 1934-1964);

G. B. Hill, ed. *Johnsonian Miscellanies*, 2 volumes (Oxford: Clarendon Press, 1897);

Aleyn Lyell Reade, *Johnsonian Gleanings*, 11 volumes (London: Privately printed for the author, 1909-1952);

Joseph Wood Krutch, *Samuel Johnson* (New York: Holt, 1944);

John Wain, *Samuel Johnson* (London: Macmillan, 1944; New York: Viking, 1975);

James L. Clifford, *Young Sam Johnson* (New York: McGraw-Hill, 1965);

The Early Biographies of Samuel Johnson, edited by O. M. Brack, Jr., and Robert E. Kelley (Iowa City: University of Iowa Press, 1974);

W. Jackson Bate, *Samuel Johnson* (New York: Harcourt Brace Jovanovich, 1977; London: Chatto & Windus, 1978);

James L. Clifford, *Dictionary Johnson: Samuel Johnson's Middle Years* (New York: McGraw-Hill, 1979; London: Heinemann, 1979).

References:

The Age of Johnson [annual], edited by Paul J. Korshin (New York: AMS Press, 1987-);

Paul K. Alkon, *Samuel Johnson and Moral Discipline* (Evanston, Ill.: Northwestern University Press, 1967);

Bertrand H. Bronson, "The Double Tradition of Dr. Johnson," *ELH: A Journal of English Literary History*, 18 (June 1951): 90-106;

Bronson, "Johnson Agonistes," in his *Johnson and Boswell: Three Essays* (Berkeley & Los Angeles: University of California Press, 1944);

Joseph Epes Brown, *The Critical Opinions of Samuel Johnson* (Princeton: Princeton University Press, 1925);

John J. Burke, Jr., and Donald Kay, eds. *The Unknown Samuel Johnson* (Madison: University of Wisconsin Press, 1983);

Chester F. Chapin, *The Religious Thought of Samuel Johnson* (Ann Arbor: University of Michigan Press, 1968);

T. S. Eliot, Introduction to *London and the Vanity of Human Wishes* (London: Etchells & Macdonald, 1930);

J. D. Fleeman, ed., *The Sale Catalogue of Samuel Johnson's Library: A Facsimile Edition*, University of Victoria English Literary Studies, no. 2 (Victoria, B.C., 1975);

Robert Folkenflik, *Samuel Johnson, Biographer* (Ithaca, N.Y.: Cornell University Press, 1978);

James Gray, *Johnson's Sermons: A Study* (Oxford: Clarendon Press, 1972);

Donald Greene, *The Politics of Samuel Johnson* (New Haven: Yale University Press, 1960; revised edition, Athens: University of Georgia Press, 1990);

Greene, *Samuel Johnson* (New York: Twayne, 1970; revised edition, Boston: Twayne, 1989);

Greene, *Samuel Johnson's Library: An Annotated Guide*, University of Victoria English Literary Studies, no. 1 (Victoria, B.C., 1975);

Greene, ed., *Samuel Johnson: A Collection of Critical Essays* (Englewood Cliffs, N.J.: Prentice-Hall, 1965);

Jean H. Hagstrum, *Samuel Johnson's Literary Criticism* (Minneapolis: University of Minnesota Press, 1952);

F. W. Hilles, ed. *The Age of Johnson: Essays Presented to C. B. Tinker* (New Haven: Yale University Press, 1949);

Hilles, ed., *New Light on Dr. Johnson* (New Haven: Yale University Press, 1959);

Benjamin B. Hoover, *Samuel Johnson's Parliamentary Reporting* (Berkeley & Los Angeles: University of California Press, 1953);

George Irwin, *Samuel Johnson: A Personality in Conflict* (Auckland, N.Z., Auckland University Press / New York: Oxford University Press, 1971);

Johnsonian News Letter [quarterly] (New York: Department of English, Columbia University, 1940-);

Thomas Kaminski, *The Early Career of Samuel Johnson* (New York: Oxford University Press, 1987);

Paul J. Korshin ed., *Johnson After Two Hundred Years* (Philadelphia: University of Pennsylvania Press, 1986);

Mary Lascelles, James L. Clifford, and others, eds., *Johnson, Boswell, and Their Circle: Essays Presented to L. F. Powell* (Oxford: Clarendon Press, 1965);

E. L. McAdam, Jr., *Dr. Johnson and the English Law* (Syracuse, N.Y.: Syracuse University Press, 1951);

Richard B. Schwartz, *Samuel Johnson and the New Science* (Madison: University of Wisconsin Press, 1971);

Schwartz, *Samuel Johnson and the Problem of Evil* (Madison: University of Wisconsin Press, 1975);

Arthur Sherbo, *Samuel Johnson, Editor of Shakespeare, with an Essay on The Adventurer* (Urbana: University of Illinois Press, 1956);

James H. Sledd and Gwin J. Kolb, *Dr. Johnson's Dictionary: Essays in the Biography of a Book* (Chicago: University of Chicago Press, 1955);

John A. Vance, *Samuel Johnson and the Sense of History* (Athens: University of Georgia Press, 1984);

Robert Voitle, *Samuel Johnson the Moralist* (Cambridge, Mass.: Harvard University Press, 1961);

W. K. Wimsatt, Jr., *Philosophic Words: A Study of Style and Meaning in the Rambler and Dictionary of Samuel Johnson* (New Haven: Yale University Press, 1948);

Wimsatt, *The Prose Style of Samuel Johnson* (New Haven: Yale University Press, 1941).

Papers:

Although Johnson's output of writing was enormous, only a relatively small amount of manuscript material has survived. The largest holding is in the Hyde Collection, Four Oaks Farm, Somerville, New Jersey, which incorporates the collection of R. B. Adam, described in four volumes (*The R. B. Adam Library Relating to Dr. Samuel Johnson and His Era*, 1929-1930); important holdings are in other private collections. The Yale University Library, the British Library, the Bodleian Library, the library of Pembroke College, Oxford, and the Johnson Birthplace Museum, Lichfield, have important manuscripts. A useful guide is J. D. Fleeman, *A Preliminary Handlist of Documents and Manuscripts of Samuel Johnson* (Oxford Bibliographical Society Occasional Publications, no. 7, 1967). This does not include the locations of manuscripts of Johnson's letters, which are listed in R. W. Chapman's edition of the letters (1952). A forthcoming new edition of the letters, in five volumes, will include newly discovered letters and new locations of previously known ones.

Henry Home, Lord Kames

(1696 - 27 December 1782)

Roger L. Emerson
University of Western Ontario

See also "Eighteenth-Century Background: Henry Home, Lord Kames," in *DLB 31: American Colonial Writers, 1735-1781.*

BOOKS: *Remarkable Decisions of the Court of Session, from 1716, to 1728,* 2 volumes (Edinburgh: Printed by T. Ruddiman, 1728);

Essays upon Several Subjects in Law (Edinburgh: Printed by R. Fleming & sold by James McEuen, 1732);

The Decisions of the Court of Session, from Its First Institution to the present Time: Abridged and Digested under proper Heads, in Form of a Dictionary, 2 volumes (Edinburgh: Printed by R. Watkins for himself, A. Kincaid, and others, 1741);

Essays upon Several Subjects concerning British Antiquities (Edinburgh: Printed for A. Kincaid, 1747; third edition, revised and enlarged, Edinburgh: Printed for A. Kincaid & J. Bell, 1763);

Essays on the Principles of Morality and Natural Religion (Edinburgh: Printed by R. Fleming for A. Kincaid & A. Donaldson, 1751; revised edition, London: Printed for C. Hitch & L. Hawes, R. & J. Dodsley, J. Rivington & J. Fletcher, and J. Richardson, 1758, third edition, corrected and enlarged, Edinburgh: Printed for John Bell & J. Murray, 1779);

Objections against the Essays on Morality and Natural Religion Examined, by Kames, possibly with passages by Robert Wallace and Hugh Blair, (Edinburgh, 1756);

Statute Laws of Scotland Abridged with Historical Notes (Edinburgh: Printed by Sands, Donaldson, Murray & Cochran for A. Kincaid & A. Donaldson, 1757);

Historical Law Tracts (2 volumes, Edinburgh: Printed for A. Millar, London, and A. Kincaid & J. Bell, Edinburgh, 1758; third edition, revised and enlarged, 1 volume Edinburgh: Printed for T. Cadell, London, and J. Bell & W. Creech, Edinburgh, 1776);

Henry Home, Lord Kames, 1794 (portrait by David Martin; Scottish National Portrait Gallery)

Principles of Equity (Edinburgh: Printed by Alexander Kincaid for A. Millar, London, and A. Kincaid & J. Bell, Edinburgh, 1760; second edition, revised and enlarged, Edinburgh: Printed for A. Millar, London, and A. Kincaid & J. Bell, Edinburgh, 1767);

Introduction to the Art of Thinking (Edinburgh: Printed for A. Kincaid & J. Bell, 1761);

Elements of Criticism (3 volumes, Edinburgh: Printed for A. Millar, London, and A. Kincaid & J. Bell, Edinburgh, 1762; second edition, revised and enlarged, Edinburgh: Printed for A. Millar, London, and A. Kincaid & J. Bell, Edinburgh, 1763; 2 volumes, third edition, revised and enlarged, Edinburgh: Printed for A. Millar, London, and A. Kincaid & J. Bell, Edinburgh, 1765; fourth edition, revised and enlarged, Edinburgh: Printed for A. Millar & T. Cadell, London, and A. Kincaid & J. Bell, Edinburgh, 1769; fifth edition, Edinburgh: Printed for A. Kincaid, 1774; sixth edition, with the author's last corrections and additions, Edinburgh: Printed for J. Bell & W. Creech and for T. Cadell & G. Robinson, London, 1785; first American edition, from the seventh London edition, Boston: From the Press of Samuel Etheridge for J. White, Thomas & Andrews, W. Spotswood, D. West, and others, 1796);

Remarkable Decisions of the Court of Session, from the year 1730 to the year 1752 (Edinburgh: A. Kincaid & J. Bell, 1766);

Progress of Flax-Husbandry in Scotland (Edinburgh: Printed by Sands, Murray & Cochran, 1766);

Sketches of the History of Man, 2 volumes (Edinburgh: Printed for W. Creech, and for W. Strahan & T. Cadell, London, 1774); republished in part as *Six Sketches on the History of Man*, 1 volume (Philadelphia: Sold by R. Bell & R. Aitken, 1776); *Sketches of the History of Man. Considerably Improved in a Second Edition*, four volumes (Edinburgh: Printed for W. Strahan & T. Cadell, London, and for W. Creech, Edinburgh, 1778; third edition, with the author's last corrections and additions; Edinburgh: Printed for A. Strahan & T. Cadell, London, and for W. Creech, Edinburgh, 1788);

The Gentleman Farmer: Being an Attempt to Improve Agriculture by Subjecting it to the Test of Rational Principles (Edinburgh: Printed for W. Creech and T. Cadell, London, 1776: second edition, revised and enlarged, Edinburgh: Printed for J. Bell, 1779; third edition, revised and enlarged, Edinburgh: Printed for J. Bell and for G. G. J. & J. Robinson, London, 1788);

Elucidations Respecting the Common and statute Law of Scotland (Edinburgh: Printed for W. Creech and sold by T. Cadell, London, 1777);

Select Decisions of the Court of Session, from the Year 1752 to the Year 1768 (Edinburgh: Printed by Neill for J. Bell, 1780);

Loose Hints upon Education, chiefly concerning the culture of the Heart (Edinburgh: Printed for J. Bell and J. Murray, London, 1781).

OTHER: "Essays on the Laws of Motion," in *Essays and Observations, Physical and Literary. Read Before a Society in Edinburgh and Published by Them* [Philosophical Society of Edinburgh], volume 1, edited by David Hume and Alexander Monro I (Edinburgh: Printed by G. Hamilton & J. Balfour, 1754), pp. 1-69;

"Observations upon the Paper Concerning Shallow Ploughing" and "On Evaporation," in *Essays and Observations, Physical and Literary. Read before the Philosophical Society in Edinburgh, and Published by Them*, volume 3, edited by Alexander Monro II (Edinburgh: Printed for John Balfour, 1771), pp. 68-79; 80-99.

Henry Home was a hardheaded but sensitive lawyer whose abilities and disciplined research took him to the top of his profession and made him for more than forty years a dominant figure in the Scottish Enlightenment. He was regarded in his own time as an original thinker whose interests spanned the range of enlightened concerns and spilled over into nearly as broad a spectrum of improving activities. A patron and companion to David Hume, Adam Smith, William Robertson, John Millar, and others who made Edinburgh a leading center of European culture in the 1760s and 1770s, Home appeared to his contemporaries as their equal and in practical affairs as a far more important man. Today he still deserves attention as a founder of Scottish Common-Sense Philosophy, as an aesthetician and rhetorician, as one of the improvers who helped to transform Scotland's economy during the late eighteenth and early nineteenth century and, finally, as the man whose interests and beliefs best exemplify the Scottish Enlightenment.

Home was born in Eccles, a parish in Berwickshire in the eastern Scottish borders. Both of his parents, Agnes Walkinshaw and George Home of Kames, had learned and illustrious forebears, and both belonged to families split into Jacobite and Episcopalian, Whig and Presbyterian branches. One of Home's distant cousins was mistress to the Pretender, Charles Edward; another was in the entourage of the mother of George III. Home's own father had suspiciously ambiguous loyalties. While he served as a major with the infantry during the 1715 rebellion, he provided Henry and his seven younger siblings with tutors (John Wingate and John Anderson) who were nonjuring Episcopalians and probably Jacobites.

Because the Homes of Kames were relatively poor, Henry was educated at home and did not attend a university. He went up to Edinburgh circa 1712 to study to become a writer (a Scottish solicitor), a lucrative profession in which he could expect to recoup the family's fortune and one sometimes preferred to the bar by Jacobites. Within a few years (about 1716?) Home left the office of his mentor, John Dickson, and directed his studies toward a career at the bar. Privately he read the classics and studied French, Italian, philosophy, and law. He is thought to have been taught law by Patrick Grant, later Lord Elchies, and is known to have attended Professor James Craig's lectures on civil law at Edinburgh University. Home was admitted to the Faculty of Advocates on 22 January 1723, after which he could practice before any court in Scotland. In these courts Home tried cases in accordance with the principles of the civil law as it had evolved in Scotland and in accordance with the somewhat less defined principles of Scottish criminal law.

Part of Home's education during these years was gained elsewhere. By about 1718 he had joined the Associated Critics, a classical, literary and antiquarian society promoted by the Jacobite scholar, printer, and librarian of the Faculty of Advocates, Thomas Ruddiman. By then, or shortly thereafter, Home belonged to a philosophical club in which religious, political, and metaphysical issues were discussed. This is said to have been the Rankenian Club, but some evidence suggests that it was another group. Home was intimate with the poet William Hamilton of Bangour and by 1724 had had philosophical correspondence with Samuel Clarke and Andrew Baxter. An interest in polite culture is further attested by his attendance at the Edinburgh Assembly (begun 1723) and by his membership in the Musical Society (1727 or 1729-1732, 1743-?, 1752-1782), a group of amateur players among whom were composers and theorists. Kames's instrument is not known, although he probably played one. His musical interests contributed to his aesthetic theories and kept him *au courant* with the controversies swirling in the musical world of the eighteenth century. The cultured Edinburgh circles in which Home moved until 1727 were rather Jacobite in orientation, but after about 1723 he probably moved toward Whiggism and the Kirk, in which he became a ruling elder, probably during the 1740s.

As a young lawyer Home had little business until after about 1730. In 1732 he unsuccessfully sought the Edinburgh Chair of Civil Law which would have subsidized the leisure he devoted to study. By 1736 Home was a well-established advocate with a lucrative general practice. After that year he was also well known because he served as the attorney for John Porteous, captain of the Edinburgh City Guard, when he was tried for the murder of rioters attempting to free convicted, but popular, smugglers. This notorious case ended badly for Porteous (he was lynched) and for the town, which could not find and punish the other rioters.

By then Home had attached himself to the Scottish political faction headed by John, Second Duke of Argyll. The duke's patronage probably secured for him the post of advocate depute (circa 1738), and in 1752 he owed his Court of Session (Scotland's supreme civil court) gown and his lawlord's title, Lord Kames, to Archibald, Third Duke of Argyll. In 1763, John Stuart, Third Earl of Bute, nephew and inheritor of the third duke's political machine, secured for Lord Kames a place on the High Court of Justiciary (Scotland's highest criminal court). In 1755 Kames was appointed to the Board of Trustees for the Encouragement of Fisheries, Arts and Manufactures of Scotland and to the Commission for the Forfeited Estates. Those were the principal government agencies interfering with the Scottish economy. Kames was active in both until his death, often as the initiator of schemes or as the patron of craftsmen and farmers. By then he was also involved with other improving activities.

As early as 1739 Kames and David Hume considered starting a literary and political periodical in Edinburgh. The project failed, but both men may have written essays intended for it. Around 1741 Home became a member of the Philosophical Society of Edinburgh, a body which discussed medical, scientific, metaphysical, and improving topics. When it was revived, circa 1748-1750, after the Jacobite uprising of 1745, Home was chosen as one of its two vice-presidents and in 1769 succeeded to its presidency, an office he retained until his death. His activity in the society brought him recognition and a cherished friendship with Benjamin Franklin, who adapted and printed one of Kames's Philosophical Society papers in the 1770 edition of *Poor Richard's Almanac*. In 1755 Kames was active as a member of the Select Society and of its improving offshoots, the Edinburgh Society for the Improvement of Arts and Sciences and the Society for Promoting the Reading and Speaking of the English Language in Scotland. As early as 1748 Home had interested himself in the cause of the second group and had helped to set up Adam Smith as an extramural lecturer in Edinburgh on rhetoric and taste. Later he patronized Robert Watson, Hugh Blair, and William Barron, who all afterward taught this subject from university chairs that he probably helped them secure.

After 1741, the year in which he inherited the estate of Kames and married Agatha Drummond, Home became much interested in agriculture and eventually was a notable improver of his wife's estate, Blair Drummond in Stirlingshire. The estate came to them in 1766. There he also laid out an American or winter garden. His interests in agricultural improvement are clear from papers on ploughing and the use of oxen that he contributed to the *Essays and Observations* in 1771 and from *Progress of Flax-Husbandry in Scotland* (1766), which also appeared in the *Scots Magazine* in 1766. Late in his life *The Gentleman Farmer* (1776) was to collect much more material of a similar sort. Reflecting his own practice, research by William Cullen, Joseph Black, and John Walker, and studies produced in England and France, this book marked a notable advance over earlier treatises in English. Kames tried to show how the application of proper methods, sound theory, the proven wisdom of experience, and better organization and cost accounting could change farming. At the same time he recognized that techniques, machinery, and practices had to be adapted to various soils, climates, and kinds of husbandry. The book called for a government "Board for Improving Agriculture" and looked forward to the inclusion of that subject in the universities. Such ideas had long circulated among Scottish improvers. Kames no doubt regarded his writings and his active involvement in the management of the Faculty of Advocates as a piece with his other improving works. One suspects that he had little time for his wife, Agatha Drummond, or for his children, George Home Drummond (1742-1819) and Jean (birth and death dates unknown). Jean divorced Patrick Heron of Kirroughtree in 1777 and was the married woman in the affair that James Boswell confessed to Jean-Jacques Rousseau.

Kames's life was so busy that it was said after his death that he lived a normal man's one hundred years. Increasingly his works were followed in the British and European press. He was honored by the Society of Citizens of Berne, which in 1762 made Kames an honorary member. In 1778 the Manchester Society of Agriculture accorded him similar recognition, as did the Society of Antiquaries of Scotland in 1781. When Kames died, John Ramsay of Ochtertyre said of him, "he did more to promote the interests of philosophy and *belles lettres* in Scotland than all the men of law had done for a century before." Ramsay could have added to Kames's good deeds many other activities ranging from the growing of turnips to helping to build a new Edinburgh Exchange, a theater, a concert hall, and an art school. Even so, that does not show the contemporary reputation of Kames the literary man.

The major portion of Kames's publications deal with the law of Scotland, which, when he began to write, had only a handful of institutional works and no more than twelve published collections of decisions. He was concerned both to shed light upon the history of Scottish law and to organize its principles into volumes which were coherent and useful. It was that latter end which he first addressed as a young man working on an assignment made by the Faculty of Advocates. Home's *Remarkable Decisions of the Court of Session from 1716, to 1728* (1728), its sequel, *Remarkable Decisions of the Court of Session from the Year 1730 to the Year 1752* (1766), and *Select Decisions of the Court of Sessions from the Year 1752 to the Year 1768* (1780) each tried to collect and classify decisions according to the rules of law being applied. The taxonomic work is thus directed to an empirical sorting out of the principles of common law actually applied by Scottish judges. The rules alone were of interest to Kames, who, like most civilians, had no high regard for mere precedents. In 1741 Home pushed this enterprise further back in time when he produced his useful *The Decisions of the Court of Session from Its First Institution to the present Time: Abridged and Digested under Proper Heads, in Form of a Dictionary*. A typical enlightenment compendium from one point of view, this volume was also meant to establish the rules recognized by Scottish lawyers from at least 1532. As he classified and clarified the rules, Home was also establishing on an empirical basis what the common law of Scotland really was— something that would remain undone and incomplete in 1782. That task required supplementation by a compendium of statute laws held to be still in force. This Kames produced in 1757 in *Statute Laws of Scotland Abridged with Historical Notes*. All of that painstaking work had brought to his attention changes in Scottish law as it had evolved

Caricature of Kames with Hugo Arnot, author of the first history of Edinburgh, and James Burnett, Lord Monboddo, a Scottish judge and pioneer anthropologist (etching by John Kay)

under the pressures of economic, religious, and social change from a feudal system to one influenced by ancient and modern Roman law systems. Scots had long been mindful of these changes that had been previously noted by Sir Thomas Craig and James Dalrymple, First Viscount Stair. Both had taught Scots to see their social evolution as a national variation on a European and universal pattern of development.

Kames was intrigued by that history. He would also have recognized that it related to the program of the elucidation of Scottish history upon which Thomas Ruddiman and others had been engaged since the 1690s. Tracing the development of Scottish institutions, of Scottish society, manners, ways of thinking and acting could be done by studying the law of Scotland. That message is clearly articulated in Home's *Essays upon Several Subjects concerning British Antiquities* (1747), a work which deals with the introduction of the feudal law, with the Scottish Parliament, with distinctions of honor and rank, and the related topics of succession to property and titles. Written during the 1745 rebellion, it shows Kames to be now no Jacobite but a defender of the Union, which had increased real freedom for Scots by less-

ening the influence of the Scottish magnates. Eleven years later Kames's *Historical Law Tracts* (1758) sought to bring together his observations on the general historical development of all law in a work of synthesis that was not, as David Hume feared it would be, a "mixture of wormwood and aloes." Here Kames recurs to other themes that had been running through his mind since 1732, when they had first appeared in *Essays upon Several Subjects in Law*. Those essays largely concern property and rights to its various species. What is new here is Home's interest in showing that property is based not upon the positive creation of states but that it has a natural basis in the feelings of men. Kinds of property might come and go, but constant human nature will always discriminate between mine and thine; society and its agencies will enforce those distinctions, albeit in different ways at different times. The *Historical Law Tracts* again takes up the problem of rooting all laws in human nature and shows that criminal laws are based in feelings of resentment and desires for revenge that have been modified over time as societies evolved from primitive to polished states. This book also contains Kames's best known plea for law as the basis for a liberal, useful, rational, and genteel education:

> The history of man is a delightful subject. A rational inquirer is no less entertained than instructed, in tracing the progress of manners, of laws, of arts, from their birth to their present maturity.... Law in particular, becomes then only a rational study, when it is traced historically, from its first rudiments among savages, through successive changes, to its highest improvements in civilized society.

That is how law should be taught and how Kames's friend, Professor John Millar, taught it at Glasgow University from a chair Kames had helped to secure. The work also has in mind a comparison of English and Scottish law, one in which the latter comes off well, but also one aimed at the convergence of the two systems in a more perfect union. This book shows Kames to be a sophisticated historian, a pioneer in comparative legal history, and a scholar able to go beyond Montesquieu in showing how institutions evolve and are modified by climate, human activities, and basic human motivations. It states no unambiguous theory of progress, but it does tend to find the most dynamic forces for social change in economics and in the reason and sensitivities of men. It is also notable as a clear statement of his hope that Scottish law could be improved. Two years later he showed how in *Principles of Equity* (1760).

In this first Scottish work on equity, Kames argues against separate rules and courts of equity, such as the English had, and for equity law as the rules of natural justice which might be applied by the common law courts, as was done in Scotland. He argues that judges free to apply the rules of natural justice would make decisions leading to the convergence of English and Scottish law and smooth the transition of Scotland into a commercial and politer era. Incidentally, he provides arguments justifying the extension of judicial authority in Scotland. Judicial discretion was very great in a realm lacking a well-defined criminal law and where judges still determined civil cases by rules of natural justice. When one adds to that the ability of Scottish lawlords to make quasilegislative findings in their Acts of Sederunt, one finds Kames justifying a program which would have satisfied many a French *parlementaire*. Here and elsewhere, Kames criticizes the law and practice of entail, and he argues for a development of Scottish law which would be more favorable to industry and commerce, more reasonable and humane, and more guided by utility and justice.

His conviction that law is rooted in morality and nature is again set forth in *Elucidations Respecting the Common and Statute Laws of Scotland* (1777). This work, whose patriotic theme is the defense of Scottish law, is compiled from essays written much earlier. It defends positions he had already enunciated, including a need to rationalize bankruptcy law and generally to modernize both procedures and the legal rules applied in them. Here he looks again for the inductive generalizations which define the rules of the system he had so long administered. He makes his last attempts to understand and to state the systematic character of a law based on natural justice which he thought best defined by judges, not by legislators. That view points to the close connections which Kames always made between morals and the law. That point of view is also adopted in a book sometimes mistakenly attributed to him, John Erskine's *Principles of the Law of Scotland* (1754).

Home's first attempt to outline a philosophic position was made in *Essays on the Principles of Morality and Natural Religion* (1751). There, as in later works, he shows himself to be a good empiricist, opposed to speculation, eager to relate all knowledge and values to human faculties and convinced of the need to argue only from critically examined facts. Part 1 of this book sets out a moral-sense theory largely borrowed from Anthony Ashley Cooper, Third Earl of Shaftesbury, Francis Hutcheson, Joseph Butler, and even David Hume, against whose philosophy much of the work is aimed.

In part 2 Home sets out arguments against skepticism which became the core of Scottish Common-Sense Philosophy. Home was a realist in epistemology, holding that men do perceive things which are taken to be the effects of causes and that the secondary properties and qualities of bodies have no real existence outside the minds which sense them or abstract them from what is perceived. The ideas we form of things are signs which cannot be equated with the things themselves. The external senses thus give us a knowledge of body, a knowledge which he examines and explores more fully in "Essays on the Laws of Motion," papers presented to the Philosophical Society circa 1751 and published by it in *Essays and Observations* in 1754. There Home argues against the Newtonian theories of the passivity of matter. He tries to show that the facts of our experience and the known operations of the mind require us to believe that matter is self-moving in predictable ways described by Newton's equations. Here, as in his moral theory, Home's views verge on determinism, and his universe looks somewhat abandoned by a creator whose providence is displayed in secondary causes. It is not surprising that the *Essays on the Principles of Morality and Natural Religion* provoked a storm of protest from the orthodox.

Between 1753 and 1757 these conservatives tried to have him and his work condemned by the General Assembly of the Church of Scotland. In 1756 Kames anonymously published a partial retraction of his views, in which he asserts, with some inconsistency, that men do make real and efficacious choices and that they know more about the probable goodness of the probably existing God than he had at first believed. The failure of the "unco guid" (or, as Robert Burns phrases it, "the rigidly righteous") to get a sentence against Kames's work or that of his distant cousins, David Hume and the Reverend Mr. John Home, marked the establishment of genuine free discussion in Scotland—an achievement managed by the government and the moderate party in the Kirk. Kames's enemies were less upset by other parts of the *Essays.* There he holds that reflection gives us a perceptual knowledge of the self, which retains its personal identity over time beyond the grave.

Introspection for him became the key to an understanding of the mind. Rational psychology, or a phenomenological account of the faculties, senses, powers, instincts, passions, or states of consciousness, Kames sets out most coherently in the *Elements of Criticism* (1762) and *Sketches of the History of Man* (1774). In volume three of the latter he published Thomas Reid's well-known critique of Aristotelian logic, with which he agreed. That work shows induction to be the most useful way of reasoning and relates the progress of knowledge to the employment of the analytical and synthetic methods of the natural philosophers described by Sir Isaac Newton, Robert Boyle, and John Locke. *Elements of Criticism* begins with an extended account of the senses and passions connected with moral and aesthetic approbation or disgust. It goes on to relate the rules governing good taste and style to the feelings engendered in the mind by imaginative works. Beauty is in the mind, but the means of raising that complex of feelings and ideas can be generally explained and taught by aestheticians and specifically by rhetoricians. Kames is also concerned to show that, while the canons of good taste and beauty are general and timeless, "the principles of the fine arts," like those of law, are differently exemplified in the progress of men from barbarism to refinement. Finally, he insists that the cultivation of taste and beauty promotes religion, sociability, morality, and civic virtue by making men sensitive to one another and appreciative of the design in nature. Kames contributed important critical concepts such as "waking dream," "ideal presence," and "organic unity" to the writers of the Romantic movement, and his *Elements of Criticism* was a staple of American education in the nineteenth century.

Kames considered his magnum opus to be *Sketches of the History of Man.* Here he discusses at length the social feelings and passions which ground sociability, morals, natural justice, and law. Tracing their interplay over time allows him to write one of the eighteenth century's great conjectural histories. Into that he worked much that he had earlier said about the evolution of law, taste, reasoning, and religion. Inspired by the works of Montesquieu, Rousseau, and his Scottish friends, Kames sets out his own unique contributions to social theory. Some of his ideas seem bizarre, such as his belief in the separate creation of American aborigines, but they also contain arguments for the polycentrism of cultures and for racial theories which in the nineteenth century inspired physical anthropologists. Kames as a sociologist was much interested in the nature of social wholes and in the reasons for their constant changes. This aspect of his work looks forward to Auguste Comte, Karl Marx, and Herbert Spencer, whose social statics and dynamics owe much to Scottish writers who, like Kames, tend to find men in conditions defined both by economic orders governed by the prevailing modes and means of production and also by characteristic ways of feeling and thinking. Kames undoubtedly saw this work as following his methodological prescriptions, and he characteristically used it to recommend reforms of many kinds. It remains a monument to eighteenth-century comparative anthropology and the search for the secular causes of social change. It was a book thirty years in the making. Today, however, it is very difficult to know just how original it was. Many of its important ideas had been stated by Hume, Millar, Smith, and others before Kames went to press. They all shared in the discussions of their lively societies and lived on terms of intimacy with one an-

The estate Kames's wife inherited in 1766 (engraving made before 1868)

other. It is not surprising that they should have held so many positions in common.

Like most of the philosophes, Kames was an educational writer touched by the works of Locke, Charles Rollin, and Rousseau. For this improving Scot, clear thinking was to be inculcated upon the young. His *Introduction to the Art of Thinking* (1761) resembles many other books in its concern with methods, habits, and exhortations to disciplined study and clarity of thought and expression. His last book, *Loose Hints on Education* (1781), is somewhat broader but in general reiterates and collects comments scattered in his works. For Kames, the cultivation of character, taste, feeling, and sensitivity is more important than learning. Both are to be conditioned by the class and sex of the student. Women can be better educated than they are, but people should not be educated beyond their real expectations in life—a harsher message than that contained in the works of most of his friends. What he says clearly relates to his experience as the husband of a bright and well-educated woman and to his experience as the father of a precocious daughter and a son with limited abilities.

Kames was very much an eighteenth-century man. His works exhibit the encyclopedic range of the learned of that time and the coher-ence which they prized. His commitments to scientism, to empiricism, and even to historicism of a sort were as common in the late eighteenth century as was his urge to improve everything. What was less common was the realism, even the harshness, and the basic conservatism of this provincial judge before whom malefactors wished not to appear. Behind the urbanity of thought was the man who spoke not English but earthy Scots. Behind the metaphysician and the skeptical inquirer, there still lurked a somewhat pessimistic, perhaps a Calvinist sense of the contingency of things and of the determined order of life. Kames was a busy and an apparently happy man but also one who was impatient, domineering, and given to sharp comments, the most famous of which is his valedictory to his fellow judges a few days before his death, "Fare ye a' weel, ye bitches."

Biographies:

William Smellie, *Literary and Characteristical Lives of John Gregory, M.D., Henry Home, Lord Kames, David Hume, Esq. and Adam Smith, L.L.D.* (Edinburgh: A. Smellie, 1800);

Alexander Fraser Tytler, Lord Woodhouselee, *Memoirs of the Life and Writings of the Honourable Henry Home of Kames, one of the Senators of the College of Justice and one of the Lords Commissioners of Justiciary in Scotland*, 2 volumes (Edinburgh: W. Creech / London: T. Cadell, 1807); supplement (Edinburgh: W. Creech 1809); second edition, revised and enlarged, 3 volumes (Edinburgh: T. Cadell & W. Davis, 1814);

John Ramsay of Ochtertyre, *Scotland and Scotsmen in the Eighteenth Century*, 2 volumes, edited by Alexander Allardyce (Edinburgh & London: Blackwood, 1888);

James Boswell, "Materials for Writing the Life of Lord Kames [c. 1778-1782]," in volume 15 of *Private Papers of James Boswell from Malahide Castle*, edited by Geoffrey Scott and F. A. Pottle, 18 volumes (Mt. Vernon, New York: Privately printed by W. E. Rudge, 1928-1934);

William C. Lehmann, *Henry Home, Lord Kames and the Scottish Enlightenment: A Study in National Character and in the History of Ideas* (The Hague: Nijhoff, 1971);

Ian Simpson Ross, *Lord Kames and the Scotland of His Day* (Oxford: Clarendon Press, 1972).

References:

Michael Barfoot, "James Gregory (1753-1821) and Scottish Scientific Metaphysics, 1750-1800," Ph.D. dissertation, University of Edinburgh, 1983, pp. 50-77;

Roger L. Emerson, "The Philosophical Society of Edinburgh 1737-1748," *British Journal for the History of Science*, 12 (July 1979): 154-191;

Emerson, "The Philosophical Society of Edinburgh 1748-1768," *British Journal for the History of Science*, 14 (July 1981): 133-176;

Emerson, "The Philosophical Society of Edinburgh 1768-1783," *British Journal for the History of Science*, 18 (November 1985): 255-303;

Duncan Forbes, "Natural Law and the Scottish Enlightenment," in *The Origins and Nature of the Scottish Enlightenment*, edited by R. H. Campbell and A. S. Skinner (Edinburgh: John Donald, 1982), pp. 186-204;

Ronald Hamowy, *The Scottish Enlightenment and the Theory of Spontaneous Order* (Carbondale & Edwardsville, Illinois: Southern Illinois University Press for the Journal of the History of Philosophy, 1987);

Wilbur Samuel Howell, *Eighteenth Century British Logic and Rhetoric* (Princeton: Princeton University Press, 1971);

David Liebermann, "The legal needs of a commercial society: the jurisprudence of Lord Kames," in *Wealth and Virtue: The Shaping of Political Economy in the Scottish Enlightenment*, edited by Istvan Hont and Michael Ignatieff (Cambridge: Cambridge University Press, 1983), pp. 203-234;

Arthur E. McGuinness, *Henry Home, Lord Kames* (New York: Twayne, 1970);

David F. Norton, *David Hume: Common-Sense Moralist, Sceptical Metaphysician* (Princeton: Princeton University Press, 1982);

Helen W. Randall, *The Critical Theory of Lord Kames*, Smith College Studies in Modern Languages, volume 22, nos. 1-4 (October 1940-July 1941) (Northampton, Mass.: Departments of Modern Languages of Smith College, 1944);

Ian Ross, "Unpublished Letters of Thomas Reid to Lord Kames, 1762-1782," *Texas Studies in Literature and Language*, 7 (Spring 1965): 17-65;

Leroy Shaw, "Henry Home of Kames: Precursor of Herder," *Germanic Review*, 35 (February 1960): 16-27;

George W. Stocking, Jr., "Scotland as the Model of Mankind: Lord Kames's Philosophical View of Civilization," in *Toward a Science of Man: Essays in the History of Anthropology*, edited by Timothy H. H. Thoresen (The Hague: Mouton, 1975), pp. 65-89;

A. A. Tait, *The Landscape Garden in Scotland, 1735-1835* (Edinburgh: Edinburgh University Press, 1980), pp. 45-47;

David M. Walker, *The Scottish Jurists* (Edinburgh: Green, 1985), pp. 220-247.

Papers:

The largest collections of Kames materials are held at the Scottish Record Office: see the Abercairny Papers; the Forfeited Estates Papers, 1745; the Records of the Board of Trustees for Manufactures and Fisheries. Isolated items exist at the other major Scottish libraries, particularly in the National Library of Scotland, Edinburgh; the university libraries in Edinburgh, Aberdeen, and Glasgow; the Mitchell Library, Glasgow; and the Edinburgh City Archives. Other collections include those at Aldourie Castle, Inverness-shire; the British Library; Yale University; and the American Philosophical Society.

Catherine Macaulay

(2 April 1731 - 22 June 1791)

Barbara Brandon Schnorrenberg

BOOKS: *The History of England, from the Accession of James I to That of the Brunswick Line*, volumes 1 and 2 (London: Printed for J. Nourse, R. & J. Dodsley, and W. Johnston, 1763-1765);

The History of England from the Accession of James I to the Elevation of the House of Hanover, volume 3 (London: Printed for the author, and sold by W. Johnston, J. Dodsley, T. Davies & T. Cadell, 1767);

Loose Remarks on Certain Positions to be found in Mr. Hobbes's Philosophical Rudiments of Government and Society. With a Short Sketch of A Democratical Form of Government, in a Letter to Signior Paoli (London: Printed for T. Davies, Robinson & Roberts, and T. Cadell, 1767);

The History of England from the Accession of James I to the Elevation of the House of Hanover, volume 4 (London: Printed for the author, and sold by W. Johnston, T. Davies, J. Almon, Robinson & Roberts, and T. Cadell, 1768);

Observations on a Pamphlet, Entitled, Thoughts on the Cause of the Present Discontents (London: Printed for Edward & Charles Dilly, 1770);

The History of England from the Accession of James I to the Elevation of the House of Hanover, volume 5 (London: Printed for Edward & Charles Dilly, 1771);

A Modest Plea for the Property of Copyright (Bath: Printed by R. Cruttwell for Edward & Charles Dilly, London, 1774);

An Address to the People of England, Ireland, and Scotland, on the Present Important Crisis of Affairs (Bath: Printed by R. Cruttwell for Edward & Charles Dilly, London, 1775; New York: Printed by John Holt, 1775);

The History of England, from the Revolution to the Present Time in a Series of Letters to the Reverend Doctor Wilson (Bath: Printed by R. Cruttwell, and sold by E. & C. Dilly, T. Cadell, and J. Walter, London, 1778);

The History of England from the Accession of James I to the Revolution, volumes 6 and 7 (London:

Printed by A. Hamilton, Jun., and sold by C. Dilly, G. Robinson, J. Walter, and R. Faulder, 1781);

The History of England from the Accession of James I to the Revolution, volume 8 (London: Printed by A. Hamilton, Jun., and sold by C. Dilly, G. Robinson, J. Walter, R. Faulder & T. Lewis, 1783);

A Treatise on the Immutability of Moral Truth (London: Printed by A. Hamilton, Jr., and sold by C. Dilly, G. Robinson, T. Cadell, T. Lewis, J. Walter, and R. Faulder, 1783);

Letters on Education, with Observations on Religious and Metaphysical Subjects (London: Printed for C. Dilly, 1790);

Observations on the Reflections of the Right Hon. Edmund Burke on the Revolution in France, in a Letter to the Earl of Stanhope (London: Printed for C. Dilly, 1790; Boston: Printed by I. Thomas & E. T. Andrews, 1791).

While scholars in the second half of the twentieth century generally recognize Catherine Macaulay as the first English woman historian, it was not her sex but her politics that made her an important figure in the eighteenth century. As one of the last Old Whigs, or Commonwealthmen, she presented in her writings views of liberty, constitutional government, and the nature of man inherited from seventeenth-century writers such as James Harrington and Sir Algernon Sidney. Her *History of England* replied to David Hume's history far more vigorously than did Tobias Smollett's. Her pamphlets most obviously argued the contemporary radical position, in many instances replying to Edmund Burke's much more conservative views.

Catherine Sawbridge was born at Olantigh, the family estate in Kent. Both her mother, Elizabeth Wanley Sawbridge, and father, John Sawbridge, came from prominent London Whig banking families. Her father lived the life of a country gentleman; after his wife's death in 1733, he largely cut himself off from society.

Catherine Macaulay as a Roman matron, frontispiece to volume 3 of her History of England

The four children, two sons and two daughters, were educated at home. Given the political inheritance of the family, the library was presumably filled not only with the usual Greek and Roman writers but also with seventeenth-century authors whose views Catherine and her brother John would later reflect. In June 1760 Catherine Sawbridge married Dr. George Macaulay, a Scots physician living in London. Macaulay was widely acquainted with both the radical Whig and Scots circles in the metropolis; through him his wife met, and became better acquainted with, men such as Tobias Smollett, William Hunter, and Thomas Hollis.

It was apparently Hollis who encouraged Mrs. Macaulay to pursue the seventeenth-century roots of their mutual political ideas, to discover what he regarded as the true English constitution and how it had been betrayed. A wealthy barrister, Hollis occupied himself with encouraging devotion to liberty. He sponsored a reprinting of John Milton's political works, collected republi-

can tracts and books, and sent copies of them to various correspondents both in Britain and North America. He supplied Mrs. Macaulay with pamphlets and guided her reading in the manuscript and printed sources of the previous century's history.

The first volume of her *History of England from the Accession of James I to that of the House of Hanover* was published in 1763. The irregular intervals at which the eight volumes appeared over the next twenty years were caused by events and diversions in the author's life. There was, however, no real change over the years in the focus or intent of Macaulay's *History of England.* It is unquestionably her most important work, and it was highly regarded by her contemporaries, including some, like Horace Walpole, who later turned against Macaulay. The *History* is significant for both its political view and its methodology.

The *History of England* is the longest and one of the most complex statements of the Old Whig view. It is antimonarchical and strongly supports liberty, reason, the people, and the perfectibility of human institutions. It answered Hume's *History of England* (1754-1762), which had presented a monarchical, Tory interpretation of the seventeenth century. Macaulay's purpose was also to remind Britons of their history so that they would beware of what many saw as the threat to the constitution by John Stuart, third Earl of Bute, and the court party of the early 1760s. The *History* reflects Macaulay's interpretation of politics, but not all her judgments are what the reader might expect. She naturally condemned the actions and motives of Charles I, but she admired his conduct in his last days. She is much more severe with Oliver Cromwell, whom she regarded as the destroyer of the Commonwealth, England's best chance to attain political perfection. She admired the political manipulations of Charles II more than the actions of traditional Whig heroes such as James Scott, Duke of Monmouth, and Anthony Ashley Cooper, first Earl of Shaftesbury. The Glorious Revolution was for her a disaster, for it merely disguised the power of the monarchy rather than replacing it with popular sovereignty. With the apparatus of placemen, infrequent elections, and a limited franchise untouched, the Crown could again seek absolute power.

Macaulay's methodology in accumulating material for her *History* is more nearly like that of the modern historian than that of most of her contemporaries. She read seventeenth-century pamphlets and manuscripts, drawing her conclusions from them. She often used extensive quotations from these sources and sometimes published documents reflecting both sides of the argument. In contrast with contemporaries such as Hume, Gibbon, or Voltaire, Macaulay was writing history mainly for a political, not a moral, purpose. She was not writing philosophy in historical terms but rather history to defend a current political position. For this effort she was recognized in her own time, and, in part for this same reason, she was later ignored as her position lost influence.

In the mid 1760s Macaulay's interests were diverted to contemporary events, probably through the influence of her brother John Sawbridge, who was active in City of London politics. Her first pamphlet, *Loose Remarks on Certain Positions to be found in Mr. Hobbes's Philosophical Rudiments of Government and Society. With a Short Sketch of A Democratical Form of Government, in a Letter to Signior Paoli* (1767), was largely a by-product of her research for the *History of England*. She had

read Thomas Hobbes and was clearly indignant about his views on the necessity of monarchy and the imperfectibility of human society. Pasquale di Paoli's Corsican revolt of 1755 had been greeted enthusiastically by all friends of liberty, and he served as the president of Corsica until his defeat by the French in 1769. Macaulay offered the island a constitution based on rational republican principles, stating for the first time her formula for securing a proper government—rotation in office, equal inheritance of property by sons, frequent elections, and universal manhood suffrage.

The return of John Wilkes to England in 1768 provided an active focus for antigovernment political activity. John Sawbridge became a leading supporter of Wilkes, who had been expelled from Parliament in 1763 and had fled to France after being charged with seditious libel for criticizing George III's speech from the throne. Catherine Macaulay was introduced into the center of radical politics. In addition to meeting Wilkes, she became particularly well acquainted with the elder William Beckford, Lord Mayor of London, and the Reverend Dr. Thomas Wilson, rector of St. Stephen Walbrook in the City.

The government was under attack from various factions; in 1770 Edmund Burke presented the views of the Rockingham Whigs in *Thoughts on the Cause of the Present Discontents*. Answering Burke in *Observations on a Pamphlet, Entitled, Thoughts on the Cause of the Present Discontents*, Macaulay said the time had come for radical solutions—that is, frequent elections, extended suffrage, and rotation in office—not piecemeal reform. *Observations* was widely read on both sides of the Atlantic and was generally considered the most effective answer to Burke. Macaulay met most of the American colonials who came to England, and she began to correspond with several American leaders, most notably John and Abigail Adams and Mercy Otis Warren. Her last Wilkite pamphlet, *An Address to the People of England, Ireland, and Scotland, on the Present Important Crisis of Affairs* (1775), discussed the American problem, warning that repression in the colonies could lead to repression at home. This work was especially well received in North America, where it was republished.

By the early 1770s Mrs. Macaulay had little to tie her to London. Dr. Macaulay had died in 1766, and Hollis retired to the country in 1770. Her health was not good, and she made frequent visits to Bath, where she finally settled in 1774. *A*

"The Auspicious Marriage," a caricature published at the time of Macaulay's elopement with William Graham,
who was her junior by twenty-six years

Modest Plea for the Property of Copyright, published that year in support of authors' claims to copyright, is her least significant pamphlet, and she apologized for it on the grounds of ill health and hasty composition. The matter of copyright was being decided that year, first in court and then by act of Parliament, and many authors rushed into print to defend their rights against the booksellers.

Macaulay remained in Bath until the end of 1778. During her years there, her personal life became the subject of extensive gossip, which became fuel for her political opponents. She moved into the house of Thomas Wilson; their relationship caused much speculation, as did their association with the quack doctor James Graham. An elaborate and well-publicized birthday party the two men staged for Macaulay in 1777 elicited much comment. The same year Wilson erected a larger-than-life-sized white marble statue of Macaulay as Clio in his church in the city; this too was the subject of much talk.

Though only five volumes of her *History* had thus far appeared, Macaulay published the first volume of a continuation, *The History of England, from the Revolution to the Present Time in a Series of Letters to the Reverend Doctor Wilson*, in 1778. This was the only volume of the new history to appear, for no one, except presumably Wilson, was impressed by it. Her thesis was unchanged: the revolution of 1688-1689 and succeeding governments had done nothing to ensure liberty and honest government; but her research was apparently limited to reading some of the periodical press. There is none of the thorough documentation here that characterizes *The History of England, from the Accession of James I*. Macaulay's unflattering accounts of men of more recent times turned many against her, among them Horace Walpole, who heartily condemned her portrait of his father, Sir Robert. The final blow to Macaulay's reputation for many contemporaries was her elopement with William Graham, the twenty-one-year-old brother of James Graham, on 17 December 1778. The marriage and her ensuing quarrel with Wilson were covered extensively in the press, both factually and in fictionalized accounts.

After her second marriage, Mrs. Macaulay Graham, as she was then usually known, and her husband lived quietly in Leicestershire. There she completed and published the remaining volumes of her *History of England, from the Accession of James I*. In spring 1784 the couple went to the United States, where they visited many of her longtime correspondents and American heroes during a fifteen-month stay. The trip culminated in a ten-day visit at Mount Vernon with George and Martha Washington in June 1785. From America they went to France, returning to London in 1787. In the following year they settled in Binfield, Berkshire, where they remained until the historian's death in 1791.

After completing the *History of England* Macaulay turned to more speculative topics. Mercy Otis Warren had suggested she write a history of the American Revolution, but the Englishwoman declined, saying she was too old to undertake such a task. Instead she published *A Treatise on the Immutability of Moral Truth* (1783), which stated her views on man, morality, and religion more plainly than her earlier political works had done. She believed that without religion there could be no morality; through the perfection of his reason and morals man and his institutions became perfect. The plan of perfection is God's; it is man's duty actively to help achieve God's ends through improving his temporal institutions. As a devout Anglican, Macaulay believed that Christianity was a necessity for good government, liberty, and the rule of reason. There was little in the *Treatise* that most English readers could take issue with; it received generally more favorable notices than any of her writings since the early volumes of the *History of England*.

If, as *A Treatise on the Immutability of Moral Truth* argued, man is capable of creating a rational society and institutions and if the right basis for this society is equality, then a crucial question is how man can be made ready for this society in which all must share responsibility. Since proper education is the answer, it is not surprising that Macaulay next tackled this subject. In 1790 she published *Letters on Education, with Observations on Religious and Metaphysical Subjects*. Part 3 of this work, the "Observations," was primarily a revision of *A Treatise on the Immutability of Moral Truth*, though more specific in its attacks on

Henry St. John, Viscount Bolingbroke, and Archbishop William King and their acceptance of the inevitability of evil. Parts 1 and 2 of the *Letters on Education* contain Macaulay's ideas on education, her reflections on the classical societies of Athens, Sparta, and Rome, and her views of how various aspects of contemporary society could be improved. She dealt with education in its broadest sense, including artistic and leisure activities as well as academic training.

The *Letters on Education* make clear that, in addition to John Locke, Macaulay had read the works of Jean-Jacques Rousseau and Félicité Ducrest de Saint-Aubin, Madame de Genlis, as well as many of the contemporary courtesy books and popular works on education, whose widely accepted ideas about education Macaulay criticized extensively. She also criticized Rousseau's ideas, especially the notion that children could not be taught a sense of right and wrong. Although her plan of education did not call for rigid formal training at an early age, she did believe that learning should start when children are young and be made interesting so that curiosity, study, and knowledge would naturally expand. The curriculum she laid out was heavy on languages, literature, history, and philosophy. She also advocated sports and outdoor activities and a simple, healthy life. None of these ideas was particularly unusual in her day. The most remarkable aspect of the *Letters on Education* is Macaulay's position on the education of women. She came to the conclusion that the only real difference between the sexes is physical: men are usually larger and stronger, but intellectually, and above all morally, men and women are equal. Therefore, Macaulay believed that they should receive the same education and should be educated together; she called for a thorough reform in the education of both sexes.

In her assessment of the innate characteristics of women and their capabilities, Macaulay attacked Burke as well as Rousseau. In his *Philosophical Enquiry into the Origins of Our Ideas of the Sublime and Beautiful* (1757) Burke had defined *feminine* in terms of weakness, smallness, timidity, imperfection, and delicacy. Macaulay argued that these characteristics were not innate in women but had been imposed by their education and society's expectation of them. Women, she argued, needed to discard these limitations and take their rightful place as rational members of society. The feminism of the *Letters on Education* is a logical outcome of Macaulay's ideas and philosophy of history, though none of the other eighteenth-century writers who were concerned with how to create a more perfect society made this leap from man as male to man as all people. None of Macaulay's earlier works reflects any sort of feminism, and there is no evidence of what led her to this position. Was it the result of her own experience, or of wide reading of works on the *querrelle des femmes*, or simply of a logical mind? The *Letters on Education* received generally favorable notice from Whig and radical periodicals, although the *Critical Review* (December 1790) did question her views on the equality of men and women. The most important notice was a fourteen-page essay by Mary Wollstonecraft in the *Analytical Review* (November 1790). The *Letters on Education* were important in the formation of Wollstonecraft's views, and she acknowledged her debt in the *Vindication of the Rights of Woman* (1792).

By the time the *Letters on Education* appeared, most people's attention was fixed on the French Revolution. Like other British radicals, Macaulay welcomed the events in France. She was one of the first to reply to Burke's *Reflections on the Revolution in France* (1790); her *Observations on the Reflections of the Right Hon. Edmund Burke on the Revolution in France* appeared in late 1790. Macaulay used her usual arguments to commend the actions of the French, who seemed to her to be trying to create a better and more rational society. She believed they were as likely to achieve this as they were to degenerate into the chaos and tyranny Burke predicted. At least the French people were acting to change their own situations, she said; what they did was their own business, not Britain's. Among the flood of replies to Burke, Macaulay's received little notice. Her arguments are largely historical, not prophetic; the *Observations on the Reflections* offers nothing in the way of general political theory that she had not said before. It is her last publication, a sort of postscript to her earlier work.

Catherine Macaulay Graham was the first woman to write serious history in English. She was the leading pamphleteer for the Wilkite radicals of the 1760s and 1770s, as well as the first English writer to advocate not just giving women the same education as men but also reforming the education of both sexes to achieve true equality. Her reputation as historian and pamphlet writer in her own time was high, but in the nineteenth century she was almost entirely ignored. Only in the late twentieth century have her writings once again been taken into consideration as important for the study of the eighteenth century.

There are several intertwined reasons for Macaulay's eclipse. In her own day her personal conduct was generally condemned, especially by many of literary and social importance, including Hannah More, Samuel Johnson, and Horace Walpole. This disapproval was reflected in her contemporaries' assessment of her works. The people who criticized her conduct were also conservatives who did not approve of Macaulay's basic political ideas; the triumph of conservatism in the period of the French Revolution further diminished her credibility. In addition Macaulay's political views were based in the thinking of the seventeenth century. By the late eighteenth century, the Enlightenment and the beginning of industrialization had made many of her arguments outmoded. She had no more to say to the nineteenth-century reformer than did, for example, James Harrington. Her *Letters on Education* were more forward-looking in their proposals, but few in the nineteenth century were likely to look favorably on someone praised by the notorious Mary Wollstonecraft as the "woman of the greatest ability, undoubtedly, that this country has ever produced."

References:

Florence S. Boos, "Catherine Macaulay's *Letters on Education* (1790): An Early Feminist Polemic," *University of Michigan Papers in Women's Studies*, 2, no. 2 (1976): 64-78;

Florence and William Boos, "Catherine Macaulay: Historian and Political Reformer," *International Journal of Women's Studies*, 3, no. 1 (1980): 49-65;

Natalie Zemon Davis, "History's Two Bodies," *American Historical Review*, 93 (February 1988): 1-30;

G. M. Ditchfield, "Some Literary and Political Views of Catherine Macaulay," *American Notes and Queries*, 12 (January 1974): 70-75;

Lucy M. Donnelly, "The Celebrated Mrs. Macaulay," *William & Mary Quarterly*, third series, 6 (April 1949): 173-207;

Claire Gilbride Fox, "Catherine Macaulay, An Eighteenth Century Clio," in *Winterthur Portfolio*, volume 4 (Charlottesville: University of Virginia Press, 1968), pp. 129-142;

Christopher and Bridget Hill, "Catherine Macaulay and the Seventeenth Century," *Welsh History Review*, 3 (December 1967): 381-402;

Barbara Brandon Schnorrenberg, "The Brood Hen of Faction: Mrs. Macaulay and Radical Politics, 1765-1775," *Albion*, 11 (Spring 1979): 32-45;

Schnorrenberg, "*Observations on the Reflections*: Macaulay vs Burke Round Three," in *The Consortium on Revolutionary Europe 1750-1850 Proceedings 1987* (Athens, Ga.: The Consortium, 1987), pp. 215-225;

Lynne E. Withey, "Catherine Macaulay and the Uses of History: Ancient Rights, Perfectionism, and Propaganda," *Journal of British Studies*, 16 (Fall 1976): 59-83.

Thomas Percy

(24 April 1729 - 30 September 1811)

Bertram H. Davis
Florida State University

BOOKS: *A Letter Describing the Ride to Hulne Abbey from Alnwick in Northumberland* (N.p.: Privately printed, 1765);

A Key to the New Testament. Giving an Account of the several Books, their Contents, their Authors, And Of the Times and Occasions, on which they were respectively written (London: Printed for L. Davis & C. Reymers, 1766);

Four Essays, as Improved and Enlarged in the Second Edition of the Reliques of Ancient English Poetry (London: Printed for J. Dodsley, 1767);

A Sermon Preached before the Sons of the Clergy, at Their Anniversary Meeting, in the Cathedral Church of St. Paul, on Thursday, May 11, 1769 (London: Printed for John & Francis Rivington, 1770);

The Hermit of Warkworth. A Northumberland Ballad. In Three Fits or Cantos (London: Printed for T. Davies & S. Leacroft, 1771);

A Sermon Preached at Christ-Church, Dublin, On the 18th of April, 1790, before His Excellency John, Earl of Westmoreland, President; and the rest of the Incorporated Society, in Dublin, for Promoting English Protestant Schools, in Ireland (Dublin: Printed by George Perrin for the Incorporated Society, 1790).

OTHER: "Cynthia, an Elegiac Poem," in *A Collection of Poems in Six Volumes. By Several Hands* (London: Printed by J. Hughs for R. & J. Dodsley, 1758), VI: 234-239;

James Grainger, *A Poetical Translation of the Elegies of Tibullus; and The Poems of Sulpicia*, 2 volumes, includes translations by Percy of Tibullus's Elegy 1 and Ovid's elegy on Tibullus (London: Printed for A. Millar, 1759);

Hau Kiou Choaan or The Pleasing History. A Translation from the Chinese Language. To Which Are Added, I. The Argument or Story of a Chinese Play, II. A Collection of Chinese Proverbs, and III. Fragments of Chinese Poetry. In Four Volumes. With Notes, edited, and partly translated, by Percy (London: Printed for R. & J. Dodsley, 1761);

The Matrons. Six Short Histories, edited, and partly translated, by Percy (London: Printed for R. & J. Dodsley, 1762);

Miscellaneous Pieces Relating to the Chinese, 2 volumes, edited, with "A Dissertation on the Language and Characters of the Chinese," by Percy (London: Printed for R. & J. Dodsley, 1762);

Five Pieces of Runic Poetry Translated from the Islandic Language (London: Printed for R. & J. Dodsley, 1763);

The Song of Solomon, Newly Translated from the Original Hebrew: with a Commentary and Annotations (London: Printed for R. & J. Dodsley, 1764);

Reliques of Ancient English Poetry: Consisting of Old Heroic Ballads, Songs, and other Pieces of our earlier Poets, (Chiefly of the lyric Kind.) Together

Thomas Percy (mezzotint by William Dickinson, after a portrait by Sir Joshua Reynolds)

with some few of later Date, 3 volumes (London: Printed for J. Dodsley, 1765);

Northern Antiquities: Or, a Description of the Manners, Customs, Religion and Laws of the Ancient Danes, and other Northern Nations; Including those of Our own Saxon Ancestors. With a Translation of the Edda, or System of Runic Mythology, and Other Pieces, from the Ancient Islandic Tongue. In Two Volumes. Translated from Mons. Mallet's Introduction a l'Histoire de Dannemarc, &.c. With Additional Notes by the English Translator, and Goranson's Latin Version of the Edda (London: Printed for T. Carnan, 1770);

The Regulation and Establishment of the Houshold of Henry Algernon Percy, the Fifth Earl of Northumberland, at His Castles of Wresill and Lekinfield in Yorkshire Begun Anno Domini 1513, includes a preface and notes by Percy (London: Privately printed, 1770);

Arthur Collins, *The Peerage of England,* fifth edition, volume 2 includes "Percy, Duke of Northumberland" by Percy (London, 1779);

Biographia Britannica, second edition, volume 3 includes an article on John Cleveland by Percy (London, 1784);

"The Life of Dr. Oliver Goldsmith," in volume 1 of *The Miscellaneous Works of Oliver Goldsmith, M.D. A New Edition in Four Volumes* (London: Printed for J. Johnson by H. Baldwin & Sons, 1801);

Ancient Songs Chiefly on Moorish Subjects Translated from the Spanish by Thomas Percy. With a Preface by David Nichol Smith (Oxford: Oxford University Press, 1932);

Ian A. Gordon, ed., *Shenstone's Miscellany, 1759-1763,* includes poems and notes by Percy (Oxford: Clarendon Press, 1952).

Thomas Percy was well known during his lifetime as a pioneer scholar, a friend and clubmate of Samuel Johnson, and a dignitary of the church. Today he is remembered for the *Reliques of Ancient English Poetry* (1765), a three-volume collection that achieved a new prominence for the popular ballads of earlier times and inspired many of the Romantic poets. Percy's *Reliques* became a household book, and Percy himself attained an eminence reserved for only the most exceptional scholars.

Percy's Shropshire beginnings were modest but not altogether humble. A great-grandfather was the brother of the poet John Cleveland, and a great-great-grandfather had served as mayor of Worcester. His mother was Jane Nott, and his father was Arthur Lowe Piercy, a wholesale grocer, maltster, and tobacconist whose variable fortunes twice won him election as one of Bridgnorth's two chief magistrates and lords of the manor, and in between plunged him to the very brink of bankruptcy. Arthur Lowe's fondness for books led him to encourage his son's reading and support his education, first at the Bridgnorth Free School and then at Newport School, where Percy progressed so rapidly that two years before he was to graduate he was awarded a scholarship for Christ Church, Oxford. With the help of still another scholarship he completed his undergraduate course in 1750 and the work for the master's degree in 1753. In 1751 he was ordained a deacon in the Church of England and began his clerical career as a curate in two churches just outside of Bridgnorth. He was ordained a priest in 1753.

As a young man, Percy was drawn to the writing of poetry, much of it addressed to "Flavia," his poetic name for a young woman whom he seems to have courted with all the ardor of first love. These and a few other surviving poems of this Bridgnorth period are not without grace and promise, though only a few of them were published in his lifetime. Together they show him variously influenced by ballads and by the poems of John Milton, Alexander Pope, and Thomas Gray, whose *Elegy Wrote in a Country Church Yard* (1751) provided him with a model for a "Post-script" to one of his Flavia poems. Perhaps the ballad influence was a consequence of his acquiring during his Bridgnorth years a folio manuscript of early ballads, romances, and lyric poems that he saw in the parlor of a Shropshire friend, Humphrey Pitt, whose maids were tearing out its leaves to light the fires. Although unaware of its value, Percy asked for the manuscript and was given it.

In 1753 Christ Church presented him with a living as vicar of Easton Maudit in Northamptonshire, but he engaged a curate to perform his new duties until George Augustus Yelverton, Earl of Sussex, lord of the manor at Easton Maudit, attracted him to Northamptonshire in 1756 by offering him a second living as curate of nearby Wilby. The year 1756 was eventful in other ways as well. The earl, only two years Percy's senior, encouraged his literary work, appointed him first his chaplain and then rector of Wilby, and introduced him at court, where the earl was master of the bedchamber to the future George III. In London Percy made the acquaintance of the physician and poet James Grainger and, through Grainger, Samuel Johnson. After a summer visit to Worcester, when he noted the practice of the city registrars and his own Worcester relations, he changed the spelling of his surname from Piercy to Percy.

On his birthday in 1759 he married Anne Gutteridge of Desborough in Northamptonshire, by whom he was to have five daughters and one son, of whom only two daughters survived to adulthood. Anne seems to have fitted the ideal he had set for his wife in a thirty-two-line "Song" written in 1755, apparently before he and Anne had met. Originally an imitation of a Scottish song, it was published in Robert Dodsley's *Collection of Poems* (1758) in an English version later praised by Robert Burns as perhaps the most beautiful of all English songs. Although still memorable for the similar opening and closing lines of its four stanzas, the poem's idea of true love seems a little one-sided: the young woman is asked if she is ready to give up, without regret, all pleasures and comforts for her love. But it struck a responsive chord in its time and was set to music in both its English and Scottish versions and frequently republished:

> O Nancy, wilt thou go with me,
>   Nor sigh to leave the flaunting town:
> Can silent glens have charms for thee,
>   The lowly cot and russet gown?
> No longer dress'd in silken sheen,
>   No longer deck'd with jewels rare,
> Say can'st thou quit each courtly scene,
>   Where thou wert fairest of the fair?

Encouraged by Grainger, who remained a close friend until his death in 1766, Percy contributed translations of Tibullus's Elegy 1 and Ovid's elegy on Tibullus to Grainger's *Poetical Translation of the Elegies of Tibullus* (1759). He had not yet gone beyond familiarizing himself with his folio manuscript of ballads and other poems, even though Johnson had suggested that he publish the best of them, and Johnson, William Shenstone, and the Anglo-Saxon scholar Edward Lye had offered their assistance. Instead he turned to a manuscript borrowed from a Northamptonshire friend, a 1719 translation of the seventeenth-century Chinese novel *Hau Kiou Choaan*, three parts of which had been rendered into English by a representative of the East India Company in Canton and the fourth into Portuguese by an unknown person. Percy did not know Chinese, but he had taught himself Portuguese, and he thus translated the fourth part and revised the rest to form a coherent narrative. The novel, which recounts the efforts of the bright and attractive Shuey-ping-sin to outwit her tireless pursuer Kho-khé-tzu, might have been expected to please an audience that had welcomed Richardson's *Pamela* (1740-1741) and *Clarissa* (1747-1749), but Robert Dodsley, who contracted for this and Percy's next five books, had difficulty selling his 1761 printing of a thousand copies, and the remainder were republished in 1774 with a new "Advertisement."

Shenstone and Ralph Griffiths, the reviewer for the *Monthly Review*, were more impressed with Percy's annotations than with the story itself, and probably this first Chinese novel printed in England was the first novel of any origin to be so thoroughly annotated. Taking his information from more than two dozen works on the Orient, particularly P. J. B. du Halde's *Description of the Empire of China and Chinese-Tartary* (1738, 1741), Percy included a preface, a bibliography, a fifteen-page index, and numerous notes that ranged from short sentences to essays of several hundred words. The novel itself, he asserted in the preface, presented "a faithful picture of Chinese manners," and it was these that he set out further to illuminate in notes to which, far removed though he was from China, he managed to give the authentic ring of firsthand accounts.

Two other works of this period seem to have been byproducts of his researches for *Hau Kiou Choaan*. In *Miscellaneous Pieces Relating to the Chinese* (1762) he brought together seven essays on China by various writers, with his own contributions confined to a preface and an introductory "Dissertation on the Language and Characters of the Chinese." The preface is marred by Percy's rash acceptance of a recent "discovery" that the Chinese characters had been derived from Egyp-

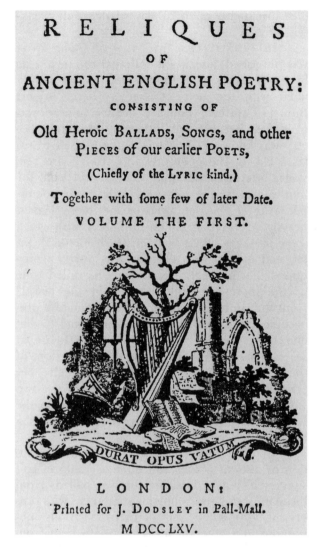

RELIQUES
OF
ANCIENT ENGLISH POETRY:
CONSISTING OF
Old Heroic BALLADS, SONGS, and other PIECES of our earlier POETS,
(Chiefly of the LYRIC kind.)
Together with some few of later Date.
VOLUME THE FIRST.

DURAT OPUS VATUM

LONDON:
Printed for J. DODSLEY in Pall-Mall.
M DCC LXV.

Title page for Percy's innovative anthology, which he modestly described as "the amusement of now and then a vacant hour"

tian hieroglyphics, but he made amends with the "Dissertation," in which he explains very clearly what was then known about the written Chinese language.

The Matrons (1762) is related to *Hau Kiou Choaan* through its story of the Chinese matron, which Percy translated anew from du Halde. The prototype of Percy's stories of widows false to their vows of fealty to their dead husbands was Petronius's tale of the Ephesian matron, which Percy also translated anew and supplemented with accounts of French, British, Turkish, and Roman matrons that he adopted without change. His only really original contribution to this slight collection was the idea for it and the half-serious "Dedication to the Matrons of Great Britain and Ireland," who were not likely to have taken much pleasure in his open display of matronly weakness.

In 1763 Percy's *Five Pieces of Runic Poetry* was published, and it was followed the next year by his translation of *The Song of Solomon*, annotated with the help of Percy's friend Robert Binnel. The first, though a slender volume, was of interest because very little of the Icelandic poetry was known in England. Percy himself translated two of the poems, mainly from Latin versions, intermediaries that made it difficult for him to capture the spirit of Nordic battle poems. *The Song of Solomon*, perhaps inevitably, leaned heavily on the King James translation, with which some passages were wholly or nearly identical. Interested in *The Song of Solomon* as poetry, Percy hoped that he might rescue what he called "one of the most beautiful pastorals in the world" from the confusion caused by commentators preoccupied with its allegorical meaning, and to that end he presented it as a dramatic eclogue in seven parts corresponding to the seven days of the Jewish nuptial week. Not surprisingly, *The Song of Solomon* is the more readable of the two works, Percy having nothing comparable to the King James Bible to draw upon for his translations of the Icelandic poems.

In 1760 he had decided to prepare an edition of ancient poems, not quite as Johnson had suggested, but by selecting the best ballads from his manuscript and supplementing them with others, including some later poems, from various publications and other manuscripts. With help from Shenstone he undertook the process of selection and of searching out ballads in other parts of Britain, particularly Scotland; and with help from Johnson he was able to conclude a contract with Robert Dodsley on 22 May 1761. He had already solicited the aid of Richard Farmer at Cambridge, and he was soon reaching out for help from Thomas Warton at Oxford, Evan Evans in Wales, and David Dalrymple in Scotland. Shenstone's help was so extensive, in fact, that Percy came to think of the collection as a joint effort, and, after Shenstone died in February 1763, Percy's first thought was to dedicate it to his memory. In April 1764, however, Elizabeth Percy, Countess of Northumberland, consented to accept the dedication, and, in June, Percy adapted the three-volume collection to its patroness by interchanging the first and third volumes so that the Northumberland ballads would stand at the beginning. In July and August Johnson, on the verge of completing his edition of Shakespeare's plays, spent nearly eight weeks with the Percys at Easton Maudit, in the course of which he wrote the graceful dedication of the *Reliques*, a role kept secret until the publication of James Boswell's *Life of Johnson* in 1791.

Reliques of Ancient English Poetry, the first of Percy's publications to bear his name, was published on 11 February 1765 and was immediately successful. Of its fifteen hundred copies, six hundred were sold by the end of March and a total of twelve hundred by the beginning of July, and it was well received by the reviews. Its effect upon Percy was incalculable. In June 1765 he was appointed tutor to Algernon Percy, the younger Northumberland son, and by September, after almost two months with the Northumberland family at Alnwick Castle, he was appointed chaplain and secretary to Hugh Smithson Percy, Earl of Northumberland, who was raised to a dukedom the next year. He was also given an apartment in Northumberland House for his use when he was in London. In 1768 he was elected to the famous literary Club established by Johnson and Sir Joshua Reynolds in 1764.

Probably much of the initial success of the *Reliques* resulted from the countess's patronage and from Percy's adroit citing in his preface of the respected persons who had provided assistance: Johnson, Shenstone, David Garrick, and others. These, Percy wrote, were the amulet to guard his book against censure. But ultimately its only certain defense lay in its poems and Percy's editing, and with these, with advice from Shenstone and Johnson, he had taken extraordinary care. Because his primary aim was to please readers of taste, he considered quality his principal criterion in selecting poems, and he had been much helped by Shenstone's assigning grades to each of the poems in numerous published collections. Both English and Scottish ballads were included. The organization was essentially chronological, but to avoid placing too many older poems together, Percy divided each volume into three parts, with the poems in each part arranged roughly in chronological order. Poems on similar subjects were grouped together—"Ballads that Illustrate Shakespeare," for example—long poems were separated by short ones; lyric poems were interspersed among the ballads; and poems that illuminated each other were placed together. When the hapless swain of "The Baffled Knight" is ducked in the castle moat in his fourth attempt on a maiden's virtue, Sir John Suckling's "Why so pale?" promptly supplies the best possible advice: "The devil take her!"

For each poem or group of poems Percy provided an introduction, and at appropriate points he inserted four essays that were themselves significant landmarks in English literary history: on the English minstrels, alliterative verse, the English romances, and the early English drama. To make the poems more attractive he also edited them by occasionally smoothing out the meter, substituting more readily comprehensible words and phrases, blending different versions of the same poem, and, when there were gaps resulting from the mutilation of his folio manuscript, filling them in from his own imagination. Rather than crowd his pages with notes, he normally called attention to changes only in a general way, through single quotation marks around a replacement or a brief comment in his introduction.

The ballads had never been taken so seriously before, nor had they been approached so comprehensively and imaginatively. Yet Percy, concerned lest his ballad work be thought inappropriate for a minister of the gospel, took frequent opportunities to minimize his effort and even to disparage the ballads themselves. At one time he likened his ballad activity to the games of whist engaged in by other clergymen, and at another he went so far as to describe the *Reliques* as "a strange collection of trash." In the *Reliques* itself he was more restrained. "This little work," he wrote in the preface, was merely "the amusement of now and then a vacant hour amid the leisure and retirement of rural life." The very modesty of the *Reliques*, William Wordsworth later observed, helped to endear it to its readers.

Before the publication of the *Reliques* in 1765, Percy had committed himself to numerous other projects, some of which were never completed. He signed contracts with the publisher Jacob Tonson in 1761 to edit the poems of Henry Howard, Earl of Surrey; in 1763 to edit the works of George Villiers, Duke of Buckingham, including the preparation of a new key to Buckingham's play *The Rehearsal* (1672); and in 1764 to edit *The Tatler*, *The Spectator*, and *The Guardian*. For Lockyer Davis he proposed an edition of *Don Quixote* (1605), and he was writing *A Key to the New Testament*; and for Thomas Carnan and John Newbery he was translating Paul Henri Mallet's *Introduction à l'Histoire de Dannemarc* (1755-1756). Of these he himself completed the work on only two, the *Key to the New Testament*, published in 1766, and the translation of Mallet, published in 1770 as *Northern Antiquities*. He turned the editions of Joseph Addison and Richard Steele's essays over to John Calder sometime before 1772, and for *Don Quixote* he settled for assisting John Bowle, whose Spanish-language edition was published in 1781. The printed sheets of the nearly completed Surrey and Bolingbroke editions languished in the warehouse after Tonson's death in 1767 and were finally destroyed in a fire that consumed John Nichols's warehouse in 1808. Only two or three copies of each have survived.

A Key to the New Testament proved to be one of Percy's most successful works. A manual of instruction written in Percy's characteristically clear and concise language, it drew for its information from the most recent scholarly works, particularly those of J. D. Michaelis and Nathaniel Lardner. With his usual modesty Percy informed George Paton that it was written for the use of his parishioners, but it found a more eager audience among university students and the clergy and went through a half-dozen editions in Percy's lifetime.

In *Northern Antiquities* Percy was responding to a kindred spirit in Mallet, who found in the early Scandinavian poetry the same graphic representation of the "manners of life and modes of thinking" that had helped to attract Percy to the ancient English and Scottish poems, and he followed Mallet with pleasure through such discussions as those on the religion of Odin and the Scandinavian conquests of northern Europe and Britain. Though otherwise favorably disposed, he concentrated in his preface, with help from Evan Evans, on a major point of disagreement, Percy concluding, as Mallet had not, that the Gothic and Celtic were distinct peoples. But the real value of Percy's eloquent translation, which included the prose *Edda*, was that it served to introduce the English public not just to Nordic history, but to Nordic mythology and folklore as well.

In 1767, after giving birth to the Percys' fifth child, Anne Percy was appointed wet nurse to the infant Prince Edward, who was to be the father of Queen Victoria, and in 1769 she was granted an annual pension of one hundred pounds for life. In that year Percy was appointed a chaplain-in-ordinary to George III with December duties that he discharged regularly for the next nine years. In 1770 Cambridge University awarded him the degree of doctor of divinity, as Oxford was to do also in 1793. Throughout the thirteen years after the publication of the *Reliques* he continued as chaplain to the duke of Northumberland, with much of his literary activity inspired by his summers at Alnwick Castle. A pamphlet, adapted from a letter to Edward Lye and known familiarly as "The Ride to Hulne Abbey," was privately printed in 1765 and routinely given to castle guests, whom Percy regularly conducted on tours to the abbey and other nearby points of interest. In 1770 Percy completed his editing of a Northumberland manuscript privately printed as *The Regulation and Establishment of the Houshold of Henry Algernon Percy*, the approximately 180 copies of which were presented by the duke to his and Percy's friends. In 1779, for the fifth edition of Collins's *Peerage of England*, Percy revised the article on "Percy, Duke of Northumberland," and about the same time he began for the duke the writing of "A Genealogical History of the Percy Family," four sheets of which were printed before he abandoned the project.

His best-known publication of the Northumberland years was *The Hermit of Warkworth* (1771), an artfully contrived poem of some two hundred ballad stanzas that Percy fitted to a mysterious hermitage carved out of the rock beside the River Coquet, about half a mile from the ruined Percy castle at Warkworth. Popular in its day, *The Hermit of Warkworth* went through two editions of five hundred copies each within a few months. But, though an interesting experiment in the extended use of the ballad stanza, it embodies a rather overwrought story, in which the elderly hermit recounts to two young lovers his own tragic love affair, climaxed by his killing his brother, whom he fails to recognize as the rescuer rather than the abductor of his love. Percy was unable to bring to his poem the fire and color that characterize the ballads of the *Reliques*—many of its verses are quite pedestrian—and it is remembered today less for itself than for the parodies with which Johnson, who thought it much overrated, ridiculed it.

Other fruits of Percy's Northumberland years were the second edition of the *Reliques* in 1767 and the third in 1775, with only minor changes in the selections but, in the second edition, a substantial revision of the essay on the English minstrels to meet objections raised by the antiquary Samuel Pegge. In 1775 Percy also virtually completed a volume containing seven of his translations of Spanish poems, two of which he had included in the *Reliques*, but for reasons now unclear he withdrew his *Ancient Songs Chiefly on Moorish Subjects* after it had been set in type and embellished with illustrations. It was finally published in 1932.

In 1778, on a recommendation of the duke of Northumberland to Frederick, Lord North, Percy was appointed dean of Carlisle, a position that he held until he was promoted to the bishopric of Dromore on 17 April 1782. In May and June 1782 he was in Ireland, where he was seated in the Irish House of Lords and paid his first visit to some of his Dromore parishes; but he did not move to Ireland with his family until July 1783, when a new see house was ready for occupancy. In April of that year the Percys lost their only son, a student at Cambridge, who Percy had hoped would someday undertake the ballad projects for which he had never found time.

Percy's twenty-nine years as bishop of Dromore were exciting ones, with Ireland's political hopes fluctuating through the repeal of England's detested Poyning's Law in 1783, the disastrous rebellion of 1798, and the uneasy union of England and Ireland in 1800. They were satisfying years for him also. He enjoyed widespread respect for his humane and efficient leadership of the diocese and his attention to civic improvements and the education of the young. With an income far exceeding that of many English bishoprics—augmented by inheritance and careful management—he was able to pay off debts that had oppressed him in Carlisle, purchase and improve his see house, transform more than a hundred acres of his four-hundred-acre demesne into a splendid garden, and provide ample dowries for the two Percy daughters.

Welcomed in Ireland as a scholar as well as a prelate, he was soon drawn into active literary work. He became a charter member of the Royal Irish Academy, was the center of a literary coterie in County Down, provided information for both Boswell's and Robert Anderson's biographies of Johnson, and encouraged young poets, two of whom dedicated volumes of verse to him. His own writing included genealogical work, occasional reviews and articles in the periodicals, an account of the poet John Cleveland for the *Biographia Britannica*, and the life of Oliver Goldsmith—the first attempt at a comprehensive biography—prefixed to the first volume of the 1801 *Miscellaneous Works of Oliver Goldsmith*.

In spite of his reluctance to have his name associated with ballad editing, intensified by his elevation to a bishopric, he was goaded by the re-

Percy's account of the founding of the Club in a 28 February 1788 letter to James Boswell (private collection; from Samuel
Johnson, 1709-84: A Bicentenary Exhibition, *The Arts Council of Great Britain, 1984)*

peated attacks of Joseph Ritson into undertaking a fourth edition of the *Reliques*, though not without concealing his role behind the nominal editorship of his nephew, Thomas Percy of St. John's College, Oxford. The edition, dated 1794, was published in 1795, once again with a major revision in the essay on the English minstrels, which had come under Ritson's attack. More difficult for him to respond to was Ritson's attack upon his editorial practice, specifically his alteration of texts without precise notice to the reader. He revised occasional lines to meet Ritson's criticism and marked conspicuously the nearly 50 of his 175 poems with which he had taken considerable liberty. But ultimately he had to rest his case on the acceptance of the *Reliques* by scholars and the general reading public, for there could be no assurance that his three volumes would have enjoyed the same success if he had approached them differently.

Percy's wife died in 1806, and he himself, blinded by cataracts in his last few years, died in 1811. Both were buried in the cathedral of Dromore. Percy's reputation as an editor of the ballads survived Ritson's assaults but suffered appreciably when John W. Hales and Frederick J. Furnivall revealed all his textual changes in *Bishop Percy's Folio Manuscript* (1867-1868). But Percy's achievement was in no way diminished by the revelations of his critics. A pioneer in just about everything he attempted, he showed the way for later scholars and authors with his translations of Icelandic and Spanish poetry and of Mallet, his work with Chinese literature, his editing of the Northumberland household book, and even his romantic Northumberland ballad. But none of his achievements was comparable to that of the *Reliques*, which inspired not only other ballad scholars and collectors but such poets as James Beattie, William Blake, William Wordsworth, Samuel Taylor Coleridge, and Walter Scott, and—as England's foremost anthology—introduced generation after generation to the wonders of English poetry. Ballads such as "Sir Patrick Spens" and "Edward, Edward," both first published in the *Reliques*, have taken their place among the best of narrative poems. The very title *Lyrical Ballads* (1798) had its origin in the *Reliques*, as did any number of Wordsworth's poems written in the manner and language of the ballads. Coleridge too drew on it for the language and supernatural elements of "The Ancient Mariner," as well as for the name of his heroine in "Christabel."

In Wordsworth's view, the *Reliques* was the absolute redemption of English poetry; and certainly few works of scholarship—perhaps few works of any kind—have exerted such an influence on succeeding generations.

Letters:

John Nichols and John Bowyer Nichols, *Illustrations of the Literary History of the Eighteenth Century*, volumes 6-8 (London: Nichols, 1831-1858);

The Percy Letters, general editors, David Nichol Smith and Cleanth Brooks; later Cleanth Brooks and A. F. Falconer:

Volume 1: *The Correspondence of Thomas Percy & Edmond Malone*, edited by Arthur Tillotson (Baton Rouge: Louisiana State University Press, 1944; second edition, New Haven: Yale University Press, 1960);

Volume 2: *The Correspondence of Thomas Percy & Richard Farmer*, edited by Brooks, 1946;

Volume 3: *The Correspondence of Thomas Percy & Thomas Warton*, edited by M. G. Robinson and Leah Dennis (Baton Rouge: Louisiana State University Press, 1951);

Volume 4: *The Correspondence of Thomas Percy & David Dalrymple, Lord Hailes*, edited by Falconer (Baton Rouge: Louisiana State University Press, 1954);

Volume 5: *The Correspondence of Thomas Percy & Evan Evans*, edited by Aneirin Lewis (Baton Rouge: Louisiana State University Press, 1957);

Volume 6: *The Correspondence of Thomas Percy & George Paton*, edited by Falconer (New Haven: Yale University Press, 1961);

Volume 7: *The Correspondence of Thomas Percy & William Shenstone*, edited by Brooks (New Haven: Yale University Press, 1977);

Volume 8: *The Correspondence of Thomas Percy & John Pinkerton*, edited by Harriet Harvey Wood (New Haven: Yale University Press, 1985);

Volume 9: *The Correspondence of Thomas Percy & Robert Anderson*, edited by W. E. K. Anderson (New Haven: Yale University Press, 1988);

Thomas Percy & John Bowle: Cervantine Correspondence, edited by Daniel Eisenberg (Exeter: Exeter Hispanic Texts, 1987).

Biographies:

Alice C. C. Gaussen, *Percy: Prelate and Poet* (London: Smith, Elder, 1908);

Bertram H. Davis, *Thomas Percy: A Scholar-Cleric in the Age of Johnson* (Philadelphia: University of Pennsylvania Press, 1989).

References:

Walter Jackson Bate, "Percy's Use of His Folio-Manuscript," *Journal of English and Germanic Philology*, 43 (July 1944): 337-348;

Elsie I. M. Boyd, "The Influence of Percy's 'Reliques of Ancient English Poetry' on German Literature," *Modern Language Quarterly* (London), 7 (1904): 80-99;

Bertram H. Davis, *Thomas Percy* (Boston: Twayne, 1981);

Albert B. Friedman, *The Ballad Revival: Studies in the Influence of Popular on Sophisticated Poetry* (Chicago: University of Chicago Press, 1961);

John W. Hales and Frederick J. Furnivall, eds., *Bishop Percy's Folio Manuscript*, 3 volumes (London: Trübner, 1867-1868);

Zinnia Knapman, "A Reappraisal of Percy's Editing," *Folk Music Journal*, 5 (1986): 202-214;

L. F. Powell, "Percy's *Reliques*," *Library*, 9 (September 1928): 113-137.

Papers:

The two major collections of Percy's voluminous and widespread papers are in the British and Bodleian libraries, but there are also numerous letters and other materials in the Houghton Library, Harvard University; the Beinecke Library, Yale University; Alnwick Castle; and the Hyde Collection, Somerville, New Jersey. Manuscripts for some of Percy's early poems are in the Huntington Library, and extensive Percy memorabilia, including letters and documents, are in the collection of Mr. Kenneth Balfour, Marlow, Buckinghamshire. Much of Percy's own library, containing frequent annotations and occasional letters, is at the Queens University of Belfast. A detailed section on Percy may be found in the *Index of English Literary Manuscripts*, volume 3, part 2.

Hester Lynch [Thrale] Piozzi

(27 January 1741 - 2 May 1821)

Martine Watson Brownley
Emory University

BOOKS: *Anecdotes of the Late Samuel Johnson, LL.D., During the Last Twenty Years of His Life* (London: Printed for T. Cadell, 1786);

Letters to and from the Late Samuel Johnson, LL.D., to which are added some Poems never before Printed, 2 volumes, letters by Johnson and Piozzi, edited by Piozzi (London: Printed for A. Strahan & T. Cadell, 1788);

Observations and Reflections Made in the Course of a Journey through France, Italy, and Germany, 2 volumes (London: Printed for A. Strahan & T. Cadell, 1789);

British Synonymy; or, an Attempt at Regulating the Choice of Words in Familiar Conversation, 2 volumes (London: Printed for G. G. & J. Robinson, 1794);

Three Warnings to John Bull before He Dies (London: Printed for R. Faulder, 1798);

Retrospection: or a Review of the Most Striking and Important Events, Characters, Situations, and Their Consequences, which the Last Eighteen Hundred Years Have Presented to the View of Mankind, 2 volumes (London: John Stockdale, 1801);

Autobiography, Letters, and Literary Remains of Mrs. Piozzi (Thrale), 2 volumes, edited by Abraham Hayward, second edition (London: Longman, Green, Longman & Roberts, 1861; Boston: Ticknor & Fields, 1861);

The French Journals of Mrs. Thrale and Dr. Johnson, edited by Moses Tyson and Henry Guppy (Manchester: Manchester University Press, 1932);

Thraliana: The Diary of Mrs. Hester Lynch Thrale (Later Mrs. Piozzi), 1776-1809, 2 volumes, edited by Katharine C. Balderson (Oxford: Clarendon Press, in co-operation with the Huntington Library, 1942; second edition, revised, 1951);

The Thrales of Streatham Park [Family Book], edited by Mary Hyde (Cambridge, Mass. & London: Harvard University Press, 1977).

Editions: *The Letters of Samuel Johnson, with Mrs. Thrale's Genuine Letters to Him,* 3 volumes, ed-ited by R. W. Chapman (Oxford: Clarendon Press, 1952);

Observations and Reflections Made in the Course of a Journey through France, Italy, and Germany, edited by Herbert Barrows (Ann Arbor: University of Michigan Press, 1967);

Anecdotes of the Late Samuel Johnson, LL.D. during the Last Twenty Years of His Life, edited by Arthur Sherbo (London: Oxford University Press, 1974).

OTHER: "The Three Warnings" and "Epistle of Boileau to his Gardener," in *Miscellanies in Prose and Verse,* by Anna Williams (London: Printed for T. Davies, 1766); "The Three Warnings" republished in *A Collection of Poems in Four Volumes. By Several Hands,* edited by George Pearch (London: Printed for G. Pearch, 1770);

"Journal of the Welsh Tour" (1744), in *Dr. Johnson and Mrs. Thrale,* edited by A. M. Broadley (London: John Lane, 1910), pp. 155-219.

Hester Lynch Piozzi's fame and notoriety as a friend of Samuel Johnson have often obscured her own literary achievements and her considerable contemporary success in publishing. The trusted confidante and society hostess was also a versatile and productive writer. A mercurial and capricious character, full of charm and contradictions, she wrote poetry all through her life, leaving behind hundreds of verses in most of the major eighteenth-century modes, from pastoral and ode to satire and fable. But her poems tend to be derivative, while the nonfictional prose works for which she is best known show both scope and originality.

Hester Lynch Salusbury's associations with literature began in her earliest years. An only child, she later explained that "although Education was a Word then unknown, as applied to Females," her parents "taught me to read, & speak, & think, & translate from the French, till I was

Hester Thrale and her daughter Queeney (Hester Maria), 1781 (portrait by Sir Joshua Reynolds; Beaverbrook Art Gallery)

half a Prodigy." She was given Ogilby's translation of Homer when she was four years old, and by the time she was seven her uncle Sir Robert Cotton joined others in sending her French books as presents. Her father, John Salusbury, was irascible, imprudent, and unsettled, and partly as a result, her parents' marriage was a stormy one. Hester learned early to use her intellectual abilities and talents to please both her father and a succession of rich relations on whom her family was dependent. With some guidance from her mother, Hester Maria Cotton Salusbury, and her aunt Lady Anna Maria Salusbury, she read widely on her own; tutors later provided formal instruction. She later depicted herself in her early teens as continually contributing pseudonymous letters as well as poems to newspapers. She recalled that a political essay, an eclogue, and a translated French fable had been especially praised, but all of her youthful intellectual endeavors and

literary pursuits elicited lavish admiration from her own small circle. Her upbringing led her to view herself as a particularly talented woman with unusual intelligence and literary prowess.

More than her talents, her prospects as a potential heiress with wealthy connections attracted various suitors. The powerful combination of her mother and her rich uncle Sir Thomas Salusbury insured the ultimate success of Henry Thrale, a handsome if somewhat phlegmatic businessman with a substantial fortune from the family brewery. After Hester married him on 11 October 1763, Mr. Thrale and Mrs. Salusbury amicably scheduled Hester's activities for their mutual convenience. Both at Henry Thrale's beautiful country estate at Streatham and at their home by the brewery in Southwark, she found herself limited to the drawing room, the bedchamber, and the nursery; Thrale himself controlled even the kitchens. To fill up her time she continued to read and write, although her husband remained unresponsive to her literary efforts, even to her verses to him. On 17 September 1764 her first child, a daughter, was born, and a succession of pregnancies, births, and, too often, deaths followed, along with occasional miscarriages. Over the next fourteen years she bore twelve children, only four of whom lived to adulthood. She was an extremely conscientious mother, energetically educating her children, strictly disciplining them, and assiduously nursing their countless ailments.

On 9 January 1765 the Thrales met Samuel Johnson at a dinner arranged by their mutual friend Arthur Murphy. Two lonely people who seemed instinctively to bring out the best in each other, Samuel Johnson, who was almost fifty-seven years old at the time, and Hester Thrale, who was almost twenty-four, struck up a friendship that transformed the worlds of both. They began translating Boethius together, and Johnson also asked her for contributions to fill a subscription volume of a friend's verses. One of Thrale's poems for Anna Williams's *Miscellanies in Prose and Verse* (1766), "The Three Warnings," later became popular through republication in other volumes, in one of which, George Pearch's 1770 collection, her name appeared for the first time as an author. In 1766 Johnson's serious emotional collapse led Henry Thrale to insist that he move with them to Streatham, and Hester nursed him back to health. Johnson in effect joined the Thrale family, with his own rooms at Streatham and in Southwark, and for the next sixteen years he lived more with them than in his own house. Throughout this period Hester mothered him, attending to his constant ailments, calming his fears, listening as she sat up nights with him and brewed pot after pot of tea until the early hours of the morning. Her own assessment of the results in the *Anecdotes of the Late Samuel Johnson* (1786) is couched in the plural, but the bulk of the sustaining psychological care of Johnson was hers alone: "To the assistance we gave him, the shelter our house afforded to his uneasy fancies, and to the pains we took to sooth or repress them, the world perhaps is indebted for the three political pamphlets, the new edition and correction of his Dictionary, and for the Poets' Lives. . . . "

In Johnson, Hester found, as she once noted in her diary, a "Friend, Father, Guardian, Confidant!" He joined her in everything from chemical experiments to Mr. Thrale's Parliamentary reelection campaigns, sharing her concerns whether in the nursery, in brewery operations, or in charitable projects. Along with offering plentiful sympathy and emotional support, he challenged her intellectually. He claimed that while she was feeding her chickens she was starving her understanding, and he set out to right the balance. Throughout her life Hester was a natural student, and in Johnson, a born educator, she found the greatest of her mentors. He read her youthful poems, urged her to write more, and praised her efforts as lavishly as her early circles had. As his friends flocked to Streatham, she blossomed as a hostess in distinguished company. A living example of literary fame, Johnson encouraged in a variety of ways the inclinations toward writing that Hester Thrale had exhibited since childhood. Indeed, after his death gave her an opportunity to publish, she proceeded to recapitulate in miniature several of the high points of his career, writing her own life of a poet in the *Anecdotes of the Late Samuel Johnson,* becoming an editor of his letters, producing a travel book and a political pamphlet, and creating her own version of a dictionary in the *British Synonymy* (1794).

Johnson also provided a major impetus for the diaries that are one of Thrale's major literary achievements. Although she had kept at least one journal earlier, she started the *Family Book* (17 September 1766 - 31 December 1778), the first of her major diaries, mainly because of Johnson's influence. Originally entitled "The Children's Book" and focused on them, it grew to encompass more, and she ultimately added *Family Book* to the title on the cover. When, a little before their thirteenth wedding anniversary, Henry Thrale presented her with six bound blank volumes to which he gave the title *Thraliana,* she began what was to become her greatest journal with Johnson's admonition on keeping a diary. He also gave her suggestions for writing it and told her that it would interest posterity. The *Thraliana* was modeled on the French anas, collections of witty sayings and anecdotes about people, but over the three decades during which she wrote in it (15 September 1776 - 30 March 1809), she widened the scope to include a variety of materials: verses and epigrams, political commentary, portraits of her friends, puns, observations on nature, literary criticism, etymologies, and all manner of other miscellaneous information. In the process she preserved for posterity a wealth of information about the people she knew and the attitudes and life-styles of several eras. Because the *Thraliana* at times functioned as a diary, it also provides valuable autobiographical records of Thrale herself. An inveterate journalizer, she kept separate diaries of trips and composed additional personal accounts at various times. In many ways she appears at her literary best in her personal writings, which did not require narrative organization, condensed expression, and other skills she lacked and which highlighted her abilities in vivid short descriptions, her lively colloquial wit, and her varied insights and interests.

Henry Thrale's failing health, after an initial stroke in 1779, and his consequent depressions were a constant concern for Hester and the whole household until his death in April 1781 began the dissolution of the golden life at Streatham. Johnson, old and ill, also continually created difficulties. Thrale's growing attraction to Gabriel Piozzi, her daughters' music master, left her floundering in indecision, for she recognized the social opprobrium that a marriage for love to an Italian musician, a Roman Catholic who was her equal neither in class nor income, would produce. Finally in 1783 she sent Piozzi away and retired to Bath with her daughters, who had never gotten along with her. But her precipitous decline led finally to Piozzi's recall, and to the horror of London society and her Bluestocking friends, she married him on 23 July 1784. For many complex reasons the association with Johnson had become impossible for her to maintain; his outraged reaction to her marriage severed all contact between them.

Abroad on her honeymoon in Italy, Hester Piozzi learned of Johnson's death in December 1784 and of the plethora of Johnsonian biographies being planned and published. She decided to begin an account of her own immediately, but in doing so she worked under several important disadvantages. Except for the *Thraliana*, which did contain a great deal of information, most of the materials she had collected over the years had been left behind in England, and she would not allow anyone to send them to her. Equally problematical were her attitudes at the time. She knew that many people who disapproved of her marriage also blamed her for what they considered her heartless abandonment of Johnson. Eager for literary fame, she wanted to write a good Johnsonian memoir, but she was also determined to justify herself and her behavior to him. The two aims were not entirely congruent, and, together with her lack of access to information,

they adversely affected both the form and content of her work.

The *Anecdotes of the Late Samuel Johnson* is an extended series of stories, vignettes, and commentary about Johnson's life and character. Like most anecdotal collections, the overall structure of the work is weak. More seriously, Piozzi's tone and her emphasis were problematical. Inaccuracies resulted as she occasionally remolded evidence to serve her own exculpatory purposes, although her limited access to materials also contributed. To vindicate herself, she often highlighted the less amiable side of Johnson's character, in order to show how difficult he had been to live with and to justify her final break with him. Yet at the same time she insistently extolled his strengths and virtues. The resulting distortions blurred the focus of the work.

Nevertheless, few in Johnson's entire life had been as close to him as Hester Piozzi was during their long friendship, and the *Anecdotes of the Late Samuel Johnson* offered her own unique angle of vision on him. In many cases the information she could provide, ranging from various stories of his childhood to identification of his minor verse, was available from no other source. She once told Johnson that she loved "the light parts of a solid character," and she had seen these aspects of his personality as no one else had; with her eye for significant detail, she could portray them appealingly. Above all she could reveal Johnson in a domestic setting—relaxed, playful, at ease romping with the Thrale children or bantering with her. For these reasons the *Anecdotes* is the most important contemporary biography of Johnson except for Boswell's great *Life of Johnson* (1791), and it has remained an invaluable source of information for scholars and critics.

The fifth account of Johnson to appear, the *Anecdotes of the Late Samuel Johnson* was a smashing success. The first edition sold out in a day, and in the evening the publisher had to borrow a copy for the king, who wanted to read it. In less than a month and a half it reached a fourth edition. It was fiercely attacked by Johnson's friends and others shocked by her frank depictions of less pleasant attributes and by her inclusion of many small personal details about him. But in both cases Piozzi made an important contribution to the development of truthful biography at a time when too many writers still hesitated to write fully and honestly about their subjects. Such advances in biographical technique and method are usually attributed entirely to Boswell,

1

It is many Years since Doctor Samuell Johnson advised me to get a little Book, and write in it all the little Anecdotes which might come to my Knowledge, all the Observations I might make or hear; all the Verses never likely to be published, and in fine every thing which struck me at the Time—. Mr. Thrale has now treated me with a Repository,—and provided it with the pompous Title of Thraliana,—I must endeavour to fill it with Nonsense new and old—. 15: September 1776.———

Bob Lloyd used to Say that a Parent or other Person devoted to the Care and Instruction of Youth, led the Life of a Finger Post; still fixed to one disagreeable Spot himself while his whole Business was only to direct others in the way.

An old man's Child says Johnson leads much the same Sort of Life as a Child's Dog. teized like that with Fondness through Folly, and exhibited like that to every Company through idle and empty Vanity.

The first two pages of Thraliana, *the journal Hester Thrale kept for more than three decades, during her marriage to Henry Thrale, her friendship with Samuel Johnson, and her marriage to Gabriel Piozzi (HM 12183; Henry E. Huntington Library and Art Gallery)*

2

I have heard Johnson observe that as Education is often compared to Agriculture, so it resembles it chiefly in this: that though no one can tell whether the Crop may answer the Culture, yet if nothing be sowed, we all see that no Crop can be obtained.

Mr. Damor a fine Gentleman about this Town, shot himself a few Weeks ago, he had bought a pair of new Pistols at noon, dined with a friend at five, and appeared chearful; it is not said where he loitered till eleven, but at that hour or near it he went to a Tavern in ~~Pallmall~~ Fleetstreet, & calling for four Wenches & a Fiddle, sate down to see them dance for some Time; He then dismissed them, but ordered the Fidler to return in five & twenty Minutes, which he accor- dingly did, & found Mr. Damor shot through the head — the Body sitting upright, & the brains blown to the Door. — Can one help thinking of the Verses in Buck- ingham's Rehearsal?

> Let us to serious Counsel now advance,
> 'Tis very fit — but first let's have a Dance.

This Man belonged to the Sçavoirvivre Club indeed — he certainly did not understand the Sçavoirmourir.

but Piozzi too has a share. Similarly, until well into the twentieth century, assessments of her achievement in the *Anecdotes* were inadequate because of the inevitable comparisons with Boswell's *Life*, which overshadowed Piozzi's very different biographical aims and approaches.

Mrs. Piozzi had initially planned the *Anecdotes* to combine a memoir of Johnson with her letters from him. Having decided in Italy to publish the letters separately, she began to edit them after she and Piozzi returned to London in March 1787. Although she omitted some of the letters she had, either on personal grounds or for their lack of general significance, she published the majority of them in the *Letters to and from the Late Samuel Johnson* (1788). Particularly interesting are Johnson's letters to her in 1773 while on his trip to the Hebrides with Boswell, which Johnson later used in composing his *Journey to the Western Islands of Scotland* (1775). Now superseded by more complete editions of Johnson's letters, Piozzi's *Letters*, like the *Anecdotes*, was a publishing sensation when it appeared. A public eager for Johnsoniana devoured them eagerly, while they were attacked with equal fervor by others, particularly Joseph Baretti, her oldest daughter's former tutor. Modern critics give Piozzi credit for fairly conscientious and sometimes innovative editing, particularly in view of the standards of the age, and her edition also increased the literary stature of the personal letter, which had been slowly growing over the eighteenth century.

As the title of the work indicates, Piozzi, urged by the publisher, had printed some of her own letters to Johnson along with his. She painstakingly reworked them for inclusion, and although two of them, a description of a regatta and a letter of advice to a young man on marriage, were republished elsewhere and became well known, most of them self-consciously reflect the dual strain of her excessive revision and of her continuing uneasiness about her relationship with Johnson. They do not presage her later success in the genre of the letter. After her second marriage she became a prolific letter writer, cultivating an artful and polished epistolary style for her many correspondents. Many of the elements of style criticized in her published works showed to great advantage in her letters, and she has always been praised for her literary skill in them.

Despite some snubs from old acquaintances, Hester Piozzi set about reestablishing a place for herself and her husband in fashionable London society. She gathered a new circle of friends around her, particularly the actress Sarah Siddons, and rapidly achieved the social success she desired. She provided prologues and epilogues for friends and wrote other ephemeral pieces. While on her protracted honeymoon tour of the Continent, she had kept two journals, and she used these, along with entries in the *Thraliana*, as the basis for a travel book drafted in two months in the summer of 1788 and revised during the fall. Published in 1789, the *Observations and Reflections Made in the Course of a Journey through France, Italy, and Germany* is in the literary tradition of the individual report of the Grand Tour, which originated in the mid seventeenth century. A combination of private diary and objective account, its strength is in its "Observations," her colorful renderings of personal experiences and insights, rather than the "Reflections," moral or philosophical generalizations that are too often gratuitous or verbose. The book was widely read, although, like the Johnsonian *Letters*, it did not go into a second London edition. In addition to a Dublin edition (1789), a German translation appeared in 1790. Many contemporary readers, including William Cowper, found it entertaining; Ann Radcliffe drew on it for some of the Italian settings in her Gothic novels. Several modern critics have considered it the best of her published books.

Like all of Piozzi's works, the *Observations* incited fierce attack. In this case criticism centered mainly on her style, particularly her colloquialism and informality, which had also been points of contention with the *Anecdotes*. Piozzi employed relaxed and natural prose as a deliberate stylistic innovator. She considered the prose of her period overly ornate and sought a less artificial alternative. Since she believed that style and character should be integrally related, the familiar and personal mode of expression that she evolved, an extension of good conversation into the literary arena, was a particularly suitable one for her. Although nineteenth-century writers would frequently draw on elements of this kind of prose, eighteenth-century critics and many members of the reading public were not ready for it. Piozzi herself exacerbated the difficulties by failing to employ the style consistently. She was not without ability in wielding the mighty Johnsonian cadence and his ponderous expression, and since she too often mixed this style with her own lighter one, the combination of two antithetical modes resulted in an awkward disparity.

Piozzi's next writing project was a book of synonyms, on which she worked in 1792 and

"Bozzy and Piozzi," Thomas Rowlandson's 1786 caricature of Hester Piozzi and James Boswell arguing over their merits as biographers of Samuel Johnson as Sir John Hawkins, another Johnson biographer, sits in judgment

1793. Only one English synonymy existed—a rather poor imitation of Gabriel Girard's French work—and Piozzi's idea for the book was a good one. She planned it to help foreigners with conversational English, differentiating similar words by including illustrative anecdotes along with definitions to establish proper usage. Unfortunately her lifelong interest in etymology led her to excessive philological speculations that seriously marred the *British Synonymy.* Its critical and popular reception was, as usual, mixed; however, parts of it were reprinted in France in 1804, and extracts appeared in the *Gentleman's Magazine* as late as 1849 and 1850. It is still a useful record for historians of the language who are interested in later eighteenth-century patterns of popular usage, although most modern readers find interesting only the anecdotes and some of the discursive definitions that elaborate Piozzi's own ideas on various topics.

Hester Piozzi had always been proud of her Welsh ancestry, and in 1795 she and her husband left London permanently to live at Brynbella, a country home they had built on her Welsh property on a hill overlooking a beautiful prospect. There Gabriel Piozzi adapted completely to the life of a typical English country squire, bothered only by increasingly severe attacks of gout. In 1798 they adopted his five-year-old Italian nephew, John Salusbury Piozzi, and brought him to England. Characteristically, Mrs. Piozzi during this period had turned once again to a new writing project, this time a popularized history of the world since the birth of Christ, to appear with the turn of the new century in 1800. In the midst of researching it, she took time off briefly to compose *Three Warnings to John Bull before He Dies* (1798), a political pamphlet opposing the radical ideas emanating from France. For her history her aim was a readable summary with anecdotes and reflections for a general audience. As with the *British Synonymy,* however, she spoiled a clever idea by her inability to execute the work she intended. The scope of *Retrospection: or a Review of the Most Striking and Important Events, Characters, Situations, and Their Consequences, which the Last Eighteen Hundred Years Have Presented to the View of Mankind* (1801) far exceeded her scholarly abilities. Nor was her style particularly suited for sustained narrative. Modern criticism has found considerable conceptual sophistication in *Retrospection,* but Piozzi's contemporaries failed to respond to it and the *Critical Review* in particular was savage ("a series of dreams by an old lady"). Her last published work, *Retrospection* was printed in an edition of 750 copies; only 516 were sold.

Bruised by the reception of *Retrospection,* Piozzi also had to devote much of her time over the next years to nursing her suffering and disabled husband. Always intellectually active, in 1805, at the age of sixty-four, she began to study Hebrew. Her second marriage had been an extremely happy and successful one, and she was devastated by Piozzi's death in 1809. Afterward she made his nephew her heir, legally changing his name to John Salusbury Piozzi Salusbury, and she signed over all of her Welsh property to him in 1814. She herself lived mainly at Bath, cultivating as usual new circles of friends, including Sir James Fellowes, Edward Mangin, and the actor William Augustus Conway. She also produced one last manuscript, "Lyford Redivivus or a Grandame's Garrulity," a compilation of nine hundred proper names and their derivations, which she again marred with abstruse philological conjectures. Lively to the end, she celebrated her seventy-ninth birthday with a splendid ball in the Bath Assembly Rooms, where she danced into the early morning hours.

Piozzi was widely recognized as a successful writer by her contemporaries. Soon after her death, however, Mrs. Thrale the friend of Johnson rapidly eclipsed Piozzi the author. Caught in a sense between two literary giants, Johnson and Boswell, she suffered from unfair comparisons with both. For more than a century, with a few notable exceptions, her writings about Johnson were consistently underrated, while the rest of her works were generally ignored. With the rise of feminist criticism and increased critical attention to nonfictional prose, long overdue assessments of her literary achievements began to appear. While never denying the unevenness in her writings, critics have traced how the pressures of female authorship and the female role in general during the period, as well as Piozzi's interests in literary innovation, must be taken into account to evaluate her works properly. Her pioneering role as one of the first women writing in England to attempt prose genres such as biography, history, and the travelogue has been recognized, as well as her considerable stature as a letter writer and diarist. A more equitable assessment of one of the most important English female writers before Jane Austen is beginning to emerge.

Letters:

Autobiography, Letters, and Literary Remains of Mrs. Piozzi (Thrale), 2 volumes, edited by Abraham Hayward, second edition (London: Longman, Green, Longman & Roberts, 1861; Boston: Ticknor & Fields, 1861);

The Intimate Letters of Hester Piozzi and Penelope Pennington, 1788-1821, edited by Oswald G. Knapp (London: John Lane, 1914);

Letters of Mrs. Thrale, edited by R. Brimsley Johnson (London: John Lane, 1926; New York: L. MacVeagh, Dial Press, 1926);

The Queeney Letters, edited by Henry William Edmund Petty FitzMaurice, Marquis of Lansdowne (London: Cassell, 1934);

The Letters of Samuel Johnson, with Mrs. Thrale's Genuine Letters to Him, 3 volumes, edited by R. W. Chapman (Oxford: Clarendon Press, 1952).

Biographies:

James L. Clifford, *Hester Lynch Piozzi (Mrs. Thrale),* second edition, revised (Oxford: Clarendon Press, 1968);

Mary Hyde, *The Thrales of Streatham Park* (Cambridge: Harvard University Press, 1977).

References:

Edward A. and Lillian D. Bloom and Joan Klingel, "Portrait of a Georgian Lady: The Letters of Hester Lynch (Thrale) Piozzi, 1784-1821," *Bulletin of the John Rylands Library,* 60 (Spring 1978): 303-338;

Morris R. Brownell, "Hester Lynch Piozzi's Marginalia," *Eighteenth-Century Life,* 3 (1977): 97-100;

Martine Watson Brownley, "Samuel Johnson and the Printing Career of Hester Lynch Piozzi," *Bulletin of the John Rylands Library,* 67 (Spring 1985): 623-640;

Brownley, "'Under the Dominion of *Some Woman*': The Friendship of Samuel Johnson and Hester Thrale," in *Mothering the Mind,* edited by Ruth Perry (New York & London: Holmes & Meier, 1984), pp. 64-79;

James L. Clifford, "Mrs. Piozzi's Letters," in *Essays on the Eighteenth Century Presented to David Nichol Smith,* edited by James Sutherland and F. P. Wilson (Oxford: Clarendon Press, 1945), pp. 155-167;

Mary Hyde, *The Impossible Friendship: Boswell and Mrs. Thrale* (Cambridge, Mass.: Harvard University Press, 1972);

William McCarthy, *Hester Thrale Piozzi: Portrait of a Literary Woman* (Chapel Hill & London: University of North Carolina Press, 1985);

John C. Riely, "Johnson's Last Years with Mrs. Thrale: Facts and Problems," *Bulletin of the John Rylands Library,* 57 (Autumn 1974): 196-212;

Patricia Meyer Spacks, "Scrapbook of a Self: Mrs. Piozzi's Late Journals," *Harvard Library Bulletin,* 18 (July 1970): 221-247.

Papers:

The John Rylands University Library of Manchester (Manchester, England) has a large collection of Piozzi manuscripts, including letters, journals, miscellaneous prose, poetry, and translations, and drafts of *Observations and Reflections.* A five-volume account of herself and her poetry that she composed from 1810 to 1814, along with "Minced Meat for Pyes," a collection of miscellaneous extracts and quotations (1796-1820), is in the Houghton Library, Harvard University. The Princeton University Library has Piozzi's letters to Penelope Pennington and Edward Mangin and the autobiography she composed in 1815 for Sir James Fellowes. The six volumes of *Thraliana* are at the Henry E. Huntington Library.

Sir Joshua Reynolds

(16 July 1723 - 23 February 1792)

Pat Rogers
University of South Florida

BOOKS: *Three Letters to the Idler* (N.p., 1761)— *The Idler,* nos. 76, 79, 82, first published in the *Universal Chronicle,* 29 September, 20 October, and 10 November 1759;

A Discourse, Delivered at the Opening of the Royal Academy, January 2, 1769, by the President (London, 1769);

A Discourse, Delivered to the Students of the Royal Academy, on the Distribution of the Prizes, December 11, 1769, by the President (London: Sold by Thomas Davies, 1769);

A Discourse, Delivered to the Students of the Royal Academy, on the Distribution of the Prizes, December 14, 1770, by the President (London: Printed for Thomas Davies, 1771);

A Discourse, Delivered to the Students of the Royal Academy, on the Distribution of the Prizes, December 10, 1771, by the President (London: Printed for Thomas Davies, 1772);

A Discourse, Delivered to the Students of the Royal Academy, on the Distribution of the Prizes, December 10, 1772, by the President (London: Printed by W. Griffin and sold by Thomas Davies, 1773);

A Discourse, Delivered to the Students of the Royal Academy, on the Distribution of the Prizes, Dec. the 10th, 1774, by the President (London: Printed for Thomas Davies, 1775);

A Discourse, Delivered to the Students of the Royal Academy, on the Distribution of the Prizes, December 10, 1776, by the President (London: Printed by Thomas Davies, 1777).

Seven Discourses Delivered in the Royal Academy by the President (London: Printed for T. Cadell, 1778);

A Discourse, Delivered to the Students of the Royal Academy, on the Distribution of the Prizes, December 10, 1778, by the President (London: Printed by T. Cadell, 1779);

A Discourse, Delivered at the Opening of the Royal Academy, October 16, 1780, by the President, published with *A Discourse, Delivered to the Students of the Royal Academy, on the Distribution of the Prizes, December 11, 1780, by the Presi-*

Sir Joshua Reynolds, self-portrait, 1773 (Royal Academy, London)

dent (London: Printed by Thomas Cadell, 1781);

A Discourse, Delivered to the Students of the Royal Academy on the Distribution of the Prizes, December 10, 1782, by the President (London: Printed by Thomas Cadell, 1783);

A Discourse, Delivered to the Students of the Royal Academy, on the Distribution of the Prizes, December 10, 1784, by the President (London: Printed by Thomas Cadell, 1785);

A Discourse, Delivered to the Students of the Royal Academy on the Distribution of Prizes, December 11, 1786, by the President (London: Printed by Thomas Cadell, 1787);

A Discourse, Delivered to the Students of the Royal Academy, on the Distribution of the Prizes, Dec. 10th, 1788, by the President (London: Printed by Thomas Cadell, 1789);

A Discourse, Delivered to the Students of the Royal Acad-emy, on the Distribution of the Prizes, Dec. 10th, 1790, by the President (London: Printed by Thomas Cadell, 1791);

The Works of Sir Joshua Reynolds, Knt. Late President of the Royal Academy, 2 volumes, edited by Edmond Malone (London: printed for T. Cadell, Jun. & W. Davies, 1797); revised and expanded edition, 3 volumes (London: Printed for T. Cadell, Jun. & W. Davies, 1798);

Portraits by Sir Joshua Reynolds, edited by Frederick W. Hilles (New York: McGraw-Hill, 1952; London: Heinemann, 1952).

Edition: *Discourses on Art*, edited by Robert R. Wark (San Marino: Huntington Library, 1959; revised edition, New Haven & London: Published for the Paul Mellon Centre for Studies in British Art by Yale University Press, 1975).

OTHER: *The Art of Painting of Charles Alphonse du Fresnoy. Translated into English Verse by William Mason M.A. with Annotations by Sir Joshua Reynolds, Knt. President of the Royal Academy* (York: Printed by A. Ward and sold by J. Dodsley, T. Cadell, R. Faulder, London, and J. Todd, York, 1783).

The chief claim of Sir Joshua Reynolds to immortality lies in his magnificent achievement as a portrait painter, and his secondary claim would probably rest on his role as the first president of the Royal Academy, from 1768 to his death in 1792. Nevertheless, he aspired to the condition of an author, and according to Hester Thrale—who knew him well—he was more pleased about the praise he received for his *Discourses* than the reputation he enjoyed as a painter. Many contemporary references describe him as successfully courting the sister arts of literature and painting. One fulsome tribute in 1777 asserted that he had "of two Arts attain'd the lawrel'd Heights; / Paints with a Pen, and with a Pencil Writes!" Today this readiness to see his activity in the two spheres as one of absolute equality seems exaggerated. However, we must not minimize the scale of his contribution to literature. Not only did he compose the first sustained body of serious art criticism in the English language; he stood at the head of a cultural group which gave primacy to literate and educated taste in belles lettres above all else. He was the chief promoter and most active member of the so-called Literary Club which gave Samuel Johnson so much space for his dictatorial formation of taste. Reynolds contributed three significant critical essays to his friend's *Idler* series as early as 1759. At the end of his life he was the subject of the heartfelt dedication in James Boswell's *Life of Johnson* (1791); and he supported the work of Edmund Burke, Charles Burney, Thomas and Joseph Warton, Edmond Malone, and others. He was, in fact, one of the most significant figures in the literature of his time, even if he produced no "creative" writing beyond some jocular character sketches of Johnson, David Garrick, and Oliver Goldsmith.

It is worth reminding ourselves at the outset that he was not always Sir Joshua Reynolds, Knight, P.R.A., rich and famous. There was a long way to travel from the schoolroom in Plympton, near the naval town of Plymouth in Devon, where he was born on 16 July 1723. In the very next year Daniel Defoe, in his *Tour* of Brit-

ain, was to describe Plympton as "a poor and thinly inhabited town, though blessed with the privilege of sending members to the Parliament." Joshua was the third son and seventh child of Theophila (Potter) Reynolds and Samuel Reynolds, the master of Plympton Grammar School, an Oxford product who struggled to support his growing family on a stipend of £120 a year. Samuel was the kind of loving but ineffective father whom fortune also bestowed on William Hogarth and Charles Dickens. His son's biographer Derek Hudson graphically describes him as "a failure of great respectability." Among his children, it was Frances, born in 1729, the youngest of three surviving girls, who was closest to Joshua. She kept his London house for him for several years, engaged in a frustrated career as artist and writer, and attracted the support of Samuel Johnson when she and her brother quarreled in later years.

Joshua himself was intended for the humble calling of a country apothecary, but talent and ambition sent him in a different direction. At the age of seventeen he moved to London as apprentice to Thomas Hudson, then in vogue as the leading portrait painter of the day. Particularly useful to the young artist were Hudson's extensive library of art books and his collection of old masters and sculptures. In addition Hudson introduced Reynolds to the world of artists centering on Old Slaughter's coffeehouse in St. Martin's Lane, where he probably met Hogarth, then at the height of his powers. Almost all accounts stress the next main phase of the artist's career—that is, the time he spent in Italy—as decisive; but it is a mistake to underestimate the period of tutelage under Hudson. This ended in 1743, and the young man passed the next few years alternately in Plymouth and in London, beginning to make a modest niche in portrait painting.

Reynolds set out from Plymouth for Italy in May 1749 and returned to London in October 1752. His opportunity to spend time in the great study center for a career in art came about as the result of a lucky break. He made the acquaintance of a naval officer named Augustus Keppel, who rose ultimately to the rank of admiral. Keppel offered to take him to the Mediterranean, and Reynolds managed to obtain funds for his sojourn in Rome from two married sisters. Most of his time in Italy was spent in the capital, though he did pay a short visit to Naples during his last summer there and then made his way home overland, stopping at Florence, Bologna,

The portrait of Augustus Keppel that helped to secure Reynolds's reputation as a painter (National Maritime Museum, Green-wich). Reynolds posed Keppel in the stance of the Apollo Belvedere, the ancient Roman statue that Reynolds established as an ideal model for eighteenth-century artists.

Venice, and Milan. He carried out intensive studies of Michelangelo, Raphael (whom he found hard to appreciate at first), Titian, Guido Reni, and others. Every page of the *Discourses* was to benefit from the concentrated attention he gave to these masters; though he later amassed a considerable collection of paintings and even operated as a dealer, it was the prolonged exposure to Renaissance art in Rome and other Italian cities which formed his taste for life and also contributed to the development of his own artistic style.

Leaving Italy in September 1752, he made a brief stop in Paris, where for the first time he met William Chambers, the rising young architect (an exact contemporary), who was to cross his path often in the years to come. After a brief holiday in Devon, he settled in London to re-

sume his practice, and by the end of 1753 was fixed in Great Newport Street, near the heart of the artists' quarter in London. His dramatic portrait of Keppel gave his reputation a major lift, and before long he was able to raise his prices to a level among the highest in England. It was important that he managed to get something of a start on his future rivals: for various reasons, none of his ultimate competitors apart from Allan Ramsay (who was himself away in Italy during the mid 1750s) was in a position to mount a challenge. The generation of Thomas Gainsborough, Johann Zoffany, Benjamin Wilson, George Stubbs, and Joseph Wright had yet to make a mark. Two of the best-established painters were Hogarth and Francis Hayman, but neither specialized in portraiture, and both were heavily involved in the complicated politics which surrounded attempts to create a major institution to support British artists. Reynolds went along with these schemes but did not divert too much of his energies into time-consuming lobbying. He was elected to the Society of Arts in 1756, as was his new friend Johnson, and it was this body which helped to mount the first public exhibition ever held in England in 1760. By this time he had also come to know Edmund Burke, David Garrick, and John Wilkes, followed soon afterward by Oliver Goldsmith. Fruits of these liaisons include the *Idler* papers which Reynolds wrote for Johnson's series (29 September, 20 October, and 10 November 1759), and moves toward the foundation of the famous Club in 1764. There was also the celebrated picture of Garrick between the muses of tragedy and comedy, shown in 1761.

For the remainder of his life Reynolds, the prime mover in the formation of the Club, remained close to the greatest figures in literature and drama. During the protracted squabbles which enveloped the competing bodies of artists in the 1760s, he kept largely aloof from day-to-day involvement, concentrating on promoting his career and relaxing among his literary friends. He kept on good terms with most of his own profession, and enjoyed a warm friendship with Angelica Kauffmann when she arrived in London in 1766. He did not seek to enroll his colleagues in the literary Club and may well have acted quietly to keep out such potential candidates for admission as William Chambers. Nevertheless, his professional reputation steadily grew, and he was the natural choice for president when the Royal Academy finally became a reality in late 1768. On 2 January 1769 he gave the first of the celebrated addresses to academy students which were published as the fifteen *Discourses* (1769-1791). These were major occasions in the artistic calendar, attended by the students and staff of the Royal Academy, but also graced by distinguished outsiders, including the luminaries of the Club. By the 1770s the Club also numbered in its midst Edward Gibbon, Charles Burney, Charles James Fox, and Richard Brinsley Sheridan. Reynolds was an assiduous theatergoer, who supported the efforts of Goldsmith and Sheridan and who admired such different actresses as Sarah Siddons and Frances Abington. At no time in history have the links between the art world and the theater been closer: Garrick alone was painted by Gainsborough, Hogarth, Kauffmann, Nathaniel Dance, Hayman, Philippe-Jacques de Loutherbourg, Jean-Etienne Liotard, Zoffany, Benjamin Wilson, and others.

The interest Reynolds took in the playhouse is part of his generally sociable and socializing habits. He went to card parties, masquerades, pleasure gardens, balloon displays, and almost anything that was available. This suave ease in the general round of human intercourse has counted against him in posthumous reputation. We find it hard to believe that a man so skilled in the amenities of ordinary life should have been a deep or inward observer of the human condition. In fact, as with Boswell, the involvement in the external world enabled him to portray Georgian society with remarkable insight. It is significant that Reynolds maintained good relations with Boswell, with whom the rest of the Club generally fell out sooner or later. It should be added that Reynolds had a large female acquaintance; we know nothing of his sex life, but his dealings with Hester Thrale, Hannah More, Fanny Burney, Elizabeth Montagu, and others show that he was capable of taking women seriously in a way that many of the club could never manage.

The *Discourses* appeared at first annually and then biennially. They take up separate topics and do not form a single unified argument. Nonetheless, their central emphasis and concerns are unmistakable. Reynolds set out to endorse the traditionally high valuation of history painting (that is, the branch of art dealing with mythological and biblical subjects), even though he was intelligent enough to realize that his own distinction as a painter lay in the lower sphere, as then conceived, of portraiture. He set out the principles of the grand style, embodied in the great masterpieces of Roman and Bolognese art of the Renaissance; the "decorative" manner of Venice and France (as well as the Flemish and Dutch schools) was ranked on a lower plane, though Reynolds had considerable admiration for Titian, Poussin, and Van Dyke, among others. He made visits to Flanders and Holland on two occasions and emerged with an increased (though not unbounded) respect for Rembrandt. Another function of the discourses was to advise students on habits of study, and on the course of preparation they should undertake for their career. Underlying all this was the desire to set art criticism on a sounder basis of intellectual principle, and equally the ambition to place the visual arts nearer to the center of British culture than they had so far lain. They were less statements of private taste than semiofficial pronouncements, liter-

Garrick between Comedy and Tragedy, *Reynolds's most-celebrated portrait of his actor friend (private collection; from Rich-ard Wendorf,* The Elements of Life: Biography and Portrait Painting in Stuart and Georgian England, *1990)*

ally ex cathedra—injunctions to the community of artists and to cultivated people generally, designed to enhance the standing of the profession and of the Royal Academy within national life. The *Discourses* helped to codify artistic theory, as Burney codified music, Johnson codified literature, Chambers codified architecture, and Gibbon codified the study of antiquity.

Each discourse appeared as a separate pamphlet within weeks of its delivery, which took place at the regular ceremony to award prizes to the academy students. The first seven were collected in 1778, after which there followed translations into Italian (1778), German (1781) and French (1787). The full series of fifteen did not appear until the collected edition of *The Works of Sir Joshua Reynolds* (1797; revised, 1798). This collection was prepared by the author's great friend Edmond Malone, but it had benefited from joint efforts the two men had made to produce an improved text, not long before Reynolds died. The

Works were to include the few other substantive works from Reynolds's pen, including the notes he appended to a 1783 translation by William Mason of Dufresnoy's *De arte graphica*, and the journal of a trip to Flanders. The only significant omission lay in some brief dialogues and character sketches of the Johnson circle, which remained unpublished in some cases until 1952, as did a brief "ironical" discourse voicing sentiments directly opposite to those of the main series.

Honors flowed in on Reynolds during middle life. He was made a member of the Florentine academy; he was awarded an honorary doctorate by the University of Oxford; he even enjoyed the sweetest reward for a small-town boy when he was elected alderman and then mayor of little Plympton. It was a measure of the distance he had traveled. Perhaps the apogee came with the grand opening of new accommodations for the Royal Academy at Somerset House, held on 16 October 1780. Chambers had designed the new rooms, with a ceiling depicting "Theory" by the president, reflecting his standing as the great spokesman for art criticism. Reynolds delivered a special lecture, the only discourse not attached to the regular prize-giving ceremonies. Around this time Reynolds was painting the other members of the Johnson circle for Mrs. Thrale's house at Streatham Park; his portraits often supply the strongest physical image we have of this distinguished gathering. Indeed, for many of the best-known figures in eighteenth-century life, it is Reynolds who provided the most characteristic study—even of Chambers, whom he did not much like, or of Laurence Sterne, whom he did not know well.

After this, the relentless drive upward and onward flagged a little. Garrick had died in 1779; Johnson followed in 1784. The picture commissioned from Reynolds by Catherine the Great was not altogether successful; younger artists such as James Barry were starting to question the president's authority (though William Blake had yet to contradict all his views). Gainsborough died in 1788, provoking a notable tribute in the penultimate discourse; but no doubt this was a reminder to Reynolds (four years senior) of his own mortality. Then in July 1789 came a sudden calamity—his eyesight was impaired and within weeks he was totally blind in his left eye. This meant the effective end of his career as a painter, and with it the activity which had underlain all his drive for success. This was the prelude to his final three sad years. A bitter quarrel erupted within the academy over a relatively minor appointment; Reynolds actually resigned the presidency in February 1790. Although he was persuaded to withdraw his resignation a few weeks later, this episode of wrangling made an unhappy backdrop to the last discourse, delivered on 10 December in that year. A more cheerful note appears briefly with the publication of Boswell's *Life of Johnson* in May 1791, dedicated in the warmest terms to the man who had been perhaps the most significant friend Johnson had possessed. (In return, Reynolds never failed to acknowledge his debt, asserting that it was Johnson who had "formed his mind.") A month later Reynolds was able to attend an academy function, but this was to be his last public appearance. The sight of his remaining eye was now threatened, and he preferred to stay at home in protective isolation. Friends such as Boswell and Fanny Burney have left depressing accounts of his solitary and self-pitying condition, all the more unsettling

because it was so unlike the purposeful energy of earlier years.

Reynolds died at his home in London on 23 February 1792, probably as the result of a malignant liver condition diagnosed too late: this disease lay at the root of his eye trouble. An impressive funeral procession set out from Somerset House on 3 March, despite the efforts of William Chambers to prevent the body from lying in state in this building, which came under his jurisdiction as government surveyor. Dukes and earls made up the line of pallbearers when the procession reached St. Paul's Cathedral. Many of the most distinguished in the land were among the congregation, headed by Burke, who had written a noble obituary for the *Morning Chronicle*. The occasion gave expression to the position Reynolds had attained within national life—the unrivaled chronicler of the good and the great in his portraits, the spokesman for high culture, the link between studios, garrets, and society drawing rooms.

Reynolds made a sustained effort to achieve distinction as a writer, a process minutely charted in the splendid survey of his literary career by F. W. Hilles. Although everything he wrote possesses some interest (not least the agreeable verbal "portraits" of his friends and fellow Clubmen), it is the *Discourses* which represent his substantial contribution to literature. In terms of ideas, they are resumptive and judicial rather than obviously innovative. Reynolds had studied the art history, biography, and criticism of the Italian Renaissance; his details often come from Vasari's accounts of the painters. He knew well the more recent French critics, including Dufresnoy (whom he annotated for the translation by William Mason, while engaged on discourse 11), Roger de Piles, and aestheticians such as Abbé Charles Batteux and the widely influential Jean-Baptiste Du Bos. His most important English predecessors were John Dryden, with his celebrated "Parallel between Poetry and Painting," also appended to a translation of Dufresnoy, and Jonathan Richardson, whose ground-breaking essays on artistic taste had first come to the attention of the youthful Joshua Reynolds in Plympton. But Reynolds is, crucially, two generations further on than Richardson. He does not make much use of Hogarth's *Analysis of Beauty*, which had appeared in 1753, but he was profoundly influenced by the new aesthetic and philosophic British criticism of the third quarter of the century. Works such as Adam Smith's *Theory of*

distance or in whatever light it is
is placed, ~~on before~~ can be shewn

It is in vain to attend to the variation
of tint, if in that attention the general
hue of flesh is lost, or to finish ever
so minutely the parts, if the masses
are not observed, or the whole not
well put together.

Vasari ~~who~~ seems to have no great
disposition to favour
~~partiality to~~ the Venetian Painters,
he
yet, every where ~~he~~ justly com-
mends   il modo di fare , la maniera

la bella pratica   that is the
admirable manner and practice of
that school, on Titian in particular
he bestows the epithets of giudicioso,
bello, e Stupendo.

Page from the manuscript for Reynolds's eleventh Discourse *(delivered in December 1782) with revisions by Samuel Johnson*
(Royal Academy, London)

Moral Sentiments (1759), Burke's *Philosophical Enquiry into the Origin of Our Ideas of the Sublime and Beautiful* (1757), and (mainly for disagreement, especially in *discourse* 6, on such matters as imitation) the pioneering *Conjectures on Original Composition* (1759) of Edward Young underlie the text in many places. Reynolds is polite but lukewarm with regard to some of Burke's ideas on the value of indistinctness in art. His principal mentor remained Samuel Johnson: the impress of *The Rambler* (1750-1752) and of the "Preface to Shakespeare" (1765) is particularly evident. Above all, the congruence of the two minds can be seen in their common desire to "establish principles: to improve opinion into knowledge" and to find "principles of judgment on unalterable and evident truth," as Johnson had expressed it.

It has already been noted that the *Discourses* lack obvious unity, in the sense that they vary in scope, in tone, in line of approach, and in the use of exemplary detail. Setting aside number 9, a short speech to commemorate the opening of new accommodations at Somerset House, we can see that the different topics call forth a wide range of rhetorical styles. Naturally number 1 is introductory and expository; at the other end of the series, number 15 ends on an assertive and innovatory note with its glowing tribute to the unique greatness of Michelangelo. Number 14 is a special case, with its carefully balanced appreciation of Gainsborough, who had died in 1788. Perhaps the weakest is number 10, on sculpture, a topic that does not call out Reynolds's most incisive writing. All in all the most impressive are number 3, on the Grand Style; numbers 6 and 11, on the currently much-discussed issue of originality and genius (this is the place where Reynolds runs into conflict with Young); and the final discourse. A lecture useful in its day, which now holds less immediate appeal, is number 12, with its essentially pedagogic concerns. The *Discourses* all contain eloquent and cogent writing, deriving from the clarity of organization, the chaste but far from dull selection of language, and the air of good temper and tolerance. Where Johnson could grow persnickety, Burke shrill, and Gibbon pompous, Reynolds contrives to remain sweetly reasonable, judicious, and calmly authoritative. This is just what his later detractors, starting with Blake and William Hazlitt, found limited and limiting in his criticism; the *Discourses* make few divagations along the road of excess.

Reynolds is important in the history of literature for several reasons. His own *Discourses* made a vital contribution to the growth of a serious body of art criticism in Britain. He encouraged and supported the work of writers in his circle, ranging from Burke and Adam Smith to Fanny Burney and Hannah More. A lifelong student of Shakespeare, he supplied some notes for Johnson's edition. He cemented the fame of figures such as Garrick, Sterne, Sarah Siddons—and above all Johnson—with his portraits, in which psychological insight is underpinned by a subtle social understanding. More generally, he operated as a kind of cultural entrepreneur and aided the careers of little-known writers such as George Crabbe. It was principally Reynolds who kept the Club in being, and without that we should lose some of the most memorable pages in Boswell. Though he lacked the literary ability of the other great Club members, he stood at the center of a group whose lasting contribution hinges on the production of great literature. Even if he had not been a great artist in his own right, this would have been a notable legacy to leave.

Letters:
Letters of Sir Joshua Reynolds, edited by F. W. Hilles (Cambridge: Cambridge University Press, 1929).

Bibliography:
F. W. Hilles, "A Bibliography of Sir Joshua's Writings," in *The Literary Career of Sir Joshua Reynolds* (Cambridge: Cambridge University Press, 1936), pp. 277-300.

Biographies:
James Northcote, *The Life of Sir Joshua Reynolds*, 2 volumes (London: H. Colburn, 1818);

Charles Robert Leslie and Tom Taylor, *Life and Times of Sir Joshua Reynolds*, 2 volumes (London: John Murray, 1865);

Derek Hudson, *Sir Joshua Reynolds: A Personal Study* (London: Bles, 1958).

References:
John Barrell, *The Political Theory of Painting from Reynolds to Hazlitt* (New Haven: Yale University Press, 1986);

W. J. Bate, *From Classic to Romantic* (Cambridge, Mass.: Harvard University Press, 1946);

E. H. Gombrich, "Reynolds's Theory and Practice of Form," in his *Norm and Form* (London: Phaidon, 1966), pp. 129-136;

F. W. Hilles, *The Literary Career of Sir Joshua Reynolds* (Cambridge: Cambridge University Press, 1936);

Lawrence Lipking, *The Ordering of the Arts in Eighteenth-Century England* (Princeton: Princeton University Press, 1970);

Nicholas Penny, *Reynolds* (London: Weidenfeld & Nicolson, 1986);

Edgar Wind, *Hume and the Heroic Portrait*, edited by J. Anderson (Oxford: Clarendon Press, 1986).

Papers:

The largest collection of Reynolds manuscripts is to be found at the Royal Academy, which holds most of his extant engagement books for various years between 1757 and 1790. The engagement book for 1755 is preserved at the Cottonian Museum in Plymouth, England. Other personal documents survive in private hands. Working drafts for the *Discourses*, mostly among the Royal Academy manuscripts, are discussed in Hilles's *The Literary Career of Sir Joshua Reynolds*.

William Robertson
(19 September 1721 - 11 June 1793)

Jeffrey Smitten
Utah State University

BOOKS: *The Situation of the World at the Time of Christ's Appearance, and Its Connexion with the Success of His Religion, Considered. A Sermon* (Edinburgh: Printed by Hamilton, Balfour & Neill, 1755);

The History of Scotland, During the Reigns of Queen Mary and of King James VI, 2 volumes (London: Printed for A. Millar, 1759; revised edition, London: Printed for T. Cadell, 1787);

Memorial Relating to the University of Edinburgh, sometimes attributed to Adam Ferguson (Edinburgh: Printed by Balfour, Auld & Smellie, 1768);

The History of the Reign of the Emperor Charles V, 3 volumes (London: Printed by W. & W. Strahan for W. Strahan, T. Cadell, and J. Balfour, Edinburgh, 1769); republished as *The History of the Reign of Charles the Fifth, Emperor of Germany and King of Spain*, 2 volumes (Philadelphia: Sold by Robert Bell, 1770 [i.e., 1771]); revised edition, *The History of the Reign of Emperor Charles V*, 4 volumes (London: Printed for A. Strahan, T. Cadell, and J. Balfour, Edinburgh, 1787);

The History of America, 2 volumes (London: Printed for W. Strahan, T. Cadell, and J. Balfour, Edinburgh, 1777; revised edition, London: Printed for A. Strahan, T. Cadell, and

William Robertson (portrait by Henry Raeburn; University of Edinburgh)

J. Balfour, Edinburgh, 1788; New York: Printed for S. Campbell, 1798);

An Historical Disquisition Concerning the Knowledge Which the Ancients Had of India (London: Printed for A. Strahan, T. Cadell and E. Balfour, Edinburgh, 1791; Philadelphia: Printed by William Young, 1792);

The History of America. Books IX and X, edited by William Robertson *secundus* (London: Printed for A. Strahan, T. Cadell, Jun. & W. Davies, and E. Balfour, Edinburgh, 1796; Philadelphia: Printed by J. Humphreys, 1799).

Edition: *The Progress of Society in Europe* [volume 1 of *The History of the Reign of the Emperor Charles V*], edited, with an introduction, by Felix Gilbert (Chicago: University of Chicago Press, 1972).

OTHER: "The General Assembly's Answer to the King's Most Gracious Letter"; "The General Assembly's Congratulatory Address to the King on the Happy Event of the Peace"; "The General Assembly's Congratulatory Address to the Queen, on the Happy Event of the Birth of the Prince of *Wales,*" in *The Principal Acts of the General Assembly of the Church of Scotland, Conveened at Edinburgh the 26th Day of May, 1763* (Edinburgh: Printed by James Davidson & Robert Fleming, 1763), pp. 5-9;

Robert Adam, *Ruins of the Palace of the Emperor Diocletian at Spalato,* includes an unsigned preface by Robertson (London: Printed for the author, 1764);

"Dedication to the King," *Transactions of the Royal Society of Edinburgh,* volume 1 (Edinburgh: Printed for J. Dickson, sold in London by T. Cadell, 1788): v-vii;

"Address of Principal Robertson on Laying the Foundation Stone of the Edinburgh College, 1791" [i.e., 1789], in *Lives of Men of Letters and Science,* 2 volumes, by Henry, Lord Brougham (London: Knight, 1845), I: 318-319.

Richard Sher and Doris Sher, eds., "William Robertson and the Glorious Revolution: An Unpublished Sermon," "Church, University, Enlightenment: The Moderate Literati of Edinburgh, 1720-1793," by Richard Sher, Ph.D. dissertation, University of Chicago, 1979, pp. 551-559.

PERIODICAL PUBLICATIONS— UNCOLLECTED: "Reasons of Dissent from the

Judgment and Resolution of the Commission, March 11, 1752," attributed to Robertson though revised by a committee, *Scots Magazine,* 14 (April 1752): 191-197;

Review of *The History of Peter the Great, Emperor of Russia* by Alexander Gordon, sometimes attributed to Robertson, *Edinburgh Review,* 1 (January-July 1755): 1-9;

Review of *Memoirs of the Affairs of Scotland* by David Moysie, sometimes attributed to Robertson, *Edinburgh Review,* 1 (January-July 1755): 23-27;

Review of *A Collection of Poems* (volume 4) edited by Robert Dodsley, sometimes attributed to Robertson, *Edinburgh Review,* 1 (January-July 1755): 58-61;

Review of *Theron and Aspasio* by James Hervey, sometimes attributed to Robertson, *Edinburgh Review,* 1 (January-July 1755): 73-75;

Review of *The History of Croesus, King of Lydia* by Walter Anderson, sometimes attributed to Robertson, *Edinburgh Review,* 2 (July 1755 - January 1756): 1-3;

Review of *A Catalogue of the Bishops of the Several Sees within the Kingdom of Scotland, down to the Year 1688* by Robert Keith, sometimes attributed to Robertson, *Edinburgh Review,* 2 (July 1755 - January 1756): 13-18;

Review of *Lettres de Louis XIV* edited by Toussaint Rose, sometimes attributed to Robertson, *Edinburgh Review,* 2 (July 1755 - January 1756): 18-21;

Review of *A Summary, Historical and Political, of the First Plantings, Progressive Improvements, and Present State of the British Settlements in North America* by William Douglas, sometimes attributed to Robertson, *Edinburgh Review,* 2 (July 1755 - January 1756): 34-44;

Review of *Historical Law-Tracts* by Henry Home, Lord Kames, sometimes attributed to Robertson, *Critical Review,* 7 (April 1759): 356-367.

Together with David Hume and Edward Gibbon, William Robertson was one of the most important historians in eighteenth-century Britain. Although he published most of his books in London, his career was centered in Edinburgh, spanning what is today called the Scottish Enlightenment, a period rich in historical writing. His interests were wide, ranging from sixteenth-century Scotland to Europe of the late Renaissance to the exploration and settlement of the

New World to the culture and trade of ancient India. Neither Hume nor Gibbon dealt with such a variety of subjects. Nor did their careers match his in terms of their public roles. Robertson was an ordained minister in the Church of Scotland (with clerical duties including regular preaching) as well as an ecclesiastical and political leader in the Kirk's general assembly; he was at the center of Edinburgh literary life, commenting on manuscripts sent to him by aspiring authors in many fields; and he served for more than a quarter century as principal of the University of Edinburgh, helping to make the university one of the most respected in Europe.

The son of William and Eleanor (Pitcairne) Robertson, William Robertson was born on 19 September 1721, approximately fifteen miles southeast of Edinburgh at Borthwick, where his father was a minister. Concerned for his son's education, his father sent him to Dalkeith Grammar School, then one of the leading schools in the country, and in 1735 enrolled him at the University of Edinburgh, as indicated by the matriculation register of the university. Robertson proceeded steadily through the curriculum, completing his studies in 1741. He worked diligently with some of the most important teachers at Edinburgh, such as John Stevenson, who developed the subject of rhetoric and belles lettres and introduced John Locke's philosophy into the curriculum, and Charles Mackie, the school's first professor of civil history, who lectured on topics ranging from Roman social history to current events. His home environment was equally influential, because here his father's traditional Calvinism mixed with the more liberal thought of the Continental Arminians, including Samuel Werenfels and J. A. Turretin, whose works were in his father's library. During these years, Robertson also formed lifelong friendships with Hugh Blair, Alexander Carlyle, and John Home, students whose political, religious, and artistic outlooks were to be closely allied to his.

Upon completion of his studies at Edinburgh, Robertson turned first to literature and philosophy. At the beginning of 1742, in an effort to perfect his English style and to develop his command of moral philosophy, he started a translation of Marcus Aurelius, but his work was preempted by a Glasgow translation published that year. This disappointment was quickly followed by more serious concerns. The death of both his parents in the autumn of 1745 meant that he was responsible for the family. Fortu-

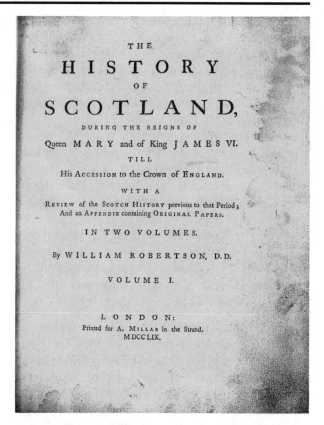

Title page for Robertson's first full-length book, which went through sixteen editions during his lifetime

nately, he had already made his choice of vocation: in June 1743 the Presbytery of Dalkeith had granted him a license to preach, and in 1744 he received from John Hope, second Earl of Hopetoun, through the influence of the Dundas family, the living of Gladsmuir, near Edinburgh, a post he held until 1758. Thus, apart from a romantic effort to volunteer on the Hanoverian side in the Jacobite uprising of 1745, Robertson settled into the life of a parish minister, attending to his siblings and parishioners, and even postponing marriage (to his cousin Mary Nisbet) until 21 August 1751 when his circumstances were more prosperous.

Edinburgh, however, was close at hand, and he eventually worked his way into its political and literary life. He began to emerge as a political figure in connection with the long-standing controversy surrounding the law of church patronage. He joined with Blair, Carlyle, Home, and others in 1751 to argue in the general assembly of the Church of Scotland against allowing local parishes to appoint ministers and to advocate that the general assembly should support the right of patrons to do the appointing. Although they lost their first debate, these men had formed the nucleus of what was to be called the Moderate party; and the views of this group strongly marked all of Robertson's subsequent work and came to have an important impact on Scottish culture and society. In 1752 the Moderates carried their arguments on church patronage (outlined in a report entitled "Reasons of Dissent from the Judgment and Resolution of the Commission, March 11, 1752," which Robertson had a large role in composing), and from this point they undertook an aggressive literary and political campaign to reshape Scottish society on more liberal Enlightenment principles. Robertson was the center of this campaign. By 1753 he had begun work on his *History of Scotland*; in 1754 he helped to found the Select Society, a group of prominent intellectuals, lawyers, and politicians that met to discuss the key issues of the day; in 1755 he published a sermon that attempted to mediate between humanist and antihumanist views of history; in 1755-1756 he wrote, along with other Moderates, for the *Edinburgh Review*, perhaps contributing as many as eight reviews to this short-lived publication intended to bring Enlightenment ideas to Scotland; in 1757, as a token of his Enlightened taste in the arts, Robertson wrote the preface to his cousin Robert Adam's *Ruins of the Palace of the Emperor Diocletian* (1764); in 1755, 1756, and 1757 he and other Moderates were involved in the so-called Three Humes Controversy, defending David Hume, John Home, and Henry Home, Lord Kames, against more conservative religious critics; and during the latter half of the 1750s he helped the Moderates wage a spirited but unsuccessful campaign on behalf of the establishment of a Scottish militia, which they believed essential to the preservation of civic integrity in Scotland.

The History of Scotland captures the essence of all this activity. From the moment of its appearance on 1 February 1759, the book was a success, with a second edition called for in April, followed by fourteen more during Robertson's lifetime. Treating primarily the reigns of Mary Stuart and James VI, Robertson concentrates on two central themes: progress and tolerance. In his interpretation this period saw the collapse of feudal and the emergence of commercial society, with the consequent displacement of divine-right monarchy and personal patronage by public assemblies and the rule of law. For Robertson, the emergence of bourgeois, commercial society clearly marks the path of progress. He presents

this view of Scottish history in a style characterized by impartiality, objectivity, and detachment— in short, tolerance, a quality he believed necessary for the improvement of Scottish civilization. His treatment of the controversial Mary, Queen of Scots, the idol of the reactionary Jacobites and the anathema of the progressive Hanoverians, is a typical example of his approach. He carefully weighs the evidence for and against her, concluding that she was not only personally guilty of complicity in the murder of Henry Stewart, Lord Darnley, but also a failure as a leader of her people. But at the same time he builds so much sympathy for her that this negative view is softened. As his friend David Hume remarked, in Robertson's treatment the queen "merits, on many accounts, our condemnation, whilst there is room left for our pity in deploring her misfortunes" (*Critical Review*, February 1759). There is no doubt about where Robertson stands, but he does not present his views as those of a committed partisan but rather as a polite arbiter.

With the publication of this highly regarded book, Robertson consolidated his social and political position. In 1758 he had received an appointment at Lady Yester's Chapel in Edinburgh as well as an honorary doctor of divinity degree from the University of Edinburgh. In 1759 he was appointed chaplain of Sterling Castle, and in 1761 he was named one of His Majesty's Chaplains in Ordinary and was translated from Lady Yester's to Old Greyfriars, a post he retained for the rest of his life. At the same time, he began to think of a university position, composing a series of lectures on Western history (now lost) for the University of Edinburgh and soliciting the support of politically influential figures. His efforts were rewarded in spring of 1762 when he was elected principal of the University of Edinburgh. A further sign of his growing influence was his election in 1763 as moderator of the general assembly, a position held only for a year but an indication of the control he and the Moderates now had in the Church of Scotland. In this same year, Robertson was appointed by the king to be historiographer royal for Scotland, an office that had not been filled since the Union of Scotland and England in 1707.

In the midst of all this social and political maneuvering, however, Robertson had not lost sight of his writing. As early as 1759 he had decided on the subject of his next book—a history of the reign of Charles V, the sixteenth-century Hapsburg emperor of Germany and king of Spain—

Page from a letter to Edward Gibbon in which Robertson asks for comments on his recently published History of America *and discusses his friendship with David Hume (Add. MS 34886, f. 98; British Library)*

though for a while in the early 1760s, perhaps to gain political advantage, he led some to believe he might write a history of England. In choosing to write on Charles V, Robertson was building on the *History of Scotland*. Having shown the transition from feudal to commercial society in Scotland, he wished now to trace the same transition in Europe. Charles V was an especially appropri-

ate subject because, in Robertson's view, he had, albeit unwittingly, helped to lay the foundations of modern society. It was during his reign that Protestantism was established and that the balance of power among European nation states emerged, and these events gave Robertson the opportunity to develop his preferred themes of progress and toleration. He first composed volumes 2 and 3, containing the detailed political narrative of Charles's reign, and then about 1765 wrote an innovative, sweeping introductory volume, showing how the Middle Ages gave way to the Renaissance. This volume, subtitled *A View of the Progress of Society in Europe, from the Subversion of the Roman Empire, to the Beginning of the Sixteenth Century*, is the hallmark of Robertson's work as an historian, capturing his themes of progress and toleration with unparalleled vigor and conciseness. Few historical works have been more eagerly awaited by the public than *The History of the Reign of the Emperor Charles V*, and the price Robertson received for the manuscript (approximately 4,000 pounds) was the highest then known for history. Upon its publication on 9 March 1769, the history was extremely successful: it saw at least six subsequent editions in Britain, it was translated into all major European languages, and it was one of the first works of the Scottish Enlightenment to be published in America.

In the preface to the history, Robertson indicated that he had intended to include an account of the exploration and settlement of the New World. He found in writing, however, that the subject was too large, and he promised a separate treatment of it. Thus, in the year *Charles V* was published he began his research for a history of Spanish, Portuguese, and British colonization of the Americas. There were no adequate comprehensive histories of this increasingly important subject, and Robertson may have believed this work could be his magnum opus. He completed the Spanish portion by 1775 and immediately began work on the British portion, but by the summer of 1776 events in America forced Robertson to put his manuscript aside and, as he wrote to Robert Waddilove in July 1778, to "wait for times of greater tranquillity, when I can write and the public read with more impartiality and better information than at present." Robertson could not write his style of polite history—with its emphasis on reasonableness, moderation, and impartiality—in the midst of open warfare abroad and political tension at home.

The Spanish portion, however, was complete, and its subject sufficiently distant from immediate British concerns. He therefore published that part on 28 May 1777, and like his previous histories, this one was an immediate success, going through six editions in his lifetime as well as translation into all major European languages. Much of the book's popularity was due to Robertson's comprehensive treatment of the New World and its native inhabitants. Although he concentrates on the exploration and conquest of the New World by Christopher Columbus, Hernán Cortés, and Francisco Pizarro, he also provides detailed, up-to-date descriptions of the Aztec, Inca, and other native American cultures that they encountered. Robertson's history reflects the growing scientific interest in primitive societies, and he tried conscientiously to gather reliable information about the native inhabitants of America, consulting eyewitness accounts, attempting to track down native artifacts, and even sending out questionnaires to correspondents in the colonies. Despite its novel subject, this history carries through Robertson's favorite themes. He studies the idea of progress, juxtaposing the Old World and the New, the civilized and the primitive, carefully weighing each one against the other. He also tries to be tolerant in his judgments of the Spanish empire. Many had condemned the Spaniards for their treatment of the Native Americans, arguing that the empire was merely an effort to get gold and land at any price. Robertson takes a more balanced view, setting the achievements of the empire against its failures. For Robertson, colonization is an inevitable and necessary part of the evolution of world history, integrating separate, isolated nations into increasingly more complex systems of interdependence.

After *The History of America*, Robertson published no major work for nearly fifteen years. During 1780-1781 he worked for a short while on his history of British colonization but laid it aside for good without plans for publication. His eldest son eventually published what Robertson had written. He seems never to have begun the Portuguese section of the project. In 1778, at the suggestion of his publisher, Robertson again contemplated writing a history of England covering the reigns of William and Mary and Queen Anne (1688-1714) as a continuation of Hume's *History of England* (1754-1762). He gathered some manuscript materials and discussed the project with friends, but it, too, was soon laid aside. The reasons for Robertson's long silence are complex and have yet to be fully explained. Illness played a large role. He noted in a letter of 8 March 1784 that his health was "shattered" for three years after the publication of *The History of America* because of the combined demands of research and writing as well as political and academic duties. But public factors may have been more important than personal ones, for Robertson found himself under strong attack by those opposed to his political and religious views; and he suddenly retired from leadership of the Moderates in 1780. Because Robertson's histories had always been closely tied to his politics, his retirement from political affairs may have made it impossible—at least for a while—for him to continue writing.

The 1780s, however, were not empty of achievement. Although Robertson may have lost stature at home, his international reputation grew, as indicated by his admission to the Academy of Sciences at Padua in 1781 and to the Russian Academy in 1783, honors matching his unanimous election as corresponding member of the Royal Academy of History at Madrid in 1777. This decade also saw the beginning of one of Robertson's major projects for the University of Edinburgh: the construction of new buildings. In 1768 he had written a *Memorial Relating to the University of Edinburgh*, mounting a fund-raising campaign to rebuild the school's shabby quarters. By 1785 he was working with his cousin James Adam on designs, and in 1789 he gave a speech on the laying of the foundation stone. Robertson was also busy developing the intellectual life of Edinburgh. He helped to found the Royal Society of Edinburgh in 1782, writing a dedication to the king in the first volume of the *Transactions*; and, throughout the decade and into the next, he was asked for advice and assistance on a wide range of literary projects, including James Hutton's geological theories, the publication of his colleague John Drysdale's sermons, and Thomas Somerville's history of England in the reign of Queen Anne. Finally, Robertson resumed his own pen. In 1788, he preached a highly regarded sermon commemorating the Glorious Revolution of 1688. Perhaps most important, from 1785 to 1787 he undertook a thorough revision of each of his three major historical works. He made numerous changes in style, especially in the *History of Scotland*, where his language became more Latinate and abstract. Always a severe critic of his own work, he also brought each of the histories up to date, testing his own facts and conclusions against those of other historians.

Somewhat to his own surprise, given his retirement from politics and writing, he also began to compose his last work, *An Historical Disquisition Concerning the Knowledge Which the Ancients Had of India*, which was published on 4 June 1791. It is uncertain when Robertson first became interested in the subject; however, because he worked hard—and successfully—in the early 1780s to se-cure military positions for his sons James and David in India and Ceylon, he obviously had for several years a strong personal interest in the area. The borrowing registers of the Edinburgh University Library indicate that beginning about 1788 Robertson was frequently withdrawing books relating to ancient history and to the East. By 1790 he had sent a finished manuscript to his publisher, though he was disappointed to find that the price for it was considerably less than that paid for *Charles V* or the *History of America*. The intervening two decades had taken their toll on Robertson's reputation. Nonetheless, Robertson felt, as he told Gibbon in a letter dated 25 August 1791, "a partial fondness for this child of my old age."

In at least two important ways, the *Disquisition* is a fitting conclusion to Robertson's literary career. First, the subject matter, the ancient world up to about 1500, complements his earlier works dealing with the modern world since 1500. The writing of the *Disquisition* may have been sparked by the 1787 revision of the *History of America*, because in the first book of that earlier history he touches upon the problem of the West's knowledge of India; and the *Disquisition* was conceived, as he remarks in its preface, as an elaboration and expansion of these earlier comments. Thus, Robertson touched upon both the ancient and modern worlds during his long career. Second, the book shows the persistence of Robertson's Moderate ideology, with its concern for progress and toleration. On the one hand Robertson envisions the incorporation of India into the British empire and therefore into the West's sphere of influence. Just as he had celebrated the establishment of the British empire in his speech as moderator in 1763 and had defended (to an extent) the Spanish empire, Robertson is here once again a spokesman for empire, seeing the spread of Western colonialism as the means of integrating the nations of the world into a higher, more complex level of existence. Colonialism is the instrument of progress. On the other hand the book is a liberal, humanitarian plea for the respect and preservation of Indian culture by the conquering British. At one point he even proposes a kind of national study center to be devoted to explaining Indian philosophy. Such deference to other traditions and cultures springs from the tolerance at the heart of Moderatism. Although the *Disquisition* received polite reviews, it did not command the attention that his previous histories did. New methods and new concerns had come to occupy historians at the end of the century. Despite its relative neglect, however, the *Disquisition* is one of the finest statements of the Moderate vision.

After the publication of his last work, Robertson's health began slowly to decline, and he died on 11 June 1793. His subsequent reputation as both a man and a writer has varied markedly. His histories held their place as major works well into the nineteenth century, but in the twentieth they have received very little critical attention. Lacking the stylistic brilliance of Gibbon's or the philosophical insights of Hume's, Robertson's histories lost their attraction as the immediate issues they addressed—progress, tolerance, and other Enlightenment ideals—began to fade. His life has been similarly ignored in this century, and lacking a complete biography, it is difficult to assess his character. Turning to the opinion of his contemporaries, we find that his enemies attacked him as being overbearing and tyrannical, and his friends, though occasionally teasing him for his air of self-importance, praised him as a model of humanity and intellectual vigor. Perhaps the most meaningful assessment of him—one that takes in both life and works—is the sermon preached at his funeral by his colleague John Erskine. They had known each other since college, and since 1767 they had held a joint appointment at Old Greyfriars, Robertson representing the Moderate faction, Erskine the evangelicals. They were not only theological opponents, but they also differed politically—Erskine, for example, supporting the American Revolution, while Robertson opposed it. Yet Erskine could declare his admiration for Robertson's genius: "Few minds were naturally so large and capacious as Dr. Robertson's; or stored by study, experience, and observation with so rich furniture." And, he could praise Robertson's character in the restrained, balanced terms that a Moderate would approve: "He enjoyed the bounties of Providence, without running into riot; was temperate, without austerity; cheerful, without levity; condescending, and affable, without meanness; and in expence, neither sordid nor prodigal. He could feel an injury or affront, and yet bridle his passion; was grave, not sullen; steady, not obstinate; friendly, not officious; prudent and cautious, not timid." Such praise from an opponent who had known Robertson through most of his life is testimony to the strength of both his character and literary achievement.

Letters:

Horace Walpole's Correspondence with Robertson, edited by C. H. Bennett and A. G. Hoover, volume 15 of *Correspondence of Horace Walpole*, edited by W. S. Lewis and others, 48 volumes (New Haven: Yale University Press, 1935-1983);

R. B. Sher and M. A. Stewart, eds., "William Robertson and David Hume: Three Letters," *Hume Studies*, 10 (1985): 69-86;

Jeremy Black, ed., "The Enlightenment Historian at Work: The Researches of William Robertson," includes six letters between Robertson and Lord Grantham, *Bulletin of Hispanic Studies*, 65 (1988): 251-260.

Biographies:

Dugald Stewart, *Account of the Life and Writings of William Robertson* (London: Printed by A. Strahan for T. Cadell, Jun. & W. Davis and E. Balfour, Edinburgh, 1801);

George Gleig, *Some Account of the Life and Writings of Robertson* (Edinburgh, 1812);

Henry, Lord Brougham, *Lives of Men of Letters and Science*, 2 volumes (London: Knight, 1845), I: 256-323.

References:

J. B. Black, *The Art of History: A Study of Four Great Historians of the Eighteenth Century* (London: Methuen, 1926);

Alexander Carlyle, *Anecdotes and Characters of the Times*, edited by James Kinsley (London: Oxford University Press, 1973);

Jeremy J. Cater, "The Making of Principal Robertson in 1762: Politics and the University of Edinburgh in the Second Half of the Eighteenth Century," *Scottish Historical Review*, 49 (April 1970): 60-84;

Ian D. L. Clark, "Moderatism and the Moderate Party in the Church of Scotland, 1752-1802," Ph.D. dissertation, Cambridge University, 1964;

Dennis R. Dean, "James Hutton on Religion and Geology: The Unpublished Preface to His *Theory of the Earth* (1788)," *Annals of Science*, 32 (May 1975): 187-193;

Mark Duckworth, "An Eighteenth-Century Questionnaire: William Robertson on the Indians," *Eighteenth-Century Life*, 11 (February 1987): 36-49;

John Erskine, "The Agency of God in Human Greatness," in his *Discourses Preached on Several Occasions*, 2 volumes (Edinburgh: Ogle,

1801-1804), I: 230-265;

Mary Fearnley-Sander, "Philosophical History and the Scottish Reformation: William Robertson and the Knoxian Tradition," *Historical Journal*, 33 (June 1990): 323-338;

D. B. Horn, "Principal William Robertson, D.D., Historian," *University of Edinburgh Journal*, 18 (Autumn 1956): 155-168;

R. A. Humphreys, *William Robertson and His History of America: A Lecture Delivered at Canning House on 11 June 1954* (London: Hispanic and Luzo-Brazilian Councils, 1954);

James L. McKelvey, "William Robertson and Lord Bute," *Studies in Scottish Literature*, 6 (April 1969): 238-247;

Manfred Schlenke, "Aus der Frühzeit des englishcen Historismus: William Robertsons Beitrag zur methodischen Grundlegung der Geschichtswissenschaft im 18. Jahrhundert," *Saeculum*, 7 (1956): 107-125;

Schlenke, "Kulturgeschichte oder politische Geschichte in der Geschichtsschreibung des 18. Jahrhunderts: William Robertson als Historiker des europäischen Staatensystem," *Archiv für Kulturgeschichte*, 37 (1955): 60-97;

Richard B. Sher, *Church and University in the Scottish Enlightenment: The Moderate Literati of Edinburgh* (Princeton: Princeton University Press, 1985);

Sher, "1688 and 1788: William Robertson on Revolution in Britain and France," in *Culture and Revolution*, edited by Paul Dukes and John Dunkley (London & New York: Pinter, 1990), pp. 98-109;

Jeffrey Smitten, "Impartiality in Robertson's *History of America*," *Eighteenth-Century Studies*, 19 (Fall 1985): 56-77;

Smitten, "Moderatism and History: William Robertson's Unfinished History of British America," in *Scotland and America in the Age of Enlightenment*, edited by Richard B. Sher and Jeffrey Smitten (Edinburgh: Edinburgh University Press, 1990), pp. 163-179;

Smitten, "Robertson's *History of Scotland*: Narrative Structure and the Sense of Reality," *Clio*, 11 (Fall 1981): 29-47;

David J. Womersley, "The Historical Writings of William Robertson," *Journal of the History of Ideas*, 47 (July-September 1986): 497-506.

Papers:

Robertson's papers, especially his letters, are widely scattered. The primary holdings are in the National Library of Scotland, the Edinburgh University Library, and the British Library. The National Library of Scotland houses the Robertson-McDonald papers, a large collection of letters and other documents from Robertson's family, including the unfinished translation of Marcus Aurelius, the manuscript of the 1788 sermon, the manuscript of the unfinished history of British America, the manuscript of the *Disquisition*, and the questionnaires used for the *History of America*. The library also has many other manuscript letters by and to Robertson in other collections. The Edinburgh University Library houses many letters as well as an essay titled "De probabilitate historica," written by Robertson for Stevenson as a school exercise in 1737. The British Library has a large collection of letters as well as manuscript materials used in writing *Charles V*. Other important collections of letters are to be found in the Scottish Record Office, the Bute papers at Mount Stuart, and Duke University Library.

Adam Smith
(5 June 1723 - 17 July 1790)

Ian Ross
University of British Columbia

BOOKS: *The Theory of Moral Sentiments* (London: Printed for A. Millar and A. Kincaid & J. Bell, Edinburgh, 1759; second edition, revised, 1761); third edition, enlarged as *The Theory of Moral Sentiments. To which is added A Dissertation on the Origin of Languages* (London: Printed for A. Millar; A. Kincaid & A. Bell, Edinburgh; and sold by T. Cadell, 1767); fourth edition, retitled *The Theory of Moral Sentiments; or, An Essay towards an Analysis of the Principles by which Men naturally judge concerning the Conduct and Character, first of their Neighbours, and afterwards of themselves* (London: Printed for W. Strahan, J. & F. Rivington, T. Longman, and T. Cadell, and for W. Creech, Edinburgh, 1774; fifth edition, 1781); sixth edition, considerably enlarged and corrected, 2 volumes (London: Printed for A. Strahan, and A. Cadell; and W. Creech and J. Bell, Edinburgh, 1790);

An Inquiry into the Nature and Causes of the Wealth of Nations, 2 volumes (London: Printed for W. Strahan, and T. Cadell, 1776; second edition, revised, 1778); third edition, with "Additions and Corrections" and index, 3 volumes (London: Printed for W. Strahan, and T. Cadell, 1784; fourth edition, London: Printed for A. Strahan, and T. Cadell, 1786; fifth edition, 1789; Philadelphia: Printed for Thomas Dobson, 1789);

Essays on Philosophical Subjects . . . To Which is prefixed An Account of the Life and Writings of the Author; by Dugald Stewart, edited by Joseph Black and James Hutton (London: Printed for T. Cadell Jun. & W. Davies and W. Creech, Edinburgh, 1795);

The Works of Adam Smith. With an Account of his Life and Writings by Dugald Stewart, 5 volumes (London: Printed for T. Cadell & W. Davies and W. Creech, Edinburgh, 1811-1812);

Lectures on Justice, Police, Revenue and Arms, Delivered in the University of Glasgow by Adam Smith, Reported by a Student in 1763, edited by Edwin Cannan (Oxford: Clarendon Press, 1896);

Lectures on Rhetoric and Belles Lettres delivered in the University of Glasgow by Adam Smith, Reported by a Student in 1762-63, edited by John M. Lothian (London: Nelson, 1963; Carbondale & Edwardsville: Southern Illinois University Press, 1971).

Edition: *The Glasgow Edition of the Works and Correspondence of Adam Smith*, 7 volumes, edited by A. S. Skinner and others (Oxford: Clarendon Press, 1976-1987).

OTHER: Preface (2 December 1748) to *Poems on Several Occasions*, by William Hamilton (Glasgow: Printed & sold by Robert & Andrew Foulis, 1748); reprinted with a dedication by Smith to "Mr. William Craufurd, Merchant in Glasgow" (Glasgow: Printed & sold by Robert & Andrew Foulis, 1758);

"Considerations concerning the first formation of Languages, and the different genius of original and compounded Languages," in *The Philological Miscellany* (London: Printed for the editor & sold by T. Beckett & P. A. Dehondt, 1761), I: 440-479.

There is something of a cult of Adam Smith at present. One devotee (George J. W. Goodman) has appropriated Smith's name to sell books about making money, others advise local and central governments in Britain and administrations in the United States of America, and some content themselves with wearing neckties of red or blue emblazoned with his head. It is not clear that Adam Smith would have approved of these enterprises. Contemporaries were disappointed that he did not leave more money in his will, but he had apparently given a great deal of it away in secret charity. His policy advice was requested by various governments, but his wisest counsel about ending the American revolutionary war was ignored. He put his privacy before public attention, and even denied David Hume's

Adam Smith, 1787 (medallion by James Tassie; Scottish National Portrait Gallery)

deathbed wish that he oversee publication of the *Dialogues Concerning Natural Religion* (1779), because he was "uneasy" about the book exciting "clamour." Nevertheless, we should attend to what he wrote. He reasoned acutely about important subjects: composition and aesthetic judgment; the history of science and that of civil society; the nature of ethical judgments; and the operation of the market economy. He wrote about and for his own time, but what he wrote has application, with appropriate adjustments, to our time, which—for good and ill—is connected with his, when individual lives and human society were changing through improvement in the food supply, the growth of manufacturing and commerce, and replacement of religious values by secular ones. Moreover, he wrote with care about these important subjects, picking and placing his words sensitively, and attending to the larger, aesthetic design of what he wrote and the thought he systematized. Though he is dismissed, on occasion, as the outmoded father of the "dismal science" of economics, a closer view finds him a tire-

less inquirer into the human condition and the champion of our capacity for sympathy and imagination as well as prudent acquisitiveness.

Posthumous son of Adam Smith, a comptroller of customs in the Fife seaport of Kirkcaldy, Adam Smith was born there on or shortly before 5 June 1723, when his baptism was recorded in the register of the burgh kirk. He survived a sickly childhood due to the attention of a remarkable mother, Margaret Douglas, with whom he lived on affectionate terms until she died, aged ninety, in 1784. Her father, Robert Douglas, was a Fife laird with army connections, and Smith told the biographer James Boswell, who was his student at Glasgow University, that his family "had cut his throat in not allowing him to be a soldier" (*London Journal*, 23 April 1763), but he found his métier as a scholar, teacher, and man of letters. Taking that direction was probably a result of his mother's encouragement and instruction at the Kirkcaldy burgh school, where an excellent master, David Miller, insisted on translation exercises from Latin and writing themes in English. Two textbooks of Smith's survive from his schooldays: *Eutropii Historiae Romanae Breviarum* (1725) and Justinus's epitome of the *Historiae Philippicae* by Pompeius Trogus, which provide a conspectus of the history of Ancient Greece, Rome, and the Orient. Smith was attracted to historical studies, and his later writings made considerable use of examples drawn from them. Kirkcaldy must also have provided him with an additional education from observing the port's trade, local industries (coal mining, salt panning, and nail making), and farming in the vicinity. Further instruction in the ways of the world came from reports of the smuggling on the Fife coast, with which his relatives in the customs service contended, and, within the law, the rise of local families who befriended Smith: the Oswalds of Dunnikier, active in the law and politics; the Adamses, who were architects; and Jardines, who served the kirk of Scotland.

At fourteen, Smith went to Glasgow University, perhaps because his father had been made a burgess of the city when he was secretary to Hugh Campbell, Earl of Loudoun, a Campbell magnate, and the Campbell interest predominated there. He displayed at first a bent for Newtonian physics and mathematics, stimulated in the latter subject by the professor, Robert Simson, who was engaged in fundamental research in Greek geometry. Latterly, Smith came under the sway of the "never to be forgotten" Francis Hutcheson, whose teaching of moral philosophy and publications profoundly influenced his thought and expression throughout his career. Hutcheson refined Shaftesbury's theory of a moral sense, arguing that our aesthetic and moral judgments rested on our feelings, not reason, and, in highly successful lectures in English at Glasgow, when he became a professor there in 1730, he stressed the benevolent side of human nature, urged moral action that would promote the greatest happiness of the greatness number, and asserted the fundamental value of natural liberty. These are all themes that reappear in Smith's writings and move him to an eloquence with Ciceronian echoes similar to that of his teacher.

Though he did not take an M.A. degree on completing his studies at Glasgow in 1740, Smith received the approval of the faculty as a "very fine boy as any we have," and was elected to a Snell Exhibition to Balliol College. He was disappointed, however, by his experience there, writing to his guardian on 24 August 1740: "it will be his own fault if anyone should endanger his

Smith's mother, Margaret Douglas Smith (artist unknown; Kirkcaldy Museum)

health at Oxford by excessive Study, our only business here being to go to prayers twice a day, and to lecture twice a week." He claimed that "In the university of Oxford, the greater part of the publick professors have, for these many years, given up altogether even the pretence of teaching," because their large emoluments came with appointment and did not depend on students' fees, so there were no incentives from competition to perform their duties. On his own Smith read widely in foreign languages, ancient and modern, and practiced translation, particularly from French, "with a view to the improvement of his own style." There is also a circumstantial story to the effect that the Balliol authorities caught him reading David Hume's *Treatise of Human Nature* (1739-1740) and disciplined him. It appears that Smith fell into ill health from prolonged, self-directed study, and he must have read or been informed about George Berkeley's *Siris* (1744), for he believed for a time that tar water had cured the "inveterate scurvy and shaking in the head" from which he suffered. He may also have been infected with skepticism from reading Hume or some other like-minded authors, since he did not take orders in the Church of England, though this was the career intended for Snell Exhibitioners, and he left Oxford in 1746 disgusted with its Tory politics and stagnation.

Following two further years of study at home with his mother in Kirkcaldy, Smith was induced by Henry Home of Kames, a leading advocate and promoter of improvement in Scotland, to give public lectures in Edinburgh on rhetoric and belles lettres. The first series was given in the winter of 1748-1749 and then repeated in the next two years to a "respectable auditory" of students and graduates in law and theology. Part of the attraction for them was that Smith's English "pronunciation and his style were much superior to what could, at that time, be acquired in Scotland only." At this time there was considerable anxiety among educated Scots over their standard of English; as Hume observed on 2 July 1757: "[we] are unhappy, in our Accent and Pronunciation, speak very corrupt Dialect of the Tongue which we make use of." Smith inspired confidence that this condition could be changed, and he gave instruction in acquiring good taste, then regarded as a badge of social cohesion among the educated classes.

It is believed that Smith repeated his Edinburgh rhetoric lectures at Glasgow when he became a professor there in 1751, since he did not have time to prepare a new series. The contents were described as follows by the university library keeper, James Wodrow, in a letter dated 28 May 1808:

> Smith delivered a set of admirable Critical Lectures on Language, not as a Grammarian but Rhetorician—on the different kinds of characteristics of Style suited to different subjects, *simple, nervous,* &c, the structuring, the natural order, & proper arrangement of the different Members of a Sentence. He characterised the Stile & Genius of some of the best ancient Writers, Poets, but especially Historians, Thucidides [*sic*], Polybius &c translating long passages of them; also the Style of the best English Classics, Ld Clarendon, Addison, Swift, Pope &c, and though his own didactic style in his last famous bouk [*Wealth of Nations*] (however suited to the subject)—the style of the former book [*The Theory of Moral Sentiments*] was much superior—was certainly not a Model for good writing, yet his remarks & rules given in the lectures I speak of, were the result of a fine taste and sound judgement, well calculated to be exceedingly useful to young Composers so

that I have often regretted that some part of them has never been published.

Contemporary opinion agreed in general with Wodrow in preferring *The Theory of Moral Sentiments* (1759) in point of style to *The Wealth of Nations* (1776), though the latter book cost Smith more pains in writing and proved to be the more influential. He continued to disseminate his ideas about aesthetic subjects, and within a year of going to Glasgow helped to found a literary society, reading to its members papers "on Taste, Composition and the History of Philosophy which he had previously delivered while a lecturer on rhetoric in Edinburgh." Two of these papers constituted parts 1 and 2 of his essay on the imitative arts, posthumously published in *Essays on Philosophical Subjects* (1795). Thus we can date back to his days as a lecturer in Edinburgh Smith's formulation that the aesthetic pleasure afforded by paintings and statuary (also by topiary) "is founded altogether upon our wonder at seeing an object of one kind represent so well an object of a very different kind, and upon our admiration of the art which surmounts so happily that disparity which Nature establishes between them." Smith also expressed the view with respect to music that the "sentiments and passions" naturally and properly imitated by that art are "of all beauties the brightest." In stressing the role of wonder and admiration in our aesthetic responses, also in drawing attention to the emotional basis of musical forms, Smith conducted at an early point in his career the kind of psychological analysis that culminated in his systems of ethics and economics.

Another stage toward that culmination was represented by the Edinburgh lectures on the "History of Philosophy." The type of history in this context is that named "conjectural" or "theoretical" by Smith's first biographer, Dugald Stewart, in discussing his subject's essays on astronomy and languages. This was a favorite form of many contributors to the Scottish Enlightenment such as David Hume, Adam Ferguson, and William Robertson. By this term Stewart meant history that, lacking evidence in the form of records and witnesses' reports, nevertheless proceeds to account for the development of beliefs, practices, and even institutions by showing how they could have arisen from what are taken to be natural causes.

Smith's own skeptical definition of philosophy was "that science which pretends to lay open the concealed connections that united the various appearances of nature." It is reasonable to suppose that the Edinburgh "History of Philosophy" lectures set out to account for the successive systems explaining the connecting principles of nature in terms of human propensities. These gave rise to systems, exploded them, and supplanted them, one after another, in a fashion that, as far as Western culture is concerned, was initiated by Greek thinkers searching for more satisfying ways of ordering appearances. Smith's history of astronomy survives in the *Essays on Philosophical Subjects* to provide a brilliant example of this procedure. Its author proposes an origin for systems of astronomy in the human emotions of wonder, surprise, and admiration. Apparently recollecting Hume's treatment of causation in the *Treatise of Human Nature*, Smith notes that when unlike objects constantly succeed each other in the same order, an association of ideas is established between them, and it becomes a habit of the imagination when one idea is presented to pass to the other. If the customary connection of objects is disrupted, and they assume an order for which the imagination is not prepared, we feel surprise and then wonder, and the imagination is exercised: "to find out something which may fill up the gap, which, like a bridge, may so far at least unite those seemingly distant objects, as to render the passage of the thought between them smooth, and natural, and easy."

In the rhetoric lectures which have come down to us, Smith draws attention to the discomfort felt in meeting a "chasm or Gap" in historical narration. It is human nature, he reckons, to avoid discomfort, and he paints the imagination achieving tranquillity, upon encountering an uncommon sequence of objects, by devising a theory or hypothetical system to glide from one object to another. Accordingly, Smith reviews the chief systems of astronomy not with an eye to their "absurdity or probability; their agreement or inconsistency with truth or reality," but through estimating their success in soothing the imagination, also in achieving coherence and enhancing our response to the objects they comprehended as the "clew that is most capable of conducting us through all the labyrinths of philosophical history." Explaining in this fashion how the Ptolemaic system fell into "complexity" and "confusion" as ever more corrections had to be made to bring it into line with the phenomena, Smith offers a definition of a system as an "imaginary machine invented to connect together in the fancy those different movements and effects

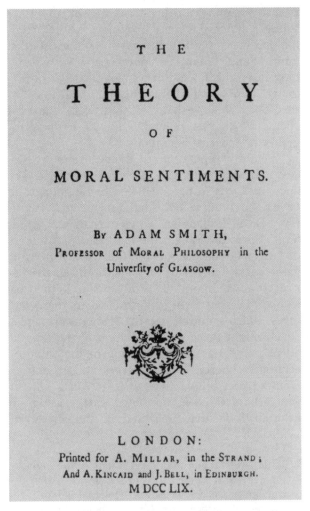

THE

THEORY

OF

MORAL SENTIMENTS.

By ADAM SMITH,
Professor of Moral Philosophy in the
University of Glasgow.

LONDON:
Printed for A. Millar, in the Strand;
And A. Kincaid and J. Bell, in Edinburgh.
M DCC LIX.

Title page for Smith's first book, which grew out of lectures he delivered at the University of Glasgow

which are in reality effected." He then argues that as later machines "with fewer wheels, and fewer principles of motion" supplant more complex earlier ones, so complex systems give place to those in which "one great connecting principle is . . . found to be sufficient to bind together all the discordant phaenomena that occur in a whole species of things." Smith provides examples in the systems of Copernicus, René Descartes, and finally Isaac Newton, who is the philosophical hero in this sequence, since he demonstrated how "gravity might be the connecting principle which joined together the movements of the Planets, [and] . . . endeavoured next to prove that it really was so." Thus Smith illustrated the "principles which lead and direct philosophical enquiries," as the title of the history of astronomy essay claims, but his conclusion does not omit a cautionary and skeptical note: "even we, while we have been endeavouring to represent all philosophical systems as mere inventions of the imagination, to connect together the otherwise disjointed and discordant phenomena of nature, have insensibly been drawn in, to make use of language expressing the connecting principles of this one [Newton's], as if they were the real chains which Nature makes use of to bind together her several operations."

Smith's reputation, of course, rests on success in inventing systems in the realm of social science, and it is to be noted that in Edinburgh he gave a third course in this field. As one of his auditors, David Callander of Westerhall, reported, Smith "privately taught the Civil Law to Students of Jurisprudence. It was the fame which he thus gained as a Teacher of Law, that induced the Patrons to invite him to the professorship in the College of Glasgow." A major theme in these lectures, which inquired into the "general principles which ought to be the foundation of the laws of all nations," was the affirmation of the value of economic liberty. This emerges in an extract from a paper Smith gave at Glasgow in 1755, but which harked back, he stated categorically, to Edinburgh lectures delivered in the winter of 1750-1751:

> Little else is requisite to carry a state to the highest degree of opulence from the lowest barbarism, but peace, easy taxes, and a tolerable administration of justice; all the rest being brought about by the natural course of things. All governments which thwart this natural course, which force things into another channel, or which endeavour to arrest the progress of society at a particular point are unnatural, and to support themselves are obliged to be oppressive and tyrannical.

Smith became concerned that his ideas were plagiarized by William Robertson in his account of the "progress of society in Europe," which constituted the first volume of his *History of the Reign of the Emperor Charles V* (1769). However, the theme of the injustice of governments interfering in trade is part of the civic humanist discourse of the period and appears, for example, in Andrew Fletcher of Saltoun's *Account of a Conversation concerning a Right Regulation of Governments for the common Good of Mankind* (1703), republished in the 1749 Glasgow edition of his *Political Works*: "all governments which put discouragements on the industry of their subjects are not upon a right foot; but violent, and consequently unjust." Perhaps

Glasgow as a rising entrepôt port favored such views and welcomed in Smith an eloquent exponent who was to incorporate them in a comprehensive system of political economy featuring access to the free market as a form of natural liberty.

When called to Glasgow University in 1751, Smith was first elected to the Chair of Logic. He soon saw the need to abandon the scholastic version of this subject derived from Aristotle, and sought to direct his pupils to "studies of a more interesting and useful sort." So reported one of them, John Millar, who became an intimate friend of Smith's, also an outstanding professor of civil law at Glasgow from 1761 until his death in 1801. His report continued:

> after exhibiting a general view of the powers of the mind, and explaining so much of the ancient logic as was requisite to gratify curiosity with respect to an artificial method of reasoning, [Smith] dedicated all the rest of his time to the delivery of a system of rhetoric and belles lettres. The best method of explaining and illustrating the various powers of the human mind, the most useful part of metaphysics, arises from an examination of the several ways of communicating our thoughts by speech, and from an attention to the principles of literary compositions which contribute to persuasion or entertainment. By these arts, every thing that we perceive or feel, every operation of our minds, is expressed and delineated in such a manner, that it may be clearly distinguished and remembered. There is, at the same time, no branch of literature more suited to youth at their first entrance upon philosophy than this, which lays hold of their taste and their feelings.

Millar expressed regret that the manuscript of these lectures had been destroyed at Smith's death, but, by a stroke of good fortune, two volumes of manuscript "Notes of Dr. Smith's Rhetorick Lectures" turned up in 1958, at a sale of an Aberdeenshire manor-house library.

Lacking a first lecture, and in the third one presenting a shortened version of Smith's essay on the first formation of languages, which was published in 1761 in *The Philological Miscellany*, the manuscript proved to be a report by a student or students of a series of rhetoric lectures running from Friday, 19 November 1762, until Friday, 18 February 1763.

The twenty-nine lectures of the series fall into the two major divisions identified by Millar: an "examination of the several ways of communicating our thoughts by speech" (nos. 2-11), and "attention to the principles of those literary compositions which contribute to persuasion or entertainment" (nos. 12-30). Smith's rhetoric is a system of a piece with his ethics, as he makes clear in the first division, which challenges the standpoint of traditional rhetoric that the expressive *force* and *beauty* of language reside in figures of speech. Smith's approach differs: "when the sentiment of the speaker is expressed in a neat, clear, plain, and clever manner, and the passion or affection he is possessed of and intends, *by sympathy*, to communicate to his hearer, is plainly and cleverly hit off, then and then only the expression has all the force and beauty that language can give it." Because the "grammarians" are confused about the role of the figures of speech, and do not appreciate the fact that, for example, the beauty of a passage "flows from the sentiment and the method of expressing it being suitable to the passion," they form their systems of rhetoric "from the consideration of these figures [of speech], and divisions and sub-divisions of them." Smith concludes, with some asperity: "they are generally a very silly set of books and not at all instructive."

From this account of Smith's lectures on rhetoric and belles lettres it can be judged how useful they were for an introductory university course. His model was followed by Hugh Blair, one of his successors at Edinburgh, who was appointed to a Regius Chair in that subject at the university on 7 April 1762. This was in effect the first English literature chair established anywhere. Blair published his lectures in 1783, acknowledging in this book his debt to Smith. Together with Henry Home of Kames's *Elements of Criticism* (1762), itself founded on the aesthetic principles of Hume and Smith, Blair's *Lectures on Rhetoric and Belles Lettres* (1783) became a standard textbook in liberal arts courses in North America, adopted, for example, at Yale in 1785 and at Harvard three years later.

Further elements of Smith's characteristic thought appear in the second division of the lectures, for instance, the importance of the pleasure principle with reference even to didactic composition. Thus, in distinguishing between the Aristotelian and Newtonian systems of science, he echoes the claim of his history of astronomy: "It gives us a pleasure to see the phaenomena which we reckoned the most unaccountable all deduced from some principle (commonly a well-known one) and all united in one chain, far superior to what we feel from the unconnected method where everything is accounted for by itself without any referen[c]e to the others."

Elsewhere he comments on the fact that, as societies become commercial and opulent, prose is cultivated, since it is "naturally the Language of Business, as Poetry is of pleasure and amusement.... No one ever made a Bargain in verse; pleasure is not what he there aims at." He also displays awareness of cultural relativism, a mark of his historical understanding of human affairs, when he reports that Athenian oratory, designed for a democracy, would not have suited Rome with its plutocratic order of government.

As matters turned out, Smith did not hold the Chair of Logic at Glasgow long, for Hutcheson's successor, Thomas Craigie, was ill and went to Lisbon in the autumn of 1751 to regain his health. Smith had to take over some of his duties, writing to a colleague on 3 September of that year: "You mention Natural Jurisprudence and Politics as the parts of [Craigie's] lectures, which it would be most agreeable for me to take upon me to teach. I shall willingly undertake both." He had just been teaching jurisprudence at Edinburgh, and that subject and government were part of Hutcheson's moral philosophy course at Glasgow, which Smith had taken as a student. When Craigie died in Lisbon on 27 November 1751, Smith was elected to his chair. John Millar is our informant again about the four-part division of Smith's treatment of moral philosophy, and how this gives rise to the great works that bear his name:

> The first contained Natural Theology; in which he considered the proofs of the being and attributes of God, and those principles of the human mind upon which religion is founded. The second comprehended Ethics, strictly so called, and consisted chiefly of the doctrines which he afterwards published in his Theory of Moral Sentiments. In the third part, he treated at more length of that branch of morality which relates to *justice*, and which, being susceptible of precise and accurate rules, is for that reason capable of a full and particular explanation.
>
> Upon this subject he followed the plan that seems to be suggested by Montesquieu; endeavouring to trace the gradual progress of jurisprudence, both public and private, from the rudest to the most refined ages, and to point out the effect of those arts which contribute to subsistence, and to the accumulation of property, in producing correspondent improvements or alterations in law and government. This important branch of his labours he also intended to give to the public; but this intention, which is mentioned in the

conclusion of the Theory of Moral Sentiments, he did not live to fulfill.

In his *Historical View of the English Government* (1787) Millar followed up some of Smith's ideas and acknowledged how much he had benefited from hearing the lectures of the third part of the moral philosophy course, which he described as dealing with the "History of Civil Society." He also declared that in this "branch of philosophy," Montesquieu was the Bacon and "Dr Smith was the Newton." Of the last part of the course, Millar wrote:

[Smith] examined those political regulations which are founded, not upon the principle of *justice*, but that of *expediency*, and which are calculated to increase the riches, the power, and prosperity of a State. Upon this view, he considered the political institutions relating to commerce, to finances, to ecclesiastical and military establishments. What he delivered on these subjects contained the substance of the work he afterwards published under the title of An Inquiry into the Nature and Causes of the Wealth of Nations.

There is every reason to believe Smith was extremely successful teaching moral philosophy along these lines, and in 1787 when he accepted election to the office of Rector of Glasgow University, he said he remembered the thirteen years of his professorship "as by far the most useful, and, therefore, the most honourable period of my life."

During this period, Smith had the benefit of the company of Glasgow merchants who shared their practical knowledge with him. He also became fast friends with Hume, and developed links with others among the Scottish literati: John Home the poet; Adam Ferguson the pioneer sociologist; Sir John Dalrymple of Cranstoun, lawyer and historian; the medical scientists William Cullen and Joseph Black; and James Hutton, trained in medicine, but well known for his work on geological theory. Smith helped with the publication of the work of the Jacobite poet William Hamilton of Bangour, and for the first issue of the first *Edinburgh Review* (26 August 1755, for 1 January - 1 July 1755), he assessed the merits and defects of Johnson's *Dictionary*, numbering among the latter the insufficiently grammatical nature of its plan. For the second issue (March 1756, for July 1755 - January 1756) he wrote a letter proposing that the review become more cosmopolitan, and he set an exam-

Engraved portrait of Smith by John Kay

ple by providing knowledgeable evaluations of the *Encyclopédie* of Denis Diderot and Jean le Rond d'Alembert, as well as the writings of "Mr Rousseau of Geneva."

The end of his professorial period came in sight with the publication of *The Theory of Moral Sentiments*. David Hume wrote on 12 April 1759 to give Smith the "melancholy News, that your Book has been very unfortunate: For the Public seem disposed to applaud it extremely . . . and the Mob of Literati are already beginning to be very loud in its Praises." Hume went on to say that the politician Charles Townshend was so impressed by the book that he wished to make its author tutor to his stepson, Henry Scott, third Duke of Buccleuch. This came about in 1764-1766, when Buccleuch was of an age to travel to France and Geneva with Smith.

As for the contents of *The Theory of Moral Sentiments*, they do not make the book a landmark in ethics, but they do constitute a sophisticated extension of the arguments of Hutcheson and Hume asserting that moral and aesthetic judgments are based on feelings. The cornerstone of the book is the ingenious account of the role of sympathy in human interactions. Smith extends the meaning of sympathy beyond, simply, the sharing of feelings of others, to an individual's awareness that he is sharing another person's feelings. This extension permits Smith to account for different kinds of moral judgment: first, the "propriety" of an action, that it is right or wrong; and second, that praise or blame is to be attached to it. For the first kind of judgment, Smith postulates sympathy with the motive of an agent, or antipathy: for example, I place myself in someone's shoes and consider such and such a thing to be the right thing to do, or the wrong thing. For the second kind of judgment: I imagine I share the feelings of someone acted upon, either those of gratitude or resentment, which leads me to consider an action praiseworthy or blameworthy. An important part of Smith's explanation of moral feelings is that it involves giving a vital role to imagination, namely, the capacity to place oneself in someone else's shoes with respect to motives or reactions. The concept of the sympathetic imagination was an attractive one to many of Smith's readers, and had its place in the development of literary theory in his time.

To be sure, Smith maintains a distinction between imagination and reality. He notes that we desire others to sympathize with us, but we realize that they cannot experience the same feelings as we do, and so we adjust the pitch of our feelings to the level "spectators" can attain. In reverse, "spectators" will strive to identify themselves more closely with those gripped by feeling. These processes encourage social bonding through the toning down of emotional excess, on the one hand, and the deepening of emotional response, on the other. At the stage of his book when he is examining kinds of ethical teaching, Smith points out that the first process leads to the virtue of self-command, and the second to that of benevolence. His own proclivity was more in the first direction, since as a student of Hutcheson he had been much stimulated by his reading of Stoic philosophers, particularly Epictetus, the Greek slave who valued freedom of the mind above all else, and guided his actions by prudence and propriety.

Beside tracing the role of sympathy in moral judgments about others, Smith's second important contribution to ethics was developing the concept of the ideal or impartial spectator to account for the formation of our judgments of ourselves. Bereft of society, we could not think of our own character, or of the propriety of our conduct, any more than we could estimate the beauty or ugliness of our faces. According to Smith, it is society that provides a mirror in which we can see these things. Aware of society's views about conduct and beauty, for example, we can become spectators of our own behavior and appearance, and so make judgments. Of course, spectators may have limited vision because they are misinformed or prejudiced. By the same token, we may be too partial toward our conduct and features because we are dominated by self-interest or self-regard. Smith's answer to this problem is an intriguing one: "This self-deceit, this fatal weakness of mankind, is the source of half the disorders of human life. If we saw ourselves in the light in which others see us, or in which they could see us if they knew all, a reformation would generally be unavoidable. We could not otherwise endure the sight." Robert Burns reflects awareness of this idea in "To a Louse": "O wad some Pow'er the giftie gie us / To see oursels as others see us!"

Smith continues by drawing attention to the role of imagination, because the phrase he often uses as he develops his argument is the "supposed impartial spectator," that is, a construct of our own thinking and not some actual onlooker who approves or disapproves of what we do. As Smith revised his book, particularly for the sixth and last edition of his lifetime (1790), he seems to have trusted the imagination more, associating it with "reason, principle, conscience," in establishing the impartiality of the "man within," and correspondingly played down the role of social attitudes.

For many years, commentators saw a conflict between *The Theory of Moral Sentiments* in stressing the importance of sympathy and *The Wealth of Nations* in focusing on self-love: this was thought to be the heart of what August Oncken called "Das Adam Smith-Problem." The ostensible conflict is resolved on noting that the first book shows how a selfish creature such as man is led by natural means to limit his passions and aspire to happiness measured by moral quality, while the second book deals with the complementary process of aspiration to happiness of a material nature. Smith is as hardheaded in the one book as in the other, and relies on the same naturalistic explanatory principles. Thus, in *The The-*

Portion of an early draft for The Wealth of Nations, *in the hand of an amanuensis with an addition and alterations in the text by Smith (from William Robert Scott,* Adam Smith as Student and Professor, *1937)*

ory of *Moral Sentiments* we read of the "natural self-ishness and rapacity" of the rich seeking to gratify "their own vain and insatiable desires" and so being "led by an invisible hand" to distribute the means to happiness for the poor. Smith resumes the same theme in the later book when he discusses how an individual "necessarily labours to render the annual revenue of the society as great as he can." Intending only to promote his own gain, "he is . . . led by an invisible hand to promote an end which was no part of his intention." In the first instance he is directing arguments against finding an origin for moral rules in utility, and in the second he is attacking monopolies and emphasizing the value for all of the unfettered market.

Among the "Mob of Literati" who praised *The Theory of Moral Sentiments* was "an Irish Gentleman, who wrote lately a very pretty Treatise on the Sublime," as Hume put it, mentioning to Smith that he had given Edmund Burke a copy of the book. Himself an ingenious student of human nature and fashioner of a striking prose style, as is revealed in *An Philosophical Enquiry into the Origin of Our Ideas of the Sublime and Beautiful* (1757), Burke wrote to Smith that his theory "founded on the Nature of man" would last, and he commended the book's manner for being

"every where lively and elegant," indeed, "often sublime . . . particularly in that fine Picture of the Stoic Philosophy . . . which is dressed out in all the grandeur and Pomp that becomes that magnificent delusion" (10 September 1759).

We might imagine Smith equally eloquent in the lecture hall and drawing there, too, on a wide range of illustrations from literature and history to reinforce his points, and we read with sympathy of his students' regret when he announced the resignation of his Glasgow chair in January 1764, prior to his departure for France with Buccleuch. He went first to stay in Toulouse, and, finding himself without introductions to good company, he announced to Hume: "I have begun to write a book in order to pass away the time" (5 July 1764). This has been taken as a reference to *The Wealth of Nations*, though John Glassford, a Glasgow merchant, writing to Smith on 5 November of the same year, expressed hopes that he was "bringing forward at [his] Leisure Hours the usefull work that was so well advanced here." Smith had in fact stated his intention of writing such a book, making clear its connection with the jurisprudence parts of his moral philosophy course, as John Millar described them, at the conclusion of *The Theory of Moral Sentiments*: "I shall in another discourse endeavour to give an account of the general principles of law and government, and of the different revolutions they have undergone in the different ages and periods of society, not only in what concerns justice, but in what concerns police, revenue, arms, and whatever else is the object of law."

A report of Smith's lectures on jurisprudence for 1762-1763 was discovered in 1876, then published by Edwin Cannan in 1896, and a fuller version dated 1766 turned up in 1958 at the same Whitehaugh library sale which yielded the lectures on rhetoric and belles lettres. As a result of this discovery, also of the survival of an early draft of *The Wealth of Nations*, probably to be dated before April 1763, and of two fragments on the topic of the division of labor, we are well informed about the progress of Smith's thinking about political economy, as he called it, that "branch of the science of a statesman or legislator" proposing to enable the people to provide a "plentiful revenue or subsistence" for themselves and provide the state with sufficient revenue for public services such as defense, justice, education, and essential works such as roads and harbors. The economic teaching outlined by Smith in his Glasgow period attacked the notion that money is the only wealth of a state and developed a theory of economic growth. Smith argued that this growth involved division of labor, production and consumption of goods, and a money supply adequate to stimulate the circulation of goods. Following up a point already made in his Edinburgh lectures, Smith stressed the importance of free trade: "prohibitions [on trade] . . . lessen the exchange of commodities, hurt the division of labour, and diminish the opulence [of trading countries]." Smith must have found similar ideas in the *Encyclopédie*, which he had recommended to his countrymen in 1756, and in Paris in 1766 he met the authors of the articles on economics: for example, François Quesnay, the leader of the Physiocrat circle, and Anne-Robert-Jacques Turgot, who was of like mind but disclaimed system building. These encounters helped Smith gain new perspectives on economic issues such as the circulation of capital and the balance between the productive and unproductive sectors of the economy.

It was one thing, of course, to project a book on these topics; it was another thing to compose and complete it, exhibiting for the admiration of readers the "beauty of a systematical arrangement of different observations connected by a few common principles" that describe and account for the rise, decline, and replacement of successive stages of social organization answerable to the "natural wants" of self-regarding man. When Smith returned to Britain from France in 1766, he struggled for ten years to bring his book to fruition, finally delaying its publication to catch the attention of Parliament. Its members were preoccupied at the time with the conflict between the mother country and the American colonists. The economic origins of the dispute in the application of the Navigation Acts are examined in the book as an example of mistaken interventions by government.

The Wealth of Nations received favorable attention from its first publication, winning from Hume, who was well aware of the difficulty of its composition, the accolade: "Euge! Belle! Mr Smith: I am much pleas'd with your Performance, and the Perusal of it has taken me from a State of great Anxiety" (1 April 1776). Smith's central idea is that wealth or economic prosperity is created by the division of labor. This development has its origin in the drive to better one's condition coupled with the "propensity to truck, barter, and exchange." Though some friends feared that the abstruse supporting economic analysis would prevent the book being understood and hold up the institutional reforms it promoted, they need not have worried. The "very violent attack" on government restrictions and economic privilege, depicted as thwarting the drive to prosperity, appealed to the rising capitalist classes. In turn, movements for reform of the tax structure, free trade, and popular education all owed something to the thrust of the book.

From a modern standpoint, however, the more durable part of the book is the analytic one, which largely defined the scope of "classical" economics until the revision of William Stanley Jevons and Alfred Marshall in the later nineteenth century: the theory of price, and of wages, rent, and profit (book 1); the discussion of macroeconomic issues in relation to "circular flow" (book 2); the comprehensive picture of the economic history of Europe from the fall of the Roman Empire (book 3); the critique of mercantilism and physiocracy (book 4); and the review of the state's role in allocating resources for defense, justice, and public works and institutions (book 5).

Perhaps intoxicated by the reception and success of its doctrine, the nineteenth-century historian Henry Buckle declared in his *History of Civili-*

Panmure House, Edinburgh, where Smith settled after his appointment as a commissioner of customs for Scotland (engraving by Joseph Pennell)

zation in England (1857-1861) that *The Wealth of Nations* "[has] done more towards the happiness of man than has been effected by the united abilities of all the statesmen and legislators of whom history has preserved an authentic account." We may believe that the book's success owed something to its comprehensive and beautiful system, presented in fluent and persuasive prose, with its high points of witty and forceful utterance: "People of the same trade seldom meet together, even for merriment and diversion, but the conversation ends in a conspiracy against the publick, or in some contrivance to raise price"; and, "All for ourselves and nothing for other people, seems, in every age of the world, to have been the vile maxim of the masters of mankind." The book also impresses the reader with the power of its realistic or pessimistic passages, contemplating, for instance, the degradation that has overtaken wealthy and complacent educational institutions where competition is lacking, and the "mental mutilation" brought to the laboring classes by the ravages of the division of labor.

Smith's eminence as a man of letters was recognized when he was made a commissioner of customs for Scotland in 1778. He settled in Edinburgh, where his Sunday suppers at Panmure House in the Canongate drew together the literati and distinguished visitors. He took his duties in the customhouse seriously, however, and attendance there, together with the onset of old age and sickness, prevented him from completing "two other great works" he declared he had "upon the anvil." As he wrote in a letter dated 1 November 1785, one was a "sort of Philosophical History of all the different branches of Literature, of Philosophy, Poetry and Eloquence," and the other a "sort of theory and History of Law and Government." Since Joseph Black and James Hutton, his literary executors, scrupulously followed his instructions to burn his manuscripts, all that we have of these works are the pieces found in *Essays on Philosophical Subjects*, including the history of astronomy so valuable for giving Smith's account of the motives and principles underlying intellectual systems. Nevertheless, Smith was able to leave behind his published works in the state he wished. He saw *The Wealth of Nations* through five editions, including a third (1784) with extensive additions, partly coming from his experience as a customs official; and *The Theory of Moral Sentiments* through six editions, of which the last (1790) had several new parts, including one dealing with the practical and political application of moral theory. This addition was inspired to some extent by news of the outbreak of the French Revolution. Smith received copies of this edition "with very great satisfaction," just before he died on 17 July 1790. A plain inscription marks his grave in the Canongate kirkyard, where his remains share a burial plot, curiously, with those of the secretary of the customs board of his time, R. E. Phillips, who lived to be 104.

Biography:

John Rae, *Life of Adam Smith* (London & New York: Macmillan, 1895); republished with "Introduction: Guide to John Rae's *Life of Adam Smith*," by John Viner, Reprints of Economic Classics (New York: Augustus M. Kelley, 1965);

References:

James Bonar, *A Catalogue of the Library of Adam Smith*, second edition, enlarged (London: Macmillan, 1932);

Maurice Brown, *Adam Smith's Economics: Its Place in the Development of Economic Thought* (London: Croom Helm, 1988);

R. H. Campbell and A. S. Skinner, *Adam Smith* (London: Croom Helm, 1982);

Campbell and Skinner, eds., *The Origins and Nature of the Scottish Enlightenment* (Edinburgh: John Donald, 1982);

T. D. Campbell, *Adam Smith's Science of Morals* (London: Allen & Unwin, 1971);

Clyde E. Dankert, *Adam Smith: Man of Letters and Economist* (Hicksville, N.Y.: Exposition Press, 1974);

Roger L. Emerson, "Conjectural History and Scottish Philosophers," *Historical Papers 1984 Communications Historiques* (Ottawa: Canadian Historical Association, 1984), pp. 63-90;

C. R. Fay, *Adam Smith and the Scotland of His Day* (Cambridge: Cambridge University Press, 1956);

Knud Haakonssen, *The Science of a Legislator: The Natural Jurisprudence of David Hume and Adam Smith* (Cambridge: Cambridge University Press, 1981);

Istvan Hont and Michael Ignatieff, eds., *Wealth and Virtue: The Shaping of Political Economy in the Scottish Enlightenment* (Cambridge: Cambridge University Press, 1983);

A. L. Macfie, *The Individual in Society: Papers on Adam Smith* (London: Allen & Unwin, 1967);

Hiroshi Mizuta, *Adam Smith's Library: A Supplement to Bonar's Catalogue* (Cambridge: Cambridge University Press, 1967);

August Oncken, "Das Adam Smith-Problem," in *Zeitschrift für Socialwissenschaft*, edited by J. Wolf, I Jahrgang (Berlin, 1898);

D. D. Raphael, *Adam Smith*, Past Masters series (Oxford: Oxford University Press, 1985);

W. R. Scott, *Adam Smith as Student and Professor*, Glasgow University Publications, no. 46 (Glasgow: Jackson, 1937);

A. S. Skinner, *A System of Social Science: Papers Relating to Adam Smith* (Oxford: Clarendon Press, 1979);

Skinner and T. Wilson, eds., *Essays on Adam Smith* (Oxford: Clarendon Press, 1975);

Richard E. Teichgraeber III, *'Free Trade' and Moral Philosophy: Rethinking the Sources of Adam Smith's Wealth of Nations* (Durham, N.C.: Duke University Press, 1986);

T. Wilson and Skinner, eds., *The Market and the State: Essays in Honour of Adam Smith* (Oxford: Clarendon Press, 1976);

Donald Winch, *Adam Smith's Politics: An Essay in Historiographic Revision* (Cambridge: Cambridge University Press, 1978);

J. C. Wood, ed., *Adam Smith: Critical Assessments*, 4 volumes (London: Croom Helm, 1984).

Papers:
Glasgow University Library has the largest collections of Smith manuscripts: family papers, letters, reports of the lectures on rhetoric and belles lettres and of jurisprudence, and fragments connected with *The Theory of Moral Sentiments* and *The Wealth of Nations*. The Scottish Record Office, H. M. General Register House, Edinburgh, has legal and customs board papers, also an early draft of part of *The Wealth of Nations* (Buccleuch Muniments). The National Library of Scotland, Edinburgh, also has letters, including one covering an extensive revision of the first edition of *The Theory of Moral Sentiments*. The William L. Clements Library, University of Michigan, Ann Arbor, has in the Wedderburn Collection a manuscript titled "Smith's Thoughts on the State of the Contest with America 1778." Smith's library is largely divided between Edinburgh University Library and that of the Faculty of Economics, Tokyo University. There is an extensive collection of Smithiana, including copies of the translations of his books, in the Kress Library of Business and Economics, Baker Library, Harvard Graduate School of Business Administration.

Tobias Smollett
(March 1721 - 17 September 1771)

Byron Gassman
Brigham Young University

See also the Smollett entry in *DLB 39: British Novelists, 1660-1800.*

BOOKS: *The Tears of Scotland* (Edinburgh? 1746?);

Advice: A Satire (London: Printed for M. Cooper, 1746);

Reproof: A Satire. The Sequel to Advice (London: Printed for W. Owen & M. Cooper, 1747);

The Adventures of Roderick Random, 2 volumes (London: Printed for J. Osborn, 1748);

The Regicide; or, James the First, of Scotland: A Tragedy (London: Printed by subscription for the benefit of the author, 1749; London: Printed for J. Osborn & A. Millar, 1749);

The Adventures of Peregrine Pickle, in Which Are Included Memoirs of a Lady of Quality, 4 volumes (London: Printed for the author & sold by D. Wilson, 1751);

An Essay on the External Use of Water in a Letter to Dr. ****, with Particular Remarks upon the Present Method of Using the Mineral Waters at Bath in Somersetshire, and a Plan for Rendering Them More Safe, Agreeable and Efficacious (London: Printed for M. Cooper & sold by D. Wilson and by Leake & Frederick, Bath, 1752);

A FAITHFUL NARRATIVE of the base and inhuman Arts That were lately practised upon the Brain of Habbakkuk Hilding, Justice, Who Now Lies at His House in Covent-Garden, in a Deplorable State of Lunacy: A Dreadful Monument of False Friendship and Delusion, as Drawcansir Alexander, Fencing Master and Philomath (London: Printed for J. Sharp, 1752);

The Adventures of Ferdinand Count Fathom, 2 volumes (London: Printed for W. Johnston, 1753);

The Reprisal; or, the Tars of Old England: A Comedy of Two Acts (London: Printed for R. Baldwin, 1757);

A Complete History of England, Deduced from the Descent of Julius Cæsar to the Treaty of Aix la Chapelle, 1748: Containing the Transactions of One Thousand Eight Hundred and Three Years,

Tobias Smollett (portrait by William Hoare; Lilly Library, Indiana University)

4 volumes (London: Printed for James Rivington & James Fletcher, 1757-1758);

Continuation of the Complete History of England, 5 volumes (London: Printed for Richard Baldwin, 1760-1765);

The Adventures of Sir Launcelot Greaves, 2 volumes (London: Printed for J. Coote, 1762);

The Briton, nos. 1-38 (London: Printed for J. Coote, 29 May 1762 - 12 February 1763);

Travels through France and Italy: Containing Observations on Character, Customs, Religion, Government, Police, Commerce, Arts and Antiquities, with a particular Description of the Town, Territory and Climate of Nice; to which Is Added a Register of the Weather, kept during a Residence of

Eighteen Months in that City, 2 volumes (London: Printed for R. Baldwin, 1766);

The History and Adventures of an Atom, 2 volumes (London: Printed for J. Almon, 1769);

The Expedition of Humphry Clinker, 3 volumes (London: Printed for W. Johnston and B. Collins, Salisbury, 1771);

Ode to Independence (Glasgow: Printed by Robert & Andrew Foulis, 1773).

Editions: *The Works of Tobias Smollett, M.D., with Memoirs of His Life*, 8 volumes, edited by John Moore (London: Printed for B. Law, J. Johnson, G. G. & J. Robinson, R. Baldwin and twelve others, 1797);

The Works of Tobias Smollett, 12 volumes, edited by George Saintsbury (London: Gibbings, 1895-1903; Philadelphia: Lippincott, 1895-1903);

The Works of Tobias Smollett, 12 volumes, edited by W. E. Henley and Thomas Seccombe (London: Constable, 1899-1901; New York: Scribners, 1899-1901);

The Novels of Tobias Smollett, Shakespeare Head Edition, 11 volumes (Oxford: Blackwell, 1925-1926; Boston: Houghton Mifflin, 1925-1926);

An Essay on the External Use of Water, edited by Claude E. Jones (Baltimore: Johns Hopkins Press, 1935);

Travels through France and Italy, introduction by Seccombe (London & New York: Oxford University Press, 1935);

The Adventures of Peregrine Pickle, edited by James L. Clifford (London: Oxford University Press, 1964); revised by Paul-Gabriel Boucé (Oxford: Oxford University Press, 1983);

The Expedition of Humphry Clinker, edited by Lewis M. Knapp (London: Oxford University Press, 1966); revised by Boucé (Oxford: Oxford University Press, 1984);

The Expedition of Humphry Clinker, edited by Angus Ross (Harmondsworth, U.K.: Penguin, 1967);

The Adventures of Ferdinand Count Fathom, edited by Damian Grant (London: Oxford University Press, 1971);

The Life and Adventures of Sir Launcelot Greaves, edited by David Evans (London: Oxford University Press, 1973);

Travels through France and Italy, edited by Frank Felsenstein (Oxford: Oxford University Press, 1979);

The Adventures of Roderick Random, edited by Boucé (London: Oxford University Press, 1979; revised, Oxford: Oxford University Press, 1981);

The Works of Tobias Smollett, Jerry C. Beasley, general editor, 3 volumes to date (Athens: University of Georgia Press, 1988-   ).

OTHER: William Smellie, *A Treatise on the Theory and Practice of Midwifery*, edited by Smollett (London: Printed for D. Wilson & T. Durham, 1752);

Smellie, *A Collection of Cases and Observations in Midwifery*, edited by Smollett (London: Printed for D. Wilson & T. Durham, 1754);

Alexander Drummond, *Travels through Different Cities of Germany, Italy, Greece and Several Parts of Asia, as Far as the Banks of the Euphrates: In a Series of Letters*, edited by Smollett (London: Printed by W. Strahan for the author, 1754);

A Compendium of Authentic and Entertaining Voyages, Digested in a Chronological Series, 7 volumes, edited by Smollett (London: Printed for R. & J. Dodsley, Jo. Rivington, Ja. Rivington & J. Fletcher, W. Johnston, W. Strahan, and T. Jefferys, 1756);

The Modern Part of an Universal History, from the Earliest Account of Time. Compiled from Original Writers. By the Authors of the Ancient Part, 44 volumes, edited by Smollett (London: Printed for S. Richardson, T. Osborne, C. Hitch, A. Millar, John Rivington, S. Crowder, P. Davey & B. Law, T. Longman, and C. Ware, 1759-1765);

Smellie, *A Collection of Preternatural Cases and Other Observations in Midwifery*, edited by Smollett (London: Printed for D. Wilson & T. Durham, 1764);

The Present State of All Nations: Containing a Geographical, Natural, Commercial, and Political History of All the Countries in the Known World, 8 volumes, edited by Smollett (London: Printed for R. Baldwin, W. Johnston, S. Crowder, and Robinson & Roberts, 1768-1769).

TRANSLATIONS: Alain-René Lesage, *The Adventures of Gil Blas of Santillane*, 4 volumes (London: Printed for J. Osborn, 1749);

Select Essays on Commerce, Agriculture, Mines, Fisheries and Other Useful Subjects (Translated from *Journal Oeconomique*) (London: Printed for

D. Wilson & T. Durham, 1754; Philadelphia: Printed by Robert Bell, 1777);

The History and Adventures of the Renowned Don Quixote, Translated from the Spanish of Miguel de Cervantes Saavedra (2 volumes, London: Printed for A. Millar, T. Osborn, T. & T. Longman, C. Hitch & L. Hawes, J. Hodges, and J. & J. Rivington, 1755; 4 volumes, Philadelphia: Published by John Conrad, M. & J. Conrad, Baltimore; Rapin, Conrad & Co., Washington; Printed by R. Groff, 1803);

The Works of M. de Voltaire: Translated from the French, with Notes, Historical and Critical, by Dr. Smollett and Others, 25 volumes, translated by Smollett and Thomas Francklin (London: Printed for J. Newbery, R. Baldwin & others, 1761-1765);

The Adventures of Telemachus, the Son of Ulysses, Translated from the French of Messire François Salignac de la Mothe Fénelon (London: Printed for S. Crowder, T. Longman, G. Robinson, R. Baldwin, and E. Johnston, 1776).

Tobias Smollett's literary reputation properly rests upon his achievements as a great novelist who in the eighteenth century helped pioneer and establish the novel as one of the most important forms of literary expression in the past three hundred years. The five novels he published in his lifetime raised him into the company of Daniel Defoe, Henry Fielding, Samuel Richardson, and Laurence Sterne as one of the preeminent founders of the English novelistic tradition. But putting his novels against the total number of printed words for which Smollett was in one way or another responsible in his lifetime will reveal that Smollett's novels are a somewhat small part of his total output as a man of letters. Scientific writer, historian, art and literary critic, reviewer, political propagandist—these are only a few of the roles Smollett assumed while busily turning out material for London booksellers from the mid 1740s until near his death in 1771.

The birthdate of Tobias George Smollett, the third child of Archibald and Barbara Cunningham Smollett, is uncertain. Presumably it was only a few days before his baptism on 19 March 1721 in the parish church of Cardross, not far from Loch Lomond in Scotland. His father, a man of property and one educated in the law, died soon after Tobias's birth, but Tobias received an excellent grammar school education at the Dumbarton school in the neighborhood of his home. In 1736, not quite fifteen years old, he

was apprenticed to William Stirling and John Gordon, well-known Glasgow surgeons. During the next few years he not only began learning the surgeon's trade but apparently broadened the classical education of his grammar-school days by studying at the University of Glasgow.

If traditional anecdotes are to be believed, during his years in Glasgow, he also commenced his literary career by writing and circulating satirical squibs against some pretentious citizens of the city. Such anecdotes are certainly credible, because, if there is one constant in all of Smollett's subsequent writing, it is his dislike of those who abuse their station by tyrannizing others and by failing to recognize and encourage merit. There is frequently a touch of defensiveness—some have called it quarrelsomeness—in Smollett's personality and in his writing that reveals his feeling that he had had to struggle too hard to gain deserved recognition. An explanation in the preface to *Roderick Random* (1748) of his purpose in writing that work, his first novel, might serve as an epigraph for the entire canon of his works: "I have attempted to represent modest merit struggling with every difficulty to which a friendless orphan is exposed, from his own want of experience, as well as from the selfishness, envy, malice, and base indifference of mankind."

In 1739 Smollett secured a release from his apprenticeship articles and left Glasgow to seek his fortune in London. With him he carried the manuscript for *The Regicide* (1749), a five-act blank-verse tragedy based on the assassination of James I of Scotland in 1437. For nearly a decade after his arrival he struggled with double-dealing playhouse managers and fickle patrons—at least such was Smollett's version of the experience—in a vain attempt to get *The Regicide* staged.

Smollett did have his mind taken off this struggle when, in March 1740, he received a warrant as a surgeon's second mate in the British navy. A few months later he found himself sailing for the New World with the ill-fated British expedition to Cartagena. For Smollett this expedition, which failed in its mission to weaken Spanish power in the Caribbean and South America, became a classic example of official incompetence and brutality. Events and circumstances he witnessed during his naval experience gave birth to important episodes in the story of Roderick Random, the writing of whose fictional adventures Smollett began sometime after his discharge from the navy.

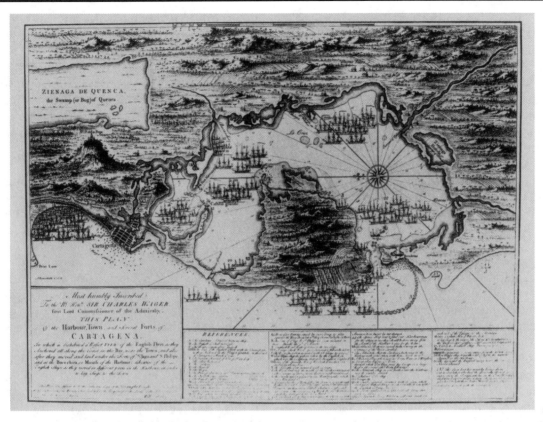

Map of the harbor at Cartagena, Colombia, where Smollett served as a surgeon's second mate during the ill-fated British naval expedition of 1741

Biographers have virtually no information on the whereabouts or activities of Smollett from late 1741 to mid 1744. It is known that in May 1744 he was settled again in London, having married a Jamaican heiress, Anne Lassells, and apparently having decided to try to establish a surgical practice. But literary ambitions soon overtook his interest in surgery. In 1746 his first significant composition, *The Tears of Scotland*, was published. Written in verse to express feelings aroused in him by the crushing of Bonnie Prince Charlie's rebellion at the Battle of Culloden (16 April 1746) and William Augustus, Duke of Cumberland's subsequent harsh pacification of the highlands of Scotland, Smollett's ode is an early expression of his indignation in the face of the brute exertion of power and position.

His indignation found further vent about the same time in the writing of *Advice* (1746), a verse satire imitative of Alexander Pope. As Pope had done in his verse satires, Smollett accuses numerous contemporaries, some by name, some by innuendo, of promoting the decadence of English society by spreading corruption and lewdness throughout the land. The same indignation

and the same themes appear in Smollett's second verse satire, *Reproof*, published in January 1747.

The publication in January 1748 of Smollett's first novel, *The Adventures of Roderick Random*, gained him his first significant popularity with the reading public. Like his creator, the picaresque Roderick serves for a time as a surgeon's mate aboard a naval vessel dispatched as part of the expedition to Cartagena. Although harshly satirical and filled with characters and events that are clearly fictional, the Cartagena section of *Roderick Random* (something less than one-sixth of the entire book) has often been taken as a valuable account of that historical episode. Eight years after the publication of *Roderick Random*, when his indignation over the sorry conduct of the leaders of the expedition had softened somewhat, Smollett found occasion to publish a more evenhanded account of the expedition in his "An Account of the Expedition against Carthagene," contained in volume 5 of *A Compendium of Authentic and Entertaining Voyages* (1756) which he edited. Skillfully made up of his own observations and extracts from reports of the expedition published by others, Smollett's account, despite its tone of factual presentation and rational judgment, makes clear his continuing contempt for the misjudgments, malfeasance, and incompetence of those officers who should have made the expedition a success.

It is typical of Smollett's versatility and energy that within the few years before and after the publication of *Roderick Random*, he was trying still to get his tragedy staged, publishing three poetic works, accepting a commission to provide the text for a dramatic spectacle, and undertaking the translation of a famous French novel. The dramatic spectacle, a production planned by the impresario John Rich, was to be based on the Greek legend of Alceste, with music by the great George Frideric Handel. Although Smollett apparently completed his part of the project and Handel set several of Smollett's lyrics to music, Rich's production never materialized. The translation Smollett undertook was that of Alain-René Lesage's *Gil Blas* (1715-1735), the well-known picaresque novel that Smollett identified in his preface to *Roderick Random* as a model for his own work. Smollett's translation, available late in 1748 or early in 1749, was immediately popular.

Being finally convinced that *The Regicide* would never gain sufficient favor with theatrical patrons and managers to get it on the stage, Smollett resorted to publishing it by subscription in 1749. For the published text, he prepared a brief preface in which he recounted the neglect, broken promises, and treacherous encouragement that had marked his efforts to get his youthful production onto the stage. The preface, marked by Smollett's narrative clarity and his sense of injury at the hands of established promoters, is much more readable than the artificial blank verse and melodramatic action of the play itself.

In spite of a few setbacks and a continuing sense that merit such as his was not being properly recognized, by the beginning of the 1750s Smollett was getting along well with the booksellers and reading public of England. A short trip to Paris in 1750 may have provided him ideas and material for his next novel, *The Adventures of Peregrine Pickle*, published in four volumes in 1751. Its scoundrelly hero, like the traditional picaro, moves about from place to place not only in England but on the Continent, finding skulduggery and charlatanism—and contributing his own share of them—everywhere he goes.

The first readers of *Peregrine Pickle* focused most attention on an extremely long interpolated narrative titled "The Memoirs of a Lady of Qual-ity," the actual memoirs of Lady Frances Anne Vane, whose troubled marriage and adultery brought her much notoriety. How and why her memoirs got into *Peregrine Pickle* is pretty much a mystery. Quite possibly Lady Vane gave Smollett her own written account of her errant life, which he then edited and recast—to what degree readers can only speculate—into the form in which it was published.

In 1751-1752 Smollett had his first experience with book reviewing by contributing three pieces to the recently begun *Monthly Review*, the first British periodical to be wholly devoted to reviewing and providing excerpts from publications regularly coming off the presses of England. Smollett's reviews, one of a novel and two of books on medical subjects, although hardly substantial enough to provide sound generalizations about his literary or medical views, presage ideas and the authoritative style that were to become important in Smollett's later reviews.

Smollett's interest in scientific and medical matters is evidenced again in his *Essay on the External Use of Water*, published in 1752. The first part of this essay merely presents Smollett's thesis that bathing in plain water is medically preferable to bathing in mineral water. In the second part, written in a more characteristic Smollettian vein, he inveighs against the unsanitary conditions of the popular health and pleasure resort of Bath. In doing so, he picks up his favorite theme, that of merit unrecognized, as he angrily defends Archibald Cleland, a surgeon who had been dismissed from the Bath Hospital presumably for making certain proposals to improve conditions in the city's medical facilities. His satiric disapproval of conditions in Bath was to emerge again years later when his Welsh travelers in *Humphry Clinker* (1771) spend several uncomfortable, disgusting days at the resort.

Smollett returned to the novel with the publication in 1753 of *The Adventures of Ferdinand Count Fathom*. One of the most unusual elements in his third novel is the dedication "TO DOCTOR * * * * * *," that is, to Doctor Smollett himself. One effect of this dedication is to carry on Smollett's satirical attacks against prejudiced patrons. More important, the dedication, which serves also as a preface to the work, contains Smollett's most pointed definition of a novel and what amounts to a brief theory of realistic fiction. With the preface to *Roderick Random* and bits and pieces that can be picked up from Smollett's review work, it constitutes a useful critical state-

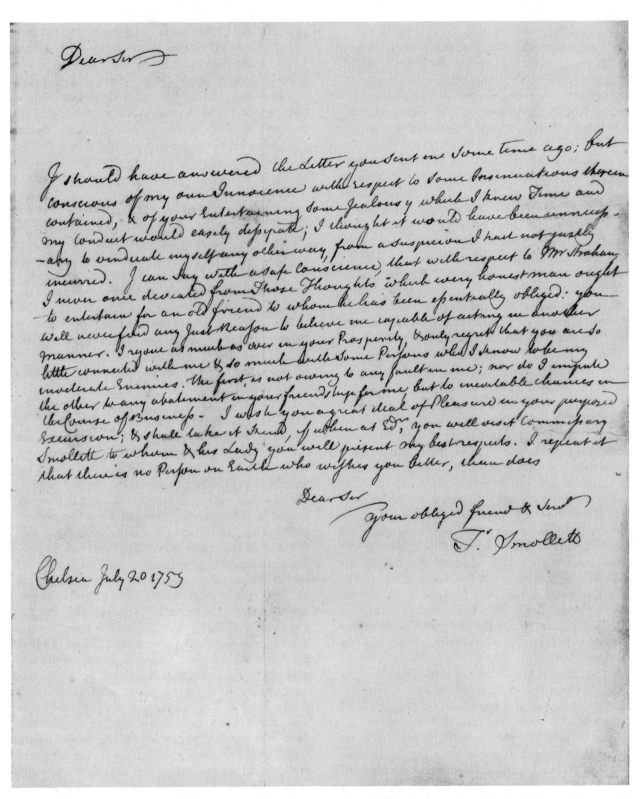

Letter to William Strahan, who had printed some of Smollett's works and lent him money but had also printed pamphlets attack-
ing Smollett by "inveterate Enemies" such as Ralph Griffiths, editor of the Monthly Review *(MA 1229; Pierpont*
Morgan Library)

ment against which Smollett's intents and achievements in his own novels can be assessed. Although certain elements of the novel have had their admirers—a couple of scenes in particular have long attracted notice for their Gothic qualities—its history has largely been one of critical neglect. Recently, however, its reputation has been rising as critics have found some intriguing psychological and moral dimensions within the book.

In December 1755 Smollett published proposals in the London newspapers "For Publishing Monthly, the Progress or Annals of Literature and the Liberal Arts." At the end of the following February, making good on his proposals, Smollett and a small group of associates published the first number of the *Critical Review*. Doubtlessly looking at the already established *Monthly Review*, which would be the main rival of the new journal, the proposals complained of having "seen the noble Art of Criticism reduced to a contemptible Manufacture subservient to the most sordid Views of Avarice and Interest, and carried on by wretched Hirelings, without Talent, Candour, Spirit, or Circumspection." The proposal then presented the platform of Smollett and his associates: "Urged by these considerations, they have resolved to task their Abilities, in reviving the true Spirit of Criticism, and exert their utmost Care in vindicating the Cause of Literature from such venal and corrupted Jurisdiction."

One doubts that English criticism had degenerated to the state Smollett describes. On the other hand, the criticism and book reviewing that Smollett supervised and did himself during the next seven years in the pages of the *Critical Review* significantly affected the book scene of England, helping to raise standards of disinterestedness among book reviewers and voicing an intelligent concern for the need of responsibility among writers and a cosmopolitan taste among readers.

Smollett's prejudices did of course show through from time to time—he became an enthusiastic promoter of the spurious Ossianic works of James Macpherson—but the real impact of the *Critical Review* on readers and writers may be gauged by the numerous attacks its sharply worded reviews provoked upon it. Smollett's best-known quarrel as a reviewer was occasioned by his brief but unrestrained review (May 1758) of a pamphlet written by Admiral Charles Knowles to justify his part in a recent unsuccessful military and naval expedition against Rochefort on the coast of France. For Smollett this pamphlet was exactly the kind of abuse of power and place that repeatedly raised his anger, and his anger led him to publish some clearly injudicious comments on Knowles and his pamphlet. Knowles replied by laying a charge of libel against Smollett. Legal proceedings dragged on for some time, but eventually Smollett was found guilty of libel and in November 1760 was sent to the King's Bench Prison for almost three months.

In spite of—or perhaps because of—such quarrels and problems, many writers and much of the reading public clearly recognized the authority of the *Critical Review* and looked to it for guidance in their adoption of ideas and their choice of books. Smollett's own reviews, numbering more than three hundred according to a checklist compiled by James G. Basker in *Tobias Smollett: Critic and Journalist* (1988), cover virtually the entire spectrum of publication, from books on specialized medical topics to items of belles lettres, from political pamphlets to treatises on agriculture. Particularly innovative are his reviews not of books, but of individual works of art and of art exhibits.

Smollett's work as editor and reviewer on the *Critical Review* must have been a full-time occupation. Even so, in 1757 he saw the staging of his two-act farce *The Reprisal* and the publication of all but the final volume of his four-volume *Complete History of England* (volume 4 appeared in January 1758). There is evidence that Smollett wrote one or more comedies soon after his disappointments with *The Regicide*, but none was staged and the text of none has survived. It must then have been particularly gratifying to Smollett to finally see a theatrical work of his presented as an afterpiece to the evening's fare at the Theatre Royal in Drury Lane on 22 January 1757. *The Reprisal; or, The Tars of Old England* is set aboard a French naval vessel, where a private English party has been taken captive but is eventually rescued by a crew of British sailors. Smollett may have conceived the work partly as propaganda to raise a patriotic spirit among the English and to belittle the French as the two nations confronted each other at the beginning of the Seven Years' War. *The Reprisal* was a modest success, having several performances during the next few years and eventually being included in a 1786 anthology titled *A Collection of the Most Esteemed Farces and Entertainments Performed on the British Stage*.

A Complete History of England, which Smollett probably wrote in little more than a year during

1755-1756, is one of the most impressive of his literary accomplishments, not least because of its bulk and comprehensiveness. Written in a straightforward but pungent and attractive style, Smollett's work covers the history of England from the days of Julius Caesar to 1748, the year of the treaty of Aix-la-Chapelle. Although it has been characterized at times, particularly during the nineteenth century, as a Tory work, it generally remains free of strong political bias. Because Smollett was almost always cynical about the motives and self-proclaimed public reputations of persons in power, there are practically no heroes in the history, neither anointed kings nor usurpers, royalists nor republicans, Whigs nor Tories. As might be expected in a work by a novelist turned historian, the verbal portraits of various historical figures are rich in detail and perceptive comment on their motives and behavior.

The first edition of *A Complete History of England* sold well. Shortly after its appearance, its publishers began bringing it out in weekly installments at six pennies each. By September 1758 Smollett could report that weekly sales for these pamphlets were more than ten thousand copies, making it the most financially rewarding of any of Smollett's literary enterprises. Its success prompted Smollett to carry his history beyond 1748. Four volumes of the *Continuation of the Complete History of England* appeared in 1760 and 1761, and a fifth volume, bringing the history down to the early years of the reign of George III, appeared in 1765. Since these volumes are a history of his own times, they provide an excellent index to Smollett's judgments on his age, in which he found much to admire but which by and large seemed to his Augustan sensibilities an era of tastelessness, corruption, and general decadence.

Smollett's history, or at least a part of it, continued to be republished and widely read well into the nineteenth century. (There is an amusing reference to it in chapter 10 of William Makepeace Thackeray's 1847-1848 novel *Vanity Fair*.) Smollett's Scottish contemporary David Hume had written and published a history of England at almost exactly the same time that Smollett had, but Hume's history ended with the Glorious Revolution of 1688. After the deaths of both Smollett and Hume, a bookseller made the rather strange decision to add Smollett's history after 1688 to Hume's history and publish it as a continuation of Hume's. In that truncated form

the history continued to be republished for its nineteenth-century readers.

While incessantly turning out work of his own during the 1750s, Smollett somehow found time to contribute to and edit medical and travel works written by others, produce a biting satire on Henry Fielding titled *A FAITHFUL NARRATIVE of the base and inhuman Arts That were lately practised upon the Brain of Habbakuk Hilding* (1752), translate *Don Quixote* into English (1755), compile and edit a seven-volume *Compendium of Authentic and Entertaining Voyages* (1756), and act as editor on what eventually turned out to be the forty-four-volume *Modern Part of an Universal History* (1759-1765) and the twenty-five-volume English translation *The Works of M. de Voltaire* (1761-1765).

There is an interesting sketch in *Humphry Clinker* related to this period of almost frantic literary activity for Smollett. Two of that novel's traveling party pay a Sunday visit to Smollett at his home in Chelsea, where he lived from 1750 to 1763. They find him hosting an odd assortment of "unfortunate brothers of the quill," with whom Smollett consults during the course of the afternoon. The sketch pictures Smollett as a well-established man of letters tolerantly encouraging, supervising, and mediating among a troublesome bunch of hack writers to whose doings he is trying to give some touch of respectability.

In 1761, still heavily involved with the *Critical Review*, Smollett took on the editorship of another new journal, the *British Magazine*. This new magazine printed a miscellany of material, such as news of the day, scientific articles, literary essays, stories, and poems. Smollett himself wrote many such items, but he also included contributions from Samuel Johnson, Oliver Goldsmith, and other noteworthy writers of the day. The most significant feature of the *British Magazine*, however, was its serialized publication of Smollett's novel *The Adventures of Sir Launcelot Greaves* in twenty-five installments (January 1760-December 1761). Smollett's serialization of *Sir Launcelot Greaves* in the *British Magazine* may be considered the opening move in establishing a practice that was to become the most common means of first publication of British novels in the Victorian age.

Sir Launcelot Greaves is Smollett's Quixote, an idealist who sets out to right the wrongs of the world. It is appropriate that *Sir Launcelot Greaves*, published in two volumes in 1762, should first appear in a magazine that often

*Caricature of Smollett holding a shield labeled "The Briton" to fend off arrows shot at a jackboot (John Stuart, Earl of Bute) by
John Wilkes, William Pitt, and others*

printed articles dealing with contemporary issues and concerns because of all Smollett's novels it is the one that seems most alert to contemporary social and political matters. Conditions in private madhouses, electioneering, and provincial law courts are three of the journalistic topics Smollett critically looks at during his telling of Sir Launcelot's adventures.

Even with responsibilities for the *Critical Review* and the *British Magazine* still heavy on his hands, Smollett was somehow persuaded in 1762 to undertake yet another journalistic project, the writing and editing of a weekly political sheet to defend John Stuart, Earl of Bute, who had replaced the popular William Pitt as the chief minister of George III. Trying to repress the opposition and garner support for his policy of bringing an end to the Seven Years' War, Bute employed his fellow-Scot Smollett to write and edit *The Briton*, which began propagandizing for the Bute ministry in May 1762. For the next nine months, Smollett fired weekly broadsides against Bute's opponents in an attempt to vilify them while supporting Bute. Soon after the first appearance of *The Briton*, Bute's opponents counterat-

tacked by sponsoring their own new weekly, *The North Briton*, under the direction of the daring, witty, and shameless John Wilkes. Until *The Briton* ceased publication in February 1763, upon the signing of the Peace of Paris, it and *The North Briton* were the loudest voices in the paper war which erupted over Bute's policy. Although he tried to maintain a tone of reasonable discourse, nowhere is Smollett's talent for satiric rhetoric and name-calling of public men more evident than in many passages of *The Briton*.

By the time Smollett discontinued *The Briton*, his health had deteriorated alarmingly. Adding to his emotional and physical exhaustion was the death of the Smolletts' only child, Elizabeth, in April 1763. Feeling terribly abused by what he considered the distortions and libels that the paper war had spread about him and his cause and, moreover, eventually feeling neglected and disregarded even by those who had sponsored *The Briton*, Smollett in the summer of 1763 gave over all his activities on the London book scene and left England with his wife for a two-year sojourn in France and Italy. Although the main object of his travels was the search for more salubrious climes, Smollett apparently soon realized that he could capitalize on his travels by gathering material for his next book. Within a few months of his return to England in 1765, he was at work compiling a collection of letters reporting the events and observations of his travels. The outcome of his work was the publication in May 1766 of *Travels through France and Italy*. Although some of the letters in the book may be based on letters Smollett wrote to actual correspondents during his time abroad, most likely Smollett simply decided to write an account of his travels by casting it in the form of letters addressed to an imaginary correspondent. (All the letters in the collection are addressed merely to "Dear Sir.") Whatever their origin, the letters are a combination of the satiric complaints of a British traveler vexed by Continental customs and the careful observations of a trained journalist reporting on the history, manners, climate, institutions, topography, and curiosities of foreign lands.

Smollett's *Travels through France and Italy* was well received by the English reading public as being both entertaining and useful. But its reputation was greatly altered by a passage that Laurence Sterne put in his *A Sentimental Journey through France and Italy* (1768). In his chapter "In the Street: Calais" Sterne satirizes Smollett as "the learned Smelfungus," who set out on his travels "with the spleen and jaundice, and every object he pass'd by was discoloured or distorted— He wrote an account of them, but 'twas nothing but the account of his miserable feelings." Sterne's characterization of Smollett and of his book soon passed for current, and the work was little regarded in the nineteenth century. Its reputation has, however, been revived in our century, and it has come to be looked upon as one of Smollett's most attractive works.

Smollett never returned to the frantic pace of writing and editing that had been his before he left for France and Italy, but his pen was not idle after his return to England. The most important project of 1767-1768 apparently was the editing and partial writing of an eight-volume world geography and current history titled *The Present State of All Nations* (1768-1769). This compilation has never earned much attention, and its only real significance seems to be the fact that the English and Scottish sections were quite likely written by Smollett himself and include material that he later reworked and incorporated into his last novel, *Humphry Clinker*.

Smollett circa 1770 (portrait by an unknown Italian artist; National Portrait Gallery, London)

Smollett's health continued to decline in the few years after his return to England. In the fall of 1768 he left England for the last time, heading for Italy, where he hoped to be eased of his physical miseries. A few months after Smollett had left for Italy, there appeared on the shelves of London booksellers a coarse political satire with the title of *The History and Adventures of an Atom* (1769). Although no author's name was attached to or associated with the book, the book world soon began to claim that Tobias Smollett was the author. Only in recent years has sufficient evidence been assembled to fix the work firmly in the Smollett canon and increase scholarly attention to it.

In the guise of a narrative history about Japanese political life, *The History and Adventures of an Atom* allegorizes the events and persons of contemporary English politics, particularly those from the period just before and after the accession of George III in 1760. In penning *The History and Adventures of an Atom* Smollett clearly was still feeling strongly the rancor of the days spent with *The Briton* at the end of the Seven Years' War.

Some of that rancor still occasionally peeks through the pages of Smollett's final literary achievement, *The Expedition of Humphry Clinker*.

Perhaps begun before he left England, but undoubtedly finished during his last years in Italy, that novel was published in London on 15 June 1771, just soon enough for Smollett to receive a few copies before his death in Leghorn on 17 September of the same year. Put together as a series of letters written by five members of a Welsh household traveling through England and Scotland, the novel is a curious assortment of travel reports, jeremiads on the sorry state of commercial, urban England (especially London and Bath), picaresque adventures, and sentimental celebrations of the idyllic life, far from the madding crowd, still to be found in Scotland and rural England. The crotchety but benevolent Matthew Bramble, head of the traveling party and writer of a good share of the letters in the novel, has often been seen as a representation of Smollett himself.

Humphry Clinker was generally welcomed by contemporary reviewers, many of whom commented on it more as a travel book and an account of its own times than as a novel. It soon became a popular favorite, early established as a classic of the eighteenth century and displaying the skills of Smollett at his best both as a novelist and as a journalist. And it has remained the most attractive and readable of all Smollett's works. William Hazlitt, in his assessment of Smollett in *Lectures on the English Comic Writers* (1819), best explained the wide appeal of *Humphry Clinker* when he called it "the most pleasant gossiping novel that ever was written."

Few works have provided a more appropriate valedictory to their author's life and career than did *Humphry Clinker* to Smollett's. Patches from practically all the concerns and endeavors of his literary life can be discovered in the fabric of this last novel, reinforcing the conviction that in the breadth of his interests, in the depth of his convictions, in his disdain for the self-serving and the intellectually irresponsible, and in his vision of an ideal society both of men and of letters, Smollett was consistently one of the most farsighted and gifted, certainly one of the most energetic and persistent, writers of his age. For twentieth-century readers who would know some of the best of what was thought and felt at the midpoint of the eighteenth century, the writings of Smollett are a good place to start.

Letters:
The Letters of Tobias Smollett, M.D., edited by

Edward S. Noyes (Cambridge: Harvard University Press, 1926);
The Letters of Tobias Smollett, edited by Lewis M. Knapp (Oxford: Clarendon Press, 1970).

Bibliographies:
Robert D. Spector, *Tobias Smollett: A Reference Guide* (Boston: G. K. Hall, 1980);
Mary Wagoner, *Tobias Smollett: A Checklist of Editions of His Works and an Annotated Secondary Bibliography* (New York: Garland, 1984).

Biographies:
David Hannay, *Life of Tobias George Smollett*, with a bibliography by John P. Anderson (London: Walter Scott, 1887);
Lewis M. Knapp, *Tobias Smollett: Doctor of Men and Manners* (Princeton: Princeton University Press, 1949).

References:
James G. Basker, *Tobias Smollett: Critic and Journalist* (Newark: University of Delaware Press, 1988);
Charles L. Batten, Jr., "*Humphry Clinker* and Eighteenth-Century Travel Literature," *Genre*, 7 (December 1974): 392-408;
Edward A. Bloom, "Neoclassic 'Paper Wars' for a Free Press," *Modern Language Review*, 56 (October 1961): 481-496;
Fred W. Boege, *Smollett's Reputation as a Novelist* (Princeton: Princeton University Press, 1947);
Paul-Gabriel Boucé, "Smollett and the Expedition against Rochefort (1757)," *Modern Philology*, 65 (August 1967): 33-38;
Robert Adams Day, "The Authorship of the *Atom*," *Philological Quarterly*, 59 (Spring 1980): 187-193;
Robin Fabel, "The Patriotic Briton: Tobias Smollett and English Politics," 1756-1771," *Eighteenth-Century Studies*, 8 (Fall 1974): 100-114;
Byron Gassman, "*The Briton* and *Humphry Clinker*," *Studies in English Literature*, 3 (Summer 1963): 397-414;
Gassman, "Smollett's *Briton* and the Art of Political Cartooning," *Studies in Eighteenth-Century Culture*, 14 (1985): 243-258;
Robert Giddings, *The Tradition of Smollett* (London: Methuen, 1967);
M. A. Goldberg, *Smollett and the Scottish School: Studies in Eighteenth-Century Thought* (Albu-

querque: University of New Mexico Press, 1959);

Morris Golden, "Travel Writing in the *Monthly Review* and *Critical Review, 1756-1775,*" *Papers on Language and Literature*, 13 (Spring 1977): 213-223;

Damian Grant, *Tobias Smollett: A Study in Style* (Manchester: Manchester University Press, 1977);

Donald Greene, "Smollett the Historian: A Reappraisal," in *Tobias Smollett: Bicentennial Essays Presented to Lewis M. Knapp*, edited by G. S. Rousseau and P.-G. Boucé (New York: Oxford University Press, 1971), pp. 25-56;

Eugène Joliat, *Smollett et la France* (Paris: Librairie Ancienne Honoré Champion, 1935);

Joliat, "Smollett, Editor of Voltaire," *Modern Language Notes*, 54 (June 1939): 429-436;

Claude E. Jones, Introduction to *An Essay on the External Use of Water by Tobias Smollett* (Baltimore: Johns Hopkins Press, 1935);

Jones, *Smollett Studies* (Berkeley & Los Angeles: University of California Press, 1942);

Jones, "Tobias Smollett (1721-1771)—the Doctor as Man of Letters," *Journal of the History of Medicine and Allied Sciences*, 12 (July 1957): 337-348;

George M. Kahrl, *Tobias Smollett: Traveler-Novelist* (Chicago: University of Chicago Press, 1945);

Philip J. Klukoff, "Smollett and the *Critical Review*: Criticism of the Novel, 1756-1763," *Studies in Scottish Literature*, 4 (October 1966): 89-100;

Lewis M. Knapp, "The Publication of Smollett's *Complete History* ... and *Continuation,*" *Library*, fourth series 16 (December 1935): 295-308;

Louis L. Martz, *The Later Career of Tobias Smollett* (New Haven: Yale University Press, 1942);

Martz, "Smollett and the Expedition to Carthagena," *PMLA*, 56 (June 1941): 428-446;

Martz, "Tobias Smollett and the *Universal History,*" *Modern Language Notes*, 56 (January 1941): 1-14;

Peter Miles, "A Semi-Mental Journey: Structure and Illusion in Smollett's *Travels,*" *Prose Studies*, 5 (May 1982): 43-60;

Daniel M. Musher, "The Medical Views of Dr. Tobias Smollett (1721-1771)," *Bulletin of the History of Medicine*, 41 (September-October 1967): 455-462;

Alice Parker, "Tobias Smollett and the Law," *Studies in Philology*, 39 (July 1942): 545-558;

Scott Rice, "The Satiric Persona of Smollett's *Travels,*" *Studies in Scottish Literature*, 10 (July 1972): 33-47;

Rice, "Smollett's *Travels* and the Genre of Grand Tour Literature," *Costerus*, 1 (1972): 207-220;

Derek Roper, "The Politics of the *Critical Review*, 1756-1817," *Durham University Journal*, 53 (June 1961): 117-122;

Roper, "Smollett's 'Four Gentlemen': The First Contributors to the *Critical Review,*" *Review of English Studies*, new series 10 (February 1959): 38-44;

John Sekora, *Luxury: The Concept in Western Thought, Eden to Smollett* (Baltimore: Johns Hopkins University Press, 1977);

John F. Sena, "Smollett's Persona and the Melancholic Traveler: An Hypothesis," *Eighteenth-Century Studies*, 1 (Summer 1968): 353-369;

Osbert Sitwell, Introduction to *Travels through France and Italy* (London: Chiltern Library, 1949), pp. v-xi;

Robert Donald Spector, "Smollett's Traveler," in *Tobias Smollett: Bicentennial Essays Presented to Lewis M. Knapp*, edited by G. S. Rousseau and P.-G. Boucé (New York: Oxford University Press, 1971), pp. 231-246;

Spector, *Tobias Smollett* (New York: Twayne, 1968);

E. Ashworth Underwood, "Medicine and Science in the Writings of Smollett," *Proceedings of the Royal Society of Medicine*, 30 (June 1938): 961-974;

Arnold Whitridge, *Tobias Smollett: A Study of His Miscellaneous Works* (New York, 1926).

Papers:
Relatively few documents and letters in Smollett's hand have survived, and many of these are privately owned. The manuscripts for his novels have all been lost. The following libraries hold small collections of Smollett papers, mostly letters: the National Library of Scotland; the University of Glasgow Library; the British Library; the Library of the Royal College of Surgeons; the Pierpont Morgan Library in New York; the Henry E. Huntington Library in San Marino, California; Harvard University Library.

Horace Walpole

(24 September 1717 - 2 March 1797)

Pat Rogers
University of South Florida

See also the Walpole entry in *DLB 39: British Novelists, 1660-1800.*

SELECTED BOOKS: *Aedes Walpolianae; or, A Description of the Collection of Pictures at Houghton-Hall in Norfolk, the Seat of the Right Honourable Sir Robert Walpole, Earl of Orford* (London, 1748);

A Letter from Xo Ho, a Chinese Philosopher at London, to His Friend Lien Chi at Peking (London: Printed for N. Middleton, 1757);

A Catalogue of the Royal and Noble Authors of England, With Lists of Their Works, 2 volumes (Strawberry Hill, 1758);

Fugitive Pieces in Verse and Prose (Strawberry Hill, 1758);

Anecdotes of Painting in England; With some Account of the principal Artists; And Incidental Notes on other Arts; Collected by the late Mr. George Vertue; And now digested and published from his original MSS., 4 volumes (Strawberry Hill: Printed by Thomas Farmer, 1762-1771 [i.e., 1780]);

The Castle of Otranto, A Story. Translated by William Marshal, Gent. From the Original Italian of Onuphrio Muralto, Canon of the church of St. Nicholas at Otranto (London: Printed for Tho. Lownds, 1765 [i.e., 1764]);

Historic Doubts on the Life and Reign of King Richard the Third (London: Printed for J. Dodsley, 1768);

The Mysterious Mother. A Tragedy (Strawberry Hill, 1768);

A Description of the Villa of Horace Walpole, Youngest Son of Sir Robert Walpole Earl of Orford, at Strawberry-Hill, near Twickenham (Strawberry Hill: Printed by Thomas Kirgate, 1774);

A Letter to the Editor of the Miscellanies of Thomas Chatterton (Strawberry Hill: Printed by T. Kirgate, 1779);

Hieroglyphic Tales (Strawberry Hill: Printed by T. Kirgate, 1785);

Postscript to the Royal and Noble Authors (Strawberry Hill, 1786);

The Works of Horatio Walpole, Earl of Orford, 5 volumes, edited by Mary Berry, as Robert Berry (London: Printed for G. G. & J. Robinson and J. Edwards, 1798);

Memoires of the Last Ten Years of the Reign of George the Second, 2 volumes, edited by Lord Holland (London: John Murray, 1822);

Memoirs of the Reign of King George the Third, 4 volumes, edited by Sir Denis Le Marchant (London: Richard Bentley, 1845);

Journal of the Reign of King George the Third, from the Year 1771 to 1783, 2 volumes, edited by John Doran (London: Richard Bentley, 1859).

Editions: *Memoirs and Portraits,* edited by Matthew Hodgart (London: Batsford, 1963);

The Castle of Otranto, edited by W. S. Lewis (London: Oxford University Press, 1969);

Hieroglyphic Tales, introduction by Kenneth W. Gross (Los Angeles: William Andrews Clark Memorial Library, 1982);

Memoirs of King George II, 3 volumes, edited by John Brooke (New Haven: Yale University Press, 1985).

Horace Walpole was a significant figure in literary history, but his reputation would stand even higher if he had excelled in what today are regarded as the "major" genres. He wrote a pioneering book which initiated the Gothic novel; he produced a high-flown tragedy which impressed the Romantics; and he composed serviceable verse satires, a favorite Augustan form. Yet none of these works represents his main achievement. It is in a category now relegated to "miscellaneous prose" that Walpole made an imperishable contribution to literature: first, in a remarkable series of historical memoirs, bequeathed to posterity at his death, and second, in some four thousand personal letters, which many consider the finest body of private correspondence in the English language. In addition Walpole, a leading virtuoso of his day, compiled the engaging *Anecdotes of Painting in England* (1762-1780); catalogued the

Horace Walpole, 1756 (portrait by Sir Joshua Reynolds; Art Gallery of Ontario, Toronto; bequest of John Paris Bickell, 1952)

productions of "Royal and Noble Authors"; and ruffled his fellow antiquarians with a novel defense of an unlikely hero in his *Historic Doubts on the Life and Reign of King Richard the Third* (1768). Walpole's shorter pieces in prose include an essay on landscape gardening, which helped to define this branch of artistic activity, some periodical essays, and diverse journalism. Finally, Walpole served as a handmaiden to literature as editor, publisher, and printer.

In the "Brief Notes" on his own life which he compiled in 1779, he tells us, "I was born on Arlington Street near St. James's London Sept. 24, 1717, O[ld] S[tyle]." He mentions his godparents, but not his parents, perhaps assuming that everyone would be able to identify his father as the great Robert Walpole, who at this date was on the brink of his long period of power as Britain's longest-serving prime minister. Young Horatio's mother, née Catherine Shorter, was the daughter of a wealthy merchant, and she had already

borne her husband five children, of whom two sons and a daughter survived along with her youngest child, Horatio, who, from his earliest years, was usually called Horace.

Recent scholarship has found no substantial evidence to support an allegation deriving ultimately from Lady Mary Wortley Montagu, to the effect that Horace was the son not of Robert Walpole but of a member of the famous Hervey family. Much more solidly authenticated is Robert Walpole's liaison with Maria Skerrett, whom he eventually married after his wife's death. Despite these infidelities, real or assumed, Horace developed a strong affection for both his parents; in his childhood he was certainly closer to his mother, but in later life he developed an almost equally passionate loyalty to the memory of his father. At the age of nine, in April 1727, the boy was sent away from home, according to the habits of his class, and entered Eton College. He stayed there until the eve of his seventeenth birthday in September 1734. He made important contacts, which is, after all, one of the purposes of attending such a school. The friends included his cousin Henry Conway, George Selwyn, a socialite later noted for his excruciating puns, and George Montagu, the recipient of many of Walpole's finest letters. In addition he formed a literary coterie known as the Quadruple Alliance, of whom the other key member was Thomas Gray.

Looking back on his school days in a letter that he wrote to Montagu from Cambridge, Walpole portrayed Eton as a site of pastoral fantasy: "Dear George, were not the playing fields of Eton food for all manner of flights? . . . As I got further into Virgil and *Clelia*, I found myself transported from Arcadia, to the garden of Italy, and saw Windsor Castle in no other view than the *capitoli immobile saxum* ('the enduring rock of the Capitol'—*Aeneid*, IX, 448) . . . I can't say I am sorry I was never quite a schoolboy; an expedition against bargemen, or a match at cricket may be very pretty things to recollect; but thank my stars, I can remember things that are very near as pretty" (6 May 1736). Thomas Gray was to depict this childhood innocence against a more somber background in his "Ode on a Distant Prospect of Eton College" (1747); his friend Walpole characteristically lays the emphasis on charm, melancholy, literary association, and private yearning.

In March 1735 Walpole moved on to King's College, Cambridge, where Gray had been a member of another college, Peterhouse, since the previous October. Walpole spent almost four years at the university without achieving much in terms of public honors (indeed, like young men of his class, he never bothered to take a degree), but indulging in the kind of undergraduate activity which may be of more ultimate significance for most students. He made an abortive attempt to study mathematics; he wrote Latin poetry; he got religion briefly, and visited prison to pray with the inmates—the kind of behavior that earned for Christopher Smart the reputation of a madman and would have done as much for Walpole if he had persisted in his ways beyond student life. He spent a good deal of time at home in London, learning to dance and fence among other things. In 1736 he made his first visit to his father's great new palace at Houghton—his first trip to Norfolk, the county of his forebears. It was the beginning of a lasting affection for the house and its fine collection of pictures, and, though Walpole affected feelings of total ennui

whenever he was forced to spend any length of time in the country, he did respond to the romantic surroundings of Houghton. The death of his mother in 1737 confirmed the end of adolescence, and the natural rite de passage for a youth entering on manhood was a Grand Tour. Gray left Cambridge in the same year; he had no obvious prospects and seemed the natural companion for his friend. In a fateful moment the decision was made, and the two young men set out from Dover on Easter Day in 1739.

The tour lasted until September 1741; it is among the best-known phases in Walpole's career owing to a variety of incidents and his justly famous letters. After some weeks of routine socializing in Paris and Rheims, the pair made their way south late in the summer. On 28 September 1739 Walpole wrote to his friend Richard West of "Precipices, mountains, torrents, wolves, rumblings, Salvator Rosa. . . . Here we are, the lonely lords of glorious desolate prospects." This letter was written from "a hamlet among the mountains of Savoy," and Walpole took pleasure in devising fantasies to match the grandeur of his surroundings near the Grande Chartreuse monastery: "Yesterday I was a shepherd of Dauphiné; today an Alpine savage; tomorrow a Carthusian monk; and Friday a Swiss Calvinist." His fondness for such playacting survived with him throughout life; the value of this tour to hallowed regions was not (as with so many callow youths) to induce a vague sense of history, but to allow Walpole to instill wilder and more exotic elements in his register of poetic tones. The opportunity expanded with a four-day crossing of the Alps in wintry conditions, en route to Turin. Walpole lamented the uncouth rocks and uncomely inhabitants of the Alps, and matters were made worse when a "cruel accident" occurred —a young wolf leapt out from a wood and carried off Walpole's pet spaniel. The anecdote can be seen as an emblem of the comfortable, easygoing, seemingly effeminate Walpole in his confrontation with savage nature: if so, the lesson was not lost on Walpole, whose imagination compassed much that was dark and forbidden amid all the serene domesticity of his later life.

The two travelers moved on, arriving in good time for the carnival at Florence, where they were the guests of Horace Mann, the British envoy; Mann was to become Walpole's most regular correspondent. In February 1740 Walpole and Gray went on to Rome, where the conclave to elect a new Pope was in session, and Jacobite in-

Strawberry Hill from the southeast (painting by Paul Sandby; Castle Museum, Nottingham)

trigues festered in the years leading up to the second Stuart rising. A trip to Naples included an obligatory visit to the recently discovered site at Herculaneum: "There is nothing of the kind known in the world; I mean a Roman city entire of that age, and that has not been corrupted with modern repairs" (letter to Richard West, 14 June 1740). Meanwhile relations between the two friends had started to fray; Walpole was worldly and sociable, whereas Gray preferred that quiet study of antiquarian relics which always excited Walpole's impatience. They managed to preserve at least a semblance of friendship for a time, but after they left Florence for Reggio on their return journey northward, the resentments boiled over into an open quarrel. In later years Walpole took the blame on himself, as having been "inattentive and insensible to the feelings of one I thought below me" (letter to William Mason, 2 March 1773); but he was the more generous in spirit of the two men, and it is hard to believe that Gray was not equally at fault. At all events, the breach was so severe that even a serious illness which brought Gray back from Venice to Walpole's bedside at Reggio did not promote a reconciliation. The two young men made their way home separately. Walpole proceeded through Venice and Genoa, thence by sea to Antibes, and then up through the south of France toward Paris. He eventually arrived back in England in the middle of September 1741.

Coming up to his twenty-fourth birthday, with his education behind him, Walpole stood poised for a glittering career: the obvious route lay through politics. Indeed, he returned to England to find that he had just been elected to Parliament by the undemanding electorate of Callington, a tiny Cornish borough, where the hundred voters were sufficiently under government control to provide the necessary majority. (Walpole and his colleague each received forty-four votes, against twenty-three and twenty-one for the two opposition candidates.) But the days of the great Sir Robert Walpole were numbered: his long hold on power was visibly slipping away, and early in 1742 he was forced to resign. The following month Horace made his maiden speech in the House of Commons, opposing a motion to appoint a special committee of inquiry into his father's administration.

Thus began a period of twenty-seven years in Parliament. Horace set out with high hopes, perhaps envisaging a resplendent political life in which he would be Walpole the Younger much as, later in the century, the younger Pitt was to succeed his eminent father. It was not to be: he was

Many of Walpole's own books, as well as poems by his friend Thomas Gray, were printed at Walpole's Strawberry Hill press, which he founded in 1757.

too obstinately loyal to his father's memory and slow to adapt to the new Whig bosses, the Pelham brothers—one of these, Thomas Pelham-Holles, Duke of Newcastle, remained his bête noire for the rest of his life. His memoirs are studded with cruel observations on Newcastle, whom he portrays as both absurd and dangerous: "He thought he possessed secrets, if he did but whisper and was whispered." Equally, Walpole clung for years to the illusion that his cousin Henry Conway would prove a considerable figure in the world of politics and would reward Horace with marks of gratitude. Neither the general nor the particular assumption turned out to have any warrant. Walpole grew steadily more disenchanted with Westminster intrigues and the charades, as he saw them, of life at court. His final departure from an active role was marked by a letter to his constituency in 1767, published in the London press. But by this time he had been for many years virtually silent in Parliament, an observer rather than a participant; he might well have anticipated Edward Lear's words, "Long ago he was

one of the singers, / But now he is one of the dumbs."

Other interests had taken over, and his literary career had started to occupy a major part of his attention. His first substantial work was a description of the pictures at Houghton, *Aedes Walpolianae*, published in 1748 with a dedication to his father dated 24 August 1743. Since Sir Robert died March 1745, this work was in effect a posthumous tribute to the glory that had been England (in Horace's view) during the years in which he grew up. A sumptuous volume in royal quarto, printed at the author's expense to be given away privately (only one hundred copies in all), it consists of a capricious and opinionated introduction, followed by a loving account of the fine collection of old masters which Walpole senior had assembled. The Raphaels, Titians, and Poussins were mostly dispersed within Horace's own lifetime, when his nephew George Walpole, third Earl of Orford, recouped his debts by selling the collection to Catherine the Great for a reputed sum of forty thousand pounds. This was a heavy blow to Horace, both as a symbolic repudiation of his father's achievement and as an irreparable artistic loss.

For the next decade Walpole wrote nothing of great moment. His attention had been diverted by the purchase and remodeling of his house near the banks of the Thames at Twickenham. It was a small and unappealing villa when Walpole first saw it in the spring of 1747; but it had marvelous views across the river to Richmond, and he saw its potential straightaway. He bought the remainder of the lease from its tenant and in 1749 put through a private act of Parliament to purchase the property outright. In the deeds he discovered the old name "Strawberry Hill" and conferred immortality on the place when he adopted this title. The original site was only five acres, but by a series of further acquisitions he gradually annexed an area almost ten times as large. The house itself was revolutionized by additions, alterations, and refurbishments. In waves of activity Walpole's building mania caused turrets, arches, and Gothic filigree to sprout in all directions. Internally the rooms were semifunctional, especially the library, but many had bestowed on them fanciful names and chivalric offices. Here began a revolution in the taste of the nation; yet it was also a kind of physical autobiography of Walpole.

His description of the scene when he first discovered Strawberry Hill is justly renowned, occurring in a letter to Conway on 8 June 1747: "It is set in enamelled meadows, with filigree hedges. . . . Two delightful roads . . . supply me continually with coaches and chaises: barges as solemn as barons of the Exchequer move under my window; Richmond Hill and Ham Walks bound my prospect; but, thank God! the Thames is between me and the Duchess of Queensbury. Dowagers as plenty as flounders inhabit all around, and Pope's ghost is just now skimming under my window by a most poetical moonlight." The progress of Strawberry Hill is recounted in a long series of wonderful letters, which set out the owner's ideals and visions as he embarked on his laborious plan to surround himself with a reincarnation of baronial splendor. To take a single instance, Walpole's letter to Horace Mann on 12 June 1753 gives a detailed picture of work in progress: "Imagine the walls covered with (I call it paper, but it is really paper painted in perspective to represent) Gothic fretwork: the lightest Gothic balustrade to the staircase, adorned with antelopes (our supporters) bearing shields; lean

windows fattened with rich saints in painted glass, and a vestibule open with three arches on the landing pace, and niches full of trophies of old coats of mail, Indian shields made of rhinoceros's hides, broadswords, quivers, long bows, arrows and spears—all *supposed* to be taken by Sir Terry Robsart in the holy wars." There is a serious aesthetic program in mind here but also a delightful sense of play which the sprightly prose beautifully conveys. Strawberry Hill became a matter for correspondence, but it was also a kind of underlying spirit in its own right. Here Walpole planned his various activities, established his press, formed his "Committee of Taste" to supervise the re-creation of the house, and coordinated his numerous ventures in literature and the visual arts. But Strawberry Hill was also the base for his monumental correspondence, and without the security of this ever-changing structure it is doubtful whether Walpole could (or would have wished to) have kept up the flow of letters.

He snatched the time for occasional bursts of literary activity. He had finally been reconciled with Gray and in 1751 saw through the press his friend's *Elegy Wrote in a Country Churchyard*. This inspired him to publish six of Gray's early poems (almost everything he had written, in fact) in 1753, with illustrations by Richard Bentley, one of the team engaged in the designs for Strawberry Hill. In turn this venture gave Walpole the idea for setting up a press of his own, an ambition to be realized with the inception of the Strawberry Hill press in 1757. Again Gray was the favored author, though the *Odes* thus introduced to the world (including "The Progress of Poesy" and "The Bard") elicited little but incomprehension among the public, a fact which probably surprised Walpole less than it did Gray.

A year later the press printed Walpole's own *Catalogue of the Royal and Noble Authors of England* in two handsome volumes. A larger edition was produced for the trade by Robert Dodsley, and the work excited some derision. The problem was, as R. W. Ketton-Cremer has observed, "He wished to write books on antiquarian subjects without becoming associated with the pedantry and dinginess of antiquaries; he vaguely thought that his books, the productions of a gentleman's leisure, ought to be exempt from the searching criticism of professionals." Such an act grew harder all the time to maintain. Walpole could reject the Society of Antiquaries, claiming that they "seldom do anything but grow an-

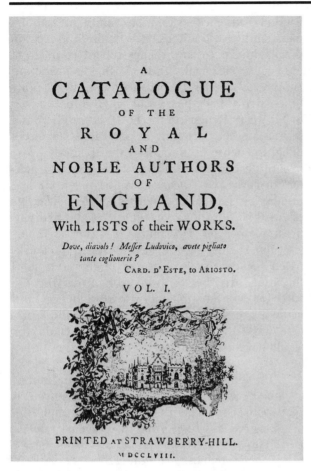

A

CATALOGUE

OF THE

R O Y A L

AND

NOBLE AUTHORS

OF

ENGLAND,

With LISTS of their WORKS.

Dove, diavolo ! Meſſer Ludovico, avete pigliato
tante coglionerie ?
CARD. D' ESTE, to ARIOSTO.

VOL. I.

PRINTED AT STRAWBERRY-HILL.
M DCC LVIII.

*Title page for the first book by Walpole to be printed at
Strawberry Hill*

tiquated themselves"; but he was in truth a learned and sensitive student of the past. As he produced more and more books and acted as midwife to many more through the activity of the press, he became a kind of professional himself.

The title of his *Fugitive Pieces* (1758) claims amateur status still, and the impression of a bare two-hundred-copy printing indicates a continuing adherence to "private" distribution. Nevertheless, the book was printed and published, not handed about in manuscript; it contains an impressive variety of poetry and prose, including essays written for the widely circulated magazine the *World* in 1753 and the highly popular *Letter from Xo Ho*, a hastily written pamphlet satirizing affairs in 1757, the low point of the Seven Years' War from a British point of view, and a year disfigured for Walpole by the execution of the hapless Admiral John Byng—"a perfect tragedy, for there were variety of incidents, villainy, murder and a hero," as he wrote to Mann on 17 March 1757. *Fugitive Pieces in Verse and Prose* confirms Walpole's aspira-

tions as a serious writer, even though the individual items are slender: it is a retrospective collection by an artist who climbed out of gentility into authorship only at the age of forty.

On 1 January 1760, with typical neatness of design, Walpole began to work on a new project: editing the papers of the engraver and antiquarian George Vertue. He had acquired a large mass of manuscripts after Vertue's death in 1756. They were full of hitherto unknown details concerning earlier English painting but had been left in considerable disarray. Walpole reduced them to order and in the process was responsible for the first major work of art history in the English language. *Anecdotes of Painting in England*, which appeared in four volumes between 1762 and 1780, remains one of his most distinguished achievements. He had help from Gray and others, but essentially Walpole had to make his own sense of Vertue's materials, which were little more than jottings and ana. The work has been seen as a crucial example of the "ordering of the arts" which was under way in a crucial period of twenty years—other key documents include Samuel Johnson's *Lives of the Poets* (1779, 1781), Thomas Warton's *History of English Poetry* (1774-1781), the histories of music by Charles Burney (1776-1789) and Sir John Hawkins (1776), and the *Discourses* (1769-1791) of Sir Joshua Reynolds. Later editions of Walpole's book included new material discovered along the way.

The book is organized chronologically, starting with misty origins in the reign of Henry III, leading through the Tudor period and major figures of the seventeenth century. The main account then concludes with the reign of Queen Anne. A catalogue of engravers and an account of Vertue's life form one appendix; the fourth volume brings the account up to the last reign, that of George II, and ends with William Kent. Walpole also incorporated his "Essay on Modern Gardening," which was sometimes republished separately. It is one of the most absorbing sections of the entire work, forming as it does the first sustained literary response to a major phenomenon in eighteenth-century taste—that is, the rise of landscape-gardening. A celebrated passage lauds the contribution of William Kent: "At that moment appeared Kent, painter enough to taste the charms of landscape, bold and opinionative enough to dare and to dictate, and born with a genius to strike out a great system from the twilight of imperfect essays. He leaped the fence, and saw that all nature was a garden." Modern readers might expect that a similar tribute would be paid to Kent's successor, Capability Brown, but Walpole simply writes, "Did living artists come within my plan, I should be glad to do justice to Mr. Brown; but he may be a gainer, by being reserved for some abler pen." The modest yet faintly ironic touch is characteristic.

Better known today is Walpole's tale of medieval (literally, early Renaissance) prodigies, set in a vague Italianate landscape—*The Castle of Otranto*, dated 1765 but published as a regular trade edition at the end of 1764, in a print run of five hundred copies, soon doubled by the scale of demand, beginning a long series of editions and translations. Simply as a work of fiction, it contributed less to the later "Gothic" genre than did Ann Radcliffe's *Mysteries of Udolpho* (1794), but it created a whole range of atmospheric devices which were to extend the bounds of the novel beyond the fairly timid realism which had dominated its early history. Above all, it was Walpole's unblushing acceptance of the supernatural which led some readers to see in it a revival of the ancient spirit of romance and to attribute to it a power equivalent to that of epic or even of Shakespearean tragedy. Exorbitant as some of this praise now seems, it is important to understand the historical significance of such comparisons: the revival of romance was a necessary first stage in the romantic revival itself, and the defense by Walpole of Shakespeare against Voltaire (in the preface to the second edition of *Otranto*, dating from April 1765) promoted one reviewer to commend "the noble spirit which Mr. W. has shewn in defence of the glory of this country." In any case the novel manages to survive, less as a major example of the art of fiction than as a full-blooded carnival of Gothic effects. Like Strawberry Hill, Otranto draws on "the gloomth of abbeys" to create a world remote from everyday reality but with its own logic of dream, vision, and miracle. "I gave my imagination free rein," said Walpole, and that is the point, as much as the precise outcome of such a process.

In 1765 Walpole began a series of visits to Paris, where he achieved a social success almost equivalent to that of David Hume, David Garrick, and Laurence Sterne in the same period. The most important contact he made was with the blind and aged Marie de Vichy-Champrond, Marquise du Deffand, a highly intelligent woman with a rich past and an immense cultural presence by reason of her famous salon, attended by many of the great figures in the Enlightenment. Despite disparities in age and background, the two established a close and lasting relationship, ended only by the death of Mme du Deffand fifteen years later. It was a relation conducted largely by correspondence, despite visits by Walpole to Paris in succeeding years, and it had a higher emotional temperature than most of his friendships. Mme du Deffand was spontaneous, touchy, resentful, and combative; she brought out in Walpole areas of vulnerability he had managed to disguise in his dealings with men and even with Englishwomen such as Mary Lady Hervey, and Anne, Countess of Upper Ossory. One generally reads the incoming side of Walpole's correspondence, where it survives, with little interest, waiting for the main performer to come back onstage. In the case of Mme du Deffand, it is different; she is eloquent in ways that Walpole, with all his sensitivity and polish, found difficult to attain. Nonetheless she elicited from him in a handful of letters some feeling and inward passages.

By this time Walpole was distancing himself from public affairs and was able to direct more of his time toward literary pursuits. The first product of this labor was his curious tract *Historic Doubts on the Life and Reign of King Richard the Third*, published by James Dodsley in February 1768. This is quite a short book, but it packs a considerable punch, as the continuing disagreement over Richard's alleged villainy would indicate. Walpole was the first person seriously to suggest that the king had been maligned by posterity, especially in the plays of Shakespeare. His crucial contention is that Richard had been innocent of the murders of the princes in the Tower, with some wilder surmises appended (one of the princes survived, he believed, to reemerge as the pretender Perkin Warbeck). The historical evidence he claimed to have dug up is not impressive; indeed some is based on misidentification of key records. As usual, his reasoning has a casual, take-it-or-leave-it air, suggesting a deliberately paradoxical or purely academic effort: the preface even proclaims the fact that "the attempt was mere matter of curiosity and speculation." But Walpole was too able a casuist to reveal the extent of his commitment, and one should be unwise to accept Walpole's protestations at face value. There are serious currents beneath the surface: the author's dislike of establishment orthodoxy, his willingness to identify with outsiders (at some level he felt himself stigmatized and misun-

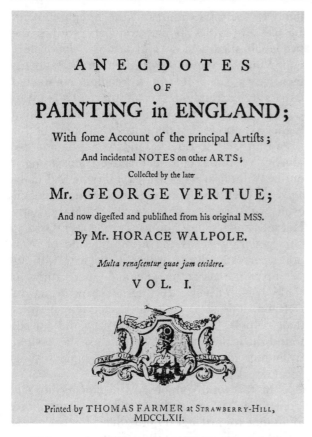

ANECDOTES

OF

PAINTING in ENGLAND;

With fome Account of the principal Artifts;

And incidental NOTES on other ARTS;

Collected by the late

Mr. GEORGE VERTUE;

And now digefted and publifhed from his original MSS.

By Mr. HORACE WALPOLE.

Multa renafcentur quae jam cecidere.

VOL. I.

Printed by THOMAS FARMER at STRAWBERRY-HILL, MDCCLXII.

Title page for the first major work of art history in the English language

derstood, like Richard), his contempt for mindless antiquarians without a real idea to set forth, his attachment to unpopular causes. Quite a furor blew up after the book was published; Walpole conducted himself with his usual sangfroid, suppressing a reply to a criticism of the book which was sent to him by Hume.

One other work dating from 1768, this one a production of the Strawberry Hill Press, is his tragedy *The Mysterious Mother*. This achieved notoriety as a result of its theme (incest), but it holds some independent interest by reason of its surprising narrative power and a dramatic tautness one would not have anticipated from the relaxed garrulity of Walpole's style as a letter writer. The blank verse is less obviously dependent on Shakespeare than is the case with most eighteenth-century attempts at poetic drama. There was little prospect that a play on such a theme could find a home on the public stage; Walpole contented himself with printing fifty copies at his own press and distributing them to selected friends. One of these went to the aristocratic artist Lady Diana Beauclerk, of whose talents Wal-

pole held a possibly exaggerated estimate. She made seven drawings to illustrate the play; Walpole was so pleased with these that he had James Essex build a special repository in order to house the drawings. The "Beauclerk Closet" was constructed in a slim Flemish turret alongside the Round Tower at Strawberry Hill. *The Mysterious Mother* did not succeed in what was its evident aim: reviving high tragedy in English. Walpole's postscript gives a rapid account of the decline of tragedy:

> Theatrical genius lay dormant after Shakespeare; walked with some bold and glorious, but irregular and often ridiculous flights in Dryden, revived in [Thomas] Otway; maintained a placid pleasing kind of dignity in [Nicholas] Rowe, and even shone in his Jane Shore. It trod in sublime and classic fetters in Cato [by Joseph Addison], but void of nature or the power of affecting the passions. In [Thomas] Southern it seemed a genuine ray of nature and Shakespeare; but falling on an age still more Hottentot, was stifled in those gross and barbarous productions, tragicomedies. It turned to tuneful nonsense in the Mourning Bride [by William Congreve]; grew stark mad in [Nathaniel] Lee.... It recovered its senses in [John] Hughes and [Elijah] Fenton.... We have not mounted again above the two last.

Despite this outmoded historical underpinning, the play is a work of some psychological interest and again a testimony of Walpole's power to surprise.

The years 1769 and 1770 were dominated by the arrival on the scene of the youthful prodigy Thomas Chatterton, an episode in Walpole's life that does not figure in the "Short Notes" of autobiography. Chatterton, then sixteen, wrote to Walpole in March 1769 to offer "Several curious Manuscripts." These proved to be the famous Rowley collection allegedly produced by a fifteenth-century priest. At first Walpole was impressed, but he was advised by Gray and William Mason to proceed cautiously and wrote back to Chatterton rejecting the authenticity of the works and less tactfully suggesting that their true author should return to his calling as an apprentice attorney. Infuriated, Chatterton attacked Walpole in the pages of a scandal sheet known as the *Town and Country Magazine*. Four months after his move to London, in August 1770, Chatterton was dead, either by suicide or by some form of accidental drug abuse. His criticism of Walpole's alleged duplicity stuck, and not even a temperate review of the case, privately printed in 1779 and then published in London in 1782, could stem the flow of opinion against Walpole. Only in recent times has a more balanced view prevailed, and while it is now possible to see Chatterton as much more than a crude forger, we can also recognize the fact that Walpole behaved with his usual meticulous propriety throughout the episode.

Some comparatively quiet years followed Chatterton's death: Walpole listed a few key events in the "Short Notes" on his life, including the entry "My nephew Lord Orford went mad, by quack medicines that he had taken for the scurvy, which by carelessness and catching cold flew up into his head." Walpole wrote a one-act farce, began publishing a series of *Miscellaneous Antiquities*, and then in 1774 brought out one of the most appropriate books ever printed at Strawberry Hill, *A Description of the Villa of Horace Walpole*. This volume includes an inventory of the choice collections built up over the years, including pictures, furniture, objects of *virtu*, and other "curiosities." Walpole spared no pains in itemizing the most minute of his acquisitions. Ketton-Cremer calls it "a fascinating compilation, in which every picture and drawing on the walls, almost every cup and saucer in the China Closet, is mentioned with affectionate particularity." A shortened version of the catalogue was prepared for the benefit of the many visitors who made regular pilgrimages to tour the house almost every day of the week. The fourth volume of *Anecdotes of Painting*, in print since 1771, was finally published in 1780. Similarly Walpole made a collection of his works to date and had them printed in two volumes around 1770, but they were never published in that form.

The last two substantial works published in Walpole's lifetime both date from 1785. The first is a translation by Louis-Jules-Barbon Mancini-Mazarini, Duc de Nivernais, of the *Essay on Modern Gardening*, published with the English text on facing pages in an edition of four hundred copies. The other is a strange collection, *Hieroglyphic Tales*, of which as few as six copies were printed at the Strawberry Hill press. The number of copies in this edition matches the number of fairy stories in the volume, fantastic narratives on the model of the *Arabian Nights* with an element of the childlike, but also an occasionally macabre humor. They have never attained the currency of *The Castle of Otranto* and might have been forgotten but for Walpole's distinction in other branches of writing. Along with the almost contemporaneous *Vathek* (1786) of William Beckford,

Mary and Agnes Berry, the sisters who befriended Walpole in his last decade of life

Hieroglyphic Tales is evidence of a vein of surreal imagination in the twilight of Augustan orthodoxy.

The last decade of Walpole's life passed quietly for the most part and without major literary output. Many of his oldest friends were dead by the late 1780s, and those who survived, including Horace Mann, dropped away one by one. His new acquaintance was headed by a pair of sisters, the Misses Mary and Agnes Berry, who moved to Twickenham in 1788. An immediate consequence was the composition of some agreeable "Reminiscences" addressed to the sisters and first published in *The Works of Horatio Walpole, Earl of Orford* (1798). These "Reminiscences" took the form of nine chapters of anecdotes, mostly concerning royal and noble personages from the earlier part of the century. Relaxed and informal, they lack the grand historiographic ambition of the main series of Walpole's memoirs, and substitute persiflage and jest, though there is still room for a thrust at the duke of Newcastle.

The Berry sisters became Walpole's chief support in his declining years. It has even been speculated that he proposed marriage to Mary, the elder and more spirited of the girls (at the time of their first meeting, when Horace was seventy, Mary was twenty-five and Agnes twenty-four). There does not seem to be any evidence to sustain this idea. Mary had an admirer, a middle-aged general, who was serving on the Continent. She was also the object of what was then an illicit if not an incomprehensible passion nurtured by Walpole's friend the sculptress Anne Damer, the daughter of a man he had once revered, Henry Conway. Walpole arranged for the Berry sisters to take over the almost adjoining property of Little Strawberry Hill, where another of his friends, the great actress Kitty Clive, had lived until her death in 1785. The relationship continued on its gentle course: it was Mary who oversaw the 1798 publication of Walpole's posthumous collection of works.

Two other events cast something of a shadow over Walpole's declining years, one personal, one public. In December 1791, at the age of seventy-four, he succeeded as fourth earl of Orford on the death of his intermittently mad and always improvident nephew. He inherited the debts, legal tangles, the "mortifying ruin" of Houghton (which he was now too frail to visit), and a whole new set of unexpected problems. As he wrote to Hannah More on the first day of 1792, "I am overwhelmed with troubles, and with business—and business that I do not understand—law, and the management of a ruined estate, are subjects ill-suited to a head that never studied anything that in worldly language is called useful. The tranquility of my remnant of life will be lost"—and so up to a point it was. A few days later, on 18 January, he wrote to Lady Ossory of his discovery that he was "the poorest Earl in England." Walpole never took his seat in the House of Lords. He was too old to make any impact as a politician, and, unlike many upper-class Englishmen with a taste for genealogy and feudal bric-a-brac, he lacked many of the attributes of vulgar snobbery.

The second crucial event of these years was the outbreak of the French Revolution, together with the ensuing Terror. Like his contemporaries Edmund Burke, Edward Gibbon, and Dr. Charles Burney, he found his former toleration sorely tested. In his own case his liberal attitude had amounted to outright Whiggery, with a kind of closet republicanism thrown in: he had been an ardent supporter of the American revolutionaries and had seen merits in a figure such as John Wilkes that were invisible to most of the ruling class. But he was appalled by the mounting tide of violence after the fall of the Bastille, including the killing of the French king and queen, and

the rattle of the tumbrils during the reign of Robespierre. Letter after letter proclaims his revulsion against the progress of events in France. "The new legislators were pedants, not politicians, when they announced the equality of all men," he told Sir David Dalrymple on 21 September 1790. He foresaw increasing anarchy in September 1791, and on the twenty-seventh he wrote to Conway, "The new Assembly will fall on the old, probably plunder the richest, and certainly disapprove of much they have done; for can eight hundred new ignorants approve of what has been done by twelve hundred almost as ignorant, and who were far from half agreeing?"

Even the death of Robespierre himself brought fresh anxieties, recounted to Lady Ossory on 4 September 1794: "Atrocious a monster as Robespierre was, I do not suppose the alleged crimes were true, or that his enemies, who had all been his accomplices, are a whit better monsters." His strongest condemnation, matching the words of Burke in fervor, comes in a letter to Lady Ossory written on 29 January 1793, after the execution of Louis XVI: "*Savages, barbarians,* etc., were terms for poor ignorant Indians and blacks and hyaenas, or, with some superlative epithets, for Spaniards in Peru and Mexico, for Inquisitors, or for enthusiasts of every creed in religious wars. It remained for the enlightened eighteenth century to baffle language and invent horrors that can be found in no vocabulary." Today one may be surprised by the virulence of this language and by the extent to which the topic dominated Walpole's later correspondence, but one must remember that he had been a creature of the ancien régime, albeit an enlightened one, and had tasted in full what Talleyrand was to call the "pleasure of living" in the prerevolutionary world.

At length Walpole's protracted life came to an end. He died at the age of seventy-nine, on 2 March 1797, at the London home in Berkeley Square which he had taken in 1778 and where he spent his final winters. He left a complex legacy. His reputation stood to fall, as he was already a figure from the past, having outlived all his friends and contemporaries. The appearance in 1798 of five sumptuous volumes in royal quarto, *The Works of Horatio Walpole, Earl of Orford,* did not change very much: Mary Berry had simply followed her instructions, and the major works already published formed the staple of the set. However, the last volume was composed of some of Walpole's letters, providing the first

26.

She appeared in the court of justice, and with some wit and infinite abuse treated the laughing public with the spectacle of a Woman who had held the reins of Empire metamorphosed into the Widow Blackacre. Her grandson in his suit demanded a sword set with diamonds given to his Grandsire by the Emperor. "I retained it, said the Beldame, lest he should pick out the diamonds & pawn them."

I will repeat but one more instance of her insolent asperity, which produced an admirable reply of the famous Lady Mary Wortley Montague. Lady Sundon had received a pair of diamond earrings as a bribe for procuring a considerable post in Queen Caroline's family for a certain Peer; & decked with those jewels, paid a visit to the old Duchess, who as soon as She was gone, said, "what an impudent creature, to come hither with her bribe in her ear!" "Madam, replied Lady Mary Wortley, who was present, how should people know where wine is sold, unless a bush is hung out?"

The Duchess of Buckingham was much elated by owing her birth to James 2d, as the Maylt was by the favour of his Daughter. Lady Dorchester, the Mother of the former, endeavoured to curb that pride, & one should have thought took an effectual method, tho one few Mothers would have practiced; "you need not be so vain, said the old Profligate, for you are not the King's Daughter, but Colonel Graham's." Graham was a fashionable Man of those days, and noted for dry humour: His legitimate Daughter the Countess of Berkshire was extremely like to the Duchess of Buckingham: "well! well! said Graham, Kings are all-powerfull, and one must not complain, but certainly the same Man begot those two Women." To discredit the Wit of both Parents the Duchess never ceased labouring to restore the House of Stuart, & to mark her filial devotion to it. Frequent were her journies to the Continent for that purpose. She always stopped at Paris, visited the Church where lay the unburied body of James, and wept over it. A poor Benedictine of the Convent observing her filial piety, took notice to her Grace that the velvet pall that covered the Coffin was become threadbare—and so it remained!

Finding all her efforts fruitless, and perhaps aware that her plots were not undiscovered by Sr Robert Walpole, who was remarkable for his intelligence, She made an artfull double, & resolved to try what might be done thro him himself. I forget how She contracted an acquaintance with Him—I do remember that more than once He received letters from the Pretender Himself, which probably were transmitted thro Her. Sr Robert always carried them to George 2d, who endorsed and returned them. That negotiation not succeeding, the Duchess made a more home push. Learning his extreme fondness for his Daughter [afterwards Lady Mary Churchill] She sent for Sr Robert and asked him if he recollected what had not been thought too great a reward to Lord Clarendon for restoring the Royal Family? He affected not to understand her—"was not he allowed, urged the zealous Duchess, to match his Daughter to the Duke of York?" Sr Robert smiled, & left Her.

Sr Robert being forced from Court, the Duchess thought the moment favorable, & took a new journey to Rome—but conscious of the danger She might run of discovery, She made over her Estate to the famous Mr Pulteney [afterwards Earl of Bath] and left the Deed in his Custody. What was her astonishment when on her return she redemanded the Instrument—It was mislaid—He could not find it—He never could find it! The Duchess grew clamorous—at last his Friend

Page from a fair copy, dated 13 January 1789, of the "Reminiscences" Walpole wrote for Mary and Agnes Berry (MA 493; Pierpont Morgan Library)

glimpse which the world at large had enjoyed of his correspondence. They elicited some mixed opinions: one commentator in 1810 admired their "playful ease, enlivened by quaint turns and occasionally sparkling with bon mots," but also deplored "a sickly fastidious delicacy, on the very verge of affectations." The poet Anna Seward was one who came on the letters with a sense of surprise: "His delightful letters have not only amused me infinitely, but filled me with contrition for the long injustice which I had done to his heart" (letter to Miss Fern, 7 February 1806). Further letters appeared in stages: those to George Montagu in 1818, to the antiquarian William Cole in the same year, to Francis Seymour Conway, Earl of Hertford (Henry Conway's elder brother), in 1825, and crucially those to Horace Mann in 1833.

The series of letters to Mann prompted the best-known appraisal of Walpole ever made—that is, the damaging, unfair, but brilliantly conducted, denunciation by Thomas Babington Macaulay of "the most eccentric, the most artificial, the most fastidious, the most capricious, of men" (*Edinburgh Review*, October 1833). In a few glittering paragraphs Macaulay defined an image of Walpole which has never been entirely obliterated, despite all the efforts of historians, scholars, and critics. A series of sharp epigrams flowed from Macaulay: "His features were covered by mask within mask.... He played innumerable parts, and over-acted them all.... He scoffed at Courts, and kept a chronicle of their most trifling scandal.... The conformation of his mind was such, that whatever was little, seemed to him great, and whatever was great, seemed to him little.... After the labours of the print-shop and the auction-room, he unbent his mind in the House of Commons.... When he was fetching and carrying the gossip of Carlton House, he fancied that he was engaged in politics, and when he recorded that gossip, he fancied that he was writing history." Such is the zest of Macaulay's belittlement that the appearance of further sets of letters—those to Lady Ossory in 1848, and those to William Mason in 1851, for example—served but to confirm this hostile estimate in the eyes of many readers.

Meanwhile, there was a further body of evidence accumulating. Walpole had left complex instructions concerning the series of historical memoirs which he had been compiling, year by year, for much of his adult life. The first set of memoirs, covering the later years of George II, were published in a somewhat mangled form in 1822; it was not until 1985 that a reliable edition appeared. These were followed by the memoirs of George III—actually, the first decade of the reign—which were published in 1845 in a slightly superior form. Finally there came the so-called last journals, first published in an unsatisfactory edition in 1859; these run from 1771 to 1783. A further section of the journal, extending from 1784 to 1791, is preserved in the Lewis Walpole Library and has never been published.

Any modern estimate of Walpole must pay due attention to the books which appeared during his lifetime. *The Castle of Otranto* has a significant place in literary history, but it cannot be regarded as a living classic in the same way as *Tom Jones* (1749), *Clarissa* (1747-1748), or *Tristram Shandy* (1759-1767). Otherwise *Anecdotes of Painting* is probably Walpole's most considerable single work, with its wealth of historical information and easy manner of relation. All the same, Walpole lives today by virtue of Strawberry Hill and of two posthumous collections—the memoirs and the letters. Walpole had a keen sense of his own limitations: it was not just mock modesty when he wrote to John Pinkerton on 27 October 1784: "I have learnt and have practised the humiliating task of comparing myself with great authors; and that comparison has annihilated all the flattery that self-love could suggest. I know how trifling my own writings are, and how far below the standard that constitutes excellence ... and he must be very modest, or easily satisfied, who can be content to glimmer for an instant a little more than his brethren glow-worms." In 1784 this was a plausible self-assessment. In the light of history, it must be revised upward by a considerable degree as we survey the report on his times which Walpole bequeathed to posterity. It is amazingly full, often highly perspicacious, constantly exhilarating in its imaginative sweep, and above all written with surpassing skill, in terms of clarity, grace, wit, and fund of allusion. Walpole's lifespan overlapped with the lives of Joseph Addison, Daniel Defoe, Jonathan Swift, Alexander Pope, Samuel Johnson, Thomas Gray, David Hume, Lady Mary Wortley Montagu, Edward Gibbon, Edmund Burke, and William Cowper, but there is a serious case to be made for him as the finest English prose writer of his age.

In the memoirs he unquestionably set out to play the role of Clarendon to his age. He opens the memoirs of George III with a declaration that he writes not out of frustrated ambition or the spirit of faction, but in order to set out the "true causes" of events in the 1760s. His task was to unfold "the secret springs of politics in which I was unwillingly a considerable actor." There ensues a characteristic passage: "How far I have been in the right or in the wrong, I leave to the judgement of posterity, who shall be impartially informed; and who may draw some benefit from the knowledge of what I have seen; though few persons, I believe, profit much from history. Times seldom resemble one another to be very applicable; and if they do, the characters of the actors are very different." Walpole's picture is not an impartial one by any means: he was led into distortions by his grudges against the Pelhams, the earl of Bute ("his plodding, methodic genius made him take the spirit of detail for ability"), and the renegade Henry Fox, a former ally; but his "characters" are masterfully composed, and do justice to the complexity of figures such as the mercurial William Pitt (later Lord Chatham) or the almost friendless William Augustus, Duke of Cumberland. Above all he draws a magnificent portrait of the duke of Newcastle, who stood at the center of British politics from the time of the South Sea Bubble until almost the eve of the American Revolution. Walpole draws his picture chiefly in terms of sharp antitheses and paradoxical detail, as on Newcastle's "busy timidity," and creates a comic identity of total conviction: "His grace retired to Claremont, where for about a fortnight he played at being a country gentleman. Guns and green frocks were bought, and at past sixty, he affected to turn sportsman; but getting wet in his feet, he hurried back to London in a fright, and his country was once more blessed with his assistance."

Some passages, especially in the memoirs of George II, achieve an eloquence which has rarely been equaled by any writer in the whole sweep of eighteenth-century history. Witness a passage on colonization, written before many people had woken up to the implications of Britain's new imperial role:

> A sea captain at first spying a rock in the fifteenth century; perhaps a cross, or a coat of arms set up to the view of a few miles of coast by an adventurer, or even by a shipwrecked crew, gave the first claims to kings and arch-pirates over an unknown tract of country. This transitory seizure sometimes obtained the venerable confirmation of an old priest at Rome (who a century or two before had in his infallibility pronounced that the existence of such a country was

> impossible). . . . Sometimes indeed, if the discoverers were conscientious, they made a legal purchase to all eternity, of empires, and posterity from a parcel of naked natives for a handful of glass beads and baubles. Maryland, I think, was solemnly acquired at the extravagant rate of a quantity of vermillion and jew's harps. I don't know whether the authentic instrument may not be recorded in the Christian depository, the court of Chancery.

Just as powerful is a passage on the rise of reason and toleration:

> Methodism made fools, but they did not arrive to be saints; and the histories of past ages describing massacres and murders, public executions of violence, and the more private though not less horrid acts of poison and daggers, began to be regarded almost as romances. Caesar Borgia seemed little less fabulous than Orlando; and whimsical tenures of manors were not more in disuse, than sanguinary methods of preserving or acquiring empires. No Prime Ministers perished on a scaffold, no heretics in the flames: a Russian princess spared her competitor; even in Turkey the bow-string had been relaxed—alas! frenzy revived in France the credibility of assassination: guilt renewed in England machinations of scarce a whiter dye.

The twentieth century may appear to have falsified this complacent view of human progress, but Walpole provides an important record of how the Enlightenment conceived its own place in history.

The great series of letters give us a rich coverage of almost every aspect of national life, from high politics to low entertainments, from Methodism to ballooning mania, from crime to philanthropy, from sport to theater, from the pursuit of pleasure to the quest for health ("They may say what they will, but it does one ten times more good to leave Bath than to go to it"). Great events are chronicled, including the Jacobite rising, the American War of Independence, and the Gordon riots: readers witness the rise of John Wilkes, the trial of Warren Hastings, and the funeral of David Garrick. There are spectacular set pieces such as the coronation of George III, with a comic bit part for Newcastle again, and graphic evocations of high society, as in a ball attended by the bigamous Elizabeth Chudleigh, Duchess of Kingston, in 1760. Walpole understood the social round so perfectly that he was able in a letter to Lord Hertford on 29 December 1763 to unroll an entire annual tableau in a few deft phrases. His account of a chilly fête champêtre at Stowe occurs in an immortal letter to Montagu dated 7 July 1770: the aged troop of guests goes "hobbling down" to an Arcadian supper in a grotto, "which is as proper to this climate, as a sea-coal fire would be in the dog days at Tivoli."

Walpole has a remarkable sense of futurity: he is constantly transporting his imagination forward to look at the present from the perspective of posterity: "I shall relate it to you to show you the manners of the age, which are always as entertaining to a person fifty miles off, as to one born an hundred and fifty years after this time." There is a constant intercourse between the distant past and the future: "Strangers visit the vestiges of the Acropolis, or may come to dig among the ruins of St. Paul's." Likewise on the course of empire: "America and France must tell us how long this exuberance of opulence is to last! The East Indies, I believe, will not contribute to it much longer. Babylon and Memphis and Rome, probably, stared at their own downfall." Walpole imagines a Jacobite takeover which will leave him "a loyal sufferer in a thread-bare coat, and shivering in an ante-chamber at Hanover." He foresees a time when aerial warfare will ravage the countryside and balloons will set off for China with a stop to pick up passengers on the top of the Monument. As early as 6 May 1770, in a letter to Mann, he predicts a day when America would grow great: "I have many visions about that country and fancy I see twenty empires and republics forming upon vast scales over all that continent, which is growing too mighty to be kept in subjection to half a dozen exhausted nations in Europe. . . . I entertain myself with the idea of a future senate in Carolina and Virginia, where their future patriots will harangue on the austere and uncorruptible virtue of the ancient English!"

Walpole had a genius for friendship, and matched his correspondence perfectly to the interests and personalities of the different recipients. Politics was dealt with chiefly in letters to Mann; literature to Gray and then William Mason; antiquarian subjects to William Cole; the social round to George Montagu and later the countess of Ossory. The last category perhaps includes the finest concentration of shrewdly observant, humane, and sane commentary on the passing scene. But each category contains its gems, and Walpole was incapable of writing a dull letter, even to the dreariest men and women among his acquaintance. Together with his memoirs, the correspondence

stands as Walpole's enduring legacy to English literature: the more we learn about the eighteenth century, decade by decade, the more apparent it becomes that Horace Walpole is a key witness to the age.

Letters:

Letters from the Hon. Horace Walpole, to George Montagu, Esq. from the Year 1736, to the Year 1770, edited by John Martin (London: Printed for Rodwell & Martin and Henry Colburn, 1818);

Letters from the Hon. Horace Walpole, to the Rev. William Cole, and Others; from the Year 1745, to the Year 1782, edited by Martin (London: Printed for Rodwell & Martin and Henry Colburn, 1818);

Letters from the Honble. Horace Walpole, to the Earl of Hertford, during His Lordship's Embassy in Paris. To Which Are Added Mr. Walpole's Letters to the Rev. Henry Zouch, edited by John Wilson Croker (London: Printed for Charles Knight, 1825);

Letters of Horace Walpole, Earl of Orford, to Sir Horace Mann, British Envoy at the Court of Tuscany, 3 volumes, edited by Lord Dover (London: R. Bentley, 1833);

The Yale Edition of Horace Walpole's Correspondence, 48 volumes, edited by W. S. Lewis (New Haven: Yale University Press, 1937-1983).

Bibliographies:

A. T. Hazen, *A Bibliography of Horace Walpole* (New Haven: Yale University Press, 1948);

Hazen, *A Bibliography of the Strawberry Hill Press*, revised edition (Folkestone & London: Dawsons of Pall Mall, 1973);

Peter Sabor, *Horace Walpole: A Reference Guide* (Boston: G. K. Hall, 1984).

Biography:

R. W. Ketton-Cremer, *Horace Walpole: A Biography*, third edition, revised (London: Methuen, 1964).

References:

Kenneth Clark, *The Gothic Revival*, revised edition (New York: Harper & Row, 1962);

J. Mordaunt Crook, "Strawberry Hill Revisited—I," *Country Life*, 154 (7 June 1973): 1598-1602;

Crook, "Strawberry Hill Revisited—II," *Country Life*, 154 (14 June 1973): 1726-1730;

Austin Dobson, "A Day at Strawberry Hill," in his *Eighteenth Century Vignettes*, first series (New York: Dodd, Mead, 1892), pp. 158-166;

Dobson, *Horace Walpole: A Memoir*, fourth edition, revised and enlarged by Paget Toynbee (London: Oxford University Press, 1927);

A. T. Hazen, *A Catalogue of Horace Walpole's Library*, 3 volumes (New Haven: Yale University Press, 1969);

G. P. Judd, *Horace Walpole's Memoirs* (New York: Bookman Associates, 1959);

W. S. Lewis, "The Genesis of Strawberry Hill," *Metropolitan Museum Studies*, 5, no. 1 (1934): 57-92;

Lewis, *A Guide to the Life of Horace Walpole (1717-1797)* (New Haven: Yale University Press, 1973);

Lewis, *Horace Walpole* (New York: Pantheon, 1961);

Lawrence Lipking, *The Ordering of the Arts in Eighteenth-Century England* (Princeton: Princeton University Press, 1970);

Thomas Babington Macaulay, Review of *Letters of Horace Walpole ... to Sir Horace Mann*, *Edinburgh Review*, 58 (October 1833): 227-258;

Peter Sabor, ed., *Horace Walpole: The Critical Heritage* (London: Routledge, 1987);

Sir Walter Scott, Introduction to *The Castle of Otranto* (Edinburgh: Printed by James Ballantyne for John Ballantyne, Edinburgh, and Longman, Hurst, Rees, Orme & Brown, London, 1811), pp. iii-xxxvi;

Warren Hunting Smith, ed., *Horace Walpole: Writer, Politician, and Connoisseur: Essays on the 250th Anniversary of Walpole's Birth* (New Haven: Yale University Press, 1967);

Paul Yvon, *La Vie d'un dilettante: Horace Walpole* (Paris: Presses Universitaires de France, 1924).

Papers:

The Lewis Walpole Library, Yale University, at Farmington, Connecticut, has an incomparable collection of manuscript material by and relating to Walpole and has photocopies of all other known Walpole manuscripts not in its possession.

William Warburton

(24 December 1698 - 7 June 1779)

Elise F. Knapp
Western Connecticut State University

SELECTED BOOKS: *Miscellaneous Translations, in Prose and Verse, from Roman Poets, Orators, and Historians* (London: Printed for Anthony Barker, 1724);

A Critical and Philosophical Inquiry into the Causes of Prodigies and Miracles, as related by Historians. With an Essay towards restoring a Method and Purity in History. In which, The Characters of the most celebrated Writers of every Age, and of the several Stages and Species of History are occasionally criticized and explained. In Two Parts (London: Printed for Thomas Corbett, 1727);

An Apology for Sir Robert Sutton (London: Printed for T. Warner, 1733);

The Alliance between Church and State, or, The Necessity and Equity of an Established Religion and a Test-law demonstrated, from the Essence and End of Civil Society, upon the fundamental Principles of the Law of Nature and Nations. In Three Parts. The First, treating of a Civil and a Religious Society: The Second, of an Established Church: and The Third, of a Test-Law (London: Printed for Fletcher Gyles, 1736);

The Divine Legation of Moses demonstrated, on the Principles of a Religious Deist, from the Omission of the Doctrine of a Future State of Reward and Punishment in the Jewish Dispensation. In Six Books. By William Warburton, A.M., Author of The Alliance between Church and State (London: Printed for Fletcher Gyles, 1738);

A Vindication of the Author of the Divine Legation of Moses, &c., from the Aspersions of the Country Clergyman's letter in The Weekly Miscellany of February 24, 1737. By William Warburton, A.M. (London: Printed for Fletcher Gyles, 1738);

A Vindication of Mr. Pope's Essay on Man, from the Misrepresentations of Mr. de Crousaz, Professor of Philosophy and Mathematicks in the University of Lausaunne. By the Author of The Divine Legation of Moses Demonstrated. In Six Letters (London: Printed for J. Robinson, 1740);

A Seventh Letter, which finishes the Vindication of Mr. Pope's Essay on Man, from the Misrepresenta-

Engraving by Thomas Burford, after a circa 1737 portrait by Charles Philips

tions of Mr. de Crousaz, Professor of Philosophy and Mathematicks in the University of Lausaunne. By the Reverend William Warburton, M.A., Chaplain to His Royal Highness the Prince of Wales (London: Printed for J. Robinson, 1740);

The Divine Legation of Moses demonstrated, on the Principles of a Religious Deist, from the Omission of the Doctrine of a Future State of Reward and Punishment in the Jewish Dispensation. The Second Volume, in Two Parts. By William Warburton, A.M., Chaplain to His Royal Highness the

Prince of Wales (London: Printed for Fletcher Gyles, 1741);

A Critical and Philosophical Commentary on Mr. Pope's Essay On Man. In which is contain'd A Vindication of the said Essay from the Misrepresentations of Mr. De Resnel, the French Translator, and of Mr. De Crousaz, Professor of Philosophy and Mathematics in the Academy of Lausaunne, the Commentator. By Mr. Warburton (London: Printed for John & Paul Knapton, 1742);

Remarks on Several Occasional Reflections: In Answer to the Rev. Dr. Middleton, Dr. Pococke, the Master of the Charter House, Dr. Richard Grey, and others. Serving to explain and justify divers Passages in the Divine Legation objected to by those Learned Writers. To which is added, A General Review of the Argument of the Divine Legation, as far as it is yet advanced: wherein is considered the Relation the several Parts bear to each other, and to the Whole. Together with an Appendix in answer to a late Pamphlet entitled, An Examination of Mr. W----s second Proposition. By Mr. Warburton (London: Printed for John & Paul Knapton, 1744);

A Sermon occasioned by the Present Unnatural Rebellion. Being an Earnest Exhortation to a Manly Defence of our Happy Constitution in Church and State. Preached in Mr. Allen's Chapel at Prior-Park near Bath, and publish'd at his Request. By William Warburton, M.A., Chaplain to His Royal Highness the Prince of Wales (London: Printed for J. & P. Knapton, 1745);

A Letter from an Author to a Member of Parliament concerning Literary Property (London: Printed for John & Paul Knapton, 1747);

A Letter to the Editor of the Letters on the Spirit of Patriotism, The Idea of a Patriot-King, and The State of Parties &c., occasioned by the Editor's Advertisement (London: Printed for J. Roberts, 1749); facsimile in *A Letter to the Editor of the Letters on the Spirit of Patriotism, &c.* [William Warburton] *(1749)* and *A Familiar Epistle to the Most Impudent Man Living* [Henry St. John, Viscount Bolingbroke] *(1749),* introduction by Donald T. Siebert, Jr., Augustan Reprint Society, Publication Number 192 (Los Angeles: William Andrews Clark Memorial Library, 1978);

Julian, or A Discourse Concerning the Earthquake and Fiery Eruption, which defeated that Emperor's Attempt to rebuild the Temple at Jerusalem. In which The Reality of a Divine Interposition is shewn; The Objections to it are answered; and The Nature of that Evidence which demands the as- sent of every reasonable man to a Miraculous fact, is considered and explained. By the Rev. Mr. Warburton, Preacher to the Hon. Society of Lincoln's Inn (London: Printed for John & Paul Knapton, 1750);

The Principles of Natural and Revealed Religion occasionally opened and explained; In a Course of Sermons preached before the Honourable Society of Lincoln's Inn. In Two Volumes. By the Rev. Mr. Warburton, Preacher to the Society (London: Printed for John & Paul Knapton, 1753, 1754);

A View of Lord Bolingbroke's Philosophy; In Four Letters to a Friend. Letters First and Second (London: Printed for John & Paul Knapton, 1754);

A View of Lord Bolingbroke's Philosophy; in Four Letters to a Friend. Letter the Third (London: Printed for John & Paul Knapton, 1755);

A View of Lord Bolingbroke's Philosophy; In Four Letters to a Friend. Letter the Fourth and Last (London: Printed for John & Paul Knapton, 1755);

Remarks on Mr. David Hume's Essay on the Natural History of Religion: Addressed to the Rev. Dr. Warburton (London: Printed for M. Cooper, 1757);

An Enquiry into the Nature and Origin of Literary Property (London: Printed for W. Flexney, 1762);

The Doctrine of Grace; or, The Office and Operations of the Holy Spirit vindicated from the Insults of Infidelity and the Abuses of Fanaticism; concluding with some Thoughts (humbly offered to the consideration of the Established Clergy) with Regard to the Right Method of defending Religion against the Attacks of either Party. In Two Volumes. By William, Lord Bishop of Gloucester (London: Printed for A. Millar and J. & R. Tonson, 1763);

Sermons and Discourses on Various Subjects and Occasions. Volume the Third. By Dr. William Warburton, Lord Bishop of Gloucester (London: Printed for J. & R. Tonson, and A. Millar: and sold by T. Cadell, 1767);

The Works of the Right Reverend William Warburton, Lord Bishop of Gloucester. In Seven Volumes, edited by Richard Hurd (London: Printed by John Nichols, and sold by T. Cadell, 1788);

Tracts by Warburton and a Warburtonian; not admitted into the Collections of their respective Works, edited by Dr. Samuel Parr (London: Printed for Charles Dilly, 1789).

OTHER: "A Supplement to the Translator's Preface," in *The Life and Exploits of the Ingenious Gentleman Don Quixote de la Mancha. Translated from the Original Spanish of Miguel Cervantes de Saavedra. By Charles Jarvis, Esq.; In two Volumes* (London: Printed for J. & R. Tonson, 1742);

Samuel Butler, *Hudibras, In Three Parts, Written in the Time of the Late Wars: Corrected and Amended. With Large Annotations, and a Preface, By Zachary Grey, LL.D. Adorn'd with a new Set of Cuts*, 2 volumes, includes notes by Warburton (Cambridge: Printed by J. Bentham for W. Innys, 1744);

Remarks upon the Principles and Reasonings of Dr. Rutherforth's Essay on the Nature and Obligations of Virtue: In Vindication of the contrary Principles and Reasonings inforced in the Writings of the late Dr. Samuel Clarke. Published by Mr. Warburton with a Preface (London: Printed for John & Paul Knapton, 1747);

A Critical Inquiry into the Opinions and Practice of the Ancient Philosophers, concerning the Nature of the Soul and a Future State, and their Method of Teaching by the Double Doctrine. In which are examin'd the Notion of Mr. Jackson and Dr. Sykes concerning these Matters. With a Preface by the Author of the Divine Legation &c. (London: Printed for C. Davis, 1747);

The Works of Shakespear in Eight Volumes. The Genuine Text (Collated with all the former Editions, and then corrected and emended) is here settled: Being restored from the Blunders of the first Editors, and the Interpolations of the two Last: With a Comment and Notes, Critical and Explanatory. By Mr. Pope and Mr. Warburton (London: Printed for John & Paul Knapton, 1747);

Paradise Lost. A Poem, In Twelve Books. The Author John Milton. A New Edition, with Notes of Various Authors, By Thomas Newton, D.D., 2 volumes, includes notes by Warburton (London: Printed for J. & R. Tonson, 1749);

The Works of Alexander Pope, Esq. In Nine Volumes Complete. With his last Corrections, Additions, and Improvements; As they were delivered to the Editor a little before his Death: Together with the Commentaries and Notes of Mr. Warburton (London: Printed for J. & P. Knapton, 1751);

Paradise Regain'd. A Poem, In Four Books. To which is added Samson Agonistes: and Poems upon Several Occasions. The Author John Milton. A New Edition, with Notes of Various Authors, By Thomas Newton, D.D., includes notes by Warburton (London: Printed for J. & R. Tonson, 1752);

The Life of Alexander Pope, Esq. Compiled from Original Manuscripts; with a Critical Essay on his Writings and Genius. By Owen Ruffhead, Esq. (London: Printed for C. Bathurst, 1769)—Warburton supplied materials for and supervised the composition of this book; he corrected and made alterations in the proof sheets (now in the Bodleian Library);

The History of the Rebellion and Civil Wars in England to which is added An Historical View of the Affairs of Ireland, By Edward, Earl of Clarendon. A New Edition, exhibiting a faithful collation of the Original MS., with all the suppressed Passages; also the unpublished Notes of Bishop Warburton, 8 volumes, volume 7 includes 142 pages of notes by Warburton (Oxford: Clarendon Press, 1826);

During the middle years of the eighteenth century, William Warburton achieved an eminence as a scholar and man of letters not surpassed by Samuel Johnson himself. Brilliant, rash, daring, intuitive, zealous in pursuit of paradox and controversy, he commanded attention and respect for his vast learning and powerful intellect. As a speculative theologian, literary historian, critic, and editor of William Shakespeare and Alexander Pope, he demonstrated a breadth of learning which compelled admiration even from writers who deplored his relish for controversy. Arrogant and aggressive in his defense of orthodox Christian doctrine, yet gentle and solicitous to his friends, he presents a complex and contradictory character driven by apparently inexhaustible energy and insatiable curiosity. Warburton was at the hub of midcentury literary activities: as an Anglican clergyman who later became bishop of Gloucester, he took part in significant clerical debates, wrote influential sermons, and drew international recognition and interest in his *Divine Legation of Moses* (1738, 1741), a powerful and ingenious work of speculative theology; as critic and editor he knew, corresponded, and worked with some of the most influential writers of the century: Pope, Richard Hurd, Henry Fielding, Laurence Sterne, Samuel Richardson, Thomas Warton, and Lewis Theobald; as a bishop he sat in the House of Lords, where he was a friend to William Pitt, Earl of Chatham, and other government leaders. He was preacher to the Honorable Society of Lincoln's Inn for many years. Warburton's literary and social activities vividly reveal the spirit of the times: its belief in the social nature of literary creation; its didactic bent; its love of controversy; its preoccupation with public morality and religion; its faith in the rational and intellectual; its astonishing degree of tolerance. In our time Warburton's nearly complete eclipse in the record of literary history points to a radical shift in expectations of writers, editors, and their readers. Romantic notions of individual and autonomous artistic inspiration widely accepted today are at odds with Warburton's conviction that the body of literature is social in nature and grows through time by communal and collaborative effort. His passionate defense of Christian orthodoxy and the great number of readers his theological works attracted reflects the central importance of religious theory in the eighteenth century. To become familiar with Warburton is to discover the astonishing variety of midcentury discourse.

Warburton's beginnings give no hint that he was to reign as "the dictator and tyrant of literature," as Edward Gibbon put it. The son of George and Elizabeth Hobman Warburton, he was born on 24 December 1698, in Newark, Nottinghamshire, into an old family that traced its origins to a companion of William the Conqueror. Like his father and grandfather before him, he chose a career in the law and was articled at the age of sixteen to John Kirke, an attorney at East Markham. Dissatisfied with the law after five years, he nevertheless remained a lawyer at heart, with an appetite for argument that endured through his career in the church. He returned to Newark, where through exhaustive study of classical and theological literature, he began his preparation for ordination in the Anglican church. At this time he made a lifelong friend of William Stukeley, a doctor of medicine, clergyman, and serious antiquarian. Warburton's letters to Stukeley, collected in the Bodleian Library and published in volume 2 of John Nichol's *Illustrations of Literature of the Eighteenth Century* (1817), suggest his mature critical attitudes and interests: he saw literature and history bound together inseparably in the social record of a culture; and he believed that damaged ancient texts could be emended satisfactorily after careful analysis of the existing fragments, followed by intuitive rearrangement. The validity of the resulting text could be tested by the force of logic.

In 1724, three years before his ordination, Warburton published his first work, a modest collection of translations entitled *Miscellaneous Trans-* *lations, in Prose and Verse, from Roman Poets, Orators, and Historians*. An elaborate Latin dedication to his patron, Sir Robert Sutton, is followed by seventy pages of translated fragments of Latin prose and poetry. Warburton's view of translation is compatible with his theory of literature: "originality" has to do with wit, or the manner of assembling ideas, not with the material itself. A writer's translation should reflect not simply the original work but other translations as well. The resulting compression and richness of effect emphasizes his literary heritage to the discerning reader.

Warburton was ordained a priest in London on 1 March 1727. During the same year he published his second book, *A Critical and Philosophical Inquiry into the Causes of Prodigies and Miracles, as Related by Historians*. Despite its forbidding title, this book is a daring attempt to reconcile belief in supernatural revelation with Baconian scientific precepts, a combination Warburton would use again in *Julian* (1750). He shared with a group of influential orthodox clergymen the notion that religious and moral experience have been progressive throughout history, that in earlier ages, when man was simpler and more credulous, God revealed himself through true miracles. In *A Critical and Philosophical Enquiry* Warburton proposes a way of identifying these true miracles and separating them from superstition. He quotes Francis Bacon's *De Augmentis Scientarum* (1623) and accepts his historical method of investigation in attempting to bring order and scientific method to the study of man, society, and literature. Warburton was among the first scholars in the eighteenth century to apply this analytical method to the social sciences. *A Critical and Philosophical Enquiry* ends with an imitation of a passage from John Milton's *Areopagitica* (1644), in which Warburton praises Cambridge University and a chair in history recently established there by George II. This passage may later have embarrassed its author, because years later when Edmund Curll, an unprincipled publisher, bought rights to republish the book, Warburton asked John and Paul Knapton, his publishers, to outbid him. The book was not republished. Warburton dismissed the entire episode in a 1757 letter to his friend Richard Hurd: "I was very much a young boy when I wrote that thing about prodigies, and I had never the courage to look into it since, so I have quite forgot all the nonsense it contains."

His loyal friend and patron, Sir Robert Sutton, presented the newly ordained Warburton with a living in Brant Broughton in Lincolnshire near Newark. Sutton's influence was also responsible for the young priest's award of an honorary Master of Arts degree at Cambridge in 1728. For the next eighteen years, he enjoyed the happiest period of his life in the rectory at Brant Broughton with his mother and sisters, spending long hours daily reading history, theology, and philosophy, in English, French, Italian, and Spanish, as well as in Greek and Latin. The learning he accumulated drew admiration from his contemporaries. Boswell reports in his *Life of Johnson* (1791) that when Samuel Johnson visited King George III in 1767, the king asked about the extent of his reading. Johnson replied that he "had not read much, compared to Dr. Warburton. Upon which the King said, that he heard Dr. Warburton was a man of such general knowledge, that you could scarce talk with him on any subject on which he was not qualified to speak; and that his learning resembled Garrick's acting in its universality."

At this time Warburton began to work on a remarkable treatise, *The Alliance between Church and State, or, the Necessity and Equity of an Established Religion and a Test-law demonstrated*. His purpose was to defend the need for a test act and an established church. The book was published anonymously in 1736 at a time when the Anglican church as an established institution was being attacked on all sides. Deists, nonconformists, Quakers, and some Anglicans themselves questioned the need for a test law, which would bar members of dissenting churches from holding civil and military office unless they took communion in the established Church of England once a year. Members of the House of Commons showed clear hostility toward the church and its clergy. At this critical moment, Warburton argued in favor of both the test act and the established church on the paradoxical ground that human liberty and social welfare generally are best protected under both. Liberty is best maintained in an orderly state where power is given, by common consent, to one well-ordered government and one established church chosen by the majority of the people. The church does not have to be Christian, but the choice must be supported by the majority. Warburton's focus is on social welfare; all institutions must serve human needs or be replaced. His faith in progress and in the positive evolution of human institutions is evident throughout *The Alliance between Church and State*. The work impressed contemporary read-

ers and, subsequently, nineteenth-century scholars. Warburton treats the origins of civil and religious societies, the need for religious tolerance, the interdependence of institutions, and the nature of social will and group psychology. In his discussion of group psychology and social will, Warburton anticipates nineteenth-century psychological theorists, pointing out that one civil population can generate many groups, each with its own personality. "The will and personality of a community is as different and distinct from the will and personality of the individuals of which it is composed, as the body is," he observes. In summary, *The Alliance between Church and State* remains significant for its breadth of theological and historical background, as well as its emphasis on the enduring importance of tolerance and human liberty, and on the idea that religious belief is a divine gift to man, who can employ it to create his own religious institutions, refining and improving them in time.

In 1736 *The Alliance between Church and State* created a powerful stir among men of letters and the clergy; it went through four editions in Warburton's lifetime. It raised him to a new position in the literary world and brought him influential connections at court, where it was a subject of lively discussion. Queen Caroline expressed interest in having conversations with its author, but she died in 1737 before Warburton could meet her. Bishop Samuel Horsley summarized contemporary opinion in claiming that *The Alliance between Church and State* was "one of the finest specimens . . . in any language, of scientific reasoning applied to a political subject," and for more than a hundred years its substance and argument were highly regarded.

Warburton promised his readers of *The Alliance between Church and State* that it was to be part of a much larger and more ambitious work. The first part of that work, *The Divine Legation of Moses demonstrated, on the Principles of a Religious Deist, from the Omission of the Doctrine of a Future State of Reward and Punishment in the Jewish Dispensation*, appeared in 1738. It immediately caused a sensation, partly because it attempted to defend Christianity in a unique way, but also because it boldly addressed a current concern that social morality would be dangerously weakened if religious belief declined. The deists had pointed to the absence of any reference to a promise of immortality in the Mosaic Law. Warburton accepted that fact and paradoxically built his refutation of their position on their own argument. Warburton reasons that the Jewish religion must have been of divine origin and protected by divine providence, specifically because there is no mention of immortality in Mosaic Law. Because a doctrine of future rewards and punishments is normally necessary for effective control of society, the Jewish state must have been protected by divine providence in order to function without it. To develop his proof Warburton drew on learning from every field of scholarship in a comprehensive study of human social, literary, and religious history. An angry and jealous scholar, Robert Lowth, described it accurately if scathingly: "it is a perfect Encyclopaedia; it includes in it self all History, Chronology, Criticism, Divinity, Law, Politics, from the Law of Moses to the late Jew-Bill, and from Egyptian Hieroglyphics to modern Rebus-writing." In *The Divine Legation of Moses* once again, Warburton uses scientific and psychological analysis to demonstrate evolutionary progressivism in the record of human history.

Part 1 of his massive work deals with a society's need, in order for it to protect its moral fabric, to believe in life after death. Much of this section had been covered earlier in *The Alliance between Church and State*. In the second part of *The Divine Legation of Moses* Warburton argues that ancient legislators cultivated, even invented, religion and the belief in life after death to maintain order and political control; Greek leaders invented the Eleusinian mysteries to strengthen belief in a future state of punishments and rewards. Using an allegorical interpretation of the sixth book of Virgil's *Aeneid* to illustrate his argument, Warburton makes an exhaustive analysis. "For the descent of Virgil's hero into the infernal regions, I presume, was no other than a figurative description of an initiation; and particularly, a very exact picture of the spectacles on the Eleusinian mysteries."

The third book examines the opinions of classical philosophers about a future state; book 4 searches for the origins of the ideas of classical philosophers and finds them in Egypt. Ancient Egypt, its language and culture, are discussed at length, including a long digression on the hieroglyphics. Books 5 and 6 consider the ancient Jewish state from a study of the biblical texts and from historical analysis. Warburton intended, after completing his treatment of the pagan and Jewish religions, to conclude his treatise with an analysis of Christianity, but he never finished the project; the work remains a fragment.

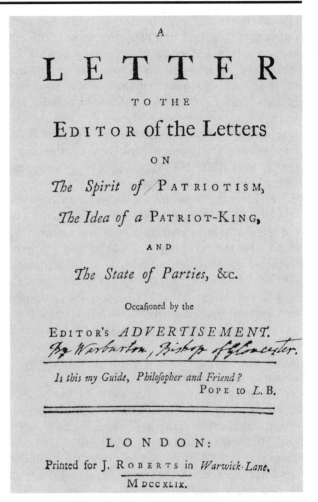

A

LETTER

TO THE

EDITOR of the Letters

ON

The Spirit of PATRIOTISM,

The Idea of a PATRIOT-KING,

AND

The State of Parties, &c.

Occasioned by the

EDITOR's *ADVERTISEMENT*.

By Warburton, Bishop of Gloucester.

Is this my Guide, Philosopher and Friend?
POPE to *L.B.*

LONDON:

Printed for J. ROBERTS in *Warwick-Lane.*
MDCCXLIX.

Title page for Warburton's defense of Alexander Pope against charges by Henry St. John, Viscount Bolingbroke, that Pope had betrayed Bolingbroke's friendship by secretly printing and circulating an incorrect version of Bolingbroke's Idea of a Patriot King

The Divine Legation of Moses excited immediate controversy in England and in France, where large portions of it were later embedded without attribution by Denis Diderot in his *Encyclopédie* (1751-1772). Dr. Johnson was delighted by the range and variety of Warburton's imagination and learning; he described the effect of such a feast for the mind and spirit: "The table is always full, Sir. He brings things from the north, and the south, and from every quarter. In his *Divine Legation*, you are always entertained. He carries you round and round, without carrying you forward to the point; but then you have no wish to be carried forward. . . . Warburton is perhaps the last man who has written with a mind full of reading and reflection."

But not every reader was so approving. Some clergymen attacked the work, and gradually Warburton allowed himself to engage in acrimonious debate and ad hominem attacks on his adversaries. The bitterness of his contempt and the arrogance he showed his opponents in controversy accounts for much of the hostility shown to him by critics and readers of later periods. His imperious tone is not the only reason for Warburton's virtual disappearance from the annals of literary history. Criticism in the nineteenth and twentieth centuries reveals the great gulf of understanding that separates them from the eighteenth. Gone are the belief that Christianity must form the moral basis for society, the unlimited faith in reason as a tool for discovering truth, and the acceptance of a loose encyclopedic form for speculative writing. The monumental size of *The Divine Legation of Moses* and its vast scope, combined with Warburton's triumphant and assured tone, have made the work seem arrogant and eccentric to later readers, for example to Leslie Stephen, who dismissed it as "an attempt to support one gigantic paradox by a whole system of paradoxes."

During the years of his work on *The Alliance of Church and State* and *The Divine Legation of Moses*, Warburton pursued other literary interests. He lived comfortably at Brant Broughton, visiting Stukeley, taking trips to places of antiquarian interest, and finding new friends with whom to share his intellectual interests, among them the philosopher David Hartley and John Towne, who became a lifelong friend. In London in 1726 Warburton met Matthew Concanen, a writer who introduced him to Lewis Theobald, then preparing his edition of Shakespeare. He and Concanen exchanged letters in which they commented on writers. In his correspondence with Concanen, and in three articles in the *Daily Journal*, Warburton made derogatory statements about Pope. "Dryden I observe borrows for want of leasure, and Pope for want of genius," he wrote, making clear that he shared Theobald's and Concanen's negative attitude toward Pope. Pope never saw the letter, and Warburton later changed his view of Pope; but this early evidence has been used to suggest that Warburton was insincere when he came to Pope's defense in 1738.

At that time Pope found himself under attack most unexpectedly by a Swiss mathematician, Jean Pierre de Crousaz, who challenged the religious and moral basis of *An Essay on Man* (1732-1734) and charged Pope with deism. Warburton, smarting from the memory of attacks on his theological orthodoxy in *The Divine Lega-*

tion of Moses, quickly rose to defend Pope, whom he had not met. In a series of six long letters in *The History of the Works of the Learned* (December 1738-May 1739)—published in 1740 as *A Vindication of Mr. Pope's Essay on Man*—Warburton argued that the beliefs and values underlying *An Essay on Man* are essentially based on Christian doctrine. Warburton argued with his customary forcefulness and conviction, handily fending off the attack. Pope was relieved and delighted; he wrote a letter of thanks to his new interpreter: "I know I meant just what you explain, but I did not explain my meaning so well as you. You understand me as well as I do myself, but you express me better than I could express myself." Correspondence between the two continued, and it led to collaboration on other literary ventures.

In 1740 the two men met in person, and Pope immediately asked his new friend to visit him at his villa in Twickenham. Later he introduced Warburton to his influential circle of friends, who were writers and patrons of the arts, among them Lords Bathurst, Burlington, Chesterfield, and Lyttelton, as well as Ralph Allen of Bath. Allen was wealthy and generous; at his mansion, Prior Park, Warburton met friends who were to change the course of his life: Henry Fielding, Samuel Richardson, Tobias Smollett, William Pitt, William Mason, and especially Richard Hurd and Charles Yorke, who were to become Warburton's close friends and correspondents. Through Allen's influence, Warburton was named bishop of Gloucester in 1760; Allen's favorite niece, Gertrude Tucker, became Warburton's wife on 25 April 1746. Pope's introduction provided Warburton with so many opportunities that King George III remarked to Samuel Johnson that Pope made Warburton a bishop. "True, Sir, (said Johnson,) but Warburton did more for Pope; he made him a Christian," referring to Warburton's ingenious comments on *An Essay on Man*.

At this time Pope cherished the plan of introducing Warburton to one of his oldest and most trusted friends, Henry St. John, Lord Bolingbroke, whose philosophy had been strongly influential in the creation of *An Essay on Man*. When the two finally met at a dinner party given by William Murray, Earl of Mansfield, in 1743, they fell into a heated disagreement about the moral aspects of divine power and soon became bitter enemies. Pope recognized both men in his will when he died in 1744: Bolingbroke was left Pope's manuscripts and unpublished papers, while Warburton was named literary executor and editor of all works previously printed, a legacy worth four thousand pounds.

During and long before these years of intimacy with Pope, Warburton had continued to study and emend Shakespearean texts. In the eighteenth century Shakespeare appealed to national pride and attracted scholars as an especially English poet. The corrupt and incomplete condition of the texts at that time challenged editors and critics. The title of Lewis Theobald's *Shakespeare Restored* (1726), suggests the goal and methods assumed by early editors. Warburton met Theobald through their mutual friend Matthew Concanen and collaborated heavily with Theobald on his new edition of Shakespeare, which came out in 1734. Many of the best notes as well as the preface were Warburton's. Their collaboration broke down when Theobald failed to acknowledge Warburton's contribution adequately. Later efforts on Warburton's part to collaborate with Sir Thomas Hanmer in editing Shakespeare collapsed for the same reason.

A different and successful collaboration took place with Thomas Birch, when Warburton contributed thirty-four pages of the section on Shakespeare in volume 9 (1740) of Birch's *General Dictionary*. Birch, in return, announced to his readers that Warburton was preparing an edition of Shakespeare. In 1747 that edition appeared with the confident title, *The Works of Shakespear in Eight Volumes. The Genuine Text (Collated with all the former Editions, and then corrected and emended) is here settled: Being restored from the Blunders of the first Editors, and the Interpolations of the two Last: with a Comment and Notes, Critical and Explanatory. By Mr. Pope and Mr. Warburton.* The dedication was, appropriately, to Mrs. Ralph Allen and was followed by Warburton's preface, then Pope's. In his preface Warburton outlines a critic's duties. The notes in the edition reflect Warburton's editorial method: collation of all the texts, study of Elizabethan English in order to clarify any obscurity, and emendation as necessary to produce a text that makes sense. Warburton regularly begins by looking for the author's intention or design in a passage. Some of his notes are brilliant and illuminating, while others tend to provide gratuitous explanations.

The reception of the edition was almost uniformly hostile. Warburton's confident tone and relentless didacticism, combined with his elaborate set of "canons" for judging passages, set him up for ridicule. In 1748 Thomas Edwards, a lawyer

and wit, published *The Canons of Criticism*, a devastating parody of Warburton's critical method as laid out meticulously in his preface. Making pompous and sweeping claims in Warburton's style, Edwards's work became instantly popular; it went through six editions in ten years, permanently damaging Warburton's reputation as a critic for most readers. Samuel Johnson, however, was not persuaded. Discussing Warburton and Edwards with friends at Jacob Tonson's, he told his listeners that "there is no proportion between the two men; they must not be named together. A fly, Sir, may sting a stately horse and make him wince; but one is but an insect, and the other is a horse still." When he came to edit Shakespeare himself, Johnson respected Warburton's edition. "I treated him with great respect both in my Preface and in my Notes," he told Dr. W. Adams of Pembroke College. Johnson's own notes depended on Warburton's in so many instances that neither he nor his compositor could work without them. Since Johnson, few critics have held Warburton in such high regard.

Critical response was much more favorable to Warburton's next significant publication, *Julian, or a Discourse Concerning the Earthquake and Fiery Eruption, which defeated that Emperor's Attempt to rebuild the Temple at Jerusalem* (1750). At a time when the accuracy of testimony regarding ancient miracles was being argued by theologians and philosophers, Warburton chose a miracle from the fourth century and examined it rigorously, especially by comparison to contemporary reports. He concluded that the central event itself was indeed miraculous but that much of the phenomena surrounding the reported rush of fire could be scientifically explained. His ingenious and brilliant argument was supported by wide references to theology, natural history, and the records of eye witnesses to the event. The work brought Warburton high praise, not only in England, but also in France, where Montesquieu wrote, "*Julian* charms me."

In the following year, 1751, Warburton published the work on which his uncertain reputation in the twentieth century is based: *The Works of Alexander Pope, Esq. In Nine Volumes Complete. With his last Corrections, Additions and Improvements: . . . Together with the Commentaries and Notes of Mr. Warburton.* Pope had died seven years earlier, in 1744, leaving Warburton as his literary executor. Pope's will had bequeathed to Warburton all printed works that he had written or should write commentaries or notes upon. Their correspondence shows that, ever since he had written his *Vindication of Mr. Pope's Essay on Man* in 1738, Warburton, at Pope's repeated requests, had become the poet's literary partner and collaborator. Pope had proposed that Warburton translate *An Essay on Man* into Latin and attach sections of his *Vindication* in the form of notes. Although this plan was never completed, it illustrates the poet's eagerness to have Warburton's help in building his literary legacy. Warburton continued to give advice on the formal and logical arrangement of ideas within the long poems, Pope's *Iliad*, for example. Warburton suggested that Pope write the fourth book of the *Dunciad* and replace Theobald with Colley Cibber as its hero. In proposing that Warburton work with him on the final edition of his work and predicting its success, Pope wrote confidently to his collaborator, "We shall take our Degree together in Fame."

The critical apparatus for the 1751 edition includes commentary, notes, variations from original manuscript readings, and Latin originals of Pope's imitations. The notes include short, often brilliant essays on myth, figurative language, aesthetic theory, philology, and design. A contemporary reader described their effect: "Our present after-supper author is Mr. Pope in Mr. Warburton's edition. . . . The notes are worth any body running over; some very wild, some very ingenious, some full of amusing anecdotes . . . and the greatest number, true commentator like, explaining what needs no explanation." Since 1751, most critical reaction to the edition has been adverse. Critics have dismissed evidence in Warburton's correspondence with Pope and have generally assumed that the bishop bullied the poet into making changes in his poems and into attaching Warburton's notes to them. Leslie Stephen, writing in the nineteenth century, viewed Warburton's commitment to Christian orthodoxy with scorn and distrust; he dubbed the editor a "pachydermatous defender of Pope." Later critics have tended to accept this judgment.

Pope was not the only writer with whom Warburton corresponded and collaborated. He encouraged his close friend Richard Hurd in writing, especially his *Letters on Chivalry and Romance* (1762). Through Hurd he met and corresponded with William Mason and Thomas Balguy. He wrote "A Supplement to the Translator's Preface" for Charles Jarvis's translation (1742) of *Don Quixote*. In this piece, with his customary concern about literary origins, he examines for the first time the origins of romance in English. Later he

wrote a preface for the fourth volume of Richardson's *Clarissa* (1747-1749), in which he traces the development of the romance from its Spanish origins to *Clarissa*.

Warburton was generous in offering notes to writers who were preparing editions of major British authors. He offered his notes on Samuel Butler's *Hudibras* (1663) to Zachary Grey and his notes on Spenser to John Jortin. His most significant contribution comprised the notes and biographical material he gave Owen Ruffhead for *The Life Of Alexander Pope. Esq.* Ruffhead's book appeared in 1769; it was almost entirely Warburton's work.

A devoted family man as well as a loyal friend, Warburton was deeply moved by his mother's death in 1749. He told Dr. Philip Doddridge it was "the greatest loss I ever had, in that of the best parent and woman that ever was." Another terrible loss came in 1775 with the death of consumption of his only child, Ralph, then nineteen. His father had called the boy "half his soul," and his death marked the father's rapid mental and physical decline. He died in 1779, leaving Richard Hurd as his editor and executor.

Warburton's career in the Church of England was marked by a succession of honors and advancements. He became chaplain to King George II in 1754 and received a Doctor of Divinity degree conferred by the archbishop of Canterbury in the same year. In 1760 he was consecrated bishop of Gloucester. Even as his preferment in the church moved forward, however, he became increasingly embroiled in theological and literary controversies. He used notes in each fresh edition of *The Divine Legation of Moses* and *The Dunciad* to excoriate his enemies. Among these were Bolingbroke, after he had quarreled with and attacked Pope; David Hume, for his analysis of the psychology of religion in *The Natural History of Religion* (1757); and Robert Lowth, a biblical scholar with whom Warburton argued regarding the origin and especially the dating of the Book of Job.

Warburton's lofty position in eighteenth-century letters, and his relegation to the footnotes of literary history today, can best be understood by noting his philosophical and literary beliefs, summarized in a pamphlet he published in 1762, *An Enquiry into the Nature and Origin of Literary Property*. Here Warburton argues the social need for public ownership of works composing our literary heritage: "The learning of the present Age may be considered a vast Superstruc-

Warburton in 1765 (portrait by William Hoare; Hurd Episcopal Library, Hartlebury)

ture, to the rearing of which the Geniusses of Past Times have contributed their Proportion of Wit and Industry; to what Purpose would they have contributed if each of them could insist that none should build on their Foundations?" This notion of literature as community property lies behind all of Warburton's literary activities. He was building on the foundations of others when he wrote notes and prefaces, strengthening and clarifying their work in order to extend the vast superstructure of literature as he saw it. Because twentieth-century critics accept the notion of separate and autonomous literary creation, they tend to agree in their condemnation of Warburton. Recent scholarship has begun to study him in the context of his own literary assumptions and has cautiously begun to acknowledge his achievement. Samuel Johnson's balanced estimate, from his

Life of Pope, shows both the gifts which brought Warburton to prominence and the destructive tendencies which developed from those very talents: "He was a man of vigorous faculties, a mind fervid and vehement, supplied by incessant and unlimited inquiry, with wonderful extent and variety of knowledge. . . . To every work he brought a memory full fraught, together with a fancy fertile of original combinations, and at once exerted the powers of the scholar, the reasoner, and the wit. But his knowledge was too multifarious to be always exact, and his pursuits too eager to be always cautious. His abilities gave him a haughty confidence, which he disdained to conceal or mollify; and his impatience of opposition disposed him to treat his adversaries with such contemptuous superiority as made his readers commonly his enemies, and excited against the advocate the wishes of some who favoured the cause."

Letters:

Letters of a Late Eminent Prelate to One of his Friends, edited by Richard Hurd (Kidderminster: Printed by George Gower for T. Cadell & W. Davies, London 1808; Boston: Munroe, Francis & Parker, 1809);

Letters from the Reverend Dr. Warburton, Bishop of Gloucester to the Hon. Charles Yorke, from 1752 to 1770 (London: Printed by the Philanthropic Society, 1812);

John Nichols, *Illustrations of the Literary History of the Eighteenth Century. Consisting of Authentic Memoirs and Original Letters of Eminent Persons; and Intended as a Sequel to The Literary Anecdotes*, volume 2 (London: Printed for the author by Nichols, Son & Bentley, 1817);

A Selection from the Unpublished Papers of the Right Reverend William Warburton, D.D., late Lord Bishop of Gloucester, edited by Francis Kilvert (London: John Bowyer Nichols & Son, 1841).

Biography:

John Selby Watson, *The Life of William Warburton, D.D., Lord Bishop of Gloucester, from 1760 to 1779: with Remarks on His Works* (London: Longman, Green, Longman, Roberts, and Green, 1863).

References:

Clifton Cherpack, "Warburton and the Encyclo-pédie," *Comparative Literature*, 7 (Summer 1955): 226-239;

Stephen J. Curry, "The Literary Criticism of William Warburton," *English Studies*, 48 (-1967): 35-48;

A. W. Evans, *Warburton and the Warburtonians: A Study in Some Eighteenth-Century Controversies* (London: Oxford University Press, 1932);

Elise F. Knapp, "Community Property: A Case for Warburton's 1751 Edition of Pope," *Studies in English Literature*, 26 (1986): 455-468;

Melvin New, "Sterne, Warburton, and the Burden of Exuburant Wit," *Eighteenth-Century Studies*, 15 (1982): 245-274;

John Nichols, *Literary Anecdotes of the Eighteenth Century: Comprizing Biographical Memoirs of William Bowyer, F.S.A., and Many of His Friends*, 9 volumes (London: Nichols & Bentley, 1812-1816);

Robert M. Ryley, *William Warburton* (Boston: Twayne, 1984);

Sir Leslie Stephen, *History of English Thought in the Eighteenth Century*, 2 volumes (London: Smith, Elder, 1876).

Papers:

The Bodleian Library, Oxford, has Warburton's letters to William Stukeley. Warburton's letters to Thomas Birch and other correspondence are at the British Library. The Gloucester Cathedral has manuscripts for sermons. The Harry Ransom Humanities Research Center, University of Texas at Austin, also has Warburton letters.

Joseph Warton

(April 1722 - 23 February 1800)

John A. Vance
University of Georgia

BOOKS: *Fashion: An Epistolary Satire to a Friend* (London: Printed for R. Dodsley & sold by T. Cooper, 1742);

The Enthusiast; or, the Lover of Nature (London: Printed for R. Dodsley & sold by M. Cooper, 1744);

Odes on Various Subjects (London: Printed for R. Dodsley & sold by M. Cooper, 1746; second edition, revised, London: Printed for R. Dodsley & sold by M. Cooper, 1747);

Ranelagh House: A Satire (London: Printed for W. Owen, 1747);

An Ode, Occasioned by Reading Mr. West's Translation of Pindar (London: Printed for W. Owen, 1749);

An Essay on the Writings and Genius of Pope (London: Printed for M. Cooper, 1756); second edition, revised as *An Essay on the Genius and Writings of Pope* (London: Printed for R. & J. Dodsley, 1762); third edition, revised (London: Printed for J. Dodsley, 1772); volume 2 (London: Printed for J. Dodsley, 1782); volumes 1 and 2, "fourth" edition, revised (London: Printed for J. Dodsley, 1782).

OTHER: *Poems on Several Occasions. By the Reverend Mr. Thomas Warton*, edited, with contributions, by Warton (London: Printed for R. Manby & H. S. Cox, 1748);

The Enthusiast, revised version, in volume 3 of *A Collection of Poems by Several Hands*, 3 volumes, edited by Robert Dodsley (London: Printed for R. Dodsley, 1748);

The Adventurer, nos. 1-140 (London: Printed for J. Payne, 7 November 1752 - 9 March 1754) —includes twenty-four numbers, signed "Z," by Joseph Warton, with the assistance of Thomas Warton & Jane Warton;

The Works of Virgil, 4 volumes, edited, with translations, by Warton (London: Printed for R. Dodsley, 1753; second edition, London: Printed for R. & J. Dodsley, 1763);

Sir Philip Sydney's Defence of Poetry, and Observations on Poetry and Eloquence, From the Discoveries

Joseph Warton (portrait by Sir Joshua Reynolds; Ashmolean Museum, Oxford)

of Ben Jonson, edited by Warton (London: Printed for G. G. & J. Robinson, 1787);

The Works of Alexander Pope, 9 volumes, edited by Warton (London: Printed for B. Law, J. Johnson, C. Dilly, G. G. & J. Robinson, J. Nichols, and others, 1797);

The Poetical Works of John Dryden, 4 volumes, edited by Warton, with the assistance of John Warton (London: F. C. & J. Rivington, 1811).

Joseph Warton was an important contributor to the dynamic literary activity in the Age of Johnson (1740-1800). His aggressive endorsement of the imagination and his refusal to accept the authority of "correct" verse and to deem Alexander Pope as the best model for contemporary poets made Warton a vigorous champion of the poetry that emerged in the 1740s. To the end of his life, Warton maintained his reputation as a literary radical, one who challenged the perceptions of noted authors and critics, such as his friend Samuel Johnson. Although his poetic output was limited roughly to a ten-year period and his literary career interrupted by a hiatus of some twenty years, Joseph Warton wrote enough to secure the distinction of being one of the most influential English writers of the eighteenth century. As a critic, poet, essayist, and editor, Warton offered works that were challenging, sound, innovative, and solidly historical. Not simply a collaborator with his brother Thomas, Joseph Warton has a significant place of his own in the history of English literature. To know Warton is to understand and appreciate the vibrant literary milieu of the mid and late eighteenth century.

Joseph Warton was born in April of 1722 (baptized on 22 April) at the vicarage of his maternal grandfather in Dunsfold, Surrey. He was the child of Elizabeth and Thomas Warton, who was then Professor of Poetry at Oxford University. A year later the family moved to Basingstoke, Hampshire—where, after a time, Thomas became headmaster at the local grammar school. While at Basingstoke, Joseph Warton witnessed the birth of his sister, Jane, in 1724 and brother, Thomas, in 1728. Warton's education continued at Winchester College (1736-1740) and at Oriel College, Oxford (1740-1744), where he took a B.A. degree. While at Winchester, Warton made the acquaintance of young William Collins—the intimacy between them having a considerable effect on Warton's literary direction.

In these years, Joseph Warton began his brief but fruitful career as a poet, writing initially satirical verse in a "Popean" vein (for example, *Fashion: An Epistolary Satire to a Friend* in 1742), but then venturing far away from any established literary models with *The Enthusiast* (1744; revised and enlarged in 1748). *The Enthusiast* is the work of an exuberant and confrontational poet, one who exults in the delights of unrefined nature, rejects the formal expectations of art, and forwards the imagination (or "Fancy") as the most crucial ingredient of true poetry. Warton also provides some stinging social commentary in the poem and advocates in his poetic reverie an abandonment of "civilization" and all its corrupting influences. Significantly, much of what Warton has to say in his poem finds expression in his later criticism. It would therefore be inaccurate to dismiss *The Enthusiast* as a youthful attempt to cut a new poetic path with the brands of hyperbole and artistic "insincerity." In addition, *The Enthusiast* has long been seen as an example of "preromantic" verse (along with poems by James Thomson, William Collins, and Thomas Gray), but it would be incorrect to categorize it as a mere historical curiosity, for the poem reflects well the course much poetry was taking in the 1740s.

In 1746 Robert Dodsley chose to publish Warton's *Odes on Various Subjects*, which continues much that was evident in *The Enthusiast*—as such poems as "Ode to Fancy," "Ode to the Nightingale," "Ode to Solitude," and "Ode to a Lady in the Spring" make clear. Occasionally marred by awkward images and an abundance of alliteration, the collection nevertheless endorses without qualification the imagination as the prime motivating force in poetry, sings the praises of unspoiled and unrefined nature, discredits rational and didactic verse, and trumpets loudly British liberty. Perhaps most impressive is Warton's short prose preface, in which he notes that the public has for too long been accustomed to moralistic, didactic, and formal poetry and prose. As a reflection of his normally sound critical judgments, Warton concedes that the public, by nature of its sensibilities, has little use for any work "where the imagination is much indulged," but Warton defies custom and public censure by offering an alternative to didactic and satiric verse and by insisting that "Invention and Imagination" are the "chief faculties of a Poet." Warton also provides a clue to his critical perspective—and that of his brother Thomas as well—when he adds that these odes should be looked upon as "an attempt to bring back Poetry into its right channel." For Warton, English poetry has been served poorly since the death of Milton. The reader is left to conclude that Dryden and particularly Pope interrupted and, owing to their influence, suppressed the flow of imaginative verse in England. Warton's bold challenge to their authority (or at least to his perception of that authority) would be a hallmark of his criticism until his death more than fifty years later.

But Warton did not ignore or reject what marked Pope and writers of similar interests, though of lesser talents. Initially there was Warton's *Ranelagh House*, a witty prose pamphlet published in the spring of 1747. In the "Manner of Monsieur Le Sage," *Ranelagh House* provides a catalogue of various fools, hypocrites, and misfits, depicted in a manner reminiscent of both Restoration comedies and Hogarth prints. Warton demonstrates a facility in conventional satire, muted to an extent by the humanity that reveals itself in the piece; and one could make an argument that he would have been a competent, though certainly a less brilliant, successor to Pope and Jonathan Swift had he so chosen. But serious editorial projects and perceptive literary criticism seemed more attractive challenges to him in the late 1740s and 1750s.

Like his literary efforts, Warton's personal life did not lack variety in this period. Having served at ministerial duties in Chelsea, Chawton, and Droxford, Warton returned to Basingstoke after the death of his father in 1745 to manage his family's affairs. He was also becoming known in literary circles. Besides Collins, Robert Dodsley and Henry Fielding would soon become literary acquaintances. In the summer of 1747 Charles Paulet, Duke of Bolton, provided Warton a much needed living at Winslade, and, with the prospects of financial security, he married Mary (Molly) Daman on 21 September. Warton would father six children with Molly Daman (who died in 1772), marrying once more in December 1773, to Charlotte Nicholas, who bore him another child. While continuing his literary work (poetry and some editing), Warton went to the south of France in 1751 specifically to marry the duke of Bolton to the actress Lavinia Fenton, even though at the time the duchess of Bolton, who was suffering from a terminal illness, had not yet died. The duchess's tenacity forced Warton to return to England before having the opportunity to perform the nuptial service for his benefactor. Back in England during the early 1750s, Warton was able to broaden further his literary friendships—most notably with Samuel Johnson, Edmund Burke, David Garrick, and Bonnell Thornton.

In 1748, owing in part to the family's precarious financial situation, Warton had brought out an edition of his father's verse—*Poems on Several Occasions. By the Reverend Mr. Thomas Warton*. Modern scholarship has revealed, however, that despite its title the volume actually includes some poems written by Joseph himself and by his brother Thomas; in fact, these "forged" verses are among the most interesting in the collection. The elder Warton's reputation, which was fairly good throughout most of this century, has therefore been considerably diminished. (He had been thought of, along with his sons, as one of the century's "preromantics.") Joseph Warton's motives for the deception were both financial and filial: he needed to offer a substantial and attractive volume for sale, and he wished to enhance the literary reputation of his father.

When he returned from France in 1751, Warton set about completing a four-volume edition of Virgil, which he had begun two years earlier. On 25 January 1753 he published the edition, comprising his translations of the *Eclogues* and the *Georgics*, along with Christopher Pitt's translation of the *Aeneid* and essays on the *Aeneid* by William Warburton, Francis Atterbury, and William Whitehead. Everything else was written by Warton: a life of the poet, notes to the entire four volumes, a postscript on the *Aeneid*, and, most importantly, essays on pastoral, didactic, and epic poetry. Other than confronting the authority of Dryden, whose translation of the *Aeneid* he did not use, Warton speaks for his own generation of writers—for example, by his including Johnson's *Rambler* 37 (24 July 1750) as the best commentary on pastoral poetry. In his three critical essays Warton evinces the same appreciation of untamed nature conspicuous in *The Enthusiast*, the same preference for the imagination over the formal requirements of art, and the same sensitivity to the pathetic in literature: "A stroke of passion is worth a hundred of the most lively and glowing descriptions. Men love to be moved, much better than to be instructed." Warton, moreover, considers those aspects of literature he knew were dear to Dryden and Pope and shows that he was not simply a literary iconoclast but rather a learned scholar who could speak with authority and perception on the usefulness of didactic poetry, even though he felt it was not in the first rank of poetic efforts. For instance, Warton argues that digressions are necessary to the didactic poet, for they may gain and then keep the reader's attention. He also writes with facility on the demands of the epic poem, and praises Virgil for the sublimity and harmony of his art.

Warton's Virgil had the respect of important literary men and women of mid century (it went into a second edition in 1763). Samuel Johnson thought highly of the effort, and it was through his growing friendship with Johnson that Warton received in March 1753 an invitation to write critical essays for *The Adventurer*, which had begun to appear in November 1752. Johnson wrote Warton that John Hawkesworth (the editor) and the publisher John Payne wished to assign the "Province of Criticism and Literature" to the "Commentator on Virgil." Until 1974, all twenty-four papers signed "Z" (Johnson signed his "T") were believed to be by Joseph Warton, but modern scholarship has offered compelling evidence that Thomas Warton not only assisted his brother with the composition of some of the papers but might have written a few on his own. (Evidence also points to Jane Warton as the author of one of the papers.) Most of the "Z" papers in *The Adventurer* series (those from April 1753 to March 1754) were by Joseph alone. In these pieces he comments on the classical epic (the *Iliad* and the *Odyssey*), the significance of the imagination in literature and formal rules in art, imitations by modern authors, the burden of the ancients on contemporary poets, English drama, satire, the state of current literary taste, and Milton's *Paradise Lost*. His contributions also include five important essays on Shakespeare, two on *The Tempest* and three on *King Lear*. Evident in all of Warton's papers is an easy, lucid style, unencumbered by a rigid allegiance to a theoretical school or by any critical timidity. Warton argues in one essay that, if books on philosophy and criticism were somehow lost to subsequent generations of writers, their loss would be inconsequential, for then writers would have to start anew, free from custom, and would have to "follow truth instead of authority" (*Adventurer* 89). Agreeing with Joseph Addison that the ancients likely surpassed the moderns in literary efforts, Warton asserts they did not succeed as well in humor and ridicule as did Pope, Nicolas Despréaux Boileau, Swift, and Addison (*Adventurers* 127, 133).

Warton's judicious remarks on Milton's *Paradise Lost* (*Adventurer* 101) are typical of his criticism in general; he is not hesitant to point out the flaws in a work he deeply respected, and his negative assessments in no way diminish the enthusiasm for that work or the validity of the critical position he assumes. He can fault the dialogue between Adam and Raphael, the esoteric allusions given to Adam by the angels, and the sketchy description of the Tree of Life—yet still mark the pathos and brilliance of the expulsion in book 12, the depiction of the fallen angels in book 1, their debate in Pandemonium in book 2, and Satan's dis-

covery of Sin and Death at the end of that book. Warton adds that Satan's speech before the temptation of Eve in book 9 is "the most natural, most spirited, and truly dramatic speech, that is, perhaps, to be found in any writer, whether ancient or modern."

The five essays on Shakespeare effectively demonstrate Warton's critical method and central positions. He holds Shakespeare accountable for his violation of the unity of time, his occasionally "obscure and turgid" diction, his plot distractions and staged violence in *Lear*—but any negative remarks are quickly varnished over by the critic's exuberant advocacy of what he believed to be the best in Shakespeare: his "lively creative imagination; his strokes of nature and passion; and his preservation of the consistency of characters." Warton finds Ariel one of Shakespeare's most brilliant creations and calls *The Tempest* a play that gives rein to the playwright's "boundless imagination." The following comment is indicative of the best of Warton's prose: Shakespeare is "a more powerful magician than his own Prospero: we are transported into fairy land; we are wrapt in a delicious dream, from which it is misery to be disturbed; all around is enchantment!" (*Adventurer* 93). In the speeches of Caliban and Miranda, Warton finds Shakespeare's words exceptional in their "appropriateness" to character (*Adventurer* 97).

Warton discovers in *King Lear* the best illustration of Shakespeare's mastery of brevity as the most poignant manner in which to present tragic moments, his effective employment of pathos, and the kind of reader response which Shakespeare's characters and speeches encourage: "I know not a speech more truly pathetic than that of Cordelia when she first sees [her father]." Of the end of the play Warton writes: "I hope I have no readers that can peruse [Lear's] answer [to Cordelia] without tears" (*Adventurer* 122). Perhaps the most significant of his comments, however, is in response to the debate regarding the authority of the general over the particular in literature. Warton advocates forcibly the minority position (at least as he views it): "General criticism is on all subjects useless and unentertaining; but is more than commonly absurd with respect to Shakespeare, who must be accompanied step by step, and scene by scene, in his gradual developments of characters and passions, and whose finer features must be singly pointed out, if we would do complete justice to his genuine beauties" (*Adventurer* 116). These five papers were the first series of connected essays dealing exclusively with Shakespearean criticism. Along with the other *Adventurer* essays and the edition of Virgil, these writings on Shakespeare established Joseph Warton, in the eyes of his contemporaries, as a leading literary critic. As John Hawkesworth remarked in a footnote to the final *Adventurer* (number 140), Warton's translation of Virgil "would alone sufficiently distinguish him as a genius and a scholar."

Joseph Warton would not move to London and join the literary establishment; he remained, except for periodic trips to the city, esconced in Winchester, raising a family and devoting a good deal of his energy to academic life. In 1755 Warton became second master at Winchester College; he received a patronage from George, Lord Lyttelton, in 1756, an M.A. degree from Oxford in 1759, and a B.D. and D.D. from Oxford in 1768. In 1766 he replaced the retired John Burton as headmaster of Winchester. Except for further editions of Virgil and his essay on Pope and a few poems, Warton brought out nothing of note for more than twenty-five years after the publication of his essay on Pope in 1756. The reputation he earned in the early and mid 1750s stayed with him throughout the hiatus. His circle of literary friendships broadened to include George Colman the Elder, Joshua Reynolds, John Wilkes, James Boswell, John Nichols, Fanny Burney, Hannah More, and Elizabeth Montagu. Warton visited these friends in London and kept up a correspondence with most of them. In 1777 he was elected to the famous Literary Club established by Johnson and Reynolds.

At Winchester College, however, events did not always run smoothly. Even though Warton was popular with his students—who enjoyed his more liberal teaching methods and philosophy—they often took advantage of Warton's laxity in matters of discipline. At least three open rebellions occurred during Warton's tenure. These chaotic moments were often more playful than threatening, and comic activities marked the rambunctiousness of the lads, but there were a few times when the activity got too far out of hand: one report has a boy throwing a Latin dictionary at Warton's head; and another, perhaps less reliable, says that Warton was knocked down by a volume of his own Virgil. During the riot of 1793, only several months before Warton retired from Winchester, the students confiscated provisions, swords, and firearms. Through it all Warton remained popular with the students, whom he was not always able to control.

Joseph Warton's major literary achievement was his *Essay on the Genius and Writings of Pope*—one of the most important books of criticism in the eighteenth century. Forwarding a proposal to Robert Dodsley early in 1755, Warton had already done some work on the essay—gathering materials rather than writing much on the project. As an indication that Warton's reputation as vigorous champion of imaginative poetry was firmly entrenched at this time, Dodsley asked him not to ignore the beauties of Pope and wrote to brother Thomas, fearing that Joseph would inordinately assail the revered Pope. The printing of the essay was done at Oxford, under the supervision of Thomas Warton, in 1755 and early 1756. Warton decided to publish two volumes of his criticism, and offered a first volume when enough copy had been completed and printed. On 2 April 1756 appeared, anonymously, *An Essay on the Writings and Genius of Pope* (subsequent editions reversed "Writings" and "Genius" in the title), and it was well received by the public. (Warton's reputation also made the identity of the author an easy guess.) The second edition of volume 1 appeared in 1762, complete with some 250 changes from the 1756 edition. The third edition (including some 70 further changes) was published in 1772, and then, in 1782 the long-awaited second volume appeared—with a two-volume fourth edition in the same year (complete with further changes in volume 1).

The extensive delay in getting out the second volume has long puzzled scholars. Some have argued that Warton did not wish to offend Pope's executor, William Warburton; others, such as Samuel Johnson, felt that Warton was frustrated at not being able to convince the literary world that Pope did not deserve a place among the very best poets; and still others suggested that Warton's tending to his family and college simply made the completion a low priority. It appears that some two hundred pages of the second volume had been printed in 1760 and likely stored by James Dodsley. Modern scholarship has also indicated that Warton worked piecemeal throughout the 1760s and 1770s, rather than beginning and then completing the second volume in the early 1780s. Finally, some have advanced the theory that the reason Warton finally completed volume 2 was the challenge offered by his friend Johnson's "Life of Pope," printed in 1781. The appearance of the second volume and the two-volume fourth edition roused several dissenting and disparaging critical responses, although *An Essay on the Genius and Writings of Pope* led to no major literary warfare. A fifth edition (both volumes) complete with index appeared after Warton's death, in 1806.

The opening pages of *An Essay on the Genius and Writings of Pope* quickly challenge the existing perception of Pope yet do not attack him indiscriminately: as Warton writes in his dedication to Edward Young: "I revere the memory of Pope; I respect and honour his abilities; but I do not think him at the head of his profession. In other words, in that species of poetry wherein Pope excelled, he is superior to all mankind: and I only say, that this species of poetry is not the most excellent one of the art." Warton argues that since the "Sublime and the Pathetic are the two chief nerves of genuine poesy," it is important to ask what is "transcendently Sublime or Pathetic in Pope?" The structure of the essay is an examination of Pope's works (in fourteen sections)—all for the purpose of deciding if Pope ranks in the first class of English poets, along with Shakespeare, Spenser, and Milton. The material specifically on Pope (roughly, only one of the two volumes) treats the poetry judiciously; there are words of praise sprinkled liberally throughout the discussions, even though the reader is aware from the outset that Warton will not find Pope worthy of a place in the pantheon of great English poets. A good number of Warton's estimations sound exactly like many of the comments offered by Pope enthusiasts. For example, Warton calls the *Essay on Criticism* a "master-piece in its kind" and the *Essay on Man* "as close a piece of argument, admitting its principles, as perhaps can be found in verse." Throughout the two volumes one finds in large supply such adjectives as *mellifluous, exquisite, lucid, brilliant,* and *ingenious.* Warton also determines *The Rape of the Lock* to be the most excellent example of the "heroi-comic," and he considers *Eloisa to Abelard* both "tender and pathetic." Of course, there are a plethora of negative and severe assessments—few of which, though, are trite or petty. Warton finds sections of many of Pope's poems "flat" and "ridiculous" and some images vulgar and offensive. He faults the *Dunciad* for "the violence and vehemence of its satire, and the excessive height to which it is carried." In the second volume, which the public waited twenty-six years to read, Warton concludes that Pope became "one of the most correct, even, and exact poets that ever wrote"—the

master of didactic, moral, and satirical verse. However, Pope lacks enough "fancy and invention" to place him in the first rank of English poets. Consequently, he is situated as first of the second rank— just above Dryden—for while Dryden is "the greater genius" Pope is "the better artist."

The other volume's worth of material is composed of Warton's many digressions on various literary topics. Background information regarding allusions in Pope's verse, for example, is occasionally taken to inordinate lengths. But these digressions also help make the volume the important achievement it is. Warton reflects in the digressive material his philosophy regarding poetic excellence and what can suppress it: he notes in several places, for instance, the debilitating effect of the formal "dictates of art." His observations on dramatic literature suggest, as do his *Adventurer* essays, that Warton was an important drama critic of midcentury. He offers interesting assessments of the newer school of poets, as well as of earlier ones—discussing more than fifty different poets and writers. But certainly Thomas Gray, Mark Akenside, James Thomson, and Edward Young are the poets Warton chiefly praises for their genius and imaginative gifts—often noting that *sections* of their works are superior to anything Pope wrote. Warton terms Young a "sublime and original genius"—a designation he refuses to give Pope—concluding, "The preference given here to Pope, above other modern English poets . . . is founded on the excellencies of his works *in general,* and *taken all together*; for there are *parts* and *passages* in other modern authors, in *Young* and *Thomson,* for instance, equal to any of Pope; and he has written nothing in a strain so truly sublime, as the *Bard* of *Gray.*" Warton does not rank the newer generation of poets, but it seems apparent that he wishes to stress that poetic genius did not die with Pope. Warton emerges from these pages as the exuberant and successful spokesman for his generation of poets and critics.

Warton came out of his literary retirement with the second volume of *An Essay on the Genius and Writings of Pope* in 1782, but it would be five years before he brought out his next effort, an edition of Sir Philip Sydney's *Defence of Poesy* (1595) and Ben Jonson's "Observations on Eloquence and Poetry" from the *Discoveries* (1640-1641). And then there was another ten-year lapse before Warton published his own nine-volume edition of Pope's poetry (three volumes contained the letters) in 1797. The notes to the edition have been criticized for being often "irrelevant" and "malicious." (To his death and beyond Warton maintained his reputation as the chief antagonist of Pope's memory.) Although he apparently merely cut up his notes from *An Essay on the Genius and Writings of Pope* and incorporated them into the edition, the new material demonstrates that with few exceptions Warton thought exactly the same about the superiority of imaginative poetry as he did when he was writing the preface to his *Odes on Various Subjects* fifty years earlier. In 1795 he wrote to a friend that "no very correct writer can be a good subject for criticism." After the completion of the edition, Warton, then in his mid seventies, turned to an edition of John Dryden, and composed notes for two volumes before his death in 1800. Two years later, his son John completed the edition, which was published in 1811.

Joseph Warton let many years go by without writing poetry or criticism or editing important texts, but his accomplishments in the years when he was busy earned him a reputation he never lost: as an exuberant, judicious, and forceful critic who believed strongly that the imagination produced the best kind of poetry. As a poet and critic Warton demonstrated a delightful form of rebellion from (at least as he perceived it) the established schools of poetry and poetic theory, lorded over by the example and memory of Pope. Well-known contemporaries valued his friendship and respected and admired his literary efforts, and some—most notably Samuel Johnson—could be both impressed and infuriated by Warton's commitment to his literary values. He was no "preromantic" to be conveniently labeled and then shelved; rather, Joseph Warton's writings represented the best literary work characteristic of the mid and late eighteenth century.

Letters:
Hugh Reid, ed., "The Correspondence of Joseph Warton," doctoral thesis, University of London, 1987.

Bibliographies:
Julia Hysham, "Joseph Warton: A Biographical and Critical Study," Ph.D. dissertation, Columbia University, 1950;

John A. Vance, *Joseph and Thomas Warton: An Annotated Bibliography* (New York: Garland, 1983).

Biographies:
John Wooll, *Biographical Memoirs of the Late Revd. Jo-*

seph Warton, D.D. (London: T. Cadell & W. Davies, 1806);

Alexander Chalmers, "Joseph Warton," in *The Works of the English Poets* (London: J. Johnson, 1810), XVIII: 75-88;

Julia Hysham, "Joseph Warton: A Biographical and Critical Study," Ph.D. dissertation, Columbia University, 1950.

References:
John Dennis, "The Wartons," *Cornhill Magazine*, 30 (November 1874): 534-547;

David Fairer, "Authorship Problems in *The Adventurer*," *Review of English Studies*, new series 25 (May 1974): 137-151;

Fairer, "The Poems of Thomas Warton the Elder?," *Review of English Studies*, new series 26 (August 1975): 287-300, 395-406; "Postscript," *Review of English Studies*, new series 29 (February 1978): 61-65;

Fairer, "The Writing and Printing of Joseph Warton's *Essay on Pope*," *Studies in Bibliography*, 30 (1977): 211-219;

Edmund Gosse, "Two Pioneers of Romanticism: Joseph and Thomas Warton," *Proceedings of the British Academy*, 7 (1915): 145-163;

Philip Mahone Griffith, "Joseph Warton's Criticism of Shakespeare," *Tulane Studies in English*, 14 (1965): 17-27;

William D. MacClintock, *Joseph Warton's Essay on Pope: A History of the Five Editions* (Chapel Hill: University of North Carolina Press, 1933);

Edith J. Morley, "Joseph Warton: A Comparison of His *Essay on the Genius and Writings of Pope* with his Edition of Pope's Works," *Essays and Studies*, 9 (1924): 98-114;

David B. Morris, "Joseph Warton's Figure of Virtue: Poetic Indirection in "The Enthusiast," *Philological Quarterly*, 50 (October 1971): 678-683;

Joan Pittock, *The Ascendancy of Taste: The Achievement of Joseph and Thomas Warton* (London: Routledge & Kegan Paul, 1973);

Pittock, "Joseph Warton and His Second Volume of the *Essay on Pope*," *Review of English Studies*, new series 18 (1967): 264-273;

Pittock, "Lives and Letters: New Wartoniana," *Durham University Journal*, 70 (June 1978): 193-203;

Christina Le Prevost, "More Unacknowledged Verse by Joseph Warton," *Review of English*

Studies, new series 37 (August 1986): 317-347;

Hoyt Trowbridge, "Joseph Warton and the Imagination," *Modern Philology*, 35 (August 1937): 73-87;

John A. Vance, *Joseph and Thomas Warton* (Boston: Twayne, 1983);

Vance, "The Samuel Johnson-Joseph Warton Friendship," *Transactions of the Johnson Society* (December 1982): 44-55;

William Youngren, "Dr. Johnson, Joseph Warton, and the 'Theory of Particularity,' " *Dispositio*, 4 (Summer-Fall 1979): 163-188.

Papers:

The largest holdings of Warton's correspondence and manuscripts are at the British Library and Winchester College.

Thomas Warton
(9 January 1728 - 21 May 1790)

John A. Vance
University of Georgia

BOOKS: *Five Pastoral Eclogues: The Scenes of which are Suppos'd to lie among the Shepherds Oppress'd by the War in Germany* (London: Printed for R. Dodsley, 1745);

The Pleasures of Melancholy. A Poem (London: Printed for R. Dodsley & sold by M. Cooper, 1747);

The Triumph of Isis, A Poem. Occasioned by Isis, An Elegy (London: Printed for W. Owen, 1750);

A Description of the City, College, and Cathedral of Winchester (London: Printed for R. Baldwin, 1750; revised edition, London: Printed for R. Baldwin; sold by T. Burdon, Winchester; B. Collins, Salisbury, 1760); third edition published as *The Winchester Guide* (Winton: Printed & sold for T. Blagden, 1796);

New-market, A Satire (London: Printed for J. Newbery, 1751);

Ode for Music, as performed at the Theatre in Oxford, on the second of July 1751 (Oxford: Printed for R. Clements & J. Barrett; W. Thurlbourne, Cambridge; R. Dodsley, London, 1751);

Observations on the Faerie Queene of Spenser (London: Printed for R. & J. Dodsley, and J. Fletcher, Oxford, 1754); revised and enlarged as *Observations on the Fairy Queen of Spenser*, 2 volumes (London: Printed for R.

& J. Dodsley and J. Fletcher, Oxford, 1762);

A Companion to the Guide and Guide to the Companion: Being a Complete Supplement to All the Accounts of Oxford Hitherto Published (London: Printed for H. Payne, 1760; second edition, corrected and enlarged, 1762?);

Mons Catharina; prope Wintoniam. Poema (London: Prostant venales apud R. & J. Dodsley, 1760);

The Life and Literary Remains of Ralph Bathurst, 2 volumes (London: Printed for R. & J. Dodsley, C. Bathurst, and J. Fletcher, Oxford, 1761);

The Life of Sir Thomas Pope, Founder of Trinity College Oxford (London: Printed for T. Davies, T. Becket, T. Walters, F. Newbery, and J. Fletcher, Oxford, 1772; revised edition, London: Printed for Thomas Cadell, 1780);

The History of English Poetry, from the Close of the Eleventh to the Commencement of the Eighteenth Century, 3 volumes (London: Printed for & sold by J. Dodsley, J. Walter, T. Becket, J. Robson, G. Robinson, J. Bew, and Messrs. Fletcher, Oxford, 1774-1781); volume 4, pp. 1-88 (N.p., 1789);

Poems. A New Edition, With Additions. By Thomas Warton (London: Printed for T. Becket, 1777); enlarged as *Poems. A New Edition* (Lon-

Thomas Warton (portrait by Sir Joshua Reynolds; Trinity College, Oxford)

don: Printed for T. Becket, 1777; third edition, corrected, 1779; fourth edition, corrected and enlarged, London: Printed for G. G. J. & J. Robinson, 1789); greatly enlarged as *Poems on Various Subjects, of Thomas Warton* (London: Printed for G. G. J. & J. Robinson, 1791);

Specimen of a Parochial History of Oxfordshire (N.p.: Privately printed, 1782); corrected and enlarged as *Specimen of a History of Oxfordshire* (London: Printed for J. Nichols, J. Robson, and C. Dilly; Mess. Fletchers, D. Prince & J. Cook, Oxford; J. Merrill, Cambridge, 1783); third edition, *The History and Antiquities of Kiddington* (London: J. Nichols, 1815);

An Enquiry into the Authenticity of the Poems Attributed to Thomas Rowley (London: Printed for J. Dodsley & sold by Mess. Fletchers, Oxford, 1782);

Verses on Sir Joshua Reynolds's Painted Window at New-College Oxford (London: Printed for J.

Dodsley & sold by Mess. Fletchers, Oxford, 1782);

A History of English Poetry: An Unpublished Continuation, edited by Rodney M. Baine, Augustan Reprint Society Publication No. 39 (Los Angeles: William Andrews Clark Memorial Library, 1953).

Edition: *The Poetical Works of the Late Thomas Warton, B.D.*, 2 volumes, edited by Richard Mant (Oxford: Oxford University Press, 1802).

OTHER: *The Union; or Select Scots and English Poems*, edited by Warton (Edinburgh [i.e., Oxford]: Printed for Archibald Monro and David Murray [i.e., Printed by William Jackson], 1753);

Inscriptionum Romanarum Metricarum Delectus, edited by Warton (London: Apud R. & J. Dodsley, 1758);

The Idler, nos. 33, 93, and 96, *Universal Chronicle*, 2 December 1758, 26 January 1760, and 16 February 1760;

The Oxford Sausage; or Select Poetical Pieces Written by the Most Celebrated Wits of the University of Oxford, edited by Warton (London: Printed for J. Fletcher, 1764);

Anthologiae Graecae à Constantino Cephala condita libri tres, edited by Warton (Oxford: E typographeo Clarendoniano, prostant venales apud Jacobum Fletcher; J. Nourse, P. Vaillant, and J. Fletcher, London, 1766);

Theocriti Syracusii Quae Supersant, 2 volumes, edited by Warton (Oxford: E typographeo Clarendoniano, 1770);

Poems Upon Several Occasions, English, Italian, and Latin, with Translations, by John Milton, edited by Warton (London: Printed for J. Dodsley, 1785; revised edition, London: Printed for G. G. J. & J. Robinson, 1791).

As a poet, critic, essayist, editor, literary historian, biographer, and antiquarian, Thomas Warton ranks as one of the most accomplished and versatile writers of the eighteenth century. In his poetry he reflected his lifelong belief that nature and the historical past should be the concerns of the truly imaginative poet. Although not a brilliant poet, Warton wrote verse that is often excellent and usually stimulating. His nine sonnets helped to renew interest in the form and to pave the way for the important sonnet writing of William Wordsworth and Samuel Taylor Coleridge. Warton's appreciation of melancholy culminated a period rich with works devoted to the pleasures of contemplation and graveyard imaginings. In addition, his editions of poetry by his contemporaries helped to advance them as significant voices in the period immediately following the death of Alexander Pope. Warton's critical work on Edmund Spenser made more popular the historical method of criticism, which asked the reader to judge a literary work from a historical perspective as well as from the critical preferences of contemporary times. Warton explored antiquities and wrote about them with facility and grace, and his examination of the Thomas Chatterton forgeries ranks as the most important response to one of the century's most intense literary debates. Moreover, Warton's monumental *History of English Poetry* (1774-1781) cast important light on the authors of the medieval period and presented to later literary historians a solid base on which to improve. Warton deserves a high place among the writers of the second rank.

Thomas Warton was born on 9 January 1728, at Basingstoke, Hampshire—the second son of Thomas and Elizabeth Warton. The elder Thomas Warton had by this time left Oxford University, where he had been the university's Professor of Poetry for the previous ten years. Enjoying a warm relationship with his elder brother, Joseph (born in 1722), and sister, Jane (born in 1724), Thomas Warton grew up with constant literary and intellectual stimulation from his family, but the boy also found pleasure and inspiration in the countryside nearby and in the antiquities dotting the landscape near his home. Following a formal education guided by his father, Thomas Warton entered Trinity College, Oxford, in 1744 and began an association that would last until his death in 1790. At Oxford he took a B.A. degree in 1747, entered holy orders soon afterward, and concluded his training with an M.A. degree in 1750. During this period, Warton established himself as a poet of some merit with some pastoral eclogues in the manner of Virgil (1745) and with *The Pleasures of Melancholy* (1747). In 1756 he became the second Thomas Warton to be named Professor of Poetry at Oxford University, serving, like his father, two five-year terms.

Warton wrote other poems dealing with natural delights and melancholy (for example, his odes "On the Approach of Summer," "The Suicide," and "The First of April"), and verses in praise of Oxford and its surrounding area, such as *The Triumph of Isis* (1750) and a bit later "On

the Marriage of the King" and "On the Birth of the Prince of Wales." Warton also wrote and would continue to write a considerable number of poems treating historical themes and including historical allusions—primarily from the medieval period, most notably "The Crusade," "The Grave of King Arthur," "Ode on Vale Royal Abbey," and *Verses on Sir Joshua Reynolds's Painted Window at New-College Oxford* (1782). Warton's nine sonnets focus on the restorative power of natural settings, on the pleasures of antiquarian study, and on historical topics. From 1785 to his death in 1790, Warton served as his country's poet laureate (part of his responsibilities being to pen two odes a year). From his first verses in the 1740s until his final laureate odes, Thomas Warton maintained an appreciation of nature, love of the past, and sensitivity for the introspective—all qualities that would come to be identified with the succeeding period of English literature.

Recent scholarship has demonstrated that Thomas Warton helped write several of the *Adventurer* papers signed "Z" and assigned to his brother, Joseph. The same evidence makes a good case for Thomas's having written a few on his own—for example, numbers 71, 76, 109, and 129, essays marked by Warton's special brand of humor, which is evident in such delightful verses as *New-market, A Satire* (1751) and "A Panegyric on Oxford Ale," and by an appreciation for the "avuncular" tale, the kind Warton wrote several years later for number 96 of Samuel Johnson's *Idler* series.

But his first major critical and historical effort was his *Observations on the Faerie Queene of Spenser* (1754), a work composed during a period of renewed critical and editorial interest in the great Elizabethan poet. Warton shared his brother's estimation of Edmund Spenser as one of the three truly imaginative English poets, but in his essay he displays none of the votary's zeal. The work is marked by a reserved approach to and a judicious estimation of its subject. The publication of the work (in one volume) prompted a letter from Samuel Johnson, who acknowledged Warton's "advancement" of the literature of his "native Country": "You have shown to all who shall hereafter attempt the study of our ancient authours the way to success, by directing them to the perusal of the books which those authours had read" (16 July 1754). Although a few spoke harshly—such as William Huggins, who took exception to Warton's comments on Ariosto—the literary world generally shared Johnson's assessment.

Warton then worked further on the *Observations*, making additions and corrections and receiving advice from Thomas Percy and Richard Hurd, and brought out a two-volume second edition in 1762.

The study is organized as a series of essays on various aspects of the *Faerie Queene* (1590, 1596)—its own organization, its relationship to Ariosto's *Orlando Furioso* (1532), its borrowings, its use of mythology and history, and its parallels to other works by Spenser. Throughout the *Observations*, Warton makes clear the importance of knowing the historical and literary context in which the *Faerie Queene* was written. Rather than a rebellious "romantic" critic, one finds an author willing to try the book by "epic rules"—even though he is quick to remind his readers that it is "absurd to think of judging either Ariosto or Spenser by precepts which they did not attend to." Warton does not always suppress the critical perspective he shared with brother Joseph: in Spenser's great work, for all its violations of rules and balance, we are attracted to something "which engages the affections, the feelings of the heart, rather than the cold approbation of the head." Warton adds, "In reading Spenser if the critic is not satisfied, yet the reader is transported." Although less stimulating than his brother's *Essay on the Genius and Writings of Pope* (1756), the *Observations on the Fairy Queen of Spenser* (enlarged edition, 1762) nevertheless stands as an important document of midcentury criticism, and for more than 150 years would be pointed to as the best work ever written on the *Faerie Queene*.

By the mid 1750s, then, Thomas Warton had become an important contributor to English literature. His poetry and criticism had been read and admired, and his circle of literary friends was expanding to include Johnson, whom Warton had entertained at Trinity College in 1754 and for whom he had helped secure an M.A. degree before publication of the *Dictionary* (1755). In this period Warton also brought out two collections of miscellaneous verse—*The Union; or Select Scots and English Poems* (1753) and *The Oxford Sausage; or Select Poetical Pieces Written by the Most Celebrated Wits of the University of Oxford* (1764). These collections included the verses of important contemporary poets, such as William Collins, Samuel Johnson, Mark Akenside, Joseph Warton, Thomas Gray, and Thomas Warton himself—and *The Oxford Sausage*, in particular, demonstrated Warton's proficiency with and appreciation of lighthearted verse. As a reflection

of his broad interests and talents, Warton published editions of classical metrical inscriptions (*Inscriptionum Romanarum Metricarum Delectus*) in 1758, of Cephalas's *Anthology* in 1766, and of Theocritus in 1770 (a two-volume project on which he had been working since at least 1758). Such efforts as these furthered Warton's reputation as a serious literary scholar.

Other than progressing with his literary history, Warton continued to write poetry and to tend to his duties at Oxford in the 1760s and 1770s. The tales of his habitual indolence at the university were delightfully exaggerated, but it seems certain that he always found time for some of his favorite relaxations: conversation, pipe smoking, imbibing ale, and telling jokes. At times Warton conducted himself in a manner befitting a subject in a William Hogarth print, but his diversions did not interrupt his literary and antiquarian labors. There did not appear to be a sustained period in which he was idle; he was always at work on a project. One aspect of these projects was biographical. In 1760 he published in *Biographia Britannica* a life of Sir Thomas Pope (1507-1559), the founder of Trinity College (the work was completed, however, by 1756). In 1772 he expanded the work to more than four hundred pages—and this version was followed by an enlarged edition in 1780. Late in the nineteenth century H. E. D. Blakiston accused Warton of plagiarism and literary fraud in this biography, but careful examination acquits Warton of these charges, even though misleading and false information did find its way into the work—the result of faulty sources, not literary fraud. In 1761 Warton brought out *The Life and Literary Remains of Ralph Bathurst*, in which Warton provides a good historical sense of Oxford in the seventeenth century as well as a worthy portrait of an earlier president of Trinity College, one of the college's most interesting luminaries. Warton's brief accounts of John Weever the antiquary, William Collins, and Samuel Johnson for Boswell's *Life of Johnson* (1791) further testify to his appreciation of and success in biographical composition. As Boswell wrote in the preface to the *Life of Johnson*, "amidst his variety of genius and learning," Warton was "an excellent Biographer."

Warton's fascination for antiquities began when he was a young boy in Basingstoke, and he always maintained an active interest in the relics and structures of the past. His friendship with Thomas Percy, especially, helped keep his knowledge and perceptions sharp, and Warton advised

Percy in the preparation of his *Reliques of Ancient English Poetry* (1765). Warton's correspondence offers a wealth of evidence suggesting his enthusiasm for the artifacts of the past (which also became subject matter for his verses). Warton kept notebooks filled with comments about the buildings and places he traveled to and passed through. (Much of this material was never published, though some of it is still accessible.) In 1750 he produced *A Description of the City, College, and Cathedral of Winchester* (revised in 1760, and in 1796 under the title *The Winchester Guide*). One guesses that had he had more leisure or a more limited sphere of literary interests, Warton might have written many such guides, but in 1782 he did find time to publish a small pamphlet relating to the history of Kiddington Parish, *Specimen of a Parochial History of Oxfordshire*. Convinced by friends that he should enlarge the work and distribute it more widely (only twenty copies of the pamphlet had been printed as gifts for friends), Warton brought out in 1783—with the assistance of John Nichols, Daniel Prince, and Richard Gough—*Specimen of a History of Oxfordshire*. (In 1815 appeared the third edition, *The History and Antiquities of Kiddington*.) In the preface we find Warton defending the occupation of the antiquarian to the general reader, one who would have read dozens of lampoons on the burrowing, bumbling antiquarian. Warton would have wanted his readers to understand the sentiment expressed in one of his sonnets: "Nor rough, nor barren, are the winding ways / Of hoar Antiquity, but strown with flowers."

Yet his commitment to antiquarian studies did not preclude his poking fun at his interest or at himself; in fact, one of Warton's most delightful personality traits was his self-effacing sense of humor. In 1760 he combined his love of a good jest and of antiquity in the pamphlet *A Companion to the Guide and Guide to the Companion*, in which he sends a playful jab at historical and architectural research, concluding that the caricature of Democritus on one of Oxford's outer walls is there to "admonish Strangers, and particularly the Young Student, that Science is not inconsistent with Good-Humour, and that Scholars are a *merrier* Sett of People than the World is apt to imagine"—a summation that nicely reflects a major aspect of Warton's personality.

On a more serious note is Warton's most important piece of antiquarian writing, *An Enquiry into the Authenticity of the Poems Attributed to Thomas Rowley* (1782)—Warton's response to the contro-

versy surrounding Chatterton's poems, a controversy that had commanded the interest of the general public as well as serious scholars since Chatterton's suicide in 1770. Battle lines were quickly drawn regarding the authenticity of the poems as fifteenth-century verses, with such men as Horace Walpole, Thomas Tyrwhitt, Jacob Bryant, George Steevens, Oliver Goldsmith, Edmond Malone, Samuel Johnson, and Thomas Percy all expressing opinions on the legitimacy of the poems. One assumes the scholarly world anticipated Thomas Warton's pronouncements on the matter, for few men were as well qualified to comment on this fascinating issue. As he would write, he believed the poems to be spurious as early as 1772, but he would not speak with certainty until he had the opportunity to study the verses in more detail. After consulting with several antiquaries, including Percy, Warton was still, almost four years later, unable to state categorically that they were forgeries; in fact, his correspondence with Percy suggests a man hopeful of finding some evidence of their authenticity. Here was a clear case of Warton's fondness for the medieval, which allowed his fancy free rein, clashing with his sober, scholarly side, which sought truth rather than excitement.

Yet by the time he finished the second volume of his *History of English Poetry*, he was ready to take a position on Chatterton's glorious forgeries. In that volume (published in 1778), he examined several of the major poems in the Rowley collection and concluded that a comparison of the verses with other medieval works and a careful consideration of internal evidence make clear that the Rowley poems are not vintage fifteenth-century literary artifacts. One senses Warton's disappointment with such a conclusion: "It is with regret that I find myself obliged to pronounce Rowlie's poems to be spurious." But this section from the *History of English Poetry* would not be enough to settle the matter or to satisfy Warton's interest in the subject; four years later he would produce *An Enquiry into the Authenticity of the Poems Attributed to Thomas Rowley*, a book of 125 pages that easily marks the climax of the long controversy over the poems.

In this book Warton systematically examines the verses and offers solid evidence of their illegitimacy. In the eight sections of his examination, Warton compares the wording, phrasing, and sentiments of the Rowley poems with those characteristic of medieval verse; examines the meter and stanzaic patterns of both; looks at the "affected and unnatural" language of the Rowley verses, concluding harshly that Chatterton seemed to "have been persuaded, that no other ingredient was necessary for his fiction than old words"; scrutinizes the historical allusions in the verses and notes the inconsistencies with actual events; compares the Rowley verses with other poems known to be by Chatterton, arguing that the same hand is well evident in both sets of works; and makes the argument that had Rowley been this good, he would have been "idolized by his age" and certainly printed by Caxton. Throughout his hard-hitting attack on Chatterton's forgeries, Warton does, however, point to the young man's poetic gifts: "We wonder at the address, the command, the facility, the versatility of mind, the accommodation of sentiment, with which in a short space of time he composed a variety of pieces, and on subjects which usually require long observation and experience." Although the matter was not "officially" settled until W. W. Skeat's 1871 edition of Chatterton, it was obvious that Warton's was the deciding blow in the controversy.

Warton's long appreciation of John Milton (like his brother, he believed that Milton was the last of his country's great imaginative poets) culminated in an edition of the poet's "shorter" works—that is, all the poems except *Paradise Lost* (1667, 1674), *Paradise Regained* (1671), and *Samson Agonistes* (1671)—published in the spring of 1785. That year was especially significant in Warton's life: he was elected Camden Professor of History at Oxford, and, more important, he was named his country's poet laureate—a position he held until his death five years later. With little question, Warton was eminently qualified to edit Milton. His affinity for the poet was a secondary qualification, for his having compiled England's first literary history was the best evidence of his fitness for the task. The edition was for the most part praised lavishly—the occasional complaining not at all representative of the edition's reception.

Earlier efforts of those such as Joseph Addison, Richard Bentley, the Jonathan Richardsons, John Callander, William Lauder, and William Warburton suggest the kind of interest the eighteenth century had for Milton's poetry, which had been published (along with *Paradise Lost*) in every decade of the century. Warton realized that the "minor" poetry had not been accorded the attention it deserved; he observes in the preface that these poems did not move the readers of the earlier eighteenth century because "public taste

was unprepared for their reception." Only recently, he argues, has fiction, "fancy," "picturesque description and romantic imagery" diluted enough of the public's taste for wit, rhyme, "sentiment and satire, polished numbers, sparkling couplets, and pointed periods." These remarks easily attest to Warton's unchanging beliefs regarding the best kind of poetry; as with his brother, advancing age did not mean critical conservatism. But the preface does take Milton to task for his politics; in this area Warton could be most "conservative"; he points out as well that a preoccupation with the "deplorable polemics of puritanism" suppressed Milton's imagination, thus depriving posterity of more examples of his poetic genius.

The texts of and commentary on *Lycidas* (1638), *L'Allegro* (1645), and *Il Pensoroso* (1645) compose some forty percent of the more than six hundred pages of the edition; many of Warton's notes read like critical essays. But Warton also paid attention to the sonnets and Latin poems. We again find a learned literary historian and historical critic at work, though one fully sensitive to the brilliance of the poet he is examining. For modern readers, the most rewarding aspect of the edition would be Warton's defense of *Lycidas* against the charges of Samuel Johnson, who found the poem too contrived, trite, and insincere. Warton places Milton in the historical context of the mid seventeenth century and champions the poet's imaginative gifts: "Milton dignifies and adorns [the] common artificial incidents with unexpected touches of picturesque beauty, with the graces of sentiment, and with the novelties of original genius." Warton rejects Johnson's conclusions that there is nothing "new" in the poem and that it has no "real passion."

The success of the volume no doubt encouraged a second edition, which would have included *Paradise Regained* and *Samson Agonistes*. Drawing on the assistance of his brother, Edmond Malone, George Steevens, and Richard Hurd, Warton worked on the second edition (a planned two-volume work) until at least the summer of 1789 (when he had finished the revisions of the 1785 volume), and he believed that the second edition would be completed by early spring of 1790. But upon his death in May 1790 there was no second volume to be published; most of the copy and notes seemed to have disappeared. (The major assumption is that Joseph Warton had them and planned to bring out the second volume, but for whatever reason his plan was not realized. Therefore, only the revision of the 1785 volume appeared in 1791.)

Warton's fecund mind frequently planned projects which he had neither time nor stamina to complete. The proposed second volume of his Milton edition is one such example; his writings on further antiquarian topics would be another. But these failures can easily be forgiven when one considers Warton's major work, *The History of English Poetry*—published in three volumes, 1774-1781. Recent investigations by David Fairer have demonstrated that Warton had been contemplating the project as far back as the early 1750s—not 1762 as was formerly believed. Between 1752 and 1754 he had been collecting materials dealing with literary history and criticism as well as with drama and poetry—material dating from the late sixteenth and early seventeenth centuries. Immersion into the works of Spenser and regular readings at the Ashmolean Museum and in catalogues such as the Harleian Collection indicate that even in his mid twenties Warton was laying the foundation for a full-scale literary history of his country. By 1762, then, Warton was simply renewing his efforts toward the project, not beginning them. The delay of some twelve years until the publication of the history's first volume may at first suggest indolence or lack of resolve—but clearly Warton's duties at Oxford, his broad interest in antiquities, and his impressive literary output better explain the delay. What also explains the lapse of time is the fact that although he had collected a considerable amount of material from the early 1750s, he still had much more to research—especially on the eleventh through the fourteenth centuries, which was the focus of the first volume. It appears that around 1769 Warton found the way clear to begin writing in earnest. (An examination of Warton's correspondence is most helpful in determining the progress of the composition of the *History*.) Warton initially believed that the first volume would go to press in the fall of 1770, but duties and other projects deterred him further.

Finally, in March 1774 appeared the first volume of *The History of English Poetry, from the Close of the Eleventh to the Commencement of the Eighteenth Century*, to which were prefixed two dissertations, "Of the Origin of Romantic Fiction in Europe" and "On the Introduction of Learning into England." Although Warton was confident that the second volume would appear shortly, distractions and commitments (one being the preparation of a volume of his own poetry) delayed the continua-

tion's appearance until the spring of 1778. An anonymous publication took issue with the second volume of *The History of English Poetry*, particularly the conclusions Warton drew about the Rowley poems—and others, such as Horace Walpole, were quick to express some dismay over the unfamiliarity of much of the material (fifteenth-century poets and drama) and over Warton's scholarly style—but the work was universally praised as an important literary and historical achievement.

The third volume, treating a literary period far more familiar to Warton's readers, elicited responses such as the following from the *Gentleman's Magazine* (May 1781): "This volume, like the former, does equal credit to Mr. Warton's taste, judgement, and erudition, and makes us impatiently desirous of more." But it also inspired the attack by Joseph Ritson, in his *Observation on the First Three Volumes of the History of English Poetry* (1782). Ritson accuses Warton, for example, of "gross and unaccountable stupidity"—asserting that Warton deserves the name of "Swindler" for writing volume after volume only to secure profit for himself. The public generally dismissed Ritson's eccentric attack, however, and looked forward to the fourth volume (the third stopped in the late sixteenth century), in which Warton had expected to continue the account up to the beginning of his own century. His 1785 edition of Milton announces the publication of a fourth volume "Speedily," but this volume never reached the public: only some eighty-eight pages were run off and published in 1789 (an unpublished continuation of several more pages was finally published by Rodney M. Baine in 1953). Again, one can explain the failure to complete the fourth volume by considering Warton's other commitments, projects, and interests; the 1780s was a busy decade for him. Some have argued that Warton lost interest in the material he would have had to cover, and one can argue that the volume of Spenser in 1754 and the edition of Milton in 1785 had both satisfied his desire to bring the history up to the end of the seventeenth century. Whatever the reason for the evaporation of the project, the literary world expected Joseph Warton to complete it, a task he originally agreed to perform but found too imposing or uninspiring actually to finish.

Thomas Warton begins the first volume of *The History of English Poetry* with a defense of the historical method of criticism and his chronological method of organization. Although he explains his unwillingness to treat the "Saxon poetry," he does discuss its influence in his first digression, "Of the Origin of Romantic Fiction in Europe." Here and throughout the volume one finds evidence of Warton's respect for the influences that made medieval literature what it was: an imaginative and boisterous depiction of real life and fancy—unrefined and often vulgar, yet still worthy of study by modern (eighteenth-century) scholars and readers. Warton discusses dialects, monasteries, the nature of learning in the Middle Ages, the state of manuscripts, the development of metrical romances, the influences of Continental literature, and the unfortunate state of so many medieval literary artifacts lying "concealed and forgotten in our manuscript libraries": "They contain . . . amusing images of antient customs and institutions, not elsewhere to be found, or at least not otherwise so strikingly delineated: and they preserve pure and unmixed, those fables of chivalry which formed that taste and awakened the imagination of our elder English classics."

His remarks on Geoffrey Chaucer are of most interest today. At a time when the appreciation of the great medieval poet was not general, Warton's assessments suggest a perceptive critic worth listening to. Remarks such as those on the "Knight's Tale" are of special note: "We are surprised to find, in a poet of such antiquity, numbers so nervous and flowing." Of the Canterbury pilgrims, Warton writes both judiciously and enthusiastically: "It is here that we view the pursuits and employments, the customs and diversions, of our ancestors, copied from life, and represented with equal truth and spirit, by a judge of mankind, whose penetration qualified him to discern their foibles or discriminating peculiarities; and by an artist, who understood that proper selection of circumstances, and those predominant characteristics, which form a finished portrait." Of Chaucer himself, Warton concludes that in "elevation, and elegance, in harmony and perspicuity of versification, he surpassed his predecessors in an infinite proportion: . . . his genius was universal, and adapted to themes of unbounded variety"; "In a word . . . he appeared with all the lustre and dignity of a true poet, in an age which compelled him to struggle with a barbarous language, and a national want of taste."

The second volume evinces a noticeable drop in the historian's enthusiasm. The fifteenth and early sixteenth centuries presented Warton his biggest challenge—and in places he is not up to the task. But it is in this volume that Warton

makes his thesis most clear: the progress in learning which swept aside the barbarism and superstition of medieval thought also brushed aside the inspiration and temperament necessary for truly imaginative verse. Other than his comments on the Rowley poems, the most engaging section in the second volume comes at the end, when he again considers the unhappy irony that advancing sophistication brought with it: "Ignorance and superstition, so opposite to the real interests of human society, are the parents of imagination." Warton laments further, "we have lost a set of manners, and a system of machinery, more suitable for the purposes of poetry, than those which have been adopted in their place." These comments summarize effectively Warton's lifelong critical position and his affinity for Shakespeare, Spenser, and Milton.

The second volume does provide the necessary examinations of such poets as John Gower, Thomas Hoccleve, John Lydgate, Alexander Barclay, William Dunbar, and John Skelton—and the section is also valuable for what it says about medieval drama. Throughout, Warton provides excerpts from the poems under discussion—primarily because many of the pieces were not easily available to readers—with the result that the work serves as a selected edition of early English works as well as a literary history. In the third volume (to which is prefaced a long dissertation on the *Gesta Romanorum*), Warton continues his survey, moving into the reign of Henry VIII and the influence of Italian poetry and concluding with the Elizabethan poets. He shares with his readers some interesting, significant, controversial, and, to our thinking, simply wrongheaded estimations—for instance, about the superiority of Henry Howard, Earl of Surrey, over Sir Thomas Wyatt: Wyatt's genius, like Pope's, was of "the moral and didactic species: and his poems abound more in good sense, satire, and observation on life, than in pathos or imagination." Regarding Christopher Marlowe's *Dr. Faustus* (written in 1592-1593), Warton writes that the drama is a "proof of the credulous ignorance which still prevailed, and a specimen of the subjects which then were thought not improper for tragedy"; it is a tale which "now only frightens children at a puppet-show in a country-town." But there is much more in the volume that reveals a thoughtful and sophisticated literary critic, a careful literary historian, and an exuberant student of early English literature. Even when the modern reader may not perhaps agree with a conclusion, such as that Spenser was a better sonneteer than Shakespeare (this estimation was published in the continuation edited by Rodney Baine in 1953), one still finds a judicious critic: although Shakespeare excels in "brilliance of imagery, quickness of thought, variety and fertility of allusion," he is still "more incorrect, indigested, and redundant."

The History of English Poetry is unquestionably an imperfect work: it contains a good number of factual errors and omissions; forwards several indefensible positions; demonstrates in places a lack of discrimination and proportion in the selection and treatment of materials; and frequently interrupts the narrative flow with scores of digressions, discussions, and historical and biographical facts. Yet its strengths and the very nature of the work testify to its significance as a major publication of the eighteenth century. First, Warton's research was impressive: he held in his hands a considerable number of unknown or little-known books and manuscripts; he provided his readers with important background information that furthered their knowledge of medieval and Renaissance society, learning, and literature; he demonstrated the effectiveness and judiciousness of the historical method of criticism while still evaluating an author by modern standards; he helped his century appreciate the genius of Geoffrey Chaucer in a manner few had tried before; and finally, as René Wellek has noted, Warton made "genuine literary history in England possible." This impressive achievement, along with his many other works, made Warton at his death in May 1790 one of England's most important and accomplished authors and scholars. To know Warton is to know well the varied and energetic activity characteristic of the Age of Johnson.

Letters:

Clarissa Rinaker, "Twenty-Six Unedited Letters from Thomas Warton to Jonathan Toup, John Price, George Steevens, Isaac Reed, William Mavor, and Edmond Malone," *Journal of English and Germanic Philology*, 14 (1915): 96-118;

"Correspondence of Thomas Warton," *Bodleian Quarterly Record*, 6 (1931): 303-307;

The Correspondence of Thomas Percy and Thomas Warton, edited by M. G. Robinson and Leah Dennis (Baton Rouge: Louisiana State University Press, 1951);

David Fairer, "The Correspondence of Thomas Warton," doctoral thesis, Oxford University, 1975.

Bibliographies:

Clarissa Rinaker, *Thomas Warton: A Biographical and Critical Study* (Urbana: University of Illinois Press, 1916);

John A. Vance, *Joseph and Thomas Warton: An Annotated Bibliography* (New York: Garland, 1983).

Biographies:

Richard Mant, Memoir of Warton, in *The Poetical Works of the Late Thomas Warton, B.D. . . . Together with Memoirs of His Life and Writings*, 2 volumes (Oxford: Oxford University Press, 1802);

Alexander Chalmers, "Thomas Warton," in *The Works of the English Poets* (London: J. Johnson, 1810), XVIII: 145-153;

Clarissa Rinaker, *Thomas Warton: A Biographical and Critical Study* (Urbana: University of Illinois Press, 1916).

References:

John Dennis, "The Wartons," *Cornhill Magazine*, 30 (November 1874): 534-547;

David Fairer, "Authorship Problems in *The Adventurer*," *Review of English Studies*, new series 25 (May 1974): 137-151;

Fairer, "The Origins of Warton's *History of English Poetry*," *Review of English Studies*, new series 32 (1981): 37-63;

Fairer, "Oxford and the Literary World," in *The History of the University of Oxford* (Oxford: Clarendon Press, 1986), V: 779-805;

Fairer, "The Poems of Thomas Warton the Elder?," *Review of English Studies*, new series 26 (August 1975): 287-300, 395-406; "Postscript," *Review of English Studies*, new series 29 (February 1978): 61-65;

Edmund Gosse, "Two Pioneers of Romanticism: Joseph and Thomas Warton," *Proceedings of the British Academy*, 7 (1915): 145-163;

Raymond D. Havens, "Thomas Warton and the Eighteenth-Century Dilemma," *Studies in Philology*, 25 (January 1928): 36-50;

Lawrence Lipking, "The Compromises of Thomas Warton and *The History of English Poetry*," in *The Ordering of the Arts in Eighteenth-Century England* (Princeton: Princeton University Press, 1970), pp. 352-404;

Leonard C. Martin, "Thomas Warton and the Early Poems of Milton," *Proceedings of the British Academy*, 20 (1934): 25-43;

Frances Schouler Miller, "The Historic Sense of Thomas Warton, Junior," *English Literary History*, 5 (March 1938): 71-92;

Joan Pittock, *The Ascendancy of Taste: The Achievement of Joseph and Thomas Warton* (London: Routledge & Kegan Paul, 1973);

Pittock, "Lives and Letters: New Wartoniana," *Durham University Journal*, 70 (June 1978): 193-203;

Pittock, "Thomas Warton and the Oxford Chair of Poetry," *English Studies*, 62 (January 1981): 14-33;

Clarissa Rinaker, "Thomas Warton's Poetry and Its Relation to the Romantic Movement," *Sewanee Review*, 23 (April 1915): 140-163;

David Nichol Smith, "Warton's History of English Poetry," *Proceedings of the British Academy*, 15 (1929): 73-99;

John A. Vance, *Joseph and Thomas Warton* (Boston: Twayne, 1983);

Vance, "Samuel Johnson and Thomas Warton," *Biography*, 9 (Spring 1986): 95-111;

René Wellek, *The Rise of English Literary History* (Chapel Hill: University of North Carolina Press, 1941), pp. 166-201.

Papers:

The largest holdings of Warton correspondence, literary fragments, and journals are in the British Library and in the Bodleian Library at Oxford University.

John Wesley

(17 June 1703 - 2 March 1791)

Richard E. Brantley
University of Florida

SELECTED BOOKS: *The Character of a Methodist* (Bristol: Printed by Felix Farley, 1742);

An Earnest Appeal to Men of Reason and Religion (Newcastle upon Tyne: Printed by J. Gooding, 1743);

A Farther Appeal to Men of Reason and Religion (London: Printed by W. Strahan, 1745);

Advice to the People Called Methodists (Newcastle, 1745);

Sermons on Several Occasions, volumes 1-3 (London: Printed by W. Strahan, sold by T. Trye and at the Foundery, 1746, 1748, 1750); volume 4 (Bristol: Printed by John Grabham, 1760); volume 3, enlarged (Bristol: Printed by William Pine, circa 1762-1770); volumes 5-8 (London: Printed and sold at the New Chapel, 1788); volume 9 (London: Printed by G. Story, sold by G. Whitfield, 1800);

Primitive Physick: or, An Easy and Natural Method of Curing Most Diseases (London: Printed, and sold by Thomas Trye, 1747);

A Letter to the Reverend Dr. Conyers Middleton, Occasioned by His Late Free Enquiry (London: Printed & sold by G. Woodfall, 1749);

A Plain Account of the People Called Methodists (Bristol: Printed by F. Farley, 1749);

The Complete English Dictionary, Explaining Most of Those Hard Words, which are Found in the Best English Writers (London: Printed by W. Strahan & sold by J. Robinson, T. Trye, T. James & G. Englefield, 1753; second edition, enlarged, Bristol: Printed by William Pine, 1764);

The Desideratum: or, Electricity Made Plain and Useful (London: Printed, and sold by W. Flexney, 1760);

A Short History of Methodism (London: Printed & sold at the Foundery, 1765);

The Witness of the Spirit (Bristol: Printed by William Pine, 1767);

The Works of the Rev. John Wesley, M.A., Late Fellow of Lincoln-College, Oxford, 32 volumes (Bristol: William Pine, 1771-1774);

John Wesley (engraving by J. Faber, after a portrait by J. Williams)

Thoughts upon Necessity (London: Printed by W. Hawes, 1774);

Thoughts upon Slavery (London: Printed by R. Hawes, 1774);

A Concise History of England, From the Earliest Times, to the Death of George II, 4 volumes (London: Printed by R. Hawes, 1776);

A Collection of Hymns, for the Use of the People Called Methodists, by John Wesley and Charles Wesley (London: Printed by J. Paramore, 1780).

Editions: *The Works of the Rev. John Wesley, A.M.*, 14 volumes, edited by Thomas Jackson (London: John Mason, 1829-1831);

The Works of John Wesley, 26 volumes, edited by Frank Baker and Richard P. Heitzenrater

(Oxford: Clarendon Press, 1975-1983; Nashville: Abingdon Press, 1984-   ).

OTHER: *A Christian Library: Consisting of Extracts from and Abridgments of the Choicest Pieces of Practical Divinity, which have been Publish'd in the English Tongue*, abridged by Wesley, 50 volumes (Bristol: Printed by F. Farley, 1749-1755);

A Survey of the Wisdom of God in the Creation: or A Compendium of Natural Philosophy, abridged by Wesley, 2 volumes (Bristol: Printed by W. Pine, 1763; Lancaster, Pa.: Hamilton, 1810);

"Extracts from Mr. Locke and Remarks upon Mr. Locke's 'Essay on Human Understanding,'" *Arminian Magazine*, 5 (1782): 27-30, 85-88, 144-146, 190-195, 247-249, 307-310, 361-363, 413-417, 476-478, 528, 534, 585-587, 646-648; 6 (1783): 30-31, 86-89, 136-138, 197-199, 254-256, 310-312, 366-368, 418-420, 480-484, 534-536, 590-594, 650-652; 7 (1784): 32-33, 91-92, 148-149, 201-202.

John Wesley, the leader of the Methodist revival, was also an intellectual and a man of letters. His two million published words feature such marks of literary craftsmanship as grasp of narrative vocabulary, the use of familiar words and aphorisms, an especially wide range of adjectives, vivid figures of speech, and a natural assimilation of scriptural idiom. His blend of theological traditions (such as the Anglican, the Dissenting, the Puritan, the Arminian, the Calvinist, the Lutheran, the Thomistic, the Catholic, and the Anglo-Catholic) emerges from his command of theme, his resonant and forceful diction, and, above all, his mastery of such formal and informal, conventional and original genres as diaries, journals, letters, advice to the Methodists, Methodist polity and principles, polemics, appeals, open letters to exponents of religion, apologetics, expositions of doctrine, biblical exegesis, homilies, devotionals, hymns, prayers, poems, editions of fiction and biography, abridgments (of works of theology, works of philosophy, and works of natural philosophy—that is, science), a medical treatise, scientific essays, history, and, clearly not least for those interested in Wesley as a literary figure, a dictionary.

John Wesley was born on 17 June 1703 at Epworth Rectory, Lincolnshire, and he was peculiarly suited by birth to start the revival that effectively retouched the various colorations of doc-

trine to be found throughout the disparate kinds of English church organization. Samuel Wesley, his father, was an Anglican vicar; his mother, Susanna, was the daughter of the well-known Presbyterian divine Samuel Annesley of London. He was therefore in a position to know at firsthand about the varieties of doctrine and organization at the beginning of his century, a time when the Anglicans and the Dissenters (Congregationalists, Baptists, and Presbyterians) went their separate ways for the most part, afraid of reopening the wounds of the seventeenth-century civil war. Nurtured in both traditions, Wesley venerated the Anglican liturgy and sacraments, and at the same time responded to the covenant organization of Nonconformist ecclesiology. As a true son of the Puritans, he may well have considered himself—as Susanna thought him after his rescue from the fire that destroyed the Epworth Rectory on 9 February 1709—"a brand snatched from the burning" or member of the Elect. Yet he often expressed his Anglican fear of the excesses of enthusiasm. Thus equipped to reconcile potentially opposing traditions, he seemed destined to remind England that her two religious heritages are not mutually exclusive: the Calvinism appropriated by the Puritans and their Nonconformist descendants can also be found in Archbishop Thomas Cranmer's *Book of Common Prayer* (1549). For that matter, the Augustinianism preserved in Anglican theology nurtured the thought of the well-educated Evangelical—Dissenter and Anglican alike. Wesley leavened Calvinism, finally, with Arminian free will, that is, with an emphasis on action and the practical in matters of religion.

After graduating from Christ Church, Oxford, in 1724 (John Locke was an earlier graduate) and his ordination as a deacon in the Church of England in 1725, Wesley was elected a fellow of Lincoln College, Oxford, on 17 March 1726 and was granted a master's degree in February 1727. As leader of the Holy Club (or Oxford Methodists as they came to be called) during the early 1730s, he inspired the few men in the Club to practice charity as well as to obey strict rules of study and religious observance. During a mission to Georgia (6 February 1736 - 22 December 1737), he met the German Moravians and proposed marriage to Sophia Hopkey, who refused him. His conversion, or what turned out to be the seed of his fifty-three-year itinerant ministry, occurred at a quarter to nine on the evening of 24 May 1738, in Aldersgate Street, London, where his heart was "strangely warmed"; and he

Wesley's parents: Reverend Samuel Wesley (engraving by R. M. Meadows, after a portrait by N. Branwhite) and Susanna Annesley Wesley (engraving by Owen, after a portrait by Williams)

began his practice of open-air preaching near Bristol on 2 April 1739, taking as his precedent the Sermon on the Mount and declaring, "the world is my parish." He dissociated himself from the Calvinism of his friend George Whitefield on 24 December 1740 (the Calvinist/Arminian controversy did not estrange him from Whitefield, but led him to found the *Arminian Magazine* in 1778), and began his organization of lay preachers, circuit riders, class meetings (for moral and spiritual inspection), and conferences (for the expression of divergent opinions) during the 1740s. He proposed marriage to Grace Murray early in 1749, but she married instead the Reverend John Bennet (on 3 October 1749). On 19 February 1751 he married Mary Vazeille (the marriage was unhappy, and she deserted him in 1776). On 2 September 1784 he ordained Thomas Coke as a superintendent of Methodism in the United States, defying Anglican church orders and paving the way for the separation of the Methodists from the Anglican church in 1795. Wesley was also a pioneer in the protest against slavery, his abhorrence of which formed the subject of the last letter he ever wrote, to William Wilberforce on 24 February 1791.

By himself or with his brother Charles, Wesley published twenty-three collections of hymns between 1737 and 1786. He "unawares became rich" (he said in 1789) through the sale of cheap books and tracts, but he gave his money away; his charities often exceeded £1,000 per year. Reading and writing on horseback, he traveled 250,000 miles and preached 40,000 sermons. As an endearing corollary to the Arminian belief that "Christ died for *all*," he entertained—rather against his usually more ironic than sentimental frame of mind—the belief in a future life for animals.

The effects of his ministry were nothing short of astonishing. His evangelistic campaign was rapid, constant, and huge in its results. By the time of his death on 2 March 1791, he had changed both Dissent, including the radical Quakers, and Anglicanism, including the Highest Churchmen. It is sometimes suggested that Evangelicalism, binding together differing religious persuasions, helped to mold the character of the British people, who gradually showed a new humanitarian spirit—or, more precisely, an Arminian practical charity—that bore no small part in doubling the population during the eighteenth

Mary Vazeille, who became Wesley's wife in 1751 (artist unknown; Methodist Church Archives and History Committee)

century. An awareness of the sociological as well as religious importance of the phenomenon may have led Thomas Babington Macaulay to be impatient with any earlier historian who neglected the revival. Its importance has never again been ignored. In the late nineteenth century, W. E. H. Lecky observed that Wesley's conversion "meant more for Britain than all the victories of Pitt by land and sea," and, more recently, Augustine Birrell declared that "No single figure influenced so many minds, no single voice touched so many hearts, no other man did such a work for England."

Samuel Johnson not only admired Wesley but espoused the kind of earnest faith that led his first modern editor, Birkbeck Hill, to conclude: "In his personal religion Johnson was, in the best sense, a Methodist." The next literary figures to respond to the revival were the first-generation Romantics, whose formative years were passed during the period when Wesley was still active and Evangelical faith was in the flush of increasing vigor.

Because the sense of a neoapostolic age was widespread, it is not surprising that Samuel Taylor Coleridge respected Wesley's leadership and wrote in his copy of Robert Southey's *Life of Wesley* (1820; a work in William Wordsworth's library too) that Arminian Methodism "has been the occasion, and even the cause, of turning thousands from their evil deeds, and . . . has made . . . bad and mischievous men peaceable and profitable neighbors and citizens." On the basis of both favorable and hostile reaction to Wordsworth's *The Excursion* (1814), one can ask whether Wordsworth himself consciously permitted the Methodists in particular, as well as the Evangelicals in general, to affect his literary practice. Charles Lamb praised the "natural methodism" in the poem, and Francis, Lord Jeffrey, in his notorious review, explicitly denounced Wordsworth's "mystical verbiage of the Methodist pulpit." Lord Jeffrey overstated his case for effect, and Lamb's phrase does not demonstrate any precise Methodist allegiances on Wordsworth's part. The phrase, however, was perhaps intended to suggest the poet's enthusiasm for nature—an enthusiasm to be found among many Evangelicals—or, more generally, his affinity for the larger movement. The word *Methodism* also suggests the religious quality of Wordsworth's thoroughgoing reliance on one's own experience as the basis for knowing the good and the true.

Methodism, after all, besides designating the devotional exercises of Wesley's Holy Club at Oxford and besides referring to the systematic practice of one's religion (naming, somehow, whatever it was that warmed the hearts and caught the imaginations of many), connotes the induction of religious knowledge from natural as well as spiritual experience. Wesley's conversion, a spiritual watershed of English cultural life, had as much to do with place, time, and the specific circumstances of his sense experience, and as much to do with his state of mind, as with his state of spirit.

Both before and after the conversion, he derived theological method from John Locke's theory of knowledge. In 1730, intrigued by an obscure follower of Locke, Wesley abridged *The Procedure, Extent, and Limits of Human Understanding* (1728), a theologizing of Locke's empiricism by Peter Browne, Bishop of Cork and Ross during the 1720s and 1730s. In 1781 Wesley wrote annotations to Locke's *Essay Concerning Human Understanding* (1690), and published them with extracts from Locke's essay in the *Arminian Magazine* during 1782-1784.

As the result of such educational enterprises as Wesley's condensations of Browne's work, which was first published in *A Survey of the Wisdom of God in the Creation: or A Compendium of Natural Philosophy* (1763), and Locke's *Essay Concerning Human Understanding*, generations of laity were at home with Lockean categories and with Browne's appropriation of Locke for theological purposes. It is especially interesting that Wesley took women seriously as philosophical and theological discussion partners, recognizing their intellectual abilities and encouraging their literary efforts as did few of his contemporaries.

As a means of placing Wesley's works historically and of approaching them as literature, it is helpful to outline their relation to Locke's *Essay Concerning Human Understanding*, for Locke's empiricism exercised a great and lasting influence on literary theory and practice. Wesley's prose, besides being scriptural, classical, and colloquial, is pervasively philosophical, for the Lockean language of experience enabled him to raise his ineffable experience of grace to graceful, cogent, and frequent expressions of methodology. Although evangelicalism is "spiritual" and empiricism is "natural," the great principle of empiricism—that one must see for oneself and be in the presence of the thing one knows—applies to evangelical faith. Each of these two codes of human methodology operates along a continuum joining emotion to intellect, and each of these two sign systems joins externality to words through "ideas/ideals of sensation," that is, through either perception itself or grace-in-perception or both. While *empiricism* refers to immediate contact with and direct impact from objects and subjects in time and place. *evangelicalism* entertains the similarly reciprocating notions that religious truth is concerned with experiential presuppositions and that experience itself need not be nonreligious. Wesley conceived of an analogy between sense perception of natural things and "sense perception" of the divine. He thought of a continuum joining scientific method and rational empiricism to natural and revealed religion; and he succeeded in spreading this "empiricism," this peculiarly English method for understanding the "spiritual sense."

Locke's view that words correspond to things, albeit through ideas, leads him to advocate a simple style, with as little as possible of the arbitrariness of metaphor, and, though more mes-

sage than intellectual treatise, Wesley's *Character of a Methodist* (1742) implies a similar view:

> The most obvious, easy, common, words, wherein our meaning can be conveyed, we prefer before others, both on ordinary occasions, and when we speak of the things of God. We never, therefore, willingly or designedly, deviate from the most usual way of speaking; unless when we express scripture truths in scripture words, which, we presume, no Christian will condemn.

This passage, describing "scripture words" as desirable, hardly excludes metaphor, but the simplicity and clarity of Wesley's writing, both here and generally, are due in part to the corollary of Locke's preference for analogy: that metaphor too easily undermines the capacity of language to communicate and represent truths whether natural or spiritual.

An Earnest Appeal to Men of Reason and Religion (1743), in its turn, is so Lockean as to suggest that Wesley had the *Essay Concerning Human Understanding* in view:

> You know . . . that before it is possible for you to form a true judgment of the things of God, it is absolutely necessary that you have a *clear apprehension* of them, and that your ideas thereof be all *fixed*, *distinct*, and *determinate*. And seeing our ideas are not innate, but must all originally come from our senses, it is certainly necessary that you have senses capable of discerning objects of this kind—not those only which are called "natural senses," which in this respect profit nothing, as being altogether incapable of discerning objects of a spiritual kind, but spiritual senses, exercised to discern spiritual good and evil. . . .
>
> And till you have these internal senses, till the eyes of your understanding are opened, you can have no apprehension of divine things, no idea of them at all. Nor consequently, till then, can you either judge truly or reason justly concerning them, seeing your reason has no ground whereon to stand, no materials to work upon.

The sensationalist diction ("materials," "ground," "eyes," "internal senses," "spiritual senses," "natural senses," "objects," and "things") constitutes perhaps the fullest statement of Wesley's "spiritual sense." The philosophical demand for empiricism, which in Locke's case is rational as well as sensationalist, is met too in Wesley's far from antirational concept of inspiration ("reason," "understanding," "discern," "ideas," "apprehen-

(78)

407. Or, Drink for a Month a Decoction of *Elm Bark*, morning and evening.

CXXIX. The LETHARGY.

408. Snuff strong *Vinegar* up the Nose,
409. Or, Powder of *White Hellebore:*
410. Or, Take half a pint of Decoction of *Savoury*, morning and evening:
411. Or, of Infusion of *Water-Cresses*.

CXXX. LICE (to kill).

412. Sprinkle *Spanish Snuff* over the Head,
413. Or, Wash it with a Decoction of *Amaranth*.

CXXXI. For one seemingly KILL'D with LIGHTNING, or a DAMP: or SUFFOCATED.

414. Plunge him immediately into *Cold Water*,
415. Or, *Blow* strongly with Bellows down his Throat.

CXXXII. LUNACY.

416. Give a Decoction of *Agrimony* four times a day,

417.

(79)

417. Or, of *Pimpernell*;
418. Or, Juice of *Ground-ivy* three Ounces daily.
419. Or, Boil Juice of *Ground-ivy* with sweet Oil and white Wine into an Ointment. Shave the Head, anoint it therewith, and chafe it in warm, every other Day for three Weeks. Bruise also the Leaves and bind them on the Head, and give three spoonfuls of the Juice warm every morning.

CXXXIII. RAGING MADNESS.

420. Keep on the Head a Cap fill'd with *Snow*, for two or three Weeks:
421. Or, Set the Patient with his Head under a Great *Water-Fall*, as long as his Strength will bear:
422. Or, Let him eat nothing but *Apples* for a Month:
423. Or, Give Juice and Decoction of *Hearts-ease* daily.

CXXXIV. The BITE of a MAD DOG.

424. Plunge into *cold Water*, and keep as long under it, as can be done without drowning.

3

425.

Pages from Primitive Physick, *Wesley's handbook of home remedies*

sion," and "judgment"). Wesley, then, as though to maintain Lockean balance between reason and its ground, implies a more than metaphorical, far from arbitrary relation between spiritual senses and rational apprehension by the spirit. Consistent with his endorsement of tabula rasa as the first principle of theology, he signals his affinity for, dependence on, Lockean method.

An Earnest Appeal to Men of Reason and Religion draws an analogy between faith and empirical observation: Faith "is with regard to the spiritual world what sense is with regard to the natural." This idea too is explicitly Lockean, or at least perspicuously so, for the precisely analogistic structure rests on a more than metaphorical,

far from arbitrary association of faith with the natural senses. Of course, in suggesting that sense perception is related to faith, Wesley avoids implying that one ever fully knows the common ground between faith and empiricism. *An Earnest Appeal to Men of Reason and Religion*, like Locke's *Essay Concerning Human Understanding*, stresses that natural understanding cannot easily apprehend spiritual truth: "What then will your reason do here? How will it pass from things natural to spiritual? From the things that are seen to those that are not seen? From the visible to the invisible world? What a gulf is here!" Nonetheless, faith is defined not simply according to scripture, but even in accordance with a balance between the sensing and the reasoning powers:

> It is the feeling of the soul, whereby a believer perceives, through the "power of the Highest overshadowing him" [see Luke 1:35] both the existence and the presence of him in whom he "lives, moves, and has his being" [see Acts 17:28], and indeed the whole invisible world, the entire system of things eternal. And hereby, in particular, he feels "the love of God shed abroad in his heart" [see Rom. 5:5].

By *feeling*, Wesley does not mean "inner trend" so much as "faith in relation to the senses"; for on the preceding page of *An Earnest Appeal to Men of Reason and Religion* he associates *faith* with sight, hearing, and taste. Wesley's definition, finally, both by its diction ("whereby a believer perceives") and by its development throughout the book, intimates his view, derived from Locke, that religious feeling, like sense data, constitutes matter for the mind to work upon: faith exists, too, in relation to reason.

A Farther Appeal to Men of Reason and Religion (1745) is concerned primarily to prove that the "technical terms" of Methodism "coincide exactly with . . . the official pronouncements of the Church of England," but this appeal, like the first, is concerned as well to use the language of Lockean method. The kind of religion Wesley espouses is not "religious madness,"

> but rational as well as scriptural; it is as pure from enthusiasm as from superstition. . . . Who will prove that it is enthusiasm . . . to rejoice in the sense of [God's] love to us?

"To this day," Wesley wrote in his letters to Mr. John Smith (written in 1745-1748), "I have abundantly more temptation . . . to be . . . a philosophical sluggard, than an itinerant Preacher." ("Smith" was probably Thomas Secker, Bishop of Oxford and later Archbishop of Canterbury.) Throughout these letters, Wesley combines evangelistic goals with his evident love of "philosophical" theology, and his Lockean method is especially perspicuous, for, even to traditional revelation, he applies Lockean as well as Cartesian skepticism: "I am as fully assured to-day, as I am of the shining of the sun, that the scriptures are of God. I cannot possibly deny or doubt of it now; yet I may doubt of it tomorrow; as I have done heretofore a thousand times, and that after the fullest assurance preceding." Thus, the mind remains open even after systematically searching

Wesley in 1789 (engraving by W. Ward, after a portrait by George Romney)

for, and apparently finding, what is not subject to doubt. The letters to "Smith," moreover, acknowledge both poles of Lockean method, for the sense-based nature of mind is implicit in Wesley's phraseology, "so far as men can judge from their eyes and ears." *The rise and progress of*, a phrase characteristic of eighteenth-century England, assumes the English philosophy of experience, and, where Wesley writes that "we are speaking, not of the progress, but of the first rise, of faith," he suggests, for one thing, that no more than knowledge does faith exist innately and, for another, that faith, like knowledge, must be datable by precise moments in personal history. Just as one knows what one experiences naturally, so one has faith in what one encounters spiritually: "it cannot be, in the nature of things, that a man should be filled with this peace, and joy, and love, by the inspiration of the Holy Spirit, without perceiving it as clearly as he does the light of the sun."

In *Primitive Physick: or, An Easy and Natural Method of Curing Most Diseases* (1747), Wesley's endorsement of empirical method is in his delightfully blunt praise of the ancient Greek healing art: "The Trial was made. The Cure was wrought. And Experience and Physick grew up together." He deplores much subsequent medical practice, in which "Men of Learning began to set Experience aside," but he rejoices that "there have not been wanting from Time to Time, some Lovers of Mankind . . . Who have laboured to explode out of [physick] all Hypotheses, and fine-spun theories, and to make it a plain intelligible Thing, as it was in the Beginning: Having no more Mystery in it than this, 'Such a Medicine removes such a Pain.'" Where he asks "Has not the Author of Nature taught us the use of many . . . Medicines?" he implies an undeistical, because intervenient, God of nature in the very process of scientific inquiry. Thus, *Primitive Physick* suggests that a theistical natural religion is not just consistent with, but even demanded by, empirical method.

In "The Great Privilege of Those that are Born of God" (1748), Wesley preaches that "the circumstances of the natural birth" provide "the most easy way to understand the spiritual." This sermon affirms a real correspondence between a universal, describable experience and experience that, though possible for all, would remain quite ineffable were it not for the linguistic instrument of analogy. The entire sermon teaches that the invisible world is familiar to twice-born people whose "spiritual sense" parallels the limited but sufficient a posteriori operation of the natural faculties. With regard to the interpenetrations of sense perception and the world of here and now, "The Great Privilege of Those that are Born of God" waxes precisely Lockean:

> no sooner is the child born into the world, than he . . . *feels* the air with which he is surrounded, and which pours into him from every side, as fast as he alternately breathes it back, to sustain the flame of life: and hence springs a continual increase of strength, of motion, and of sensation; all the bodily senses being now awakened, and furnished with their proper objects.

In this passage the mind's wakeful involvement with sense data is just as clear as in whole sections of the *Essay Concerning Human Understanding* where Locke insists that the mind's response to sense experience is almost at one with what one needs to know about the world. The sermon's description of "*senses*, whereby alone we can *discern* the things of God" (emphasis added) bespeaks a vital interaction: what is "continually received" is "continually rendered back." At the mental level and by analogy with the senses, spiritual experi-

ence is depicted as a coalescence at least, and at most as an almost total identification, with the condescensions of God. The alternation, and indeed the oscillation, between rational diction and sensationalist diction signifies, again and again, that through immediate revelation God and man are ensphered, or rather that a clear intercourse occurs not only between man as object and God as subject, but also between man as subject and God as object.

A Letter to the Reverend Dr. Conyers Middleton (1749) expresses a theology of immediate revelation:

> Traditional evidence is of an extremely complicated nature, necessarily including so many and so various considerations, that only men of a strong and clear *understanding* can be *sensible* of its full force. On the contrary, how plain and simple is this; and how level to the lowest *capacity*! Is not this the sum: "One thing I *know*; I was blind, but now I *see*"? [see John 9:25]. An argument so plain, that a peasant, a woman, a child, may feel all its force.
>
> The traditional evidence of Christianity stands, as it were, a great way off; and therefore, although it speaks loud and clear, yet makes a less lively *impression*. It gives us an account of what was transacted long ago, in far distant times as well as places. Whereas the inward evidence is intimately present to all persons, at all times, and in all places [emphasis added].

The diction here, at once sensationalist and rational, signals again the analogy between sense perception and immediate revelation, for, although Wesley is careful to manifest reticence about how much one knows even from "spiritual sense" and spiritual discernment, his relative confidence in immediate revelation is especially clear in this fully epistemological tone. Indeed, the letter to Middleton rises to an especially characteristic height where it presents experiential faith as full counterpart to a skeptical, though courageous, "empiricism":

> Is it not so? Let impartial reason speak. Does not every thinking man want a window, not so much in his neighbour's, as in his own, breast? He wants an opening there, of whatever kind, that might let in light from eternity. He is pained to be thus feeling after God so darkly and uncertainly; to know so little of God, and indeed so little of any beside material objects. He is concerned, that he must see even that little, not directly, but in the dim, sullied glass of sense;

and consequently so imperfectly and obscurely, that it is all a mere enigma still.

Now, these very desiderata faith supplies. It gives a more extensive knowledge of things invisible, showing what eye had not seen, nor ear heard, neither could it before enter into our heart to conceive [see I Cor. 2:9]. And all these it shows in the clearest light, with the fullest certainty and evidence. For it does not leave us to receive our notices of them by mere reflection from the dull glass of sense; but resolves a thousand enigmas of the highest concern by giving faculties suited to things invisible.

This statement, couched in the doubly "empirical" context of a telescope metaphor (for example, "resolves a thousand enigmas") and a quasi-philosophic allusion to the Bible, is more than in keeping with the *Essay Concerning Human Understanding*, for the statement epitomizes Wesley's at once spiritual and natural mode of knowing and of speaking.

During the 1740s Wesley completed his formulation of method, for he not only drew an analogy between sense perception and revelation, but also attempted to bridge the gap between natural religion and revealed religion. At once theological and philosophical, his methodology operated throughout his mind's long history: after the 1740s, to be sure, he wrote increasingly with his followers in mind; but he remained as rigorous as ever. The later works, more often sermons than not, include many nonhomiletical and intellectually ambitious titles intended not only for Methodist readers but for readers in general, and these typically "public," less narrowly directed writings of his fullest literary maturity are very often either simultaneously theological and philosophical or all but exclusively philosophical. The following works, for example, are overwhelmingly philosophical, and even specifically Lockean: the preface to *The Desideratum: or, Electricity Made Plain and Useful* (1760), the preface to and the conclusion of *A Survey of the Wisdom of God in the Creation: or A Compendium of Natural Philosophy* (1763), *Thoughts upon Necessity* (1774), "Remarks upon Mr. Locke's 'Essay on Human Understanding'" (1782-1784), "The Case of Reason Impartially Considered" (1788), and "The Imperfection of Human Knowledge" (1788). *A Short History of Methodism* (1765) and *A Concise History of England* (1776), moreover, reflect an emphasis on experience reminiscent of Locke, and even of David Hume. Finally, the following sermons of Wesley's maturity are obviously pertinent to the "empiri-

cal" dimension of religion: *The Witness of the Spirit* (1767); "The Witness of our Own Spirit" (1746); "The Means of Grace" (1746); "The Marks of the New Birth" (1748); "On a Single Eye" (*Arminian Magazine*, November-December 1790); "Walking by Sight, and Walking by Faith" (*Arminian Magazine*, January-February 1790); and, clearly not least (in view of Locke's pioneering theories in the area), "On the Education of Children" (*Arminian Magazine*, November-December 1783). Far from sacrificing quality of thought to broad appeal, Wesley's later discourse respects the common reader's intellect, for the sermons—like such mass-audience matter for the mind as the popularizations of electrical science and natural philosophy, the reviews of philosophical books, and the annotations to the *Essay Concerning Human Understanding*—reflect a consistently functioning, often explicit theologizing of Locke's empiricism.

Thus, Wesley's works disseminated empiricism as well as evangelicalism, and their influence underscores his importance in the world of letters. His determination to make challenging books available in brief and handy, yet attractive and durable form means, among other things, that he was a Mortimer J. Adler: his abridgments in particular amount to a *synopticon* of many "great books of the Western world." *A Christian Library: Consisting of Extracts from and Abridgments of the Choicest Pieces of Practical Divinity, which have been Publish'd in the English Tongue* (1749-1755) is a logical product of his prolific editorial pen; but his scientific encyclopedia for the common reader, *A Survey of the Wisdom of God in the Creation: or A Compendium of Natural Philosophy*, is also typical of him; and these collections of abridgments were read as companion sets, as an interdisciplinary vade mecum, for more than one hundred years.

Wesley, moreover, was something of a DeWitt Wallace: without diluting the works with which he challenged the common reader and while abjuring mere topicality, he otherwise anticipated the *Reader's Digest*; for by condensing a variety of works and by keeping the cost of his volumes down, he aimed for a large audience. His audience was large, even after his death, or especially then. The Methodist Episcopal church in America grew from a membership of less than ten thousand in 1780, to more than five hundred thousand by 1830. A similar pattern obtained in England; although Methodists made up only about five percent of the adult British population

Wesley preaching near Gwennap, Cornwall (nineteenth-century print)

in 1840, they were the largest and most influential element in a much wider constituency. By 1851 there were more than two million Sunday-school scholars in England alone, six hundred thousand of whom were Methodists, and they represented seventy-six percent of working-class children between the ages of five and fifteen. The second half of the nineteenth century and at least the first part of the twentieth belonged to the evangelicals, who, even when their numbers were small, represented an especially significant Anglo-American trend, not least because their "social contract" originated in the decidedly "Lockean" as well as simply Christian "societies" that flourished among Methodists on both sides of the Atlantic during the eighteenth century. "Reading Christians," declared Wesley, "will be knowing Christians." The statement suggests a twofold ambition: first, to make the rising middle class of the Anglo-American world literate and second, to educate that class about science as well as theology. By insuring the "spiritual sense" of transatlantic culture, he insured, as well, a continuing unity of it, for epistemology and ontology, however esoteric, filter down to those who live within a worldview, distinct from those who create it (witness the analogy of "Freudians" who do not read Sigmund Freud).

Insofar as Wesley shaped an eighteenth- and even nineteenth-century mode of thought and feeling, a mode in which sense perception of natural things formed the model for "sense perception" of the divine, the evangelical and the Lockean understandings of experience came together for, and in, the Anglo-American middle class. An Anglo-American character arising from the empirical as well as evangelical emphasis of the eighteenth century finds mature expression in the vital synthesis, the complex entity, of British and American letters. *Locke, Wesley, and the Method of English Romanticism* (1984) seeks to demonstrate that Wesley absorbed and spiritualized the epistemology of Locke and then, through a sometimes direct but more often indirect and rather complex process of cultural osmosis, passed on to William Blake, William Wordsworth, Samuel Taylor Coleridge, Percy Bysshe Shelley, and John Keats a method for both their natural observation and their "spiritual experience." British authors such as Thomas Carlyle, George Eliot, and Alfred, Lord Tennyson, and American authors such as Ralph Waldo Emerson, Herman Melville, and Emily Dickinson descend spiritually and intellectually from Wesley insofar as all of them theologize empiricism, ground transcendentalism in mind and world, balance religious myths and religious morality with scientific reverence for fact and detail, ally empirical assumptions with spiritual discipline, and share, above all, the simultaneously rational and sensationalist reliance on experience as the avenue to knowledge, both natural and spiritual.

Letters:

The Letters of the Rev. John Wesley, A.M., Sometime Fellow of Lincoln College, Oxford, 8 volumes, edited by John Telford (London: Epworth Press, 1931);

Letters I-II, edited by Frank Baker, volumes 25 and 26 of *The Works of John Wesley*, edited by Baker and Richard P. Heitzenrater (Oxford: Clarendon Press, 1980).

Bibliographies:

Frank Baker, *A Union Catalogue of the Publications of John and Charles Wesley* (Durham, N.C.: Divinity School, Duke University, 1966);

Samuel J. Rogal, "The Wesleys: A Checklist of Critical Commentary," *Bulletin of Bibliography*, 28 (April 1971): 22-35;

Richard Green, *The Works of John and Charles Wesley*, revised edition (New York: AMS Press, 1976);

Kenneth E. Rowe, *United Methodist Studies: Basic Bibliographies* (Nashville: Abingdon Press, 1987).

Biographies:

Robert Southey, *The Life of Wesley; and Rise and Progress of Methodism*, 2 volumes (London: Printed for Longman, Hurst, Rees, Orme & Brown, 1820); third edition, with notes by Samuel Taylor Coleridge and remarks on Wesley by Alexander Knox, edited by Charles Cuthbert Southey (London: Longman, Brown, Green & Longmans, 1846);

Luke Tyerman, *The Life and Times of the Rev. John Wesley*, 3 volumes (London: Hodder & Stoughton, 1870, 1871; New York: Harper, 1872);

V. H. H. Green, *The Young Mr. Wesley: A Study of John Wesley and Oxford* (New York: St. Martin's Press, 1961);

Martin Schmidt, *John Wesley: A Theological Biography*, 2 volumes (New York: Abingdon Press, 1961);

Richard P. Heitzenrater, *The Elusive Mr. Wesley* (Nashville: Abingdon Press, 1984).

References:

Henry Abelove, *The Evangelist of Desire: John Wesley and the Methodists* (Stanford: Stanford University Press, 1991);

Richard E. Brantley, "The Common Ground of Wesley and Edwards," *Harvard Theological Review*, 83 (forthcoming 1991);

Brantley, "Johnson's Wesleyan Connection," *Eighteenth-Century Studies*, 10 (Winter 1976/1977): 143-168;

Brantley, "Keats's Method," *Studies in Romanticism*, 22 (Fall 1983): 389-405;

Brantley, *Locke, Wesley, and the Method of English Romanticism* (Gainesville: University of Florida Press, 1984);

Brantley, *Wordsworth's "Natural Methodism"* (New Haven: Yale University Press, 1975);

Richard Carwardine, *Transatlantic Revivalism: Popular Evangelicalism in Britain and America, 1790-1865* (Westport, Conn.: Greenwood Press, 1978);

Valentine Cunningham, *Everywhere Spoken Against: Dissent in the Victorian Novel* (Oxford: Clarendon Press, 1975);

Donald Davie, *A Gathered Church: The Literature of the English Dissenting Interest* (London & Henley: Routledge, 1978);

Frederick Dreyer, "A 'Religious Society under Heaven': John Wesley and the Identity of Methodism," *Journal of British Studies*, 25 (January 1986): 62-83;

Martha England and John Sparrow, *Hymns Unbidden: Donne, Herbert, Blake, Emily Dickinson, and the Hymnographers* (New York: New York Public Library, 1966);

F. C. Gill, *The Romantic Movement and Methodism: A Study of English Romanticism and the Evangelical Revival* (London: Epworth Press, 1937);

James L. Golden, "John Wesley on Rhetoric and Belles Lettres," *Speech Monographs*, 28 (November 1961): 250-264;

A. W. Harrison, "Romanticism and Religious Revivals," *Hibbert Journal*, 31 (July 1933): 579-591;

Grace Elizabeth Harrison, *Haworth Parsonage: A Study of Wesley and the Brontës* (London: Wesley Historical Society, 1937);

F. Brompton Harvey, "Methodism and the Romantic Movement," *London Quarterly and Holborn Review*, 159 (July 1934): 289-302;

David Hempton, *Methodism and Politics in British Society 1750-1850* (Stanford: Stanford University Press, 1984);

T. Walter Herbert, *John Wesley as Editor and Author* (Princeton: Princeton University Press, 1940);

Elisabeth Jay, *The Religion of the Heart: Anglican Evangelicalism and the Nineteenth-Century Novel* (Oxford: Clarendon Press, 1979);

T. W. Laquer, *Religion and Respectability: Sunday Schools and Working Class Culture 1780-1850* (New Haven: Yale University Press, 1976);

George Lawton, *John Wesley's English: A Study of His Literary Style* (London: Allen & Unwin, 1962);

Kenneth MacLean, *John Locke and English Literature of the Eighteenth Century* (New Haven: Yale University Press, 1936);

Mark A. Noll, "Romanticism and the Hymns of Charles Wesley," *Evangelical Quarterly*, 46 (1974): 195-223;

Bernard Semmel, *The Methodist Revolution* (New York: Basic Books, 1973);

T. B. Shepherd, *Methodism and the Literature of the Eighteenth Century* (London: Epworth Press, 1940);

G. H. Vallins, *The Wesleys and the English Language* (London: Epworth Press, 1957).

Papers:
The major collection of Wesley materials is at the John Rylands University Library of Manchester, which houses the vast Methodist Archives. Other important collections are at the British Library; Perkins Library, Duke University; Beinecke Library, Yale University; the Emory University Library; and the Southern Methodist University Library.

Mary Wollstonecraft

(27 April 1759 - 10 September 1797)

Gary Kelly
University of Alberta

See also the Wollstonecraft entry in *DLB 39: British Novelists, 1660-1800.*

BOOKS: *Thoughts on the Education of Daughters: With Reflections on Female Conduct, in the More Important Duties of Life* (London: Printed for J. Johnson, 1787);

Mary, A Fiction (London: Printed for J. Johnson, 1788); facsimile, introduction by Gina Luria (New York & London: Garland, 1974);

Original Stories, from Real Life; with Conversations, Calculated to Regulate the Affections, and Form the Mind to Truth and Goodness (London: Printed for J. Johnson, 1788; revised, 1791);

A Vindication of the Rights of Men, in a Letter to the Right Honourable Edmund Burke (London: Printed for J. Johnson, 1790; second edition, revised, 1790); facsimile of second edition, introduction by Eleanor Louise Nicholes (Gainesville: Scholars' Facsimiles & Reprints, 1959);

A Vindication of the Rights of Woman: with Strictures on Political and Moral Subjects (London: Printed for J. Johnson, 1792; Boston: Printed by Peter Edes for Thomas & Andrews, 1792; Philadelphia: Printed & sold by William Gibbons, 1792; second edition, revised London: Printed for J. Johnson, 1792); facsimile of the Boston edition, introduction by Luria (New York & London: Garland, 1974);

An Historical and Moral View of the Origin and Progress of the French Revolution; and the Effect It Has Produced in Europe. By Mary Wollstonecraft. Volume the First [no more published] (London: Printed for J. Johnson, 1794); republished as *An Historical and Moral View of the French Revolution, and the Effect It Has Produced in Europe* (Philadelphia: Printed by Thomas Dobson, 1795); facsimile of 1794 edition, introduction by Janet Todd (Delmar, N.Y.: Scholars' Facsimiles & Reprints, 1975);

Mary Wollstonecraft, 1792 (portrait by an unknown artist; Walker Art Gallery, Liverpool)

Letters Written During a Short Residence in Sweden, Norway, and Denmark (London: Printed for J. Johnson, 1796; Wilmington, Del.: Printed for and sold by J. Wilson & J. Johnson, 1796);

Posthumous Works of the Author of A Vindication of the Rights of Woman, 4 volumes, edited by William Godwin (London: Printed for J. Johnson and G. G. & J. Robinson, 1798); facsimile, introduction by Luria (New York & London: Garland, 1974);

Maria; or, The Wrongs of Woman: A Posthumous Fragment (Philadelphia: Printed by James Carey, 1799).

Editions: *A Vindication of the Rights of Woman,* edited by Carol H. Poston (New York: W. W.

350

Norton, 1975; second edition expanded, 1988);

Letters Written During a Short Residence in Sweden, Norway, and Denmark, edited by Poston (Lincoln & London: University of Nebraska Press, 1976);

Mary and *The Wrongs of Woman*, edited by Gary Kelly (London: Oxford University Press, 1976);

A Critical Edition of Mary Wollstonecraft's A Vindication of the Rights of Woman: With Strictures on Political and Moral Subjects, edited by Ulrich H. Hardt (Troy, N.Y.: Whitston Publishing, 1982);

A Short Residence in Sweden, Norway and Denmark, with William Godwin, *Memoirs of the Author of the Rights of Woman*, edited by Richard Holmes (Harmondsworth, U.K.: Penguin Books, 1987);

The Collected Works of Mary Wollstonecraft, 7 volumes edited by Marilyn Butler, Janet Todd, and Emma Rees-Mogg (London: Pickering & Chatto, 1989).

OTHER: *The Female Reader*, edited, with contributions, by Wollstonecraft as Mr. Cresswick (London: Printed for J. Johnson, 1789); facsimile, introduction by Moira Ferguson (Delmar, N.Y.: Scholars' Facsimiles & Reprints, 1980).

TRANSLATIONS: Jacques Necker, *Of the Importance of Religious Opinions. Translated from the French of Mr. Necker* (London: Printed for J. Johnson, 1788);

Maria Geertruida van de Werken de Cambon, *Young Grandison: A Series of Letters from Young Persons to their Friends. Translated from the Dutch of Madame de Cambon, with Alterations and Improvements*, 2 volumes (London: Printed for J. Johnson, 1790);

Christian Gotthilf Salzmann, *Elements of Morality, for the Use of Children; With an Introductory Address to Parents. Translated from the German of the Rev. C. G. Salzmann*, 3 volumes (London: Printed for J. Johnson, 1790-1791; 1 volume, Providence, R.I.: Printed by Carter and Wilkinson, 1795).

Mary Wollstonecraft's achievement as a prose writer is twofold. She was the most notable arguer for women's equality in her time. She also explored new ways of arguing for such equality as a woman in domains and discourses domi-

nated by men. She looked for ways of arguing and uses of style and genre that would answer both to her claims for women and to her own position as a woman, writing and arguing in political and literary terrain from which women were to be excluded.

She lived in an age of increasing social conflict and change, conflicts and changes she knew well from family and personal experience. Wollstonecraft was born the second of seven children to a family of London master weavers and small-scale rentiers. But her father, Edward John Wollstonecraft, decided to attempt the jump from trade, however successful, to gentleman farmer—a significant rise up the social scale. Unfortunately, his aspirations to gentility also involved him in the extravagance, personal and financial, to which landed gentry were thought susceptible.

The family moved several times before ending up in Beverley, Yorkshire, in 1768, where Mary Wollstonecraft passed through early adolescence and first experienced a wider social world of gentrified and intellectual middle classes. More moves followed—back to London, to Wales, and back to London again. The dwindling family resources were devoted to preparing Wollstonecraft's older brother, Edward, for a profession, the law. The younger children, Mary, Elizabeth, Everina, James, and Charles, were left to do the best they could (another brother, Henry, did not live long). Wollstonecraft's father became an alcoholic, and Wollstonecraft took on the role of protecting the family, especially her mother, Elizabeth Dickson Wollstonecraft, from him. On more than one occasion she lay all night in front of her mother's bedroom, to protect her mother from her father's abuse or penitent affection.

Meanwhile, in London, Wollstonecraft had been befriended by two of the many substitute parents of her early life, the Clares. She also formed one of several important female friendships to mark her life, with Fanny Blood. Disgusted with a family life in which she bore increasing responsibility, Wollstonecraft left home in 1778, not yet out of her teens. By then she had seen, been personally implicated in, and been permanently wounded by, the social conflict between middle and upper classes, the role of women in the marriage market as a scramble for upward social mobility, the inferior education allotted to women in order to put them on that market, and the oppression of girls and women in the late eighteenth-century middle-class family.

She also knew that there were few vocations besides wife for a respectable woman of some education and no money. Her first employment was in one of the few, as a lady's companion. This position took her to Bath and into the fringes of fashionable society, but she was called home to nurse her mother through a long last illness. She found herself increasingly responsible for her younger brothers and sisters, and in January 1784 intervened in her sister Eliza's marriage, helping Eliza and her daughter to run away from Eliza's husband. To form a self-supporting community, she, her sisters, and Fanny Blood opened a school at Newington Green, a center for Nonconformists and home of the leader of the Nonconformist Enlightenment, Richard Price, whom she met and admired. The next year, in November 1785, she traveled to Portugal to assist Fanny Blood, who had gone there to marry an English businessman, in the last stages of her pregnancy. When Fanny and her child died, Wollstonecraft returned to London.

Her absence had accelerated the decline of the school at Newington Green. Again forced to seek employment, she found teaching posts for her two sisters and went herself to Ireland in 1786 as governess to the daughters of Robert King, Viscount Kingsborough, and Caroline Fitzgerald, Lady Kingsborough. With them she did see upper-class fashionable society, but she also met and befriended some gentlemen of letters, including Henry Gabell and George Ogle. She continued her self-education in the literature of sensibility and the social thought of the Enlightenment, especially as combined in the work and the character of Jean-Jacques Rousseau. She traveled with the Kingsboroughs to Bath but was dismissed by them in August 1787 because their daughter was growing too attached to Wollstonecraft.

Fortunately, Wollstonecraft had already met the publisher Joseph Johnson and had begun to write. She was about to become, as she put it, "the first of a new genus," a professional woman writer. In the nine years since she first left home to work she had read a great deal, met and talked with leading figures of the late eighteenth-century Enlightenment, traveled on her own, fended for herself, and helped friends and family. She also saw a good deal of upper-class fashionable society, their professional middle-class dependents, the commercial bourgeoisie, and the lower classes in Portugal, London, and Ireland.

This intellectual and social experience prepared her well to become an Enlightenment social critic, as her many interesting letters show. But as an author she first ventured in the acceptably feminine, and subliterary, terrain of educational writing and fiction. Her first book, *Thoughts on the Education of Daughters* (1787), is in the line of eighteenth-century conduct books for females, a line that sought to establish the domestic and feminine character of girls and women within emergent bourgeois culture. In this line Wollstonecraft is a liberal, showing influence from Enlightenment materialism as well as Nonconformist moralism. She shows that she has read some Lockean epistemology, and such books as Hester Chapone's *Letters on the Improvement of the Mind, Addressed to a Young Lady* (1773), James Burgh's *The Dignity of Human Nature* (1754; a new edition was published by Wollstonecraft's publisher in 1787), John and Anna Lætitia Aikin's *Miscellaneous Pieces, In Prose* (1773), Rousseau's *Emile* (1762), and Catharine Talbot's *Works* (1780).

Wollstonecraft's concern is with education as a process of constructing an independent, autonomous moral and intellectual being. This concern was part of a broad middle-class interest in the subjective self, divinely validated, as the source of meaning and value to set against the merely social self of aristocratic or plebeian culture. Within this ideology of subjectivity Wollstonecraft works on the special problems of girls and mothers. Her method of discourse is designed for women readers, and uses the series of brief essays, a recognized "feminine" way of writing. Certain features of her own prose style are already present, too. There is the tendency to rely on personal observation, or "I"-centered discourse; setting forth an argument in desultory, repetitive form rather than cumulatively or connectedly; reliance on forceful comparisons, especially metaphors, from ordinary life; using certain key words and phrases again and again (*reason, passion, candour, simplicity, prejudice, partial, exercise*); relying on aphoristic turn of phrase or statement; use of autobiographical reference, in a sentimental mode; occasional passages of religious piety; and occasional recourse to lyrical self-expressiveness. Wollstonecraft's early novel, *Mary: A Fiction* (1788), exhibits a more critical, proto-feminist attitude to the education and socialization of upper-middle-class women, the same mix of social and cultural cri-

Mʀˢ GODWIN.

Engraving of Wollstonecraft wearing a hat like those worn by female French revolutionaries

tique (including critique of the "female" genre of the novel) and sentimentalism. It, too, is highly autobiographical, figural, and aphoristic.

Wollstonecraft's next work, *Original Stories, from Real Life* (1788), was the most successful in her lifetime. It continues the educational topics of *Thoughts on the Education of Daughters* but combines essay and fictitious narrative, thus leaving the form of Chapone's *Letters on the Improvement of the Mind* or the Aikins' *Miscellaneous Pieces* for the form of Sarah Trimmer's highly successful *Fabulous Histories*, published only two years earlier. There are also points of resemblance to Trimmer's *An Easy Introduction to the Knowledge of Nature* (1782) and to Dorothy Kilner's classic *Perambulation of a Mouse* (1783-1784). In *Original Stories* a Mrs. Mason (an aptly named moral and social builder) supervises two girls who have been miseducated by ignorant servants and undereducated

by merely fashionable parents. Mrs. Mason re-educates Mary and Caroline in a series of walks and dialogues, using objects and events along the way in order to teach morality and conduct through questioning. The topics include treatment of animals, the danger of giving way to passions, moral versus physical beauty, the importance of foresight and self-discipline, prayer and religious devotion, the proper character of girls and women, the distinction between generosity and extravagance, the value of hard work—in short, an introduction to properly middle-class moral self-culture and social practices, especially as applied to girls and women. Incorrect values and immoral conduct are clearly those derived from either the improvident, irrational lower classes or the merely fashionable, decadent upper classes. The narrative in *Original Stories*, like that in *Mary, A Fiction*, is omniscient third person; but Wollstonecraft still manages to personalize the narrative, to give intimations of autobiography, identification of author-narrator and chief protagonist, and personal reflections and aphorisms, that derive authority from the self of the author.

Wollstonecraft was now a professional writer, for better and for worse. For the better were her regular contacts with the artists, intellectuals, and writers in the circle of her publisher, Joseph Johnson. Johnson's circle resembled and surpassed the famous dissenting academies, such as Warrington and Hoxton, which were centers of the English Nonconformist Enlightenment and hotbeds of political and religious debate. Wollstonecraft was a rare woman in Johnson's "academy," but as yet she was a professional writer in a narrow sense, turning out books to earn a mere living. Johnson set her to work translating Joachim Heinrich Campe's *New Robinson Crusoe* in 1788, but a rival translation was published first. The same thing happened when she undertook to translate Johann-Kaspar Lavater's *Physiognomy* (1775-1778). Johnson gave her a poor translation of Maria Geertruida van de Werken de Cambon's *Young Grandison* to revise; it was published in 1790.

Under the nom de plume "Mr. Cresswick, teacher of elocution," she produced *The Female Reader* (1789)—a feminine companion to the highly successful anthologies of prose and verse extracts edited by William Enfield and others. Significantly, the readers for boys and young men featured texts to be read aloud, as preparation for public and professional life. The readers for females relied on texts for private reading, moral self-schooling, self-domestication. Wollstonecraft also fought her way through translations of books in the moralizing, educational line—Jacques Necker's *On the Importance of Religious Opinions* (1788), and C. G. Salzmann's *Elements of Morality* (1790-1791).

She was also reviewing for Johnson's new critical magazine, the *Analytical Review*. These pieces, often signed "M." or "W.," are on a variety of topics of interest to her, including music, aesthetics, education, moral philosophy, treatment of the insane, Portugal, and novels. Her style as a reviewer exhibits the personal tone and reference found in her books and soon to become characteristic of Romantic reviewers. The reviews, from 1788 to the mid 1790s, show glimpses of her developing intellectual, literary, and political values. They also state her belief in the individual, or even individualistic style of "genius," as understood at that time. She approves of vigor, energy, force, candor, and simplicity in writing, and shows in general a belief in the new, "sentimental" canons of prose style described in such writers as Hugh Blair (*Lectures on Rhetoric and Belles Lettres*, 1783) and exemplified in such writers as Rousseau. At the same time, she condemns sensibility of theme or style when it seems to be merely an appropriation of decadent aristocratic literary culture. She continues to push the same aggressively middle-class ideas of reason, virtue, simplicity, and candor in literature as in social practice, advocated in her educational writing.

These values and the kind of prose style Wollstonecraft felt properly exemplified them were given a political direction in her first important book, published in late 1790—*A Vindication of the Rights of Men*. Wollstonecraft, like many in Joseph Johnson's circle, welcomed the French Revolution as the opening up of the political and state structure in a way they had long wished to see in Britain. One of Wollstonecraft's mentors in particular, Richard Price, was a leading figure linking British reform and civil liberty to the French Revolution in 1789. Wollstonecraft had also formed a close relationship with the German Swiss painter and literary man Henry Fuseli, also a member of Johnson's academy. Fuseli was deeply read in Enlightenment and sentimental literature; he was an admirer of Rousseau; and he had a forceful personality. He was a proponent of a new kind of writing, validated, legitimized, or authenticated by the exhibition of its author's mind by stylistic, rhetorical means. In early life destined for the ministry, he was also well read in rhetorical the-

ory and practice. This knowledge and experience were available for Wollstonecraft when the publication of Edmund Burke's *Reflections on the Revolution in France* at the beginning of November 1790 crystallized Wollstonecraft's social criticism into a noble indignation, seconded by Fuseli, Johnson, and others in Johnson's circle, and inspired by Price as man and as moral and political writer. Wollstonecraft plunged into writing a reply to Burke, stalled part way through, and was maneuvered by Johnson into finishing her book. It appeared anonymously, was well received, and was reprinted, with her name on the title page. She had emerged as a writer in the fully public, political domain, a transformation in her identity as a woman that was of fundamental importance for her, for other women writers of her time, and for the nature of public political imagining in the 1790s and after.

She chooses to reply to Burke by the rhetorical strategy of turning the tables. To Burke's emotive language and expressive, personal style, she opposes her own. To Burke's ad hominem attack on Price she opposes her own on Burke. Against Burke's appeal to history, tradition, custom, and property she opposes "reason," "virtue," moral-intellectual equality (or merit), and citizenship. In particular, she accuses Burke of sentimentality and effeminacy in thought and morals, an accusation that would be more effective when Wollstonecraft revealed her identity as a woman by affixing her name to the title page of the second edition. Like Thomas Paine, Wollstonecraft opposes Burke's emphasis on the Parisians' march on Versailles (October 1789) as the representative revolutionary event. She emphasizes the passing of the Declaration of the Rights of Man and Citizen in August 1789 (hence Wollstonecraft's title). Burke's prose style is self-authenticating in its practice of the middle style, its copiousness, rich allusiveness, and its management of figures representing the culture of the professionalized gentry, whom Burke, the attorney's son, had joined and whom he equated with the political nation. Wollstonecraft eschews this style, and the "nervousness," aphoristic turns, personal tone, sarcasm, and recourse to "immutable principles" in her style implies a different kind of self-authentication of argument—that of the "genius" or unique individual. Her style implies a different political nation, determined by moral and intellectual, expressly personal merit. This is the political nation of the professional intellectuals, liberal Dissenters, men (and women) of letters so despised by Burke. However, it would be true to say that, effective as Wollstonecraft's argumentative and stylistic counter to Burke is, especially as far as members of Johnson's circle were concerned, it does not show that she understood his point of view, except as that of a lackey to court society and aristocratic culture, one of the emulative rather than independent middle classes.

Nevertheless, the success of *A Vindication of the Rights of Men* freed Wollstonecraft from her acceptably feminine work in fiction, educational writing, and minor belles lettres, to write her second *Vindication*, published just over a year after the first, early in 1792. *A Vindication of the Rights of Woman* is her most famous and influential work. In it she moves to incorporate the feminine and female discourses and issues of her earlier writing career into the public political domain broached by her in *A Vindication of the Rights of Men*.

A Vindication of the Rights of Woman continues the work of the first *Vindication* in being a critique of court culture, especially in its discourse of gender and especially as that discourse is incorporated in professional, middle-class ideology, values, and social practice. The point of contact with her reply to Burke would be through the courtly "gallantry" he exhibited, she felt, in the notorious "ten thousand swords" passage in *Reflections on the Revolution in France*, exculpating the decadent court society and politics around Marie Antoinette and appealing to "antient chivalry."

The specific occasion for *A Vindication of the Rights of Woman* was the proposal for a system of national education in France, one which excluded females. The book is also informed by a close reading of Catherine Macaulay Graham's *Letters on Education* (1790), which Wollstonecraft reviewed in the *Analytical Review* for November 1790. Now Wollstonecraft applies to women the professional middle-class ideology of *A Vindication of the Rights of Men*: that of the moral-intellectual self as foundation of social practice and the state. Relying on a transcendental yet irreducibly subjective first cause—the equality of souls—she argues for a more or less equal education for women, greater (though not equal) access for (middle-class) women to professions appropriate for them, and purging of courtly "gallantry" and "coquetry" from middle-class—indeed, any class's—social practice. In these ways, she argues, women will be best able to fulfill the central role as essentially domestic beings allotted to them in the new social order and state.

She accepts gender difference, but attempts to equalize the effects of difference by incorporating it into the emergent liberal bourgeois critique of court culture and proposals to refound the state and the national culture on the private and domestic individual. She first discusses "the rights and the duties of mankind," and goes on to consider prevailing views of gender difference and the resulting moral, intellectual, social, and legal degradation of women. She then looks at writers who have promulgated these false views and gives a critique of such false social conventions and principles of education as feminine modesty, reputation, and feminine "nature." She considers social inequality as the foundation of many social evils, questions the family power structure, and weighs the advantages of different schemes of education. She closes with a sarcastic description of the bad effects of improper education of girls and women and discusses the benefits to be derived from a correct education and its accompanying "revolution in female manners." Insofar as this critique and these proposals were, as she thought, central to the early, pre-Jacobin phase of the French Revolution, as well as to reformist politics in Britain, Wollstonecraft's feminism could be described as revolutionary.

In this second *Vindication*, however, Wollstonecraft again faces the problem of authority insofar as she is inserting herself into the public and political domain of discourse, one in which women were generally assumed to have no legitimate place. Authority is also a problem because of her individualist politics, politics resting on "natural" rights, "principles of reason," and ideas of "innate virtue." Having rejected tradition, custom, and false consciousness, she is faced with making a political text that will grant her (and women like her) political existence, but she must make her political text out of herself, a self not yet existing politically. Her text must create the self that validates the text. Again, she fell back on frequent recourse to her own experience, in an I-centered discourse; a personal tone; an oppositional posture toward writers of conduct books, Rousseau, and other bourgeois writers who argued for a courtly kind of female; use of figures and examples from common, domestic life rather than from learned literature or elite culture; lyrical and expressive passages; critical use of language, defining words for her own use; recourse to aphorism in order to close or to generalize a passage of personal statement; and a desultory, repetitive, and rhythmic way of proceeding, rather

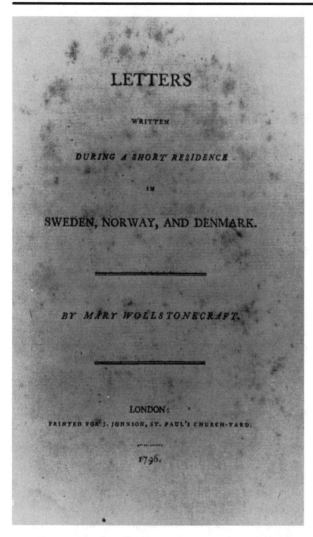

Title page for the book that resulted from Wollstonecraft's summer 1795 visit to Scandinavia

than a forensic, cumulative, or highly structured and subdivided one. In the context of the repertory of discourses available in her time, Wollstonecraft's self-vindication of the rights of woman was original, admirably consistent, and successful.

From writing revolutionary feminism Wollstonecraft moved to enact it. She wished to make her intellectual relationship with Fuseli a more intimate one yet also to resituate it in a more open political scene. Thus she planned to go to Paris with him, and set off once, only to turn back at news of fresh disturbances there. When he dropped out of the plan she finally went alone, in December 1792. Her chief contacts in Paris were with the Girondin faction around Marie Roland and her husband, and with various Americans and British reformers, such as Helen Maria Williams, Joel Barlow, Thomas Christie, Thomas

Paine, and A. H. Rowan. But the revolution reached a critical phase with the execution of Louis XVI, war between Britain and France, and the Jacobins' coup d'état. She fell in love with Gilbert Imlay, an American, former army officer, author, and land speculator. To protect herself, as an alien, she had herself registered as his wife, though they were not married. Opposition to marriage was part of a self-consciously revolutionary hostility to tradition and property as false bases for relationships. A year later, in May 1794, their daughter Fanny was born. Wollstonecraft had entered the romance of revolution, already described with such intensity by Helen Maria Williams. in her series of influential books on the Revolution and by Marie Roland in her *Memoirs* (1795).

Wollstonecraft, meanwhile, wrote her own book on the revolution, one still very characteristic of a member of Joseph Johnson's academy, and probably inspired by Williams's success. Another influence may have been the kind of "philosophical history" being written by Wollstonecraft's close friend William Roscoe, a Liverpool lawyer. "Volume one" of Wollstonecraft's *An Historical and Moral View of the Origin and Progress of the French Revolution* was published late in 1794. It was very much a book of its time, for a British readership. The impulse is to account for the degeneration of the revolution from the Girondist bourgeois liberalism of its early phases to the Jacobin terror. The explanation is the usual one offered by those British reformers, such as the ones in Johnson's circle, who had much in common with the Girondins: the corruption and tyranny of the ancien régime were so great that a countervailing revolutionary momentum had, temporarily, gone too far. Wollstonecraft's *View* is also in the line of Enlightenment social critique as "philosophical history." In particular Wollstonecraft looks critically at the court culture and politics that were, she thought, the ground of all subsequent events. Here is the connection with her reply to Burke and her critique of the courtly practices of gender difference, and Wollstonecraft makes Marie Antoinette the emblem of what the revolution had to sweep away. On the other hand, the *View* lacks the strong personal element that was a central part of her rhetorical strategy in most of her other work. That rhetoric—the female "voice" in public-political debate—had already been preempted, as far as accounts of the Revolution were concerned, by Helen Maria Williams in her *Letters* from France of 1790 and

1792. It may be, too, that Wollstonecraft's dangerous situation in Paris (Williams was actually arrested), her increasing involvement in Imlay's concerns, and her caution in the face of the preeminently male discourse of political historiography inclined her to a more "philosophical" voice in her *Historical and Moral View of the French Revolution*.

Her personal life turned her in the right direction, but almost at the cost of her life. Imlay had become preoccupied with business interests, supplying the beleaguered French economy with essential imports from neutral Scandinavian countries. This preoccupation and the separations it necessitated between Imlay and Wollstonecraft hardened her long-standing contempt for the merely commercial bourgeoisie, a contempt that was probably an aspect of her upbringing. When Imlay relocated to London, Wollstonecraft followed him there, only to find that he had been unfaithful. She attempted suicide, but was persuaded by Imlay to visit Scandinavia on his behalf to recover money owed him. She went in the summer of 1795, with her infant daughter and a French woman servant.

The product of this impulsive and hazardous voyage was her best book, *Letters Written During a Short Residence in Sweden, Norway, and Denmark*, published early in 1796. Here she successfully adapts to her own purpose the female literary tradition of familiar letters and the tradition of the female travelogue. Helen Maria Williams had done this, too, in her successful series of *Letters* from France, the latest and best of which had been published in 1795. Williams and Wollstonecraft both aim to fuse the personal and the "philosophical" (or analytical and critical) into a woman's kind of political writing on public affairs as experienced at the individual, familial, and community levels. Both make the move into the public and political domain from acceptably feminine discourses of education, the domestic, and the affective and subjective. Both aim to reveal the relationship between large social structures, political institutions, and economic practices and the local, particular, immediate, and quotidian. If Wollstonecraft's *Letters* are superior, it is because they are less diffuse, more detailed and particular in their observations, more rigorously analytical, more convincingly epistolary, more intense, and less self-consciously sentimental and "feminine" than Williams's *Letters*. Wollstonecraft was moving toward a critique of the politics of everyday life, in tune with the young

Romantic poets' interest in the "domestic affections" and the "trivial sublime" and linking social critique with personal experience. As reaction against the French Revolution and its English supporters hardened, she moved away from polemical, nonfiction writing as the most effective medium for her social critique.

Soon she shifted her formal ground again. When she returned from Scandinavia she had found Imlay living with a young actress and again attempted suicide. She had seen for herself, in her failing relationship with Imlay, how well courtly "mistress system," "gallantry," and "coquetry" and merely commercial bourgeois values could penetrate even liberal, reformist, prorevolutionary attitudes and practices. A few months later, about the time *Letters Written During a Short Residence in Sweden, Norway, and Denmark* was published, she met again the leading philosophical anarchist and novelist William Godwin. He later claimed that *Letters* would make a man fall in love with its author; after courtship that was hesitant on both sides they became lovers in late summer 1796. Wollstonecraft became pregnant; they married on 29 March 1797, having decided that their principled opposition to marriage had to give way to their desire for domestic peace and social usefulness. Once Wollstonecraft married Godwin, it was obvious she had not been married to Imlay and some people dropped her.

As a writer on the politics of class and gender in everyday life, Wollstonecraft had to be influenced by the Godwin circle's great interest in the then subliterary form of the novel as a vehicle for such political critiques. Wollstonecraft's close friend Mary Hays shared this interest. In 1792 Wollstonecraft had intended to publish further volumes of *A Vindication of the Rights of Woman* dealing with "the laws relative to women, and the consideration of their peculiar duties," as she said in the advertisement in the first edition. She took this material, combined it with her general concern for the penetration of courtly gender practices into middle-class life, as "gallantry" but also as "sensibility," and informed it with her own social experience and observation. Moving with the Godwin circle, she chose not polemical prose or political travelogue, but the novel, the most widely distributed form of print (except newspapers) and a genre especially, and damagingly, associated with women authors and readers at that time. With an eye on the model set by Godwin's *Things As They Are; or, The Adventures of Caleb Williams* (1794), she began work on *The Wrongs of*

Wollstonecraft in 1797 (portrait by John Opie; National Portrait Gallery, London)

Woman; or, Maria. She would use a prose form particularly associated with the intellectual, cultural, and social inferiority of women in order to expose the causes of that inferiority and thus to end it. She would do what she had done in her *Vindication of the Rights of Woman* and her *Letters* from Scandinavia—join the political and the private, give her argument the intensity of the autobiographical mode (first-person narratives in the novel), yet generalize the personal through the novel form and through particular details from contemporary life and from historical analogies.

But Wollstonecraft was not to complete this new experiment in feminist writing. Her daughter Mary, born on 30 August, later became the wife of the poet Percy Bysshe Shelley and a novelist in her own right, practicing a similar form, if different politics, to that of her mother's *Wrongs of Woman.* On 10 September Wollstonecraft died of puerperal fever. Godwin, grief-stricken, worked on her literary remains and in January 1798 published *Posthumous Works of the Author of A Vindication of the Rights of Woman,* thus equating her with her writing, in an appropriate gesture. These volumes contain the unfinished *Wrongs of Woman*; a small book of "Lessons" for a child, modeled on Anna Lætitia Barbauld's *Early Lessons*

(1778-1779); some letters to Imlay and Joseph Johnson; a letter on France dated 15 February 1793, probably in imitation of Williams's *Letters*; incomplete "Letters on the Management of Infants"; an incomplete philosophical tale, "The Cave of Fancy," probably written in 1787; an essay, "On Poetry, and Our Relish for the Beauties of Nature"; and "Hints" for the second part of *A Vindication of the Rights of Woman,* actually a series of aphorisms, suggesting that she did indeed build her texts on aphoristic statements. Along with the *Posthumous Works* Godwin published a memoir of Wollstonecraft, clearly setting forth her principles and actions, in the spirit of English Jacobin candor, and thus representing Wollstonecraft as a female hero in private and public life. But the reaction against English Jacobinism and revolutionary feminism was opening into full spate, and the *Memoir,* one of the best biographies of the period, ironically did much to damn Wollstonecraft as woman, writer, and feminist, in official opinion.

Letters:

Collected Letters of Mary Wollstonecraft, edited by Ralph M. Wardle (Ithaca, N.Y. & London: Cornell University Press, 1979).

Bibliography:

Janet M. Todd, *Mary Wollstonecraft: An Annotated Bibliography* (New York & London: Garland, 1976).

Biographies:

William Godwin, *Memoirs of the Author of a Vindication of the Rights of Woman* (London: Printed for J. Johnson and G. G. & J. Robinson, 1798); republished as *Memoirs of Mary Wollstonecraft,* edited by W. Clark Durant (London: Constable / New York: Greenberg, 1927); republished in *A Short Residence in Sweden, Norway and Denmark,* edited by Richard Holmes (Harmondsworth: Penguin Books, 1987);

Ralph Wardle, *Mary Wollstonecraft: A Critical Biography* (Lawrence: University of Kansas Press, 1951);

Eleanor Flexner, *Mary Wollstonecraft: A Biography* (New York: Coward, McCann & Geoghegan, 1972);

Claire Tomalin, *The Life and Death of Mary Wollstonecraft* (New York & London: Harcourt Brace Jovanovich, 1974);

Emily W. Sunstein, *A Different Face: The Life of Mary Wollstonecraft* (New York: Harper & Row, 1975);

Margaret Tims, *Mary Wollstonecraft: A Social Pioneer* (London: Millington, 1976);

William St Clair, *The Godwins and the Shelleys* (New York & London: Norton, 1989).

References:

James T. Boulton, *The Language of Politics in the Age of Wilkes and Burke* (London: Routledge & Kegan Paul, 1963), pp. 167-176;

Diana H. Coole, *Women in Political Theory: From Ancient Misogyny to Contemporary Feminism* (Sussex: Wheatsheaf Books / Boulder, Col.: Rienner, 1988);

A Defence of the Character and Conduct of the Late Mary Wollstonecraft Godwin (London: James Wallis, 1803);

Moira Ferguson and Janet Todd, *Mary Wollstonecraft* (Boston: Twayne, 1984);

Elissa Guralnick, "Radical Politics in Mary Wollstonecraft's *A Vindication of the Rights of Woman*," *Studies in Burke and His Time*, 18 (Autumn 1977): 155-166; republished in *A Vindication of the Rights of Woman*, edited by Carol H. Poston, second edition, expanded (New York & London: W. W. Norton, 1988), pp. 308-317;

Guralnick, "Rhetorical Strategy in Mary Wollstonecraft's *A Vindication of the Rights of Woman*," *Humanities Association Review*, 30 (Summer 1979): 174-185;

Cora Kaplan, "Pandora's Box: Subjectivity, Class and Sexuality in Socialist Feminist Criticism," in *Making a Difference: Feminist Literary Criticism*, edited by Gayle Greene and Coppélia Kahn (London & New York: Methuen, 1985), pp. 146-176;

Gary Kelly, *Revolutionary Feminism: The Mind and Career of Mary Wollstonecraft* (London: Macmillan, 1991);

Mitzi Myers, "Impeccable Governesses, Rational Dames, and Moral Mothers: Mary Wollstonecraft and the Female Tradition in Georgian Children's Books," *Children's Literature*, 14 (1986): 31-59;

Myers, "Mary Wollstonecraft's *Letters Written . . . in Sweden*: Toward Romantic Autobiogra-

phy," in *Studies in Eighteenth-Century Culture*, edited by Roseann Runte (Madison: University of Wisconsin Press, 1979), VIII: 165-185;

Myers, "Reform or Ruin: 'A Revolution in Female Manners,'" in *Studies in Eighteenth-Century Culture*, edited by Harry C. Payne (Madison: University of Wisconsin Press, 1982), XI: 119-216; reprinted in *A Vindication of the Rights of Woman*, edited by Poston, second edition, expanded (New York: W. W. Norton, 1988), pp. 328-343;

Myers, "Sensibility and the 'Walk of Reason': Mary Wollstonescraft's Literary Reviews as Cultural Critique," in *Sensibility in Transformation: Creative Resistance to Sentiment from the Augustans to the Romantics: Essays in Honor of Jean H. Hagstrum*, edited by Syndy McMillen Conger (Rutherford, N. J. : Fairleigh Dickinson University Press, 1989);

Paule Penigault-Duhet, *Mary Wollstonecraft-Godwin 1759-1797* (Lille: Atelier National Reproduction des Thèses Université Lille III / Paris: Didier Erudition, 1984);

Mary Poovey, *The Proper Lady and the Woman Writer: Ideology as Style in the Works of Mary Wollstonecraft, Mary Shelley, and Jane Austen* (Chicago & London: University of Chicago Press, 1984), pp. 48-82;

Timothy J. Reiss, "Revolution in Bounds: Wollstonecraft, Women, and Reason," in *Genre and Theory: Dialogues on Feminist Criticism*, edited by Linda Kauffman (Oxford: Blackwell, 1989), pp. 11-50;

Virginia Woolf, "Mary Wollstonecraft," in her *The Second Common Reader* (New York: Harcourt Brace, 1932), pp. 141-148;

Patricia Yaeger, *Honey-Mad Women: Emancipatory Strategies in Women's Writing* (New York: Columbia University Press, 1988).

Papers:

The principal collections of Wollstonecraft's letters are at the Bodleian Library, Oxford, and in the Carl H. Pforzheimer Collection, New York Public Library.

Books for Further Reading

Anderson, Howard, Philip B. Daghlian, and Irvin Ehrenpreis, eds. *The Familiar Letter in the Eighteenth Century*. Lawrence: University of Kansas Press, 1966.

Battestin, Martin C. *The Providence of Wit: Aspects of Form in Augustan Literature and the Arts*. Oxford: Clarendon Press, 1974.

Becker, Carl L. *The Heavenly City of the Eighteenth-Century Philosophers*. New Haven: Yale University Press, 1932.

Black, J. B. *The Art of History: A Study of Four Great Historians of the Eighteenth Century*. New York: F. S. Crofts, 1926.

Bredvold, Louis I. *The Brave New World of the Enlightenment*. Ann Arbor: University of Michigan Press, 1961.

Bredvold. *The Natural History of Sensibility*. Detroit: Wayne State University Press, 1962.

Butt, John. *The Augustan Age*, third edition, revised. New York: Norton, 1966.

Clifford, James. *Eighteenth-Century Literature: Modern Essays in Criticism*. New York: Oxford University Press, 1959.

Damrosch, Leopold, Jr. *Fictions of Reality in the Age of Hume and Johnson*. Madison: University of Wisconsin Press, 1989.

Damrosch. *Modern Essays on Eighteenth-Century Literature*. New York: Oxford University Press, 1988.

Engell, James. *The Creative Imagination: Enlightenment to Romanticism*. Cambridge: Harvard University Press, 1981.

Engell. *Forming the Critical Mind: Dryden to Coleridge*. Cambridge: Harvard University Press, 1989.

Fussell, Paul, Jr. *The Rhetorical World of Augustan Humanism: Ethics and Imagery from Swift to Burke*. Oxford: Clarendon Press, 1965.

Gay, Peter. *The Enlightenment: An Interpretation*, 2 volumes. New York: Knopf, 1966, 1969.

Greene, Donald. *The Age of Exuberance: Backgrounds to Eighteenth-Century English Literature*. New York: Random House, 1970.

Humphreys, A. R. *The Augustan World: Life and Letters in Eighteenth-Century England*. London: Methuen, 1954.

Jones, Richard Foster. *Ancients and Moderns: A Study of the Rise of the Scientific Movement in Seventeenth-Century England*. Washington University Studies, New Series, Language and Literature, no. 6. St. Louis, 1936.

Lipking, Lawrence. *The Ordering of the Arts in Eighteenth-Century England*. Princeton: Princeton University Press, 1970.

Lovejoy, A. O. *The Great Chain of Being*. Cambridge: Harvard University Press, 1936.

Marshall, Dorothy. *Eighteenth-Century England*. London: Longmans, Green, 1962.

Monk, Samuel Holt. *The Sublime: A Study of Critical Theories in XVIIIth-Century England*. New York: Modern Language Association of America, 1935.

Moore, C. A. *Backgrounds of English Literature, 1700-1760*. Minneapolis: University of Minnesota Press, 1953.

Pocock, J. G. A. *The Machiavellian Moment: Florentine Political Thought and the Atlantic Republican Tradition*. Princeton: Princeton University Press, 1975.

Pocock. *Virtue, Commerce, and History: Essays on Political Thought and History, Chiefly in the Eighteenth Century*. Cambridge: Cambridge University Press, 1985.

Price, Martin. *To the Palace of Wisdom: Studies in Order and Energy from Dryden to Blake*. Garden City, N.Y.: Doubleday, 1964.

Richetti, John J. *Philosophical Writing: Locke, Berkeley, Hume*. Cambridge: Harvard University Press, 1983.

Rogers, Pat, ed. *The Context of English Literature: The Eighteenth Century*. London: Methuen, 1978; New York: Holmes & Meier, 1978.

Sambrook, James. *The Eighteenth Century: The Intellectual and Cultural Context of English Literature, 1700-1789*. London & New York: Longman, 1986.

Sherburn, George, and Donald F. Bond. *The Restoration and Eighteenth Century (1660-1789). A Literary History of England*, volume 3, edited by Albert C. Baugh, second edition. New York: Appleton-Century-Crofts, 1967.

Stephen, Leslie. *History of English Thought in the Eighteenth Century*, 2 volumes. London: Smith, Elder, 1876; New York: Putnam's, 1876.

Turberville, A. S., ed. *Johnson's England*, 2 volumes. Oxford: Clarendon Press, 1933.

Willey, Basil. *The Eighteenth-Century Background: Studies on the Idea of Nature in the Thought of the Period*. London: Chatto & Windus, 1940.

Willey, *The English Moralists*. New York: Norton, 1964.

Williamson, George. *The Senecan Amble: A Study in Prose Forms from Bacon to Collier*. London: Faber & Faber, 1951.

Contributors

Richard E. Brantley...*University of Florida*
Martine Watson Brownley...*Emory University*
John J. Burke, Jr. ....*University of Alabama*
Patricia B. Craddock..*University of Florida*
Bertram H. Davis ....*Florida State University*
Roger L. Emerson...*University of Western Ontario*
Byron Gassman ....*Brigham Young University*
Donald Greene ....*University of Southern California*
Gary Kelly...*University of Alberta*
James King..*McMaster University*
Elise F. Knapp ....*Western Connecticut State University*
Elizabeth R. Lambert...*Gettysburg College*
Donald Livingston ....*Emory University*
Alan T. McKenzie..*Purdue University*
Pat Rogers...*University of South Florida*
Ian Ross...*University of British Columbia*
Barbara Brandon Schnorrenberg...*Birmingham, Alabama*
Jeffrey Smitten ....*Utah State University*
John A. Vance ....*University of Georgia*
Samuel H. Woods, Jr. ....*Oklahoma State University*

Cumulative Index

Dictionary of Literary Biography, Volumes 1-104
Dictionary of Literary Biography Yearbook, 1980-1989
Dictionary of Literary Biography Documentary Series, Volumes 1-8

Cumulative Index

DLB before number: *Dictionary of Literary Biography,* Volumes 1-104
Y before number: *Dictionary of Literary Biography Yearbook,* 1980-1989
DS before number: *Dictionary of Literary Biography Documentary Series,* Volumes 1-8

A

B

C

D

E

F

H

I

J

L

M

O

S

T

Y

Z

80: *Restoration and Eighteenth-Century Dramatists*, First Series, edited by Paula R. Backscheider (1989)

81: *Austrian Fiction Writers, 1875-1913*, edited by James Hardin and Donald G. Daviau (1989)

82: *Chicano Writers*, First Series, edited by Francisco A. Lomelí and Carl R. Shirley (1989)

83: *French Novelists Since 1960*, edited by Catharine Savage Brosman (1989)

84: *Restoration and Eighteenth-Century Dramatists*, Second Series, edited by Paula R. Backscheider (1989)

85: *Austrian Fiction Writers After 1914*, edited by James Hardin and Donald G. Daviau (1989)

86: *American Short-Story Writers, 1910-1945*, First Series, edited by Bobby Ellen Kimbel (1989)

87: *British Mystery and Thriller Writers Since 1940*, First Series, edited by Bernard Benstock and Thomas F. Staley (1989)

88: *Canadian Writers, 1920-1959*, Second Series, edited by W. H. New (1989)

89: *Restoration and Eighteenth-Century Dramatists*, Third Series, edited by Paula R. Backscheider (1989)

90: *German Writers in the Age of Goethe, 1789-1832*, edited by James Hardin and Christoph E. Schweitzer (1989)

91: *American Magazine Journalists, 1900-1960*, First Series, edited by Sam G. Riley (1990)

92: *Canadian Writers, 1890-1920*, edited by W. H. New (1990)

93: *British Romantic Poets, 1789-1832*, First Series, edited by John R. Greenfield (1990)

94: *German Writers in the Age of Goethe: Sturm und Drang to Classicism*, edited by James Hardin and Christoph E. Schweitzer (1990)

95: *Eighteenth-Century British Poets*, First Series, edited by John Sitter (1990)

96: *British Romantic Poets, 1789-1832*, Second Series, edited by John R. Greenfield (1990)

97: *German Writers from the Enlightenment to Sturm und Drang, 1720-1764*, edited by James Hardin and Christoph E. Schweitzer (1990)

98: *Modern British Essayists*, First Series, edited by Robert Beum (1990)

99: *Canadian Writers Before 1890*, edited by W. H. New (1990)

100: *Modern British Essayists*, Second Series, edited by Robert Beum (1990)

101: *British Prose Writers, 1660-1800*, First Series, edited by Donald T. Siebert (1991)

102: *American Short-Story Writers, 1910-1945*, Second Series, edited by Bobby Ellen Kimbel (1991)

103: *American Literary Biographers*, First Series, edited by Steven Serafin (1991)

104: *British Prose Writers, 1660-1800*, Second Series, edited by Donald T. Siebert (1991)

Documentary Series

1: *Sherwood Anderson, Willa Cather, John Dos Passos, Theodore Dreiser, F. Scott Fitzgerald, Ernest Hemingway, Sinclair Lewis*, edited by Margaret A. Van Antwerp (1982)

2: *James Gould Cozzens, James T. Farrell, William Faulkner, John O'Hara, John Steinbeck, Thomas Wolfe, Richard Wright*, edited by Margaret A. Van Antwerp (1982)

3: *Saul Bellow, Jack Kerouac, Norman Mailer, Vladimir Nabokov, John Updike, Kurt Vonnegut*, edited by Mary Bruccoli (1983)

4: *Tennessee Williams*, edited by Margaret A. Van Antwerp and Sally Johns (1984)

5: *American Transcendentalists*, edited by Joel Myerson (1988)

6: *Hardboiled Mystery Writers*, edited by Matthew J. Bruccoli and Richard Layman (1989)

7: *Modern American Poets*, edited by Karen L. Rood (1989)

8: *The Black Aesthetic Movement*, edited by Jeffrey Louis Decker (1991)

Yearbooks

edited by Karen L. Rood, Jean W. Ross, and Richard Ziegfeld (1981)

edited by Karen L. Rood, Jean W. Ross, and Richard Ziegfeld (1982)